DIGITAL COMPUTER FUNDAMENTALS

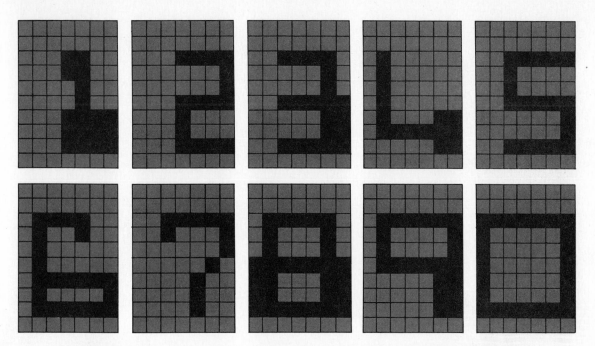

DIGITAL COMPUTER FUNDAMENTALS
SIXTH EDITION

THOMAS C. BARTEE

Harvard University

McGRAW-HILL BOOK COMPANY

New York | St. Louis | San Francisco | Auckland | Bogotá | Hamburg
Johannesburg | London | Madrid | Mexico | Montreal | New Delhi
Panama | Paris | São Paulo | Singapore | Sydney | Tokyo | Toronto

DIGITAL COMPUTER FUNDAMENTALS

234567890 DOCDOC 898765

ISBN 0-07-003899-6

This book was set in Times Roman by Waldman Graphics, Inc.
The editors were Sanjeev Rao and J. W. Maisel; the designer was Nicholas Krenitsky;
the production supervisor was Diane Renda.
New drawings were done by J & R Services, Inc.
R. R. Donnelley & Sons Company was printer and binder.

Library of Congress Cataloging in Publication Data

Bartee, Thomas C.
Digital computer fundamentals.

Bibliography: p.
Includes index.
1. Electronic digital computers. I. Title.
TK7885.B317   1985   621.3819'58   84-10054
ISBN 0-07-003899-6

CONTENTS

PREFACE xi

1
COMPUTER OPERATION 1

4
LOGIC DESIGN 135

5
THE ARITHMETIC-LOGIC UNIT 193

6
THE MEMORY ELEMENT 261

7
INPUT-OUTPUT DEVICES 323

APPENDIXES
A

PREFACE

The purpose of this book is to present, as clearly as possible, the principles of modern digital computers. Many questions—a number of which are entirely new—are included in a separate section of each chapter; answers to selected odd-numbered questions are given at the end of the book.

In the sixth edition, there are more changes than there have been in any edition since publication. No part of the book has been left untouched, and the latest technology will be found throughout the book. I have incorporated suggestions from users of the book in many places.

Chapter 1 describes the uses of the computer in business, industry, and science. It also presents a brief introduction to programming. Some historical material is included, as well as some basic concepts relating to computer usage.

Chapters 2 through 4 introduce some of the basic ideas and principles which are used in all digital computers and also in digital instruments, digital communications systems, digital control systems, and, in fact, in all digital devices. These chapters describe number systems, Boolean algebra, and logic design. The sections on counters and logic design using NAND and NOR gates have been expanded in this edition. Also, PLAs and PALs are carefully covered and the principles of state machines are presented in this section of the book.

Chapters 5, 6, 7, and 8 treat arithmetic operations, memories, input-output devices, and interfaces. The material on arithmetic operations first explains how arithmetic is performed in computers and then how arithmetic-logic units in computers are organized. The chapter on memories discusses integrated circuit memories and disk, tape, bubbles, CCD, and other storage devices. Coverage of the latest developments in this area concerning floppy disks, Winchester drives, and streaming tape drives is included here. The chapter on input and output describes the major input-output devices and also includes new expanded material on analog-to-digital converters, digital-to-analog converters, terminals, modems, etc. Some material on computer organization and the general principles of buses is presented as is an explanation of how to interface a keyboard and a printer to a microcomputer bus.

The two final chapters, Chapters 9 and 10, first discuss the control unit in modern computers, including a description of the conventional logic design of control circuitry and then of microprogramming for computer control. The overall organization of computers is then discussed, as are the major topics in computer architecture—addressing techniques, interrupt servicing, etc. Existing computers are used as examples of the ideas presented. Emphasis is placed on microcomputers and the latest micros but the classic micros are also discussed. There is an appendix on digital circuits.

The block diagram symbols in this book are those that have been adopted by the American National Standards Institute and also the Military Standards.

I have had considerable help and advice during the preparation of the various editions of this book. The first edition was written at M.I.T. Lincoln Laboratory; I will always be indebted to M.I.T. and the laboratory members for the considerable support provided me.

Many friends and users of the books have contributed to later editions. I regret that I cannot name them all. Certainly Professors Glen Goff, W. W. Peterson, M. A. Miller, Robert Carroll, Irving Reed, and Irwin Lebow should be singled out. I must also thank the teaching assistants in my courses for their many suggestions.

I am indebted to Thomas Quentin Bartee for his work on the manuscript. His help was essential to its preparation.

THOMAS C. BARTEE

DIGITAL COMPUTER FUNDAMENTALS

COMPUTER OPERATION

The computer industry continues to grow at record speeds. Computer shipments exceeded $25 billion in 1983, and the rapid growth in personal computer sales will push this number still higher each year.

Well over a million people now work in the computer industry, and this does not encompass the millions who work with computers indirectly, including bank clerks who put all their transactions into computers, airlines and motel employees who work with computers to make reservations, and machinists who use computer-controlled power tools.

In fact, computers now route long-distance telephone calls, process and issue the checks in banks, schedule planes and trains, make weather forecasts, predict and process the elections, and figure in so many things that entire books will be (and have been) written just documenting the types of applications.

Computers now use the major share of the electronics components being manufactured, and this share will continue to rise. The need for computer personnel in all areas continues to grow: over a quarter of a million new programmers are needed each year; the federal government's Department of Labor continues to maintain business machine service personnel and electronic computer operating personnel in first and second place in a list of five fastest-growing employment areas.

OBJECTIVES

1   This chapter first presents some background and historical information on the development of computer science. Early calculators and the first digital computer projects are described briefly.

**COMPUTER
OPERATION**

2   How a computer is used to solve a scientific problem or how an office procedure might be organized for computer usage is discussed.

3   An overview of several general categories of computer systems is presented including interactive systems, batch processing, and timeshared systems.

4   The general breakdown of a computer into five sections is discussed: these are input, control, memory, the arithmetic-logic unit, and output.

5   Programming and programming languages are defined and some basic concepts in this area introduced. A brief introduction to assembly language is followed by a discussion of a higher-level language, Pascal.

ELECTRONIC DIGITAL COMPUTERS

1.1   The history of attempts to make machines that could perform long sequences of calculations automatically is fairly long. The best known early attempt was made in the 19th century by Charles Babbage, an English scientist and mathematician. Babbage attempted to mechanize sequences of calculations, eliminating the operator and designing a machine so that it would perform all the necessary operations in a predetermined sequence. The machine designed by Babbage used cardboard cards with holes punched in them to introduce both instructions and the necessary data (numbers) into the machine. The machine was to perform the instructions dictated by the cards automatically, not stopping until an entire sequence of instructions had been completed. The punched cards used to control the machine already had been used to control the operation of weaving machines. Surprisingly enough, Babbage obtained some money for his project from the English government and started construction. Although he was severely limited by the technology of his time and the machine was never completed, Babbage succeeded in establishing the basic principles on which modern computers are constructed. There is even some speculation that if he had not run short of money, he might have constructed a successful machine. Although Babbage died without realizing his dream, he had established the fundamental concepts which were used to construct machines elaborate beyond even his expectations.

By the 1930s, punched cards were in wide use in large businesses, and various types of punched-card-handling machines were available. In 1937 Howard Aiken, at Harvard, proposed to IBM that a machine could be constructed (by using some of the parts and techniques from the punched-card machines) which would automatically sequence the operations and calculations performed. This machine used a combination of electromechanical devices, including many relays. The machine was in operation for some time, generating many tables of mathematical functions (particularly Bessel functions), and was used for trajectory calculations in World War II.

Aiken's machine was remarkable for its time, but was limited in speed by its use both of relays rather than electronic devices and of punched cards for sequencing the operations. In 1943 S. P. Eckert and J. W. Mauchly, of the Moore School of Engineering of the University of Pennsylvania, started the Eniac, which used electronic components (primarily vacuum tubes) and therefore was faster, but which also used switches and a wired plug board to implement the programming of operations. Later Eckert and Mauchly built the Edvac, which had its program stored in the computer's memory, not depending on external sequencing. This was an important innovation, and a computer that stores its list of operations, or program, internally is called a *stored-program computer*. Actually the Edsac, at the University of Manchester, started later but completed before Edvac, was the first operational stored-program computer.

A year or so later, John Von Neumann, at the Institute for Advanced Study (IAS) in Princeton, started the IAS in conjunction with the Moore School of Engineering, and this machine incorporated most of the general concepts of parallel binary stored-program computers.

The Univac I was the first commercially available electronic digital computer, and it was designed by Eckert and Mauchly at their own company, which was later bought by Sperry Rand. The U.S. Board of the Census bought the first Univac. (Later Univac and half of Aiken's machine were placed in the Smithsonian Institution, where they may now be seen.) IBM entered the competition with the IBM 701, a large machine, in 1953 and in 1954 with the IBM 650, a much smaller machine which was very successful. The IBM 701 was the forerunner of the 704–709–7094 series of IBM machines, the first "big winners" in the large-machine category.

Quite a few vacuum-tube electronic computers were available and in use by the late 1950s, but at this time an important innovation in electronics appeared— the transistor. The replacement of large, expensive (hot) vacuum tubes with small, inexpensive, reliable, comparatively low heat-dissipating transistors led to what are called *second-generation computers*. The size and importance of the computer industry grew at amazing rates, while the costs of individual computers dropped substantially.

By 1965 a third generation of computers was introduced. (The IBM Corporation, in introducing the 360 series, used the term *third-generation* as a key phrase in their advertising, and it remains a catchword in describing all machines of this era.) The machines of this period began making heavy use of *integrated circuits* in which many transistors and other components are fabricated and packaged together in a single small container. The low prices and high packing densities of these circuits plus lessons learned from prior machines led to some differences in computer system design, and these machines proliferated and expanded the computer industry to its present multibillion-dollar size.

Present-day computers are less easily distinguished from earlier generations. There are some striking and important differences, however. The manufacture of integrated circuits has become so advanced as to incorporate hundreds of thousands of active components in volumes of a fraction of an inch, leading to what is called *large-scale integration* (LSI) and *very large-scale integration* (VLSI). This has led to small-size, lower-cost, large-memory, ultrafast computers.

APPLICATION OF COMPUTERS TO PROBLEMS

1.2 For many years large office forces have been employed in the accounting departments of business firms. The clerks employed by these businesses spend most of their time performing arithmetic computations and then entering results

4

COMPUTER OPERATION

into company books and on paychecks, invoices, order forms, etc. Most of the arithmetic consists of repetitious sequences of simple calculations which the clerks perform over and over on different sets of figures. Few decisions are required, since rules usually have been defined covering almost all problems that might arise.

A typical task in a payroll office is the processing of paychecks for company employees who work at an hourly rate.[1] This job involves calculating total earnings by multiplying each employee's hourly wage rate by the number of hours worked, taking into consideration any overtime; figuring and then deducting taxes, insurance, contributions to charity, etc.; then making out the necessary check and entering a record of all figures. Figure 1.1 is a flowchart of a possible procedure. Flowcharts such as this are standard tools of business and are used often by the computing industry. Such flowcharts are very useful in reducing problems to the necessary steps required and are an invaluable aid in the field of programming. The example given deliberately omits overtime rates, irregular taxes such as FICA, and other such complicating features. The procedure followed by a clerk in performing this sequence of computations might be as follows:

1 The clerk looks up the employee's daily work record and adds the number of hours worked each day, obtaining the total number of hours worked during the week.

2 The total number of hours worked is multiplied by the pay rate, and the total earnings for the week are obtained.

3 The total earnings are multiplied by the tax rate for the employee, and the amount of withholding tax is found.

4 The withholding tax is subtracted from the total earnings.

5 Any regular deductions such as insurance are subtracted.

6 A record of each of the above operations is entered in the company books, and a check is made out for the correct amount.

Clearly almost all the above procedures can be mechanized by a machine which can be made to add, multiply, and subtract in the correct sequence. The machine also must have the following less obvious features:

1 The ability to remember the intermediate results that have been obtained. For instance, the total amount earned must be remembered while the tax is being figured. It is also convenient to keep the employee's pay rate, rate of withholding tax, insurance rates, and the amount regularly given to charity in the machine.

2 The ability to accept information. The records of time worked, changes in pay rates, deduction amounts, etc., must be entered into the machine.

3 The ability to print out the results obtained.

---

[1] It is interesting that 95 percent of the checks issued by the federal government are made out by computers.

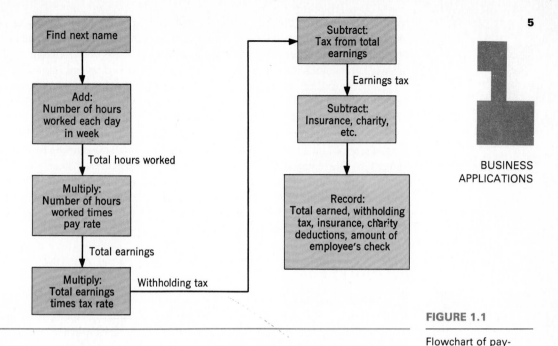

FIGURE 1.1

Flowchart of pay-
check calculation.

The widespread acceptance of digital computers in payroll offices is largely due to the repetitious type of work normally done there. Mechanization of such tasks is straightforward, although often complicated; but the additional accuracy and speed, as well as the lower operating costs, which electronic business machines make possible, has made their use especially popular in this field.

BUSINESS APPLICATIONS

1.3   The main difference between the use of digital machines in business and in scientific work lies in the ratio of operations performed to total data processed. While the business machine performs only a few calculations using each datum, a great volume of data must be processed. The scientific problem generally starts with fewer data, but a great many calculations are performed using each datum. Both types of machines still fall under the heading of digital computers, and either type of work may be done on all computers, although some machines may be better adapted to one or the other type of problem.

The description of the use of a computer in figuring payrolls (Sec. 1.2) is an example of a business application and illustrates the similarity in programming the operation of a computer and figuring out employee office procedures. First, the problem to be solved is reduced to a series of simple operations: finding the name of the next employee whose wages are to be computed, figuring how many hours he or she has worked, and multiplying this figure by the hourly rate of pay. After the procedure to be used has been worked out and explained to the clerk, the clerk is provided with the necessary numerical information, such as pay rates, insurance rates, etc. If the operations are further simplified, each step in Fig. 1.1 may be performed by a different clerk. For instance, the first clerk may find the employee's

record and send it to the second clerk, who computes the total number of hours worked and presents it to the next clerk, who multiplies by the wage rate, and so on, until all the operations have been performed. Thus the breaking down of business procedures into basic steps is a very old practice indeed.

The procedure for preparing a list of instructions for a digital computer is basically the same. All the operations the computer is to perform are written in flowchart form (Fig. 1.1). Then the problem is broken down into a list of instructions to the computer which specify exactly how the solution is to be obtained. After the problem has been programmed, the list of instructions is read into the computer. The computer automatically performs the required steps. Notice that once the procedure has been established and the programmed steps have been read in, the programming is finished until a change in procedure is desired. Changes in rates, for instance, can be inserted by simply reading the new pay rates into the machine. This does not affect the procedure.

SCIENTIFIC APPLICATIONS

1.4 Modern science and engineering use mathematics as a language for expressing physical laws in precise terms. The electronic digital computer is a valuable tool for studying the consequences of these laws. Often the exact procedure for solving a problem has been found, but the time required to perform the necessary calculations manually is prohibitive. Sometimes it is necessary to solve the same problem many times with different sets of parameters, and the computer is especially useful for solving problems of this type. Not only is the computer able to evaluate types of mathematical expressions at high speeds; but also if a set of calculations is performed repeatedly on different sets of numerical values, the computer can compare the results and determine the optimum values that were used.

An algebraic formula is an expression of a mathematical relationship. Many of the laws of physics, electronics, chemistry, etc., are expressed in this form, in which case digital computers may be easily used, because algebraic formulas may be directly changed to the basic steps they represent. Figure 1.2 is a flowchart illustrating the steps necessary to evaluate the expression $ax^3 + bx^2 + cx + d$, given numerical values for a, b, c, d, and x. The required steps are as follows:

1 Multiply a times x, yielding ax.

2 Add b, yielding $ax + b$.

3 Multiply this by x, forming $ax^2 + bx$.

4 Add c, yielding $ax^2 + bx + c$.

5 Multiply this by x: $x(ax^2 + bx + c)$, or $ax^3 + bx^2 + cx$.

6 Add d, obtaining $ax^3 + bx^2 + cx + d$.

It would take several minutes to perform the calculations necessary to evaluate this algebraic expression for a single set of values by using manually operated calculators, but practically any computer could perform this series of operations

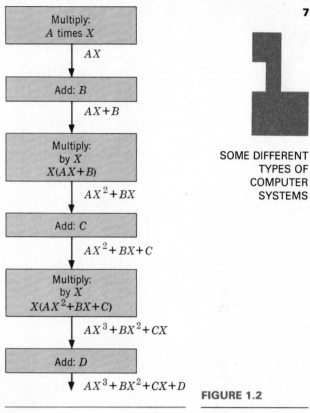

The flowchart shows:

Multiply:
A times X

AX

Add: B

$AX+B$

Multiply:
by X
$X(AX+B)$

AX^2+BX

Add: C

AX^2+BX+C

Multiply:
by X
$X(AX^2+BX+C)$

AX^3+BX^2+CX

Add: D

AX^3+BX^2+CX+D

FIGURE 1.2

Flowchart of evaluation of expression.

several thousand times per second. Although the algebraic expression shown is certainly much simpler than many formulas encountered by members of the engineering and scientific professions, the value of using a computer for certain types of problems may be readily seen.

SOME DIFFERENT TYPES OF COMPUTER SYSTEMS

1.5 A familiar early use of computers is in operating programs punched into cards (or perhaps recorded on paper or magnetic tape) and run by a computer which then prepares printouts, checks, or some form of data presentation recording the results. This is an example of *batch processing*. When a computer is used in this way, the input data (and often the program) are introduced to the computer and processed automatically, generally without operator intervention. Often many different jobs (or sets of data) are processed, one right after the other, or even at the same time, but without any interaction from the system's user during program operation. For instance, the keypunch operators may punch many decks of cards containing data on customers and claims. Then these cards are stacked and transported to a large computer which processes the cards, issuing checks, sending out bills, printing records for the company, etc. This is batch processing.

Similarly, the user of a computer in a scientific laboratory may submit program cards and data cards as a *job,* with an elastic band around these, along with

COMPUTER
OPERATION

any notes to the operators of the machine. A number of these decks of cards are collected, stacked, and finally run by the computer. Later the results are printed and, perhaps even the next day, delivered to the individual users. This is also batch processing.

In other types of systems, users interact with the computer directly, inserting and receiving the data as desired. For instance, an airline ticket agent wishes to make a reservation. The agent types the desired aircraft flight number and passenger identification on a special typewriter which communicates, via the telephone lines, with a computer. The computer looks in its memory; sees whether the flight is full, and, if not, enters the passenger's name on its list for the flight; and then communicates this fact back to the airline ticket agent. If no seats are available, the computer sends this information to the ticket agent, who attempts to interest the passenger in another flight. In this way an airline connects all its ticket agents, keeping a constant record of flights, passengers, and payments and doing all the bookkeeping. The terminals where the ticket agents are located are scattered throughout the world, but communicate with the computer via telephone lines. Motels, hotels, stockbrokers, and many businesses have similar systems for reservations, information transferral, and bookkeeping.

All these are called *interactive* systems, for the users of the system com-

FIGURE 1.3

(*a*) Personal computer with CRT display. (*b*) Computer terminal with a printer. (*DEC, Inc.*)

(*a*)

municate directly with the computer, and the computer responds directly. The development of these systems has progressed in parallel with the development of keyboard input devices, as well as output devices for users of various types, including cathode-ray tube (CRT) displays, printers, and other data display devices.

Interactive systems are widely employed in scientific applications where users operate their programs at a terminal connected to the computer, perhaps by telephone lines, trying changes and variations at will. Experimenters can try a set of inputs and study the results, then try other inputs and study these results. The technique of interactive computing is used by circuit designers, architects, and chemists, and in almost any area, including medical systems for hospital use.

Personal, or home, computers are also examples of interactive systems since the user communicates directly with the computer, inputting data and sometimes programs, and directly receiving results. Fig. 1.3(*a*) shows a personal computer with a keyboard and CRT display.

A widely used input-output device is the *terminal,* shown in Fig. 1.3(*b*). This is an example of a keyboard which is typewriterlike, generating a printed record when used, but also generating electric signals that can be used as computer input. Similarly, electronic signals from a computer can be used to control the

(*b*)

**COMPUTER
OPERATION**

terminal, and the terminal's printer will type, under the computer's control, the results of calculations.

Terminals are sometimes used in systems in which the console terminal is some distance from the computer. A special attachment called a *modem* is used, which makes it possible to transmit the electric signals generated by the terminal to the computer and receive the computer's response back over telephone lines. At the computer another modem is located which also can transmit or receive, and this allows communication in both directions over telephone lines. The user of the terminal simply dials the number at which the computer is located, establishes a connection and the user's identity and right to use the computer (the computer generally checks a password), and then proceeds to use the computer.

Terminal characteristics are fairly well standardized, and the same terminals often can use several different computers, when available. Now many companies provide computer service to users who have terminals at their disposal. The users simply dial the computer they prefer.

Figure 1.4 shows a terminal with a CRT display which is similar to a television, thus providing a temporary display (instead of *hard copy,* which is the printed page). This type of output device enables the computer to draw pictures or make graphs as well as use printed characters.

The computer terminal in Fig. 1.4 is portable. An attachment on the rear called an *acoustic coupler* which holds a telephone handset is provided so that

FIGURE 1.4

Portable computer terminal with CRT display. (*Logitron, Inc.*)

Oscilloscope display

Keyboard

when the telephone handset is placed in the attachment, a computer can be dialed. Once the connection is made, the terminal then generates audio tones into the handset when keys are depressed on the keyboard. The terminal receiver also decodes coded tones representing characters generated by the computer, displaying the information received on the CRT display device. In this way the user of a terminal can "converse," or communicate, with any compatible computer connected to the telephone system.

An acoustic coupler generates and receives audio signals from the handset while a modem uses electric signals and is connected directly into a telephone jack. For this reason acoustic couplers are often used in portable terminals.

When a number of users share a computer, using the computer, sometimes via telephone lines, at the same time, the computer is said to be *timeshared*. By timesharing is meant that the computer is able to alternate and interweave the running of its programs so that several jobs or users can be on at the same time. This makes for more efficient use, and the airline, motel, and hotel reservation systems and most online systems use timesharing.

COMPUTERS IN CONTROL SYSTEMS

1.6 The ability of digital computers to make precise calculations and decisions at high speeds has made it possible to use them as parts of control systems. The Air Traffic Control System used at airports is an example of computer usage in a control system. In this system, data from a network of radar stations, which are used to detect the positions of all aircraft in the area, are fed via communication links into a high-speed computer. The computer stores all the incoming positional information from the radar stations and from this calculates the future positions of the aircraft, their speed and altitude, and all other pertinent information. A number of other types of information are also relayed into the computer, including information from picket ships, AEW aircraft, Ground Observer Corps aircraft spotters, flight plans for both military and civilian aircraft, and weather information.

A computer receives all this information and from it calculates a composite picture of the complete air situation. The computer then generates displays on special oscilloscopes which are used by air traffic controllers. By means of radio links, the computer automatically guides aircraft in and out of airports.

A system of this sort is called a *real-time control system* because information must be processed and decisions must be made in real time. When a computer is used to process business data or to perform most scientific calculations, time is not as critical a factor. In real-time systems, the computer must "keep up," processing all data at high speeds in order to be effective.[2]

Other examples of real-time control applications include oil refineries and other manufacturing areas which use the computer to control the manufacturing processes automatically. Digital computers are used to guide machine tools which perform precision-machining operations automatically, as shown in Fig. 1.5. Fur-

---

[2]Most reservation systems would be considered real-time systems by their operators, since delays of any consequence would be detrimental to business.

Reporting terminal
with hand-held scanner

FIGURE 1.5

Computer-controlled
machine tools with
interactive terminal-
based plant commu-
nication system.
(IBM.)

ther, both staffed and nonstaffed space vehicles carry digital computers which perform the necessary guidance functions, while a network of computers on the ground monitors and directs the progress of the flight.

Most real-time control systems require an important device known as an *analog-to-digital (A/D) converter*. The inputs to these systems in many cases are in the form of *analog quantities* such as mechanical displacements (for instance, shaft positions) or temperatures, voltages, pressures, etc. Since the digital computer operates on digital rather than analog data, a fundamental "language" problem arises which requires the conversion of the analog quantities to digital representations. The A/D converter does this.

The same problem occurs at the computer output, where it is often necessary to convert numerical output data from the computer to mechanical displacements or analog-type electric signals. For instance, a "number" output from the computer might be used to rotate a shaft through the number of revolutions indicated by the output number. A device which converts digital-type information to analog quantities is called a *digital-to-analog (D/A) converter*. A description of both A/D and D/A converters is found in Chap. 7.

The basic elements of a control system using a digital computer consist of (1) the data-gathering devices which perform measurements on the external environment and, if necessary, also perform analog-to-digital conversion on the data from the system to be controlled; (2) the digital computer itself, which performs calculations on the data supplied and makes the necessary decisions; and (3) the means of communication with, or control over, certain of the elements in the external environment. If no person aids the computer in its calculations or decisions, the system is considered to be fully automatic; if a human being also enters the control loop, the system is defined as semiautomatic.

Figure 1.5 shows a computer being used in a manufacturing application. Because of their high speed, computers, often operating unattended, can measure, test, analyze, and control manufacturing functions as they occur. Computers can handle shop floor control, quality control testing, materials handling, and production monitoring. The typewriterlike station to the left in Fig. 1.5 is used to communicate with the system.

BASIC COMPONENTS OF A DIGITAL COMPUTER

1.7   The block diagram in Fig. 1.6 illustrates the five major operational divisions of an electronic digital computer. Although presently available machines vary greatly in the construction details of various components, the overall system concepts remain roughly the same.

A digital computer may be divided into the following fundamental units:

1   *Input*   The input devices read the necessary data into the machine. In most general-purpose computers, the instructions that constitute the program must be read into the machine along with all the data to be used in the computations. Some of the more common input devices are keyboards, punched-card and punched-paper-tape readers, magnetic-tape readers, and various manual input devices such as toggle switches and pushbuttons.

2   *Control*   The control section of a computer sequences the operation of the computer, controlling the actions of all other units. The control circuitry interprets

FIGURE 1.6

Block diagram of typical digital computer.

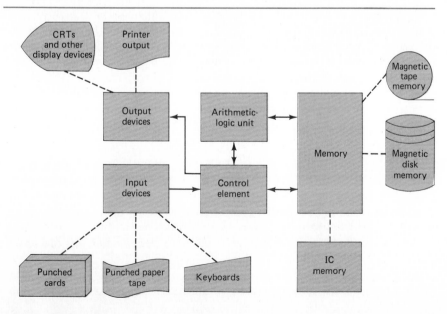

**COMPUTER
OPERATION**

the instructions which constitute the program and then directs the rest of the machine in its operation.

3   *Memory*   The memory, or storage, section of the computer consists of the devices used to store the information that will be used during the computations. The memory section of the computer is also used to hold both intermediate and final results as the computer proceeds through the program. Memory devices are constructed so that it is possible for the control unit to obtain any information in the memory. The time required to obtain information may vary somewhat, however, and is determined by the type of device used to store the information. Common storage devices are integrated-circuit memories, magnetic tape, and magnetic disks.

4   *Arithmetic-logic unit*   The arithmetic-logic units of most computers are capable of performing addition, subtraction, division, and multiplication as well as some "logical operations" which are described later. The control unit tells the arithmetic-logic unit which operation to perform and then sees that the necessary numbers are supplied. The arithmetic element can be compared to the calculating machines described previously in that the numbers to be used are inserted, and it is then directed to perform the necessary operations.

5   *Output*   The output devices are used to record the results obtained by the computer and present them to the outside world. Most output devices are directed by the control element, which also causes the necessary information to be supplied to them. Common output devices are CRT displays, printers, card-punching machines, and magnetic-tape drives. There are also many other types of output devices, such as lights, buzzers, and loudspeakers.

CONSTRUCTION OF MEMORY

1.8   The inner, or high-speed, memory is broken into a number of addresses, or locations. At each address a group of digits is stored and is handled by the computer as a unit. The group of digits stored at each address in memory is generally referred to as a memory *word*.[3] Each address in memory is assigned a number, and then the address is referred to by that number. We say that address 100 contains the value 300 or that address 50 contains an instruction word. In most computers, instruction words may be stored in the same locations as number or data words, which makes the memory more flexible. Notice also that instruction words, when stored in the computer, consist of a group of digits.

The time it takes to obtain a word from a storage device is called the *access*

---

[3]There are actually two ways of organizing a memory now in general use. One way is to store enough bits for a character at each address (a character is a 1 or 2, an A or B, etc.). These systems are called *character-addressable* or byte-addressable, systems. The second way is to store a complete *operand*, or instruction word, at each address. These systems are called *word-addressable* systems. As might be guessed, word-addressable systems have more information at each address. The character-addressable systems are more used, but we simplify the initial description by assuming that each successive address contains a word, as in word-addressable systems, and describe other systems later.

time. The access time of the storage devices used in a machine has a profound effect on the speed of the computer. One factor which for a long time impeded the construction of high-speed computers was the lack of reliable storage devices with short access times. The development of storage devices (such as integrated-circuit memories) with very short access times plus the ability to store information for an indefinite time was a great forward step.

INSTRUCTIONS

1.9 Computers can make simple logical decisions. Many of these decisions are based on numbers and so are quantitative rather than qualitative. The sort of numerical decision the computer might make is whether one number is larger than another or whether the result of some series of calculations is positive or negative. However, most decisions made by clerical workers and scientists are also based on figures. For instance, once physical phenomena have been expressed in formulas, the solutions to specific problems are expressed by means of numbers.

As mentioned, the digital computer does not figure out its own solution to problems, but must be told exactly how to solve any given problem as well as how to make all decisions. Preparing a list of instructions which tells the computer how to perform its calculations is called programming. The procedure for programming a problem generally consists of two separate steps. The first step, planning the program, involves determining the sequence of operations required to solve the problem. It sometimes consists in breaking the problem down into flow diagrams such as those illustrated earlier. Once the problem has been reduced to this form, it is ready to be *coded;* this is the second step. *Coding* consists in writing the steps outlined in the flowchart in a special language which can be interpreted by the computer. The final coded program consists of a list of instructions to the computer, written in a special format which details the operations the computer is to perform.[4]

We now describe a type of computer language called *assembly language*. The instruction words which direct the computer are stored in the computer in numerical form. The programmer rarely writes instructions in numerical form, however; instead, each instruction to the computer is written by using a letter code to designate the operation to be performed, plus the address in memory of the number to be used in this step of the calculation.[5] Later the alphabetic section of the instruction word is converted to numerical form by a computer program called an *assembler*. This is described later.

An instruction word as written by the programmer consists of two parts: (1) the *operation-code* part, which designates the operation (addition, subtraction, multiplication, etc.) to be performed, and (2) the *address* of the number to be used.

---

[4]The instructions described are typical instructions for a *single-address* computer. Computers are also constructed which use two or more addresses in each computer instruction word. These computers are described in Chap. 10. The single-address type of instruction is very straightforward and is used in the illustrations in this chapter.

[5]The following is a description of *machine-language* or *assembly-language,* programming. Applications are often written in a *high-level* language such as BASIC, Fortran, or Pascal which then must be translated to machine language before the computer can run the program.

16

COMPUTER
OPERATION

A typical instruction word written by the programmer is

ADD 535

This instruction word is divided into two main parts: first, the operation-code part, consisting of the letters ADD, which directs the computer to perform the arithmetic operation of addition; and second, the address part, which tells the computer the address in storage of the number to be used.

Note that the second section of the instruction word gives only the location (address) in storage of the number to be added. The number 535 in the instruction shown is not the actual number to be added, but only tells the computer where to find the desired number. To what is the number at address 535 added? It is to be added to the number which is already in the arithmetic-logic unit in a storage device, or register, called an *accumulator*. If the accumulator contains zero before the instruction is executed, the accumulator will contain the number which is stored at address 535 after the instruction has been performed. If the accumulator contains the number 500 before the instruction is performed and if the number stored at address 535 is 200, then the number stored in the accumulator after the ADD operation will be 700. To illustrate this principle more fully, several more instructions are explained in Table 1.1.

TABLE 1.1

INSTRUCTION WORD		FUNCTION PERFORMED BY INSTRUCTION
OPERATION CODE	ADDRESS PART	
CLA	430	The accumulator is emptied of all previous numbers, and the number at address 430 is added to it. After the instruction is performed, the accumulator contains the number in storage at address 430. CLA is a mnemonic code for "clear and add."
ADD	530	The number located at address 530 is added to the number in the accumulator. After the instruction, the accumulator contains the sum of the number it previously contained and the number in address 530.
SUB	235	The number located at address 235 in the memory is subtracted from the number in the accumulator, and the difference is placed in the accumulator.
STO	433	The number in the accumulator is stored at address 433. Any information previously in this address is destroyed. The number which was in the accumulator before the instruction was performed remains in the accumulator. This is generally referred to as a STORE instruction.
HLT	000	The machine is ordered to stop. The number in the accumulator remains.

TABLE 1.2

| ADDRESS IN MEMORY | INSTRUCTION WORD | | CONTENTS OF ACCUMULATOR AFTER INSTRUCTION IS PERFORMED |
	OPERATION CODE	ADDRESS PART	
1	CLA	6	200
2	ADD	7	500
3	ADD	8	900
4	STO	9	900
5	HLT	0	900
6 contains the number 200			
7 contains the number 300			
8 contains the number 400			

A short program which adds three numbers by using these instructions is shown in Table 1.2.

The program operates as follows: The control section starts with the instruction word at address 1, which clears the accumulator and then adds the number at address 6 into it. The instruction at address 2 adds the number at address 7 to the number already in the accumulator. This produces the sum of 200 + 300, or 500. The third instruction adds the contents of address 8 to this sum, giving 900 in the accumulator. This number is then stored in memory at location 9 in the memory. The machine is ordered to halt. Notice that the machine is stopped before it reaches the data. This is to prevent the control element from picking up the data, for instance, the number 200, which is at address 6, and trying to use it as an instruction.

There is no difference between a number and an instruction as far as storage is concerned. Both are stored in the same basic form. So the instructions are generally placed in a different section of the memory from the data to be used. The computer progresses through the instructions and is stopped before it reaches the data. The fact that either instructions or data may be stored at all addresses makes the machine more flexible. Either a large amount of data and a few instructions, or many instructions and few data, can be used as long as the total amount of storage available is not exceeded.

MULTIPLICATION INSTRUCTION

1.10 By adding another instruction, multiplication, it will be possible to write more sophisticated programs (see Table 1.3).

TABLE 1.3

| INSTRUCTION WORD | | |
OPERATION CODE	ADDRESS PART	FUNCTION
MUL	400	The number at address 400 is multiplied by the number already in the accumulator, and the product is placed in the accumulator.

	INSTRUCTION WORD		
ADDRESS IN MEMORY	OPERATION CODE	ADDRESS PART	CONTENTS OF ACCUMULATOR AFTER INSTRUCTION IS PERFORMED
1	CLA	22	a
2	MUL	26	ax
3	ADD	23	$ax + b$
4	MUL	26	$x(ax + b)$ or $ax^2 + bx$
5	ADD	24	$ax^2 + bx + c$
6	MUL	26	$x(ax^2 + bx + c)$ or $ax^3 + bx^2 + cx$
7	ADD	25	$ax^3 + bx^2 + cx + d$
8	STO	27	$ax^3 + bx^2 + cx + d$
9	HLT	000	$ax^3 + bx^2 + cx + d$

TABLE 1.4

22 contains a
23 contains b
24 contains c
25 contains d
26 contains x
27 contains 0

The program in Table 1.4 evaluates the expression $ax^3 + bx^2 + cx + d$. The actual quantities for a, b, c, d, and x are stored in memory at locations 22, 23, 24, 25, and 26, respectively. Notice that the program shown evaluates the expression for any values which might be read into these locations. The expression could be evaluated for any number of values for x by running the program for one value of x, then substituting the succeeding values of x into register 26, and re-running the program for each value. In practice, it is possible to have the program automatically repeat itself by means of special instructions. All the various desired values for x can be stored and the equation solved for each x without stopping the computer.

It can be seen from Table 1.4 that very complicated algebraic functions can be evaluated by using only a very few instructions. The program shown can be performed by a high-speed computer in less than 1/1,000,000 second(s). The value of such speed in the solution of the more complex problems encountered in engineering and science may be readily seen. Computers are making possible engineering techniques which were previously unusable because of the high costs in time and money of lengthy computations.

BRANCH, SKIP, OR JUMP INSTRUCTIONS

1.11   All the instructions explained so far have been used to perform problems in simple arithmetic. However, the computer is able to repeat the same sequence of instructions without being stopped and restarted. This facility is provided by a group of instructions referred to as *branch*, *skip*, or *jump* instructions. These instructions tell the computer not to perform the instruction at the address following that of the instruction being performed, but to skip to some other instruction. Some branch instructions are *unconditional* in nature and cause the computer to skip regardless of what the conditions may be. Other branch instructions are *conditional* and tell the computer to skip only if certain things are true. Branch instructions

TABLE 1.5

OPERATION CODE	ADDRESS PART	FUNCTION
BRA	420	This instruction tells the computer to perform the instruction at address 420 next. The computer will skip or branch from the instruction it would have performed and perform instruction 420 instead. Then the computer will perform instruction 421, followed by 422, etc.
BRM	420	The computer will branch to instruction 420 only if the number in the accumulator is negative. If the number is positive or zero, the computer will not branch, but will perform the instruction stored at the next address in memory. BRM is a mnemonic code for "branch on minus."

BRANCH, SKIP, OR JUMP INSTRUCTIONS

enable the computer to make logical choices which alter its future actions. Two typical instructions are shown in Table 1.5.

The short program shown in Table 1.6 illustrates several very important principles. The purpose of the program is to add all the even integers from 2 to 100. The program is of the repetitious sort where a few short orders are used to generate a program which runs for some time by repeating the same sequence of instructions. The program illustrates how the ability to branch on a negative number can be used to form a counter that will determine how many times a part of a program is repeated.

The number stored in location 39 increases by 2 each time the program runs through. The total of these numbers is stored in address 43 which, after the program has halted, contains the total of all the numbers that have been in location 39. The number stored at address 40 decreases in magnitude by 1 each time the program

TABLE 1.6

	INSTRUCTION WORD		CONTENTS OF ACCUMULATOR		
ADDRESS	OPERATION CODE	ADDRESS PART	1ST TIME	2D TIME	LAST TIME
1	CLA	39	0	2	98
2	ADD	41	2	4	100
3	STO	39	2	4	100
4	ADD	43	2	6	$2 + 4 + 6 + \cdots + 100$
5	STO	43	2	6	$2 + 4 + 6 + \cdots + 100$
6	CLA	40	-50	-49	-1
7	ADD	42	-49	-48	$+0$
8	STO	40	-49	-48	$+0$
9	BRM	1	-49	-48	$+0$
10	HLT	000			

39 contains 000
40 contains -50
41 contains 2
42 contains 1
43 contains 0

runs through, until the number stored at 40 is no longer negative. When the program "falls through" the BRANCH WHEN MINUS (BRM) instruction, it performs the next instruction in sequence, which is a HALT instruction. Zero is considered to be a positive number, although this varies with different machines. Notice that the first section of the program will cycle a number of times equal to the negative number stored in register 40. A simulated counter is formed by the −50 stored at address 40, the 1 stored in location 42, and the instructions at addresses 6 through 9. Any sequence of instructions which precedes a counter of this sort will be run through the number of times determined by the counter. This is an especially useful device for iterative schemes when the number of iterations required is known.

PROGRAMMING SYSTEMS

1.12   The preceding discussion showed a basic procedure for writing an assembly-language program. There are, however, various types of *programming languages* which greatly facilitate the actual writing of programs. One of the first things the programming profession discovered was that the greatest aid to programming was the computer itself. It was found to be capable of translating written programs from a language which was straightforward and natural for the programmer to computer, or machine, language.

As a result, programs were written whose purpose was to read other programs written in a language natural for the programmer and to translate them into the computer's language. The program systems now in use are primarily of two types: *assemblers* and *compilers*.[6] The assembler and the compiler are intended for the same basic purpose: Each is a program designed to read a program written in a programming language and to translate it. The assembler or compiler is read into the computer first and then is followed by the program to be translated. After translation the assembler or compiler generally stores the machine-language program on magnetic disks or tape or in some other kind of memory so that it can be performed when desired.

The purpose of this procedure is to enable programmers to write the operations they want the computer to perform in a manner that is simpler than machine language. The language which the programmer writes is called a *programming language,* and a program written in such a language is called a *source program.* The translated program in machine (or some intermediate) language is called an *object program.*

To return to the subject of the translator programs, an assembly language differs from a compiler language in that most assembly languages closely resemble machine languages, primarily because each instruction to the computer in assembly language is translated to a single computer word. In compiler systems, a single instruction to the computer may be converted to many computer words.

---

[6]There is also a translator type of program that translates one line or statement at a time, called an *interpreter,* and is used with such programming languages as BASIC. Each statement is run by the computer after translation. Interpreters perform the some general functions as compilers but need not translate an entire program before operation.

1.13 Each instruction to the computer in a programming language is called a *statement*. The basic characteristic which most distinguishes an assembly language is that each statement is translated by the assembly program to a single machine instruction word.[7] As a result, an assembly language resembles machine language. The facilities offered the programmer are substantial, however, and generally include the following:

1   *Mnemonic operation codes*   The programmer can write instructions to the computer using letters instead of binary numbers, and the letters which designate a given operation are arranged into a mnemonic code that conveys the ''sense'' of the instruction. In the preceding example of coding, the mnemonic codes ADD, MUL, CLA, etc., were used. The assembler would translate these mnemonic codes to the correct machine binary numbers and ''package'' these into the instruction words constituting the object program.

2   *Symbolic referencing of storage addresses*   One of the greatest facilities offered the programmer is the ability to name the different pieces of data used in the program and to have the assembler automatically assign addresses to each name.

If we wish to evaluate the algebraic expression $y = ax^3 + bx^2 + cx + d$ as in Sec. 1.10, the program can appear as shown in Table 1.7.

Notice that the address of the first instruction was simply given the name FST, consisting of three letters, and that no further addresses in memory were specified. If we tell the assembler that FST $= 1$, the assembler will see that the instructions are placed in memory as in the program in Sec. 1.10. Notice also that the operands were simply given the variable names X, A, B, C, and D, as in the equation, instead of assigning addresses in memory to them. The assembly program will assign addresses to these names of variables, and if it assigns A to 22, B to 23, C to 24, etc., the final program will look as in Sec. 1.10.

---

[7]This is not, of course, strictly the case (sometimes a single statement may be translated to several words), but generally translation is into a single instruction word that can require one or more memory locations or words.

TABLE 1.7	INSTRUCTION WORD	
ADDRESS IN MEMORY	OPERATION	OPERAND
FST	CLA	A
	MUL	X
	ADD	B
	MUL	X
	ADD	C
	MUL	X
	ADD	D
	STO	Y
	HLT	

The assembler will also see that actual arithmetic values for X, A, B, C, and D are placed in the correct locations in memory when the data are read into the computer.

3 *Convenient data representation* This simply means that the programmer can write input data as, for instance, decimal numbers or letters, or perhaps in some form specific to the problem, and that the assembly program will convert the data from this form to the form required for machine computation.

4 *Program listings* An important feature of most assemblers is their ability to print for the programmer a listing of the source program and the object program, which is in machine language. A study of these listings will greatly help the programmer in finding any errors made in writing the program and in modifying the program when this is required.

5 *Error detection* An assembler program will notify the programmer if an error has been made in the usage of the assembly language. For example, the programmer may use the same variable name, for instance, X, twice and then give X two different values; or the programmer may write illegal operation codes, etc. This sort of diagnosis of a program's errors is very useful during the checking out of a new program.

Assemblers provide many other facilities which help the programmer, such as the ability to use programs which have already been written as part of a new program and the ability to use routines from these programs as part of a new program. Often programmers have a set of different programs which they will run together in different combinations. This is made possible simply by specifying to the assembler the variable names in the different programs which are to be the same variable, the entry and exit points for the programs, etc. Thus programs written in an assembly language can be linked together in various ways

Let us consider the short program in Table 1.6 which sums the even integers from 0 to 100. This will illustrate the use of symbolic names for addresses when a branch instruction is used. The assembly-language program is shown in Table 1.8.

TABLE 1.8			
	INSTRUCTION WORDS		
ADDRESS	OPERATION	OPERAND	COMMENTS
A	DEC	0	
B	DEC	-50	
C	DEC	2	
D	DEC	1	
E	DEC	0	
N	CLA	A	Last value of integer
	ADD	C	
	STO	A	Stores sum for next time
	ADD	E	
	STO	E	
	CLA	B	
	ADD	D	
	STO	B	
	BRM	N	
	HLT		

Notice that the values of the variables were specified before the program was begun; DEC indicates that the values given for A, B, C, D, and E are in decimal. This enables the assembler to locate the variables in the memory and assign values to them.[8] Also note that the transfer instruction BRM was to the symbolic address N.

If the assembler were told to start the program at address 1 in the memory, conversion to object or machine language would make it look similar to the one in Sec. 1.10, provided the assembler decided to store A, B, C, D, and E in locations 39 through 43.

HIGH-LEVEL LANGUAGES

1.14 More advanced types of programming languages are called *compiler languages, high-level languages,* or *problem-oriented languages*. These are the simplest languages to use for most problems and are the simplest to learn. These languages often reveal very little about the digital machines on which they are run, however. The designer of the language generally concentrates on specifying a programming language that is simple enough for the casual user of a digital computer and yet has enough facilities to make the language and its associated compiler valuable to professional programmers. In fact, many languages are almost completely computer-independent, and programs written in one of these languages may be run on any computer that has a compiler or translator for the language in its program library.

Certain languages have been very successful and have found extremely wide usage in the computer industry. The best known are Fortran, Pascal, BASIC, and Cobol. A program written in these langauges can be run on most computers that have a memory size large enough to accommodate a compiler, because most manufacturers will prepare a compiler for each of these for their computer.

The following section gives an introduction to a specific high-level language. Those who are familiar with languages such as BASIC, Fortran, or Cobol may omit it. The text is arranged so that subsequent material in the book does not depend on the following section, and this section can be omitted or studied at a later time.

A SHORT INTRODUCTION TO PASCAL

*1.15[9] The distinguishing feature of a compiler and its associated programming language is that a single statement which the programmer writes can be converted by the compiler to a number of machine-language instructions. In Pascal, for instance, a single statement to the computer can generate quite a number of instructions in object, or machine, language. As a result, the language is not particularly dependent on the structure of the computer on which the program is run, and the following programs may be run on any computer with a Pascal compiler.

---

[8]In a sense, the operation code DEC says "assign the decimal value in the operand column to the variable name in the address column."

[9]All sections marked with an asterisk can be omitted on a first reading without loss of continuity or of overall understanding.

The Pascal compiler is written in assembly or machine language, and a Pascal program is ultimately run in machine language. For this reason, knowledge of the computer and its organization can be of great use to those writing and checking out programs. Further, for the systems programmers (those who maintain, modify, and prepare the compilers, assemblers, load programs, etc.) a knowledge of the computer on which the program is operated is indispensable. The fact that compilers and computers are backed up by an army of technical personnel—from systems programmers through design and maintenance engineers, technicians, and computer operators—is often overlooked by the user of the machine whose program is miraculously debugged and operated. Like most electronic devices, digital computers are not as independent and self-supporting as they may appear to casual users.

Thus forewarned, let us examine the structure of Pascal in a little detail, leaving a more complete exposition to one of the references.

To begin, consider the following simple complete Pascal program:

```
PROGRAM ADDNUMS;
VAR
    A, B, Y: INTEGER;
BEGIN
    A := 50;
    B :=20;
    Y := A + B
END.
```

The first line of any Pascal program must begin with the word PROGRAM, followed by the name of the program. The name of the above program is ADDNUMS. The section of program

```
VAR
    A, B, Y: INTEGER;
```

is called a *variable declaration section*. This declares the variables A, B, and Y to be of type INTEGER, specifying that A, B, and Y may assume integral values. The words BEGIN and END specify the starting and ending points of the section of the program which is ultimately run. The three lines

```
A := 50;
B := 20;
Y := A + B
```

are program *statements*. The statements specify the actions to be taken by the computer. When the program is run, the statements are executed in order, starting with the first statement after BEGIN and ending with the statement before END. Note that a semicolon is placed after each statement except the final END statement. Semicolons are used to separate statements in Pascal.

The three statements of this program are called *assignment* statements. An assignment statement acts to change the value of a given variable. The assignment operator is the ":=" sign. The variable name on the left side of the := symbol is the variable whose value is to be changed. The right side of the := symbol is an *expression* that determines the new value which the variable is to assume. For example, when writing Y := A + B; we mean "replace the current value of Y with that of A + B." Thus, after the three statements

$$A := 50;$$
$$B := 20;$$
$$Y := A + B$$

are executed, A will be equal to 50, B to 20, and Y to 70. As a further example, we can increase, decrease, or otherwise change the current value of Y by adding to or subtracting from it. Consider

A SHORT
INTRODUCTION
TO PASCAL

$$Y := 30;$$
$$A := 40;$$
$$Y := Y + A$$

After these statements are executed, Y will have the value of 70; that is, the location in memory that has been used to store Y will have the value 70 in it. Here is one further example:

$$Y := 20;$$
$$Z := 50;$$
$$W := Y + Z;$$
$$M := W - 30$$

After these statements are run, W will have the value 70 and M the value 40.

In Pascal, the addition symbol is the familiar plus sign; the subtraction symbol is the usual minus sign. Multiplication is indicated by an asterisk. Thus A * B means "multiply A by B." Therefore the program statements

$$A := 20;$$
$$B := 30;$$
$$C := A * B$$

give a value of 600 for C.

Let us examine one simple way to form a loop in the program, that is, to repeat a sequence of instructions until we desire to stop. This can be accomplished through use of the WHILE statement:

```
WHILE X <= Y DO
    BEGIN
        <sequence of statements>
    END;
```

The WHILE statement says "execute the set of statements between BEGIN and END while X is less than or equal to Y." In other words, repeat the sequence of

statements until Y is greater than X. If we write the statements

```
T := 0;
M := 4;
N := 2;
P := 6;
WHILE N <= M DO
  BEGIN
    S := P * N;
    T := T + S;
    N := N + 1
  END;
Y := T * 2;
```

then the statements between BEGIN and END will be repeated until N is greater than M. Since N starts with the value 2 (and as 1 is added each time) while M starts with the value 4, N will take the values 2, 3, 4, 5. But when N equals 5, it will be greater than M, and the program will proceed with the instruction Y: = T * 2. The statements between BEGIN and END, therefore, will be repeated three times. The first time S will equal P times N, or 12; T will be equal to 0 + S, or 12; and N will be increased from 2 to 3. The second time S will equal P times N, or 6 times 3, which is 18; T will be equal to 12 + 18, or 30; and N will be increased to 4. The third time S will equal 6 times 4, or 24; T will take the value 30 + 24, or 54; and N will be increased to 5. Then N will be greater than M, and the next statement after END; will be operated. Now T, which has the value 54, will be multiplied by 2, giving 108, and Y will be assigned this value.

Let us examine two other features. To read data, we simply write

$$READ \ (X, \ Y, \ Z);$$

This will tell the compiler to arrange for reading the values of X, Y, and Z from a keyboard and continue with the values read as the current values of X, Y, and Z. So we must supply values of X, Y, and Z from the keyboard. The advantage is that we can change the values of X, Y, and Z by simply typing new values each time the program is run. If we write

$$READ \ (X, \ Y, \ Z);$$
$$M := X + (Y * Z);$$

and input the values X = 20, Y = 30, and Z = 2, we have M = 80. If we change our input values to read X = 5, Y = 3, and Z = 4, then we have M = 17 after we run the above.

To print out data, we write the statement

$$WRITE \ (X, \ Y, \ Z, \ A);$$

and the computer will print out the current values of X, Y, Z, A.

Note that the READ and WRITE statements assume that the programmer will be satisfied with the standard format for the input data and print statements. Assuming that this is the case, we can write the following statements which will first evaluate the equation $y = ax^3 + bx^2 + cx + d$ for values of A, B, D, and X which are read in from the terminal and for C = 1. If the value of Y for these particular values is greater than 2000, the value of Y will be printed as calculated and also the value C + 1. If, however, Y is less than or equal to 2000, the statements will calculate the smallest positive integer which, when substituted into C, will make $ax^3 + bx^2 + cx + d$ greater than 2000. The WRITE statement will print this value of C and the value of $ax^3 + bx^2 + cx + d$ associated with the value of C.

```
READ (A, B, D, X);
C := 0;
Y := 0;
WHILE Y < = 2000 DO
  BEGIN
    C := C + 1;
    Y := A * X * X * X + B * X * X + C * X + D;
  END;
WRITE (C, Y);
```

We have only touched on the power of this language. It is not possible in a short exposition to do more than show several statements and give a general idea of how such a language operates. Nevertheless, a clever programmer could do quite a lot with the limited vocabulary we have introduced.

There is a Pascal microprocessor version of Pascal which is widely used; it was written at the University of California at San Diego (UCSD). The translators (compilers) for UCSD Pascal produce machine language that can be run on a microprocessor.

SUMMARY

1.16 Although the electronic computer is the newest and most important technological development in the last fifty years, the history of the computer extends back to the 19th century, when computers were first designed. The modern electronic digital computer is made possible by more recent developments in solid-state physics and engineering, however, and dates only to the 1940s and 1950s.

In order to use a computer to solve a scientific problem or implement an office procedure, it is necessary to organize the problem into clearly defined steps. A flowchart is most useful in organizing these steps. Then the procedure can be programmed, which consists of writing down the steps to be taken by the computer in a special language developed for computer usage.

The two most used classes of computer languages are *assembly language* and *higher-level,* or *application-oriented,* language. Assembly language resembles true machine language, mirroring the internal structure of the computer for which it is written. The higher-level languages such as Fortran, BASIC, Pascal, and Cobol are translated by a computer to the particular machine-language representation

COMPUTER
OPERATION

which the computer can run. The higher-level languages are specifically designed to facilitate their use by the programmer. Assembly languages also provide many aids to the programmer, but they basically correspond in structure to the specific computer on which they will run.

The five sections of a computer and typical devices that might be used in these sections were described. Detailed descriptions of the operation of these sections and devices are presented in the following chapters.

One thing which should become apparent from this brief introduction is that once the statement types and details of a high-level language are learned, the job of programming a given problem is greatly facilitated.

QUESTIONS

1.1 Discuss possible applications of microprocessors in real-time control systems.

1.2 The computer's ability to translate languages such as Pascal and Fortran greatly simplifies programming. Comment on the difficulty a computer might have in translating English. What about ambiguities? Must programming languages avoid them?

1.3 Sometimes the same computer is used by several different companies during the day, and the computer is timeshared between these companies. Discuss problems which might arise in billing the companies for the computer's services.

1.4 Discuss interactive computer systems and give examples of businesses and industries that might use interactive systems.

1.5 Discuss batch processing and give several examples of businesses and industries that might use it.

1.6 Give examples of industries that might use real-time control systems for manufacturing.

1.7 Values for X, Y, and Z are stored at memory addresses 40, 41, and 42, respectively. Using the instructions for the generalized single-address computer described in Secs. 1.9 to 1.11, write a program that will form the sum $X + Y + Z$ and store it at memory address 43.

1.8 Explain the difference between the *address* of a word in memory and the *word* itself.

1.9 Given that values for X, Y, and Z are stored in locations 20, 21, and 22, respectively, use the instructions for the computer given in Secs. 1.9 to 1.11 to write a program that will form $X^2 + Y^2 + Z^2$ and store this at memory address 40.

1.10 The program in Table 1.4 is run with the following values when it is started: 5 in address 22, 4 in address 23, 6 in address 24, 4 in address 25, and 2 in address 26. What value will be in address 27 after the program has been run?

1.11 Convert the flowchart in Fig. 1.2 to a computer assembly-language program, using the instructions described in the chapter.

1.12 If the program in Table 1.4 is started with location 22 containing 4, location 23 containing 4, location 24 containing 4, location 25 containing 1, and location 26 containing 2, what number will be stored in location 27 after the program is run?

1.13 Write a program that will store $X^5 + X$ in register 40, using the assembly language in Secs. 1.9 to 1.11, given that X is in register 20. Use fewer than 20 instructions. Now rewrite this program, using the assembly language in Sec 1.15.

1.14 If the program in Table 1.6 were operated but the number at address 40 were -30 instead of -50 when the program started, the number at address 43 would be the sum of all even integers from 2 to __ instead of 2 to 100.

1.15 Draw a flowchart for the program in Sec. 1.11.

1.16 Given that a value for X is stored at address 39, write a program that will form X^4 and store it at address 42, using the assembly language in Secs. 1.9 to 1.11.

1.17 Draw a flowchart showing how to find the largest number in a set of five numbers stored at locations 30, 31, 32, 33, and 34 in memory.

1.18 Values for X and Y are stored at addresses 30 and 31. Write a program that will store the larger of the two values at address 40, using the assembly language in Secs. 1.9 to 1.11.

1.19 Given three different numbers, determine whether they are in ascending or descending order. Draw a flowchart for the problem, and write a program, using the assembly language in Secs. 1.9 to 1.11. Assume that the numbers are stored in memory locations 30, 31, and 32.

1.20 A value for Y is stored at location 55 and a value for A at location 59. Write an assembly-language program to store AY^3 at location 40.

1.21 Write a program to find $ax^2 + by + cz^2$, with A in location 20, B in location 21, C in location 22, X in location 23, Y in location 24, and Z in location 25. Store your result in location 40.

1.22 A value for X is stored at address 40. Write a program that will store X^9 at address 45, using fewer than 10 instruction words.

1.23 Using the assembly language described in Secs. 1.9 to 1.11, write a program that will branch to location 300 if the number stored in memory register 25 is larger than the number stored in register 26 and which will transfer or branch to location 400 if the number at address 26 is equal to or larger than the number at address 25.

1.24 Write a program that will produce the value $Y - X$ or X, whichever is larger, in both the assembly language in Secs. 1.9 to 1.11 and the compiler language in Sec. 1.15. Store this value in location 300 for the assembly program, and assign the variable B to this value for the program written in the compiler language. For the assembly program, assume that X is in location 100 and Y in 101.

1.25 Calculate the largest of the three numbers A, B, and C and assign the largest

QUESTIONS

of the numbers to the variable X, using the assembly language in Sec. 1.13 to write the program.

1.26 Write a Pascal program that will assign the value 40 to variable C and the value 60 to variable D. Define C and D as being of type INTEGER.

1.27 Write a program in Pascal that will assign the value of 10 to A, 20 to B, and 5 to C, and which will then calculate the value $(A \times B)^C$ and assign this value to variable D. Declare A, B, C, and D to be of type INTEGER.

1.28 In Pascal what will be the value of D if we execute the statement D: = X + (Y * Z); when X has value 5, Y has value 2, and Z has value 2?

1.29 If the Pascal program which was used to illustrate the WHILE command is run with P having value 4, but with T, M, and N as in the program in the text, what will be the value of Y after the program is run?

1.30 Suppose that the final Pascal program in the text is run with values of 4 for A, 3 for B, 2 for D, and 2 for X. What values of C and Y will the program cause to be printed?

1.31 Modify the program in Sec. 1.11 so that it will sum all the odd numbers from 1 through 79.

1.32 We have 30 numbers stored in successive registers in our memory, starting at location 300. Write a program that will convert any negative numbers in the 30 to positive form. That is, write a program that will take the 30 numbers, convert each number to its positive value without changing its magnitude, and restore it in the same location. Use assembly language.

1.33 Write a program, using the assembly language in Secs. 1.9 to 1.11, which will rearrange five numbers stored in addresses 200 through 204 so that they are in descending order (for example, 10, 3, 0, −5, −7).

Additional questions on Pascal

1.34 In a nonparenthesized section of a given statement, the Pascal language performs first multiplication and division and then addition and subtraction. Within this hierarchy, statements are evaluated from left to right. Thus the statement A = ((B/C) − (D * E))/(C * D) can be written as A = (B/C − D * E)/(C * D). The following are four more examples of the way in which the compiler evaluates arithmetic statements:

(1) $(c \cdot d) + (e/f)$ can be written C * D + E/F.

(2) $(a \cdot b \cdot c) + (g/h)$ can be written A * B * C + G/H.

(3) $\dfrac{a \cdot b \cdot c}{d \cdot e}$ must be written (A * B * C)/(D * E).

(4) $(a \cdot b) + (c/d) + (e \cdot f)$ is written A * B + C/D + E * F.

Find the value of X in the following statements if A = 5, B = 2, C = 20, and D = 15:

(a) X = A * B + C   (b) X = C + D * B + A

(c) X = A * C * B   (d) X = C + D * B/A + A

1.35 In Pascal it is possible to write mathematical statements with subscripted variables, which are called *array variables;* that is, if we have a set of variables X_1, X_2, X_3, and X_4, we can write these in Pascal as X[1], X[2], X[3], and X[4]. Notice that the brackets do not indicate multiplication, but rather the fact that the variable is an array variable or a subscripted variable. Now, if we write in a program X[K], whether this indicates X[1] or X[2] or X[3] or X[4], for instance, depends on the value of the variable K at that particular time. What are the values of X in each of the following statements if A[1] = 3, A[2] = 4, A[3] = 5, and K = 1?

(*a*) X = A[1] + A[2]   (*b*) Y = A[2] * A[1] + A[3]

(*c*) X = A[K] + A[2] * A[3]   (*d*) Y = A[K + 2] + A[K]

QUESTIONS

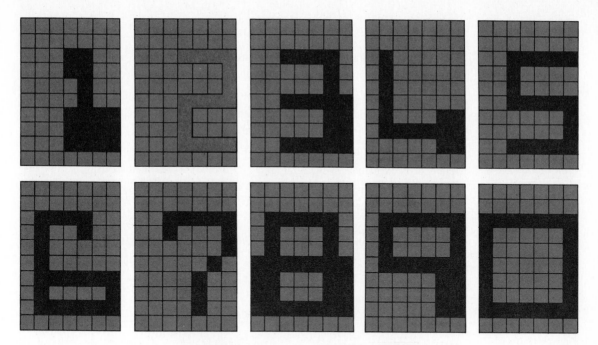

NUMBER SYSTEMS

It is India that gave us the ingenious method
of expressing all numbers by means of ten symbols,
each symbol receiving a value of position as well as an absolute
value; a profound and important idea which appears so simple
to us now that we ignore its true merit.

Marquis de Laplace

As a mathematician, Laplace could well appreciate the decimal number system. He was fully aware of the centuries of mental effort and sheer good luck which had gone into the development of the number system we use, and he was in a position to appreciate its advantages. Our present number system provides modern mathematicians and scientists with a great advantage over those of previous civilizations and is an important factor in our rapid advancement.

Since hands are the most convenient tools nature has provided, human beings have always tended to use them in counting. So the decimal number system followed naturally from this usage.

An even simpler system, the binary number system, has proved the most natural and efficient system for computer use, however, and this chapter develops this number system along with other systems used by computer technology.

NUMBER SYSTEMS

OBJECTIVES

1   An explanation of positional notation is given, and the idea of the base, or radix, of a number system is presented.

2   The binary number system is explained as well as how to add, subtract, multiply, and divide in this system. Then techniques for converting from binary to decimal and decimal to binary are given.

3   Negative numbers are represented in computers by using a sign bit, and this concept is explained. Negative numbers are often represented by using a complemented form rather than a signed-magnitude form. The two major complemented forms, true complement and radix minus one, are described.

4   The representation of decimal numbers using bistable devices can be accomplished with a binary-coded-decimal (BCD) system, and several of these are explained.

5   The octal and hexadecimal number systems are widely used in computer literature and manufacturer's manuals. These number systems are explained along with conversion techniques to and from decimal and binary.

DECIMAL SYSTEM

2.1   Our present system of numbers has 10 separate symbols, 0, 1, 2, 3, . . . , 9, which are called Arabic numerals. We would be forced to stop at 9 or to invent more symbols if it were not for the use of *positional notation*. An example of earlier types of notation can be found in Roman numerals, which are essentially additive: III = I + I + I, XXV = X + X + V. New symbols (X, C, M, etc.) were used as the numbers increased in value: thus V rather than IIIII is equal to 5. The only importance of position in Roman numerals lies in whether a symbol precedes or follows another symbol (IV = 4, while VI = 6). The clumsiness of this system can be seen easily if we try to multiply XII by XIV. Calculating with roman numerals was so difficult that early mathematicians were forced to perform arithmetic operations almost entirely on abaci, or counting boards, translating their results back to Roman numeral form. Pencil-and-paper computations are unbelievably intricate and difficult in such systems. In fact, the ability to perform such operations as addition and multiplication was considered a great accomplishment in earlier civilizations.

Now the great beauty and simplicity of our number system can be seen. It is necessary to learn only the 10 basic numerals and the *positional notational system* in order to count to any desired figure. After memorizing the addition and multiplication tables and learning a few simple rules, we can perform all arithmetic operations. Notice the simplicity of multiplying 12 × 14 by using the present system:

$$
\begin{array}{r}
14 \\
\underline{12} \\
28 \\
\underline{14} \\
168
\end{array}
$$

The actual meaning of the number 168 can be seen more clearly if we notice that it is spoken as "one hundred and sixty-eight." Basically, the number is a contraction of $1 \times 100 + 6 \times 10 + 8$. The important point is that the value of each digit is determined by its position. For example, the 2 in 2000 has a different value than the 2 in 20. We show this verbally by saying "two thousand" and "twenty." Different verbal representations have been invented for numbers from 10 to 20 (eleven, twelve, . . .), but from 20 upward we break only at powers of 10 (hundreds, thousands, millions, billions). Written numbers are always contracted, however, and only the basic 10 numerals are used, regardless of the size of the integer written. The general rule for representing numbers in the decimal system by using positional notation is as follows: $a_{n-1} 10^{n-1} + a_{n-2} 10^{n-2} + \cdots + a_0$ is expressed as $a_{n-1} a_{n-2} \cdots a_0$, where n is the number of digits to the left of the decimal point.

The *base,* or *radix,* of a number system is defined as the number of different digits which can occur in each position in the number system. The decimal number system has a base, or radix, of 10. Thus the system has 10 different digits (0, 1, 2, . . . , 9), any one of which may be used in each position in a number. History records the use of several other number systems. The quinary system, which has 5 for its base, was prevalent among Eskimos and North American Indians. Examples of the duodecimal system (base 12) may be seen in clocks, inches and feet, and dozens or grosses.

BISTABLE DEVICES

2.2 The basic elements in early computers were relays and switches. The operation of a switch, or relay, can be seen to be essentially bistable, or binary in nature; that is, the switch is either on (1) or off (0). The principal circuit elements in more modern computers are transistors. The desire for reliability led designers to use these devices so that they were always in one of two states, fully conducting or nonconducting. A simple analogy may be made between this type of circuit and an electric light. At any given time the light (or transistor) is either on (conducting) or off (not conducting). Even after a bulb is old and weak, it is generally easy to tell whether it is on or off.

Because of the large number of electronic parts used in computers, it is highly desirable to utilize them in such a manner that slight changes in their characteristics will not affect their performance. The best way of accomplishing this is to use circuits which are basically *bistable* (having two possible states).

COUNTING IN THE BINARY SYSTEM

2.3 The same type of positional notation is used in the binary number system as in the decimal system. Table 2.1 lists the first 20 binary numbers.

Although the same positional notation system is used, the decimal system uses powers of 10, and the binary system powers of 2. As was previously explained, the number 125 actually means $1 \times 10^2 + 2 \times 10^1 + 5 \times 10^0$. In the binary system, the same number (125) is represented as 1111101, meaning $1 \times 2^6 + 1 \times 2^5 + 1 \times 2^4 + 1 \times 2^3 + 1 \times 2^2 + 0 \times 2^1 + 1 \times 2^0$.

NUMBER SYSTEMS

TABLE 2.1

DECIMAL		BINARY	DECIMAL		BINARY
1	=	1	11	=	1011
2	=	10	12	=	1100
3	=	11	13	=	1101
4	=	100	14	=	1110
5	=	101	15	=	1111
6	=	110	16	=	10000
7	=	111	17	=	10001
8	=	1000	18	=	10010
9	=	1001	19	=	10011
10	=	1010	20	=	10100

To express the value of a binary number, therefore, $a_{n-1} 2^{n-1} + a_{n-2} 2^{n-2} + \cdots + a_0$ is represented as $a_{n-1} a_{n-1} \cdots a_0$, where a_i is either 1 or 0 and n is the number of digits to the left of the binary (radix) point.

The following examples illustrate the conversion of binary numbers to the decimal system:

$$
\begin{aligned}
101 &= 1 \times 2^{3-1} + 0 \times 2^{3-2} + 1 \times 2^{3-3} \\
&= 1 \times 2^2 + 0 \times 2^1 + 1 \times 2^0 \\
&= 4 + 1 = 5 \\
1001 &= 1 \times 2^{4-1} + 0 \times 2^{4-2} + 0 \times 2^{4-3} + 1 \times 2^{4-4} \\
&= 1 \times 2^3 + 0 \times 2^2 + 0 \times 2^1 + 1 \times 2^0 \\
&= 8 + 1 = 9 \\
11.011 &= 1 \times 2^{2-1} + 1 \times 2^{2-2} + 0 \times 2^{2-3} + 1 \times 2^{2-4} + 1 \times 2^{2-5} \\
&= 1 \times 2^1 + 1 \times 2^0 + 0 \times 2^{-1} + 1 \times 2^{-2} + 1 \times 2^{-3} \\
&= 2 + 1 + \tfrac{1}{4} + \tfrac{1}{8} \\
&= 3\tfrac{3}{8}
\end{aligned}
$$

Note that fractional numbers are formed in the same general way as in the decimal system. Just as

$$
0.123 = 1 \times 10^{-1} + 2 \times 10^{-2} + 3 \times 10^{-3}
$$

in the decimal system,

$$
0.101 = 1 \times 2^{-1} + 0 \times 2^{-2} + 1 \times 2^{-3}
$$

in the binary system.

BINARY ADDITION AND SUBTRACTION

2.4 Binary addition is performed in the same manner as decimal addition. Actually, binary arithmetic is much simpler to learn. The complete table for binary addition is as follows:

$$0 + 0 = 0$$
$$0 + 1 = 1$$
$$1 + 0 = 1$$
$$1 + 1 = 0 \quad \text{plus a carry-over of 1}$$

BINARY
MULTIPLICATION
AND DIVISION

"Carry-overs" are performed in the same manner as in decimal arithmetic. Since 1 is the largest digit in the binary system, any sum greater than 1 requires that a digit be carried over. For instance, 100 plus 100 binary requires the addition of the two 1s in the third position to the left, with a carry-over. Since $1 + 1 = 0$ plus a carry-over of 1, the sum of 100 and 100 is 1000. Here are three more examples of binary addition:

DECIMAL	BINARY	DECIMAL	BINARY	DECIMAL	BINARY
5	101	15	1111	$3\frac{1}{4}$	11.01
6	110	20	10100	$5\frac{3}{4}$	101.11
11	1011	35	100011	9	1001.00

Subtraction is the inverse operation of addition. To subtract, it is necessary to establish a procedure for subtracting a larger from a smaller digit. The only case in which this occurs with binary numbers is when 1 is subtracted from 0. The remainder is 1, but it is necessary to borrow 1 from the next column to the left. This is the binary subtraction table.

$$0 - 0 = 0$$
$$1 - 0 = 1$$
$$1 - 1 = 0$$
$$0 - 1 = 1 \quad \text{with a borrow of 1}$$

A few examples will make the procedure for binary subtraction clear:

DECIMAL	BINARY	DECIMAL	BINARY	DECIMAL	BINARY
9	1001	16	10000	$6\frac{1}{4}$	110.01
-5	-101	-3	-11	$-4\frac{1}{2}$	-100.1
4	100	13	1101	$1\frac{3}{4}$	1.11

BINARY MULTIPLICATION AND DIVISION

2.5 The table for binary multiplication is very short, with only four entries instead of the 100 necessary for decimal multiplication:

$$0 \times 0 = 0$$
$$1 \times 0 = 0$$
$$0 \times 1 = 0$$
$$1 \times 1 = 1$$

The following three examples of binary multiplication illustrate the simplicity of each operation. It is only necessary to copy the multiplicand if the digit in the multiplier is 1 and to copy all 0s if the digit in the multiplier is a 0. The ease with which each step of the operation is performed is apparent.

NUMBER SYSTEMS

DECIMAL	BINARY	DECIMAL	BINARY	DECIMAL	BINARY
12	1100	102	1100110	1.25	1.01
×10	×1010	×8	×1000	×2.5	×10.1
120	0000	816	1100110000	625	101
	1100			250	1010
	0000			3.125	11.001
	1100				
	1111000				

Binary division is, again, very simple. As in the decimal system (or in any other), division by zero is meaningless. The complete table is

$$0 \div 1 = 0$$
$$1 \div 1 = 1$$

Here are two examples of division:

```
        DECIMAL          BINARY
            5              101
        5)25          101)11001
                           101
                           101
                           101
```

```
        DECIMAL              BINARY
        2.416···          10.011010101···
     12)29.0000        1100)11101.00
        24                   1100
        50                  10100
        48                   1100
        20                  10000
        12                   1100
        80                  10000
        72                   1100
         8                   ···
```

To convert the quotient obtained in the second example from binary to decimal, we would proceed as follows:

$$
\begin{aligned}
10.011010101 = 1 \times 2^{1} &= 2.0 \\
0 \times 2^{0} &= 0.0 \\
0 \times 2^{-1} &= 0.0 \\
1 \times 2^{-2} &= 0.25 \\
1 \times 2^{-3} &= 0.125 \\
0 \times 2^{-4} &= 0.0 \\
1 \times 2^{-5} &= 0.03125 \\
0 \times 2^{-6} &= 0.0 \\
1 \times 2^{-7} &= 0.0078125 \\
0 \times 2^{-8} &= 0.0 \\
1 \times 2^{-9} &= 0.001953125 \\
\hline
&\,2.416015625
\end{aligned}
$$

Therefore, 10.011010101 binary equals approximately 2.416 decimal.

2.6 There are several methods for converting a decimal number to a binary number. The first and most obvious method is simply to subtract all powers of 2 which can be subtracted from the decimal number until nothing remains. The highest power of 2 is subtracted first, then the second highest, etc. To convert the decimal integer 25 to the binary number system, first the highest power of 2 which can be subtracted from 25 is found. This is $2^4 = 16$. Then $25 - 16 = 9$. The highest power of 2 which can be subtracted from 9 is 2^3, or 8. The remainder after subtraction is 1, or 2^0. The binary representation for 25 is, therefore, 11001.

CONVERTING
DECIMAL NUMBERS
TO BINARY

This is a laborious method for converting numbers. It is convenient for small numbers when it can be performed mentally, but is less used for larger numbers. Instead, the decimal number is repeatedly divided by 2, and the remainder after each division is used to indicate the coefficients of the binary number to be formed. Notice that the binary number derived is written from the bottom up.

$$125 \div 2 = 62 + \text{remainder of } 1$$
$$62 \div 2 = 31 + \text{remainder of } 0$$
$$31 \div 2 = 15 + \text{remainder of } 1$$
$$15 \div 2 = 7 + \text{remainder of } 1$$
$$7 \div 2 = 3 + \text{remainder of } 1$$
$$3 \div 2 = 1 + \text{remainder of } 1$$
$$1 \div 2 = 0 + \text{remainder of } 1$$

The binary representation of 125 is, therefore, 1111101. Checking this result gives

$$1 \times 2^6 = 64$$
$$1 \times 2^5 = 32$$
$$1 \times 2^4 = 16$$
$$1 \times 2^3 = 8$$
$$1 \times 2^2 = 4$$
$$0 \times 2^1 = 0$$
$$1 \times 2^0 = \underline{1}$$
$$125$$

This method will not work for mixed numbers. If similar methods are to be used, first it is necessary to divide the number into its whole and fractional parts; that is, 102.247 would be divided into 102 and 0.247. The binary representation for each part is found, and then the two parts are added.

The conversion of decimal fractions to binary fractions may be accomplished by using several techniques. Again, the most obvious method is to subtract the highest negative power of 2 which may be subtracted from the decimal fraction. Then the next highest negative power of 2 is subtracted from the remainder of the first subtraction, and this process is continued until there is no remainder or to the desired precision.

$$0.875 - 1 \times 2^{-1} = 0.875 - 0.5 = 0.375$$
$$0.375 - 1 \times 2^{-2} = 0.375 - 0.25 = 0.125$$
$$0.125 - 1 \times 2^{-3} = 0.125 - 0.125 = 0$$

NUMBER SYSTEMS

Therefore, 0.875 decimal is represented by 0.111 binary. A much simpler method for longer fractions consists of repeatedly "doubling" the decimal fraction. If a 1 appears to the left of the decimal point after a multiplication by 2 is performed, a 1 is added to the right of the binary fraction being formed. If after a multiplication by 2, a 0 remains to the left of the decimal point of the decimal number, a 0 is added to the right of the binary number. The following example illustrates the use of this technique in converting 0.4375 decimal to the binary system:

	BINARY REPRESENTATION
$2 \times 0.4375 = 0.8750$	0.0
$2 \times 0.875 = 1.750$	0.01
$2 \times 0.75 = 1.50$	0.011
$2 \times 0.5 = 1.0$	0.0111

The binary representation of 0.4375 is, therefore, 0.0111.

NEGATIVE NUMBERS

2.7 A standard convention adopted for writing negative numbers consists of placing a *sign symbol* before a number that is negative. For instance, negative 39 is written as -39. If -39 is to be added to $+70$, we write

$$+70 + (-39) = 31$$

When a negative number is subtracted from a positive number, we write $+70 - (-39) = +70 + 39 = 109$. The rules for handling negative numbers are well known and are not repeated here, but since negative numbers constitute an important part of our number system, the techniques used to represent negative numbers in digital machines are described.

In binary machines, numbers are represented by a set of bistable storage devices, each of which represents one binary digit. As an example, given a set of five switches, any number from 00000 to 11111 may be represented by the switches if we define a switch with its contacts closed as representing a 1 and a switch with open contacts as representing a 0. If we desire to increase the total range of numbers that we can represent so that it will include the negative numbers from 00000 to -11111, another bit (or switch) will be required. We then treat this bit as a *sign bit* and place it before the magnitude of the number to be represented.

Generally, the convention is adopted that when the sign bit is a 0, the number represented is positive, and when the sign bit is a 1, the number is negative. If the previous situation, where five switches are used to store the magnitude of a number, is extended so that both positive and negative numbers may be stored, then a sixth switch will be required. When the contacts of this switch are open, the number will be a positive number equal to the magnitude of the number stored in the other five switches; and if the switch for the sign bit is closed, the number represented by the six switches will be a negative number with a magnitude determined by the other five switches. An example is shown in Fig. 2.1.

Sets of storage devices which represent a number or are handled as an entity

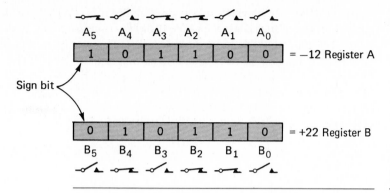

FIGURE 2.1

Example of negative-number representation.

are referred to as *registers,* and they are given names such as register A, register B, register C, etc. We can then write that register A contains − 12 and register B contains + 22. In writing a signed number in binary form, the sign bit is set apart from the magnitude of the number by means of an underscore, so that $\underline{0}0111$ represents +0111, or positive 7 decimal, and $\underline{1}0111$ represents −0111, or negative 7 decimal.

The use of the an underscore to mark the sign bit does not indicate that there is any difference between this bit and the other bits as the number is stored in a computer. Each and every binary bit is simply stored in a separate bistable device. A symbol other than the underscore could be used to separate the sign and magnitude bits, such as a hyphen, period, or a star. Then, − 1011 (negative 11 decimal) could be written 1-1011 or 1∗1011 or 1.1011 and +1100 as 0-1100 or 0∗1100 or 0.1100. In fact, no marking whatever could be used, but it is felt that some indication makes for easier reading of signed numbers which use a sign bit.

USE OF COMPLEMENTS TO REPRESENT NEGATIVE NUMBERS

2.8   The convention of using a sign bit to indicate whether a stored number is negative or positive has been described. The magnitude of the number stored is not always represented in normal form, however, but quite often negative numbers are stored in *complemented form*. By using this technique, a machine can be made to both add and subtract, using only circuitry for adding. The actual technique involved is described in Chap. 5.

There are two basic types of complements which are useful in the binary and decimal number systems. In the decimal system the two types are referred to as the 10s *complement* and the 9s *complement*.

The 10s complement of any number may be formed by subtracting each digit of the number from 9 and then adding 1 to the least significant digit of the number thus formed. For instance, the 10s complement of 87 is 13, and the 10s complement of 23 is 77.

To subtract[1] one positive number (the minuend) from another (the subtra-

---

[1]The number of digits in each number must be the same. If one number has fewer digits than the other, then 0s can be added to the left until the number of digits is the same.

hend), first the 10s complement of the subtrahend is formed, and then this 10s complement is added to the minuend. If there is a carry from the addition of the most significant digits, then it is discarded, the difference is positive, and the result is correct. If there is no carry, the difference is negative, the 10s complement of this number is formed, and a minus sign is placed before the result.

Here are some examples.

NORMAL SUBTRACTION	10s COMPLEMENT SUBTRACTION
89	89 89
− 23	− 23 = + 77
66	166
	the carry is dropped
98	98 98
− 87	− 87 = + 13
11	111
	the carry is dropped
49	49
− 62	+ 38
− 13	87 no carry, so result is negative
	10s complement, or − 13
54	54
− 81	+ 19
− 27	73 no carry, so result is negative
	10s complement, or − 27

The 9s complement of a decimal number is formed by subtracting each digit of the number from 9. For instance, the 9s complement of 23 is 76, and the 9s complement of 87 is 12. When subtraction[2] is performed by using the 9s complement, the complement of the subtrahend is added as in 10s complement subtraction, but any carry generated must be added to the rightmost digit of the result. As is the case with 10s complement subtraction, if no carry is generated for the addition of the most significant digits, then the result is negative, the 9s complement of the result is formed, and a minus sign is placed before it.

NORMAL SUBTRACTION	9s COMPLEMENT SUBTRACTION
89	89 89
− 23	− 23 = + 76
66	165
	1
	66
98	98 98
− 87	− 87 = + 12
11	110
	1
	11

---

[2]The number of digits in the subtrahend and minuend must be the same. If one number has more digits than the other, zeros are added to the left of the shorter number until it has the same number of digits.

$$\begin{array}{r} 15 \\ -37 \\ \hline -22 \end{array} \qquad \begin{array}{rr} 15 & 15 \\ -37 = & +62 \\ \hline & 77 \end{array}$$

no carry, so difference is negative 9s complement, which is -22

$$\begin{array}{r} 27 \\ -44 \\ \hline -17 \end{array} \qquad \begin{array}{rr} 27 & 27 \\ -44 = & +55 \\ \hline & 82 \end{array}$$

no carry, so difference is negative 9s complement, which is -17

Complete rules for handling signs during the subtraction process and for handling all combinations of positive and negative numbers are explained in Chap. 5. If this seems, at first, to be an unwieldy technique, note that the majority of computers now being constructed subtract by using a complemented number.

COMPLEMENTS IN OTHER NUMBER SYSTEMS

2.9 There are two types of complements for each number system. Since now only binary and BCD machines are being constructed in quantity, only these number systems are explained in any detail. The two types of complements and the rules for obtaining them are as follows:

1 *True complement* This is formed by subtracting each digit of the number from the radix minus one of the number system and then adding 1 to the least significant digit of the number formed. The true complement of a number in the decimal system is referred to as the 10s complement and in the binary system as the 2s complement.

2 *Radix-minus-one complement* The radix minus one is 9 for the decimal system and 1 for the binary system. The complement in each system is formed by subtracting each digit of the number from the radix minus one. For instance, the radix-minus-one complement of decimal 72 is 27.

BINARY NUMBER COMPLEMENTS

2.10 According to the rule in the preceding section, the 2s complement of a binary number is formed by simply subtracting each digit (bit) of the number from the radix minus one and adding a 1 to the least significant bit. Since the radix in the binary number system is 2, each bit of the binary number is subtracted from 1. The application of this rule is actually very simple; every 1 in the number is changed to a 0 and every 0 to a 1. Then a 1 is added to the least significant bit of the number formed. For instance, the 2s complement of 10110 is 01010, and the 2s complement of 11010 is 00110. Subtraction using the 2s complement system involves forming the 2s complement of the subtrahend and then adding this "true

2

complement'' to the minuend. For instance,

$$\begin{array}{r} 11011 \\ -10100 \\ \hline 00111 \end{array} = \begin{array}{r} 11011 \\ +01100 \\ \hline 1\ 00111 \end{array} \quad \text{and} \quad \begin{array}{r} 11100 \\ -00100 \\ \hline 11000 \end{array} = \begin{array}{r} 11100 \\ +11100 \\ \hline 1\ 11000 \end{array}$$

carry is dropped   dropped

Subtraction using the 1s complement system is also straightforward. The 1s complement of a binary number is formed by changing each 1 in the number to a 0 and each 0 in the number to a 1. For instance, the 1s complement of 10111 is 01000, and the 1s complement of 11000 is 00111.

When subtraction is performed in the 1s complement system, any end-around carry is added to the least significant bit. For instance,

$$\begin{array}{r} 11001 \\ -10110 \\ \hline 00011 \end{array} = \begin{array}{r} 11001 \\ +01001 \\ \hline 1\ 00010 \end{array} \quad \text{and} \quad \begin{array}{r} 11110 \\ -01101 \\ \hline 10001 \end{array} = \begin{array}{r} 11110 \\ +10010 \\ \hline 1\ 10000 \end{array}$$

$$\underrightarrow{\qquad} 1 \qquad\qquad \underrightarrow{\qquad} 1$$
$$\overline{00011} \qquad\qquad\qquad \overline{10001}$$

BINARY-CODED-DECIMAL NUMBER REPRESENTATION

2.11   Since most of the electronic circuit elements used to construct digital computers are inherently binary in operation, the binary number system is the most natural number system for a computer. Also, computers constructed with the binary number system require a smaller amount of circuitry and so are more efficient than machines operating in other number systems. However, the decimal system has been used for a long time, and there is a natural reaction to performing calculations in a binary number system. Also, since checks, bills, tax rates, prices, etc., are all figured in the decimal system, the values of most things must be converted from decimal to binary before computations can begin. For these and other reasons, most of the early machines operated in binary-coded-decimal number systems. In such systems a coded group of binary bits is used to represent each of the 10 decimal digits. For instance, an obvious and natural code is a simple *weighted binary code,* as shown in Table 2.2.

TABLE 2.2	
BINARY CODE	DECIMAL DIGIT
0000	0
0001	1
0010	2
0011	3
0100	4
0101	5
0110	6
0111	7
1000	8
1001	9

This is known as a *binary-coded-decimal 8, 4, 2, 1* code, or simply BCD. Notice that 4 binary bits are required for each decimal digit, and each bit is assigned a weight; for instance, the rightmost bit has a weight of 1, and the leftmost bit in each code group has a weight of 8. By adding the weights of the positions in which 1s appear, the decimal digit represented by a code group may be derived. This is somewhat uneconomical since $2^4 = 16$, and thus the 4 bits could actually represent 15 different values. But the next lesser choice, 3 bits, gives only 2^3, or 8, values, which are insufficient. If the decimal number 214 is to be represented in this type of code, 12 binary bits are required as follows: 0010 0001 0100. For the decimal number 1246 to be represented, 16 bits are required: 0001 0010 0100 0110.

This is a very useful code and has been much used. One difficulty with the code, however, lies in forming the complements of numbers in this system. It is common practice to perform subtraction in a computer by adding the complement of the subtrahend; however, when the BCD 8, 4, 2, 1 system is used, the most natural complement of the number stored is not useful because the most direct way for a computer to complement a number is simply to change each 0 to a 1 and each 1 to a 0. However, the natural complement of 0010 (2 decimal) is 1101, which is 13, and not an acceptable BCD character in this system. To get around this difficulty, several other codes have been used. One of the first, a code that was used in the early Mark machines built at Harvard and has been used a good deal since, is known as the *excess-3* code and is formed by adding 3 to the decimal number and then forming the binary-coded number in the normal weighted binary code. For instance, to form the excess-3 representation for 4, first 3 is added, yielding 7, and then the "normal" BCD is used, which is 0111. Therefore, 0111 is the excess-3 code for the decimal digit 4. Table 2.3 shows all 10 decimal digits and the code for each.

By complementing each digit of the binary code representing a decimal digit, the 9s complement of that digit may be formed. For instance, the complement of 0100 (1 decimal) is 1011, which is 8 decimal.

The decimal number 243 coded in the excess-3 system would be 0101 0111 0110, and the decimal number 347 would be 0110 0111 1010. The 9s complement of 243 is 756 decimal, or 1010 1000 1001 binary. Table 2.4 lists the excess-3 code representation for each of the 10 decimal digits along with the 9s complements

TABLE 2.3	
EXCESS-3 CODE	
DECIMAL	BINARY CODE
0	0011
1	0100
2	0101
3	0110
4	0111
5	1000
6	1001
7	1010
8	1011
9	1100

NUMBER SYSTEMS

TABLE 2.4

DECIMAL DIGIT	EXCESS-3 CODE	9s COMPLEMENT
0	0011	1100
1	0100	1011
2	0101	1010
3	0110	1001
4	0111	1000
5	1000	0111
6	1001	0110
7	1010	0101
8	1011	0100
9	1100	0011

TABLE 2.5   **2, 4, 2, 1, CODE**

| | CODED BINARY | | | |
| | WEIGHT OF BIT | | | |
DECIMAL	2	4	2	1
0	0	0	0	0
1	0	0	0	1
2	0	0	1	0
3	0	0	1	1
4	0	1	0	0
5	1	0	1	1
6	1	1	0	0
7	1	1	0	1
8	1	1	1	0
9	1	1	1	1

listed. Note the 9s complement of each code group may be formed by changing each 0 to a 1 and each 1 to a 0 in the code group.

The excess-3 code is not a weighted code, however, because weights cannot be assigned to the bits so that their sum equals the decimal digits represented.

A weighted code in which the 9s complement may be formed by complementing each binary digit is the 2, 4, 2, 1 code (see Table 2.5). If each bit of a code group is complemented, the 9s complement of the decimal digit represented is formed. For instance, 0010 (2 decimal) complemented is 1101 (7 decimal), and 1011 (5 decimal) complemented is 0100 (4 decimal). This code is widely used in instruments and electronic calculators.

The following convention is generally adopted to distinguish binary from decimal. A binary number is identified by a subscript of 2 placed at the end of the number (00110_2), and a decimal number by the subscript 10 (for instance, decimal 948 may be written 948_{10}). So we may write 0111_2 as 7_{10}. We use this convention when necessary.

OCTAL AND HEXADECIMAL NUMBER SYSTEMS

2.12 Two other number systems are very useful in the computer industry: the octal number system and the hexadecimal number system.

The octal number system has a base, or radix, of 8; eight different symbols

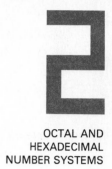

TABLE 2.6			
OCTAL	DECIMAL	OCTAL	DECIMAL
0	0	11	9
1	1	12	10
2	2	13	11
3	3	14	12
4	4	15	13
5	5	16	14
6	6	17	15
7	7	20	16
10	8	21	17

are used to represent numbers. These are commonly 0, 1, 2, 3, 4, 5, 6, and 7. We show the first octal numbers and their decimal equivalents in Table 2.6.

To convert an octal number to a decimal number, we use the same sort of polynomial as was used in the binary case, except that we now have a radix of 8 instead of 2. Therefore, 1213 in octal is $1 \times 8^3 + 2 \times 8^2 + 1 \times 8^1 + 3 \times 8^0 = 512 + 128 + 8 + 3 = 651$ in decimal. Also, 1.123 in octal is $1 \times 8^0 + 1 \times 8^{-1} + 2 \times 8^{-2} + 3 \times 8^{-3}$, or $1 + \frac{1}{8} + \frac{2}{64} + \frac{3}{512} = 1\frac{83}{512}$ in decimal.

There is a simple trick for converting a binary number to an octal number. Simply group the binary digits into groups of 3, starting at the octal point, and read each set of three binary digits according to Table 2.7.

Let us convert the binary number 011101. First, we break it into 3s (thus 011 101). Then, converting each group of three binary digits, we get 35 in octal. Therefore 011101 binary = 35 octal. Here are several more examples:

$$111110111_2 = 767_8$$
$$110110101_2 = 665_8$$
$$11011_2 = 33_8$$
$$1001_2 = 11_8$$
$$10101.11_2 = 25.6_8$$
$$1100.111_2 = 14.7_8$$
$$1011.1111_2 = 13.74_8$$

Conversion from decimal to octal can be performed by repeatedly dividing the decimal number by 8 and using each remainder as a digit in the octal number

TABLE 2.7	
000	0
001	1
010	2
011	3
100	4
101	5
110	6
111	7

NUMBER SYSTEMS

being formed. For instance, to convert 200_{10} to an octal representation, we divide as follows:

$$200 \div 8 = 25 \qquad \text{remainder is } 0$$
$$25 \div 8 = 3 \qquad \text{remainder is } 1$$
$$3 \div 8 = 0 \qquad \text{remainder is } 3$$

Therefore, $200_{10} = 310_8$.

Notice that when the number to be divided is less than 8, we use 0 as the quotient and the number as the remainder. Let us check this:

$$310_8 = 3_{10} \times 8_{10}^2 + 1_{10} \times 8_{10}^1 + 0_{10} \times 8_{10}^0 = 192_{10} + 8_{10} = 200_{10}$$

Here is another example. We wish to convert 3964_{10} to octal:

$$3964 \div 8 = 495 \qquad \text{with a remainder of } 4$$
$$495 \div 8 = 61 \qquad \text{with a remainder of } 7$$
$$61 \div 8 = 7 \qquad \text{with a remainder of } 5$$
$$7 \div 8 = 0 \qquad \text{with a remainder of } 7$$

Therefore, $7574_8 = 3964_{10}$. Checking, we find

$$7574_8 = 7_{10} \times 8_{10}^3 + 5_{10} \times 8_{10}^2 + 7_{10} \times 8_{10} + 4_{10}$$
$$= 7_{10} \times 512_{10} + 5_{10} \times 64_{10} + 7_{10} \times 8_{10} + 4_{10} \times 1_{10}$$
$$= 3584_{10} + 320_{10} + 56_{10} + 4_{10}$$
$$= 3964_{10}$$

There are several other techniques for converting octal to decimal and decimal to octal, but they are not used very frequently manually, and tables prove to be of about as much value as anything in this process. Octal-to-decimal and decimal-to-octal tables are readily available in a number of places, including the manuals distributed by manufacturers of binary machines.

An important use for octal is in listings of programs and for memory "dumps" for binary machines, thus making the printouts more compact. The manuals for several of the largest manufacturers use octal numbers to represent binary numbers because of ease of conversion and compactness.

The hexadecimal number system is useful for the same reasons. Most minicomputers and microcomputers have their memories organized into sets of *bytes*, each consisting of eight binary digits. Each byte either is used as a single entity to represent a single alphanumeric character or is broken into two 4-bit pieces. (We examine the coding of alphanumeric characters using bytes in Chap. 7.) When the bytes are handled in two 4-bit pieces, the programmer is given the option of declaring each 4-bit character as a piece of a binary number or as two BCD numbers. For instance, the byte 00011000 can be declared a binary number, in which case it is equal to 24 decimal, or as two BCD characters, in which case it represents the decimal number 18.

When the machine is handling numbers in binary but in groups of four digits,

TABLE 2.8		
BINARY	HEXADECIMAL	DECIMAL
0000	0	0
0001	1	1
0010	2	2
0011	3	3
0100	4	4
0101	5	5
0110	6	6
0111	7	7
1000	8	8
1001	9	9
1010	A	10
1011	B	11
1100	C	12
1101	D	13
1110	E	14
1111	F	15

OCTAL AND
HEXADECIMAL
NUMBER SYSTEMS

it is convenient to have a code for representing each of these sets of four digits. Since 16 possible different numbers can be represented, the digits 0 through 9 will not suffice; so the letters A, B, C, D, E, and F are used also (see Table 2.8).

To convert binary to hexadecimal, we simply break a binary number into groups of four digits and convert each group of four digits according to the preceding code. Thus $10111011_2 = BB_{16}$, $10010101_2 = 95_{16}$, $11000111_2 = C7_{16}$, and $10001011_2 = 8B_{16}$. The mixture of letters and decimal digits may seem strange at first, but these are simply convenient symbols, just as decimal digits are.

The conversion of hexadecimal to decimal is straightforward but time-consuming. For instance, BB represents $B \times 16^1 + B \times 16^0 = 11 \times 16 + 11 \times 1 = 176 + 11 = 187$. Similarly,

$$
\begin{aligned}
AB6_{16} &= 10_{10} \times 16^2_{10} + 11_{10} \times 16_{10} + 6_{10} \\
&= 10_{10} \times 256_{10} + 176_{10} + 6_{10} \\
&= 2560_{10} + 176_{10} + 6_{10} \\
&= 2742_{10}
\end{aligned}
$$

To convert, for instance, $3A6_{16}$ to decimal:

$$
\begin{aligned}
3A6_{16} &= 3_{10} \times 16^2_{10} + 10_{10} \times 16_{10} + 6_{10} \\
&= 3_{10} \times 256_{10} + 10_{10} \times 16_{10} + 6_{10} \\
&= 768_{10} + 160_{10} + 6_{10} \\
&= 934_{10}
\end{aligned}
$$

Again, tables are convenient for converting hexadecimal to decimal and decimal to hexadecimal. Table 2.9 is useful for converting in either direction.

The chief use of the hexadecimal system is in connection with byte-organized machines. And since most computers are now byte-organized, a knowledge of hexadecimal is essential to using manufacturers' manuals and to reading the current literature.

TABLE 2.9   HEXADECIMAL-TO-DECIMAL CONVERSION TABLE

A. INTEGER CONVERSION

HEX	DEC	HEX	DEC	HEX	DEC	HEX	DEC	EXAMPLE: 2322_{16} is $8192_{10} + 768_{10} + 32_{10} + 2_{10}$ = 8994.0.
0	0	0	0	0	0	0	0	
1	4,096	1	256	1	16	1	1	
2	8,192	2	512	2	32	2	2	
3	12,288	3	768	3	48	3	3	
4	16,384	4	1,024	4	64	4	4	
5	20,480	5	1,280	5	80	5	5	
6	24,576	6	1,536	6	96	6	6	
7	28,672	7	1,792	7	112	7	7	
8	32,768	8	2,048	8	128	8	8	
9	36,864	9	2,304	9	144	9	9	
A	40,960	A	2,560	A	160	A	10	
B	45,056	B	2,816	B	176	B	11	
C	49,152	C	3,072	C	192	C	12	
D	53,248	D	3,328	D	208	D	13	
E	57,344	E	3,584	E	224	E	14	
F	61,440	F	3,840	F	240	F	15	
Hexadecimal positions	4		3		2		1	

B. FRACTIONAL CONVERSION

HEX	0 1 2 3 DEC	HEX	4 5 6 7 DECIMAL	HEX	0 1 2 3 DECIMAL	HEX	4 5 6 7 DECIMAL EQUIVALENT
.0	.0000	.00	.0000 0000	.000	.0000 0000 0000	.0000	.0000 0000 0000 0000
.1	.0625	.01	.0039 0625	.001	.0002 4414 0625	.0001	.0000 1525 8789 0625
.2	.1250	.02	.0078 1250	.002	.0004 8828 1250	.0002	.0000 3051 7578 1250
.3	.1875	.03	.0117 1875	.002	.0007 3242 1875	.0003	.0000 4577 6367 1875
.4	.2500	.04	.0156 2500	.004	.0009 7656 2500	.0004	.0000 6103 5156 2500
.5	.3125	.05	.0195 3125	.005	.0012 2070 3125	.0005	.0000 7629 3945 3125
.6	.3750	.06	.0234 3750	.006	.0014 6484 3750	.0006	.0000 9155 2734 3750
.7	.4375	.07	.0273 4375	.007	.0017 0898 4375	.0007	.0001 0681 1523 4375
.8	.5000	.08	.0312 5000	.008	.0019 5312 5000	.0008	.0001 2207 0312 5000
.9	.5625	.09	.0351 5625	.009	.0021 9726 5625	.0009	.0001 3732 9101 5625
.A	.6250	.0A	.0390 6250	.00A	.0024 4140 6250	.000A	.0001 5258 7890 6250
.B	.6875	.0B	.0429 6875	.00B	.0026 8554 6875	.000B	.0001 6784 6679 6875
.C	.7500	.0C	.0468 7500	.00C	.0029 2968 7500	.000C	.0001 8310 5468 7500
.D	.8125	.0D	.0507 8125	.00D	.0031 7382 8125	.000D	.0001 9836 4257 8125
.E	.8750	.0E	.0546 8750	.00E	.0034 1796 8750	.000E	.0002 1362 3046 8750
.F	.9375	.0F	.0585 9375	.00F	.0036 6210 9375	.000F	.0002 2888 1835 9375
Hexidecimal positions	1		2		3		4

Quite a large number of questions have been included for this chapter. For those desiring to study octal and hexadecimal number systems further, Questions 2.58 through 2.67 contain information and exercises on octal addition and multiplication, and Questions 2.68 through 2.72 can be used to supplement the study of the hexadecimal system.

2.13 The individual memory cells used in computers are bistable in operation and capable of storing a single binary bit. Therefore, it is most practical to use the binary number system to represent numbers, and this system was explained along with conversion techniques to and from decimal.

Negative numbers are represented in computers by using a sign bit which is a 1 when the number is negative and a 0 for positive numbers. Negative numbers are often represented by using 1s or 2s complement form, and this was described along with examples showing how mixed numbers represented in that form can be added or subtracted.

The direct representation of decimal numbers can be accomplished by using a binary-coded-decimal (BCD) representation. This was explained, and examples were given.

The octal and hexidecimal number systems were described. These are useful in representing binary numbers in a compact form and to facilitate communication of values in written presentations. Computers are often organized with numbers represented in groups of 8 bits which makes hexadecimal particularly useful at this time.

QUESTIONS

QUESTIONS

2.1 Convert the following decimal numbers to equivalent binary numbers:
- (a) 43
- (b) 64
- (c) 4096
- (d) 0.375
- (e) $\frac{27}{32}$
- (f) 0.4375
- (g) 512.5
- (h) 131.5625
- (i) 2048.0625

2.2 Convert the following numbers to the equivalent binary numbers:
- (a) 14
- (b) 0.25
- (c) $2\frac{1}{8}$
- (d) 6.25
- (e) $2\frac{3}{8}$
- (f) 0.625

2.3 Convert the following binary numbers to equivalent decimal numbers:
- (a) 1101
- (b) 11011
- (c) 1011
- (d) 0.1011
- (e) 0.001101
- (f) 0.001101101
- (g) 111011.1011
- (h) 1011011.001101
- (i) 10110.0101011101

2.4 Convert the following binary numbers to equivalent decimal numbers:
- (a) 1011
- (b) 11000
- (c) 100011
- (d) 11011
- (e) 111001
- (f) 1011010

2.5 Convert the following binary numbers to equivalent decimal numbers:
- (a) 1011
- (b) 100100
- (c) 10011
- (d) 0.1101
- (e) 0.1001
- (f) 0.0101
- (g) 1011.0011
- (h) 1001.1001
- (i) 101.011

2.6 Convert the following binary numbers to equivalent decimal numbers:
- (a) 0.111
- (b) 0.11011
- (c) 1.011
- (d) 111.1011
- (e) 0110.0101
- (f) 101.101011

2.7 Perform the following additions and check by converting the binary numbers to decimal:

    (*a*) 1001.1 + 1011.01   (*b*) 100101 + 100101
    (*c*) 0.1011 + 0.1101   (*d*) 1011.01 + 1001.11

2.8 Perform the following additions and check by converting the binary numbers to decimal and adding:

    (*a*) 1011 + 1110   (*b*) 1010 + 1111   (*c*) 10.11 + 10.011
    (*d*) 1101.11 + 1.11   (*e*) 11111.1 + 10010.1   (*f*) 101.1 + 111.11

2.9 Perform the following additions and check by converting the binary numbers to decimal:

    (*a*) 1101.1 + 1011.1   (*b*) 101101 + 1101101
    (*c*) 0.0011 + 0.1110   (*d*) 1100.011 + 1011.011

2.10 Perform the following subtractions in binary and check by converting the numbers to decimal and subtracting:

    (*a*) 1101 − 1000   (*b*) 1101 − 1001   (*c*) 1011.1 − 101.1
    (*d*) 1101.01 − 1011.1   (*e*) 111.11 − 101.1   (*f*) 1101.1 − 1010.01

2.11 Perform the following subtractions in the binary number system:

    (*a*) 64 − 32   (*b*) 127 − 63
    (*c*) 93.5 − 42.75   (*d*) $84\frac{9}{32} - 48\frac{5}{16}$

2.12 Perform the following subtractions in the binary number system:

    (*a*) 128 − 32   (*b*) $\frac{1}{8} - \frac{1}{16}$ (*c*) $2\frac{1}{8} - 4\frac{3}{32}$
    (*d*) $31 - \frac{5}{8}$ (*e*) $62 - 31\frac{1}{16}$ (*f*) 129 − 35

2.13 Perform the following subtractions in the binary number system:

    (*a*) 37 − 35   (*b*) 128 − 64
    (*c*) 94.5 − 43.75   (*d*) 255 − 127

2.14 Perform the following multiplications and divisions in the binary number system:

    (*a*) 16 × 8   (*b*) 31 × 14   (*c*) 23 × 3.525
    (*d*) 15 × 8.625   (*e*) 6 ÷ 2   (*f*) 16 ÷ 8

2.15 Perform the following multiplications and divisions in the binary number system:

    (*a*) 24 × 12   (*b*) 18 × 14   (*c*) 32 ÷ 8
    (*d*) 27 ÷ 18   (*e*) 49.5 × 51.75   (*f*) 58.75 ÷ 23.5

2.16 Perform the following multiplications and divisions in the binary number system:

    (*a*) 16 × 2.75   (*b*) 19 ÷ 6   (*c*) $256\frac{1}{2} \div 128\frac{1}{4}$
    (*d*) 31.5 ÷ 15.75   (*e*) $3 \div \frac{5}{8}$ (*f*) $2\frac{5}{8} \times 1\frac{5}{8}$

2.17 Perform the following multiplications and divisions in the binary number system:

    (*a*) 15 × 13   (*b*) 10 × 15   (*c*) 44 ÷ 11
    (*d*) 42 ÷ 12   (*e*) 7.75 × 2.5   (*f*) 22.5 × 4.75

2.18 Convert the following decimal numbers to both their 9s and 10s complements:

    (*a*) 9   (*b*) 19   (*c*) 8
    (*d*) 24   (*e*) 25   (*f*) 99

2.19 Convert the following decimal numbers into both their 9s and 10s complements:

    (*a*) 5436   (*b*) 1932   (*c*) 45.15   (*d*) 18.293

2.20 Convert the following decimal numbers into both their 9s and 10s complements:

    (*a*) 95   (*b*) 79   (*c*) 0.83
    (*d*) 0.16   (*e*) 298.64   (*f*) 332.52

2.21 Convert the following decimal numbers to both their 9s and 10s complements:

    (*a*) 3654   (*b*) 2122   (*c*) 54.19   (*d*) 37.263

2.22 Convert the following binary numbers to both their 1s and 2s complements:
    (*a*) 1101   (*b*) 1010   (*c*) 1111
    (*d*) 1110   (*e*) 1011   (*f*) 1011

2.23 Convert the following binary numbers to both their 1s and 2s complements:
    (*a*) 1011   (*b*) 11011   (*c*) 1011.01   (*d*) 11011.01

2.24 Convert the following binary numbers to both their 1s and 2s complements:
    (*a*) 1011   (*b*) 1101   (*c*) 0.0111
    (*d*) 0.101   (*e*) 11.101   (*f*) 101.011

2.25 Convert the following binary numbers to both their 1s and 2s complements:
    (*a*) 101111   (*b*) 100100
    (*c*) 10111.10   (*d*) 10011.11

2.26 Perform the following subtractions, using both 9s and 10s complements:
    (*a*) 8 − 4   (*b*) 16 − 8   (*c*) 198 − 124
    (*d*) 28.5 − 23.4   (*e*) 27.6 − 23.4   (*f*) 0.55 − 0.42

2.27 Perform the following subtractions, using both 9s and 10s complements:
    (*a*) 948 − 234   (*b*) 347 − 263
    (*c*) 349.5 − 245.3   (*d*) 412.7 − 409.2

2.28 Perform the following subtractions, using both 9s and 10s complements:
    (*a*) 14 − 9   (*b*) 15 − 9   (*c*) 0.5 − 40.24
    (*d*) 0.41 − 0.4   (*e*) 0.434 − 0.33   (*f*) 1.2 − 0.34

2.29 Perform the following subtractions, using both 9s and 10s complements:
    (*a*) 1024 − 913   (*b*) 249 − 137
    (*c*) 24.1 − 13.4   (*d*) 239.3 − 119.4

2.30 Perform the following subtractions of binary numbers, using both 1s and 2s complements:

    (*a*) 1010 − 1011   (*b*) 110 − 10   (*c*) 110 − 0.111
    (*d*) 0.111 − 0.1001   (*e*) 0.1111 − 0.101   (*f*) 11.11 − 10.111

2.31 Perform the following subtractions, using both 1s and 2s complements:
(a) 1011 − 101   (b) 11011 − 11001
(c) 10111.1 − 10011.1   (d) 11011 − 10011.11

2.32 How many different numbers can be stored in a set of four switches, each having three different positions (four three-position switches)?

2.33 How many different binary numbers can be stored in a register consisting of six switches?

2.34 How many different BCD numbers can be stored in 12 switches? (Assume two-position, or on-off switches.)

2.35 How many different BCD numbers can be stored in a register containing 12 switches using an 8, 4, 2, 1 code? Using an excess-3 code?

2.36 Write the first 12 numbers in the base 4 (or *quaternary*) number system.

2.37 Write the first 10 numbers in the quaternary number system, which has a base, or radix, of 4. Use the digits 0. 1, 2, and 3 to express these numbers.

2.38 Write the first 20 numbers in the base 12 (or *duodecimal*) number system. Use A for 10 and B for 11.

2.39 Write the first 25 numbers in a base 11 number system, using the digits 0, 1, 2, 3, 4, 5, 6, 7, 8, 9, and A to express the 25 numbers that you write. (Decimal 10 = A, for instance.)

2.40 Perform the following subtractions in the binary number system, using 1s complements:
(a) 1111 − 1001   (b) 1110 − 1011
(c) 101.11 − 101.01   (d) 111.1 − 100.1

2.41 Using the 1s complement number system, perform the following subtractions:
(a) 0.1001 − 0.0110   (b) 0.1110 − 0.0110
(c) 0.01111 − 0.01001   (d) 11011 − 11001
(e) 1110101 − 1010010

2.42 Perform the following subtractions in the binary number system, using 2s complements:
(a) 1111 − 110   (b) 1110 − 1100
(c) 1011.11 − 101.001   (d) 111.1 − 110.1

2.43 Using the 2s complement number system, perform the following subtractions and represent the answers as decimal fractions:
(a) 0.101010 − 0.010101   (b) 0.11001 − 0.00100
(c) 0.111000 − 0.000111   (d) 0.101100 − 0.010011

2.44 Convert the following hexadecimal numbers to decimal numbers:
(a) 15   (b) B8   (c) AB4
(d) 9.B   (e) 9.1A

2.45 Convert the following hexadecimal numbers to decimal:
(a) B6C7   (b) 64AC   (c) A492   (d) D2763

2.46 Convert the following octal numbers to decimal:
(a) 15   (b) 125   (c) 115
(d) 124   (e) 156   (f) 15.6

2.47 Convert the following octal numbers to decimal:
(a) 2376   (b) 2473   (c) 276431   (d) 22632

2.48 Convert the following binary numbers to octal:
(a) 110   (b) 111001   (c) 111.111
(d) 0.11111   (e) 10.11   (f) 1111.1101

2.49 Convert the following binary numbers to octal:
(a) 101101   (b) 101101110   (c) 10110111
(d) 110110.011   (e) 011.1011011

2.50 Convert the following octal numbers to binary:
(a) 54   (b) 44   (c) 232.2
(d) 232.4   (e) 453.45   (f) 31.234

2.51 Convert the following octal numbers to binary:
(a) 7423   (b) 3364   (c) 33762
(d) 3232.14   (e) 3146.52

2.52 Convert the following decimal numbers to octal:
(a) 17   (b) 8   (c) 19
(d) 0.55   (e) 0.625   (f) 2.125

2.53 Convert the following decimal numbers to octal:
(a) 932   (b) 332   (c) 545.375
(d) 632.97   (e) 4429.625

2.54 Convert the following hexadecimal numbers to binary:
(a) 9   (b) 1B   (c) 0.A1
(d) 0.AB   (e) AB   (f) 12.B

2.55 Convert the following hexadecimal numbers to binary:
(a) CD   (b) 6A9   (c) A14
(d) AA.1A   (e) AB2.234

2.56 Convert the following binary numbers to hexadecimal:
(a) 1101.0110   (b) 11011110   (c) 1111
(d) 11101   (e) 11110.01011   (f) 1011.11010

2.57 Convert the following binary numbers to hexadecimal:
(a) 10110111   (b) 10011100   (c) 1001111
(d) 0.01111110   (e) 101101111010

2.58 A simple rule for multiplying two digits in any radix is simply to multiply the two digits in decimal. If the product is less than the radix, take it; if greater, divide (in decimal) by the radix and use the remainder as the first, or least significant, position and the quotient as the carry, or most significant, digit. In base 6, then 2 × 2 = 4, 3 × 1 = 3, etc.; however, 2 × 4 = 8, and

$$6\overline{)8}^{1}$$

So $2_6 \times 4_6 = 12_6$. Similarly, in base 7, then, $3 \times 4 = 12$ and

$$7\overline{)12} \begin{array}{r} 1 \\ \underline{7} \\ 5 \end{array}$$

So $3_7 \times 4_7 = 15_7$. Using this rule, perform, in base 7, the following:

(a) $2_7 \times 3_7$ (b) $2_7 \times 2_7$

(c) $4_7 \times 4_7$ (d) $4_7 \times 3_7$

2.59 Using the rule in Question 2.58, perform:

(a) $3_6 \times 4_6$ (b) $3_6 \times 3_6$ (c) $3_9 \times 4_9$

(d) $4_9 \times 5_9$ (e) $5_9 \times 15_9$

2.60 An addition table for octal is as follows:

+	0	1	2	3	4	5	6	7
0	0	1	2	3	4	5	6	7
1	1	2	3	4	5	6	7	10
2	2	3	4	5	6	7	10	11
3	3	4	5	6	7	10	11	12
4	4	5	6	7	10	11	12	13
5	5	6	7	10	11	12	13	14
6	6	7	10	11	12	13	14	15
7	7	10	11	12	13	14	15	16

Using this table, we add in octal:

$$\begin{array}{r} 1\,1 \leftarrow \text{carries} \\ 1\,2\,6 \\ \underline{3\,5\,7} \\ 5\,0\,5 \end{array}$$

Perform the following additions:

(a) $7_8 + 7_8$ (b) $6_8 + 5_8$ (c) $7_8 + 16_8$

(d) $5_8 + 4_8$ (e) $5_8 + 14_8$

2.61 Using the table in Question 2.60, perform:

(a) $15_8 + 14_8$ (b) $24_8 + 36_8$ (c) $126_8 + 347_8$

(d) $67_8 + 45_8$ (e) $136_8 + 636_8$

2.62 Make up a hexadecimal addition table.

2.63 Using the table in Question 2.62, perform:

(a) $6_{16} + A1_{16}$ (b) $7_{16} + 17_{16}$ (c) $8_{16} + 28_{16}$

(d) $A16A_{16} + B16A_{16}$ (e) $A84_{16} + A83_{16}$

2.64 Perform the additions in Question 2.63 in binary and convert back to hexadecimal.

2.65 Perform the additions in Question 2.61 in binary and convert back to octal.

2.66 To multiply two numbers in octal, we use the rule given in Question 2.58 and then proceed as follows:

$$6 \times 27 = 6 \times 20 + 6 \times 7$$
$$= 140 + 52 = 212$$

Multiply the following in octal:

    (*a*) 6 × 7   (*b*) 6 × 10   (*c*) 5 × 14

2.67 To multiply numbers of more than one digit, proceed as in Question 2.66 and then add in octal. Multiply the following octal numbers:

    (*a*) 3 × 14   (*b*) 23 × 12   (*c*) 11 × 22
    (*d*) 22 × 44   (*e*) 13 × 13   (*f*) 14 × 15

2.68 Perform the following multiplications of hexadecimal numbers:

    (*a*) A × 8   (*b*) 9 × 14   (*c*) A1 × 8
    (*d*) A11 × 9   (*e*) A12 × 6   (*f*) A13 × 2B

2.69 Using the rule in Question 2.58, perform the following multiplications of hexadecimal numbers:

    (*a*) 15 × B   (*b*) 14 × B   (*c*) 11 × A
    (*d*) 142 × A   (*e*) 13 × 14

2.70 Perform the multiplications in Question 2.68 in binary, then convert back to hexadecimal.

2.71 Perform the multiplications in Question 2.69 in binary, then convert back to hexadecimal.

2.72 In converting decimal numbers to hexadecimal, it is convenient to go first to octal, then to binary, then to hexadecimal. For instance, to convert 412_{10} to hexadecimal, we go first to octal:

```
     51              6
  8)412           8)51
    40              48
    12               3
     8                 ↖2d digit    6 ← 1st digit
     4
      ↖3d digit
```

Now $412_{10} = 634_8$; converting this to binary gives

$$634_8 = \underbrace{110}_{6}\ \underbrace{011}_{3}\ \underbrace{100}_{4}$$

2

Then regrouping yields

$$\underbrace{1}_{1}\ \underbrace{1001}_{9}\ \underbrace{1100}_{C}$$

So

$$412_{10} = 19C$$

Convert the following decimal numbers to hexadecimal:

(a) 24   (b) 397   (c) 1343
(d) 513   (e) 262

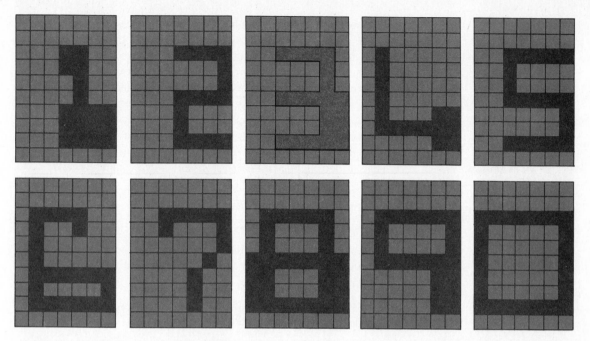

BOOLEAN ALGEBRA AND GATE NETWORKS

Modern digital computers are designed and maintained, and their operation is analyzed, by using techniques and symbology from a field of mathematics called *modern algebra*. Algebraists have studied for over a hundred years mathematical systems called *boolean algebras*. Nothing could be more simple and normal to human reasoning than the rules of boolean algebra, for these originated in studies of how we reason, what lines of reasoning are valid, what constitutes proof, and other allied subjects.

The name *boolean algebra* honors a fascinating[1] English mathematician, George Boole, who in 1854 published a classic book, *An Investigation of the Laws of Thought, on Which Are Founded the Mathematical Theories of Logic and Probabilities*. Boole's stated intention was to perform a mathematical analysis of logic.

Starting with his investigation of the laws of thought, Boole constructed a "logical algebra." This investigation into the nature of logic and ultimately of mathematics led subsequent mathematicians and logicians into several new fields of mathematics. Two of these, known as the *calculus of propositions* and the *algebra of sets,* were based principally on Boole's work. In this book we designate the algebra now used in the design and maintenance of logical circuitry as *boolean algebra*.[2]

---

[1]George Boole was the son of a shoemaker. His formal education ended in the third grade. Despite this, he was a brilliant scholar, teaching Greek and Latin in his own school, and an accepted mathematician who made lasting contributions in the areas of differential and difference equations as well as in algebra.

[2]This algebra is sometimes called *switching algebra*. It is, in fact, only one of several realizations of what modern algebraists call boolean algebra.

60

**BOOLEAN ALGEBRA
AND GATE
NETWORKS**

There are several advantages in having a mathematical technique for the description of the internal workings of a computer. For one thing, it is often far more convenient to calculate with expressions used to represent switching circuits than it is to use schematic or even logical diagrams. Further, just as an ordinary algebraic expression may be simplified by means of the basic theorems, the expression describing a given switching circuit network may be reduced or simplified. This enables the logical designer to simplify the circuitry used, achieving economy of construction and reliability of operation. Boolean algebra also provides an economical and straightforward way of describing the circuitry used in computers. In all, a knowledge of boolean algebra is indispensable in the computing field.

OBJECTIVES

1   The design and maintenance of digital computers are greatly facilitated by the use of boolean algebra and block diagrams. Both of these are explained, as is their usage in designing networks using logic gates.

2   The major types of gates now in use are AND, OR, NOR, and NAND gates. These are explained, and design procedures using these gates are presented.

3   To simplify the construction of computers, the gate networks are simplified as much as possible. Both algebraic techniques and graphical (map) techniques exist which can be used; both are discussed with emphasis on the map minimization procedures.

4   Logic networks are generally laid out in a two-level form such as AND-OR, NAND-NAND, etc. These forms are described, and design procedures for the forms are presented.

5   There are several special characteristics of gates which can influence logic design (such as wired OR and wired AND gates). These are described, as are special forms such as NAND-AND and NOR-OR.

6   Integrated-circuit (IC) manufacturing techniques now make it possible to package many gates in a single IC package (chip). Often these arrays of gates are laid out in some regular form for large-scale integration and typical forms are presented, including those for programmable logic arrays, programmable array logic, and gate array logic.

FUNDAMENTAL CONCEPTS OF BOOLEAN ALGEBRA

3.1   When a variable is used in an algebraic formula, it is generally assumed that the variable may take any numerical value. For instance, in the formula $2X - 5Y = Z$, we assume that X, Y, and Z may range through the entire field of real numbers.

The variables used in boolean equations have a unique characteristic, however; they may assume only one of two possible values. These two values may be

---

†Or T and F, or $+$ and $-$, etc. However, 0 and 1 are almost universally used in computer work.

represented by the symbols 0 and 1.† If an equation describing logical circuitry has several variables, it is still understood that each of the variables can assume only the value 0 or 1. For instance, in the equation $X + Y = Z$, each of the variables X, Y, and Z may have only the values 0 or 1.

This concept will become clearer if a symbol is defined, the + symbol. When the + symbol is placed between two variables, say X and Y, since both X and Y can take only the role 0 or 1, we can define the + symbol by listing all possible combinations for X and Y and the resulting values of $X + Y$.

The possible input and output combinations may be arranged as follows:

$$0 + 0 = 0$$
$$0 + 1 = 1$$
$$1 + 0 = 1$$
$$1 + 1 = 1$$

This is a *logical* addition table and could represent a standard binary addition table except for the last entry. When both X and Y represent 1s, the value of $X + Y$ is 1. The + symbol, therefore, does not have the "normal" meaning, but is a logical addition or logical OR symbol. The equation $X + Y = Z$ can be read "X or Y equals Z" or "X plus Y equals Z." This concept may be extended to any number of variables. For instance, in the equation $A + B + C + D = E$, even if A, B, C, and D all had the value of 1, E would represent only a 1.

To avoid ambiguity, a number of other symbols have been recommended as replacements for the + sign. Some of these[3] are $\cup$, **v**, and **V**. Computer people still use the + sign, however, which was the symbol originally proposed by Boole.

LOGICAL MULTIPLICATION

3.2   A second important operation in boolean algebra we call *logical multiplication* or the *logical* AND *operation*.[4] The rules for this operation can be given by simply listing all values that might occur:

$$0 \cdot 0 = 0$$
$$0 \cdot 1 = 0$$
$$1 \cdot 0 = 0$$
$$1 \cdot 1 = 1$$

Thus, for instance, if we write $Z = X \cdot Y$ and find $X = 0$ and $Y = 1$, then $Z = 0$. Only when X and Y are both 1s would Z be a 1.

Both + and $\cdot$ obey a mathematical rule called the *associative law*. This law says, for +, that $(X + Y) + Z = X + (Y + Z)$ and, for $\cdot$, that $X \cdot (Y \cdot Z) = (X \cdot Y) \cdot Z$. This means that we can write $X + Y + Z$ without ambiguity, for no matter in what order the operation is performed, the result is the same. That is,

---

[3]The preceding equation might then be written $A \cup B \cup C \cup D = E$.

[4]It is necessary to know both the terms *logical addition* and *OR operation* for the + symbol and the terms *logical multiplication* and *AND operation* for the $\cdot$ symbol since all these terms are actively used in computer manuals, technical journals, and trade magazines. The term $X + Y$ is called a *sum term* or *OR term* in computer literature, for example.

BOOLEAN ALGEBRA
AND GATE
NETWORKS

ORing X and Y and then ORing Z gives the same result as ORing Y and Z and then ORing X. We can test this for both $+$ and $\cdot$ by trying all combinations.

Note that while either $+$'s or $\cdot$'s can be used freely, the two cannot be mixed without ambiguity in the absence of further rules. For instance, does $A \cdot B + C$ mean $(A \cdot B) + C$ or $A \cdot (B + C)$? The two form different values for $A = 0$, $B = 0$, and $C = 1$, for then we have $(0 \cdot 0) + 1 = 1$ and $0 \cdot (0 + 1) = 0$, which differ. (Always operating from left to right will alleviate this. This technique is used in some programming languages, but not usually by algebraists or computer designers or maintenance personnel.) The rule which is used is that $\cdot$ is always performed before $+$. Thus $X \cdot Y + Z$ is the same as $(X \cdot Y) + Z$, and $X \cdot Y + X \cdot Z$ means the same as $(X \cdot Y) + (X \cdot Z)$.

AND GATES AND OR GATES

3.3 The $+$ and $\cdot$ operations are physically realized by two types of electronic circuits, called *OR gates* and *AND gates*. We treat these as "black boxes," deferring until later any discussion of how the actual circuitry operates.

A *gate* is simply an electronic circuit which operates on one or more input signals to produce an output signal. One of the simplest and most frequently used gates is called the OR gate, and the block diagram symbol for the OR gate is shown in Fig. 3.1, as is the table of combinations for the inputs and outputs for the OR gate. Since the inputs X and Y are signals with values either 0 or 1 at any given time, the output signal Z can be described by simply listing all values for X and Y and the resulting value for Z. A study of the table in Fig. 3.1 indicates that the OR gate ORs or logically adds its inputs.

Similarly, the AND gate in Fig. 3.2 ANDs or logically multiplies input values, yielding an output Z with value $X \cdot Y$, so that Z is a 1 only when both X and Y are 1s.

Just as the $+$ and $\cdot$ operations could be extended to several variables by using the associative law, OR gates and AND gates can have more than two inputs. Figure 3.3 shows three input OR and AND gates and the table of all input combinations for each. As might be hoped, the OR gate with input X, Y, and Z has a 1 output if X or Y or Z is a 1, so that we can write $X + Y + Z$ for its output.

FIGURE 3.1

OR gate.

INPUT		OUTPUT
X	Y	Z
0	0	0
0	1	1
1	0	1
1	1	1

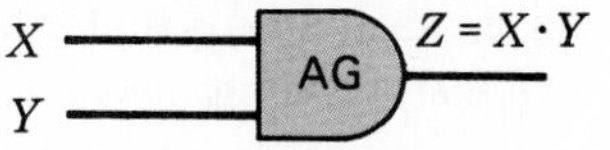

$$X \quad \xrightarrow{\quad} \boxed{AG} \quad Z = X \cdot Y$$
$$Y \quad \xrightarrow{\quad}$$

INPUT		OUTPUT	
X	Y	Z	
0	0	0	$0 \cdot 0 = 0$
0	1	0	$0 \cdot 1 = 0$
1	0	0	$1 \cdot 0 = 0$
1	1	1	$1 \cdot 1 = 1$

COMPLEMENTATION AND INVERTERS

FIGURE 3.2

AND gate.

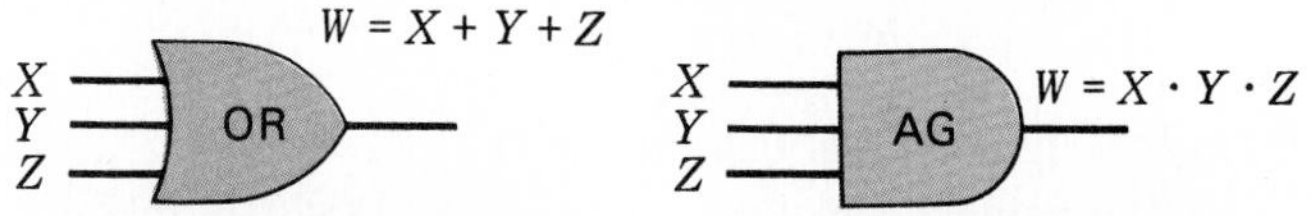

$$W = X + Y + Z$$

$$\begin{array}{c} X \\ Y \\ Z \end{array} \quad \boxed{OR} \quad \xrightarrow{\quad}$$

$$\begin{array}{c} X \\ Y \\ Z \end{array} \quad \boxed{AG} \quad W = X \cdot Y \cdot Z$$

INPUT	OUTPUT
X Y Z	W
0 0 0	0
0 0 1	1
0 1 0	1
0 1 1	1
1 0 0	1
1 0 1	1
1 1 0	1
1 1 1	1

INPUT	OUTPUT
X Y Z	W
0 0 0	0
0 0 1	0
0 1 0	0
0 1 1	0
1 0 0	0
1 0 1	0
1 1 0	0
1 1 1	1

FIGURE 3.3

Three-input OR and AND gates.

Also, the output of the AND gate with inputs, X, Y, and Z is a 1 only when all three of the inputs are 1s, so that we can write the output as $X \cdot Y \cdot Z$.

The above argument can be extended. A four-input OR gate has a 1 output when any of its inputs is a 1, and a four-input AND gate has a 1 output only when all four inputs are 1s.

It is often convenient to shorten $X \cdot Y \cdot Z$ to XYZ, and we sometimes use this convention.

COMPLEMENTATION AND INVERTERS

3.4 The two operations defined so far have been what algebraists would call *binary operations* in that they define an operation on two variables. There are also *singular* or *unary*, *operations*, which define an operation on a single variable. A

BOOLEAN ALGEBRA
AND GATE
NETWORKS

familiar example of unary operation is $-$, for we can write -5 or -10 or $-X$, meaning that we are to take the negative of these values. (The $-$ is also used as a binary operation symbol for subtraction, which makes it a familiar but ambiguous example.)

In boolean algebra we have an operation called *complementation,* and the symbol we use is $^{-}$. Thus we write $\overline{X}$, meaning "take the complement of X," or $(\overline{X + Y})$, meaning "take the complement of $X + Y$." The complement operation can be defined quite simply:

$$\overline{0} = 1$$
$$\overline{1} = 0$$

The complement of a value can be taken repeatedly. For instance, we can find $\overline{\overline{\overline{X}}}$: For $X = 0$ it is $\overline{\overline{\overline{0}}} = \overline{\overline{1}} = \overline{0} = 1$, and for $X = 1$ it is $\overline{\overline{\overline{1}}} = \overline{\overline{0}} = \overline{1} = 0$.

A useful rule is based on the fact that $\overline{\overline{X}} = X$. Checking, we find that $\overline{\overline{0}} = \overline{1} = 0$ and $\overline{\overline{1}} = \overline{0} = 1$. [This rule—that double complementation gives the original value—is an important characteristic of a boolean algebra which does not generally hold for most unary operations. For instance, the rule does not hold for the operation of squaring a real number: $(3^2)^2 = 81$, not 3.]

The complementation operation is physically realized by a gate or circuit called an *inverter.* Figure 3.4(*a*) shows an inverter and the table of combinations for its input and output. Figure 3.4(*b*) shows also that connecting two inverters in series gives an output equal to the input, and this is the gating counterpart to the law of double complementation, $\overline{\overline{X}} = X$.

Several other symbols have been used for the complementation symbol. For instance, $\sim$ is often used by logicians who write $\sim X$ and read this "the negation of X." The symbol $'$ has been used by mathematicians and computer people; thus X' is the complement of X in these systems. The overbar symbol is now used by the American National Standards Institute and military standards, as well as by most journals and manufacturers, and we use it.

FIGURE 3.4

(*a*) Block diagram of an inverter. (*b*) Two inverters in series.

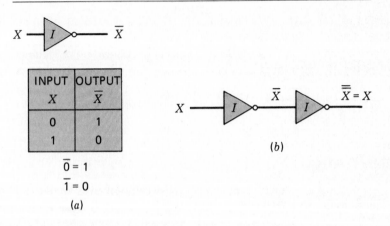

INPUT	OUTPUT
X	$\overline{X}$
0	1
1	0

$\overline{0} = 1$

$\overline{1} = 0$

(*a*)

(*b*)

3.5 The tables of values for the three operations just explained are sometimes called *truth tables,* or *tables of combinations.* To study a logical expression, it is very useful to construct a table of values for the variables and then to evaluate the expression for each of the possible combinations of variables in turn. Consider the expression $X + Y\overline{Z}$. There are three variables in this expression: X, Y, and Z, each of which can assume the value 0 or 1. The possible combinations of values may be arranged in ascending order,[5] as in Table 3.1.

One of the variables, Z, is complemented in the expression $X + Y\overline{Z}$. So a column is now added to the table listing values of $\overline{Z}$ (see Table 3.2).

A column is now added listing the values that $Y\overline{Z}$ assumes for each value of X, Y, and Z. This column will contain the value 1 only when both Y is a 1 and $\overline{Z}$ is a 1 (see Table 3.3).

Now the ORing, or logical addition, of the values of X to the values which have been calculated for $Y\overline{Z}$ is performed in a final column (see Table 3.4).

The final column contains the value of $X + Y\overline{Z}$ for each set of input values which X, Y, and Z may take. For instance, when $X = 1$, $Y = 0$, and $Z = 1$, the expression has the value of 1.

EVALUATION
OF LOGICAL
EXPRESSIONS

---

[5]Note that the variables in each row of this table may be combined into a binary number. The binary numbers will then count from 000 to 111 in binary, or from 0 to 7 decimal. Sometimes each row is numbered in decimal according to the number represented. Then reference may be made to the row by using the decimal number. For instance, row 0 has values of 0, 0, 0, for X, Y, and Z, row 6 has values of 1, 1, 0, and row 7 has values of 1, 1, 1.

TABLE 3.1

X	Y	Z
0	0	0
0	0	1
0	1	0
0	1	1
1	0	0
1	0	1
1	1	0
1	1	1

TABLE 3.2

X	Y	Z	$\overline{Z}$
0	0	0	1
0	0	1	0
0	1	0	1
0	1	1	0
1	0	0	1
1	0	1	0
1	1	0	1
1	1	1	0

66

BOOLEAN ALGEBRA
AND GATE
NETWORKS

TABLE 3.3

X	Y	Z	$\overline{Z}$	$Y\overline{Z}$
0	0	0	1	0
0	0	1	0	0
0	1	0	1	1
0	1	1	0	0
1	0	0	1	0
1	0	1	0	0
1	1	0	1	1
1	1	1	0	0

TABLE 3.4

X	Y	Z	$\overline{Z}$	$Y\overline{Z}$	$X + Y\overline{Z}$
0	0	0	1	0	0
0	0	1	0	0	0
0	1	0	1	1	1
0	1	1	0	0	0
1	0	0	1	0	1
1	0	1	0	0	1
1	1	0	1	1	1
1	1	1	0	0	1

EVALUATION OF AN EXPRESSION CONTAINING PARENTHESES

3.6 The following example illustrates the procedure for constructing a truth table for the expression $X + Y(\overline{X} + \overline{Y})$. There are only two variables in the expression, X and Y. First a table of the values which X and Y may assume is constructed (see Table 3.5).

Now, since the expression contains both $\overline{X}$ and $\overline{Y}$, two columns are added listing complements of the original values of the variables (see Table 3.6).

The various values of $\overline{X} + \overline{Y}$ are now calculated (see Table 3.7).

The values for $\overline{X} + \overline{Y}$ are now multiplied (ANDed) by the values of Y in the table, forming another column representing $Y(\overline{X} + \overline{Y})$ (see Table 3.8).

Finally the values for $Y(\overline{X} + \overline{Y})$ are added (ORed) to the values for X which are listed, forming the final column and completing the table (see Table 3.9).

Inspection of the final column of the table indicates that the values taken by the function $X + Y(\overline{X} + \overline{Y})$ are identical with the values found in the table for ORing X and Y. This indicates that the function $X + Y(\overline{X} + \overline{Y})$ is equivalent to

TABLE 3.5

X	Y
0	0
0	1
1	0
1	1

TABLE 3.6

X	Y	$\overline{X}$	$\overline{Y}$
0	0	1	1
0	1	1	0
1	0	0	1
1	1	0	0

TABLE 3.7

X	Y	$\overline{X}$	$\overline{Y}$	$\overline{X} + \overline{Y}$
0	0	1	1	1
0	1	1	0	1
1	0	0	1	1
1	1	0	0	0

TABLE 3.8

X	Y	$\overline{X}$	$\overline{Y}$	$\overline{X} + \overline{Y}$	$Y(\overline{X} + \overline{Y})$
0	0	1	1	1	0
0	1	1	0	1	1
1	0	0	1	1	0
1	1	0	0	0	0

TABLE 3.9

X	Y	$\overline{X}$	$\overline{Y}$	$\overline{X} + \overline{Y}$	$Y(\overline{X} + \overline{Y})$	$X + Y(\overline{X} + \overline{Y})$
0	0	1	1	1	0	0
0	1	1	0	1	1	1
1	0	0	1	1	0	1
1	1	0	0	0	0	1

the function $X + Y$. This equivalence has been established by trying each possible combination of values in the variables and noting that both expressions then have the same value. This is called a *proof by perfect induction*. If a logic circuit were constructed for each of the two expressions, both circuits would perform the same function, yielding identical outputs for each combination of inputs.

BASIC LAWS OF BOOLEAN ALGEBRA

3.7 Some fundamental relations of boolean algebra have been presented. A complete set of the basic operations is listed below.[6] Although simple in appearance,

---

[6]Actually, a number of possible sets of postulates may be used to define the algebra. The particular treatment of boolean algebra given here is derived from that of E. V. Huntington and M. H. Stone. The author would also like to acknowledge the influence of I. S. Reed and S. H. Caldwell on this development of the concepts of the algebra.

BOOLEAN ALGEBRA
AND GATE
NETWORKS

TABLE 3.10   BOOLEAN ALGEBRA RULES

1 $0 + X = X$
2 $1 + X = 1$
3 $X + X = X$
4 $X + \overline{X} = 1$
5 $0 \cdot X = 0$
6 $1 \cdot X = X$
7 $X \cdot X = X$
8 $X \cdot \overline{X} = 0$
9 $\overline{\overline{X}} = X$
10 $X + Y = Y + X$
11 $X \cdot Y = Y \cdot X$
12 $X + (Y + Z) = (X + Y) + Z$
13 $X(YZ) = (XY)Z$
14 $X(Y + Z) = XY + XZ$
15 $X + XZ = X$
16 $X(X + Y) = X$
17 $(X + Y)(X + Z) = X + YZ$
18 $X + \overline{X}Y = X + Y$
19 $XY + YZ + \overline{Y}Z = XY + Z$

these rules may be used to construct a boolean algebra,[7] determining all the relations that follow:

$$\text{If } X \neq 0, \quad \text{then } X = 1$$

and

$$\text{If } X \neq 1, \quad \text{then } X = 0$$

OR OPERATION (LOGICAL ADDITION)	AND OPERATION (LOGICAL MULTIPLICATION)	COMPLEMENT RULES
$0 + 0 = 0$	$0 \cdot 0 = 0$	$\overline{0} = 1$
$0 + 1 = 1$	$0 \cdot 0 = 0$	$\overline{1} = 0$
$1 + 0 = 1$	$1 \cdot 0 = 0$	
$1 + 1 = 1$	$1 \cdot 1 = 1$	

A list of useful relations is presented in Table 3.10. Most of the basic rules by which boolean algebra expressions may be manipulated are contained in this table. Each rule may be proved by using the proof by perfect induction. An example of this proof for rule 3 in Table 3.10 is as follows: The variable X can have only the value 0 or 1. If X has the value 0, then $0 + 0 = 0$; if X has the value 1, then $1 + 1 = 1$. Therefore $X + X = X$.

---

[7]These rules are used to construct an *example*, or *realization*, of a boolean algebra. We note that, strictly speaking, this boolean algebra consists of a set B of two elements which we call 0 and 1, an addition operation $+$, a multiplication operation $\cdot$, and a complement operation ‾ . There are other boolean algebras (an infinite number), but this was Boole's original algebra. This algebra is sometimes called *switching algebra* to identify it more closely, but it is the same as propositional calculus, for instance.

The same basic technique may be used to prove the remainder of the rules. Rule 9 states that double complementation of a variable results in the original variable. If X equals 0, then the first complement is 1 and the second will be 0, the original value. If the original value for X is 1, then the first complement will be 0 and the second 1, the original value. Therefore $X = \bar{\bar{X}}$.

Rules 10 and 11, which are known as the *commutative laws,* express the fact that the order in which a combination of terms is performed does not affect the result of the combination. Rule 10 is the commutative law of addition, which states that the order of addition or ORing does not affect the sum $(X + Y = Y + X)$. Rule 11 is the commutative law of multiplication $(XY = YX)$, which states that the order of multiplication or ANDing does not affect the product.

Rules 12 and 13 are the *associative laws.* Rule 12 states that in the logical addition of several terms, the sum which will be obtained if the first term is added to the second and then the third term is added will be the same as the sum obtained if the second term is added to the third and then the first term is added $[X + (Y + Z) = (X + Y) + Z]$. Rule 13 is the associative law of logical multiplication, stating that in a product with three factors, *any* two may be multiplied, followed by the third $[X(YZ) = (XY)Z]$.

Rule 14, the *distributive law,* states that the product of a variable (X) times a sum $(Y + Z)$ is equal to the sum of the products of the variable multiplied by each term of the sum $[X(Y + Z) = XY + XZ]$.

The three laws, commutative, associative, and distributive, may be extended to include any number of terms. For instance, the commutative law for logical addition states that $X + Y = Y + X$. This may be extended to

$$X + Y + Z + A = A + Y + Z + X$$

The commutative law for logical multiplication also may be extended: $XYZ = YZX$. These two laws are useful in rearranging the terms of an equation.

The terms also may be combined:

$$(X + Y) + (Z + A) = (A + Y) + (X + Z)$$

and $(XY)(ZA) = (XA)(ZY)$. These two laws are useful in regrouping the terms of an equation.

The distributive law may be extended in several ways:

$$X(Y + Z + A) = XY + XZ + XA$$

If two sums, such as $W + X$ and $Y + Z$, are to be multiplied, then one of the sums is treated as a single term and multiplied by the individual terms of the other sum. The results are then multiplied according to the distributive law. For instance.

$$(W + X)(Y + Z) = W(Y + Z) + X(Y + Z) = WY + WZ + XY + XZ$$

BOOLEAN ALGEBRA
AND GATE
NETWORKS

3.8   Notice that, among others, rule 17 does not apply to "normal" algebra. The rule may be obtained from the preceding rules as follows:

$$
\begin{aligned}
(X + Y)(X + Z) &= XX + XZ + XY + YZ &&\text{where } XX = X, \text{ rule 7} \\
&= X + XZ + XY + YZ \\
&= X + XY + XZ + YZ \\
&= X(1 + Y) + Z(X + Y) &&\text{where } 1 + Y = 1, \text{ rule 2} \\
&= X + Z(X + Y) \\
&= X + XZ + YZ \\
&= X(1 + Z) + YZ &&\text{where } 1 + Z = 1, \text{ rule 2} \\
&= X + YZ
\end{aligned}
$$

Therefore

$$(X + Y)(X + Z) = X + YZ$$

Since rule 17 does not apply to normal algebra, it is interesting to test the rule by using the proof by perfect induction. It will be necessary to construct truth tables for the right-hand $(X + YZ)$ and left-hand $[(X + Y)(X + Z)]$ members of the equation and compare the results (see Tables 3.11 and 3.12).

The last column of the table for the function $X + YZ$ is identical with the last column of the table for $(X + Y)(X + Z)$. This proves (by means of the proof by perfect induction) that the expressions are equivalent.

Rules 15 and 16 are also not rules in normal algebra. The following is a

TABLE 3.11

X	Y	Z	YZ	X + YZ
0	0	0	0	0
0	0	1	0	0
0	1	0	0	0
0	1	1	1	1
1	0	0	0	1
1	0	1	0	1
1	1	0	0	1
1	1	1	1	1

TABLE 3.12

X	Y	Z	X + Y	X + Z	(X + Y)(X + Z)
0	0	0	0	0	0
0	0	1	0	1	0
0	1	0	1	0	0
0	1	1	1	1	1
1	0	0	1	1	1
1	0	1	1	1	1
1	1	0	1	1	1
1	1	1	1	1	1

proof of rule 15 using preceding rules:

$$X + XZ = X(1 + Z) \qquad \text{distributive law}$$

And since $1 + Z = 1$ by rule 2,

$$X + XZ = X(1) \qquad \text{and} \qquad X(1) = X \qquad \text{by rule 6}$$

Therefore

$$X + XZ = X$$

It is worthwhile to try to prove rule 15 by using the proof by perfect induction at this point. Here is a proof of rule 16 that uses rules that precede it:

$$
\begin{aligned}
X(X + Y) &= XX + XY & &\text{distributive law} \\
&= X + XY & &(\text{since } XX = X) \\
&= X(1 + Y) & &\text{where } 1 + Y = 1, \text{ rule 2} \\
&= X
\end{aligned}
$$

It is instructive to prove this rule also by perfect induction at this point.

SIMPLIFICATION OF EXPRESSIONS

3.9   The rules given may be used to simplify boolean expressions, just as the rules of normal algebra may be used to simplify expressions. Consider the expression

$$(X + Y)(X + \overline{Y})(\overline{X} + Z)$$

The first two terms consist of $X + Y$ and $X + \overline{Y}$; these terms may be multiplied and, since $X + X\overline{Y} + XY = X$ and $Y\overline{Y} = 0$, reduced to X.

The expression has been reduced now to $X(\overline{X} + Z)$, which may be expressed as $X\overline{X} + XZ$ (rule 14). And since $X\overline{X}$ is equal to 0, the entire expression $(X + Y)(X + \overline{Y})(\overline{X} + Z)$ may be reduced to XZ.

Another expression that may be simplified is $XYZ + X\overline{Y}Z + XY\overline{Z}$. First the three terms $XYZ + X\overline{Y}Z + XY\overline{Z}$ may be written $X(YZ + \overline{Y}Z + Y\overline{Z})$, by rule 14. Then, by using rule 14 again, $X[Y(Z + \overline{Z}) + \overline{Y}Z]$; and since $Z + \overline{Z}$ equals 1, we have $X(Y + \overline{Y}Z)$.

The expression $X(Y + \overline{Y}Z)$ may be further reduced to $X(Y + Z)$ by using rule 18. The final expression can be written in two ways: $X(Y + Z)$ or $XY + XZ$. The first expression is generally preferable if the equation is to be constructed as an electronic circuit, because it requires only one AND circuit and one OR circuit.

DE MORGAN'S THEOREMS

3.10   The following two rules are known as De Morgan's theorems:

$$
\begin{aligned}
\overline{(X + Y)} &= \overline{X} \cdot \overline{Y} \\
\overline{(X \cdot Y)} &= \overline{X} + \overline{Y}
\end{aligned}
$$

The complement of any boolean expression, or a part of any expression, may be found by means of these theorems. In these rules, two steps are used to form a complement:

1 The + symbols are replaced with · symbols and · symbols with + symbols.

2 Each of the terms in the expression is complemented.

The use of De Morgan's theorem may be demonstrated by finding the complement of the expression $X + YZ$. First, note that a multiplication sign has been omitted and the expression could be written $X + (Y \cdot Z)$. To complement this, the addition symbol is replaced with a multiplication symbol and the two terms are complemented, giving $\overline{X} \cdot \overline{(Y \cdot Z)}$; then the remaining term is complemented, $\overline{X}(\overline{Y} + \overline{Z})$. The following equivalence has been found: $\overline{(X + YZ)} = \overline{X}(\overline{Y} + \overline{Z})$.

The complement of $\overline{W}X + Y\overline{Z}$ may be formed by two steps:

1 The addition symbol is changed.

2 The complement of each term is formed:

$$(\overline{\overline{W} \cdot X})(\overline{Y \cdot \overline{Z}})$$

This becomes $(W + \overline{X})(\overline{Y} + Z)$.

Since W and Z were already complemented, they become uncomplemented by the theorem $\overline{\overline{X}} = X$.

It is sometimes necessary to complement both sides of an equation. This may be done in the same way as before:

$$WX + YZ = 0$$

Complementing both sides gives

$$\overline{(WX + YZ)} = \overline{0}$$
$$(\overline{W} + \overline{X})(\overline{Y} + \overline{Z}) = 1$$

BASIC DUALITY OF BOOLEAN ALGEBRA

3.11 De Morgan's theorem expresses a basic duality which underlies all boolean algebra. The postulates and theorems which have been presented can all be divided into pairs. For example, $(X + Y) + Z = X + (Y + Z)$ is the *dual* of $(XY)Z = X(YZ)$, and $X + 0 = X$ is the dual of $X \cdot 1 = X$.

Often the rules or theorems are listed in an order which illustrates the duality of the algebra. In proving the theorems or rules of the algebra, it is then necessary to prove only one theorem, and the dual of the theorem follows necessarily. For instance, if you prove that $X + XY = X$, you can immediately add the theorem $X(X + Y) = X$ to the list of theorems as the dual of the first expression.[8] In effect, all boolean algebra is predicated on this two-for-one basis.

---

[8]When the first expression, $X + XY = X$, has been complemented, $\overline{X}(\overline{X} + \overline{Y}) = \overline{X}$ is obtained. Then uncomplemented variables may be substituted on both sides of the equation without changing the basic equivalence of the expression.

TABLE 3.13

INPUTS		OUTPUT
X	Y	Z
0	0	1
0.	1	0
1	0	1
1	1	1

DERIVATION OF A BOOLEAN EXPRESSION

3.12   When designing a logical circuit, the logical designer works from two sets of known values: (1) the various states which the inputs to the logical network can take and (2) the desired outputs for each input condition. The logical expression is derived from these sets of values.

Consider a specific problem. A logical network has two inputs X and Y and an output Z. The relationship between inputs and outputs is to be as follows:

1   When both X and Y are 0s, the output Z is to be 1.

2   When X is 0 and Y is 1, the output Z is to be 0.

3   When X is 1 and Y is 0, the output Z is to be 1.

4   When X is 1 and Y is 1, the output Z is to be 1.

These relations may be expressed in tabular form, as shown in Table 3.13.

It is now necessary to add another column to the table. This column will consist of a list of *product terms* obtained from the values of the input variables. The new column will contain each of the input variables listed in each row of the table, with the letter representing the respective input complemented when the input value for this variable is 0 and not complemented when the input value is 1. The terms obtained in this manner are designated as product terms. With two input variables X and $Y,$ each row of the table will contain a product term consisting of X and $Y,$ with X or Y complemented or not, depending on the input values for that row (see Table 3.14).

Whenever Z is equal to 1, the X and Y product term from the same row is removed and formed into a *sum-of-products* expression. Therefore, the product terms from the first, third, and fourth rows are selected. These are $\overline{X}\overline{Y}$, $X\overline{Y}$, and XY.

TABLE 3.14

INPUTS		OUTPUT	PRODUCT TERMS
X	Y	Z	
0	0	1	$\overline{X}\overline{Y}$
0	1	0	$\overline{X}Y$
1	0	1	$X\overline{Y}$
1	1	1	XY

TABLE 3.15

X	Y	$\overline{Y}$	$X + \overline{Y}$
0	0	1	1
0	1	0	0
1	0	1	1
1	1	0	1

There are now three terms, each the product of two variables. The logical sum of these products is equal to the expression desired. This type of expression is often referred to as a *canonical expansion* for the function. The complete expression in normal form is

$$\overline{X}\overline{Y} + X\overline{Y} + XY = Z$$

The left-hand side of the expression may be simplified as follows:

$$\overline{X}\overline{Y} + X\overline{Y} + XY = Z$$
$$\overline{X}\overline{Y} + X(\overline{Y} + Y) = Z$$
$$\overline{X}\overline{Y} + X = Z$$

and finally, by rule 18 in Table 3.10, $X + \overline{Y} = Z$.

The truth table may be constructed to check the function that has been derived (see Table 3.15). The last column of this table agrees with the last column of the truth table of the desired function, showing that the expressions are equivalent.

The expression $X + \overline{Y}$ may be constructed in one of two ways. If only the inputs X and Y are available, as might be the case if the inputs to the circuit were from another logical network or from certain types of storage devices, an inverter would be required to form $\overline{Y}$. Then the circuit would require an inverter plus an OR gate. Generally the complement of the Y input would be available, however, and only one OR gate would be required for the second way the expression would be constructed.

Another expression, with three inputs (designated X, Y, and Z), will be derived. Assume that the desired relationships between the inputs and the output have been determined, as shown in Table 3.16.

TABLE 3.16

INPUTS			OUTPUT
When $X = 0$,	$Y = 0$,	$Z = 0$	1
0	0	1	0
0	1	0	1
0	1	1	0
1	0	0	1
1	0	1	0
1	1	0	1
1	1	1	0

TABLE 3.17

INPUTS			OUTPUT
X	Y	Z	A
0	0	0	1
0	0	1	0
0	1	0	1
0	1	1	0
1	0	0	1
1	0	1	0
1	1	0	1
1	1	1	0

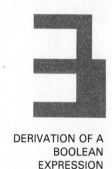

DERIVATION OF A
BOOLEAN
EXPRESSION

1 A truth table is formed (see Table 3.17).

2 A column is added listing the inputs, X, Y, and Z according to their values in the input columns (see Table 3.18).

3 The product terms from each row in which the output is a 1 are collected $(\overline{X}\overline{Y}\overline{Z}, \overline{X}Y\overline{Z}, X\overline{Y}\overline{Z},$ and $XY\overline{Z})$, and the desired expression is the sum of these products $(\overline{X}\overline{Y}\overline{Z} + \overline{X}Y\overline{Z} + X\overline{Y}\overline{Z} + XY\overline{Z})$. Therefore, the complete expression in standard form for the desired network is

$$\overline{X}\overline{Y}\overline{Z} + \overline{X}Y\overline{Z} + X\overline{Y}\overline{Z} + XY\overline{Z} = A$$

This expression may be simplified as shown below:

$$\overline{X}\overline{Y}\overline{Z} + \overline{X}Y\overline{Z} + X\overline{Y}\overline{Z} + XY\overline{Z} = A$$
$$\overline{X}(\overline{Y}\overline{Z} + Y\overline{Z}) + X(\overline{Y}\overline{Z} + Y\overline{Z}) = A$$
$$\overline{X}\,[\overline{Z}(\overline{Y} + Y)] + X[\overline{Z}(\overline{Y} + Y)] = A$$
$$\overline{X}\overline{Z} + X\overline{Z} = A$$
$$\overline{Z} = A$$

Thus the function can be performed by a single inverter connected to the Z input. Inspection of the truth table will indicate that the output A is always equal to the complement of the input variable Z.

TABLE 3.18

INPUTS			OUTPUT	PRODUCT TERMS
X	Y	Z	A	
0	0	0	1	$\overline{X}\,\overline{Y}\overline{Z}$
0	0	1	0	$\overline{X}\,\overline{Y}Z$
0	1	0	1	$\overline{X}\,Y\overline{Z}$
0	1	1	0	$\overline{X}\,YZ$
1	0	0	1	$X\,\overline{Y}\overline{Z}$
1	0	1	0	$X\,\overline{Y}Z$
1	1	0	1	$X\,Y\overline{Z}$
1	1	1	0	$X\,YZ$

3.13 The OR gates, AND gates, and inverters described in Secs. 3.3 and 3.4 can be interconnected to form *gating,* or *logic, networks.* (Those who study switching theory would also call these *combinational networks.*) The boolean algebra expression corresponding to a given gating network can be derived by systematically progressing from input to output on the gates. Figure 3.5(a) shows a gating network with three inputs X, Y, and Z and an output expression $(X \cdot Y) + \overline{Z}$. A network that forms $(X \cdot Y) + (\overline{X} \cdot \overline{Y})$ and another network that forms $(X + Y) \cdot (\overline{X} + \overline{Y})$ are shown in Fig. 3.5(b) and (c).

We can analyze the operation of these gating networks by using the boolean algebra expressions. For instance, in troubleshooting a computer, we can determine which gates have failed by examining the inputs to the gating network and the outputs and seeing whether the boolean operations are properly performed. The bookkeeping for computer circuitry is done by means of block diagrams, as in Fig.

FIGURE 3.5

Three gating networks.

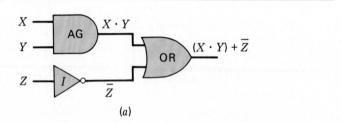

(a)

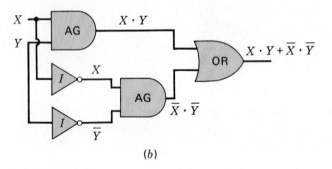

(b)

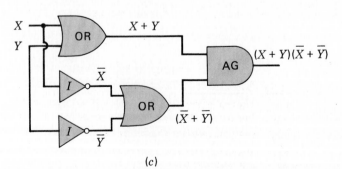

(c)

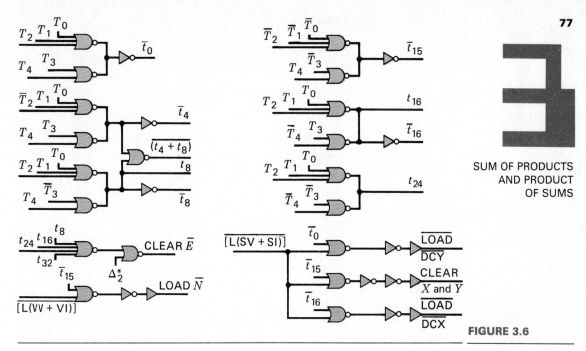

SUM OF PRODUCTS
AND PRODUCT
OF SUMS

FIGURE 3.6

Block diagram from a
computer.

3.6, which shows a typical print. The use of boolean algebra is spread completely throughout the computer industry.

SUM OF PRODUCTS AND PRODUCT OF SUMS

3.14 An important consideration in dealing with gating circuits and their algebraic counterparts is the *form* of the boolean algebra expression and the resulting form of the gating network. Certain types of boolean algebra expressions lead to gating networks which are more desirable from most implementation viewpoints. We now define the two most used and usable forms for boolean expressions.

First let us define terms:

1   *Product term*   A product term is a single variable or the logical product of several variables. The variables may or may not be complemented.

2   *Sum term*   A sum term is a single variable or the sum of several variables. The variables may or may not be complemented.

For example, the term $X \cdot Y \cdot Z$ is a product term; $X + Y$ is a sum term; X is both a product term and a sum term; $X + Y \cdot Z$ is neither a product term nor a sum term; $X + \overline{Y}$ is a sum term; $X \cdot \overline{Y} \cdot \overline{Z}$ is a product term; $\overline{Y}$ is a both a sum term and a product term. (*Comment:* Calling single variables sum terms and product terms is disagreeable but necessary. Since we must suffer with it, remember that some apples are red, round, and shiny, that is, more than one thing.)

BOOLEAN ALGEBRA
AND GATE
NETWORKS

We now define two most important types of expressions.

1 *Sum-of-products expression* A sum-of-products expression is a product term or several product terms logically added.

2 *Product-of-sums expression* A product-of-sums expression is a sum term or several sum terms logically multiplied.

For example, the expression $\overline{X}\cdot Y + X\cdot\overline{Y}$ is a sum-of-products expression; $(X + Y)(\overline{X} + \overline{Y})$ is a product-of-sums expression. The following are all sum-of-products expressions:

$$X$$
$$X\cdot Y + Z$$
$$\overline{X}\cdot\overline{Y} + \overline{X}\cdot\overline{Y}\cdot\overline{Z}$$
$$X + Y$$

The following are product-of-sums expressions:

$$(X + Y)\cdot(X + \overline{Y})\cdot(\overline{X} + \overline{Y})$$
$$(X + Y + Z)\cdot(X + \overline{Y})\cdot(\overline{X} + \overline{Y})$$
$$X + Z$$
$$\overline{X}$$
$$(X + Y)X$$

One prime reason for liking sum-of-products or product-of-sums expressions is their straightforward conversion to very nice gating networks. In their purest, nicest form they go into *two-level networks,* which are networks for which the longest path through which a signal must pass from input to output is two gates.

Note: In the following discussion we assume that when a variable X is available, its complement $\overline{X}$ is also available; that is, no inverters are required to complement inputs. This is quite important and quite realistic, since most signals come from flip-flops, which we study later, and which provide both an output and its complement.

Figure 3.7 shows several gating networks. Figure 3.7(*a*) shows sum-of-products networks, and Fig. 3.7(*b*) shows product-of-sums networks. The gating networks for sum-of-products expressions in "conventional" form—that is, expressions with at least two product terms and with at least two variables in each product term—go directly into an AND-to-OR gate network, while conventional product-of-sums expressions go directly into OR-to-AND gate networks, as shown in the figure.

DERIVATION OF PRODUCT-OF-SUMS EXPRESSIONS

3.15 The sequence of steps described in Sec. 3.12 derived a sum-of-products expression for a given circuit. Another technique, really a dual of the first, forms the required expression as a product-of-sums. The expression derived in this manner is made up, before simplification, of terms each consisting of sums of variables

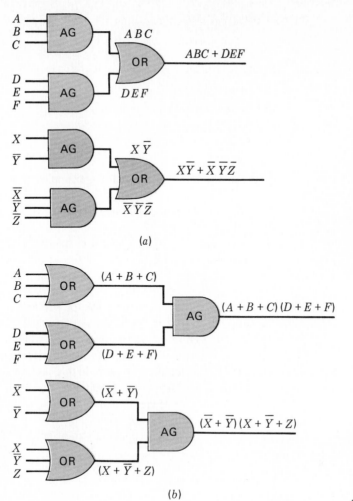

(a)

(b)

FIGURE 3.7

(a) AND-to-OR gate networks. (b) OR-to-AND gate networks.

such as $(X + Y + Z)$ $\cdots$. The final expression is the product of these sum terms and has the form $(X + Y + Z)(X + Y + \overline{Z})$ $\cdots$ $(\overline{X} + \overline{Y} + \overline{Z})$.

The method for arriving at the desired expression is as follows:

1 Construct a table of the input and output values.

2 Construct an additional column of sum terms containing complemented and uncomplemented variables (depending on the values in the input columns) for each row of the table. In each row of the table, a sum term is formed. However, in this case, if the input value for a given variable is 1, the variable will be complemented; and if 0, not complemented.

3 The desired expression is the product of the sum terms from the rows in which the output is 0.

TABLE 3.19

INPUTS		OUTPUT
X	Y	Z
0	0	1
0	1	0
1	0	0
1	1	1

The use of these rules is illustrated by working examples in this and the following sections.

Table 3.19 contains the input and output values which describe a function to be realized by a logical network.

A column containing the input variables in sum-term form is now added in each row. A given variable is complemented if the input value for the variable is 1 in the same row and is not complemented if the value is 0 (see Table 3.20). Each sum term is, therefore, simply the complement of the product term which occurs in the same row in the previous table for sum-of-products expressions. Notice that the sum term $\overline{X} + Y$ in the third row of Table 3.20 is the complement of the product term $X\overline{Y}$ used in the sum-of-products derivation.

A product-of-sums expression is now formed by selecting those sum terms for which the output is 0 and multiplying them. In this case, 0s appear in the second and third rows, showing that the desired expression is $(X + \overline{Y})(\overline{X} + Y)$. A sum-of-products expression may be found by multiplying the two terms of this expression, yielding $XY + \overline{X}\overline{Y}$. In this case the same number of gates would be required to construct circuits corresponding to both the sum-of-products and the product-of-sums expressions.

DERIVATION OF A THREE-INPUT-VARIABLE EXPRESSION

3.16 Consider Table 3.21, expressing an input-to-output relationship for which an expression is to be derived. Two columns will be added this time, one containing the sum-of-products terms and the other the product-of-sums terms (see Table 3.22). The two expressions may be written in the following way:

Sum-of-products:

$$\overline{X}Y\overline{Z} + \overline{X}YZ + XY\overline{Z} = A$$

TABLE 3.20

INPUTS		OUTPUT	SUM TERMS
X	Y	Z	
0	0	1	$X + Y$
0	1	0	$X + \overline{Y}$
1	0	0	$\overline{X} + Y$
1	1	1	$\overline{X} + \overline{Y}$

TABLE 3.21

INPUTS			OUTPUT
X	Y	Z	A
0	0	0	0
0	0	1	0
0	1	0	1
0	1	1	1
1	0	0	0
1	0	1	0
1	1	0	1
1	1	1	0

DERIVATION OF A
THREE-INPUT-
VARIABLE
EXPRESSION

Product-of-sums:

$$(X + Y + Z)(X + Y + \overline{Z})(\overline{X} + Y + Z)(\overline{X} + Y + \overline{Z})(\overline{X} + \overline{Y} + \overline{Z}) = A$$

The two expressions may be simplified as shown:

SUM OF PRODUCTS

$$(\overline{X}Y\overline{Z}) + (\overline{X}YZ) + (XY\overline{Z}) = A$$
$$\overline{X}(Y\overline{Z} + YZ) + (XY\overline{Z}) = A$$
$$\overline{X}Y + XY\overline{Z} = A$$
$$Y(\overline{X} + X\overline{Z}) = A$$
$$\overline{X}Y + Y\overline{Z} = A$$

PRODUCT OF SUMS

$$(X + Y + Z)(X + Y + \overline{Z})(\overline{X} + Y + Z)(\overline{X} + Y + \overline{Z})(\overline{X} + \overline{Y} + \overline{Z}) = A$$
$$(X + Y)(\overline{X} + Y)(\overline{X} + \overline{Z}) = A$$
$$Y(\overline{X} + \overline{Z}) = A$$

The two final expressions clearly can be seen to be equivalent. Notice, however, that the shortest sum-of-products expression, which is $\overline{X}Y + Y\overline{Z}$, requires two AND gates and an OR gate (Fig. 3.8), while the shortest product-of-sums expression, $Y(\overline{X} + \overline{Z})$, requires only a single AND gate and a single OR gate. In some cases the minimal sum-of-products expression will require fewer logical elements to construct, and in other instances the construction of the minimal product

TABLE 3.22

INPUTS			OUTPUT	PRODUCT TERMS	SUM TERMS
X	Y	Z	A		
0	0	0	0	$\overline{X}\,\overline{Y}\,\overline{Z}$	$X + Y + Z$
0	0	1	0	$\overline{X}\,\overline{Y}\,Z$	$X + Y + \overline{Z}$
0	1	0	1	$\overline{X}\,Y\,\overline{Z}$	$X + \overline{Y} + Z$
0	1	1	1	$\overline{X}\,Y\,Z$	$X + \overline{Y} + \overline{Z}$
1	0	0	0	$X\,\overline{Y}\,\overline{Z}$	$\overline{X} + Y + Z$
1	0	1	0	$X\,\overline{Y}\,Z$	$\overline{X} + Y + \overline{Z}$
1	1	0	1	$X\,Y\,\overline{Z}$	$\overline{X} + \overline{Y} + Z$
1	1	1	0	$X\,Y\,Z$	$\overline{X} + \overline{Y} + \overline{Z}$

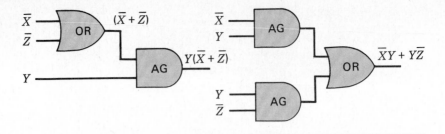

FIGURE 3.8

FIGURE 3.8

Networks for $Y(\bar{X} + \bar{Z})$ and $\bar{X}Y + Y\bar{Z}$.

of sums will require fewer elements. If the sole criterion is the number of logical elements, it is necessary to obtain both a minimal sum-of-products expression and a minimal product-of-sums expression to compare the two. It is possible first to derive the canonical expansion expression for the network to be designed in one of the forms—for instance, product of sums—to simplify the expression, and then to convert the simplified expression to the other form, by using the distributive laws. Then any additional simplification which is required can be performed. In this way, minimal expressions in each form may be obtained without deriving both canonical expansions, although this may be desirable.

The simplification techniques which have been described are algebraic and depend on judicious use of the theorems that have been presented. The problem of simplifying boolean expressions so that the shortest expression is always found is quite complex. However, it is possible, by means of the repeated use of certain algorithms, to derive minimal sum-of-products and product-of-sums expressions. We examine this problem in following sections.

NAND GATES AND NOR GATES

3.17 Two other types of gates, NAND gates and NOR gates, are often used in computers. It is fortunate that the boolean algebra which has been described can be easily used to analyze the operation of these gates.

A NAND gate is shown in Fig. 3.9. The inputs are A, B, and C, and the output from the gate is written $\bar{A} + \bar{B} + \bar{C}$. The output will be a 1 if A is a 0 or B is a 0 or C is a 0, and the output will be a 0 only if A and B and C are all 1s.

The operation of the gate can be analyzed using the equivalent block diagram circuit shown in Fig. 3.9, which has an AND gate followed by an inverter. If the

FIGURE 3.9

NAND gate.

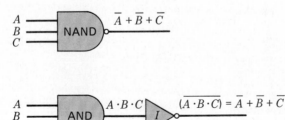

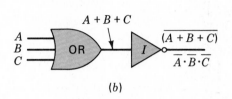

$\overline{(A + B + C)} = \overline{A} \cdot \overline{B} \cdot \overline{C}$

(a)

$A + B + C$

$\overline{(A + B + C)}$

$\overline{A} \cdot \overline{B} \cdot \overline{C}$

(b)

INPUT			OUTPUT
A	B	C	
0	0	0	1
0	0	1	0
0	1	0	0
0	1	1	0
1	0	0	0
1	0	1	0
1	1	0	0
1	1	1	0

FIGURE 3.10

(a) Block diagram symbol for a NOR gate. (b) OR gate and inverter equivalent circuit to NOR gate.

inputs are A, B, and C, the output of the AND gate will be $A \cdot B \cdot C$, and the complement of this is $\overline{(A \cdot B \cdot C)} = \overline{A} + \overline{B} + \overline{C}$, as shown in the figure.

The NOR gate can be analyzed in a similar manner. Figure 3.10 shows the NOR gate block diagram symbol with inputs, A, B, C and output $\overline{ABC}$. This shows the NOR gate's output will be a 1 only when all three inputs are 0s. If any input represents a 1, the output of a NOR gate will be a 0.

Below the NOR gate block diagram symbol in Fig. 3.10 is an equivalent circuit showing an OR gate and an inverter.[9] The inputs A, B, and C are ORed by the OR gate, giving $A + B + C$, which is complemented by the inverter, yielding $\overline{(A + B + C)} = \overline{A}\overline{B}\overline{C}$.

Multiple-input NAND gates can be analyzed similarly. A four-input NAND gate with inputs, A, B, C, and D has an output $\overline{A} + \overline{B} + \overline{C} + \overline{D}$, which says that the output will be a 1 if any one of the inputs is a 0 and will be a 0 only when all four inputs are 1s.

Similar reasoning will show that the output of a four-input NOR gate with inputs A, B, C, and D can be represented by the boolean algebra expression $\overline{A}\overline{B}\overline{C}\overline{D}$, which will be equal to 1 only when A, B, C, and D are all 0s.

If one of the two input lines to a two-input NAND gate contained the input $A + B$ and the other contained $C + D$, as shown in Fig. 3.11(a), the output from the NAND gate would be

$$\overline{[(A + B)(C + D)]} = \overline{A}\overline{B} + \overline{C}\overline{D}$$

We can show this by noting that the NAND gate first ANDs the inputs (in this case $A + B$ and $C + D$) and then complements this.

If one of the input lines to a two-input NOR gate contained the signal $A \cdot B$ and the other input line contained the signal $C \cdot D$, the output from the NOR gate would be $\overline{(A \cdot B + C \cdot D)} = (\overline{A} + \overline{B})(\overline{C} + \overline{D})$, as shown in Fig. 3.11(b).

---

[9] The "bubble," or small circle, on the output of the NAND and NOR gates represents complementation. The NAND can be seen to be an AND symbol followed by a complementer, and the NOR can be analyzed similarly.

BOOLEAN ALGEBRA
AND GATE
NETWORKS

The OR-to-NAND network:

$$\overline{[(A + B)(C + D)]} = \overline{A}\overline{B} + \overline{C}\overline{D}$$

(a)

The AND-to-NOR network:

$$\overline{(AB + CD)} = (\overline{A} + \overline{B})(\overline{C} + \overline{D})$$

(b)

FIGURE 3.11

Two types of gating networks. (*a*) OR-to-NAND gate network. (*b*) AND-to-NOR gate network.

Notice that we can make an AND gate from two NAND gates, using the trick shown in Fig. 3.12, and a two-input OR gate from three NAND gates, as is also shown in the figure. A set of NAND gates can thus be used to make any combinational network by substituting the block diagrams shown in Fig. 3.12 for the AND and OR blocks. (Complementation of a variable, when needed, can be obtained from a single NAND gate by connecting the variable to all inputs.)

The NOR gate also can be used to form any boolean function which is desired, and the fundamental tricks are shown in Fig. 3.13.

Actually, it is not necessary to use the boxes shown in Figs. 3.12 and 3.13 to replace AND and OR gates singly, for a two-level NAND gate network yields the same function as a two-level AND-to-OR gate network, and a two-level NOR gate network yields the same function as a two-level OR-to-AND gate network. This is shown in Fig. 3.14. Compare the output of the NAND gate network with that in Fig. 3.7, for example. In Secs. 3.21 and 3.22 design procedures for NAND and NOR gate networks are given.

MAP METHOD FOR SIMPLIFYING EXPRESSIONS

*3.18[10] We have examined the derivation of a boolean algebra expression for a given function by using a table of combinations to list desired function values. To derive a sum-of-products expression for the function, a set of product terms was listed, and those terms for which the function was to have a value 1 were selected and logically added to form the desired expression.

The table of combinations provides a nice, natural way to list all values of a boolean function. There are several other ways to represent or list function values, and the use of certain kinds of maps, which we will examine, also permits minimization of the expression formed in a nice graphic way.

The particular type of map we use is called the *Karnaugh map* after its originator.[11] Figure 3.15 shows the layouts for Karnaugh maps of two to four

---

[10]Sections with asterisks can be omitted in a first reading without the loss of continuity.
[11]Similar maps are sometimes called *Veitch diagrams*.

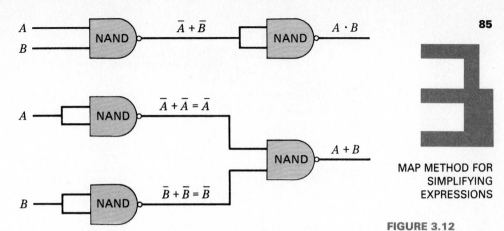

FIGURE 3.12

AND or OR operations from NAND gates.

variables. The diagram in each case lists the 2^n different product terms which can be formed in exactly n variables, each in a different square. For a function of n variables, a product term in exactly these n variables is called a *minterm*. Thus for three variables X, Y, and Z there are 2^3, or 8, different *minterms*, which are $\overline{X}\overline{Y}\overline{Z}$, $\overline{X}\overline{Y}Z$, $\overline{X}Y\overline{Z}$, $\overline{X}YZ$, $X\overline{Y}\overline{Z}$, $X\overline{Y}Z$, $XY\overline{Z}$, and XYZ. For four variables there are 2^4, or 16, terms; for five variables there are 32 terms; etc. As a result, a map of n variables will have 2^n squares, each representing a single minterm. The minterm in each box, or cell, of the map is the product of the variables listed at the abscissa and ordinate of the cell. Thus $\overline{X}Y\overline{Z}$ is at the intersection of $\overline{X}Y$ and $\overline{Z}$.

Given a Karnaugh map form, the map is filled in by placing 1s in the squares, or cells, for each term which leads to a 1 output.

As an example, consider a function of three variables for which the following input values are to be 1:

$$X = 0, Y = 1, Z = 0$$
$$X = 0, Y = 1, Z = 1$$
$$X = 1, Y = 1, Z = 0$$
$$X = 1, Y = 1, Z = 1$$

FIGURE 3.13

AND and OR gates from NOR gates.

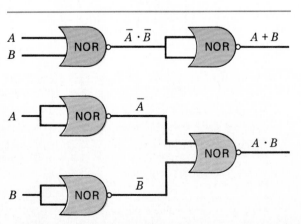

BOOLEAN ALGEBRA
AND GATE
NETWORKS

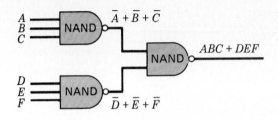

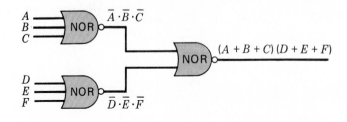

FIGURE 3.14

NAND and NOR
gates in two-level
networks.

This function is shown in Fig. 3.16(*a*) in both table-of-combinations and Karnaugh map form. Another function of four variables is shown in Fig. 3.16(*b*).

As a means for displaying the values of a function, the Karnaugh map is convenient and provides some "feeling" for the function because of its graphic

FIGURE 3.15

Karnaugh maps for
(*a*) two, (*b*) three, and
(*c*) four variables.

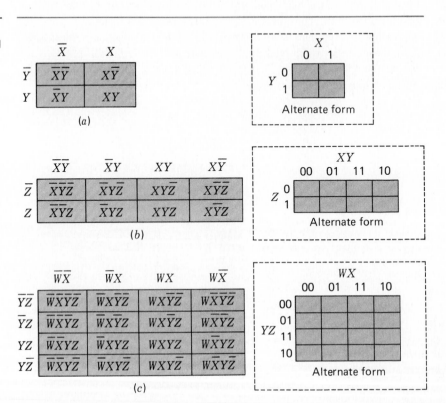

X	Y	Z	FUNCTION VALUES
0	0	0	0
0	0	1	0
0	1	0	1
0	1	1	1
1	0	0	0
1	0	1	0
1	1	0	1
1	1	1	1

	$\overline{X}\overline{Y}$	$\overline{X}Y$	XY	$X\overline{Y}$
$\overline{Z}$	0	1	1	0
Z	0	1	1	0

(a)

MAP METHOD FOR SIMPLIFYING EXPRESSIONS

W	X	Y	Z	FUNCTION VALUES
0	0	0	0	1
0	0	0	1	1
0	0	1	0	0
0	0	1	1	0
0	1	0	0	0
0	1	0	1	1
0	1	1	0	1
0	1	1	1	0
1	0	0	0	0
1	0	0	1	1
1	0	1	0	1
1	0	1	1	0
1	1	0	0	0
1	1	0	1	0
1	1	1	0	0
1	1	1	1	1

	$\overline{W}\overline{X}$	$\overline{W}X$	WX	$W\overline{X}$
$\overline{Y}\overline{Z}$	1	0	0	0
$\overline{Y}Z$	1	1	0	1
YZ	0	0	1	0
$Y\overline{Z}$	0	1	0	1

(b)

FIGURE 3.16

Two Karnaugh maps. (a) Map of boolean expression $\overline{X}Y\overline{Z} + \overline{X}YZ + XY\overline{Z} + XYZ$. (b) Map of four-variable function.

presentation. Its chief use, however, is due to the arrangement of cells. Each cell differs from its adjacent cell by having exactly one variable complemented in the minterm in one cell which is not complemented in the minterm in the adjacent cell.

As an example, consider the four-variable map in Fig. 3.16 and the minterm $\overline{W}X\overline{Y}Z$. There are four cells adjacent to the cell containing $\overline{W}X\overline{Y}Z$. These contain (1) $WX\overline{Y}Z$, which differs in the variable W; (2) $\overline{W}\overline{X}\overline{Y}Z$, which differs from $\overline{W}X\overline{Y}Z$ in X; (3) $\overline{W}XYZ$, which differs from $\overline{W}X\overline{Y}Z$ in Y; and (4) $\overline{W}X\overline{Y}\overline{Z}$, which differs from $\overline{W}X\overline{Y}Z$ in Z.

One trick should be noted at this point. The maps are considered to be

"rolled," or continuous, so that top and bottom edges or left and right side edges are touching. For the three-variable map, consider the left side edge and the right side edge to be touching, so that the map is considered to be rolled like a hoop horizontally on the page. This places the cell containing $\overline{X}\overline{Y}Z$ next to $X\overline{Y}Z$, as well as to $\overline{X}\overline{Y}\overline{Z}$ and $\overline{X}YZ$. Also, for this map it places $\overline{X}\overline{Y}Z$ next to $X\overline{Y}Z$, which touches because of the rolling, as well as to $\overline{X}Y\overline{Z}$ and $\overline{X}\overline{Y}\overline{Z}$.

For the four-variable map, the map is rolled so that the top edge touches the bottom edge, and the left side touches the right side. The touching of top and bottom places $\overline{W}X\overline{Y}\overline{Z}$ next to $\overline{W}X\overline{Y}Z$, and the left side to the right side edges touching places $W\overline{X}YZ$ next to $\overline{W}\overline{X}YZ$.

A good rule to remember is that there are two minterms adjacent to a given minterm in a two-variable map; there are three minterms next to a given minterm in a three-variable map; there are four minterms next to a given minterm in a four-variable map; etc.

SUBCUBES AND COVERING

3.19 A *subcube* is a set of exactly 2^m adjacent cells containing 1s. For $m = 0$ the subcube consists of a single cell (and thus of a single minterm). For $m = 1$ a subcube consists of two adjacent cells; for instance, the cells containing $\overline{X}\overline{Y}Z$ and $\overline{X}YZ$ form a subcube, as shown in Fig. 3.17(a), as do $X\overline{Y}\overline{Z}$ and $\overline{X}\overline{Y}\overline{Z}$ (since the map is rolled).

For $m = 2$ a subcube has four adjacent cells, and several such subcubes are shown in Fig. 3.17(c). Notice that here we have omitted 0s for clarity and filled in only the 1s for the function. This policy will be continued.

Finally, subcubes containing eight cells (for $m = 3$) are shown in Fig. 3.17(d).

(It is sometimes convenient to call a subcube containing two cells a 2 cube, a subcube of four cells a 4 cube, a subcube of eight cells an 8 cube, etc., and this is done often.)

To demonstrate the use of maps and subcubes in minimizing boolean algebra expressions, we need to examine a rule of boolean algebra:

$$AX + A\overline{X} = A$$

In the above equation, A can stand for more than one variable. For instance, let $A = WY$; then we have

$$(WY)X + (WY)\overline{X} = WY$$

Or let $A = W\overline{Y}\overline{Z}$; then we have

$$W\overline{Y}\overline{Z}\overline{X} + W\overline{Y}\overline{Z}X = W\overline{Y}\overline{Z}$$

The basic rule can be proved by factoring

$$AX + A\overline{X} = A(X + \overline{X})$$

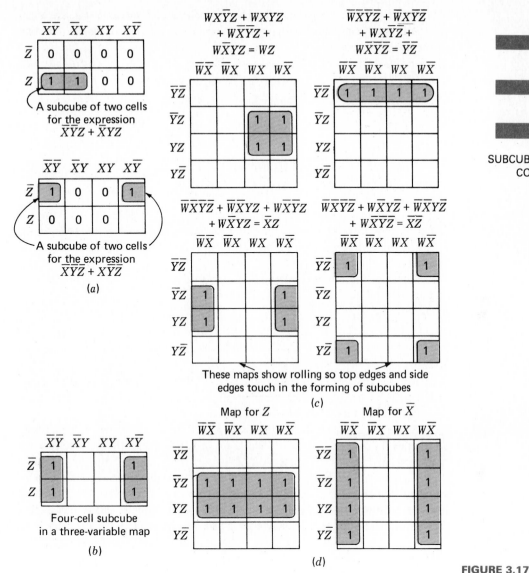

A subcube of two cells for the expression $\overline{X}\overline{Y}Z + \overline{X}YZ$

A subcube of two cells for the expression $\overline{X}\,\overline{Y}\,\overline{Z} + X\overline{Y}\,\overline{Z}$

(a)

$W\overline{X}\,\overline{Y}Z + WXYZ + W\overline{X}YZ + WXYZ = WZ$

$\overline{W}\overline{X}\overline{Y}\overline{Z} + \overline{W}X\overline{Y}\overline{Z} + WX\overline{Y}\overline{Z} + W\overline{X}\overline{Y}\overline{Z} = \overline{Y}\overline{Z}$

$\overline{W}\,\overline{X}\overline{Y}Z + \overline{W}X\overline{Y}Z + \overline{W}X Y Z + W\overline{X}YZ = \overline{X}Z$

$\overline{W}\overline{X}\overline{Y}\overline{Z} + WX\overline{Y}Z + \overline{W}\overline{X}Y\overline{Z} + W\overline{X}\overline{Y}\overline{Z} = \overline{X}\overline{Z}$

These maps show rolling so top edges and side edges touch in the forming of subcubes

(c)

Four-cell subcube in a three-variable map

(b)

Map for Z

Map for $\overline{X}$

(d)

FIGURE 3.17

Subcubes with two, four, and eight cells. Blank cells are assumed to contain 0s.

Then since $X + \overline{X} = 1$, we have

$$AX + A\overline{X} = A(X + \overline{X}) = A \cdot 1 = A$$

Each of the examples given can be checked similarly; for instance,

$$W\overline{Y}\,\overline{Z}\,\overline{X} + W\overline{Y}\,\overline{Z}X = W\overline{Y}\,\overline{Z}(\overline{X} + X) = W\overline{Y}\,\overline{Z} \cdot 1 = W\overline{Y}\,\overline{Z}$$

This rule can be extended. Consider

$$WX\overline{Y}\,\overline{Z} + W X\overline{Y}Z + W X Y\overline{Z} + W X Y Z$$

There are four terms here, each with two variables WX constant while the other two variables Y and Z take all possible values. The term WX is equal to the sum of the other terms, for

$$WX\bar{Y}\bar{Z} + WX\bar{Y}Z + WXY\bar{Z} + WXYZ = WX\bar{Y}(\bar{Z} + Z) + WXY(Z + \bar{Z})$$
$$= WX\bar{Y} + WXY$$
$$= WX(\bar{Y} + Y)$$
$$= WX$$

Thus WX could be substituted for the other four terms in an expression without changing the values the expression takes for any input values to the variables, that is, $WX = WX\bar{Y}\bar{Z} + WX\bar{Y}Z + WXY\bar{Z} + WXYZ$.

On a map the above algebraic moves may be performed easily. Since a subcube of two cells has both cells with a single variable differing, a product term in just those variables which do not differ will cover (can be substituted for) the two minterms in the two cells.

Consider the subcube of two cells for $\bar{X}\bar{Y}Z$ and $\bar{X}YZ$ on the three-variable map in Fig. 3.17(a). The single product term $\bar{X}Z$ is equal to the sum of these two minterms; that is,

$$\bar{X}\bar{Y}Z + \bar{X}YZ = \bar{X}Z$$

Similarly, the two cells containing minterms $\bar{X}\bar{Y}\bar{Z}$ and $X\bar{Y}Z$ form a subcube of two cells, as shown in Fig. 3.17(a), from which we form $\bar{Y}Z$, which can be substituted for $\bar{X}\bar{Y}Z + X\bar{Y}Z$ in an expression.

Similarly, the subcube of four cells in a three-variable map [Fig. 3.17(b)] with terms $\bar{X}\bar{Y}\bar{Z}$, $\bar{X}\bar{Y}Z$, $X\bar{Y}\bar{Z}$, $X\bar{Y}Z$ has a single-variable constant $\bar{Y}$. Therefore we have $\bar{Y} = \bar{X}\bar{Y}\bar{Z} + \bar{X}\bar{Y}Z + X\bar{Y}\bar{Z} + X\bar{Y}Z$.

In general, a subcube with 2^m cells in an n-variable map will have $n - m$ variables, which are the same in all the minterms, and m variables which take all possible combinations of being complemented or not complemented. Thus for a four-variable map for $m = 3$, any eight adjacent cells which form a subcube will have $4 - 3 = 1$ variable constant and three variables which change complementation from cell to cell. Therefore, a subcube of eight cells in a four-variable map can be used to determine a single variable which can be substituted for the sum of the minterm in all eight cells.

As an example, in Fig. 3.17(d) we find a subcube of eight cells with the minterms $\bar{W}\bar{X}YZ$, $\bar{W}X\bar{Y}Z$, $\bar{W}X\bar{Y}Z$, $\bar{W}XYZ$, $W\bar{X}\bar{Y}Z$, $W\bar{X}\bar{Y}Z$, $WX\bar{Y}Z$, and $WXYZ$. The sum of these will be found to be equivalent to Z.

The set of minterms in an expression does not necessarily form a single subcube, however, and there are two cases to be dealt with. Call a *maximal subcube* the largest subcube that can be found around a given minterm. Then the two cases are as follows:

1 All maximal subcubes are nonintersecting; that is, no cell in a maximal subcube is a part of another maximal subcube. Several examples are shown in Fig. 3.18.

Figure 3.18(a):

	$\overline{W}\overline{X}$	$\overline{W}X$	WX	$W\overline{X}$
$\overline{Y}\overline{Z}$	1			
$\overline{Y}Z$	1		1	
YZ	1		1	
$Y\overline{Z}$	1			

$\uparrow$ $\overline{W}\overline{X}$ $\qquad$ $\uparrow$ WXZ

Figure 3.18(b):

	$\overline{W}\overline{X}$	$\overline{W}X$	WX	$W\overline{X}$
$\overline{Y}\overline{Z}$	1			1
$\overline{Y}Z$		1	1	
YZ		1	1	
$Y\overline{Z}$				

Figure 3.18(c):

	$\overline{W}\overline{X}$	$\overline{W}X$	WX	$W\overline{X}$
$\overline{Y}\overline{Z}$		1	1	
$\overline{Y}Z$	1			1
YZ	1			1
$Y\overline{Z}$		1	1	

(a) $\qquad\qquad$ (b) $\qquad\qquad$ (c)

FIGURE 3.18

Maps with disjoint subcubes. (*a*) Map for $\overline{W}\overline{X} + WXZ$. (*b*) Map for $XZ + \overline{X}\,\overline{Y}\overline{Z}$. (*c*) Map for $X\overline{Z} + \overline{X}Z$.

2 The maximal subcubes intersect; that is, cells in one maximal subcube are also in other maximal subcubes. Figure 3.19 shows examples of this.

Case 1 is the more easily dealt with. In this case, the product terms corresponding to the maximal subcubes are selected, and the sum of these forms a minimal sum-of-products expression. (In switching theory, the product term corresponding to a maximal subcube is called a *prime implicant*.)

Figure 3.18(*a*) shows an example of this in four variables. There is a subcube of two cells containing $WXYZ$ and $WX\overline{Y}Z$ which can be covered by the product term WXZ. There is also a subcube of four cells containing $\overline{W}\overline{X}\overline{Y}\overline{Z}$, $\overline{W}\overline{X}\overline{Y}Z$, $\overline{W}\overline{X}YZ$, and $\overline{W}\overline{X}Y\overline{Z}$ which can be covered by $\overline{W}\overline{X}$. The minimal expression is, therefore, $\overline{W}\overline{X} + WXZ$.

Two other examples are shown in Fig. 3.18(*b*) and (*c*). In each case the subcubes do not intersect or share cells, and so the product term (prime implicant) which corresponds to a given maximal subcube can be readily derived, and the sum of these for a given map forms the minimal expression.

When the subcubes intersect, the situation can be more complicated. The first principle to note is this: *Each cell containing a 1 (that is, each 1 cell) must be contained in some subcube which is selected.*

Figure 3.19(*a*) shows a map with an intersecting pair of subcubes plus another subcube. The minimal expression is, in this case, formed by simply adding the three product terms associated with the three maximal subcubes. Notice that a

FIGURE 3.19

Intersecting subcubes. (*a*) $\overline{W}XZ + XYZ + \overline{X}Y\overline{Z}$. (*b*) $XZ + W\overline{Y}Z$. (*c*) $Y\overline{Z} + WX\overline{Z}$.

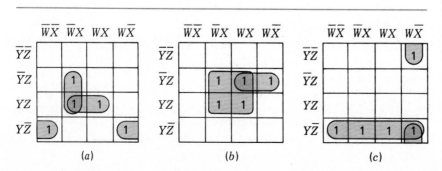

(a) $\qquad\qquad$ (b) $\qquad\qquad$ (c)

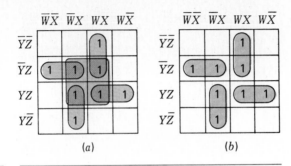

(a)   (b)

FIGURE 3.20

Intersecting subcubes
and solution. (a) *XZ*
+ *WYZ* + *W̄YZ* +
W̄XY + *WXȲ*.
(b) *WXȲ* + *WYZ* +
W̄XY + *W̄YZ*.

single term, *W̄XYZ*, is shared between two subcubes and, because of this, is effectively in the minimal expression twice. This is permissible because of the idempotent rule of boolean algebra, $A + A = A$, which states that repetition of terms does not change functional equivalence.

Two other examples of intersecting maximal subcubes are shown in Fig. 3.19(*b*) and (*c*).

As long as the maximal subcubes can be readily found and there are no options in subcube selection, the minimization problem is straightforward. In some cases the problem is more complicated. Figure 3.20 shows an expression with a subcube of four cells in the center of the map, which is maximal. The selection of this maximal subcube does not lead to a minimal expression, however, because the four cells with 1s around this subcube must be covered also. In each case these 1 cells can be found to have a single adjacent cell and so to be part of maximal subcubes consisting of 2 cells. In Fig. 3.20(*a*), *W̄XȲZ* is in a cell adjacent to only *W̄XYZ* and so forms part of a 2 cell. Figure 3.20(*b*) shows another way to form subcubes for the map, and this leads to the minimal expression *WXȲ* + *WYZ* + *W̄XY* + *W̄YZ*.

The finding of minimal expressions for such maps is not direct, but follow these rules:

1 Begin with cells that are adjacent to no other cells. The minterms in these cells cannot be shortened and must be used as they are.

2 Find all cells that are adjacent to only one other cell. These form subcubes of two cells each.

3 Find those cells that lead to maximal subcubes of four cells. Then find subcubes of eight cells, etc.

4 The minimal expression is formed from a collection of as few cubes as possible, each of which is as large as possible, that is, each of which is a maximal subcube.

Figure 3.21 shows an example of a difficult map. The maximal subcubes can be selected in several ways so that all cells are covered. The figure shows three maps, of which only one leads to a minimal expression. Practice with various maps will lead to skill in finding minimal expressions.

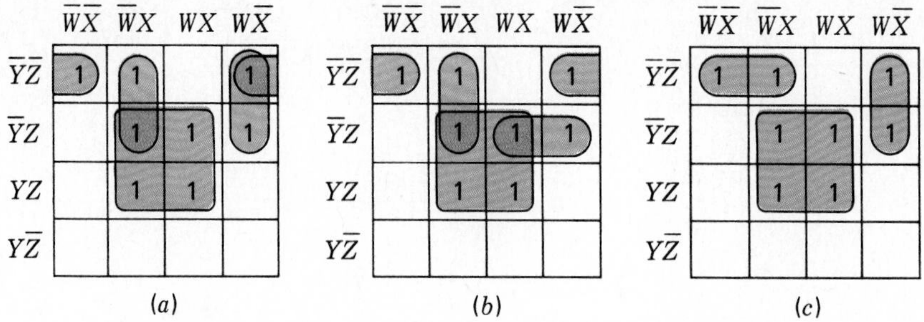

(a)   (b)   (c)

FIGURE 3.21

Three coverings of the same map. (a) $XZ + \overline{X}\overline{Y}\overline{Z} + W\overline{X}Y + \overline{W}X\overline{Y}$. (b) $XZ + \overline{X}\overline{Y}\overline{Z} + \overline{W}X\overline{Y} + W\overline{Y}\overline{Z}$. (c) $XZ + \overline{W}\overline{Y}\overline{Z} + W\overline{X}Y$.

PRODUCT-OF-SUMS EXPRESSIONS—DON'T-CARES

3.20   The technique for product-of-sums expressions is almost identical with the design procedure using sum-of-products expressions. The basic rule can be stated quite simply: *Solve for 0s, then complement the resulting expression.*

Let us take an example. Figure 3.22(*a*) shows a table of combinations and a Karnaugh map for a four-variable problem. In Fig. 3.22(*a*) the sum-of-products expression is derived and in minimal form is found to be $\overline{X}\overline{Y} + YZ + WY$.

In Fig. 3.22(*b*) the same problem is solved for the 0s, which gives $X\overline{Y} + \overline{W}Y\overline{Z}$. Since we have solved for 0s, we have solved for the complement of the desired problem. If the output is called F, then we have solved for $\overline{F}$. We then write $\overline{F} = X\overline{Y} + \overline{W}Y\overline{Z}$.

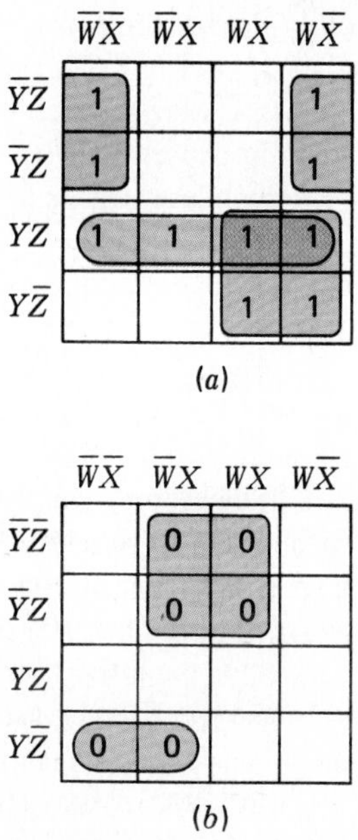

FIGURE 3.22

Solving for product of sums. (a) $\overline{X}\overline{Y} + YZ + WY$. (b) $(\overline{X} + Y)(\overline{W} + \overline{Y} + Z)$.

INPUTS				FUNCTION VALUES
W	X	Y	Z	
0	0	0	0	1
0	0	0	1	1
0	0	1	0	0
0	0	1	1	1
0	1	0	0	0
0	1	0	1	0
0	1	1	0	0
0	1	1	1	1
1	0	0	0	1
1	0	0	1	1
1	0	1	0	1
1	0	1	1	1
1	1	0	0	0
1	1	0	1	0
1	1	1	0	1
1	1	1	1	1

(a)

(b)

BOOLEAN ALGEBRA AND GATE NETWORKS

W	X	Y	Z	
0	0	0	0	1
0	0	0	1	0
0	0	1	0	0
0	0	1	1	1
0	1	0	0	1
0	1	0	1	0
0	1	1	0	0
0	1	1	1	1
1	0	0	0	1
1	0	0	1	0
1	0	1	0	d
1	0	1	1	d
1	1	0	0	d
1	1	0	1	d
1	1	1	0	d
1	1	1	1	d

(a)

	$\overline{W}\,\overline{X}$	$\overline{W}X$	WX	$W\overline{X}$
$\overline{Y}\,\overline{Z}$	1	1	d	1
$\overline{Y}Z$			d	
YZ	1	1	d	d
$Y\overline{Z}$			d	d

(a) $\overline{Y}\,\overline{Z} + YZ$

(b)

	$\overline{W}\,\overline{X}$	$\overline{W}X$	WX	$W\overline{X}$
$\overline{Y}\,\overline{Z}$			1	1
$\overline{Y}Z$			1	d
YZ	d	d		
$Y\overline{Z}$			1	d

(b) $W\overline{Z} + W\overline{Y}$

FIGURE 3.23

Don't-care conditions. (a) Map for table with don't cares. (b) Solving another map with don't-cares.

Now, what is wanted is F; so both sides of this expression are complemented, and we have

$$F = (\overline{X} + Y)(W + \overline{Y} + Z)$$

This expression is in product-of-sums form and is somewhat simpler than the sum-of-products expression.

If sum-of-products and product-of-sums expressions are equally easy to implement, then a given problem must be solved in both forms and the simpler solution chosen. There is no way to determine which will be simpler other than by a complete working of the problem.

There is another frequently encountered situation in which certain outputs are not specified in a problem. Such outputs are called *don't-care* outputs, for the designer does not care what the outputs are for these particular inputs.

Figure 3.23(a) shows such a problem with 6 of the possible 16 output values listed as d's (don't cares). This is a part of a BCD translator, and so these particular six input combinations are never used.

Since don't care output values are of no importance, they may be filled in with 1s and 0s in any way that is advantageous. Figure 3.23(a) shows a Karnaugh map of the table of combinations in the figure, with d's in the appropriate places. In solving this table, a d may be used as either a 1 or a 0; so the d's are used to enlarge or complete a subcube whenever possible, but otherwise are ignored (that is, made 0). *The d's need not be covered by the subcubes selected, but are used only to enlarge subcubes containing 1s, which must be covered.*

In Fig. 3.23(a), the vertical string of four d's in the WX column is of use twice, once in filling out, or completing, the top row of 1s and once in completing the third row. These subcubes give the terms $\overline{Y}\overline{Z}$ and YZ; so the minimal sum-of-products expression is $\overline{Y}\overline{Z} + YZ$. Notice that if all the d's were made 0s, the solution would require more terms.

Another problem is worked in Fig. 3.23(b). For this problem the solution is $W\overline{Z} + W\overline{Y}$. Notice that two of the d's are made 0s. In effect, the d's are chosen so that they lead to the best solution.

DESIGN USING NAND GATES

3.21   Section 3.17 introduced NAND gates and showed the block diagram symbol for the NAND gate. NAND gates are widely used in modern computers, and an understanding of their use is invaluable.

Any NAND gate network can be analyzed by using boolean algebra, as previously indicated. Sometimes it is convenient, however, to substitute a functionally equivalent block diagram symbol for the conventional NAND gate symbol in order to analyze a block diagram. Figure 3.24 shows a gate symbol that consists of an OR gate symbol with "bubbles" (inverters) at each input. The two block diagram symbols in Fig. 3.24 perform the same function on inputs, as shown, for the NAND gate yields $\overline{A} + \overline{B} + \overline{C}$ on these inputs A, B, and C, as does the functionally equivalent gate.

As an example of the use of an equivalent symbol to simplify the analysis of a NAND gate network, we examine Fig. 3.25(a). This shows a two-level NAND-to-NAND gate network with inputs A, B, C, D, E, and F. Figure 3.25(b) shows the same network, but with the rightmost NAND gate replaced by the functionally equivalent block diagram symbol for a NAND gate previously shown in Fig. 3.24. Notice that the output function is the same for Fig. 3.25(b) as for Fig. 3.25(a), as it should be. Finally, an examination of the fact that the bubbles in Fig. 3.25(b) always occur in pairs, and so can be eliminated from the drawing from a functional viewpoint (since $\overline{\overline{X}} = X$), leads to Fig. 3.25(c), which is an AND-to-OR gate network. This shows that the NAND-to-NAND gate network in Fig. 3.25(a) yields the same function as the AND-to-OR gate network in Fig. 3.25(c).

The substitution of the equivalent symbols followed by the removal of the "double bubbles" in Fig. 3.25 is a visual presentation of the following use of De Morgan's rule, which should be compared with the transformation in the figure:

$$\overline{(\overline{A \cdot B}) \cdot (\overline{C \cdot D}) \cdot (\overline{E \cdot F})} = \overline{\overline{(A \cdot B)}} + \overline{\overline{(C \cdot D)}} + \overline{\overline{(E \cdot F)}} = A \cdot B + C \cdot D + E \cdot F$$

Study of the above will show that the same principle applies to NAND-to-NAND gates in general. As a further example, Fig. 3.26 shows another NAND-

FIGURE 3.24

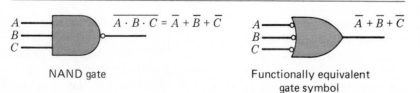

NAND gate

Functionally equivalent
gate symbol

NAND gate and functionally equivalent
gate.

BOOLEAN ALGEBRA
AND GATE
NETWORKS

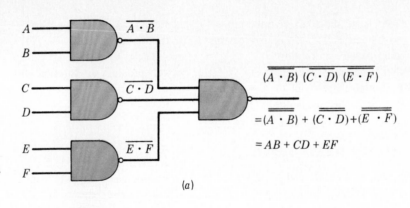

$$\overline{(\overline{A \cdot B}) \ (\overline{C \cdot D}) \ (\overline{E \cdot F})}$$

$$= (\overline{\overline{A \cdot B}}) + (\overline{\overline{C \cdot D}}) + (\overline{\overline{E \cdot F}})$$

$$= AB + CD + EF$$

(a)

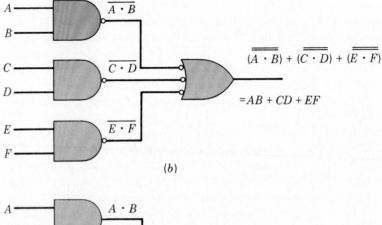

$$(\overline{\overline{A \cdot B}}) + (\overline{\overline{C \cdot D}}) + (\overline{\overline{E \cdot F}})$$

$$= AB + CD + EF$$

(b)

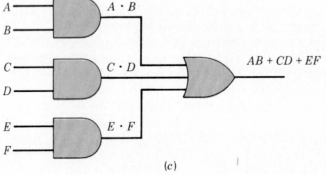

$$AB + CD + EF$$

(c)

FIGURE 3.25

NAND-to-NAND gate
analysis. (a) NAND
gate network. (b) Net-
work in (a) with
equivalent gates.
(c) AND-to-OR gate
network.

to-NAND gate network and the transformation to an AND-to-OR gate network. The algebraic moves equivalent to the symbology substitutions also are shown.

A question may arise as to why drawings of NAND gate networks in computer diagrams do not use either the equivalent symbol (as in Fig. 3.24) or even the AND-to-OR gate symbols in Figs. 3.25 and 3.26. There are several reasons. First, the industrial and military specifications call for gate symbols to reflect the actual circuit operation. Therefore, if a circuit ANDs the inputs and then complements the result, the circuit is a NAND gate and, strictly speaking, the original NAND gate symbol should be used. Also, if the circuits used are contained in

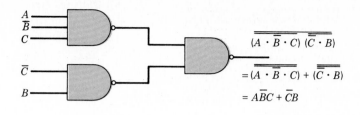

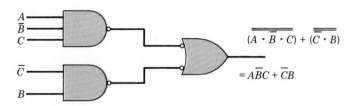

$$\overline{\overline{(A \cdot \overline{B} \cdot C)} \ \overline{(\overline{C} \cdot B)}}$$

$$= (A \cdot \overline{B} \cdot C) + (\overline{C} \cdot B)$$

$$= A\overline{B}C + \overline{C}B$$

**DESIGN USING
NAND GATES**

$$\overline{\overline{(A \cdot \overline{B} \cdot C)}} + \overline{\overline{(\overline{C} \cdot B)}}$$

$$= A\overline{B}C + \overline{C}B$$

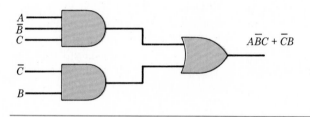

$$A\overline{B}C + \overline{C}B$$

FIGURE 3.26

NAND-to-NAND and
AND-to-OR gate
transformation.

integrated-circuit packages and the computer drawing calls out the part number for the IC packages, an examination of the manufacturer's IC package drawings will show NAND gate symbols (if NAND gates are in the IC package). In the next chapter we show such packages and clarify this. In any case, substitution of symbols might easily lead to confusion, and it seems best to use the NAND gate symbol when NAND gates are used.

The above analysis of two-level NAND gate networks leads to a direct procedure for designing a NAND-to-NAND gate network.

DESIGN RULE

To design a two-level NAND-to-NAND gate network, use the table-of-combinations procedure for a sum-of-products expression. Simplify this sum-of-products expression by using maps, as has been shown. Finally, draw a NAND-to-NAND gate network in the two-level form, and write the same inputs as would have been used in an AND-to-OR gate network, except use NAND gates in place of the AND and OR gates.

BOOLEAN ALGEBRA
AND GATE
NETWORKS

TABLE 3.23			
INPUTS			OUTPUT
For: $A = 0$ $B = 0$ $C = 0$			1
0	0	1	1
0	1	0	0
0	1	1	1
1	0	0	0
1	0	1	0
1	1	0	1
1	1	1	1

For example, let us design a NAND-to-NAND gate network for a problem with three inputs *A, B,* and *C* and the problem definition in Table 3.23. The table of combinations for this function, map, simplified expression, and NAND-to-NAND gate network is shown in Fig. 3.27. (It would be possible to go directly to the map from the above specification. The table of combinations is shown for completeness.)

An adjustment is necessary if the simplified expression contains a single variable as a product term. For instance, if the simplified expression is $A + BC + \overline{B}\overline{C}$, then the "natural" network is as shown in Fig. 3.28(*a*). Notice, however, that the NAND gate at the *A* input is unnecessary if *A* is available, and this leads to the form shown in Fig. 3.28(*b*), which eliminates this gate. [The same simplification could be repeated if several single variables occur (as product terms) in the simplified expression.]

DESIGN USING NOR GATES

3.22 NOR gates are used often in computers because current IC technology yields NOR gates in efficient, fast circuit designs. Fortunately the design of a NOR-to-NOR gate network, which is the fastest form in which all functions can be realized by using only NOR gates, follows naturally from previous design techniques, as will be shown.

First note that a symbol functionally equivalent to the NOR gate exists and is shown in Fig. 3.29. The change of the block design symbols mirrors De Morgan's rule:

$$\overline{A + B + C} = \overline{A} \cdot \overline{B} \cdot \overline{C}$$

Figure 3.30(*a*) shows a NOR-to-NOR gate network having the output function $(A + B)(C + D)(E + F)$. To analyze this network, we substitute the functionally equivalent symbol for the rightmost NOR gate, as shown in Fig. 3.30(*b*). This yields the same function, but an examination of Fig. 3.30(*b*) shows the bubbles occurring in pairs. Since $\overline{\overline{X}} = X$, these can be eliminated as shown in Fig. 3.30(*c*), which is for OR-to-AND gate networks.

Inputs A	B	C	Output	Product terms		
0	0	0	1	$\overline{A}$	$\overline{B}$	$\overline{C}$
0	0	1	1	$\overline{A}$	$\overline{B}$	C
0	1	0	0	$\overline{A}$	B	$\overline{C}$
0	1	1	1	$\overline{A}$	B	C
1	0	0	0	A	$\overline{B}$	$\overline{C}$
1	0	1	0	A	$\overline{B}$	C
1	1	0	1	A	B	$\overline{C}$
1	1	1	1	A	B	C

$$\overline{A}\overline{B}\overline{C} + \overline{A}\overline{B}C + \overline{A}BC + AB\overline{C} + ABC$$

DESIGN USING NOR GATES

A simplified expression is $\overline{A}\overline{B} + \overline{A}C + AB$

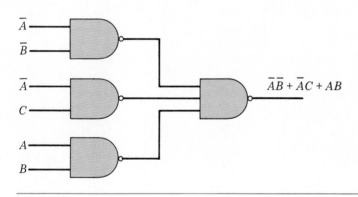

$$\overline{A}\overline{B} + \overline{A}C + AB$$

FIGURE 3.27

Design of two-level NAND-to-NAND gate.

The transformation in the block diagrams of Fig. 3.30 from (a) to (b) to (c) mirrors the following boolean algebra moves:

$$\overline{(\overline{A + B}) + (\overline{C + D})(\overline{E + F})} = \overline{(\overline{A + B})}\ \overline{(\overline{C + D})}\ \overline{(\overline{E + F})}$$
$$= (A + B)(C + D)(E + F)$$

This shows that a NOR-to-NOR gate network is functionally equivalent to an OR-to-AND gate network. Figure 3.31 shows another example of this. A NOR-to-NOR gate network is transformed to an OR-to-AND gate network, and the corresponding algebraic transformations are shown.

BOOLEAN ALGEBRA
AND GATE
NETWORKS

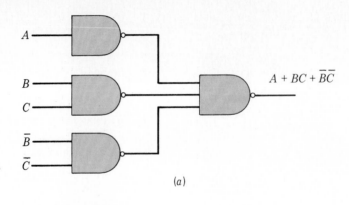

$A + BC + \overline{B}\overline{C}$

(a)

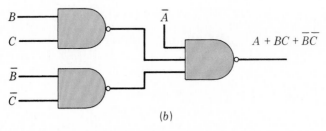

$\overline{A}$

$A + BC + \overline{B}\overline{C}$

(b)

FIGURE 3.28

Equivalent NAND-to-
NAND gate designs.
(a) Natural NAND-to-
NAND gate design.
(b) Equivalent NAND-
to-NAND gate net-
work.

Examination of the above leads to a rule for the design of a NOR-to-NOR gate network, given the input-output specifications.

DESIGN RULE

To design a NOR-to-NOR gate network, use the procedures for designing an OR-to-AND gate network. Simplify, using maps as for the OR-to-AND gate networks. Finally, draw the block diagram in the same form as for the OR-to-AND gate networks, but substitute NOR gates for the OR and AND gates.

Figure 3.32 shows two examples of NOR-to-NOR gate designs, including the simplification of networks where a single variable occurs as sum term.

FIGURE 3.30

NOR gate symbol
and equivalent gate.

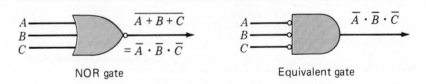

$\overline{A + B + C}$

$= \overline{A} \cdot \overline{B} \cdot \overline{C}$

NOR gate

$\overline{A} \cdot \overline{B} \cdot \overline{C}$

Equivalent gate

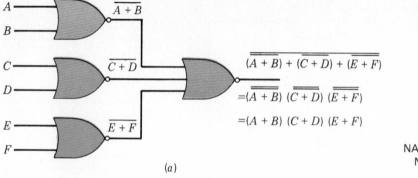

$$\overline{A + B}$$

$$\overline{C + D}$$

$$\overline{E + F}$$

$$\overline{(\overline{A + B}) + (\overline{C + D}) + (\overline{E + F})}$$

$$=\overline{(\overline{A + B})}\ \overline{(\overline{C + D})}\ \overline{(\overline{E + F})}$$

$$=(A + B)\ (C + D)\ (E + F)$$

(a)

NAND-TO-AND AND
NOR-TO-OR GATE
NETWORKS

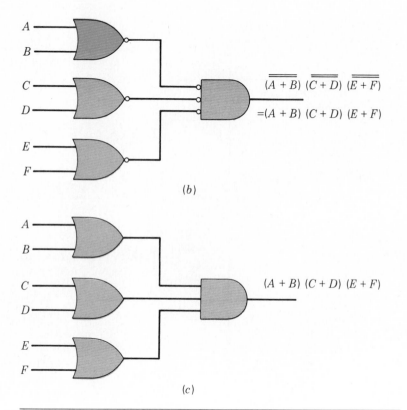

$$\overline{\overline{(A + B)}}\ \overline{\overline{(C + D)}}\ \overline{\overline{(E + F)}}$$

$$=(A + B)\ (C + D)\ (E + F)$$

(b)

$$(A + B)\ (C + D)\ (E + F)$$

(c)

FIGURE 3.29

NOR-to-NOR gate
network analysis.

NAND-TO-AND AND NOR-TO-OR GATE NETWORKS

3.23 In the two preceding sections, we showed how to analyze and design
networks using NAND and NOR gates in NAND-to-NAND and NOR-to-NOR
forms. Two other forms are in common usage: the NAND-to-AND and the NOR-
to-OR forms.

Since NAND gates are quite popular and since the outputs from NAND gates

**BOOLEAN ALGEBRA
AND GATE
NETWORKS**

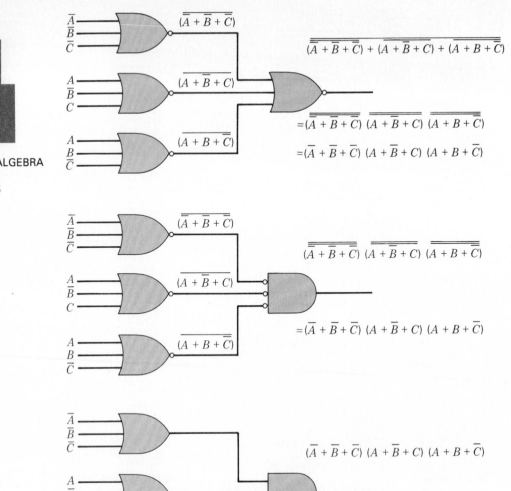

FIGURE 3.31

NOR gate network
analysis.

sometimes can be ANDed by a simple connection, as we show later, we first present
the analysis and design procedures for NAND-to-AND gate networks.

Figure 3.33(a) shows a NAND-to-AND gate network with inputs A, B, C,
D, and E. Figure 3.33(b) shows the same configuration but with the NAND gates
replaced by the equivalent NAND gate symbol from Fig. 3.24. This shows a
NAND-to-AND network functions like an OR-to-AND network with each input
complemented and leads to this design rule.

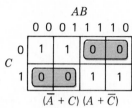

A	B	C	OUTPUT	SUM TERMS
0	0	0	1	$A + B + C$
0	0	1	0	$A + B + \overline{C}$
0	1	0	1	$A + \overline{B} + C$
0	1	1	0	$A + \overline{B} + \overline{C}$
1	0	0	0	$\overline{A} + B + C$
1	0	1	1	$\overline{A} + B + \overline{C}$
1	1	0	0	$\overline{A} + \overline{B} + C$
1	1	1	1	$\overline{A} + \overline{B} + \overline{C}$

NAND-TO-AND AND NOR-TO-OR GATE NETWORKS

AB

	0 0	0 1	1 1	1 0
C 0	1	1	0	0
1	0	0	1	1

$(\overline{A} + C)\ (A + \overline{C})$

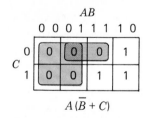

$\overline{A}$
C
$(\overline{A + C})$

A
$\overline{C}$
$(\overline{A + \overline{C}})$

$\overline{\overline{(A + C)} + \overline{(A + \overline{C})}}$

$= \overline{\overline{(A + C)}} \cdot \overline{\overline{(A + \overline{C})}}$

$= (\overline{A} + C)\ (A + \overline{C})$

A	B	C	OUTPUT	SUM TERMS
0	0	0	0	$A + B + C$
0	0	1	0	$A + B + \overline{C}$
0	1	0	0	$A + \overline{B} + C$
0	1	1	0	$A + \overline{B} + \overline{C}$
1	0	0	1	$\overline{A} + B + C$
1	0	1	1	$\overline{A} + B + \overline{C}$
1	1	0	0	$\overline{A} + \overline{B} + C$
1	1	1	1	$\overline{A} + \overline{B} + \overline{C}$

AB

	0 0	0 1	1 1	1 0
C 0	0	0	0	1
1	0	0	1	1

$A\,(\overline{B} + C)$

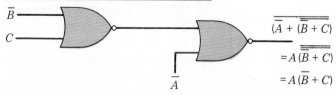

$\overline{B}$
C
$\overline{\overline{A} + \overline{(B + C)}}$

$\overline{A}$

$= A\,\overline{\overline{(B + C)}}$

$= A\,(\overline{B} + C)$

FIGURE 3.32

Two NOR gate designs.

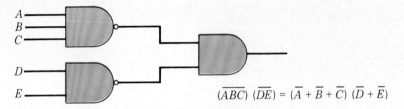

$$(\overline{ABC})\,(\overline{DE}) = (\overline{A} + \overline{B} + \overline{C})\,(\overline{D} + \overline{E})$$

a. Conventional NAND to AND gate network

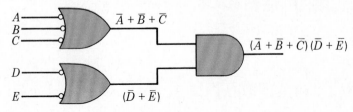

b. NAND-to-AND in (a) but with equivalent gates substituted for NANDs.

FIGURE 3.33

NAND-to-AND gate network. (*a*) Conventional NAND-to-AND gate network. (*b*) NAND-to-AND with equivalent gates substituted.

DESIGN RULE

To design a NAND-to-AND gate network, use the procedure for deriving a simplified expression in product-of-sums form for an OR-to-AND gate network. Then draw the block diagram, using a NAND-to-AND form, with a NAND gate for each sum term in the simplified expression. To form inputs to the NAND gates, complement each variable in the simplified product-of-sums expression.

Example

Design a NAND-to-AND gate network for the input-output values in Table 3.24. We add a sum-term column (Table 3.25) and then AND the sum terms where 0s appear in the output values. Our product-of-sums expression is thus $(A + B +$

TABLE 3.24			
A	*B*	*C*	OUTPUT
0	0	0	1
0	0	1	0
0	1	0	0
0	1	1	1
1	0	0	0
1	0	1	0
1	1	0	1
1	1	1	1

TABLE 3.25

A	B	C	OUTPUT	SUM TERM
0	0	0	1	$A + B + C$
0	0	1	0	$A + B + \overline{C}$
0	1	0	0	$A + \overline{B} + C$
0	1	1	1	$A + \overline{B} + \overline{C}$
1	0	0	0	$\overline{A} + B + C$
1	0	1	0	$\overline{A} + B + \overline{C}$
1	1	0	1	$\overline{A} + \overline{B} + C$
1	1	1	1	$\overline{A} + \overline{B} + \overline{C}$

NAND-TO-AND AND NOR-TO-OR GATE NETWORKS

$\overline{C})(A + \overline{B} + C)(\overline{A} + B + C)(\overline{A} + B + \overline{C})$. This must be simplified. The simplified expression is $(A + \overline{B} + C)(\overline{A} + B)(B + \overline{C})$. The rule states that we must now form a NAND-to-AND gate network, but that each input should be complemented. This means each variable in $(A + \overline{B} + C)(\overline{A} + B)(B + \overline{C})$ must be complemented. The inputs for one NAND gate thus will be $\overline{A}$, B, and $\overline{C}$ which are from the first sum term $(A + \overline{B} + C)$. The inputs to the second NAND gate will be A and $\overline{B}$ from the term $\overline{A} + B,$ and the third NAND gate will have as inputs $\overline{B}$ and C from the sum term $(B + \overline{C})$. The resulting block diagram is seen in Fig. 3.34.

NOR-to-OR gate networks are also widely used because NORs are the natural gates for emitter-coupled logic (ECL) circuits, a major circuit line. Figure 3.35(*a*) shows a NOR-to-OR gate network with four inputs and the output boolean algebra expressions. Figure 3.35(*b*) shows the same configuration but with equivalent gates from Fig. 3.29 substituted for the NOR gates. This shows that the basic form for the boolean expression realized is AND-to-OR but with each input variable complemented. Thus the design rule for a NOR-to-OR gate network is as follows:

FIGURE 3.34

Design of a NAND-to-AND network.

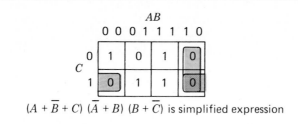

$(A + \overline{B} + C)\, (\overline{A} + B)\, (B + \overline{C})$ is simplified expression

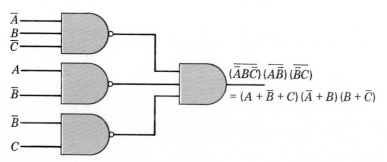

BOOLEAN ALGEBRA
AND GATE
NETWORKS

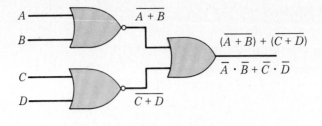

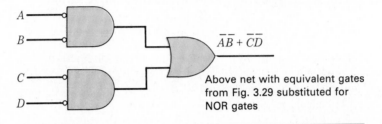

Above net with equivalent gates
from Fig. 3.29 substituted for
NOR gates

FIGURE 3.35

NOR-to-OR gate net-
work and equivalent
network.

DESIGN RULE

To design a NOR-to-OR gate network, develop and simplify the
sum-of-products expression for the described function. Then draw
a NOR-to-OR gate network with a NOR gate for each product term,
but complement each input in the sum-of-products expression to
form the input to the NOR gates.

Table 3.26 shows a table of combinations to be realized as a NOR-to-OR
gate network. The product terms are added to the table, and then the boolean
algebra expression is derived for the problem: $\overline{A}\overline{B}\overline{C} + \overline{A}B\overline{C} + A\overline{B}\overline{C} + AB\overline{C} + ABC$. This expression is then simplified, giving $AB + BC + \overline{A}C$.

The design rule says that to realize a NOR-to-OR gate network we use the
above expression but complement each input. This means the first NOR gate will

TABLE 3.26				
A	B	C	OUTPUT	PRODUCT TERMS
0	0	0	1	$\overline{A}\overline{B}\overline{C}$
0	0	1	0	$\overline{A}\overline{B}C$
0	1	0	1	$\overline{A}B\overline{C}$
0	1	1	0	$\overline{A}BC$
1	0	0	0	$A\overline{B}\overline{C}$
1	0	1	1	$A\overline{B}C$
1	1	0	1	$AB\overline{C}$
1	1	1	1	ABC

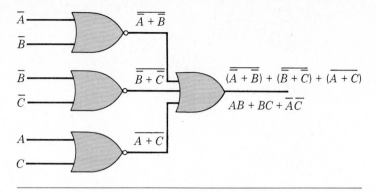

FIGURE 3.36

Design for NOR-to-OR gate network.

have as inputs $\overline{A}$ and $\overline{B}$ from the product term AB; the second NOR gate will have as inputs $\overline{B}$ and $\overline{C}$ from the product term BC; and the third NOR gate will have as inputs A and C from the product term $\overline{A}\overline{C}$. Figure 3-36 shows this design.

WIRED OR AND WIRED AND GATES

*3.24 In certain integrated-circuit technologies, it is possible to form OR and AND gates by means of a simple connection. Figure 3.37(a) shows a NAND-to-AND gate combination in which the AND gate is formed by simply connecting the NAND gate outputs. The wired AND gate in Fig. 3.37(a) requires no additional circuitry beyond that required for the NAND gates. This is shown by the dotted lines used in the NAND symbol.

Only certain NAND gates can have their outputs connected in this way and still form an AND gate. The designer of the NAND gates arranges for this feature, and the manufacturer will indicate on the specification sheet when this can be done. For example, when transistor-transistor logic (TTL) circuits are used, the specification sheets sometimes refer to the gates as having ''open collectors,'' which means they can be formed into NAND-to-AND nets by simply connecting their outputs. In effect, the circuits are designed so that the output level of all gates when the gates are connected will be the lowest level any gate would output if the gates were operated singly.

Figure 3.37(b) and (c) shows examples of NAND-to-wired-AND nets which correspond in function to those in Figs. 3.33 and 3.34. Again, we emphasize that not all NAND gates can be wire-ANDed by using a simple connection. When this is possible, however, the saving in circuitry and speed improvement makes the configuration desirable.

An important observation should be made here: If inputs are wire-ANDed by using a simple connection, a single variable cannot be tied to the AND connection. A single input NAND gate (inverter) must be used. Refer to Fig. 3.38, which shows a design where a single variable B occurs in the minimal expression.

To explain this problem, if in Fig. 3.38 A and C are each 1 and B is 0, then the NAND gate output should be 0, while the value of $\overline{B}$ is 1. What would the value at the wired AND junction be? Will the NAND gate output pull $\overline{B}$ down, or

BOOLEAN ALGEBRA AND GATE NETWORKS

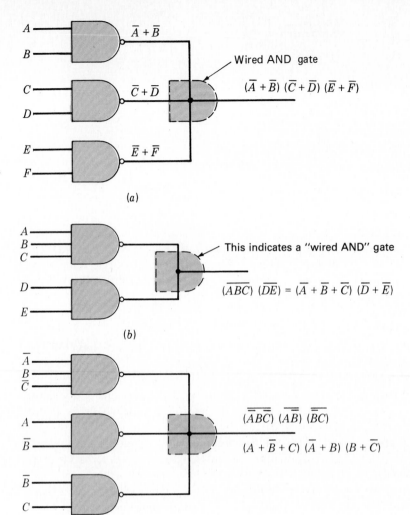

FIGURE 3.37

NAND to wired AND networks. (*a*) NAND-to-AND with wired AND gate. (*b*) NAND-to-AND with wired AND for Fig. 3.33(*a*). (*c*) NAND to wired AND for Fig. 3.34.

will the 1 on $\bar{B}$ force the level up? The situation is to use an AND gate, not a wired AND, or to use a NAND gate with the ability to have its output wire-ANDed, as shown in Fig. 3.38.

Some NOR gates will form an OR gate at their output when they are connected. Figure 3.39 shows a NOR-to-wired-OR net with output function $\overline{(A + B)} + \overline{(C + D)} = \bar{A} \cdot \bar{B} + \bar{C} \cdot \bar{D}$. This expression, $\bar{A} \cdot \bar{B} + \bar{C} \cdot \bar{D}$, shows us that the NOR-to-OR gate network functions as an AND-to-OR gate network but with each variable complemented. Again, the dotted symbol shows the gate is wired OR.

The above result shows that we can design for NOR-to-wired-OR networks just as for NOR-to-OR networks.

Again, note that only certain NOR gates can be connected at their outputs to

A	B	C	OUTPUT
0	0	0	1
0	0	1	1
0	1	0	0
0	1	1	0
1	0	0	1
1	0	1	0
1	1	0	0
1	1	1	0

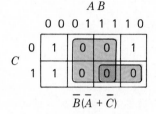

$$\overline{B}(\overline{A} + \overline{C})$$

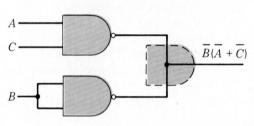

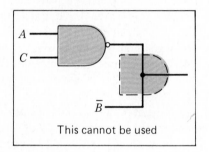

This cannot be used

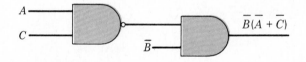

FIGURE 3.38

NAND-to-AND gate design with single variable.

form wired ORs. Some ECL circuits make this possible, and the manufacturer notes this on the specification sheets.

PLAs AND PALs

*3.25 When a design has been made for a gate network, the next step is to implement the design using integrated circuits. As has been mentioned, the most used IC line for gate networks has been a line called *transistor-transistor-logic* (TTL). Figure 3.40(*a*) shows an IC container, and Fig. 3.40(*b*) shows the gate layout in that container. This is called the *pin-out* for the IC package. The package in Fig. 3.40(*b*) is one of several hundred different gate layouts from which a designer can choose. By using this particular IC package, the NAND-to-NAND gate network for $A\overline{B} + BC$ can be realized by connecting the pins of the package as shown in Fig. 3.40(*c*). These connections are often made as conducting metallic strips on printed-circuit boards on which the IC containers are mounted.

110

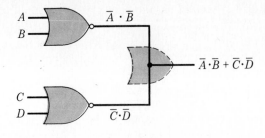

FIGURE 3.39

NOR-to-wired-OR gate network.

As the number of gates in a network increases, more IC packages such as that in Fig. 3.40 are required. To decrease the number of IC packages required and simplify interconnecting the packages, IC manufacturers have evolved manufacturing processes which greatly increase the number of gates that can be placed in a single IC container. This large-scale integration leads to several basic design problems, however. For example, the inputs and outputs to the gates in Fig. 3.40 are all available and the gates can be interconnected in any desired manner, but if more gates are placed in a single container, the number of pins in the IC container must be increased. This increases the cost of the container substantially and decreases the ability of the designer to select just the right combination of gates for the network. Also connections must still be made outside the IC container. If the same connections are made inside the container (on the IC chip), they would cost less and be more reliable. This leads to the idea of a chip with a specific gate layout in which the gates are interconnected on the chip. An IC chip with a specific gate layout made for a particular design is called a *custom* chip. Unfortunately,

FIGURE 3.40

Integrated-circuit container and pin-out. (a) Integrated circuit container. (b) Pin-out showing gate layout in container in (a). (c) NAND-to-NAND gate set realizing $A\bar{B} + BC$.

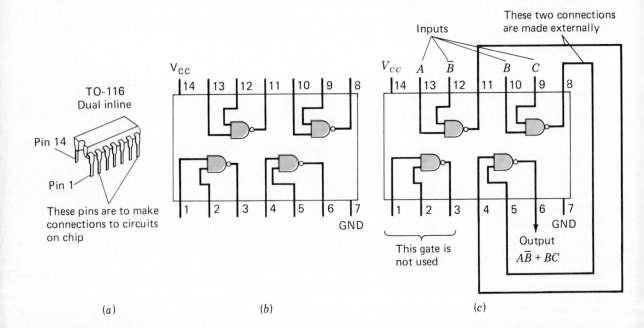

(a)   (b)   (c)

generating a complete design for a new individual custom IC chip[12] can be very expensive (costs can be from $50 to several hundreds of thousands of dollars). This means that start-up costs for a computer design that requires a number of custom chips can be very high. Once custom chips are made, however, for large runs, the cost per manufactured chip is low.

The high start-up costs for custom chips have caused designers to use IC packages with only a few gates per package, as in Fig. 3.40, and form the gate networks by interconnecting the gates outside the IC packages (using a printed-circuit board, as previously noted), particularly when small numbers of the design are to be made. However, although this approach is practical and economical for small production runs, it does not utilize the level of integration[13] possible for present ICs.

PLAs AND PALs

To aid designers in using fewer chips, IC manufacturers make *semicustom* chips in IC containers in which a basic two-level gate network with many gates is produced and the gates can be interconnected on the chip as desired. These are called *programmable logic arrays* (PLAs) or *programmable array logic* (PALs).[14] Figure 3.41 shows a layout for a small PLA. This particular array has three AND gates and two OR gates. (In actual practice, an array would have several hundred or more gates.) Note that the connections from inputs A, B, C, to the AND gates are not complete and that the AND gate outputs are not connected to the OR gates. These connections are made as desired by the gate network designer.

Figure 3.42 shows a design which uses the PLA in Fig. 3.41 and which realizes the two boolean algebra expressions $AB\overline{C} + \overline{A}B$ (for output 1) and $\overline{A}\overline{B} + AC$ (for output 2).

These PLAs are manufactured in two different ways. In the first, the manufacturer places a fused connection at every intersection point in the PLA between the inputs and the AND gates and between the AND and OR gates. Thus every possible connection is made when the PLA is manufactured, and then the undesired connections are removed by blowing the fuses.[15] This type of PLA is often called a *field-programmable logic array* (FPLA).

In the second manufacturing technique, the desired connections are made during manufacture. The manufacturer originally makes the IC array layout so that any desired connections can be made, and the logic designer tells the manufacturer which connections to make for a particular design. Then the manufacturer creates a *mask*, which generates the desired connections when layers of metallization are added to the chip during manufacture. Setting up this mask costs far less (several hundred dollars or less) than designing an entire new chip with the precise logic

---

[12]A custom IC chip is one made from scratch for a particular purpose. A particular gate configuration can be manufactured into a chip by developing the masks used to produce the chip design.

[13]The level of integration is the complexity of the chip in terms of gates per chip. *Small-scale integration* (SSI) is roughly 1 to 20 gates per chip, *medium-scale integration* (MSI) is 20 to 100 gates per chip, *large-scale integration* (LSI) is 100 to 1000 gates per chip, and *very large-scale integration* (VLSI) is more than 1000 gates.

[14]PAL is a registered trademark of Monolithic Memories.

[15]The fuses are blown by selecting a fuse using logic levels at the inputs and then applying a relatively high voltage to a pin on the IC container. Electronic instruments can be purchased which blow selected fuses on a PLA. This is called *programming* the PLA.

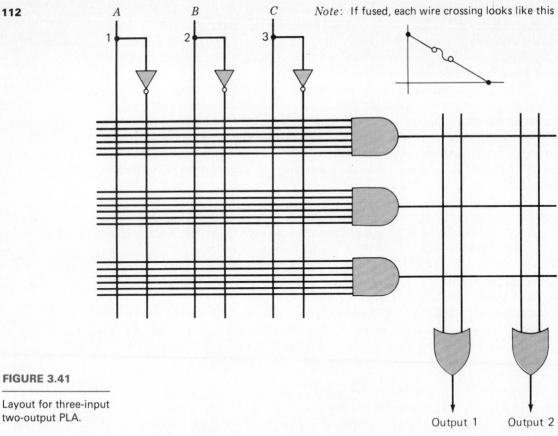

FIGURE 3.41

Layout for three-input
two-output PLA.

Output 1   Output 2

array desired by the logic designer. And production runs of these chips are inexpensive.

Note that the AND gate which generates $\overline{AB}$ in Fig. 3.42 has its output connected to two OR gates. This is sometimes a useful and desirable feature for PLAs enabling a single AND gate to be used for two outputs.

Most larger PLAs contain several hundred gates, 15 to 25 inputs, and 5 to 15 outputs. This offers the logic designer great flexibility. The low cost per unit of these IC gate networks has led to widespread use of PLAs.

To design these large arrays, a simplifying symbology has proved useful. Figure 3.43 shows this for the array in Fig. 3.42. The crosses drawn on the function indicate ANDs, and the squares indicate ORs. The figure also shows that the AND can be realized by a single semiconductor junction (called a *diode*), and the OR can be realized by a single junction pointed the other way. In practice, the manufacturer lays out the chip with junctions at every intersection of the lines, and only the desired diode connections are made.[16] Note: This is simply a redrawing of Fig.

---

[16]For field-programmable logic arrays (FPLAs) the diodes are fused so they can be blown by an instrument called an *array programmer*. This sets the FPLA as desired.

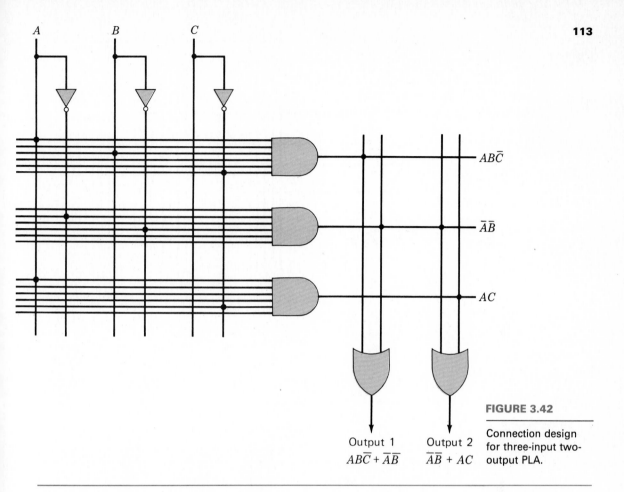

FIGURE 3.42

Connection design for three-input two-output PLA.

Output 1
$AB\overline{C} + \overline{A}\,\overline{B}$

Output 2
$\overline{A}\,\overline{B} + AC$

$AB\overline{C}$

$\overline{A}\overline{B}$

AC

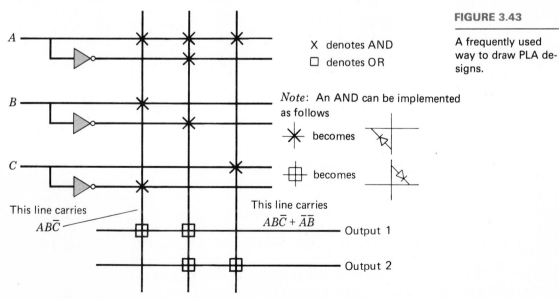

FIGURE 3.43

A frequently used way to draw PLA designs.

X denotes AND

□ denotes OR

Note: An AND can be implemented as follows

✳ becomes

⊞ becomes

This line carries $AB\overline{C}$

This line carries $AB\overline{C} + \overline{A}\overline{B}$

Output 1

Output 2

**BOOLEAN ALGEBRA
AND GATE
NETWORKS**

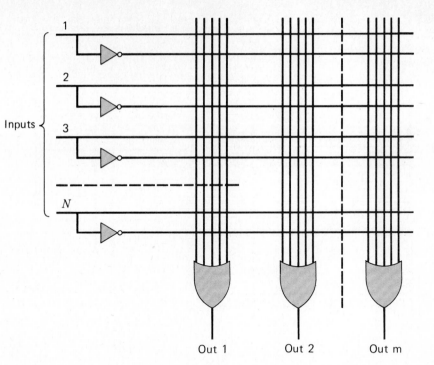

FIGURE 3.44

Layout for PAL.

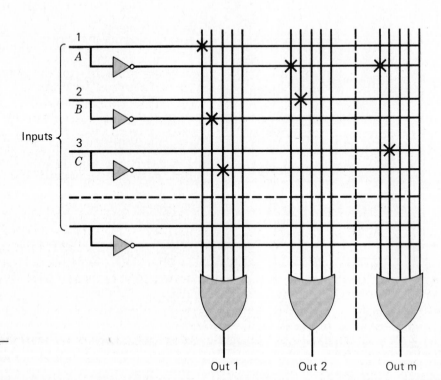

FIGURE 3.45

PAL design for $A\overline{B}\overline{C}$
$+ \overline{A}B + \overline{A}C$.

16X48X8 FPLA PROGRAM TABLE

PROGRAM TABLE ENTRIES

INPUT VARIABLE			OUTPUT FUNCTION		OUTPUT ACTIVE LEVEL	
Im	Ïm	Don't Care	Prod. Term Present in Fp	Prod. Term Not Present in Fp	Active High	Active Low
H	L	— (dash)	A	• (period)	H	L

NOTE

Enter '—' for unused inputs of used P-terms

NOTES

1 Entries independent of output polarity
2 Enter A for unused outputs of used P-terms

NOTES

1 Polarity programmed once only
2 Enter 'H' for all unused outputs

| NO | \multicolumn{16}{c}{PRODUCT TERM¹ — INPUT VARIABLE} | \multicolumn{8}{c}{ACTIVE LEVEL¹ — OUTPUT FUNCTION} |

NO	15	14	13	12	11	10	9	8	7	6	5	4	3	2	1	0	7	6	5	4	3	2	1	0
0																								
1																								
2																								
3																								
4																								
5																								
6																								
7																								
8																								
9																								
10																								
11																								
12																								
13																								
14																								
15																								
16																								
17																								
18																								
19																								
20																								
21																								
22																								
23																								
24																								
25																								
26																								
27																								
28																								
29																								
30																								
31																								
32																								
33																								
34																								
35																								
36																								
37																								
38																								
39																								
40																								
41																								
42																								
43																								
44																								
45																								
46																								
47																								

(1) Input and Output fields of unused P-terms can be left blank. Unused inputs and outputs are FPLA terminals left floating

THIS PORTION TO BE COMPLETED BY SIGNETICS

CF (XXXX)

CUSTOMER SYMBOLIZED PART #

DATE RECEIVED

COMMENTS

CUSTOMER NAME

PURCHASE ORDER #

SIGNETICS DEVICE #

TOTAL NUMBER OF PARTS

PROGRAM TABLE #

REV ____ DATE

FIGURE 3.46

Program table for a PLA.

BOOLEAN ALGEBRA
AND GATE
NETWORKS

I,N PACKAGE*

FE†	1	28	V_{CC}
I_7	2	27	I_8
I_6	3	26	I_9
I_5	4	25	I_{10}
I_4	5	24	I_{11}
I_3	6	23	I_{12}
I_2	7	22	I_{13}
I_1	8	21	I_{14}
I_0	9	20	I_{15}
F_7	10	19	$\overline{CE}$
F_6	11	18	F_0
F_5	12	17	F_1
F_4	13	16	F_2
GND	14	15	F_3

*I = Ceramic
N = Plastic
†Open during normal operation

FIGURE 3.47

Pin-out for PLA. (*Signetics Corp.*)

3.42 with a different symbology. This symbology becomes very useful when there are many inputs and gates, however.

Figure 3.44 shows the layout for a version of the PLA which has become popular and which is called *programmable array logic*. The PALs are very similar to PLAs except that the OR gates are fixed and permanently connected to a set of AND gate output lines. As a result, AND gates cannot be shared, but the fixed OR gate connections lead to an ease of manufacture which has proved popular. Figure 3.45 shows a PAL design using the AND symbology (crosses) at intersections as in Fig. 3.43.

The current nomenclature calls the version of Fig. 3.44 in which the AND element connections are fused a PAL, but calls the version in which the manufacturer makes the connections *hard array logic* (HAL).

EXAMPLE OF DESIGN USING A PLA

3.26 Since PLAs and PALs are widely used because of their economy and speed of operation, we examine the design of a small network employing a widely used table listing.

16X48X8 FPLA PROGRAM TABLE

PROGRAM TABLE ENTRIES						
INPUT VARIABLE			OUTPUT FUNCTION		OUTPUT ACTIVE LEVEL	
Im	$\overline{Im}$	Don't Care	Prod Term Present in Fp	Prod Term Not Present in Fp	Active High	Active Low
H	L	— (dash)	A	• (period)	H	L
NOTE Enter (—) for unused inputs of used P-terms			NOTES 1 Entries independent of output polarity 2 Enter (A) for unused outputs of used P-terms		NOTES 1 Polarity programmed once only 2 Enter (H) for all unused outputs	

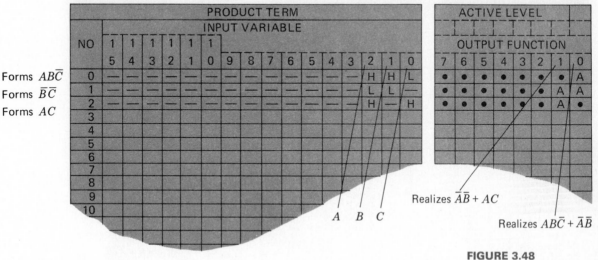

Realizes $\overline{A}\overline{B} + AC$

Realizes $AB\overline{C} + \overline{A}\overline{B}$

FIGURE 3.48

Program table for PLA design in Fig. 3.42.

Figure 3.46 shows a program table for a PLA manufactured by Signetics. This PLA has 16 input variables and 8 outputs from OR gates. Also, 48 AND gates can be formed on the chip. This PLA is packaged in a 28-pin IC container, and the pin-out is shown in Fig. 3.47.

The table in Fig. 3.46 can be filled out to describe a particular gate network and then mailed to an IC manufacturer, who will then produce chips with a gate network corresponding to the table. Although a Signetics table is used here, the table is typical and other manufacturers provide the same service.

The table is filled out as follows:

First, the logic input variables are identified with the INPUT VARIABLE number 0 to 15 on the table. We fill out the table for Fig. 3.42 as a (small) example. To do this, we identify A with input 2, B with input 1, and C with input 0 on the program table. We now wish to form the product terms $AB\overline{C}$, $\overline{A}\overline{B}$, and AC. The rule is that if an input is not complemented (inverted), an H is written in the table; if the input is to be complemented, an L is written; and if the input is not used, a — is written. To form $AB\overline{C}$, then, we form a row in the table containing dashes everywhere except in INPUT VARIABLE columns 2, 1, and 0, and in these we write H, H, and L. This is shown in Fig. 3.48.

The OR gate inputs are written as follows:

If the AND term in a particular row is to be used in an OR output, an A (for

117

16X48X8 FPLA PROGRAM TABLE

PROGRAM TABLE ENTRIES						
INPUT VARIABLE			OUTPUT FUNCTION		OUTPUT ACTIVE LEVEL	
Im	$\overline{\text{Im}}$	Don't Care	Prod Term Present in Fp	Prod Term Not Present in Fp	Active High	Active Low
H	L	– (dash)	A	• (period)	H	L
NOTE Enter (–) for unused inputs of used P-terms			NOTES 1 Entries independent of output polarity 2 Enter (A) for unused outputs of used P-terms		NOTES 1 Polarity programmed once only 2 Enter (H) for all unused outputs	

NO	15	14	13	12	11	10	9	8	7	6	5	4	3	2	1	0		7	6	5	4	3	2	1	0
	PRODUCT TERM – INPUT VARIABLE																	ACTIVE LEVEL / OUTPUT FUNCTION							
0	—	—	—	—	—	—	—	—	—	—	—	—	H	—	—	—		•	•	•	•	•	•	•	A
1	—	—	—	—	—	—	—	—	—	—	—	—	—	H	H	—		•	•	•	•	•	•	A	A
2	—	—	—	—	—	—	—	—	—	—	—	—	L	—	L	H		•	•	•	•	•	A	•	A
3	—	—	—	—	—	—	—	—	—	—	—	—	H	H	—	—		•	•	•	•	•	•	A	•
4	—	—	—	—	—	—	—	—	—	—	—	—	H	L	L	H		•	•	•	•	•	A	A	•
5	—	—	—	—	—	—	—	—	—	—	—	—	—	L	L	—		•	•	•	•	•	A	•	•
6	—	—	—	—	—	—	—	—	—	—	—	—	H	—	H	—		•	•	•	•	•	A	•	•
7																									
8																									
9																									
10																									
11																									
12																									
13																									

Output 0 = $A + BC + \bar{A}\bar{C}D$

Output 1 = $BC + AB + A\bar{B}\bar{C}D$

Output 2 = $\bar{A}\bar{C}D + A\bar{B}\bar{C}D + \bar{B}\bar{C} + AC$

Note: Input variable 3 = A, 2 = B, 1 = C, 0 = D

FIGURE 3.49

Program table for three AND-to-OR gate networks.

active) is written in the row; if not, a • is written. In Fig. 3.48, the OUTPUT FUNCTION line 0 in the table is associated with OUTPUT 1 in Fig. 3.42 and OUTPUT FUNCTION line 1 is associated with OUTPUT 2 in Fig. 3.42.

A final example is shown in Fig. 3.49. In this case, there are three output lines 0, 1, and 2. We associated A with INPUT VARIABLE 3 on the table, B with 2, C with 1, and D with 0. The functions formed are

$$\text{OUTPUT LINE } 0 = A + BC + \bar{A}\bar{C}D$$
$$\text{OUTPUT LINE } 1 = AB + BC + A\bar{B}\bar{C}D$$
$$\text{OUTPUT LINE } 2 = \bar{B}\bar{C} + \bar{A}\bar{C}D + A\bar{B}\bar{C}D + AC$$

Clearly PLAs provide a convenient way to fabricate IC chips with gate networks. The fact that field-programmable arrays with a given design can be made by blowing selected fuses and then the computer design can be tested by using these trial chips is very convenient. Later, for production runs, the chips made by a manufacturer from the table can be used.

This part of the IC business is sufficiently developed that PLA designs can be punched into cards and sent to a manufacturer, punched into tapes and sent to a manufacturer, and even sent over the telephone line from a terminal connected to a tape reader. (Manufacturers will provide a long-distance number you can call to phone in designs.)

SUMMARY

3.27 This chapter presented the basic idea of a gate and showed how gates can be interconnected to form logic networks. The basic types of gates were introduced: AND, OR, NAND, and NOR gates and inverters.

The design of logic networks for computers is greatly facilitated by boolean algebra. This subject was introduced, and tables of combination, theorems of the algebra, and algebraic reduction of expressions were all explained.

The map method for simplifying boolean algebra expressions was presented. This makes it possible to minimize boolean expressions, thereby also simplifying the logic networks that realize these expressions. The various network forms such as AND-to-OR, NAND-to-NAND, OR-to-AND, NOR-to-NOR, NAND-to-AND, and NOR-to-OR networks were explained, and the design procedure for each was presented.

Gating networks can now be made with many gates in a single container by using LSI manufacturing techniques. The general layout for several such integrated circuits was presented, as was a special representation which is commonly used. This makes possible design of relatively large arrays of gates using PLAs, PALs, and HALs.

QUESTIONS

3.1 Prepare a truth table for the following boolean expressions:
(a) $XYZ + \overline{XYZ}$
(b) $ABC + A\overline{BC} + \overline{ABC}$
(c) $A(B\overline{C} + \overline{B}C)$
(d) $(A + B)(A + C)(\overline{A} + \overline{B})$

3.2 Prepare a table of combinations for the following boolean algebra expressions:
(a) $\overline{XY} + \overline{X}Y$
(b) $XY\overline{Z} + \overline{X}YZ$
(c) $\overline{X}Y\overline{Z} + X\overline{Y}$
(d) $\overline{XYZ} + X\overline{Y}Z + \overline{X}YZ$
(e) $\overline{X}Y + \overline{Y}Z$
(f) $\overline{AB}(\overline{ABC} + \overline{BC})$

3.3 Prepare a truth table for the following boolean expressions:
(a) $A\overline{B} + \overline{A}B$
(b) $A\overline{B} + B\overline{C}$
(c) $A\overline{C} + \overline{A}C$
(d) $\overline{ABC} + AB\overline{C} + \overline{A}BC$
(e) $AB(A\overline{B}C + \overline{AB}\overline{C} + AB\overline{C})$

3.4 Prepare a table of combinations for the following boolean algebra expressions:
(a) $X(\overline{Y} + \overline{Z}) + X\overline{Y}$
(b) $X\overline{Y}(Z + \overline{YZ}) + \overline{Z}$
(c) $[X(Y + \overline{Y}) + \overline{X}(\overline{Y} + Y)]\cdot\overline{Z}$
(d) $AB(\overline{AB} + \overline{A}B)$
(e) $A[(\overline{B} + C) + \overline{C}]$
(f) $\overline{ABC}\,(\overline{ABC} + \overline{ABC})$

3.5 Prepare a table of combinations for the following boolean algebra expressions:
(a) $XY + \overline{XY}Z$
(b) $ABC + \overline{AB} + \overline{A}B$
(c) $ABC + \overline{AC}$

BOOLEAN ALGEBRA
AND GATE
NETWORKS

3.6 Prepare a table of combinations for the following boolean algebra expressions:
(a) $A\overline{B}\overline{C} + \overline{A}B$ (b) $\overline{A}\overline{B}\overline{C} + AC + AB$
(c) $XZ + X\overline{Y} + \overline{X}Z$

3.7 Simplify the following expressions, and draw a block diagram of the circuit for each simplified expression, using AND and OR gates. Assume the inputs are from flip-flops.
(a) $A\overline{B}\overline{C} + \overline{A}\overline{B}\overline{C} + \overline{A}B\overline{C} + \overline{A}\overline{B}C$
(b) $ABC + \overline{A}B\overline{C} + A\overline{B}\overline{C} + AB\overline{C} + A\overline{B}C + \overline{A}BC + \overline{A}\overline{B}C$
(c) $A(A + B + C)(\overline{A} + B + C)(A + \overline{B} + C)(A + B + \overline{C})$
(d) $(A + B + C)(A + \overline{B} + \overline{C})(A + B + \overline{C})(A + \overline{B} + C)$

3.8 Simplify the expressions in Question 3.4 and draw block diagrams of gating networks for your simplified expressions, using AND gates, OR gates, and inverters.

3.9 Simplify the following expressions:
(a) $ABC(A\overline{B}\overline{C} + A\overline{B}C + \overline{A}BC)$ (b) $AB + A\overline{B} + \overline{A}C + \overline{A}\overline{C}$
(c) $XY + XY\overline{Z} + XYZ + XZY$ (d) $XY(\overline{X}Y\overline{Z} + X\overline{Y}Z + \overline{X}\overline{Y}Z)$

3.10 Simplify the expressions in Question 3.6 and draw block diagrams of gating networks for your simplified expressions, using AND gates, OR gates, and inverters.

3.11 Form the complements of the following expressions. For instance, the complement of $(XY + XZ)$ is equal to $\overline{(XY + XZ)} = (\overline{X} + \overline{Y})(\overline{X} + \overline{Z}) = \overline{X} + \overline{Y}\overline{Z}$.
(a) $(A + BC + AB)$ (b) $(A + B)(B + C)(A + C)$
(c) $AB + \overline{B}C + CD$ (d) $AB(\overline{C}D + \overline{B}C)$
(e) $A(B + C)(\overline{C} + \overline{D})$

3.12 Complement the following expressions (as in Question 3.11):
(a) $\overline{X}\overline{Y} + X\overline{Y}$ (b) $X\overline{Y}Z + \overline{X}Y$
(c) $\overline{X}(Y + \overline{Z})$ (d) $X(Y\overline{Z} + \overline{Y}Z)$
(e) $XY(\overline{Y}Z + X\overline{Z})$ (f) $XY + \overline{X}\overline{Y}(Y\overline{Z} + \overline{X}\overline{Y})$

3.13 Prove the two basic De Morgan theorems, using the proof by perfect induction.

3.14 Prove the following rules using the proof by perfect induction:
(a) $X\overline{Y} + XY = X$
(b) $X + \overline{X}Y = X + Y$

3.15 Convert the following expressions to sum-of-products form:
(a) $(A + B)(\overline{B} + C)(\overline{A} + C)$
(b) $(\overline{A} + C)(\overline{A} + \overline{B} + \overline{C})(A + \overline{B})$
(c) $(A + C)(A\overline{B} + AC)(\overline{A}\overline{C} + B)$

3.16 Convert the following expressions to sum-of-products form:
(a) $(\overline{A} + \overline{B})(\overline{C} + B)$ (b) $\overline{A}B(\overline{B}C + \overline{B}C)$
(c) $(A + B\overline{C})(A\overline{B} + \overline{A}B)$ (d) $AB(A\overline{B}\overline{C} + \overline{A}C)$
(e) $(\overline{A} + B)[A\overline{C} + (B + C)]$ (f) $(\overline{A} + C)(AB + \overline{A}B + AC)$

3.17 Which rule is the dual of rule 12 in Table 3.10?

3.18 Give a dual of the rule of $X + \overline{X}Y = X + Y$.

3.19 Multiply the following sum terms, forming a sum-of-products expression in each case. Simplify while multiplying when possible.

    (a) $(A + C)(B + D)$
    (b) $(A + C + D)(B + D + C)$
    (c) $(AB + C + DC)(AB + BC + D)$
    (d) $(A\overline{B} + \overline{A}B + A\overline{C})(\overline{A}\overline{B} + A\overline{B} + A\overline{C})$

3.20 Convert the following expressions to product-of-sums form:

    (a) $A + \overline{A}B + \overline{A}\overline{C}$ (b) $BC + \overline{A}B$
    (c) $A\overline{B}(\overline{B} + \overline{C})$ (d) $\overline{A}\overline{B}(\overline{B}\overline{C} + \overline{B}C)$
    (e) $(A + \overline{B} + C)(AB + \overline{A}C)$ (f) $(\overline{A} + \overline{B})A\overline{B}C$

3.21 Write the boolean expression (in sum-of-products form) for a logic circuit that will have a 1 output when $X = 0$, $Y = 0$, $Z = 1$ and $X = 1$, $Y = 1$, $Z = 0$; and a 0 output for all other input states. Draw the block diagram for this circuit, assuming that the inputs are from flip-flops.

3.22 Convert the following to product-of-sums form

    (a) $AB + \overline{A}(B + \overline{C})(D + \overline{B})$
    (b) $(B + C)[(\overline{B} + \overline{C})(A + \overline{C})(B + C)]$

3.23 Convert the following to product-of-sums form

    (a) $AB\overline{C} + A\overline{B}C + \overline{A}BC$
    (b) $ABC + \overline{B}\overline{C}(A + CD)(B + C)$

3.24 Prove the following theorem, using the rules in Table 3.10:

$$(X + Y)(X + \overline{Y}) = X$$

3.25 Write the boolean expression (in sum-of-products form) for a logic network that will have a 1 output when $X = 1$, $Y = 0$, $Z = 0$; $X = 1$, $Y = 1$, $Z = 0$; $X = 1$, $Y = 1$, $Z = 0$; and $X = 1$, $Y = 1$, $Z = 1$. The circuit will have a 0 output for all other sets of input values. Simplify the expression derived and draw a block diagram for the simplified expression.

3.26 Derive the boolean algebra expression for a gating network that will have outputs 0 only when $X = 1$, $Y = 1$, $Z = 1$; $X = 0$, $Y = 0$, $Z = 0$; $X = 1$, $Y = 0$, $Z = 0$. The outputs are to be 1 for all other cases.

3.27 Prove rule 18 in Table 3.10, using the proof by perfect induction.

3.28 Develop sum-of-products and product-of-sums expressions for F_1, F_2, and F_3 in Table 3.27.

3.29 Develop both the sum-of-products and the product-of-sums expressions that describe Table 3.28. Then simplify both expressions. Draw a block diagram for logical circuitry that corresponds to the simplified expressions, using only NAND gates for the sum-of-products and NOR gates for product-of-sums expression.

TABLE 3.27

	INPUTS			OUTPUTS	
X	Y	Z	F_1	F_2	F_3
0	0	0	0	0	1
0	0	1	0	1	1
0	1	0	1	1	1
0	1	1	1	1	0
1	0	0	1	0	0
1	0	1	0	1	0
1	1	0	1	1	1
1	1	1	1	0	1

TABLE 3.28

	INPUTS		OUTPUT
X	Y	Z	A
0	0	0	0
0	0	1	1
0	1	0	1
0	1	1	0
1	0	0	0
1	0	1	1
1	1	0	1
1	1	1	0

3.30 Draw block diagrams for the F_1, F_2, and F_3 in Question 3.28, using only NAND gates.

3.31 Write the boolean algebra expressions for Tables 3.29 to 3.31, showing expressions in sum-of-products form. Then simplify the expressions and draw a block diagram of the circuit corresponding to each expression.

3.32 Draw block diagrams for the F_1, F_2, and F_3 in Question 3.28, using only NOR gates.

3.33 Draw block diagrams for F_1, F_2, and F_3 in Question 3.28, using OR-to-NAND networks.

3.34 Draw block diagrams for F_1, F_2, and F_3 in Question 3.28, using AND-to-NOR gate networks.

3.35 Draw Karnaugh maps for the expressions in Question 3.2.

3.36 Draw Karnaugh maps for the expressions in Question 3.3.

3.37 For a four-variable map in W, X, Y, and Z draw the subcubes for:
(a) $WX\overline{Y}$ (b) WX (c) $XY\overline{Z}$ (d) Y

3.38 For a four-variable map in W, X, Y, and Z draw the subcubes for:
(a) $\overline{W}X\overline{Y}\overline{Z}$ (b) $W\overline{Z}$ (c) $\overline{W}Z$ (d) $\overline{Y}$

TABLE 3.29

INPUTS			OUTPUT
A	B	C	Z
0	0	0	0
0	0	1	1
0	1	0	1
0	1	1	0
1	0	0	1
1	0	1	1
1	1	0	0
1	1	1	0

3.39 Draw maps of the expressions in Question 3.40; then draw the subcubes for the shortened terms you found.

3.40 Apply the rule $AY + A\overline{Y} = A$, where possible, to the following expressions:
(a) $X\overline{Y} + \overline{X}\overline{Y}$ (b) $\overline{A}\overline{B}\overline{C} + A\overline{B}\overline{C}$
(c) $A\overline{B}C + ABC$ (d) $ABC + A\overline{B}\overline{C} + A\overline{B}C + AB\overline{C}$
(e) $ABC + \overline{A}\overline{B}C + A\overline{B}C$ (f) $ABC + \overline{A}BC + \overline{A}\overline{B}C$

Note: There is a technique for writing minterms that is widely used. It consists in writing the letter *m* (to represent *minterm*) along with the value of the binary number given by the row of the table and combinations in which the minterm lies. For instance, in the variables *X, Y, Z* we have the unfinished table of combinations given in Table 3.32.

TABLE 3.30

INPUTS			OUTPUT
A	B	C	Z
0	0	0	1
0	0	1	0
0	1	0	0
0	1	1	1
1	0	0	1
1	0	1	0
1	1	0	0
1	1	1	1

TABLE 3.31

INPUTS			OUTPUT
X	Y	Z	P
0	0	0	1
0	0	1	1
0	1	0	1
0	1	1	1
1	0	0	1
1	0	1	0
1	1	0	0
1	1	1	0

TABLE 3.32

INPUT			OUTPUT	PRODUCT TERMS	DESIGNATION AS m_i
X	Y	Z			
0	0	0		$\overline{X}\overline{Y}\overline{Z}$	m_0
0	0	1		$\overline{X}\overline{Y}Z$	m_1
0	1	0		$\overline{X}Y\overline{Z}$	m_2
0	1	1		$\overline{X}YZ$	m_3
1	0	0		$X\overline{Y}\overline{Z}$	m_4
1	0	1		$X\overline{Y}Z$	m_5
1	1	0		$XY\overline{Z}$	m_6
1	1	1		XYZ	m_7

BOOLEAN ALGEBRA
AND GATE
NETWORKS

For this table $m_0 = \overline{X}\overline{Y}\overline{Z}$, $m_1 = \overline{X}\overline{Y}Z$, $m_2 = \overline{X}Y\overline{Z}$, $m_3 = \overline{X}YZ$, and so to $m_7 = XYZ$. Now we can substitute m_i's for actual terms and shorten the writing of expressions. For instance, $m_1 + m_2 + m_4$ means $\overline{X}\overline{Y}Z + \overline{X}Y\overline{Z} + X\overline{Y}\overline{Z}$. Similarly, $m_0 + m_3 + m_5 + m_7$ means $\overline{X}\overline{Y}\overline{Z} + \overline{X}YZ + X\overline{Y}Z + XYZ$.

This can be extended to four or more variables. An expression in W, X, Y, Z can be written as $m_0 + m_{13} + m_{15} = \overline{W}\overline{X}\overline{Y}\overline{Z} + WX\overline{Y}Z + WXYZ$. Or $m_2 + m_5 + m_9 = \overline{W}\overline{X}Y\overline{Z} + \overline{W}X\overline{Y}Z + W\overline{X}\overline{Y}Z$. As can be seen, to change a minterm to its m_i, simply make uncomplemented variables 1s and complemented variables 0s. Thus $\overline{W}XY\overline{Z}$ would be 0110, or 6 decimal; $\overline{W}\overline{X}Y\overline{Z}$ would be 0010, or 2 decimal. These two terms would then be written m_6 and m_2. (Notice that we must know how many variables a minterm is in.)

3.41 Draw the Karnaugh maps in X, Y, Z for:

(a) $m_0 + m_1 + m_5 + m_7$ (b) $m_1 + m_3 + m_5 + m_4$
(c) $m_1 + m_2 + m_3 + m_5$ (d) $m_0 + m_5 + m_7$

3.42 Draw the subcubes for a three-variable map in X, Y, Z for:

(a) $m_1 + m_3 + m_5 + m_0$ (b) $m_4 + m_7$ (c) $m_0 + m_3$

3.43 Find the maximal subcubes for the maps drawn for Question 3.42.

3.44 Find minimal expressions for the maps drawn in Question 3.42.

3.45 Using maps, simplify the following expressions in four variables, W, X, Y, and Z:

(a) $m_2 + m_3 + m_5 + m_6 + m_7 + m_9 + m_{11} + m_{13}$
(b) $m_0 + m_2 + m_4 + m_8 + m_9 + m_{10} + m_{11} + m_{12} + m_{13}$

3.46 Using maps, simplify the following expressions in four variables W, X, Y, and Z:

(a) $m_1 + m_3 + m_5 + m_7 + m_{12} + m_{13} + m_8 + m_9$
(b) $m_0 + m_5 + m_7 + m_8 + m_{11} + m_{13} + m_{15}$

3.47 Using maps, derive minimal product-of-sums expressions for the functions given in Question 3.46.

3.48 Using maps, derive minimal product-of-sums expressions for the functions given in Question 3.42.

3.49 Using maps, simplify the following expressions, using sum-of-products form:

$\overbrace{}^{\text{don't-cares}}$

(a) $\overline{A}\overline{B}\overline{C} + A\overline{B}\overline{C} + \overline{ABC + \overline{A}B\overline{C} + \overline{A}\overline{B}C}$

$\overbrace{}^{\text{don't-cares}}$

(b) $ABC + \overline{A}\overline{B}\overline{C} + \overline{AB\overline{C} + A\overline{B}C}$

$\overbrace{}^{\text{don't-cares}}$

(c) $ABCD + \overline{A}\overline{B}C\overline{D} + \overline{A}BC\overline{D} + \overline{A\overline{B}CD + \overline{A}\overline{B}CD + ABC\overline{D}}$

3.50 Using maps, derive minimal product-of-sums expressions for the functions given in Question 3.49.

3.51 Using maps, simplify the following expressions, using sum-of-products form:

$$\text{(a) } ABC + \overline{A}\overline{B}C + \overset{\overbrace{\text{don't-cares}}}{\overline{A}BC + A\overline{B}C} + AB\overline{C}$$

$$\text{(b) } ABCD + \overline{A}\overline{B}CD + \overset{\overbrace{\text{don't-cares}}}{\overline{A}BCD + A\overline{B}CD} + \overline{A}\overline{B}\overline{C}\overline{D}$$

$$\text{(c) } A\overline{B}C\overline{D} + A\overline{B}CD + \overset{\overbrace{\text{don't-cares}}}{\overline{A}B\overline{C}D + \overline{A}BCD}$$

3.52 (a) Design an AND-to-OR gate combinational network for the boolean algebra expression

$$ABCD + AB\overline{C}\overline{D} + \overline{A}BCD + \overline{A}B\overline{C}D + ABC\overline{D} + \overline{A}BCD$$

Use as few gates as you can.

(b) Design a NOR gate combinational network for the boolean algebra function in part (a), again using as few gates as you can.

3.53 The following is a NAND-to-NAND gate network. Draw a block diagram for a NOR-to-NOR gate network that realizes the same function, using as few gates as possible.

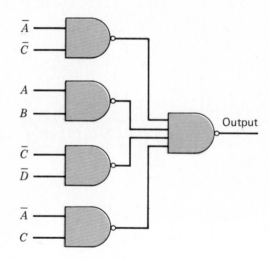

FIGURE Q3.53

3.54 (a) Derive a boolean algebra expression for the output Y of the network shown.

(b) Convert the expression for Y derived in (a) to product-of-sums form.

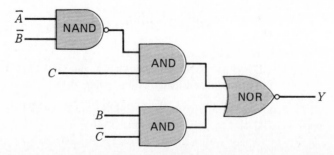

FIGURE Q3.54

3.55 (*a*) Design an OR-to-AND gate combinational network for the boolean algebra expression

$$ABCD + \overline{A}B\overline{C}\overline{D} + \overline{A}B\overline{C}D + \overline{A}BC\overline{D} + (\overline{A}\,\overline{B}\,\overline{C}\,\overline{D} + \overline{A}\,\overline{B}CD)$$

The two terms in parentheses are don't-care terms.

   (*b*) Using only NAND gates, design a combinational network for the boolean algebra function given in part (*a*).

3.56 (*a*) Design an OR-to-AND gate combinational network for the boolean algebra expression

$$\overline{A}BCD + \overline{A}BC\overline{D} + \overline{A}B\overline{C}D + \overline{A}B\overline{C}\overline{D} + \overline{A}\,\overline{B}CD)$$

The two terms in parentheses are don't-care terms.

   (*b*) Using only NOR gates, design a combinational network for the boolean algebra function given in part (*a*).

3.57 The following NAND-to-AND gate network is to be redesigned using a NOR-to-OR gate configuration. Make the change, using as few gates as possible.

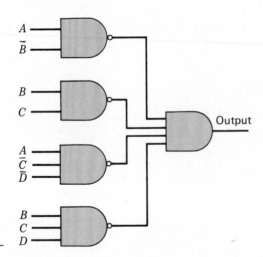

3.58 (*a*) Design an AND-to-OR gate combinational network for the boolean algebra expression

$$ABCD + AB\overline{C}D + \overline{A}\,\overline{B}C\overline{D} + AB\overline{C}\,\overline{D} + ABC\overline{D} + \overline{A}B\overline{C}\,\overline{D}$$

Use as few gates as you can.

   (*b*) Design a NOR gate combinational network for the boolean algebra function in part (*a*), again using as few gates as you can.

3.59 Convert the following NOR-to-OR gate network to a NAND-to-AND gate network. Use as few gates as possible.

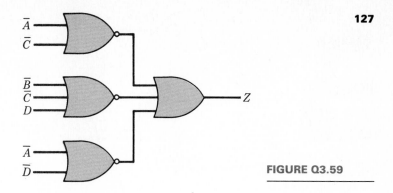

3.60 (*a*) Design an AND-to-OR gate combinational network for the boolean algebra expression

$$\overline{A}\overline{B}CD + AB\overline{C}D + \overline{A}\overline{B}CD + AB\overline{C}D + \overline{A}\overline{B}\overline{C}D + \overline{A}BCD$$

Use as few gates as you can.

(*b*) Design a NOR-to-NOR gate combinational network for the boolean algebra function in part (*a*), again using as few gates as you can.

3.61 A combinational network has three control inputs C_1, C_2, and C_3; three data inputs A_1, A_2, and A_3; and a single output Z. (And $\overline{A}_1$, $\overline{A}_2$, $\overline{A}_3$, $\overline{C}_1$, $\overline{C}_2$, and $\overline{C}_3$ are also available as inputs.) Each input is a binary-valued signal. Only one of the control inputs can be a 1 at any given time, and all three can be 0s simultaneously. When C_1 is a 1, the value of Z is to be the value of A_1; when C_2 is a 1, the value of Z is to be the value of A_2; and when C_3 is a 1, the value of the output is to be the value of A_3. If C_1, C_2, and C_3 are 0s, the output Z is to have value 0. Design this network, using only NOR gates. Make the network have two levels, and use as few gates as possible.

3.62 The following NAND-to-AND gate network is to be redesigned by using a NOR-to-OR gate configuration. Make the change, using as few gates as possible.

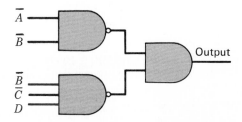

3.63 Convert the following NOR-to-NOR gate network to a NAND-to-AND gate network. Use as few gates as possible.

**BOOLEAN ALGEBRA
AND GATE
NETWORKS**

FIGURE Q3.63

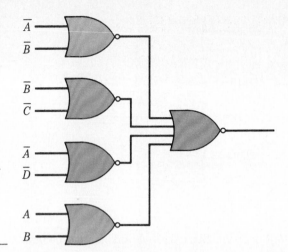

3.64 Will the minimal expression of the function in Table 3.33 require fewer NAND gates or NOR gates? (d means don't-care.) Assume complements are available. How many gates for each? Give your minimal expressions.

3.65 The following NAND-to-AND gate network must be converted to a NOR-to-OR gate network. Make the conversion, using as few gates as possible in your final design.

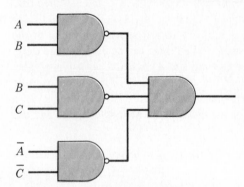

FIGURE Q3.65

3.66 Will the minimal expression for the function in Table 3.34 require fewer NAND gates or NOR gates? (d means don't-care.) Assume complements are available. How many gates for each? Give your minimal expressions.

3.67 Simplify:

(a) $\overline{(\overline{W} + \overline{X} + Y + Z)(\overline{W} + X + \overline{Y} + Z)(\overline{W} + X + Y + Z)}$

$$\overbrace{(W + X + \overline{Y} + Z)(W + \overline{X} + Y + Z)(\overline{W} + \overline{X} + Y + \overline{Z})}^{\text{don't-cares}}$$

$(W + X + Y + Z)$

(b) $\overline{A}\overline{B}\overline{C}\overline{D} + \overline{A}\overline{B}CD + ABC\overline{D} +$

$$\overbrace{\overline{A}\overline{B}CD + \overline{A}BCD + ABCD + \overline{A}BC\overline{D} + A\overline{B}C\overline{D}}^{\text{don't-cares}}$$

(c) For parts (a) and (b), design block diagrams for the logical circuitry of

TABLE 3.33

X_1	X_2	X_3	X_4	OUTPUT
0	0	0	0	0
0	0	0	1	1
0	0	1	0	1
0	0	1	1	0
0	1	0	0	0
0	1	0	1	d
0	1	1	0	1
0	1	1	1	d
1	0	0	0	d
1	0	0	1	1
1	0	1	0	0
1	0	1	1	0
1	1	0	0	d
1	1	0	1	0
1	1	1	0	d
1	1	1	1	0

TABLE 3.34

X_1	X_2	X_3	X_4	OUTPUT
0	0	0	0	0
0	0	0	1	1
0	0	1	0	1
0	0	1	1	0
0	1	0	0	0
0	1	0	1	0
0	1	1	0	1
0	1	1	1	d
1	0	0	0	d
1	0	0	1	1
1	0	1	0	1
1	0	1	1	0
1	1	0	0	d
1	1	0	1	0
1	1	1	0	1
1	1	1	1	0

the simplified expressions, using either NAND gates only or NOR gates only. Assume that complements of the inputs are available. The same type gates do not have to be used for both (*a*) and (*b*).

3.68 Write a boolean algebra expression in sum-of-products form for a gating network with three inputs A, B, and C (and their complements $\overline{A}$, $\overline{B}$, and $\overline{C}$) that is to have a 1 output only when two or three of the inputs have a 1 value. Implement, using a NAND-to-wired-AND gate network.

3.69 Draw a block diagram for a gate network having a NOR-to-OR gate network with three inputs, A, B, and C (and their complements) that have a 1 output only when two or three of the inputs have a 1 value, as in Question 3.68.

3.70 Will the minimal expression for the function in Table 3.35 require fewer NAND gates or NOR gates? (d means don't-care.) Assume that complements are available. How many gates for each? Give your minimal expressions.

TABLE 3.35				
X_1	X_2	X_3	X_4	OUTPUT
0	0	0	0	0
0	0	0	1	1
0	0	1	0	1
0	0	1	1	0
0	1	0	0	d
0	1	0	1	0
0	1	1	0	1
0	1	1	1	d
1	0	0	0	d
1	0	0	1	1
1	0	1	0	1
1	0	1	1	d
1	1	0	0	d
1	1	0	1	0
1	1	1	0	1
1	1	1	1	0

3.71 The following is a NAND-to-NAND gate network. Draw a block diagram for a NOR-to-NOR gate network that realizes the same function, using as few gates as possible.

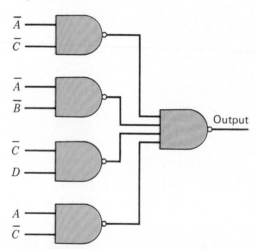

3.72 Convert the following NOR-to-OR gate network to a NAND-to-NAND gate network. Use as few gates as possible.

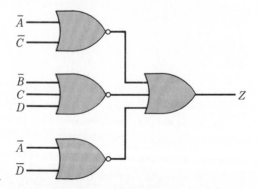

3.73 (*a*) Design an AND-to-OR gate combinational network for the boolean algebra function.

$$F = \overline{WX}\,\overline{YZ} + W\overline{XY}Z + W\overline{X}\,\overline{YZ} + W\overline{X}YZ + \overline{WX}\,\overline{YZ}$$

Use as few gates as you can.

     (*b*) Design a NOR gate combinational network for the boolean algebra function in part (*a*), again using as few gates as you can.

3.74 This chapter has explained a number of two-level networks that can be used to implement all possible functions of a given number of variables. There are also two-level networks that can implement only a few of the many functions possible. For instance, an AND-to-AND gate network is only the AND function as shown below:

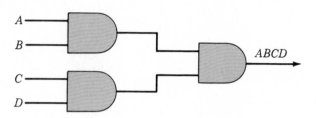

FIGURE Q3.74a

Similarly, a NAND-to-OR implements only an OR function with complemented inputs as shown below:

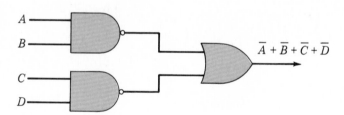

FIGURE Q3.74b

     In all, 8 of the possible 16 two-level network arrangements that can be made with NOR, NAND, OR, and AND gates will realize all functions, while 8 are degenerate and yield only a few of the functions. Identify the degenerate forms and the forms that will yield all functions.

3.75 This chapter did not treat the two-level AND-to-NOR form. Derive a rule for designing AND-to-NOR gate networks, and show how it works for a problem of your choice.

3.76 This chapter did not treat OR-to-NAND gate networks, although all boolean functions can be realized by using that configuration. Derive a sample network, using your rule.

3.77 Show how the NOR-to-NAND gate network shown at the top of page 132 can be replaced by a single gate.

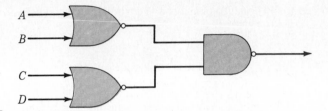

FIGURE Q3.77

3.78 Convert the following NAND-to-NAND gate network to a (two-level) NOR-to-OR gate network:

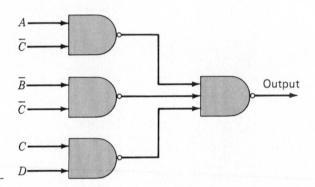

FIGURE Q3.78

3.79 Using as few gates as possible, design a NAND-to-AND gate network that realizes the following boolean algebra expression:

$$\overline{AB}\overline{C}D + AB\overline{C}\overline{D} + \overline{A}\overline{B}C\overline{D} + ABC\overline{D} + A\overline{B}\overline{C}D$$

3.80 Convert the following NAND-to-NAND gate network to a (two-level) NOR-to-OR gate network:

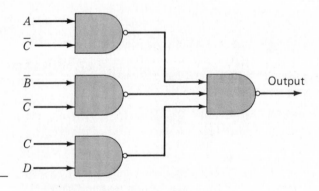

FIGURE Q3.80

3.81 Convert the following NAND-to-NAND gate network to a NOR-to-NOR gate network:

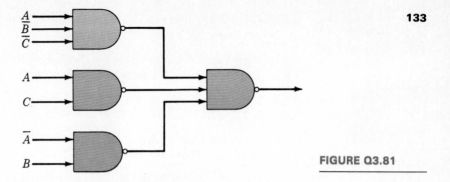

FIGURE Q3.81

3.82 Convert the following NOR-to-OR gate network to a NAND-to-AND gate network. Use as few gates as possible.

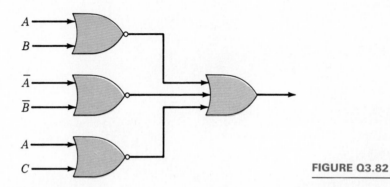

FIGURE Q3.82

3.83 Convert the following NAND-to-AND gate network to a NOR-to-OR gate network. Use as few gates as possible.

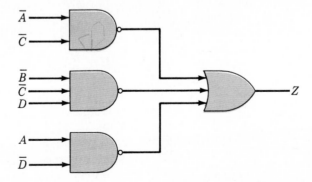

FIGURE Q3.83

3.84 Using a PLA table as in Fig. 3.46, design a three-input, six-output gate network that squares each input. (Inputs and outputs are unsigned binary integers.)

3.85 Using a PLA table as in Fig. 3.46, design a network that forms the 9s complement of a BCD number in 2, 4, 2, 1 form.

3.86 Using the PAL in Fig. 3.44, design a three-input gate network which finds the 2s complement of a positive input number.

3.87 Using the PLA symbology in Fig. 3.43, design a logic network that converts a BCD number in 2, 4, 2, 1 form to 8, 4, 2, 1 form.

3.88 Using a PLA table as in Fig. 3.46, design a four-input, five-output circuit that adds 3 to a BCD number in 8, 4, 2, 1 form.

3.89 Using the PLA in Fig. 3.41, show how to form the two outputs $X = \overline{A}\overline{B}C + A\overline{B}\overline{C}$ and $Y = \overline{A}\overline{B}C + AB$.

3.90 Using the symbology in Fig. 3.43, form a design for a PLA with two outputs $X = AB\overline{C} + A\overline{B}$ and $Y = AB\overline{C} + A\overline{B}C + \overline{A}B$.

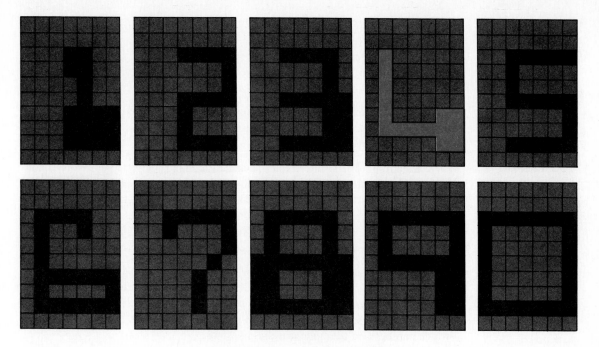

LOGIC DESIGN

Chapter 3 described gates and the analysis of gating networks by using boolean algebra. The basic devices used in the operational or calculating sections of digital computers consist of gates and devices called *flip-flops*. It is remarkable that even the largest of computers is primarily constructed of these devices. Accordingly, this chapter first describes flip-flops and their characteristics. From an intuitive viewpoint, flip-flops provide memory and gates provide operations on, or functions of, the values stored in these memory devices.

Following the introduction to flip-flops, the use of flip-flops and gates to perform several of the most useful functions in computers is presented. The particular functions described include counting in binary and binary-coded decimal, transferring values, and shifting or scaling values stored in flip-flops.

Several other names have been used instead of *flip-flop*. These include *binary* and *toggle*, but flip-flop has been the most frequently used. Also, there are several other types of memory devices in computers, and these are studied in Chap. 6. For actual operations, flip-flops remain dominant, however, because of their high speed, the ease with which they can be set or read, and the natural way gates and flip-flops can be interconnected.

This chapter also contains a section on clocks in digital computers. Computers do not run by taking steps at random times, but proceed from step to step at intervals precisely controlled by a clock which provides a carefully regulated time base for all operations. Some knowledge of the uses of clocks in computers is indispensable, and the subject is introduced here.

OBJECTIVES

LOGIC DESIGN

1   The basic memory cells in the operational part of a digital computer are electronic circuits called flip-flops. The operation of these devices is described, as are the details of clocks and how clocks are used to initiate flip-flop operation.

2   Binary counters consist of flip-flops and gates and count up (or down) at the direction of a clock and (sometimes) control inputs. The basic types of binary and BCD counters are described.

3   Electronic digital circuits are packaged in small integrated-circuit (IC) containers. The number of gates and flip-flops in a single package determines the level of integration for the package, and the various levels of integration are discussed. (The number of gates and flip-flops on a chip is sometimes called the *packing density*.) Several actual IC packages from the most used IC lines are presented. Then a shift register with feedback is designed using these packages.

4   Two representation techniques for digital design and analysis are called *state tables* and *state diagrams*. These are described, as is a procedure for designing a particular arrangement of flip-flops and gates called a *state machine*. Several design examples are presented, followed by an introduction to a class of integrated circuits which can be used to implement these designs.

FLIP-FLOPS

4.1   The basic circuit for storing information in a digital machine is called a *flip-flop*. There are several fundamental types of flip-flops and many circuit designs. However, two characteristics are shared by all flip-flops.

1   The flip-flop is a bistable device, that is, a circuit with only two stable states, which we designate the 0 state and the 1 state.

The flip-flop circuit can remember, or store, a binary bit of information because of its bistable characteristic. The flip-flop responds to inputs. If an input causes it to go to its 1 state, it will remain there and "remember" a 1 until some signal causes it to go to the 0 state. Similarly, once placed in the 0 state, the flip-flop will remain there until it is told to go to the 1 state. This simple characteristic, the ability of the flip-flop to retain its state, is the basis for information storage in the operating or calculating sections of a digital computer.

2   The flip-flop has two output signals, one of which is the complement of the other.

Figure 4.1 shows the block diagram for a particular type of flip-flop, the *RS flip-flop*. There are two inputs, designated S and R, and two outputs, marked with X and $\overline{X}$. To describe and analyze flip-flop operation, there are several conventions that are standard in the computer industry.

1   Each flip-flop is given a "name." Convenient names are letters, such as X or Y or A or B; or letter-number combinations, such as A_1 or B_2; or sometimes,

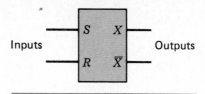

Inputs | Outputs

FIGURE 4.1

RS flip-flop.

because of difficulty in subscripting on typewriters or printers, simply $A1$ or $B2$. The flip-flop in Fig. 4.1 is called X. It has two outputs, the X output and the $\overline{X}$ output.

The X and $\overline{X}$ output lines are always complements; that is, if the X output line has a 1 signal, the $\overline{X}$ output line has a 0 signal; and if the X output line has a 0 signal, output line $\overline{X}$ has a 1 signal.

2 The state of the flip-flop is taken to be the state of the X output. Thus if the output line X has a 1 signal on it, we say that "flip-flop X is in the 1 state." Similarly, if the X line contains a 0 signal, we say that "flip-flop X is in the 0 state."

These conventions are very important and convenient. Note that when flip-flop X is in the 1 state, the output line $\overline{X}$ has a 0 on it; and when flip-flop X is in the 0 state, the output line $\overline{X}$ has a 1 on it.

There are two input lines to the RS flip-flop. These are used to control the state of the flip-flop. The rules are as follows:

1 As long as both input lines S and R carry 0 signals, the flip-flop remains in the same state, that is, it does not change state.

2 A 1 signal on the S line (the SET line) and a 0 signal on the R line cause the flip-flop to "set" to the 1 state.

3 A 1 signal on the R line (the RESET line) and a 0 signal on the S line cause the flip-flop to "reset" to the 0 state.

4 Placing a 1 on the S and a 1 on the R lines at the same time is forbidden. If this occurs, the flip-flop can go to either state. (This is, in effect, an ambiguous input in that it is telling the flip-flop to both SET and RESET at the same time.)

An example of a possible sequence of input signals and the resulting state of the flip-flop is as follows:

S	R	X	
			X is the state of the flip-flop after inputs S and R are applied.
1	0	1	
0	0	1	Flip-flop remains in same state.
0	0	1	
0	1	0	Flip-flop is reset.
0	0	0	
0	0	0	
0	1	0	Flip-flop is told to reset but is already reset.
0	0	0	
1	0	1	Flip-flop is set.
0	0	1	

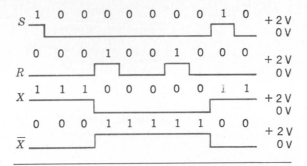

FIGURE 4.2

RS flip-flop wave-forms.

Although the above conventions may seem formidable at first, they can be simply summarized by seeing that a 1 on the S line causes the flip-flop to SET (that is, assume the 1 state) and a 1 on the R line causes the flip-flop to RESET (that is, assume the 0 state). The flip-flop does nothing in the absence of 1 inputs and would be hopelessly confused by 1s on both S and R inputs.

It is very convenient to be able to draw graphs of the inputs and outputs from computer circuits to show how they act as inputs vary. We assume the convention that a 1 signal is a positive signal and a 0 signal a ground, or 0-V, signal. This is conventional in most present-day circuits and is called *positive logic*. Figure 4.2 shows several signals as they progress in time, with the current binary values of each signal written above it. The signals in Fig. 4.2 are the sequence of signals given in the list above along with both the X and $\overline{X}$ output line signals from the flip-flop. We have arbitrarily chosen $+2$ V for the 1 state of the signals and 0 V for the 0 state because these are very frequently used levels. Notice that the flip-flop changes only when the input levels command it to, and that it changes at once. (Actually, there would be a slight delay from when the flip-flop is told to change states and when it changes, since no physical device can respond instantly; so we assume that the flip-flop's delay in responding is quite small, perhaps a small fraction of a microsecond.)

TRANSFER CIRCUIT

4.2 The RS flip-flop, although simple in operation, is adequate for all purposes and is a basic flip-flop circuit. Let us examine the operation of this flip-flop in a configuration called a *transfer circuit*. Figure 4.3 shows two sets of flip-flops named X_1, X_2, and X_3 and Y_1, Y_2, and Y_3. The function of this configuration is to transfer the states, or *contents*, of Y_1 into X_1, Y_2 into X_2, and Y_3 into X_3 upon the TRANSFER command which consists of a 1 on the TRANSFER line.

Assume that Y_1, Y_2, and Y_3 have been set to some states that we want to remember, or store, in X_1, X_2, and X_3, while the Y flip-flops are used for further calculations. Placing a 1 on the TRANSFER line will cause this desired transfer of information. Understanding the transfer of the state of Y_1 into X_1 depends on seeing that if Y_1 is in the 0 state, the Y_1 output line has a 0 on it, and so the input line connected to the AND gate will be a 0 and the AND gate will place a 0 on the S input line of X_1, while the $\overline{Y}_1$ output from Y_1 will be a 1, causing, in the presence of a 1 on the TRANSFER line, a 1 on the R input of X_1. Similar reasoning

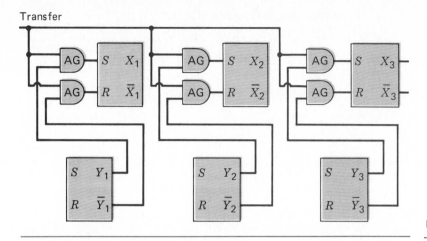

FIGURE 4.3

Transfer circuit.

will show that a 1 in Y_1 will cause a 1 to be placed in X_1 in the presence of a 1 on the TRANSFER line. As long as the TRANSFER line is a 0, both inputs to the X flip-flops will be 0s, and the flip-flop will remain in the last state it assumed.

The above simple operation, the *transfer operation,* is quite important. Related sets of flip-flops in a computer are called *registers,* and the three flip-flops Y_1, Y_2, and Y_3 would be called simply *register Y,* and the three flip-flops, X_1, X_2, and X_3 would be called *register X.* Then a 1 on the TRANSFER line would transfer the contents of register Y into register X. This is an important concept.

CLOCKS

4.3 A very important fact about digital computers is that they are clocked. This means that there is some "master clock" somewhere sending out signals which are carefully regulated in time. These signals initiate the operations performed.

There are excellent reasons why computers are designed this way. The alternative way, with operations triggering other operations as they occur, is called *asynchronous operation* (the clocked way is called *synchronous operation*) and leads to considerable difficulty in design and maintenance. As a result, genuinely asynchronous operation is rarely used.

The clock is, therefore, the mover of the computer in that it carefully measures time and sends out regularly spaced signals which cause things to happen. We can examine the operation of the flip-flops and gates before and after the clock "initiates an action." Initiating signals are often called, for historical reasons, *clock pulses.*[1]

Figure 4.4 shows a typical clock waveform. The clock waveform in Fig. 4.4(*a*) and (*b*) is called a *square wave.* The figure shows two important portions of a square wave: the *leading edge,* or *rising edge,* or sometimes *positive-going edge;* and the *falling edge,* or *negative-going edge.* These are particularly important

---

[1]The term *clock pulse* has a historical origin. The early computers used short electric pulses to initiate operations, and these were naturally called *clock pulses.* Few circuits still use these narrow pulses, and the majority of circuits now respond to edges of square waves as in Fig. 4.4.

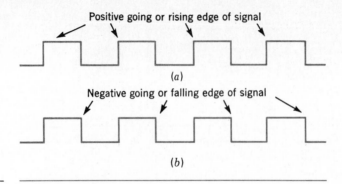

Positive going or rising edge of signal

(a)

Negative going or falling edge of signal

(b)

FIGURE 4.4

Clock waveforms.

since most flip-flops now in use respond to either (but not both) a falling edge or a rising edge. In effect, a system which responds to rising edges of the clock "rests" between such edges and changes state only when such positive-going edges occur. (The reason for the rest periods is to give the circuits time to assume their new states and to give all transients time to die down. The frequency at which such edges occur is generally determined by the speed with which the circuits can go to their new states, the delay times for the gates which must process the new signals, etc.)

Since clock signals are used to initiate flip-flop actions, a clock input is included on most flip-flops. This input is marked with a small triangle, as shown in Fig. 4.5(a). A clocked flip-flop can respond to either the positive-going edge of the clock signal or the negative-going edge.[2] If a given flip-flop responds to the positive-going edge of the signal, there is no "bubble" at the triangle or clock input on the block diagram, as in Fig. 4.5(a). If the flip-flop responds to a negative-going edge, or signal, a bubble is placed at the clock input, as in Fig. 4.5(b).

Sometimes the clock input is simply marked with a CL instead of the triangle. Manufacturers who adopt this practice will explain whether the flip-flop is or is not edge-triggered in the specifications sheet for the flip-flop.

It is important to understand the above convention because most clocked flip-flops actually respond to a *change* in clock input level, not to the level itself. This is shown in Fig. 4.5(c) and (d). The flip-flop in Fig. 4.5(a) responds to positive-going clock edges (positive shifts), and a typical set of signals for the *clocked RS flip-flop* in Fig. 4.5(a) is shown in Fig. 4.5(c).

The flip-flop is operated according to these rules:

1 If the S and R inputs are 0s when the clock edge (pulse) occurs, the flip-flop does not change states but remains in its present state.

2 If the S input is a 1 and the R input is a 0 when the clock pulse (positive-going edge) occurs, the flip-flop goes to the 1 state.

[2]A flip-flop which responds to a rising or falling clock signal (as opposed to responding to a dc level) is called an *edge-triggering*, or *master-slave*, flip-flop for reasons that will be explained.

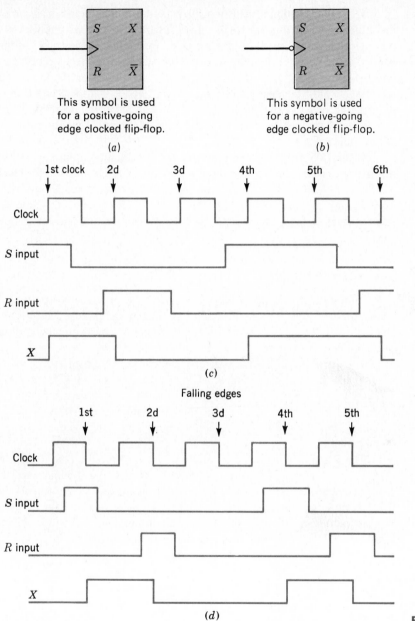

This symbol is used
for a positive-going
edge clocked flip-flop.

(a)

This symbol is used
for a negative-going
edge clocked flip-flop.

(b)

CLOCKS

(c)

(d)

FIGURE 4.5

Clocked flip-flops and
waveforms. (*a*) Posi-
tive-edge-triggering
flip-flop. (*b*) Negative-
edge-triggering flip-
flop. (*c*) Waveforms
for positive-edge-trig-
gering flip-flop in (*a*).
(*d*) Waveforms for
flip-flop in (*b*).

3 If the *S* input is a 0 and the *R* input a 1 when the clock pulse occurs, the flip-flop is cleared to the 0 state.

4 Both the *S* and *R* inputs should not be 1s when the clock signal's positive-going edge occurs.

LOGIC DESIGN

Of course, nothing happens to the flip-flop's state between occurrences of the initiating positive-going clock signal. Figure 4.5(*c*) shows this with a square-wave clock signal. The flip-flop is set to a 1 by the first clock positive-going edge and a 0 at the occurrence of the second clock signal. No change occurs at the third positive-going clock edge. The flip-flop is set to 1 again on the fourth edge and remains a 1 until the sixth clock edge occurs. Notice that the *S* and *R* inputs can be anything between the clock edges without affecting the operation of the flip-flop. (They can even both be 1s without effect, except when the positive-going edge occurs.)

Figure 4.5(*d*) shows typical waveforms for the flip-flop in Fig. 4.5(*b*). This flip-flop is *negative-edge triggering* because it responds to shifts in the clock level which are negative-going. The rules of operation are as before: 0s on *S* and *R* lead to no change; a 1 on *S* sets the flip-flop; and a 1 on *R* clears the flip-flop. The flip-flop responds to the *S* and *R* inputs only at the precise time the clock input goes negative.

FLIP-FLOP DESIGNS

4.4 Flip-flops can be made from gates; in fact, this is a common practice. Figure 4.6 shows two NOR gates cross-coupled to form an *RS* flip-flop. The cross-coupled NOR gates in Fig. 4.6(*a*) have two inputs, *S* and *R,* and two outputs, *Q*, and $\overline{Q}$. This configuration realizes the *RS* flip-flop in Fig. 4.6(*b*).

The operation of the NOR gates is as follows: Consider both *S* and *R* to be 0s. If *Q* is a 1, then the rightmost NOR gate has a 1 and a 0 input and its output will be a 0. This places a 0 on the $\overline{Q}$ output and two 0s at the input to the leftmost NOR gate which will have a 1 output, and the configuration will be stable. Similar reasoning will show that the configuration will be stable with a 1 on $\overline{Q}$ and a 0 on *Q*.

The *S* and *R* inputs work as follows: If a 1 is placed on the *R* input and a 0 on the *S* input, this will force the leftmost NOR gate to a 0 output, and this will cause the rightmost NOR gate to have two 0s as inputs and a 1 output. The flip-flop has now been cleared with a 0 on the *Q* output and a 1 on the $\overline{Q}$ output. Similar reasoning will show that a 1 on the *S* input and a 0 on the *R* input will force the NOR gate flip-flop to the 1 state with *Q* a 1 and $\overline{Q}$ a 0.

GATED FLIP-FLOP

4.5 Just as Fig. 4.6 showed that two NOR gates can be used to form an *RS* flip-flop, Fig. 4.7 shows that two NAND gates can be used to form an *RS* flip-flop

FIGURE 4.6

RS flip-flop formed by cross-coupling NOR gates. (*a*) Cross-coupled NOR gates. (*b*) *RS* flip-flop corresponding to (*a*).

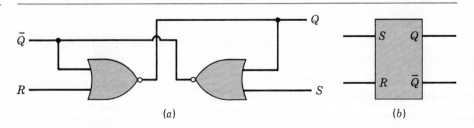

(*a*)

(*b*)

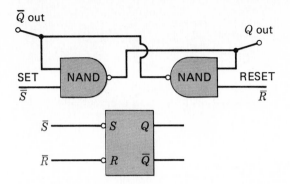

$\overline{S}$	$\overline{R}$	NEXT STATE
0	0	NOT USED
0	1	1
1	0	0
1	1	NO CHANGE

FIGURE 4.7

Two NAND gates used to form an *RS* flip-flop.

(however, the inputs are complemented). In this case the inputs operate as follows: When both $\overline{S}$ and $\overline{R}$ are 1s, the flip-flop will remain in its present state, that is, it will not change states. If, however, the $\overline{R}$ input goes to a 0, the NAND gate connected to $\overline{R}$ will have a 1 output regardless of the other feedback input to the NAND gate. This will force the flip-flop to the 0 state (provided the $\overline{S}$ input is kept high or a 1).

Similar reasoning shows that making the $\overline{S}$ input a 0 will cause the NAND gate at the $\overline{S}$ input to have a 1 output, forcing the flip-flop to the 1 state (again provided the $\overline{R}$ input is kept high or 1).

If both inputs $\overline{R}$ and $\overline{S}$ are made 0s, the next state will depend on which input is returned to 1 first. If both are returned to 1 simultaneously, the resulting state of the flip-flop will be indeterminate. As a result, this is a "forbidden," or "restricted," input combination.

The block diagram in Fig. 4.7 shows the flip-flop to be a conventional *RS* flip-flop, except that the two inputs are inverted. This is shown by the two bubbles at the $\overline{R}$ and $\overline{S}$ inputs. The circuit is activated by 0s and inputs are normally at 1.

A limited form of clocked flip-flop called a *latch* can be formed by using four NAND gates, as shown in Fig. 4.8(*a*). The circuit has an *R* and an *S* input and also a clock input CL. This latch flip-flop is activated by a positive level on the clock input, and not by a positive transition. Thus the flip-flop "takes" its input levels during the positive portion of clock signals, not changes in clock levels. Let us see how the circuit works. If the clock signal is at the 0 level, both NAND gates *A* and *B* will have 1 outputs, and so the NAND gate inputs to *C* and *D* will be a 1 and, as before, the flip-flop will remain in its present state with either *C* or *D* on. (Both cannot be on because of the cross-coupling.)

If the clock signal goes to the 1 level and both inputs *R* and *S* are at the 0 level, the NAND gate outputs of *A* and *B* will still be 1s, and the flip-flop will remain in the same state.

If the *R* input is a 1 and the *S* input a 0, when the clock input goes positive (a 1), the NAND gate connected to *R* will have a 0 output and the NAND gate connected to *S* a 1 output, forcing the flip-flop consisting of *C* and *D* to the 0 state.

Similarly, a 1 at the *S* input and a 0 at the *R* input will cause the *S* input gate *A* to have a 0 output and the *R* input gate *B* a 1 output, forcing the flip-flop to the 1 state.

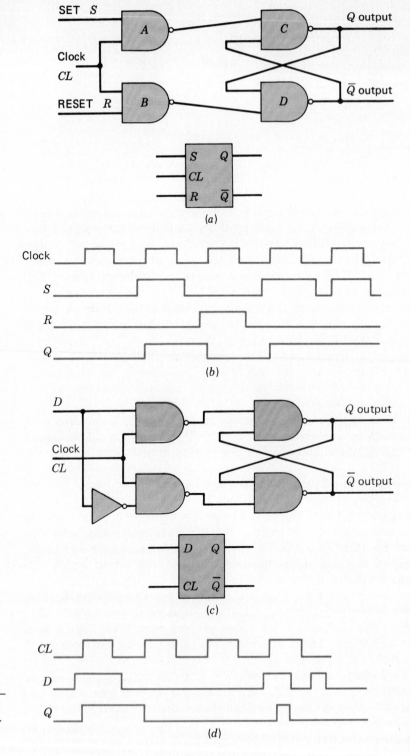

FIGURE 4.8

Latches. (a) *RS* latch.
(b) *RS* flip-flop wave-
forms. (c) *D* latch.
(d) Waveforms for *D*
latch.

If both S and R are 1s and a clock pulse (0 level to 1 level and back to 0) occurs, the next state of the circuit is indeterminate.

A major problem with this circuit is that the R and S inputs should remain unchanged during the time the clock is a 1. This considerably limits the use of the circuit, leading to more complicated circuits that can offer the designer more flexibility. The primary value of the circuit is its simplicity.

The block diagram for a latch is the same as for an edge-triggered flip-flop except for the small triangle at the clock input for edge-triggered flip-flops and a CL for the latch.

Often designers specifically identify latches on block diagrams so that users will realize that the state taken by the flip-flop is determined by the R and S inputs during the positive clock level, and not at the edge of the clock signal.

Manufacturers often put a number of latches in a single IC package. In this case, a special kind of flip-flop called the D flip-flop is often used. A D-type latch flip-flop is shown in Fig. 4.8(c). The advantage of this is the single D input. The D flip-flop takes the value at its D input whenever the clock pulse input is high. It will effectively "track" input levels as long as the clock input is high, as shown in Fig. 4.8(d). If the clock input is lowered, the state will be the last state the flip-flop had when the clock input was high. If the clock input returns to 0 just before or during a transition in the input to the D latch, the final state the flip-flop takes will depend on the delay time for the flip-flop. Allowing input transitions during the time period when the clock is high is dangerous, unless there is assurance that the D input will not change for a safe period before the clock input is lowered.

MASTER-SLAVE FLIP-FLOP

4.6 To eliminate problems which arise with the latch type of flip-flop, more complicated flip-flop designs are used. The most popular uses edge triggering from the clock to initiate changes in the flip-flop's output and is based on the use of two single or latch flip-flops to form a single edge-triggered flip-flop.

The basic flip-flop design is shown in Fig. 4.9. Figure 4.9(a) shows that an edge-triggering RS flip-flop consists of two flip-flops plus some gating. The two flip-flops are called the master and slave. An expanded logic diagram for Fig. 4.9(a) is shown in Fig. 4.9(b) in which the master flip-flop is composed of the leftmost NAND gates and the slave flip-flop of the rightmost NAND gates.

The expanded diagram in Fig. 4.9(b) can be used to explain the flip-flop's operation. The flip-flop's output changes on the negative-going edge of the clock pulse. The basic timing is shown in Fig. 4.9(b). First, on the positive-going edge and during the positive section of the clock pulse, the master flip-flop is loaded by the two leftmost NAND gates. Then, during the negative-going edge of the clock signal, the two rightmost NAND gates load the contents of the master flip-flop into the slave flip-flop just after the two-input NAND gates are disabled. This means that the master flip-flop will not change in value while the clock is low (0); so the slave remains attached to a stable flip-flop, with a value taken during the positive section of the clock pulse.

A more detailed account of the action of the flip-flop is as follows: If the clock signal is low, the two-input NAND gates both have 1 outputs; so the master

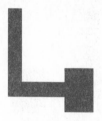

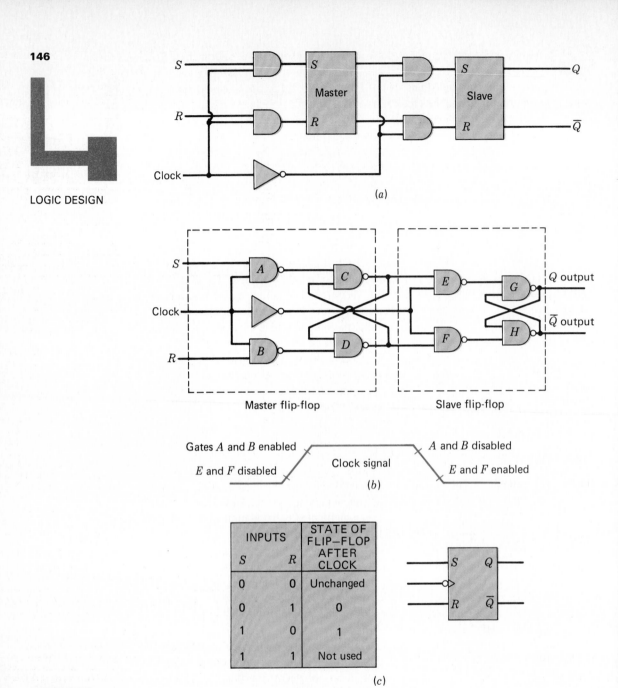

(a)

Master flip-flop   Slave flip-flop

Gates A and B enabled A and B disabled

E and F disabled   Clock signal E and F enabled

(b)

INPUTS		STATE OF FLIP–FLOP AFTER CLOCK
S	R	
0	0	Unchanged
0	1	0
1	0	1
1	1	Not used

(c)

FIGURE 4.9

(a) *RS* clocked edge-triggering flip-flop.
(b) Gate arrangement for master-slave flip-flop. (c) Master-slave flip-flop state table and symbol.

flip-flop does not change states since it is a NAND gate flip-flop and can be set or cleared only by 0 inputs.

At the same time, as long as the clock signal is low (a 0), the inverter causes the inputs to the E and F NAND gates to force the value of the master flip-flop into the slave flip-flop. The situation is stable. The master cannot change, and the output flip-flop is "slaved" to the master.

When the clock starts positive, however, the E and F NAND gates are disabled, and the NAND gates A and B to the master flip-flop are then enabled.

When the input clock signal is a 1, then the master flip-flop will accept information from the S and R inputs, and the slave flip-flop is now isolated from the master and will not change states regardless of changes in the master.

The operation of the master flip-flop is according to the following rules when the clock level is a 1:

1   If both S and R are at 0 levels, the two input NAND gates will have 1 outputs and the master flip-flop will not change values.

2   If the S input is a 1 and the R input a 0, the master flip-flop will go to its 1 state, with the upper master NAND gate having a 1 output.

3   If the S input is a 0 and the R input a 1, the master flip-flop will go to its 0 state, with the upper NAND gate having a 0 output.

4   If both R and S are 1s, the final state is indeterminate.

When the clock signal goes negative to its 0 level, first the input NAND gates to the master flip-flop are disabled, that is, each output goes to a 1; then the E and F NAND gates are enabled (by the inverted clock signal). This causes the state of the master flip-flop to be transferred into the slave flip-flop.

The effects of all this are shown in the next-state table in Fig. 4.9(c), which indicates that the flip-flop is an RS flip-flop activated by a negative-going clock signal.

An edge-triggering flip-flop which triggers on positive edges can be made by adding an inverter at the CL input.

SHIFT REGISTER

4.7   Figure 4.10 shows a *shift register*. This circuit accepts information from some input source and then shifts this information along the chain of flip-flops, moving it one flip-flop each time a positive-going clock signal occurs.

Figure 4.10 also shows a typical sequence of input signals and flip-flop signals in the shift register. The input value is taken by X_1 when the first positive-going clock signal arrives.[3] Anything in this and the remaining flip-flops is shifted right at this time. We have assumed that all the flip-flops are initially in their 0 states. In the figure, the input waveform is at 1 when the first clock occurs; so X_1 goes to the 1 state.

---

[3]There is some delay from the time the positive-going edge of the clock signal tells a flip-flop to "go" until the flip-flop's outputs are able to change values. The clock signal itself will also require some small amount of time to rise, for physical reasons. For present systems the rise time on the clock signals, that is, the time to rise 90 percent of total rise, ranges from about 1×10^{-9} to about 50×10^{-9} s. The delay from the clock-signal change until a flip-flop's output changes 90 percent, which is called the *delay time*, ranges from 10.5×10^{-9} to 50×10^{-9} s for most circuits.

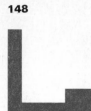

LOGIC DESIGN

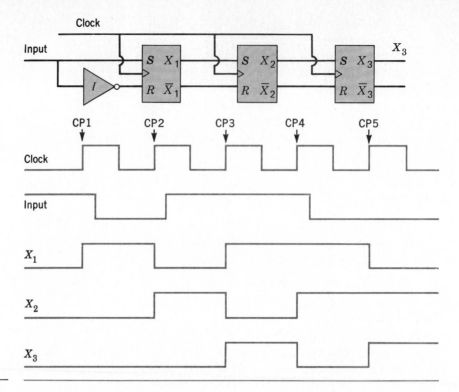

FIGURE 4.10

Shift register with waveforms.

When the second positive-going clock signal arrives, the input is at 0; so X_1 goes to the 0 state, but the 1 in X_1 is shifted into X_2. When the third clock edge appears, the input is a 1; so X_1 takes a 1, the 0 previously in X_1 is shifted into X_2, and the 1 in X_2 goes into X_3. This process continues. The values in X_3 are simply dropped off the end of the register.

Notice that each flip-flop takes the value in the flip-flop on its left when the shift register is stepped. The reasoning is as follows: If, for instance, X_1 is in the 1 state, then its X output line is a 1 and thus the S input to X_2 will be a 1; and the $\overline{X}$ output of X_1 will be a 0, and so the R input of X_2 will be a 0. This causes X_2 to take its 1 state when the clock pulse occurs. A 0 in X_1 will cause X_2 to go to 0 when the clock pulse occurs, and the reason for this should be analyzed.

There is one problem that could occur if certain design precautions were not taken with the flip-flops. If the flip-flop outputs changed too fast or if latches were used, a state could ripple, or race, down the chain. This is called the *race problem*. It is handled by designing the flip-flops so that they take the value at their inputs just as the clock positive-going edge occurs and not slightly after the clock's rise time. This leads to the complexity in flip-flop design, which has been discussed. Edge-triggered (master-slave) flip-flops are necessary for proper operation.

BINARY COUNTER

4.8 Inasmuch as the binary counter is one of the most useful of logical circuits, there are many kinds. The fundamental purpose of the binary counter is to record

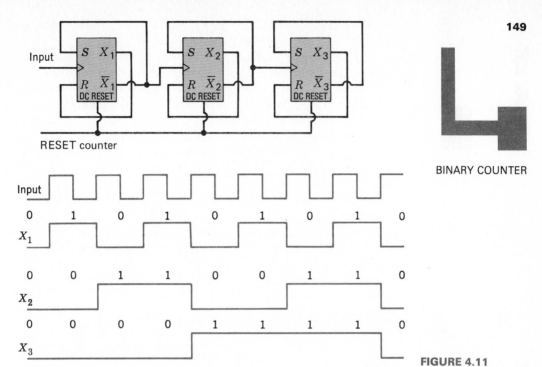

RESET counter

BINARY COUNTER

FIGURE 4.11

Binary counter.

the number of occurrences of some input. This is a basic function, that of counting, and it is used over and over.

The first type of binary counter to be explained is shown in Fig. 4.11. This counter records the number of occurrences of a positive-going edge (or pulse) at the input.

It is desirable to start this counter with 0s in all three flip-flops; so one further line is added to each flip-flop, a DC RESET line. This line is normally at the 0 level; when it goes positive, or 1, it places a 0 in the flip-flop. This action does not depend on the clock. When a DC RESET line is at the 1 level, the flip-flop goes to 0 regardless of any other input and in the absence or presence of a clock pulse.

It is quite common for flip-flops to have a DC RESET line. Notice that this input ''overrides'' all other inputs when it is a 1, forcing the flip-flop to the 0 state. A 0 on this line, however, does not affect flip-flop operation in any way.

Before counting begins, then, a 1 is placed temporarily on the RESET COUNTER line, and the three flip-flops are cleared to 0. The RESET COUNTER line is then returned to 0.

When the first clock positive edge occurs, the flip-flop X_1 goes to its 1 state. This is because when the flip-flop X_1 is in the 0 state, the $\overline{X}_1$ output is high, or 1, placing a 1 on the S input (refer to Fig. 4.11), and the X_1 output is low, or 0, placing a 0 on the R input; so a 1 goes into flip-flop X_1.

Flip-flops X_2 and X_3 are not affected by this change, for although the $\overline{X}_1$ output is connected to the clock input of X_2, the signal has gone from 1 to 0. This is a negative shift, which does nothing to X_2.

The counter now has $X_3 = 0$, $X_2 = 0$, $X_1 = 1$, or binary 001; so the first input clock edge has stepped the counter from 000 to 001.†

The occurrence of the second positive-going clock edge causes flip-flop X_1 to go from the 1 state to the 0 state. The reasoning is as follows: When X_1 is a 1, the X_1 output is a 1 and is connected to the R input, and the $\overline{X}_1$ output is a 0 and is connected to the S input. This tells the flip-flop to "go to 0," and when the second clock pulse occurs, it goes.

This is important: When a flip-flop is cross-coupled, that is, when its uncomplemented output is connected to its R input and its complemented output to its S input, the occurrence of a clock edge will always cause it to *complement*, or change values.

The change of value from 1 to 0 of flip-flop X_1 causes X_2 to change from a 0 to a 1. This is because $\overline{X}_1$'s output is connected to the CL input of X_2 and has gone from 0 to 1, a positive shift; and since X_2 is cross-coupled, it will complement (change values) and go from 0 to 1. This does not affect X_3, because the CL input of X_3 has gone from 1 to 0, a negative shift.

The counter has now progressed to $X_1 = 0$, $X_2 = 1$, and $X_3 = 0$; so the sequence of states has been 000, 001, 010.

Reasoning of this type will show that the progression of states by the counter will be as follows:

X_3	X_2	X_1
0	0	0
0	0	1
0	1	0
0	1	1
1	0	0
1	0	1
1	1	0
1	1	1
0	0	0
0	0	1
0	1	0

This is a list of binary numbers from 0 to 7, which repeats over and over. After five input pulses the counter contains 101, or binary 5; after seven pulses the counter contains 111, or binary 7. The maximum number of pulses this counter can handle, without ambiguity, is 7. After eight pulses the counter contains 0; after nine pulses, 1; etc. In the trade this is called a *modulo 8,* or *three-stage,* counter.

The counter can be extended by another flip-flop, X_4, which is cross-coupled and which has its CL input connected to the output of flip-flop $\overline{X}_3$. This forms a *four-stage,* or *modulo 16,* counter, which can handle up to 15 counts. A fifth flip-flop would form a counter which would count to 31, a sixth to 63, etc.

We now consider a *gated-clocked binary counter.* This is an exceedingly popular counter in modern computers, and it demonstrates the fact that most oper-

---

†Note that the binary numbers are written in the opposite direction from the block diagram layout, which has the least significant bit on the left. This makes for a neater block diagram and is frequently used. The standards, in fact, ask for left-to-right signal flow.

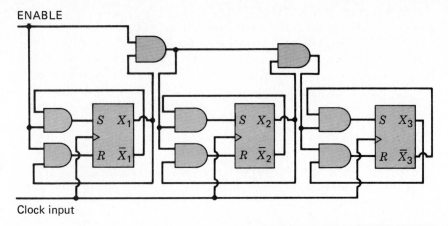

Clock input

FIGURE 4.12

Gated-clocked binary counter.

ations are *enabled* by logic levels and activated by clock signals. The preceding counter is called a *ripple counter* because changes ripple down the flip-flop chain.

In Fig. 4.12 the ENABLE input to the first flip-flop in the chain X_1 goes to two AND gates, which also have the outputs of the flip-flop as inputs. Note: if the ENABLE signal is a 0, the two AND gates will have 0 outputs and X_1 will remain in the same state regardless of how many clock pulses occur.

When the ENABLE signal is a 1, however, the outputs from flip-flop X_1 cause that flip-flop to always change values when a clock pulse occurs. Thus the counter records the number of clock pulses that occur while the ENABLE is on. Then the flip-flop X_2 will change only when X_1 is a 1, the ENABLE signal is a 1, and a positive-going clock signal occurs. Similarly, X_3 will change states only when X_1 and X_2 are 1s, the ENABLE is a 1, and a clock positive edge occurs.

The two AND gates combined with an *RS* flip-flop in Fig. 4.12 are so useful that most popular lines of flip-flops contain in a single integrated-circuit container the flip-flop and its two AND gates, as shown in Fig. 4.13(*a*).

Figure 4.13(*b*) shows another very popular and useful flip-flop, which consists of the *RS* flip-flop and its two AND gates, but with the AND gates having the cross-coupling already permanently made. In this form the two lines taken outside are called *J* and *K*, and the flip-flop is called a *JK flip-flop*. Analysis of this flip-flop indicates that the *J* and *K* inputs act just as *RS* inputs for two 0 inputs— in this case the flip-flop never changes states. Also, with a 0 on *J* and a 1 on *K*, the flip-flop goes to the 0 state when a clock positive edge appears; and with a 1 on *J* and a 0 on *K*, the flip-flop goes to 1 when a clock positive edge appears. The significant fact is that when both *J* and *K* are 1s, the flip-flop always changes states when a clock positive edge appears.

The flip-flops in Fig. 4.13(*a*) and (*b*) both have DC RESET and DC SET inputs. The bubbles at the input on the block diagram indicate that these are activated by 0 inputs and are normally held at a 1 level. When, for instance, a 0 is placed on the DC SET input, the flip-flop goes to a 1 level regardless of the clock or other inputs. DC SET and DC RESET should not be 0s at the same time, because this is forbidden and leads to an undetermined next state.

It is a general rule that bubbles, or small circles, at the DC SET and DC RESET inputs mean that these inputs are activated by 0 levels. The absence of

LOGIC DESIGN

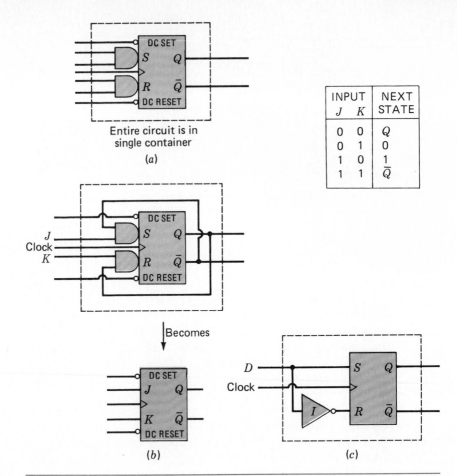

Entire circuit is in
single container

(a)

| INPUT | | NEXT |
J	K	STATE
0	0	Q
0	1	0
1	0	1
1	1	$\bar{Q}$

Becomes

(b)   (c)

FIGURE 4.13

JK and *D* flip-flops.
(*a*) *RS* flip-flop with
AND gates. (*b*) How a
JK flip-flop is made
from an *RS* flip-flop.
(*c*) *D* flip-flop.

these bubbles would mean that the inputs were activated by 1 levels and were normally at 0.

There is one other type of edge-triggered flip-flop now in general use, the *D flip-flop*. This flip-flop simply takes the value at its input when a clock pulse appears and remains in its same state until the next clock pulse appears. As shown in Fig. 4.13(*c*), the *D* flip-flop can be made from an *RS* flip-flop and an inverter. The operation is essentially the same as that of the *D* latch previously explained, except the *D* flip-flop operates on a clock edge and the latch is activated by a clock level.

The *D* flip-flop is very useful because when clocked, it takes the state on its input and holds it until clocked again. Only a single input line is needed for a transfer, whereas the *RS* or *JK* flip-flops require two input lines.

An example of the use of *JK* flip-flops is shown in Fig. 4.14(*a*) and (*b*). Figure 4.14(*a*) shows the simplicity of a gated binary counter with *JK* flip-flops. Figure 4.14(*b*) shows a block diagram for a *binary up-down counter*. When the UP ENABLE line is high or a 1, the counter will count up, that is, 0, 1, 2, 3,

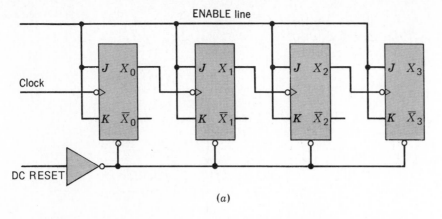

ENABLE line

Clock

DC RESET

(a)

BCD COUNTERS

UP ENABLE

HI

DOWN
ENABLE

Clock
DC RESET

(b)

FIGURE 4.14

Binary counters with
JK flip-flops. (*a*)
Gated ripple counter.
(*b*) Up-down counter.

4, ... When the DOWN ENABLE line is a 1, the counter will count down, that is, 6, 5, 4, ... In general, the counter will increase its value by 1 if the UP ENABLE line is a 1 and a clock pulse arrives, or will decrease its value by a 1 if the DOWN ENABLE input is a 1 and a clock pulse occurs.

A RESET line is provided which is used to DC RESET the counter to 0. This is activated by a 1 on the RESET line.

BCD COUNTERS

4.9 The binary counters considered so far all count to their limit before resetting to all 0s. Often it is desired to have counters count in binary-coded decimal (BCD). Figure 4.15(*a*) shows a typical BCD counter. Examination of this counter shows that it counts normally until it reaches 1001; that is, the sequence until that time is as follows:

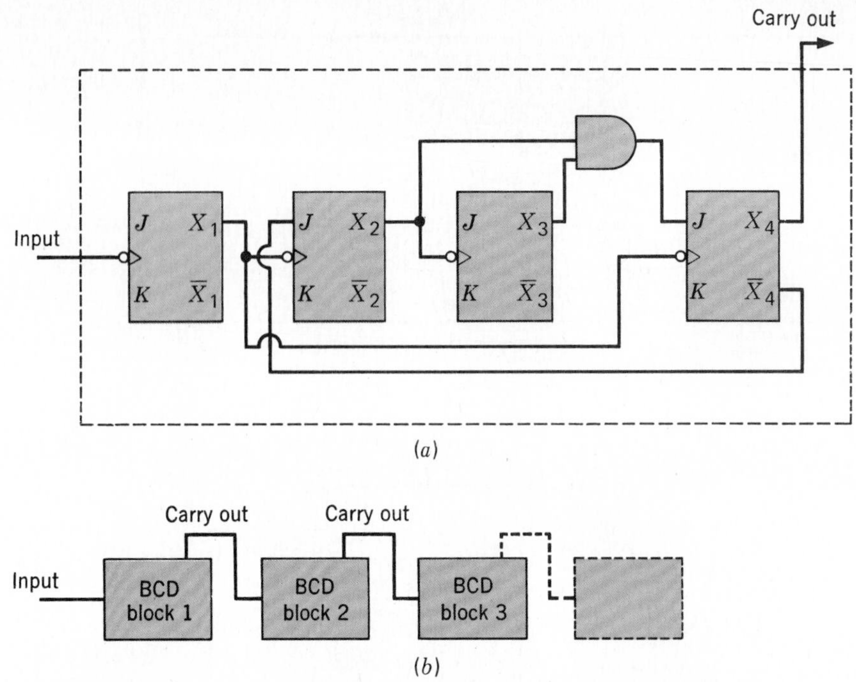

Carry out

(a)

Input

LOGIC DESIGN

Carry out   Carry out

Input | BCD block 1 | BCD block 2 | BCD block 3 |

(b)

FIGURE 4.15

BCD counters. (*a*) Decade, or BCD, counter. (*Note:* Unconnected inputs are 1s.) (*b*) Cascading BCD counter blocks.

X_4	X_3	X_2	X_1
0	0	0	0
0	0	0	1
0	0	1	0
0	0	1	1
0	1	0	0
0	1	0	1
0	1	1	0
0	1	1	1
1	0	0	0
1	0	0	1

When the next negative-going edge at the input occurs, however, the BCD counter returns to all 0s. At the same time (that is, during the interval when the counter goes from 9 to 0) a negative-going signal edge occurs at the CARRY output. This CARRY output can be connected to the INPUT of another BCD counter, which will then be stepped by 1 when the first BCD stage goes from 9 to 0. This is shown in Fig. 4.15(*b*); where several four-flip-flop BCD stages are combined to make a large counter.

If we consider just two of the "BCD boxes," we find the sequence to be as follows:

8 Y_4	4 Y_3	2 Y_2	1 Y_1	8 X_4	4 X_3	2 X_2	1 X_1	value of bits
0	0	0	0	0	0	0	0	
0	0	0	0	0	0	0	1	
0	0	0	0	0	0	1	0	
0	0	0	0	0	0	1	1	
0	0	0	0	0	1	0	0	
0	0	0	0	0	1	0	1	
0	0	0	0	0	1	1	0	
0	0	0	0	0	1	1	1	
0	0	0	0	1	0	0	0	
0	0	0	0	1	0	0	1	
0	0	0	1	0	0	0	0	
0	0	0	1	0	0	0	1	
.	.	.	.	.	.	.	.	
0	0	0	1	1	0	0	1	
0	0	1	0	0	0	0	0	
0	0	1	0	0	0	0	1	
.	.	.	.	.	.	.	.	

INTEGRATED
CIRCUITS

Here we have counted to 21. This would continue until the counter reached 99, when the Y part would put out a signal which could be used to gate another stage to form a counter that could count to 999.

This sort of repetition of various "boxes," or "modules," such as a BCD counter, is facilitated by manufacturers placing an entire four-stage BCD counter in a single integrated-circuit container.

One thing should again be noted about the block diagram in Fig. 4.15(a). The flip-flops are activated by negative-going shifts in input levels at the input. This is indicated by the small circles or bubbles at the inputs. As a result, a flip-flop such as X_3 is activated when X_2 goes from a 1 to a 0, that is, when the 1 output makes a negative transition.

Also note that unconnected inputs, such as the K inputs of all the flip-flops and the J inputs of X_1 and X_3 are at 1 levels. This is due to the circuit construction.

INTEGRATED CIRCUITS

4.10 The flip-flops and gates used in modern computing machines—which range from calculators and microcomputers through the large high-speed computers—are constructed and packaged by using what is called *integrated-circuit technology*. When integrated circuits are used, one or more complete gates or flip-flops are packaged in a single integrated-circuit (IC) container. The IC containers provide input and output pins or connections which are then interconnected by plated strips on circuit boards, wires, or other means to form complete computing devices.

In earlier computers, flip-flop and gate circuits were constructed by using discrete electrical components such as resistors, capacitors, transistors, and, before that, vacuum tubes and relays. Individual components were interconnected to form

flip-flops and gates which were then interconnected to form computers. With the present-day IC technology, flip-flops and gates are fabricated in containers, and only the IC containers (or "cans") need be interconnected.

Two typical IC containers are shown in Fig. 4.16(*a*). One is called a *dual inline package* (in the trade it is called a "coffin," or a DIP), and this particular package has 14 pins which provide for external connections. For years this 14-pin package was a standard in the industry, and plastic and ceramic DIPs of this sort were the largest-selling IC package for some years.

There has been a tendency as IC technology improved, however, to increase the number of pins per package. Packages with 16 to 40 pins are becoming popular, and up to 100 pins per package can now be found in some IC manufacturers' products.

Figure 4.16(*b*) through (*e*) shows how several gates and flip-flops are packaged in a single container. The inputs and outputs are numbered, and each number refers to an external pin on the IC container. A ground connection and a positive power voltage are both required for each container, so that only 12 pins remain to be used for the actual inputs and outputs to gates and flip-flops. (For these circuits, each V_{CC} pin is connected to a 5.5-V power supply and GND to 0 V or system ground.)

The particular circuits in Fig. 4.16 are called *transistor-transistor logic* (TTL) circuits and are widely used high-speed circuits. These circuits have a 3.5-V level for a 1 and 0.2-V level for a 0. The particular configurations shown with identical pin connections are manufactured by just about every major IC manufacturer, and packages from one manufacturer can be fairly easily substituted for another manufacturer's packages (provided the speed requirements or loading capabilities are not violated). There are many other packages with, for instance, three three-input NAND gates, two *RS* flip-flops, exclusive OR gates, etc.

To illustrate the use of IC packages in logic design, we now examine an implementation of Fig. 4.17, using the packages shown in Fig. 4.16. The logic circuit in Fig. 4.17 is called a *shift register with feedback,*[4] for it consists of four flip-flops connected in a shift-register configuration and "feedback" from these

---

[4]This particular type of shift register with feedback is so widely used that complete books have been written about it. It is sometimes called a *linear shift register,* a *random sequence generation,* or a *linear recurring sequence generator*. With similar feedback connections, a register can be made with as many flip-flops as desired, thus forming counters with sequences of $2^N - 1$ for any reasonable N (where N is the number of flip-flops).

Consider the set of consecutive states taken by X_4 in the shift register in Fig. 4.17 to be its output sequence. Each nonzero 4-tuple occurs once in any 15-bit segment of this sequence, each nonzero 3-tuple occurs twice, etc. Adding a 15-bit segment of this sequence to another 15-bit segment bit by bit mod 2 (exclusive OR) will give still another 15-bit segment. These sequences are used in instruments to form random number generators and to generate bandpass noise; in radar for interplanetary observations; in communications systems to generate noise and encode or encrypt; and for many other purposes. See Birkhoff and Bartee for more information and references.

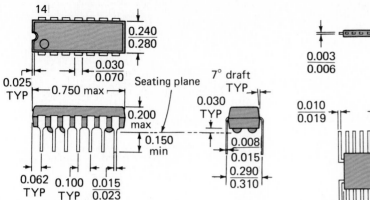

INTEGRATED
CIRCUITS

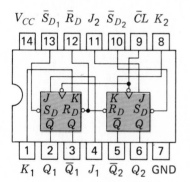

TO-116
Dual inline

(a)

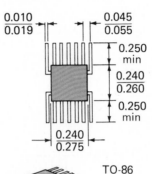

TO-86
Flat pack

V_{CC} $\bar{S}_{D_1}$ $\bar{R}_D$ J_2 $\bar{S}_{D_2}$ $\bar{CL}$ K_2

| 14 | 13 | 12 | 11 | 10 | 9 | 8 |

| 1 | 2 | 3 | 4 | 5 | 6 | 7 |

K_1 Q_1 $\bar{Q}_1$ J_1 $\bar{Q}_2$ Q_2 GND

(b)

Note:
R_D is DC RESET
and
S_D is DC SET.

TOP VIEWS

J_1 Q_1 $\bar{Q}_1$ GND K_2 Q_2 $\bar{Q}_2$

| 14 | 13 | 12 | 11 | 10 | 9 | 8 |

| 1 | 2 | 3 | 4 | 5 | 6 | 7 |

CL_1 R_{D_1} K_1 V_{CC} CL_2 R_{D_2} J_2

(c)

V_{CC} NC

| 14 | 13 | 12 | 11 | 10 | 9 | 8 |

| 1 | 2 | 3 | 4 | 5 | 6 | 7 |

NC GND

(d)

V_{CC}

| 14 | 13 | 12 | 11 | 10 | 9 | 8 |

| 1 | 2 | 3 | 4 | 5 | 6 | 7 |

GND

(e)

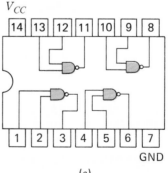

FIGURE 4.16

IC containers and flip-flop and gate circuits. (a) Dual inline and flat-pack IC containers. (b) Dual *JK* flip-flop with common clock and resets and separate sets. (c) Dual *JK* flip-flop with separate resets and clocks. (d) Dual four-input NAND gates. (e) Quadruplex two-input NAND gates.

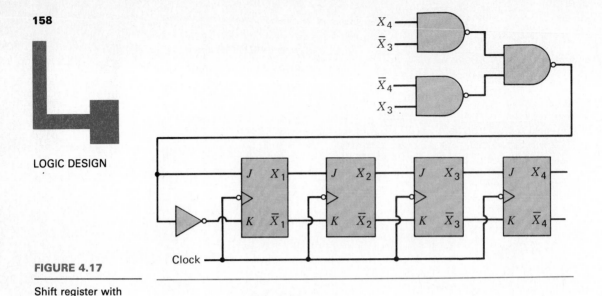

LOGIC DESIGN

FIGURE 4.17

Shift register with feedback.

four flip-flops to the first flip-flop's inputs. This particular counter is started by setting a 1 in X_1 and 0s in X_2, X_3, and X_4. The sequence of states taken is then

$$
\begin{array}{cccc}
1 & 0 & 0 & 0 \\
0 & 1 & 0 & 0 \\
0 & 0 & 1 & 0 \\
1 & 0 & 0 & 1 \\
1 & 1 & 0 & 0 \\
0 & 1 & 1 & 0 \\
1 & 0 & 1 & 1 \\
0 & 1 & 0 & 1 \\
1 & 0 & 1 & 0 \\
1 & 1 & 0 & 1 \\
1 & 1 & 1 & 0 \\
1 & 1 & 1 & 1 \\
0 & 1 & 1 & 1 \\
0 & 0 & 1 & 1 \\
0 & 0 & 0 & 1 \\
1 & 0 & 0 & 0 \\
0 & 1 & 0 & 0
\end{array}
\right\} \text{basic sequence which repeats}
$$

Notice that this sequence contains 15 of the 16 possible 4-bit numbers that might be taken by this circuit. (Only the all-0 combination is excluded.) This is a widely used sequence which occurs in many instruments and has many uses in radar systems, sonar systems, coding encryption boxes, etc.

Quite often the sequence of states taken by a logic circuit is written in a *counter table*. The counter table for the above sequence is

X_1	X_2	X_3	X_4
1	0	0	0
0	1	0	0
0	0	1	0
1	0	0	1
1	1	0	0
0	1	1	0
1	0	1	1
0	1	0	1
1	0	1	0
1	1	0	1
1	1	1	0
1	1	1	1
0	1	1	1
0	0	1	1
0	0	0	1

INTEGRATED
CIRCUITS

In the counter table, the flip-flops' names are first listed, followed by the starting states. Then the successive states taken are listed in order, and the final line contains the state preceding the starting state.

There is a straightforward technique for designing a logic circuit to realize a counter table; this technique is developed in Sec. 4.12. For now we return to the implementation of the counter in Fig. 4.17.

In order to implement this counter, we require four flip-flops and a gate circuit which will yield the $\overline{X}_3 X_4 + X_3 \overline{X}_4$. As shown, this can be made with a NAND-to-NAND gate network with three two-input NAND gates. An inverter is also required. (A NAND gate can be used for this by connecting both inputs.)

One problem remains: We need to start the counter with X_1 in state 1 and the other three flip-flops in state 0. Since DC RESET inputs are connected on the flip-flops [see Fig. 4.16(*b*)], it is necessary to use a trick for flip-flop X_1. This simply involves renaming the *J* and *K* inputs and the two outputs so that *J* becomes *K*, *K* becomes *J*, and the two output names are reversed. The DC RESET input then becomes a DC SET input for the new (renamed) flip-flop.

Figure 4.18 shows the circuit as finally designed. Notice how X_1 differs in connections from X_2 and X_3.

The logic circuit in Fig. 4.18 could be implemented by using a printed-circuit board to make the connections between IC containers. Or the connections could be made by individual wires by using any of a number of interconnection boards manufactured by various companies. Placing a 0 (ground) on the DC RESET input sets the flip-flops to the desired starting conditions, and the circuit will then step through the desired states.

There are several major lines of integrated circuits now being produced in substantial quantities. Table 4.1 lists several basic lines and gives some of the characteristics of each line. The first three IC lines in the table are called *bipolar logic* because they utilize conventional transistors in the IC packages, and the next three of the lines use what are called *field-effect transistors* (FETs) and are fabricated by using metal-oxide semiconductor (MOS) technology. IIL is also bipolar

LOGIC DESIGN

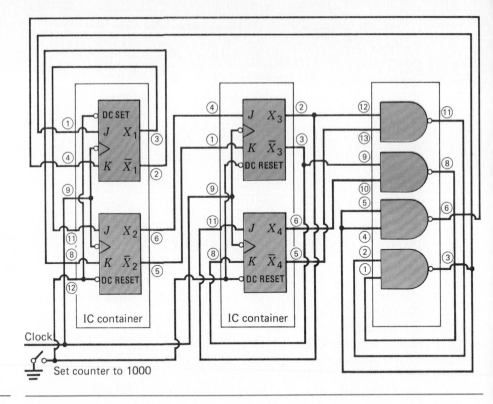

Clock

Set counter to 1000

FIGURE 4.18

Design of shift register in Fig. 4.17 using TTL. Circled numbers are pin numbers on IC containers.

but nonstandard in operation. The bipolar logic lines are widely used for constructing configurations on circuit boards which realize high-speed logic. Generally there are not so many gates and flip-flops in a package using bipolar logic, but these lines are fast and can be interconnected more readily than the MOS lines. The reason is that the bipolar logic lines use more power (primarily more current) for each gate or flip-flop and can, as a result, produce more current drive and therefore drive long cables, long wires, and, in general, more other circuits.

Associated with each gate and flip-flop in a line of integrated circuits are data concerning the gates or flip-flop's ability to drive other circuits and be driven by other circuits. Typically the manufacturer gives data concerning the delays through the circuit, rise and fall times for output waveforms, the circuit's ability to drive other electrical loads, circuits, and long wires or cables. The manufacturer also generally provides information on how many other inputs to gates of a similar type a given gate can drive. In its simplest form, every input to every gate and flip-flop is the same, and the manufacturer simply stipulates how many inputs can be connected to a given output. Each input is then called a *standard load,* and an output is said to be able to drive, for instance, eight standard loads. For some circuit lines, different gates and flip-flop inputs present different loads, and so an input to a particular kind of gate might have a number such as 2 or 3 associated with it and an output drive number such as 12. Then the designer must see that the sum of the input loads does not exceed the output drive number for a given output.

TABLE 4.1   INTEGRATED-CIRCUIT LINES

NAME OF CIRCUIT LINE	ACRONYM	SPEED (DELAY PER GATE), NS	POWER PER GATE	GOOD FEATURES	PROBLEMS
Transistor-transistor logic	TTL	3 (1 ns for Schottky clamped)	10 mW (20 mW for Schottky clamped)	Very popular line at present. Easy to interconnect; fast, wide selection of circuits available, MSI packages available, inexpensive.	Generates noise spikes, relatively high power dissipation, modest packing density.
Low-power transistor-transistor logic	LPTTL	10	1 mW	A low-power-per-gate TTL developed for space and other portable applications, easy to use and interconnect.	Low speed.
Emitter-coupled logic	ECL	0.3	60 mW	Highest speed, generates little noise internally.	Difficult to interconnect. Low packing density. Difficult to cool.
p-channel metal-oxide silicon	PMOS	25	0.1 mW	Low power, good packing density, easy to manufacture, inexpensive.	Slow and delicate, has limited ability to drive lines and to interface with other circuit lines.
n-channel metal-oxide silicon	NMOS	7	0.1 mW	Faster than PMOS, relatively low power, good packing density, inexpensive and relatively easy to manufacture.	Has limited ability to drive lines and to interface with other circuits.
Complementary metal-oxide silicon	CMOS	7	10 nW	Very low standby power required. Modest speed and packing density, reasonably priced.	Power consumption increases when switched at high speeds.
Integrated injection logic	IIL	1	0.1 mW	Fast, low power.	Difficult to manufacture. Non-standard logic gate formations.

Note: In this table W stands for watts, n for nano ($= 10^{-9}$), m for milli ($= 10^{-3}$), and s for seconds.

161

Figure 4.19 shows a binary counter which is packaged in a single IC container with 16 pins. The counter has several features:

1 The counter counts up (from 0000 to 1111) if $U/\overline{D}$ is a 1 and down (from 1111 to 0000) if $U/\overline{D}$ is a 0.

2 The four flip-flops can be "loaded" from the four DATA inputs by making the LOAD line a 1 when a clock pulse occurs (the LOAD line is normally a 0, so making it a 1 causes the upper DATA input values to be taken by the upper flip-flops, etc.).

3 The counter can be gated on or off by the two ENABLE lines.

MEDIUM-, LARGE-, AND VERY LARGE-SCALE INTEGRATION

4.11 Most circuits are now fabricated by using the general technology of integrated circuitry. In this case the transistors, diodes, resistors, and any other components are fabricated together, by using solid-state physics techniques, in a single container. In the most common technology, called *monolithic integrated circuitry,* a single semiconductor wafer is processed by photomasking, etching, diffusions, and other steps, thus producing a complete array of diodes, transistors, and resistors already interconnected to form one or more logic gates or flip-flops.

When more than a few flip-flops or a few gates are packaged in a single container, the process is called *medium-scale integration* (MSI). Notice that medium-scale integration still refers to integrated circuits, except that even more circuits are housed in a single container. There are no fixed specific rules, but generally if more than 10 but less than 100 gates or flip-flops are in a single package, the manufacturer will refer to it as MSI.

When more than 100 gates or flip-flops are manufactured in a single small container, the process is called *large-scale integration* (LSI). Some ideas of the complexity of arrays of this sort are found in later chapters where memories and arithmetic-logic units consisting of thousands of flip-flops and gates in a single package are studied.

Finally, there is very large-scale integration (VLSI) in which 50,000 to several hundred thousand gates and flip-flops are packaged in a single package. The memories and microprocessors in later chapters will illustrate this.

Despite the various levels of integration, the circuits are surprisingly similar in principle, except that VLSI tends to use a technology based on MOS, while MSI, LSI, and "conventional" integrated circuits use "conventional" *npn* and sometimes *pnp* transistors fabricated on silicon chips. There are good reasons for this. MOS circuits require very small areas on a chip and use very little power, which is quite important given the volume/complexity factor. However, conventional bipolar circuits are faster and more readily interconnected. As a result, the MOS technology is used more often for larger arrays which can be treated only as complete single units rather than on a circuit-by-circuit basis. MOS is more likely to be used in large memories and microprocessors, for example.

Figure 4.20(*a*) shows a typical MSI package containing a complete BCD counter. This counter steps from 0 to 9 and then resets to 0 when X_1 (which is pin

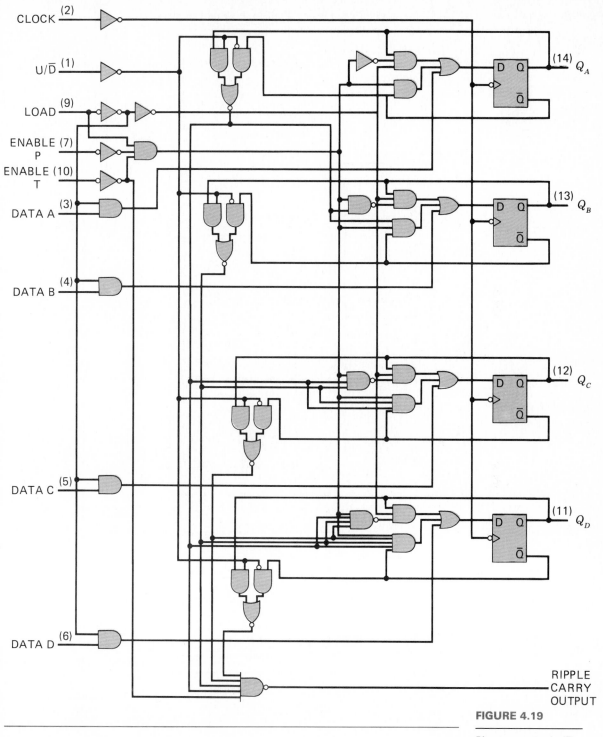

FIGURE 4.19

Binary counter in IC container.

163

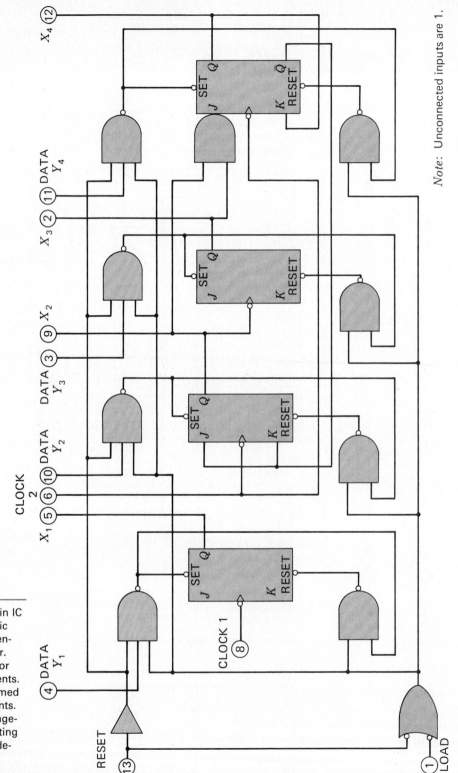

Note: Unconnected inputs are 1.

(*a*)

FIGURE 4.20

(*a*) BCD counter in IC package. (*b*) Logic diagram for seven-segment decoder. (*c*) Designation for the seven segments. (*d*) Numbers formed by seven segments. (*e*) General arrangement for connecting seven-segment decoder. (*Fairchild Semiconductor.*)

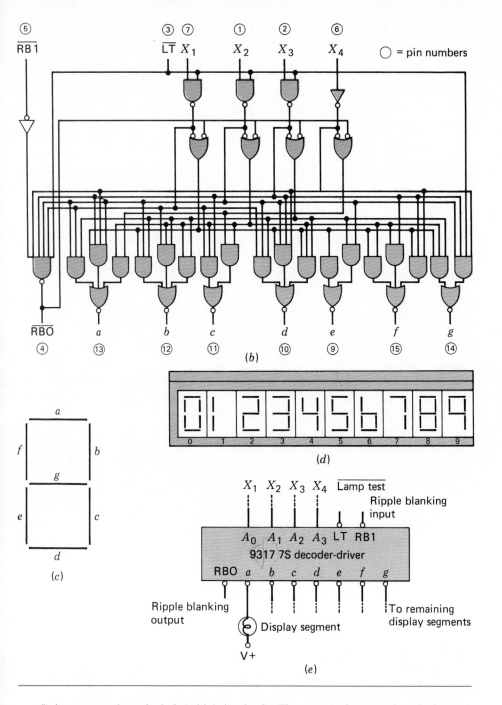

(b)

(c)

(d)

(e)

5) is connected to clock 2 (which is pin 6). The counter is stepped each time an input clock waveform connected to clock 1 (pin 8) goes negative (on negative edges). The counter can be reset to the all 0s by connecting a 0 to the reset line (pin 13). Data from four input wires connected to Y_1, Y_2, Y_3, and Y_4 will be loaded into flip-flops X_1, X_2, X_3, and X_4, respectively, if the LOAD input is pulled down to a 0. (It is normally a 1.)

An example of gate networks in MSI packages is shown in Fig. 4.20(*b*), which shows a *seven-segment decoder*. When decimal numbers are to be read from a digital calculator, instrument, microcomputer, etc., display devices using light-emitting diodes (LEDs) or liquid crystals are often used. Each digit of the display is formed from seven segments, each consisting of one light-emitting diode or crystal which can be turned on or off. A typical arrangement is shown in Fig. 4.20(*c*) which assigns the letters *a* through *g* to the segments. To make the digit 5, for example, segments *a, f, g, c,* and *d* are turned on. The set of digits as formed by these segments is shown in Fig. 4.20(*d*).

The seven-segment decoder in Fig. 4.20(*b*) can be connected to the outputs of the four flip-flops in the BCD counter in (*a*) by connecting the X_1, X_2, X_3, and X_4 outputs from (*a*) to the X_1, X_2, X_3, and X_4 inputs of (*b*). If the seven outputs *a* through *f* of Fig. 4.20(*b*) are then connected to a decimal digital display device, a counter with a decimal digit display, such as those in the familiar calculator, will be formed.

The BCD counter in Fig. 4.20(*a*) can be extended to several digits by connecting the X_4 output from one digit to the clock 1 input of the next-highest-order digit in the counter.

The seven-segment decoder in Fig. 4.20(*b*) has the ability to blank leading zeros in a multidigit display, which is commonly done on calculators. Consider that a multistage BCD counter has been connected to several seven-segment decoders with one decoder per BCD counter stage. If the ripple blanking output (RBO) of each seven-segment decoder is connected to the ripple blanking input (RBI) of the seven-segment decoder of the next-higher-order digit in the counter, and if the ripple blanking input of the most significant digit's seven-segment decoder is connected to a 0 input, then a blanking circuit will be formed. Then, for instance, in a four-stage counter the number 0014 will have the leading two 0s turned off, or *blanked*; the number 0005 will be displayed as simply 5, with the 0 displays not turned on, etc. In effect, the circuit tests for a 0 value at its input. If the value is 0 and all the digits to its left are 0, then it turns off all seven segments and generates a blanking signal for the next rightmost digit's light driver. The light test (LT) input can be used to test all seven segments simultaneously. Notice that making the light test input a 0 will cause all seven segments to go on.

In the MSI products of some manufacturers, both a four-stage BCD counter and a seven-segment decoder are placed in the same package complete with a blanking input and output for each digit. This gives some feeling for the more complex MSI packages.

COUNTER DESIGN

*4.12[5] The design of a counter to sequence through a given set of states is straightforward, using the technique to be shown. First, a counter table is made up that lists the states to be taken. Assume that we wish a counter using three flip-flops to sequence as follows:

---

[5]Sections marked with asterisks can be omitted on a first reading without loss of continuity.

	A	B	C	
Starting state →	0	0	0	⎞
	1	1	1	⎟
	1	0	1	⎟ this repeats
	1	1	0	⎟
	0	0	1	⎟
	0	1	0	⎠
	0	0	0	
	1	1	1	
	1	0	1	
	•	•	•	
	•	•	•	

COUNTER DESIGNS

This table shows that if the counter is in the state $A = 0$, $B = 0$, $C = 0$ and a clock pulse (edge) is applied, then the counter is to step to $A = 1$, $B = 1$, $C = 1$. As another example, if $A = 0$, $B = 1$, and $C = 0$ and a clock pulse occurs, then the counter is to step to $A = 0$, $B = 0$, $C = 0$. As can be seen, the counter "cycles" because after taking the state 010 it returns to 000 and then goes to 111, as before. If clock pulses continue, the counter will cycle through the six different states shown indefinitely.

We use RS flip-flops for our first design. Now each flip-flop has two inputs, an R input and an S input. So we give the R input to A the name A^R, the S input to A the name A^S, the R input to B the name B^R, and so on through C^S.

The problem is now to derive boolean algebra expressions for each of the six inputs to the flip-flops. To do this, we place the state table in a *counter design table,* listing the three flip-flops and their states and also listing the six inputs to the flip-flops. This is shown in Fig. 4.21(a).

The values for A^R, A^S, B^R, B^S, C^R, C^S are then filled in by using the following rule.

DESIGN RULE

Consider a row in the table and a specific flip-flop:

1 If the flip-flop's state is a 0 in the row and a 0 in the next row, place a 0 in the S input column and a d in the R input column for the flip-flop inputs.

2 If the flip-flop is a 1 in a row and a 1 in the next row, place a 0 in the R input column and a d in the S input column.

3 If the flip-flop is a 0 in a row and changes to a 1 in the next row, place a 1 in the S column and a 0 in the R column.

4 If the flip-flop is a 1 in a row and changes to a 0 in the next row, place a 1 in the R column and a 0 in the S column.

LOGIC DESIGN

| Counter States | | | Outputs | | | | | |
A	B	C	A^S	A^R	B^S	B^R	C^S	C^R
0	0	0	1	0	1	0	1	0
1	1	1	d	0	0	1	d	0
1	0	1	d	0	1	0	0	1
1	1	0	0	1	0	1	1	0
0	0	1	0	d	1	0	0	1
0	1	0	0	d	0	1	0	d

(a)

$A^S = \bar{B}\bar{C}$

	AB			
C	00	01	11	10
0	1	0	0	d
1	0	d	d	d

Map for A^S

$A^R = B\bar{C}$

	AB			
C	00	01	11	10
0	0	d	1	d
1	d	d	0	0

Map for A^R

$B^S = \bar{B}$

	AB			
C	00	01	11	10
0	1	0	0	d
1	1	d	0	1

Map for B^S

$B^R = B$

	AB			
C	00	01	11	10
0	0	1	1	d
1	0	d	1	0

Map for B^R

$C^S = AB + \bar{B}\bar{C}$

	AB			
C	00	01	11	10
0	1	0	1	d
1	0	d	d	0

Map for C^S

$C^R = \bar{B}C$

	AB			
C	00	01	11	10
0	0	d	0	d
1	1	d	0	1

Map for C^R

(b)

FIGURE 4.21

Designing a counter using *RS* flip-flops.

As an example, consider flip-flop A in Fig. 4.21(a). The flip-flop has value 0 in the first row and changes to a 1 in the second row. We therefore place a 1 in A^S in row 1 and a 0 in A^R in row 1. In row 2, A has value 1 and remains a 1 in row 3. So we fill in a d in A^S and a 0 in A^R.

The reasoning behind these rules is as follows: Suppose that flip-flop A is in the 0 state and should stay in the 0 state when the next clock pulse is applied. The S input must then be 0, and the R input can be a 1 *or* a 0. Thus we must have 0 at A^S, but can place a d (for don't-care) at the A^R input.

If A is a 0 and should change to a 1, however, the S input to A must be a 1 and the R input a 0 when the next clock pulse is applied. So a 1 is placed in A^S and 0 in A^R.

It is instructive to examine several of the entries in the counter table in Fig. 4.21(a) to see how this rule applies.

Our goal is to generate the flip-flop inputs (A^R, A^S, etc.) in a *given* row so that when the counter is in the state in that row, each input will take the value listed. Then the next clock pulse will cause the counter to step to the state in the next row below in the counter table.

The design of the counter now progresses as a boolean algebra expression is formed from this table for A^R, A^S, B^R, B^S, C^R, and C^S, the inputs to the flip-flops, and then each expression is minimized. This is shown in Fig. 4.21(b), which gives the maps for the flip-flops' inputs. Notice that any unused counter states can be included as d's in the map because the counter never uses them. The minimal expressions are shown beside each map.

The final step is to draw the block diagram for the counter using the minimal expressions. The final design for this counter is shown in Fig. 4.22.

Now suppose that we desire to design the above counter, using JK flip-flops. The procedure will be basically the same, except that the rules for filling in the counter design using JK flip-flops will be different.

COUNTER DESIGNS

FIGURE 4.22

Counter with *RS* flip-flops.

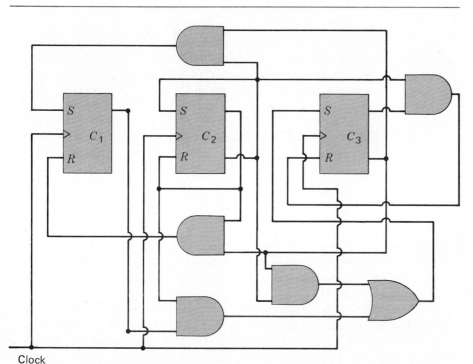

Clock

The inputs will now be A^J, A^K, B^J, B^K, C^J, and C^K. The rules for JK flip-flops are as follows:

DESIGN RULE

For a given flip-flop in a selected row, the J and K inputs to the flip-flop are filled in as follows:

1 If the flip-flop is a 0 in a row and remains a 0 in the next row, place a 0 in the J input column and a d in the K input column.

2 If the flip-flop is a 1 in a row and remains a 1 in the next row, place a 0 in the K input column and a d in the J input column.

3 If the flip-flop is a 0 in a row and changes to a 1 in the next row, place a 1 in the J input column and a d in the K input column.

4 If the flip-flop is a 1 in a row and changes to a 0 in the next row, place a d in the J input column and a 1 in the K input column.

The reasoning behind the above rules is as follows: Suppose that a given flip-flop, say A, is in the 0 state and should stay in the same state when the next clock pulse occurs. The input A^K must be a 0 at that time, but A^J can be either a 0 at that time or a 1, so that A^J input is essentially a d (or don't-care) input. If A must go from a 0 to a 1, however, the A^K input *must* be a 1, but the A^J input can be either a 0 or a 1 (since the flip-flop will change states if both inputs are 1s). Notice that there are more d's in the rules for JK flip-flops than for RS flip-flops because of the ability of the flip-flops to change states when both inputs are 1s.

The maps for each input to the flip-flops A^J, A^K, B^J, B^K, C^J, and C^K are drawn as before, the expression for each flip-flop's input is minimized, and the block diagram for the counter is then drawn as in Fig. 4.23. Notice that fewer gates are used for the counter in Fig. 4.23 than for that in Fig. 4.22. This is because of the additional d's in the maps, and it will generally, although not always, be the case. (Sometimes the RS and JK designs will be the same; JK flip-flops cannot require more gates for a given counter sequence.)

STATE DIAGRAMS AND STATE TABLES

4.13 A set of interconnected gates with inputs and outputs is called a *combinational network*. The outputs from a combinational network at a given time are completely determined by the inputs at that time. As a result, the function of a combinational network can be described by using a table of combinations that simply lists the input-output values.

When flip-flops are combined with gates, a more complicated situation arises because the flip-flops progress through various states—depending on inputs—and the output can depend on the previous as well as the preceding inputs.

A	B	C	A^J	A^K	B^J	B^K	C^J	C^K
0	0	0	1	d	1	d	1	d
1	1	1	d	0	d	1	d	0
1	0	1	d	0	1	d	d	1
1	1	0	d	1	d	1	1	d
0	0	1	0	d	1	d	d	1
0	1	0	0	d	d	1	0	d

STATE DIAGRAMS AND STATE TABLES

$A^J = \bar{B}\bar{C}$

AB
C	00	01	11	10
0	1	0	d	d
1	0	d	d	d

$A^K = \bar{C}$

AB
C	00	01	11	10
0	d	d	1	d
1	d	d	0	0

$B^J = 1$

AB
C	00	01	11	10
0	1	d	d	d
1	1	d	d	1

$B^K = 1$

AB
C	00	01	11	10
0	d	1	1	d
1	d	d	1	d

$C^J = A + \bar{B}$

AB
C	00	01	11	10
0	1	0	1	d
1	d	d	d	d

$C^K = \bar{B}$

AB
C	00	01	11	10
0	d	d	d	d
1	1	d	0	1

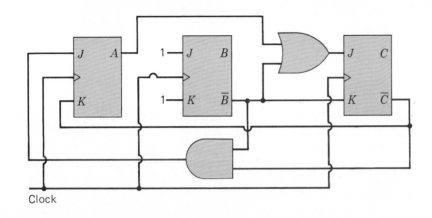

Clock

FIGURE 4.23

Design for a *JK* flip-flop counter.

To analyze and design with both flip-flops and gates, several techniques have been developed. The best known involves the use of *state diagrams* and *state tables,* which are the subject of this section.

A simple design problem which requires flip-flops as well as gates is the design of a *binary sequence detector.* A binary sequence detector has a single input line that it examines. The sequence detector looks for some specified sequence of inputs on this input line and outputs a 1 when this sequence is found.[6] An example of a specified sequence would be three consecutive 1s. In this case, if the sequence detector is present with the inputs 1001011101, the sequence detector will output a 0 at all times except immediately following the third 1, when it will output a 1. This is shown in Fig. 4.24. The sequence detector is like a lock which unlocks (outputs a 1) only when the combination (in this case, three consecutive 1s) appears. Sequence detectors can be designed to detect any specified sequence such as 11011 or 1110101 or any other.

Figure 4.25(a) shows a state diagram which describes a binary sequence detector that detects three consecutive 1s. A state diagram is formed from what mathematicians call a *directed graph.* State diagrams have *nodes,* which are the circles in Fig. 4.25(a), and *links,* which are the curved lines with arrowheads at one end. There are four nodes in Fig. 4.25(a) and eight links.

The nodes in a state diagram correspond to flip-flop states in the final design and so are also called *states* and given names. For Fig. 4.25(a), the states are named $A, B, C,$ and $D.$ To the right of each state name there is a comma, followed by the output value for that state. This corresponds to the output from the detector in Fig. 4.24. For this diagram, if the present state is $A,$ the output is 0; if the state is $D,$ the output is 1; etc. Each link of the graph is labeled with the input values $X = 1$ or $X = 0.$ These links show how transitions are made from state to state. This X input in Fig. 4.25(a) corresponds to the X input in Fig. 4.24.

The interpretation of the state diagram corresponding to Fig. 4.25(a) is as follows. The machine is started in state $A,$ at which time the output is a 0. If the input X is 0 when the first clock pulse arrives, the detector stays in state A and continues to output a 0. This is shown by the loop connected to A and labeled $X = 0.$

---

[6]The sequence of 1s and 0s on the input line occurs in time, and each 1 and 0 is generally clocked into the flip-flops.

FIGURE 4.24

Input and output waveforms for binary sequence detector.

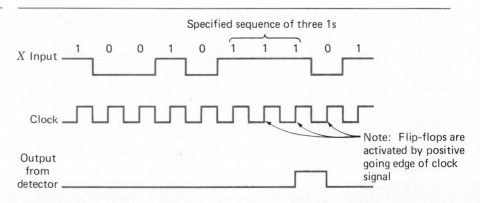

If the detector is in state A and a 1 is input (when the clock pulse arrives), the system goes to state B and continues to output a 0.

With the detector in state B, if a 0 is input, the detector goes back to state A and continues to output a 0. If a 1 is input with the detector in state B, the detector goes to C and continues to output a 0.

This analysis of the detector's operation can be continued. The important thing is that if the detector is in state C and an input of 1 is given, the detector goes to state D and outputs a 1. If more 1s are input with the machine in state D, it remains in that state and continues to output a 1. If a 0 is input, the detector returns to A.

As can be seen, the detector outputs a 0 until three successive 1s are input, at which time it outputs a 1 and this 1 output is continued until a 0 is input.

Figure 4.25(b) is a *state table* which represents the same sequence detector as the state diagram in Fig. 4.25(a). There are three major columns in the table: Present state, Output, and Next state. The interpretation of this table is as follows. If the detector is in present state A and a 0 is input, the next state will be A and a 0 will be output. If the system is in state A and a 1 is input, the detector will go to state B and a 0 will be output while in that state.

If the detector is in state A and two successive 1s are input, the resulting state will be C. If another 1 is input, the detector will go to the D state and a 1 will be output. While in D, the 1 inputs will keep the system in D and the outputs will continue to be 1s until a 0 is input; then the next state will be A and a 0 will be output. The state diagram in Fig. 4.25(a) and the state table in Fig. 4.25(b) should be compared to see how they describe the same operations.

Having described the sequence detector by using a state diagram and a state table, we now make a design using flip-flops and gates which will realize the state diagram and table and which can be constructed by using integrated circuits.

Since flip-flops are to take states corresponding to states A, B, C, and D in the state diagram and table, two flip-flops will be required to take the four states. We can make a preliminary drawing of the layout for the sequence detector. Figure 4.25(c) shows the overall layout with two flip-flops, a set of gates, and an input X and an output Z. What remains is to design the gate network in Fig. 4.25(c). First, however, it is necessary to assign values to the flip-flops for each of states A, B, C, and D.

A natural assignment of flip-flop values is to let $Q_1 = 0$, $Q_2 = 0$ represent state A; $Q_2 = 0$, $Q_2 = 1$ represent B; $Q_1 = 1$, $Q_2 = 0$ represent C; and $Q_1 = 1$, $Q_2 = 1$ represent D. Replacing the A, B, C, and D in Fig. 4.25(b) with this assignment of values leads to the table in Fig. 4.25(d), which is otherwise the same as Fig. 4.25(b).

It is now possible to design the actual gate structure. There are three inputs to the gating network: Q_1 and Q_2, the flip-flop outputs, and the X input. There are also three outputs from the gate network: the D inputs to Q_1 and Q_2 and the Z output. Since there are three outputs, three maps are required. The maps for D_1 and D_2 (the inputs to Q_1 and Q_2) will have three inputs, Q_1, Q_2, and X. However, the map for the output has only two inputs, Q_1 and Q_2, since the output Z is determined by the present state of the system and not the current input.

The maps for the system in Fig. 4.25(a) through (d) are shown in Fig. 4.25(e), and the complete design is seen in Fig. 4.25(f). A RESET has been added

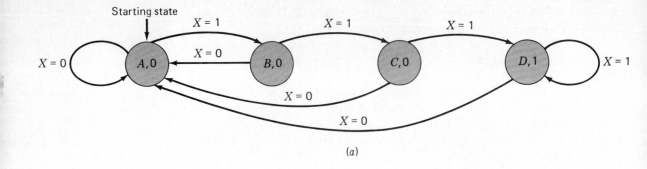

(a)

Present state	Output Z	Next state Input X	
		0	1
A	0	A	B
B	0	A	C
C	0	A	D
D	1	A	D

(b)

(c)

Present state $Q_1\ Q_2$	Output Z	Next state Input X	
		0	1
00	0	00	01
01	0	00	10
10	0	00	11
11	1	00	11

(d)

$Q_1\ Q_2$

X	00	01	11	10
0	0	0	0	0
1	0	1	1	1

$D_1 = Q_1 X + Q_2 X$

$Q_1\ Q_2$

X	00	01	11	10
0	0	0	0	0
1	1	0	1	1

$D_2 = Q_1 X + \overline{Q}_2 X$

Q_1

Q_2	0	1
0	0	0
1	0	1

$Z = Q_1 Q_2$

(e)

174

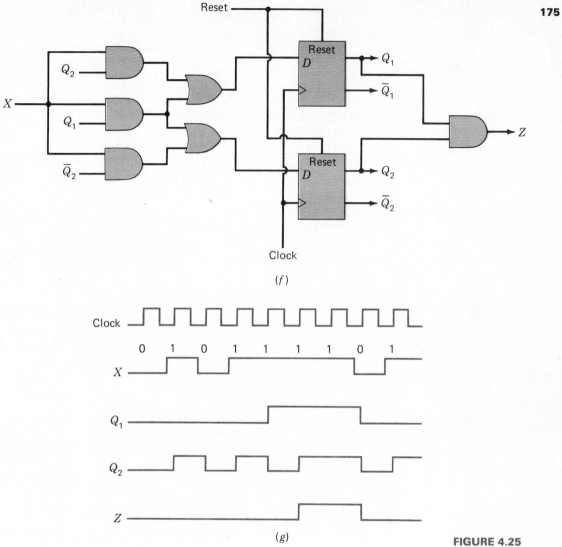

(f)

(g)

FIGURE 4.25

(a) State diagram. (b) State table. (c) Circuit for (a) and (b). (d) State table with assigned values to state flip-flops. (e) Maps for design. (f) Gates and flip-flops for sequence detector. (g) Waveforms for design.

which can be used to start the machine. The operation of this design should be checked by noting the resulting states of the flip-flops for several sequences of X inputs. Figure 4.25(f) shows a set of waveforms.

The design in Fig. 4.25(f) is an example of a state machine.[7] The same procedure involving state diagrams and state tables can be used to design many things, including interfaces and sections of a computer. In general, a state machine is simply a collection of interconnected flip-flops and gates with a set of inputs and

---

[7]State machines are often called *finite* state machines in computer science literature, but computer designs and IC manufacturers now generally use the shorter form, *state machine*.

LOGIC DESIGN

outputs. This is a very general concept, and in following section we treat it in more detail.

DESIGN OF A SEQUENTIAL MAGNITUDE COMPARATOR

4.14 In the preceding section we described the design of a state machine with a single input and output. The same technique can be used to design a state machine with several inputs and outputs.

Consider the design of a *sequential comparator* which is to determine which of two binary numbers A and B, having the same number of bits, is larger. The most significant bits of each number are input to the comparator, followed by the second most significant bits and then the next most significant bits until finally the least significant bits are presented. (The numbers A and B could be stored in two shift registers.) There are to be two outputs, Z_1 and Z_2. If $A > B$, then Z_1 is to be a 1; if $A < B$, then Z_2 is to be a 1; and if $A = B$, then both Z_1 and Z_2 are to be 0s. Figure 4.26 shows a block diagram of the comparator and a set of waveforms for inputs and outputs.

The design of this comparator will be made by first developing a state diagram.

The most significant bits of A and B are to be presented first. If the most significant bit of A is 1 and of B is 0, then $A > B$. So we can draw a starting node K and a link to a state L with the input value 10 (for $A = 1$, $B = 0$); see Fig. 4.27(a). The output for the starting state will be $Z_1 = 0$, $Z_2 = 0$, or simply 00; and the output for state L will be $Z_1 = 1$ and $Z_2 = 0$.

If the most significant bit of A is 0 and of B is 1, then $A < B$ and so a third state M is added with a link with inputs $AB = 01$ going to it from state K.

If the machine is in state L, then no sequence of inputs can change the fact that $A > B$. So a loop with 00, 01, 10, 11 is added to L, indicating it will stay in that state regardless of the inputs. Similarly, if the comparator is in state M, then $A < B$ and no sequence of inputs can change this relation. Thus 00, 01, 10, and 11 are placed on a loop leading from M to M.

FIGURE 4.26

Sequential comparator and waveforms. (*a*) Block diagram. (*b*) Waveforms for two 7-bit binary numbers $A = 0101011$ and $B = 0100100$.

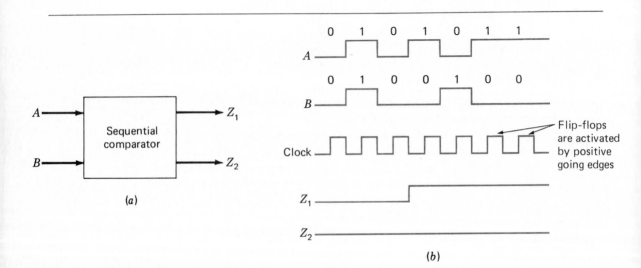

(b)

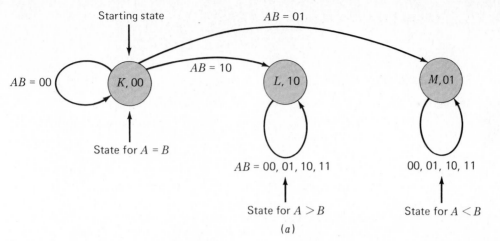

Starting state

$AB = 01$

$AB = 00$ $AB = 10$

K, 00   L, 10   M,01

State for $A = B$

$AB = 00, 01, 10, 11$ 00, 01, 10, 11

State for $A > B$ State for $A < B$

(a)

Present state	Output $Z_1 Z_2$		Next state inputs AB			
			00	01	10	11
K	0	0	K	M	L	K
L	0	1	L	L	L	L
M	1	0	M	M	M	M

(b)

Present state $Q_1 Q_2$	Output Z_1 Z_2	Next state inputs A,B			
		00	01	10	11
00	00	00	01	10	00
01	01	01	01	01	01
10	10	10	10	10	10

(c)

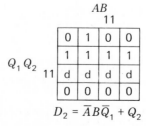

A

B

Gates

D Q_1 Z_1
$>$CLK

D Q_2 Z_2
$>$CLK

Clock

(d)

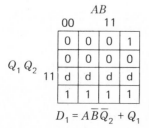

AB
00   11

0	0	0	1
0	0	0	0
d	d	d	d
1	1	1	1

$Q_1 Q_2$ 11

$D_1 = A\bar{B}\bar{Q}_2 + Q_1$

AB
11

0	1	0	0
1	1	1	1
d	d	d	d
0	0	0	0

$Q_1 Q_2$ 11

$D_2 = \bar{A}B\bar{Q}_1 + Q_2$

(e)

FIGURE 4.27

Design for sequential comparator. (*a*) State diagram. (*b*) State table for (*a*). (*c*) State table for sequential comparator with flip-flop values assigned. (*d*) Block diagram of layout for comparator. (*e*) Maps for sequential comparator. (*f*) Gate and flip-flop design for sequential comparator.

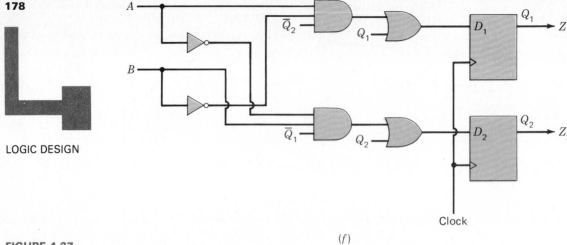

(f)

LOGIC DESIGN

FIGURE 4.27

(*Continued*)

If the most significant bits of A and B are the same, then the numbers can be equal or either A or B can be larger. So for inputs of $A = 0$ and $B = 0$, or $A = 1$ and $B = 1$, the comparator has next state K and outputs $Z_1 Z_2 = 00$. We now see that this process will continue for the next significant bits used and all those which follow. So the state diagram is complete. As an example, if $A_2 A_1 A_0 = 101$, then A has value decimal 5 and if $B_2 B_1 B_0 = 110$, then B has value decimal 6, and the state diagram will output an 01 after the second bits arrive.

A state table can be made for the state diagram in Fig. 4.27(a). This table is shown in Fig. 4.27(b).

To design an actual logic network to realize the state table and state diagram for Fig. 4.27(a) and (b), it is necessary to use flip-flops. Since there are three states, two flip-flops, Q_1 and Q_2, will be used. A natural assignment of states to Q_1 and Q_2 is to let them have the same state as the outputs Z_1 and Z_2. Then no gates are required to produce Z_1 and Z_2 since the Q_1 and Q_2 outputs can be used for this purpose.

The resulting state table is shown in Fig. 4.27(c). The overall block diagram for the design is shown in Fig. 4.27(d). Only the gating network for the two D inputs to Q_1 and Q_2 needs to be designed since Z_1 and Z_2 are simply outputs from Q_1 and Q_2. The maps for these two inputs are shown in Fig. 4.27(e), and the final design is seen in Fig. 4.27(f).

COMMENTS—MEALY MACHINES

4.15 What have here been called state machines are also called *sequential machines*, *sequential systems*, *sequential circuits*, and *finite-state machines*. Many results in the theory of computing about what can and cannot be computed are concerned with what finite-state machines can compute. A finite-state machine

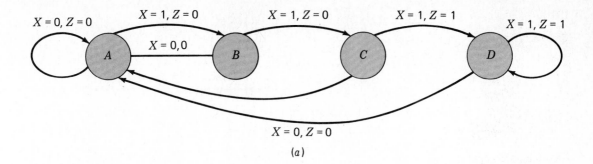

$X = 0, Z = 0$ $X = 1, Z = 0$ $X = 1, Z = 0$ $X = 1, Z = 1$ $X = 1, Z = 1$

$X = 0,0$

$X = 0, Z = 0$

(a)

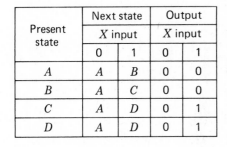

Present state	Next state		Output	
	X input		X input	
	0	1	0	1
A	A	B	0	0
B	A	C	0	0
C	A	D	0	1
D	A	D	0	1

(b)

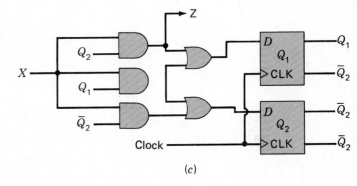

(c)

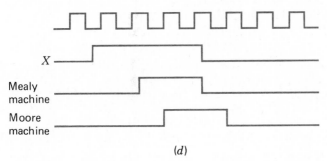

Mealy machine

Moore machine

(d)

FIGURE 4.28

Mealy machine design. (a) State diagram. (b) State table. (c) Design for Mealy version of sequence detector. (d) Waveforms for Mealy and Moore machine designs.

which can read a tape and write on it is called a *Turing machine*. If the supply of tape for this Turing machine is limitless (the tape is potentially infinite in length), there are many interesting results concerning what the machine can compute, some of which are due to Turing, a brilliant early 20th-century mathematician. The references discuss these results.

There are several variations on the state diagrams and design procedures which have been described. When the outputs are determined by only the state of the flip-flops, as in the two previous designs, the machine is called a *Moore machine,* in honor of Edward Moore. When the outputs are determined by the input value as well as the internal state, the machine is called a *Mealy machine.* Figure 4.28 shows a Mealy machine state diagram, state table, block diagram, and some

179

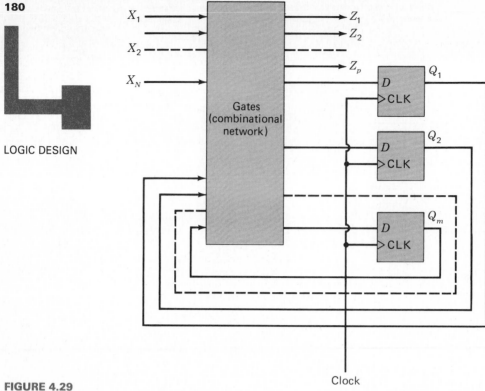

Clock

FIGURE 4.29

Block diagram of a
state machine.

output waveforms for a machine which is a sequential detector that looks for three
1s (as in Fig. 4.24). Note the output values are on the links, not the nodes, in Fig.
4.28(*a*).

Occasionally it is possible to reduce the number of states in a first design.
For completely specified tables, a technique for doing this was discovered by
Edward Moore. If not all next states and outputs are specified, the problem is much
harder, but Steve Unger solved this problem.[8]

The assignment of values to the flip-flops in the final design can influence
the number of gates used, but no one knows how to make the best assignment
short of trying every possible assignment. This is called the *assignment problem*.

PROGRAMMABLE ARRAYS OF LOGIC

*4.16   Integrated-circuit manufacturers have found natural ways to implement
layouts for state machines on IC chips. The regular shape of the state machine
with its gating array preceding the flip-flops makes for a rectangular and ordered

---

[8]Edward Moore did his work at Bell Laboratories and George Mealy at IBM. Both have changed jobs
but are still around, as is Steve Unger who is at Columbia. Detailed descriptions of their work can be
found in Birkhoff and Bartee or in Ed McClusky's book on switching theory.

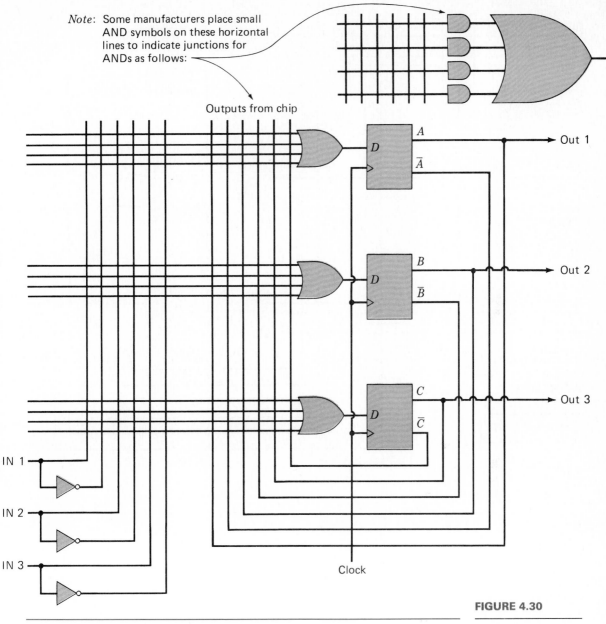

Note: Some manufacturers place small AND symbols on these horizontal lines to indicate junctions for ANDs as follows:

Outputs from chip

IN 1
IN 2
IN 3
Clock

Out 1
Out 2
Out 3

FIGURE 4.30

Programmable array of logic cells.

design for an integrated circuit. As a result, chips are available which can be used to implement state machine designs on a single chip (in a single IC package).

The basic idea is to present the designer with a layout for a design which is sufficiently flexible that most actual designs can be fabricated on this layout.

Figure 4.29 shows the basic block diagram for a state machine. What is needed is a set of flip-flops and a set of gates so that this general structure can be realized for many different designs. Figure 4.30 shows a programmable array of

181

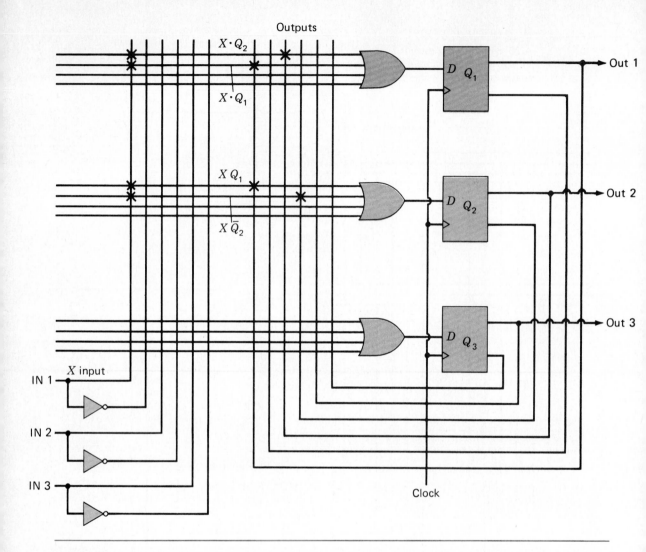

FIGURE 4.31

Design for state machine in Fig. 4.24 using PAL.

logic cells such that a state machine is formed by forming AND gates at the junctions of the vertical lines and connecting the horizontal lines to the OR gates. The particular array shown has three inputs, three flip-flops, and outputs from the flip-flops. The AND-to-OR gate networks are formed in the same way as for the PAL in Fig. 3.44; in fact, this particular array is called a PAL.

Figure 4.31 shows the design using the PAL in Fig. 4.30 for the sequence detector in Fig. 4.25. Since there are three flip-flops and three inputs in Fig. 4.31, only part of the logic in the figure is used. The idea, however, is that by working from a framework such as Fig. 4.31, most designs can be realized. Thus the manufacturer volume for the chip will be great enough that the cost per chip will be low enough to cost less than assembling a given design from several IC packages with fewer gates and flip-flops per package.

The actual IC packages on the market at present have several hundred gates and flip-flops per package. Sometimes there are several arrays in a single package and, therefore, the possibility to form several machines in a single IC container. Figure 4.32 shows a PAL layout for a state machine from a particular manufacturer.

The gating connection required for a particular design using the layout in Fig. 4.32 can be implemented in two ways: (1) The manufacturer works from a design submitted by the designer, in which case a particular mask or pattern is made for the design and is used for each chip manufactured. (2) The chip can be a user-programmable chip in which every possible connection is made and undesired connections are destroyed by the user (using high currents) blowing fuses in the undesired connections.[9]

Arrays of logic cells such as shown in Fig. 4.32 are becoming increasingly popular and frequently are used in commercial and laboratory equipment. Such *semicustom fabrication processes* are very popular in IC manufacture because of the very high cost of designing and manufacturing completely original, or custom, chips.

SUMMARY

4.17 Flip-flop operation was described along with the operation of the clocks used to initiate operations in computers. Often used flip-flops are the *RS, JK*, and *D* flip-flops; each was discussed. Latches were introduced.

Binary counters perform many useful functions in digital machines, and these were discussed in some detail. Also, BCD counters were covered.

The various classes of integrated circuits—medium-scale, large-scale, very large-scale—were described and the circuit lines used in IC packages listed along with their characteristics. A design for a shift register with feedback was implemented by using ICs from a very popular circuit line, TTL.

Sometimes flip-flops are made from gates. We detailed how this can be done for several kinds of flip-flops, including the *JK* edge-triggered flip-flop.

A counter which will count through a given sequence of states can be designed by using the procedure which was presented along with several example designs.

The design and analysis of state machines are facilitated by the use of state tables and state diagrams. A design procedure which can be used to implement a given state table or state diagram was presented.

Some integrated circuits are now being manufactured which are widely used to implement state machine designs because of their particular layout. These ICs enable designers to implement a given design by programming chips (1) by removing undesired connections by blowing fuses in the connections or (2) by submitting a design to a manufacturer, who then implements the design (using IC metallization masks which result in the desired connections being made). This class of ICs has a much higher packing density than IC packages with a few gates or flip-flops per package, costs are lower than for an original design using custom IC packages.

---

[9]This is called *programming* the chip. There are instruments made which allow the introduction of a particular design into a chip by blowing the selected fuses.

LOGIC DESIGN

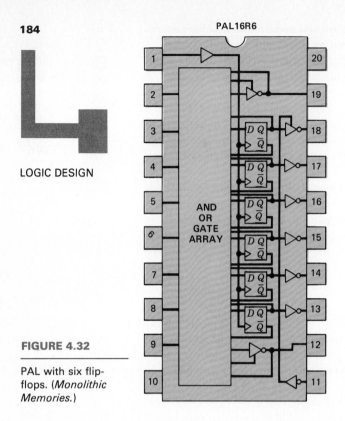

FIGURE 4.32

PAL with six flip-
flops. (*Monolithic
Memories.*)

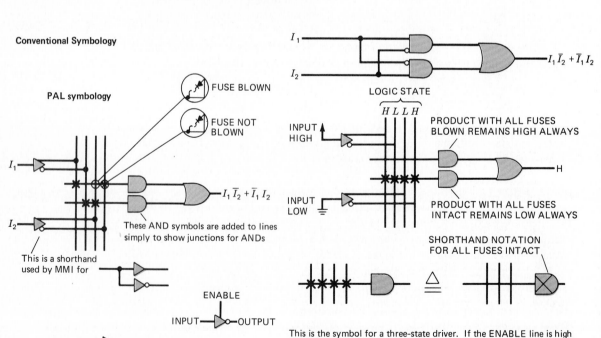

Conventional Symbology

PAL symbology

FUSE BLOWN

FUSE NOT
BLOWN

I_1

I_2

$I_1 \bar{I}_2 + \bar{I}_1 I_2$

These AND symbols are added to lines
simply to show junctions for ANDs

This is a shorthand
used by MMI for

In general a ▷ symbol represents
an amplifier which passes a larger signal at
the same level but with increased current drive.

ENABLE

INPUT ─▷○─ OUTPUT

I_1

I_2

$I_1 \bar{I}_2 + \bar{I}_1 I_2$

LOGIC STATE

$H\ L\ L\ H$

INPUT
HIGH

PRODUCT WITH ALL FUSES
BLOWN REMAINS HIGH ALWAYS

H

INPUT
LOW

PRODUCT WITH ALL FUSES
INTACT REMAINS LOW ALWAYS

SHORTHAND NOTATION
FOR ALL FUSES INTACT

This is the symbol for a three-state driver. If the ENABLE line is high
the OUTPUT will be the complement of the INPUT. If ENABLE is low
the OUTPUT will be at a high impedance and can be driven to any value
by another three-state driver. These are used on buses (see Chap. 8)

Logic diagram PAL16R6

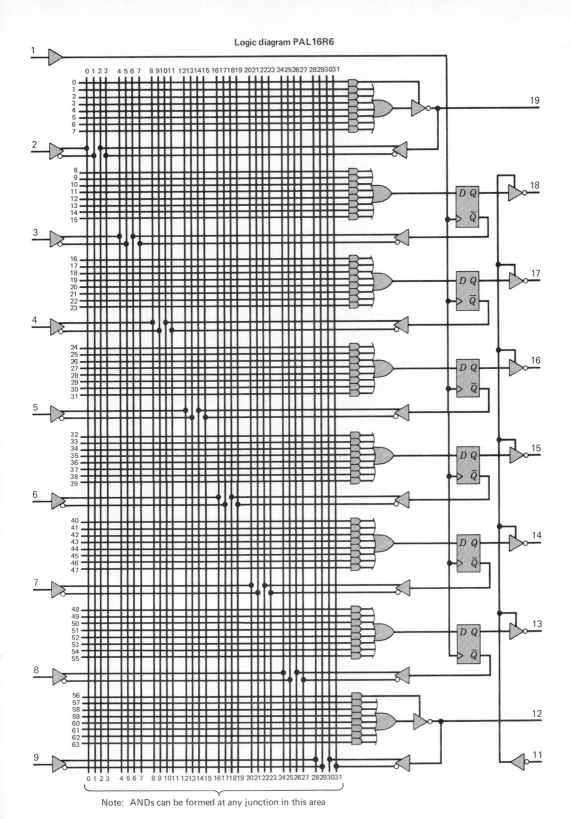

Note: ANDs can be formed at any junction in this area

4.1   Draw a set of waveforms for S and R and X and $\overline{X}$ (as in Fig. 4.2) so that the flip-flop in Fig. 4.1 will have the output signals 0011010 on the output line.

4.2   If the AND gate connected to the R input of X_1 in Fig. 4.3 fails so that its output is always 1, we would expect, after a few transfers, that X_1 would always be in what state? Why?

4.3   Draw a set of waveforms for S and R (as in Fig. 4.2) so that the flip-flop in Fig. 4.1 will have the output signals 101110001 on the X output line.

4.4   If the $\overline{X}$ output of flip-flop X is connected to an inverter, the inverter's output will always be the same as the X output of the flip-flop. True or false? Why?

4.5   Draw a set of waveforms as in Fig. 4.5(d) for the flip-flop in Fig. 4.5(b) so that the flip-flop will have the output signals 0010110 on its Y output line.

4.6   In Fig. 4.10 if flip-flop X_2 "sticks" (that is, fails) in its 0 state, will X_3 have a 1 output after (a) clock pulse 1, (b) clock pulse 2, (c) clock pulse 3 and for each clock pulse thereafter?

4.7   Draw an input waveform as in Fig. 4.10 so that X_3 will have the output signal 010011010 if X_1, X_2, and X_3 are started in the 0 state.

4.8   Draw a set of waveforms as in Fig. 4.5(c) for the flip-flop in Fig. 4.5(a) so that the flip-flop will have the output signals 10111001 on its X output line.

4.9   The binary counter in Fig. 4.11 uses flip-flops which act on positive transitions. Draw a block diagram of a binary counter with bubbles on the clock inputs (that is, with flip-flops which act on *negative*-going clock inputs).

4.10   If the X_3 line (the output of X_3) is connected to the input line in Fig. 4.10, a *ring counter* is formed. If this circuit is started with $X_1 = 0$, $X_2 = 1$, and $X_3 = 1$, draw the waveform at X_1, X_2, and X_3 for six clock pulses.

4.11   Redraw Fig. 4.11 as it is, but place bubbles on each clock input to X_1, X_2, and X_3 [that is, make the same drawing, but use the flip-flop in Fig. 4.5(b) instead of that in Fig. 4.5(a)]. Redraw the waveforms in Fig. 4.11 for this circuit.

4.12   Does the counter in Question 4.11 count up or down?

4.13   Make a single change in Fig. 4.11 by connecting the output of flip-flop X_2 to the clock input of X_3 instead of the $\overline{X}_2$ output of X_2. Now redraw the waveforms in Fig. 4.11 for this changed configuration.

4.14   After answering Question 4.13, using the flip-flop in Fig. 4.5(a), design a counter that counts as follows:

X_3	X_2	X_1
0	0	0
0	1	1
0	1	0
1	0	1
1	0	0
1	1	1
1	1	0
0	0	1
0	0	0
0	1	1
0	1	0
1	0	1
.	.	.

4.15 After answering Question 4.13, using only the flip-flop in Fig. 4.5(*a*), design a counter that counts as follows:

X_3	X_2	X_1
0	0	0
1	1	1
1	1	0
1	0	1
1	0	0
0	1	1
0	1	0
0	0	1
0	0	0
1	1	1

This counter counts *down*. Figure 4.11 counts *up*.

4.16 For Fig. 4.14(*b*) draw UP ENABLE, DOWN ENABLE, and clock waveforms so that the counter starts at 000 and counts as follows:

X_3	X_2	X_1
0	0	0
0	0	1
0	1	0
0	1	1
1	0	0
0	1	1
0	1	0
0	1	1

4.17 In Fig. 4.14(*a*), when the ENABLE line is a 1, the counter counts at the occurrence of a negative-going clock edge. Draw the output waveforms for FF0, FF1, and FF2 for these waveforms. Start the flip-flops at 0.

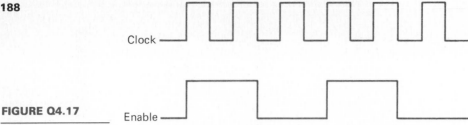

Clock

FIGURE Q4.17

Enable

4.18 Draw a clock waveform and waveforms for the output of the AND gate connected to the S input of X_1, the R input of X_2, and the 1 output of X_1, X_2, and X_3 for Fig. 4.12.

4.19 Suppose that the AND gate in Fig. 4.15(a) fails, so that its output is always a 0. Write the sequence or show the waveform through which this counter will go in response to clock signals.

4.20 Suppose that the AND gate's output in Fig. 4.15(a) is connected to the K input of X_4 instead of the J input. How will the computer count?

4.21 For Fig. 4.15(b), the carry-out from block 1 to block 2 goes from 1 to 0 every _____ clock pulses. The carry-out from block 3 to block 4 goes from 1 to 0 every _____ clock pulses.

4.22 (a) If we replace block 2 in Fig. 4.15(b) with the four-stage ripple counter in Fig. 4.14(a), using the 1 output of FF3 in that counter as the carry-out line, the carry-out line from block 2 will go from 1 to 0 after how many clock pulses?

(b) For the configuration in (a), after how many clock pulses will the carry-out from block 2 go from 0 to 1?

4.23 Using the circuits in Fig. 4.16, design a gated-clocked binary counter.

4.24 Design a BCD counter using the flip-flops in Fig. 4.16.

4.25 Using the circuits in Fig. 4.16, design a gating network with inputs A, B, and C which will have output 1 when $\overline{A}\overline{B}C$ or $AB\overline{C}$ are 1s.

4.26 Using the circuits in Fig. 4.16, design a BCD counter.

4.27 Using the circuits in Fig. 4.16, design a gate network with inputs A, B, and C and output $A\overline{B} + \overline{A}C$.

4.28 Does a four-input NAND gate, as in Fig. 4.16, with the third input held at 1, act as a three-input gate would if only two inputs were used? Explain your answer.

4.29 Design the counter in Fig. 4.12, using the blocks in Fig. 4.16.

4.30 Give the states of the flip-flops in the following circuit after each of the first five clock signals (pulses) are applied. The circuit is started in the state $A_1 = 0$, $A_2 = 0$, $A_3 = 1$.

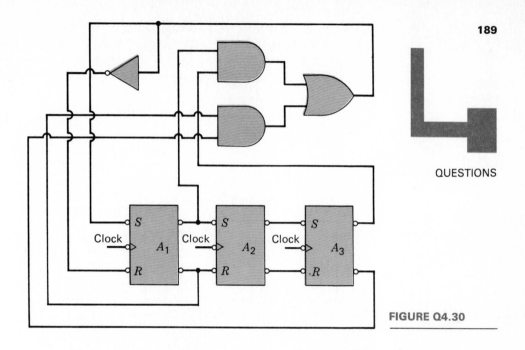

FIGURE Q4.30

4.31 Redesign the following circuit, using only *RS* flip-flops and NOR gates:

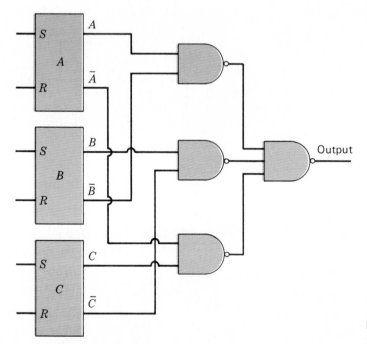

FIGURE Q4.31

4.32 The gate block in the following circuit is an "equal to" combinational network realizing the boolean function $\overline{X_3}\overline{X_2} + X_3X_2$. If this set of three flip-flops is started in $X_1 = 1$, $X_2 = 0$, and $X_3 = 0$, what will the sequence of internal states be? As a start, the first three states can be listed as follows:

X_1	X_2	X_3	
1	0	0	
1	1	0	after first clock pulse
0	1	1	after second clock pulse
.	.	.	(you are to continue this list)

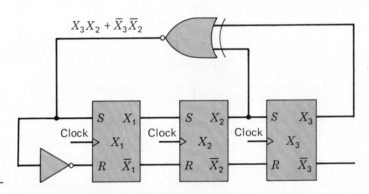

FIGURE Q4.32

4.33 The following circuit is started in $C_1 = 1$ and $C_2 = 0$. The circuit divides the number of positive-going input edges (positive pulses) by what number? (That is, every _____ input pulses the output will return to 0.) Justify your answer.

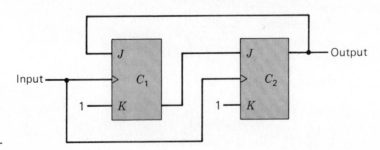

FIGURE Q4.33

4.34 In Fig. 4.9, write 0s and 1s for all gate inputs and outputs when the clock input is 1, R is a 1, S is a 1, and the flip-flop is in the 1 state.

4.35 In Fig. 4.9, why are E and F enabled at a lower level than A and B?

4.36 In Fig. 4.9, if the feedback connection from the C NAND gate output to the input of the D NAND gate is broken (open), in what state will we probably find the flip-flop?

4.37 Using your result from Question 4.34, explain how the flip-flop in Fig. 4.9 operates when R and S are 0s and a negative edge appears.

4.38 The following sequence is to be realized by a counter consisting of three *RS* flip-flops. Use AND and OR gates in your design.

	A_1	A_2	A_3	
	0	0	0	starting state
	0	1	0	
Sequence repeats after this segment	0	1	1	
	0	0	1	
	1	0	0	
	1	1	0	
	0	0	0	
	.	.	.	

4.39 Design a counter, using only *JK* flip-flops, AND gates, and OR gates which counts in the following sequence:

0	0	0	
0	1	0	
0	1	1	this repeats
1	0	0	
0	0	0	
0	1	0	
0	1	1	
1	0	0	
0	0	0	

4.40 Design a counter, using three *JK* flip-flops X_1, X_2, and X_3 and whatever gates you would like, which counts as follows:

X_1	X_2	X_3	
0	0	0	starting state
0	1	1	after first clock pulse
0	1	0	after second clock pulse
1	1	1	after third clock pulse
1	0	1	after fourth clock pulse
0	0	0	after fifth clock pulse
0	1	1	
0	1	0	

4.41 The following sequence is to be realized by a counter consisting of three *JK* flip-flops. Use AND and OR gates in your design.

	A_1	A_2	A_3	
	0	0	0	starting state
	0	1	1	
	0	1	0	
Sequence repeats after this segment	0	0	1	
	1	0	1	
	1	1	0	
	0	0	0	

4.42 If the *S* and *R* inputs to Fig. 4.7 are both made 0s and the *S* is made a 1 followed by *R*, what will be the resulting state of the flip-flop?

4.43 The NAND gate flip-flop in Fig. 4.7 will have what outputs on the 0 and 1 lines if both SET and RESET are made 0s?

4.44 Design a counter, using three JK flip-flops X_1, X_2, and X_3 and whatever gates you would like, which counts as follows:

X_1	X_2	X_3	
0	0	1	starting state
0	1	1	after first clock pulse
0	1	0	after second clock pulse
1	1	1	after third clock pulse
1	0	1	after fourth clock pulse
0	0	1	after fifth clock pulse
0	1	1	
0	1	0	

4.45 The rules for designing counters using JK and RS flip-flops have been given. Derive the rules for designing a counter using D flip-flops.

4.46 Design a counter using D flip-flops which counts in the same manner as the example given for JK and RS flip-flops.

4.47 Design a binary sequence detector which recognizes four consecutive 1s. Display the state diagram, state table, and final design.

4.48 Using the PAL in Fig. 4.30, design a state machine which realizes this state diagram:

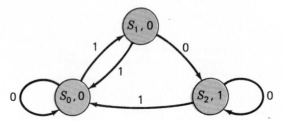

FIGURE Q4.48

4.49 Design a state machine which realizes this state diagram:

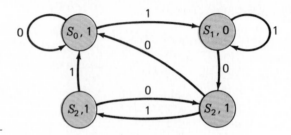

FIGURE Q4.49

4.50 Design a two-input magnitude comparator, but use the Mealy configuration instead of the Moore configuration shown in Figure 4.28.

THE ARITHMETIC-LOGIC UNIT

The arithmetic-logic unit (ALU) is the section of the computer that performs arithmetic and logical operations on the data. This section of the machine can be relatively small, consisting of as little as a part of a large-scale integration (LSI) chip, or, for large "number crunchers" (scientific-oriented computers), it can consist of a considerable array of high-speed logic components. Despite the variations in size and complexity, the small machines perform their arithmetic and logical operations using the same principles as the large machines. What changes is the speed of the logic gates and flip-flops used; also, special techniques are used for speeding up operations and performing several operations in parallel.

Although many functions can be performed by the ALUs of present-day machines, the basic arithmetic operations—addition, subtraction, multiplication, and division—continue to be "bread-and-butter" operations. Even the literature gives evidence of the fundamental nature of these operations, for when a new machine is described, the times required for addition and multiplication are always included as significant features. Accordingly, this chapter first describes the means by which a computer adds, subtracts, multiplies, and divides. Other basic operations, such as shifting, logical multiplication, and logical addition, are then described.

Remember that the control unit directs the operation of the ALU. What the ALU does is to add, subtract, shift, etc., when it is provided with the correct sequence of input signals. It is up to the control element to provide these signals, and it is the function of the memory units to provide the arithmetic element with the information that is to be used. These sections of the computer are discussed in Chaps. 6 and 9.

**THE ARITHMETIC-
LOGIC UNIT**

1   Most arithmetic operations are based on the use of a full-adder module which can add pairs of binary bits and initiate and propagate any carries that arise. The full-adder is explained, and several examples are given, including several popular IC adders.

2   The addition and subtraction of binary numbers can be effected by using adders and gates correctly connected. The layouts for 2s complement and 1s complement addition-subtraction units are shown and the general principles explained.

3   Binary-coded-decimal (BCD) adders and subtracters use a different layout than straight binary, and this subject is explained. Serial-parallel addition and subtraction using only a single BCD adder is often used in computers, and this subject is explained and examples are shown.

4   Multiplication and division are generally performed using three flip-flop registers and a sequence of addition, subtraction, and shift operations. The procedures for the operations are explained and examples given. High-speed multiplication using gate networks is covered also.

5   Arithmetic-logic units which can add, subtract, and perform logical operations form the backbone for the arithmetic and control operations in computers. The organization of these units is explained.

6   To perform scientific calculations, the floating-point number system is often used, particularly when high-level languages are written by the programmer. The structure of floating-point number systems is shown, and several example systems are explained.

CONSTRUCTION OF THE ALU

5.1   The information handled in a computer is generally divided into ''words,'' each consisting of a fixed number of bits.[1] For instance, the words handled by a given binary machine may be 32 bits in length. In this case, the ALU would have to be capable of adding, subtracting, etc., words 32 bits in length. The operands used are supplied to the ALU, and the control element directs the operations that are performed. If addition is to be performed, the addend and augend will be supplied to the ALU which must add the numbers and then, at least temporarily, store the results (sum).

   To introduce several concepts, let us consider the construction of a typical computer ALU. The storage devices will consist of a set of flip-flop *registers,* each of which consists of one or more flip-flops. For convenience, the various registers of the ALU are generally given names such as X register, B register, MQ register, etc., and the flip-flops are then given the same names, so that the X register would contain flip-flops X_1, X_2, X_3, etc.

   Many computers (especially microprocessors) have a register called an *accumulator* which is the principal register for arithmetic and logical operations. This

---

[1]Some computers also provide the ability to handle variable-length operands.

register stores the result of each arithmetic or logical operation, and gating circuitry is attached to the register so that the necessary operations can be performed on its contents and any other registers involved.

An accumulator is a basic storage register of the arithmetic element. If the machine is instructed to *load* the accumulator, the control element will first clear the accumulator of whatever may have been stored in it and then put the operand selected in storage into the accumulator register. If the computer is instructed to *add,* the number stored in the accumulator will represent the augend. Then the addend will be located in memory, and the computer's circuitry will add this number (the addend) to the number previously stored in the accumulator (the augend) and store the sum in the accumulator. Notice that the original augend will no longer be stored in the accumulator after the addition. Furthermore, the sum may either remain in the accumulator or be transferred to memory, depending on the type of computer. In this chapter we deal only with the processes of adding, subtracting, etc., and not the process of locating the number to be added in memory or the transferring of numbers to memory. These operations are covered in the following chapters.

There is now a tendency for computers to have more than one accumulator. When a computer has more than one, they are often named, for example, accumulator *A* and accumulator *B* (as in the 6800 microprocessor) or ACC1, ACC2, etc. (as in the Data General Corporation computers). When the number of registers provided to hold operands becomes larger than four, however, the registers are often called *general registers,* and individual registers are given names and numbers such as general register 4, general register 8, etc.

INTEGER REPRESENTATION

5.2 The numbers used in digital machines must be represented by using such storage devices as flip-flops. The most direct number representation system for binary-valued storage devices is an integer representation system. Figure 5.1(a) shows a register of four flip-flops, X_3, X_2, X_1, and X_0, used to store numbers.

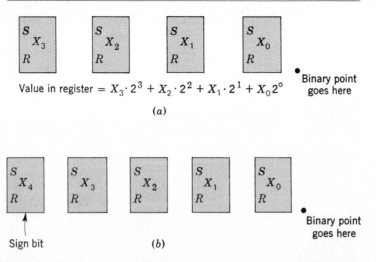

FIGURE 5.1

Representation systems. (*a*) Integer representation. (*b*) Sign-plus-magnitude system.

Value in register = $X_3 \cdot 2^3 + X_2 \cdot 2^2 + X_1 \cdot 2^1 + X_0 2^0$ Binary point goes here

(*a*)

Sign bit   (*b*)   Binary point goes here

THE ARITHMETIC-
LOGIC UNIT

Simply writing the values or states of the flip-flops gives the number in integer form. Thus $X_3 = 1, X_2 = 1, X_1 = 0, X_0 = 0$ gives 1100, or decimal 12, whereas $X_3 = 0, X_2 = 1, X_1 = 0, X_0 = 1$ gives 0101, or decimal 5.

It is generally necessary to represent both positive and negative numbers; so an additional bit is required, called the *sign bit*. This is generally placed to the left of the magnitude bits. In Fig. 5.1(*b*) X_4 is the sign bit, and so X_3, X_2, X_1, and X_0 will give the magnitude. A 0 in X_4 means that the number is positive, and a 1 in X_4 means that the number is negative (this is the usual convention).[2] So $X_4 = 0$, $X_3 = 1, X_2 = 1, X_1 = 0$, and $X_0 = 1$ gives positive 1101, or $+13$ in decimal; and $X_4 = 1, X_3 = 1, X_2 = 1, X_1 = 0$, and $X_0 = 1$ gives negative 1101, or -13 in decimal.

This system is called the *signed-integer binary system,* or *signed-magnitude binary integer system*. If a register contains eight flip-flops, a signed binary number in the system would have 7 magnitude, or integer, bits and a single sign bit. So 00001111 would be $+15$, and 10001111 would be -15, since the leading 0 and 1 indicate the plus and minus signs only.

The magnitude of numbers which can be stored in the two representation systems in Fig. 5.1 are as follows:

1   For binary integer representation, an *n*-flip-flop register can store from (decimal) 0 to $2^n - 1$. A 6-bit register can therefore store from 000000 to 111111, where 111111 is 63, which is $2^6 - 1$, or $64 - 1$.

2   The signed binary integer representation system has a range of $-(2^{n-1} - 1)$ to $+(2^{n-1} - 1)$ for a binary register. For instance, a seven-flip-flop register can store from -111111 to $+111111$, which is -63 to $+63$ [$(2^6 - 1)$ to $+ (2^6 - 1)$].

In the following sections we learn how to perform various arithmetic and logical operations on registers.

BINARY HALF-ADDER

5.3   A basic module used in binary arithmetic elements is the *half-adder*. The function of the half-adder is to add two binary digits, producing a sum and a carry according to the binary addition rules shown in Table 5.1. Figure 5.2 shows a design for a half-adder. There are two inputs to the half-adder, designated X and Y in Fig. 5.2, and two outputs, designated S and C. The half-adder performs the binary addition operation for two binary inputs shown in Table 5.1. This is arithmetic addition, not logical or boolean algebra addition.

As shown in Fig. 5.2, there are two inputs to the half-adder and two outputs. If either of the inputs is a 1 but not both, then the output on the S line will be a 1. If both inputs are 1s, the output on the C (for carry) line will be a 1. For all

---

[2]Some companies number registers with the sign bit A_0 the most significant bit A, and so on to the least significant bit A_n is a register with $n + 1$ bits. IBM does this for some of its computers, for example.

TABLE 5.1	
INPUT	SUM BITS
0 + 0	0
0 + 1	1
1 + 0	1
1 + 1	0 with a carry of 1

FULL-ADDER

other states, there will be a 0 output on the CARRY line. These relationships may be written in boolean form as follows:

$$S = X\overline{Y} + \overline{X}Y$$
$$C = XY$$

A *quarter-adder* consists of the two inputs to the half-adder and the S output only. The logical expression for this circuit is, therefore, $S = X\overline{Y} + \overline{X}Y$. This is also the *exclusive OR* relationship for boolean algebra (refer to Chap. 3).

FULL-ADDER

5.4 When more than two binary digits are to be added, several half-adders will not be adequate, for the half-adder has no input to handle carries from other digits.

Consider the addition of the following two binary numbers:

$$
\begin{array}{r}
1011 \\
+\ 1110 \\
\hline
11001\ =\ \text{sum}
\end{array}
\qquad
\begin{array}{r}
1011 \\
+\ 1110 \\
\hline
0101\ =\ \text{partial sum} \\
1\ 1\ =\ \text{carry bits} \\
\hline
11001\ =\ \text{complete sum}
\end{array}
$$

FIGURE 5.2

Half-adder.

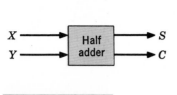

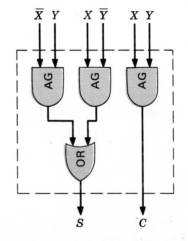

THE ARITHMETIC-
LOGIC UNIT

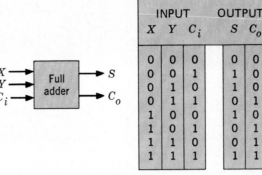

INPUT			OUTPUT	
X	Y	C_i	S	C_o
0	0	0	0	0
0	0	1	1	0
0	1	0	1	0
0	1	1	0	1
1	0	0	1	0
1	0	1	0	1
1	1	0	0	1
1	1	1	1	1

$$S = \overline{X}\,\overline{Y}C_i + \overline{X}Y\overline{C}_i + X\overline{Y}\,\overline{C}_i + XYC_i$$
$$C_o = \overline{X}YC_i + X\overline{Y}C_i + XY\overline{C}_i + XYC_i$$
or
$$C_o = XC_i + XY + YC_i$$

FIGURE 5.3

Full-adder.

As shown, the carries generated in each column must be considered during the addition process. Therefore adder circuitry capable of adding the contents of two registers must include provision for handling carries as well as addend and augend bits. So there must be three inputs to each stage of a multidigit adder—except the stage for the least significant bits—one for each input from the numbers being added and one for any carry that might have been generated or propagated by the previous stage.

The block diagram symbol for a *full binary adder,* which will handle these carries, is illustrated in Fig. 5.3, as is the complete table of input-output relationships for the full-adder. There are three inputs to the full-adder: the X and Y inputs from the respective digits of the registers to be added and the C_i input, which is for any carry generated by the previous stage. The two outputs are S, which is the output value for that stage of the addition, and C_o, which produces the carry to be added into the next stage.[3] The boolean expressions for the input-output relationships for each of the two outputs are also presented in Fig. 5.3, as is the expression for the C_o output in simplified form.

A full-adder may be constructed of two half-adders, as illustrated in Fig. 5.4. Constructing a full-adder from two half-adders may not be the most economical technique, however; generally full-adders are designed directly from the input-output relations illustrated in Fig. 5.3.

A PARALLEL BINARY ADDER

5.5 A 4-bit parallel binary adder is illustrated in Fig. 5.5. The purpose of this adder is to add two 4-bit binary integers. The addend inputs are named X_0 through X_3, and the augend bits are represented by Y_0 through Y_3.[4] The adder shown does

---

[3]C_i is for *carry-in* and C_o for *carry-out*.
[4]These inputs would normally be from flip-flop registers X and Y, and the adder would add the number in X to the number in Y, giving the sum, or S_0 through S_3.

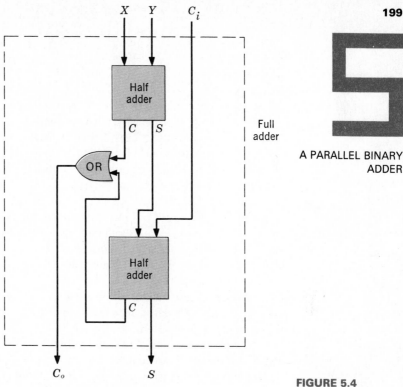

A PARALLEL BINARY
ADDER

FIGURE 5.4

Half-adder and full-
adder relations.

not possess the ability to handle sign bits for the binary words to be added, but
only adds the magnitudes of the numbers stored. The additional circuitry needed
to handle sign bits is dependent on whether negative numbers are represented in
true magnitude or in the 1s or 2s complement systems, and this problem is described
later.

FIGURE 5.5

Parallel adder.

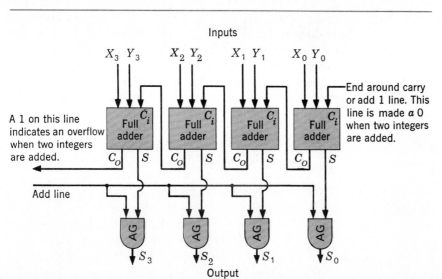

Consider the addition of the following two 4-bit binary numbers:

$$0111 \quad \text{where } X_3 = 0, X_2 = 1, X_1 = 1, \text{ and } X_0 = 1$$
$$0011 \quad \text{where } Y_3 = 0, Y_2 = 0, Y_1 = 1, \text{ and } Y_0 = 1$$
$$\text{Sum} = 1010$$

The sum should therefore be $S_3 = 1$, $S_2 = 0$, $S_1 = 1$, and $S_0 = 0$.

The operation of the adder may be checked as follows. Since X_0 and Y_0 are the least significant digits, they cannot receive a carry from a previous stage. In the problem above, X_0 and Y_0 are both 1s, their sum is therefore 0, and a carry is generated and added into the full-adder for bits X_1 and Y_1. Bits X_1 and Y_1 are also both 1s, as is the carry input to this stage. Therefore, the sum output line S_1 carries a 1, and the CARRY line to the next stage also carries a 1. Since X_2 is a 1, Y_2 is a 0, and the carry input is 1, the sum output line S_2 will carry a 0, and the carry to the next stage will be a 1. Both inputs X_3 and Y_3 are equal to 0, and the CARRY input line to this adder stage is equal to 1. Therefore, the sum output line S_3 will represent a 1, and the CARRY output line, designated as "overflow" in Fig. 5.5, will have a 0 output.

The same basic configuration illustrated in Fig. 5.5 may be extended to any number of bits. A 7-bit adder may be constructed by using 7 full-adders, and a 20-bit adder by using 20 full-adders.

Note that the OVERFLOW line could be used to enable the 4-bit adder in Fig. 5.5 to have a 5-bit output. This is not generally done, however, because the addend and augend both come from storage, and so their length is the length of the basic computer word, and a longer word cannot be readily stored by the machine. It was explained earlier that a machine with a word length of n bits (consisting of sign bit and $n - 1$ bits to designate the magnitude) could express binary numbers from $-2^{n-1} + 1$ to $2^{n-1} - 1$. A number within these limits is called *representable*. Since the simple 4-bit adder in Fig. 5.5 has no sign bit, it can represent only binary integers from 0 to 15. If 1100 and 1100 are added in the adder illustrated in Fig. 5.5, there will be a 1 output on the OVERFLOW line because the sum of these two numbers is 11000. This number is 24 decimal and cannot be represented in this system. Such a number is referred to as *nonrepresentable* for this particular very small register. When two integers are added such that their sum is nonrepresentable (that is, contains too many bits), then we say the sum *overflows,* or an *overflow* occurs and a 1 on the CARRY line for the full-adder connected to the most significant digits indicates this.

The AND gates connected to the S output lines from the four adders are used to gate the sum into the correct register.

POSITIVE AND NEGATIVE NUMBERS

5.6 When numbers are written in the decimal system, the common practice is to write the number as a magnitude preceded by a plus or minus sign, which indicates whether the number is positive or negative. Hence $+125$ is positive and -125 is negative. The same practice is generally used with binary numbers: $+111$ is positive 7, and -110 is negative 6. To handle both positive and negative numbers, the computer must have some means of distinguishing a positive from a negative number. And, as previously explained, the computer word usually contains a sign bit, generally adjacent to the most significant bit in the computer word. In the systems to be described, a 1 in the sign bit will indicate a negative number and a 0 in the sign bit a positive number.

We have examined the representation of numbers in Sec. 5.1 by using a signed-integer magnitude representation system. Two other representation systems, however, are used more often—the 1s and 2s complement systems. (The 2s complement system is the most frequently used at present.) The advantage of these systems is that both positive and negative numbers can be added or subtracted by using only an adder of the type already explained.

Here are the three basic systems.

1   Negative numbers may be stored in their *true magnitude form*. Thus the binary number -0011 will be stored as $\underline{1}0011$, where the $\underline{1}$ indicates that the number stored is negative and the 0011 indicates the magnitude of the number.[5]

2   The *1s complement* of the magnitude may be used to represent a negative number. The binary number -0111 will, therefore, be represented as $\underline{1}1000$, where the $\underline{1}$ indicates that the number is negative and 1000 is the 1s complement of the magnitude. (The 1s complement is formed by simply complementing each bit of the positive magnitude.)

3   The *2s complement* may be used to represent a negative binary number. For instance, -0111 would be stored as $\underline{1}1001$, where the 1 in the sign bit indicates that the number is negative and the 1001 is the 2s complement of the magnitude of the number. (The 2s complement is formed by 1s-complementing the magnitude part 0111, giving 1000, and then adding 1 to the least significant digit, giving 1001.)

ADDITION IN THE 1S COMPLEMENT SYSTEM

5.7   The 1s complement system for representing negative numbers is often used in parallel binary machines. The main reason is the ease with which the 1s complement of a binary number may be formed, since only complementing each bit of a binary number stored in a flip-flop register is required. Before we discuss the implementations of an adder for the 1s complement system, we note the four possible basic situations which may arise in adding combinations of positive and negative numbers in the 1s complement system:

1   When a positive number is added to another positive number, the addition of all bits, including the sign bit, is straightforward. Since both sign bits will be

---

[5]Again we note that an underscore __ is used to separate the sign bit from the magnitude bits. Thus $\underline{0}011$ is $+3$. The sign bit is simply stored in a flip-flop in the computer as are the other bits; so this is simply a notational convention and is used to indicate signed numbers.

THE ARITHMETIC-
LOGIC UNIT

0s, no sum or carry will be generated in the sign-bit adder and the output will remain 0. Here is an example of the addition of two 4-bit positive numbers.[6]

	NORMAL NOTATION	COMPUTER WORD
	$+0011$	$\underline{0}0011$
	$+0100$	$\underline{0}0100$
	$+0111$	$\underline{0}0111$

2   When a positive and a negative number are added, the sum may be either positive or negative. If the positive number has a greater magnitude, the sum will be positive; and if the negative number is greater in magnitude, the sum will be negative. In the 1s complement system, the answer will be correct as is if the sum of the two numbers is negative in value. In this case no overflow will be generated when the numbers are added. For instance,

$$
\begin{array}{cc}
+0011 & \underline{0}0011 \\
-1100 & \underline{1}0011 \\
\hline
-1001 & \underline{1}0110
\end{array}
$$

In this case, the output of the adder will be 10110, the last 4 bits of which are the 1s complement of 1001, the correct magnitude of the sum. The 1 in the sign bit is also correct, indicating a negative number.

3   If the positive number is larger than the negative number, the sum before the end-around carry is added will be incorrect. The addition of the end-around carry will correct this sum. There will be a 0 in the sign bit, indicating that the sum is positive.

$$
\begin{array}{cccc}
+1001 = \underline{0}1001 & \qquad & +0011 = \underline{0}0011 \\
-0100 = \underline{1}1011 & \qquad & -0010 = \underline{1}1101 \\
\hline
+0101 \quad \underline{0}0100 & & +0001 \quad \underline{0}0000 \\
\quad\quad \longrightarrow 1 & & \quad\quad \longrightarrow 1 \\
\hline
\underline{0}0101 & & \underline{0}0001
\end{array}
$$

Notice what happens when two numbers of equal magnitude but opposite signs are added:

$$
\begin{array}{cccc}
+1011 = \underline{0}1011 & \qquad & +0000 = \underline{0}0000 \\
-1011 = \underline{1}0100 & \qquad & -0000 = \underline{1}1111 \\
\hline
0000 \quad \underline{1}1111 & & 0000 \quad \underline{1}1111
\end{array}
$$

The result in these cases will be a negative zero ($\underline{1}1111$), which is correct.

4   When two negative numbers are added, an end-around carry will always be generated, as will a carry from the adder for the first bits of the magnitudes of the numbers. This will place a 1 in the sign bit.

---

[6]In this, and in all discussions that follow, we assume that the result (sum) does not exceed the capacity of the number of digits being used. This is discussed later.

$$
\begin{array}{llll}
-0011 = & \underline{1}1100 & -0100 = & \underline{1}1011 \\
-1011 = & \underline{1}0100 & -0111 = & \underline{1}1000 \\
\hline
-1110 \quad & \underline{1}0000 & -1011 \quad & \underline{1}0011 \\
& \xrightarrow{\qquad} 1 & & \xrightarrow{\qquad} 1 \\
& \underline{1}0001 & & \underline{1}0100
\end{array}
$$

The output of the adder will be in 1s complement form in each case, with a 1 in the sign-bit position.

From the above we see that in order to implement an adder which will handle 4-bit magnitude signed 1s complement numbers, we can simply add another full-adder to the configuration in Fig. 5.5. The sign inputs will be labeled X_4 and Y_4, and the C_o output from the adder connected to X_3 and Y_3 will be connected to the C_i input of the new full-adder for X_4 and Y_4. The C_o output from the adder for X_4 and Y_4 will be connected to the C_i input for the adder for X_0 and Y_0. The S_4 output from the new adder will give the sign digit for the sum. (Overflow will not be detected in this adder; additional gates are required.)

ADDITION IN THE 2S COMPLEMENT SYSTEM

5.8 When negative numbers are represented in the 2s complement system, the operation of addition is very similar to that in the 1s complement system. In parallel machines, the 2s complement of a number stored in a register may be formed by first complementing the register and then adding 1 to the least significant bit of the register. This process requires two steps and so is more time-consuming[7] than the 1s complement system. However, the 2s complement system has the advantage of not requiring an end-around carry during addition.

Four situations may occur in adding two numbers when the 2s complement system is used:

1   When both numbers are positive, the situation is completely identical with that in case 1 in the 1s complement system.

2   When one number is positive and the other negative, and the large number is the positive number, a carry will be generated through the sign bit. This carry may be discarded, since the outputs of the adder are correct, as shown below:

$$
\begin{array}{llll}
+0111 = & \underline{0}0111 & +1000 = & \underline{0}1000 \\
-0011 = & +\underline{1}1101 & -0111 = & +\underline{1}1001 \\
\hline
+0100 \quad & \underline{0}0100 & +0001 \quad & \underline{0}0001 \\
& \text{carry is discarded} & & \text{carry is discarded}
\end{array}
$$

3   When a positive and negative number are added and the negative number is the larger, no carry will result in the sign bit, and the answer will again be correct as it stands:

---

[7]Generally this 1 is "sneaked in" during calculation, as will be shown.

$$\begin{array}{rl} +0011 = & \underline{0}0011 \\ -0100 = & \underline{1}1100 \\ \hline -0001 & \underline{1}1111 \end{array} \qquad \begin{array}{rl} +0100 = & \underline{0}0100 \\ -1000 = & \underline{1}1000 \\ \hline -0100 & \underline{1}1100 \end{array}$$

Note: A 1 must be added to the least significant bit of a 2s complement negative number in converting it to a magnitude. For example,

$$\begin{array}{rll} \underline{1}0011 = & 1100 & \text{form the 1s complement} \\ & \underline{0001} & \text{add 1} \\ \hline & -1101 & \end{array}$$

When both numbers are the same magnitude, the result is as follows:

$$\begin{array}{rl} +0011 = & \underline{0}0011 \\ -0011 = & \underline{1}1101 \\ \hline 0000 & \underline{0}0000 \end{array}$$

When a positive and a negative number of the same magnitude are added, the result will be a positive zero.

4   When two negative numbers are added, a carry will be generated in the sign bit and also in the bit to the right of the sign bit. This will cause a 1 to be placed in the sign bit, which is correct, and the carry from the sign bit may be discarded.

$$\begin{array}{rl} -0011 = & \underline{1}1101 \\ -0100 = & \underline{1}1100 \\ \hline -0111 & \text{┌}\underline{1}1001 \end{array} \qquad \begin{array}{rl} -0011 = & \underline{1}1101 \\ -1011 = & \underline{1}0101 \\ \hline -1110 & \text{┌}\underline{1}0010 \end{array}$$
$$\qquad\qquad\quad \text{└►carry is discarded} \qquad\qquad \text{└►carry is discarded}$$

For parallel machines, addition of positive and negative numbers is quite simple, since any overflow from the sign bit is simply discarded. Thus for the parallel adder in Fig. 5.5 we simply add another full-adder, with X_4 and Y_4 as inputs and with the CARRY line C_o from the full-adder, which adds X_3 and Y_3, connected to the carry input C_i to the full-adder for X_4 and Y_4. A 0 is placed on the C_i input to the adder connected to X_0 and Y_0.

This simplicity in adding and subtracting has made the 2s complement system the most popular for parallel machines. In fact, when signed-magnitude systems are used, the numbers generally are converted to 2s complement before addition of negative numbers or subtraction is performed. Then the numbers are changed back to signed magnitude.

ADDITION AND SUBTRACTION IN A PARALLEL ARITHMETIC ELEMENT

5.9   We now examine the design of a gating network which will either add or subtract two numbers. The network is to have an ADD input line and a SUBTRACT input line as well as the lines that carry the representation of the numbers to be added or subtracted. When the ADD line is a 1, the sum of the numbers is to be on the output lines; and when the SUBTRACT line is a 1, the difference is to be on the output lines. If both ADD and SUBTRACT are 0s, the output is to be 0.

First we note that if the computer is capable of adding both positive and negative numbers, subtraction may be performed by complementing the subtrahend and then adding. For instance, $8 - 4$ yields the same result as $8 + (-4)$, and $6 - (-2)$ yields the same result as $6 + 2$. Subtraction therefore may be performed by an arithmetic element capable of adding, by forming the complement of the subtrahend and then adding. For instance, in the 1s complement system, four cases may arise:

205

ADDITION AND
SUBTRACTION IN A
PARALLEL
ARITHMETIC
ELEMENT

TWO POSITIVE NUMBERS

$$\begin{array}{r} \underline{0}0011 \\ -\underline{0}0001 \end{array}$$

complementing the subtrahend and adding

$$\begin{array}{r} \underline{0}0011 \\ \underline{1}1110 \\ \hline 00001 \\ \text{carry } 1 \\ \hline \underline{0}0010 \end{array}$$

TWO NEGATIVE NUMBERS

$$\begin{array}{r} \underline{1}1101 \\ -\underline{1}1011 \end{array}$$

complementing

$$\begin{array}{r} \underline{1}1101 \\ \underline{0}0100 \\ \hline 00001 \\ \text{carry } 1 \\ \hline \underline{0}0010 \end{array}$$

POSITIVE MINUEND,
NEGATIVE SUBTRAHEND

$$\frac{\underline{0}0010}{-\underline{1}1101} = \frac{\underline{0}0010}{\underline{0}0010} \\ \overline{\underline{0}0100}$$

NEGATIVE MINUEND,
POSITIVE SUBTRAHEND

$$\frac{\underline{1}0101}{-\underline{0}0010} = \begin{array}{r} \underline{1}0101 \\ \underline{1}1101 \\ \hline 10010 \\ \text{carry } 1 \\ \hline \underline{1}0011 \end{array}$$

The same basic rules apply to subtraction in the 2s complement system, except that any carry generated in the sign-bit adders is simply dropped. In this case the 2s complement of the subtrahend is formed, and then the complemented number is added to the minuend with no end-around carry.

We now examine the implementation of a combined adder and subtracter network. The primary problem is to form the complement of the number to be subtracted. This complementation of the subtrahend may be performed in several ways. For the 1s complement system, if the storage register is composed of flip-flops, the 1s complement can be formed by simply connecting the complement of each input to the adder. The 1 which must be added to the least significant position to form a 2s complement may be added when the two numbers are added by connecting a 1 at the CARRY input of the adder for the least significant bits.

A complete logical circuit capable of adding or subtracting two signed 2s complement numbers is shown in Fig. 5.6. One number is represented by X_4, X_3, X_2, X_1, and X_0, and the other number by Y_4, Y_3, Y_2, Y_1, and Y_0. There are two

THE ARITHMETIC-
LOGIC UNIT

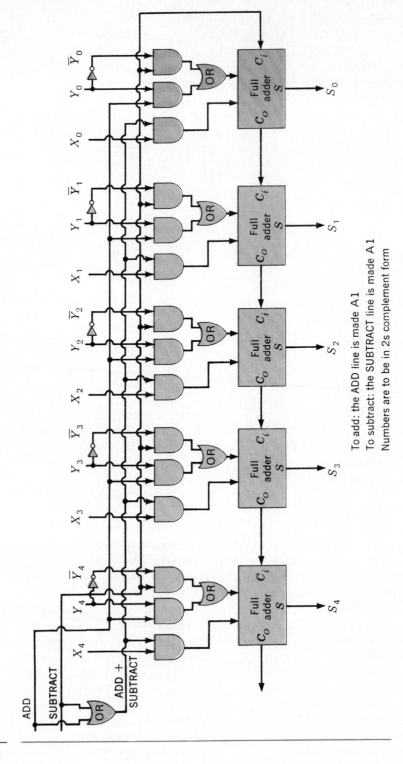

To add: the ADD line is made A 1
To subtract: the SUBTRACT line is made A 1
Numbers are to be in 2s complement form

FIGURE 5.6

Parallel addition and
subtraction.

control signals, ADD and SUBTRACT. If neither control signal is a 1 (that is, both are 0s), then the outputs from the five full-adders, which are S_4, S_3, S_2, S_1, and S_0, will all be 0s. If the ADD control line is made a 1, the sum of the number X and the number Y will appear as S_4, S_3, S_2, S_1, and S_0. If the SUBTRACT line is made a 1, the difference between X and Y (that is, $X - Y$) will appear on S_4, S_3, S_2, S_1, and S_0.

Notice that the AND-to-OR gate network connected to each Y input selects either Y or $\overline{Y}$, so that, for instance, an ADD causes Y_1 to enter the appropriate full-adder, while a SUBTRACT causes $\overline{Y}_1$ to enter the full-adder.

To either add or subtract, each X input is connected to the appropriate full-adder. When a subtraction is called for, the complement of each Y flip-flop is gated into the full-adder, and a 1 is added by connecting the SUBTRACT signal to the C_i input of the full-adder for the lowest order bits X_0 and Y_0. Since the SUBTRACT line will be a 0 when we add, a 0 carry will be on this line when addition is performed.

The simplicity of the operation of Fig. 5.6 makes 2s complement addition and subtraction very attractive for computer use, and it is the most frequently used system.[8]

The configuration in Fig. 5.6 is the most frequently used for addition and subtraction because it provides a simple, direct means for either adding or subtracting positive or negative numbers. Quite often the S_4, S_3, . . . , S_0 lines are gated back into the X flip-flops, so that the sum or difference of the numbers X and Y replaces the original value of X.

An important consideration is overflow. In digital computers, an *overflow* is said to occur when the performance of an operation results in a quantity beyond the capacity of the register (or storage register) which is to receive the result. Since the registers in Fig. 5.6 have a sign bit plus 4 magnitude bits, they can store from $+15$ to -16 in 2s complement form. Therefore, if the result of an addition or a subtraction were greater than $+15$ or less than -16, we would say that an overflow had occurred. Suppose we add $+8$ to $+12$; the result should be $+20$, and this cannot be represented (fairly) in 2s complement on the lines S_4, S_3, . . . , S_0. The same thing happens if we add -13 and -7 or if we subtract -8 from $+12$. In each case, logical circuitry is used to detect the overflow condition and signal the computer control element. Various options are then available, and what is done can depend on the type of instruction being executed. (Deliberate overflows are sometimes used in double-precision routines. Multiplication and division use the results as are.) We defer this topic to Chap 9. except that one of the questions at the end of the chapter asks for a circuit to test for overflow.

The parallel adder-subtracter configuration in Fig. 5.6 is quite important, and it is instructive to try adding and subtracting several numbers in 2s complement form, using pencil and paper and this logic circuit.

207

ADDITION AND
SUBTRACTION IN A
PARALLEL
ARITHMETIC
ELEMENT

---

[8]A 1s complement parrallel adder-subtracter can be made by connecting the CARRY-OUT line for the X_0, Y_0 adder to the CARRY-IN line for the X_4, Y_4 adder (disconnecting the SUBTRACT line to this full-adder, of course).

THE ARITHMETIC-
LOGIC UNIT

5.10 The full-adder is a basic component of an arithmetic element. Figure 5.3 illustrated the block diagram symbol for the full-adder, along with a table of combinations for the input-output values and the expressions describing the SUM and CARRY lines. Succeeding figures and text described the operation of the full-adder. Notice that a parallel addition system requires one full-adder for each bit in the basic word.

There are, of course, many gate configurations for full binary adders. Examples of an IBM adder and an MSI package containing two full-adders follow.

1 *Full binary adder* Figure 5.7 illustrates the full binary adder configuration used in several IBM general-purpose digital computers. There are three inputs to the circuit: The X input is from one of the storage devices in the accumulator, the Y input is from the corresponding storage device in the register to be added to the accumulator register, and the third input is the CARRY input from the adder for the next least significant bit. The two outputs are the SUM output and the CARRY output. The SUM output will contain the sum value for this particular digit of the output. The CARRY output will be connected to the CARRY input of the next most significant bit's adder (refer to Fig. 5.5).

FIGURE 5.7

Full-adder used in
IBM machines.

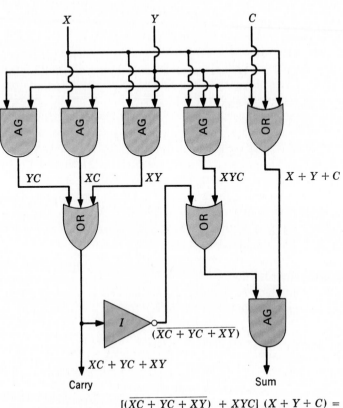

$$[(\overline{XC + YC + XY}) + XYC](X + Y + C) =$$
$$\overline{X}\,\overline{Y}C + \overline{X}Y\overline{C} + X\overline{Y}\,\overline{C} + XYC$$

The outputs from the three AND gates connected directly to the X, Y, and C inputs are logically added by the OR gate circuit directly beneath. If either the X and Y, X and C, or Y and C input lines contain a 1, there should be a carry output. The output of this circuit, written in logical equation form, is shown on the figure. This may be compared with the expression derived in Fig. 5.3.

The derivation of the SUM output is not so straightforward. The CARRY output expression $XY + XC + YC$ is first inverted (complemented), yielding $(\overline{XY + XC + YC})$. The logical product of X, Y, and C is formed by an AND gate and is logically added to this, forming $(\overline{XY + XC + YC}) + XYC$. The logical sum of X, Y, and C is then multiplied times this, forming the expression

$$[(\overline{XY + XC + YC}) + XYC](X + Y + C)$$

When it is multiplied out and simplified, this expression will be $\overline{X}\,\overline{Y}C + \overline{X}Y\overline{C} + X\overline{Y}\,\overline{C} + XYC$, the expression derived in Fig. 5.3. Tracing through the logical operation of the circuit for various values will indicate that the SUM output will be 1 when only one of the input values is equal to 1 or when all three input values are equal to 1. For all other combinations of inputs, the output value will be a 0.

2 *Two full-adders in an IC container* Figure 5.8 shows two full-adders. This package was developed for integrated circuits using transistor-transistor logic (TTL). The entire circuitry is packaged in one IC container. The maximum delay from an

FIGURE 5.8

Two full-adders in an IC container. (*Texas Instruments.*)

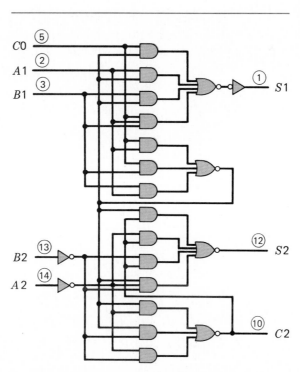

THE ARITHMETIC-
LOGIC UNIT

input change to an output change for an S output is on the order of 8 nanoseconds (ns).[9] The maximum delay from any input to the $C2$ output is about 6 ns.

The amount of delay associated with each carry is an important figure in evaluating a full-adder for a parallel system, because the time required to add two numbers is determined by the maximum time it takes for a carry to propagate through the adders. For instance, if we add 01111 to 10001 in the 2s complement system, the carry generated by the 1s in the least significant digit of each number must propagate through four carry stages and a sum stage before we can safely gate the sum into the accumulator. A study of the addition of these two numbers by using the configuration in Fig. 5.5 will make this clear. The problem is called the *carry-ripple problem*.

A number of techniques are used in high-speed machines to alleviate this problem. The most used is a bridging, or carry-look-ahead, circuit which calculates the carry-out of a number of stages simultaneously and then delivers this carry to the succeeding stages. (This is covered in a later section.)

BINARY-CODED-DECIMAL ADDER

5.11　Arithmetic units which perform operations on numbers stored in BCD form must have the ability to add 4-bit representations of decimal digits. To do this, a BCD adder is used. A block diagram symbol for an adder is shown in Fig. 5.9. The adder has an augend digit input consisting of four lines, an addend digit input of four lines, a carry-in and a carry-out, and a sum digit with four output lines. The augend digit, addend digit, and sum digit are each represented in 8, 4, 2, 1 BCD form.

The purpose of the BCD adder in Fig. 5.9 is to add the augend and addend digits and the carry-in and produce a sum digit and carry-out. This adder could be designed by using the techniques described in Chap. 3 and the rules for decimal

---

[9]1 ns $= 10^{-9}$ s.

FIGURE 5.9

Serial-parallel addition.

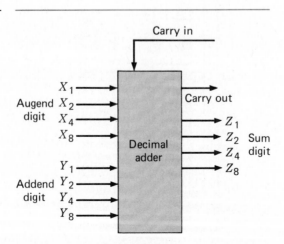

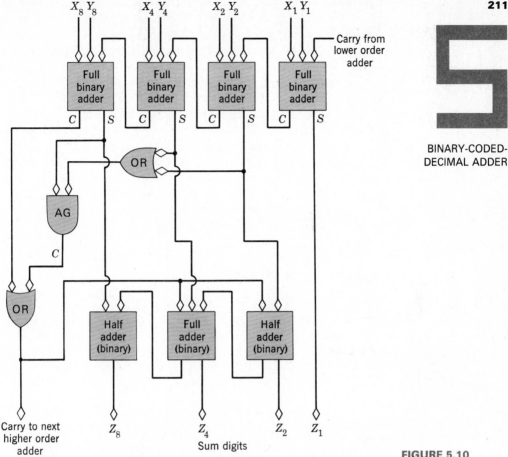

FIGURE 5.10

BCD adder.

addition. It is also possible to make a BCD adder by using full-adders and AND or OR gates. An adder made in this way is shown in Fig. 5.10.

There are eight inputs to the BCD adder; four X_i, or augend, inputs; and four Y_i, or addend, digits. Each input will represent a 0 or a 1 during a given addition. If 3 (0011) is to be added to 2 (0010), then $X_8 = 0$, $X_4 = 0$, $X_2 = 1$, and $X_1 = 1$; $Y_8 = 0$, $Y_4 = 0$, $Y_2 = 1$, and $Y_1 = 0$.

The basic adder in Fig. 5.10 consists of the four binary adders at the top of the figure and performs base-16 addition when the intent is to perform base-10 addition. Thus some provision must be made to (1) generate carries and (2) correct sums greater than 9. For instance, if 3_{10} (0011) is added to 8_{10} (1000), the result should be 1_{10} (0001) with a carry generated.

The actual circuitry which determines when a carry is to be transmitted to the next most significant digits to be added consists of both the full binary adder to which sum (S) outputs from the adders for the 8, 4, 2 inputs are connected and the OR gate to which the carry (C) from the eight-position bits is connected. An examination of the addition process indicates that a carry should be generated when

the 8 AND 4, or 8 AND 2, or 8 AND 4 AND 2 sum outputs from the base-16 adder represent 1s, or when the CARRY output from the eight-position adder contains a 1. (This occurs when 8s or 9s are added.)

Whenever the sum of two digits exceeds 9, the CARRY TO NEXT HIGHER ORDER ADDER line contains a 1 for the adder in Fig. 5.10.

A further difficulty arises when a carry is generated. If 7_{10} (0111) is added to 6_{10} (0110), a carry will be generated, but the output from the base-16 adder will be 1101. This 1101 does not represent any decimal digit in the 8, 4, 2, 1 system and must be corrected. The method used to correct this is to add 6_{10} (0110) to the sum from the base-16 adders whenever a carry is generated. This addition is performed by adding 1s to the weight 4 and weight 2 position output lines from the base-16 adder when a carry is generated. The two half-adder and the full-adders at the bottom of Fig. 5.10 perform this function. Essentially, then, the adder performs base-16 addition and corrects the sum, if it is greater than 9, by adding 6. Several examples of this are shown below.

$$8 + 7 = 15 \qquad 1000 + 0111 =$$

$$
\begin{array}{cccc}
(8) & (4) & (2) & (1) \\
1 & 1 & 1 & 1 \\
+\,0 & 1 & 1 & 0 \\
\hline
\end{array}
$$

$1 \quad 0 \quad 1 \quad 0 \quad 1 \; = 5$

└─with a carry generated

$$9 + 5 = 14$$

$$
\begin{array}{cccc}
(8) & (4) & (2) & (1) \\
1 & 0 & 0 & 1 \\
0 & 1 & 0 & 1 \\
\hline
1 & 1 & 1 & 0 \\
+\,0 & 1 & 1 & 0 \\
\hline
\end{array}
$$

$1 \quad 0 \quad 1 \quad 0 \quad 0 \; = 4$

└─with a carry generated

Figure 5.11 shows a complete BCD adder in an IC package.[10] The inputs are digits A and digits B, and the outputs are S. A carry-in and a carry-out are included. The circuit line used is CMOS.

POSITIVE AND NEGATIVE BCD NUMBERS

5.12 The techniques for handling BCD numbers greatly resemble those for handling binary numbers. A sign bit is used to indicate whether the number is positive or negative, and there are three methods of representing negative numbers which must be considered. The first and most obvious method is, of course, to represent a negative number in true magnitude form with a sign bit, so that -645 is rep-

---

[10]The IC packages in Figs. 5.11, 5.13, 5.14, and 5.15 are typical BCD MSI packages. The notation $A1, A2, A3, A4$ (instead of X_1, X_2, X_4, X_8) is often used for the 4 bits of a BCD digit, and the weights 1, 2, 4, 8 are understood. Thus a BCD digit in $B1, B2, B3, B4$ would have weight 1 on $B1$, weight 2 on $B2$, weight 4 on $B3$, and weight 8 on $B4$.

POSITIVE AND
NEGATIVE BCD
NUMBERS

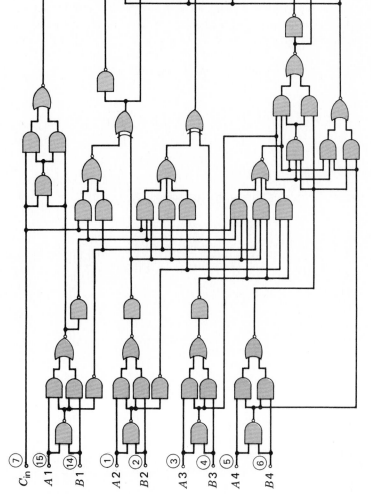

FIGURE 5.11

Complete BCD adder
in an IC package.

THE ARITHMETIC-
LOGIC UNIT

resented as $\underline{1}645$. The other two possibilities are to represent negative numbers in a 9s or a 10s complement form, which resembles the binary 1s and 2s complement forms.

ADDITION AND SUBTRACTION IN THE 9S COMPLEMENT SYSTEM

5.13 When decimal numbers are represented in a binary code in which the 9s complement is formed when the number is complemented, the situation is roughly the same as when the 1s complement is used to represent a binary number. Four cases may arise: Two positive numbers may be added; a positive and negative number may be added, yielding a positive result; a positive and negative number may be added, yielding a negative result; and two negative numbers may be added. Since there is no problem when two positive numbers are added, we illustrate the three latter situations.

NEGATIVE AND POSITIVE NUMBER—POSITIVE SUM

$$
\begin{array}{rcl}
+692 & = & \underline{0}692 \\
-342 & = & \underline{1}657 \\
\hline
+350 & & \underline{0}349 \\
& & \underline{1} \\
\hline
& & \underline{0}350
\end{array}
$$

POSITIVE AND NEGATIVE NUMBER—NEGATIVE SUM

$$
\begin{array}{rcl}
-631 & = & \underline{1}368 \\
+342 & = & \underline{0}342 \\
\hline
-289 & & \underline{1}710 = -289
\end{array}
$$

TWO NEGATIVE NUMBERS

$$
\begin{array}{rcl}
-248 & = & \underline{1}751 \\
-329 & = & \underline{1}670 \\
\hline
-577 & & \underline{1}421 \\
& & \underline{1} \\
\hline
& & \underline{1}422 = -577
\end{array}
$$

The rules for handling negative numbers in the 10s complement system are the same as those for the binary 2s complement system in that no carry must be ended-around. Therefore, a parallel BCD adder may be constructed by using only the full BCD adder as the basic component, and all combinations of positive and negative numbers may be handled thus.

There is an additional complexity in BCD addition, however, because the 9s complement of a BCD digit cannot be formed by simply complementing each bit in the representation. As a result, a gating block called a *complementer* must be used.

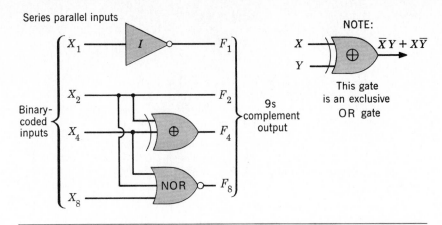

Series parallel inputs

Binary-coded inputs

9s complement output

NOTE:

$$\overline{X}Y + X\overline{Y}$$

This gate is an exclusive OR gate

FIGURE 5.12

Logic circuit for forming 9s complement of 8, 4, 2, 1 BCD digits.

To illustrate the type of circuit which may be used to form complements of the code groups for BCD numbers, a block diagram of a logical circuit which will form the 9s complement of a code group representing a decimal number in 8, 4, 2, 1 BCD form is shown in Fig. 5.12. There are four inputs to the circuit, X_1, X_2, X_4, and X_8. Each input carries a different weight: X_1 has weight 1, X_2 has weight 2, X_4 has weight 4, and X_8 has weight 8. If the inputs represent a decimal digit of the number to be complemented, the outputs will represent the 9s complement of the input digit. For instance, if the input is 0010 (decimal 2), the output will be 0111 (decimal 7), the 9s complement of the input.

Figure 5.13 shows a complete 9s complementer in an IC package. When the COMP input is a 1, the outputs $F1$–$F4$ represent the complement of the digit on $A1$–$A4$; but if COMP is a 0, the $A1$–$A4$ inputs are simply placed in $F1$–$F4$ without change.

By connecting the IC packages in Figs. 5.11 and 5.13, a BCD adder-subtracter can be formed as shown in Fig. 5.14. This shows a two-digit adder-subtracter IC package. To add the digits on the inputs, the ADD-SUBTRACT input is made a 1; to subtract, this signal is made a 0. (Making the ZERO input a 1 will cause the value of B to pass through unchanged.)

BCD numbers may be represented in parallel form, as we have shown, but a mode of operation called *series-parallel* is often used. If a decimal number is written in binary-coded form, the resulting number consists of a set of code groups, each of which represents a single decimal digit. For instance, decimal 463 in a BCD 8, 4, 2, 1 code is 0100 0110 0011. Each group of 4 bits represents one decimal digit. It is convenient to handle each code group which represents a decimal digit as a unit, that is, in parallel. At the same time, since the word lengths for decimal computation are apt to be rather long, it is desirable to economize in the amount of equipment used.

The *series-parallel* system provides a compromise in which each code group is handled in parallel, but the decimal digits are handled sequentially. This requires four lines for each 8, 4, 2, 1 BCD character, each input line of which carries a different weight. The block diagram for an adder operating in this system is shown

THE ARITHMETIC-
LOGIC UNIT

TRANSMISSION GATE

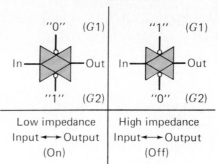

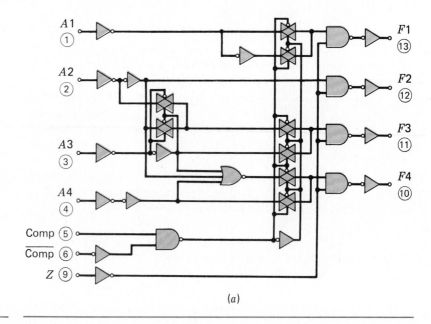

FIGURE 5.13

9s complementer in
IC package. (a) Logic
diagram. (b) Table of
combinations.

(a)

in Fig. 5.15. There are two sets of inputs to the adder; one consists of the four input lines which carry the coded digit for the addend, and the other four input lines carry a coded augend digit. The sets of inputs arrive sequentially from the A and B registers, each of which consists of four shift registers; the least significant addend and augend BCD digits arrive first, followed by the more significant decimal digits.

If the 8, 4, 2, 1 code is used, let 324 represent the augend and 238 the addend. The ADD signal will be a 0. First the adder will receive 0100 on the augend lines, and at the same time it will receive 1000 on the addend lines. After the first clock pulse, these inputs will be replaced by 0010 on the augend lines and

DECIMAL EQUIVALENT INPUT	A4	A3	A2	A1	DECIMAL EQUIVALENT OUTPUT	F1	F2	F3	F4
0	0	0	0	0	9	1	0	0	1
1	0	0	0	1	8	1	0	0	0
2	0	0	1	0	7	0	1	1	1
3	0	0	1	1	6	0	1	1	0
4	0	1	0	0	5	0	1	0	1
5	0	1	0	1	4	0	1	0	0
6	0	1	1	0	3	0	0	1	1
7	0	1	1	1	2	0	0	1	0
8	1	0	0	0	1	0	0	0	1
9	1	0	0	1	0	0	0	0	0
10	1	0	1	0	7	0	1	1	1
11	1	0	1	1	6	0	1	1	0
12	1	1	0	0	5	0	1	0	1
13	1	1	1	1	4	0	1	0	0
14	1	1	1	0	3	0	0	1	1
15	1	1	1	1	2	0	0	1	0

Illegal BCD input codes (rows 10–15)

(b)

FIGURE 5.13 (Cont.)

FIGURE 5.14

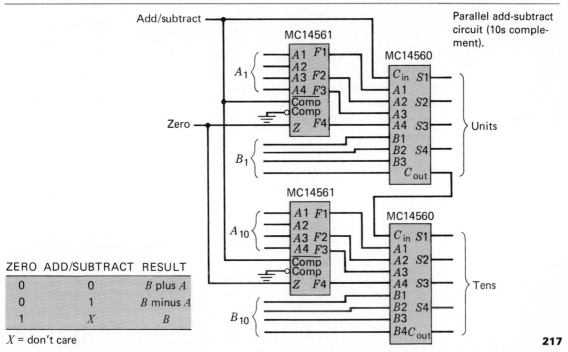

Parallel add-subtract circuit (10s complement).

ZERO	ADD/SUBTRACT	RESULT
0	0	B plus A
0	1	B minus A
1	X	B

X = don't care

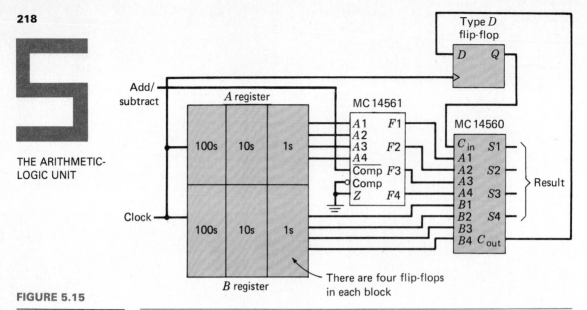

THE ARITHMETIC-LOGIC UNIT

FIGURE 5.15

Series-parallel BCD adder-subtracter using shift register.

0011 on the addend lines. Before the first clock signal, the sum lines should contain 0010; and before the second, 0110. A carry will be generated during the addition of the first two digits; this will be delayed and added in using the D flip-flop. The process will continue until each of the three digits has been added. To subtract B from A, we have only to make the ADD-SUBTRACT input a 1 and then apply the clocks.

SHIFT OPERATION

5.14 A *shift operation* is an operation which moves the digits *stored* in a register to new positions in the register. There are two distinct shift operations: a shift-left operation and a shift-right operation. A *shift-left operation* moves each bit of information stored in a register to the left by some specified number of digits. Consider the six binary digits 000110, which we assume to be stored in a parallel binary register. If the contents of the register are shifted left 1, afterward the shift register will contain 001100. If a shift right of 1 is performed on the word 000110, afterward the shift register will contain 000011. The shifting process in a decimal register is similar: if the register contains 001234, after a right shift of 1 the register will contain 000123, or after a left shift of 1 the register will contain 012340. The shift operation is used in the MULTIPLY and the DIVIDE instructions of most machines and is provided as an instruction which may be used by programmers. For instance, a machine may have instructions SHR and SHL, where the letters represent in mnemonic form the order for SHIFT RIGHT and SHIFT LEFT instructions.

A block diagram of logic circuitry for a single stage (flip-flop) in a register which can be shifted either left or right is shown in Fig. 5.16. As can be seen, the

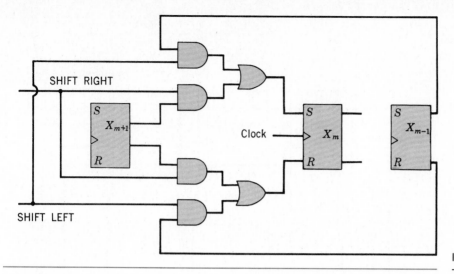

FIGURE 5.16

Shift-left and shift-right stages of register.

bit to the left is shifted into X when SHIFT RIGHT is a 1, and the bit to the right is shifted into X when SHIFT LEFT is a 1.

Figure 5.17 shows an MIS package which contains four flip-flops and gating circuitry so that the register can be shifted right or left and so that the four flip-flops can be parallel-loaded from four input lines W, X, Y, and Z. The circuits are TTL circuits and are clocked in parallel. By combining modules such as this one, a register of a chosen length can be formed which can be shifted left or right or parallel-loaded.

BASIC OPERATIONS

5.15 The arithmetic-logic unit of a digital computer consists of a number of registers in which information can be stored and a set of logic circuits which make it possible to perform certain operations on the information stored in the registers and between registers.

As we have seen, the data stored in a given flip-flop register may be operated on in the following ways:

1 The register may be reset to all 0s.

2 The contents of a register may be complemented to either 1s or 2s complement form for binary or to 9s or 10s complement form for decimal.

3 The contents of a register may be shifted right or left.

4 The contents of a register can be incremented or decremented.

Several operations between registers have been described. These include

1 Transferring the contents of one register to another register

**THE ARITHMETIC-
LOGIC UNIT**

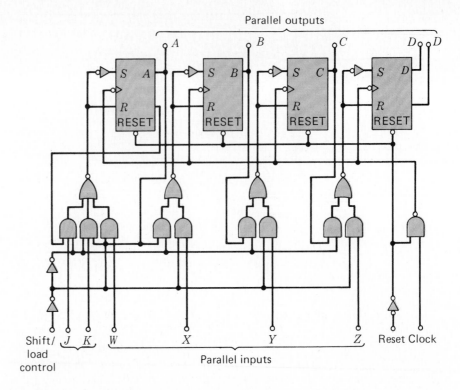

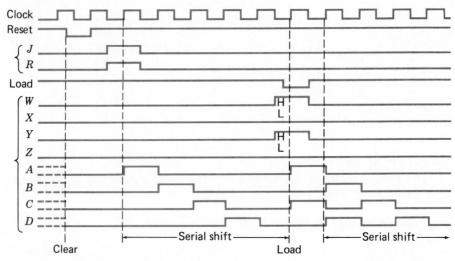

FIGURE 5.17

Shift register (model
SN74195) with paral-
lel-load ability. (*Texas
Instruments.*)

2 Adding to or subtracting from the contents of one register the contents of
another register

Most arithmetic operations which an ALU performs consist of these or sequenced sets of these two types of operations. Complicated instructions, such as
multiplication and division, can require a large number of these operations, but

these instructions may be performed by using only sequences of the simple operations already described.

One other important point needs to be made. Certain operations which occur within instructions are *conditional;* that is, a given operation may or may not take place, depending on the value of certain bits of the numbers stored. For instance, it may be desirable to multiply using only positive numbers. In this case, the sign bits of the two numbers to be multiplied will be examined by control circuitry and if either is a 1, the corresponding number will be complemented before the multiplication begins. This operation, complementing of the register, is a conditional one.

Many different sequences of operations can yield the same result. For instance, two numbers could be multiplied by simply adding the multiplicand to itself the number of times indicated by the multiplier. If this were done with pencil and paper, 369×12 would be performed by adding 369 to itself 12 times. This would be a laborious process compared with the easier algorithm which we have developed for multiplying, but we would get the same result. The same principle applies to computer multiplication. Two numbers could be multiplied by transferring one of the numbers into a counter which counted downward each time an addition was performed, and then adding the other number to itself until the counter reached zero. This technique has been used, but much faster techniques are also used and will be explained.

Many algorithms have been used to multiply and divide numbers in digital computers. Division, especially, is a complicated process; and in decimal computers in particular, many different techniques are used. The particular technique used by a computer is generally based on the cost of the computer and the premium on speed for the computer. As in almost all operations, speed is expensive, and a faster division process generally means a more expensive computer.

To explain the operations of binary multiplication and division, we use a block diagram of a generalized binary computer. Figure 5.18 illustrates, in block diagram form, the registers of an ALU. The computer has three basic registers: an accumulator, a Y register, and a B register. The operations which can be performed have been described:

1 The accumulator can be cleared.

2 The contents of the accumulator can be shifted right or left. Further, the accumulator and the B register may be formed into one long shift register. If we then shift this register right two digits, the two least significant digits of the accumulator will be shifted into the first two places of the B register. Several left shifts will shift the most significant digits of the B register into the accumulator. Since there are 5 bits in the basic computer word, there are five binary storage devices in each register. A right shift of five places will transfer the contents of the accumulator into the B register, and a left shift of five places will shift the contents of the B register into the accumulator.

3 The contents of the Y register can be either added to or subtracted from the accumulator. The sum or difference is stored in the accumulator register.

4 Words from memory may be read into the Y register. To read a word into the accumulator, it is necessary to clear the accumulator, to read the word from memory into the Y register, and to add the Y register to the accumulator.

THE ARITHMETIC-LOGIC UNIT

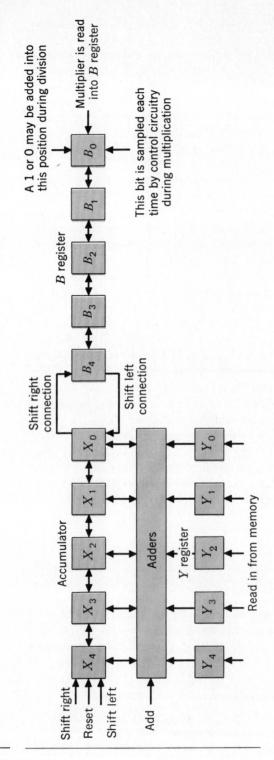

FIGURE 5.18

Generalized parallel arithmetic element.

An arithmetic element which can perform these operations on its registers can be sequenced to perform all arithmetic operations. It is, in fact, possible to construct a machine using fewer operations than these, but most general-purpose computers usually have an arithmetic element with at least these capabilities.

BINARY MULTIPLICATION

5.16   The process of multiplying binary numbers may be best examined by writing out the multiplication of two binary numbers:

$$
\begin{array}{r}
1001 \quad = \text{multiplicand} \\
\underline{1101} \quad = \text{multiplier} \\
1001 \\
0000 \\
1001 \\
\underline{1001} \\
1110101 \quad = \text{product}
\end{array}
$$

partial products

The important thing to notice in this process is that there are really only two rules for multiplying a single binary *number* by a binary *digit:* (1) If the multiplier digit is a 1, the multiplicand is simply copied. (2) If the multiplier digit is a 0, the product is 0. The above example illustrates these rules as follows: The first digit to the right of the multiplier is a 1; therefore, the multiplicand is copied as the first partial product. The next digit of the multiplier to the left is a 0; so the partial product is a 0. Each time a partial product is formed, it is shifted one place to the left of the previous partial product. Even if the partial product is a 0, the next partial product is shifted one place to the left of the previous partial product. This process is continued until all the multiplier digits have been used, and then the partial products are summed.

The three operations which the computer must be able to perform to multiply in this manner are, therefore, (1) to sense whether a multiplier bit is either a 1 or a 0, (2) to shift partial products, and (3) to add the partial products.

It is not necessary to wait until all the partial products have been formed before they are summed. They may be summed two at a time. For instance, starting with the first two partial products in the above example, we have

$$
\begin{array}{r}
1001 \\
\underline{0000} \\
01001
\end{array}
$$

Then the next partial product may be added to this sum, displacing it one position to the left:

$$
\begin{array}{r}
01001 \\
\underline{1001} \\
101101
\end{array}
$$

**THE ARITHMETIC-
LOGIC UNIT**

And finally,

$$
\begin{array}{r}
101101 \\
1001 \\
\hline
1110101
\end{array}
$$

A multiplier can be constructed in just this fashion. By sampling each bit of the multiplier in turn, adding the multiplicand into some register, and then shifting the multiplicand left each time a new multiplier bit is sampled, a product could be formed of the sum of the partial products. In fact, the process of multiplying in most binary machines is performed in a manner very similar to this.

To examine the typical technique for multiplying, the generalized arithmetic elements in Fig. 5.18 are used. Let the multiplier be stored in the B register, and the multiplicand in the Y register; the accumulator contains all 0s as shown:

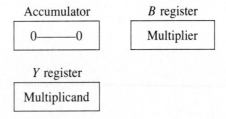

Let us also assume that both multiplier and multiplicand are positive. If either is negative, it must be converted to positive form before the multiplication begins. The sign bits will therefore be 0s.

The desired result format is shown, with the product being the combined accumulator and B register:

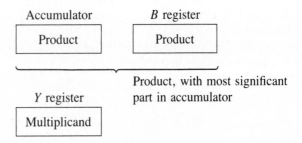

A multiplication requires *n basic steps,* where *n* is the number of bits in the magnitude of the numbers to be multiplied, and a final right shift to position the product. Each basic step is initiated by the control circuitry examining the rightmost bit in the B register. The basic step is as follows.

BASIC STEP

If the rightmost bit in the *B* register is a 0, the combined accumulator and *B* register is shifted right one place. If the rightmost bit in the *B* register is a 1, the number in the *Y* register is added to the contents of the accumulator, and then the combined accumulator and *B* register is shifted right one place.

After each basic step, the new rightmost bit of the *B* register is examined again, and the next of the *n* steps is initiated.

Let us consider the same multiplication that was used in the previous example, that is, 1101×1001, where 1101 is the multiplier. In the beginning the accumulator contains 00000, the *B* register 01101, and the *Y* register 01001 (the leftmost 0s are sign bits). Four steps and a final shift will be required.

1   Since the rightmost bit of the *B* register contains a 1 (the least significant bit of the multiplier), during the first step the contents of the *Y* register are added to the accumulator, and the combined accumulator and *B* register are shifted to the right. The second least significant bit of the multiplier now occupies the rightmost bit of the *B* register and controls the next operation. The *Y* register still contains the multiplicand 01001, the contents of the accumulator are 00100, and the contents of the *B* register are 10110.

2   The rightmost bit of the *B* register is a 0, and since it controls the next operation, a SHIFT RIGHT signal is initiated and the accumulator and *B* register are shifted right, giving 00010 in the accumulator and 01011 in the *B* register.

3   A 1 is now in the rightmost bit of the *B* register. So the *Y* register is added to the accumulator again, and the combined accumulator and *B* register are shifted right, giving 00101 in the accumulator and 10101 in the *B* register.

4   The least significant bit of the *B* register is another 1; so the *Y* register is added to the accumulator and the accumulator is shifted right. After the above shift right, the combined accumulator and *B* register contain 0011101010. A final right shift gives 0001110101, the correct product for our integer number system. The most significant digits are stored in the accumulator, and the least significant digits in the *B* register.

ACCUMULATOR	*B* REGISTER	
00000	01101	At beginning
00100	10110	After step 1
00010	01011	After step 2
00101	10101	After step 3
00111	01010	After step 4
00011	10101	After shift right

THE ARITHMETIC-
LOGIC UNIT

Now the reason for the combined accumulator and *B* register can be seen. The product of two 5-bit signed numbers can contain up to nine significant digits (including the sign bit); and so two 5-bit registers, not one, are required to hold the product. The final product is treated like a 10-bit number extending through the two registers with the leftmost bits (most significant bits) in the left register, the rightmost bits (least significant bits) in the right register, and the least significant binary digit in the rightmost bit. Thus our result in the two combined registers is 0001110101, which is + 117 in decimal.

The control circuitry is designed to perform the examination of the multiplier bits, then either shift or add and shift the correct number of times, and stop. In this case, the length of the multiplier, or *Y* register, is 4 bits plus a sign bit; so four such steps are performed. The general practice is to examine each bit of the computer word except the sign bit, in turn. For instance, if the basic computer word is 25 bits (that is, 24 bits in which the magnitude of a number is stored plus a sign bit), each time a multiplication is performed, the computer will examine 24 bits, each in turn, performing the add-and-shift or just the shift operation 24 times. This makes the multiplication operation longer than such operations as add or subtract. Some parallel computers double their normal rate of operation during multiplication: if the computer performs such operations as addition, complementation, transfers, etc., at a rate of 4 MHz/s for ordinary instructions, the rate will be increased to 8 MHz for the add-and-shift combinations performed during multiplying. Some computers are able to shift right while adding; that is, the sum of the accumulator and *Y* register appears shifted one place to the right each time, and the shift-right operation after each addition may be omitted.

The sign bits of the multiplier and multiplicand may be handled in a number of ways. For instance, the sign of the product can be determined by means of control circuitry before the multiplication procedure is initiated. This sign bit is stored during the multiplication process, after which it is placed into the sign bit of the accumulator, and then the accumulator is complemented, if necessary. Therefore, the sign bits of the multiplier and multiplicand are examined first. If they are both 0s, the sign of the product should be 0; if both are 1s, the sign of the product should be 0; and if either but not both are a 1, the sign of the product should be 1. This information, retained in a flip-flop while the multiplication is taking place, may be transferred into the sign bit afterward. If the computer handles numbers in the 1s or 2s complement system, both multiplier and multiplicand may be handled as positive magnitudes during the multiplication. And if the sign of either number is negative, the number is complemented to a positive magnitude before the multiplication begins. Sometimes the multiplication is performed on complemented numbers by using more complicated algorithms. These are described in the Bibliography.

DECIMAL MULTIPLICATION

5.17   Decimal multiplication is a more involved process than binary multiplication. Whereas the product of a binary digit and a binary number is either the number or 0, the product of a decimal digit and decimal number involves the use of a multiplication table plus carrying and adding. For instance,

$$7 \times 24 = 7 \times 4 + 7 \times 20 = 28 + 140 = 168$$

Even the multiplying of two decimal digits may involve two output digits; for instance, 7×8 equals 56. In the following discussion we call the two digits which may result when a decimal digit is multiplied by a decimal digit the *left-hand* and the *right-hand digits*. Thus for 3×6 we have 1 for the left-hand digit and 8 for the right-hand digit. For 2×3 we have 0 for the left-hand digit and 6 for the right-hand digit.

Except for simply adding the multiplicand to itself the number of times indicated by the multiplier, a simple but time-consuming process, the simplest method for decimal multiplication involves loading the rightmost digit of the multiplier into a counter that counts downward and then adding the multiplicand to itself and simultaneously indexing the counter until the counter reaches 0. The partial product thus formed may be shifted right one decimal digit, the next multiplier digit loaded into the counter, and the process repeated until all the multiplier digits have been used. This is a relatively slow but straightforward technique.

The process may be speeded up by forming products using the multiplicand and the rightmost digit of the multiplier as in the previous scheme, except by actually forming the left-hand and right-hand partial products obtained when a digit is multiplied by a number and then summing them. For instance, 6×7164 would yield 2664 for the right-hand product digits and 4032 for the left-hand product digits. The sum would be

$$
\begin{array}{r}
2664 \\
+ \quad 4032 \\
\hline
42984
\end{array}
$$

Decimal-machine multiplication is, in general, a complicated process if speed is desired, and there are almost as many techniques for multiplying BCD numbers as there are types of machines.[11] IC packages are produced that contain a gate network having two BCD characters as inputs which produce the two-digit output required. The Questions and Bibliography explore this in more detail.

DIVISION

*5.18[12]   The operation of division is the most difficult and time-consuming that the ALU of most general-purpose computers performs. Although division may appear no more difficult than multiplication, several problems in connection with the division process introduce time-consuming extra steps.

Division, using pencil and paper, is a trial-and-error process. For instance, if we are to divide 77 into 4610, we first notice that 77 will not "go" into 46; so we attempt to divide 77 into 461. We may guess that it will go six times; however,

---

[11]Several systems use table look-up techniques for forming products, where the product of each pair of digits is stored in the memory.

[12]Sections with asterisks can be omitted on a first reading with no loss in continuity.

$$
\begin{array}{r}
6 \\
77\overline{)4610} \\
462 \\
\hline
-1
\end{array}
$$

Therefore we have guessed too high and must reduce the first digit of the quotient, which we will develop, to 5.

The same problem confronts the computer when it attempts to divide in this manner. It must "try" a subtraction each step of the process and then see whether the remainder is negative. Consider the division of 1111 by 11:

$$
\begin{array}{r}
101 \\
11\overline{)1111} \\
11 \\
\hline
0011 \\
11 \\
\hline
00
\end{array}
$$

It is easy to determine visually at any step of the process whether the quotient is to be a 1 or a 0, but the computer cannot determine this without making a trial subtraction each time. After a trial quotient has been tried and the divisor subtracted, if the result is negative, either the current dividend must be "restored" or some other technique for dividing used.

There are several points to be noted concerning binary fixed-point integer-value division. The division is generally performed with two signed binary integers of the same fixed length. The result, or quotient, is stored as a number, with as many digits as the divisor or dividend, and the remainder is also stored as a number of the same length.[13]

Using the registers shown in Fig. 5.18, we show how to divide a number stored in the accumulator by a number in the Y register. Then the quotient is stored in the B register and the remainder in the accumulator. This is the most common division format.

Assume the B and Y registers in Fig. 5.18 are 5 bits in length (4 bits plus a sign bit) and the accumulator is also 5 bits in length. Before we start the procedure, the dividend is read into the accumulator, and the divisor into the Y register. After the division, the quotient is stored in the B register, and the remainder is in the accumulator. Both divisor and dividend are to be positive.

The following shows an example. The accumulator (dividend) originally contains 11 (decimal) and the Y register (divisor) contains 4. The desired result then gives the quotient 2 in the B register and the remainder 3 in the accumulator.

---

[13]If we divide one integer into another, both the quotient and remainder will be integers. The rule is as follows: If a is the dividend, y the divisor, b the quotient, and r the remainder, then $a = y \times b + r$.

Accumulator	B register
01011	00000

At beginning
of division

Y register
00100

DIVISION

Accumulator	B register
00011	00010

After division

Y register
00100

There are two general techniques for division for binary machines: the *restoring* and the *nonrestoring* techniques. Our first example illustrates the restoring technique.

Just as in multiplication, the restoring technique for division requires that a *basic step* be performed repeatedly (in this case as many times as there are significant bits in the subtrahend).

BASIC STEP

A "trial division" is made by subtracting the *Y* register from the accumulator. After the subtraction, one of the following is executed.

1 If the result is negative, the divisor will not "go"; so a 0 is placed in the rightmost bit of the *B* register, and the dividend (accumulator) is restored by adding the divisor to the result of the subtraction. The combined *B* register and accumulator are then shifted left.

2 If the result of a subtraction is positive or zero, there is no need to restore the partial dividend in the accumulator for the trial division has succeeded. The accumulator and *B* register are both shifted left, and then a 1 is placed in the rightmost bit of the *B* register.

The computer determines whether the result of a trial division is positive or negative by examining the sign bit of the accumulator after each subtraction.

THE ARITHMETIC-
LOGIC UNIT

TABLE 5.2			
B REGISTER	ACCUMULATOR	Y REGISTER	REMARKS
00000	00110	00011	We divide 6 by 3.
00000	00110	00110	Y register is shifted left once, aligning 1s in accumulator and Y register. The basic step must be performed two times.
00000	00000	00110	Y register has been subtracted from accumulator. The result is 0, so B register and accumulator are shifted left, and a 1 is placed in the rightmost bit of B register.
00001	00000	00110	
00001	11010	00110	Y register is subtracted from accumulator.
00010	00000	00110	Y register is added to accumulator, and B register and accumulator are shifted left 1. A 0 is placed in B register's last bit.
00010	00000	00110	Accumulator must now be shifted right two times, but it is 0 so no change results. The quotient in B register is 2, and the remainder in accumulator is 0.

To demonstrate the entire procedure, first it is necessary to explain how to initiate the division and how to start and stop performing the basic steps. Unfortunately these are complicated procedures, just as determining the position of the decimal point and how to start and stop the division is complicated for ordinary division.

1 As described above, if the divisor is larger than the dividend, then the quotient should be 0, and the remainder is the value of the dividend. (For instance, if we attempt to divide 7 by 17, the quotient is 0, and the remainder is 7.) To test this, the dividend in Y can be subtracted from the accumulator. If the result is negative, all that remains is to restore the accumulator by adding the Y register to the accumulator. The B register now has value 0 which is right for the quotient, and the accumulator has the original value which is the remainder.

2 After the above test is made, it is necessary both to align the leftmost 1 bit in the divisor with the leftmost 1 bit in the dividend by shifting the divisor left and then recording the number of shifts required to make this alignment. If the number of shifts is M, then the basic step must be performed $M + 1$ times.[14]

3 The basic step is now performed the necessary $M + 1$ times.

---

[14]This can be accomplished by making Y a shift register and providing a counter to count the shifts until the first 1 bit of Y is aligned with the 1 bit of the accumulator. Both the accumulator and Y could be shifted left until there is a 1 bit in their first position, but the remainder will have to be adjusted by moving it right in the accumulator.

TABLE 5.3

B REGISTER	ACCUMULATOR	Y REGISTER	REMARKS
00000	01101	00011	We divide 13 by 3.
00000	01101	00110	Shift Y register left.
00000	01101	01100	Shift Y register left. Leftmost 1 bits in accumulator and Y register are aligned. Basic step will be performed three times.
00000	00001	01100	Y register has been subtracted from accumulator. Result is positive.
00001	00010	01100	B register and accumulator are shifted left, and 1 is placed in B register.
00001	10110	01100	Y register is subtracted from accumulator. Result is negative.
00010	00100	01100	Y register is added to accumulator. Then both are shifted left, and a 0 is placed in B register.
00010	11000	01100	Y register is subtracted from accumulator. Result is negative.
00100	01000	01100	Y register is added to accumulator. Accumulator and B register are shifted left. A 0 is placed in B register's bit.
00100	00001	01100	Accumulator has been shifted right three times. The quotient is 4, and the remainder is 1.

5

DIVISION

4   Finally, to adjust the remainder, the accumulator must be shifted right $M + 1$ times after the last basic step is performed. Examples are shown in Tables 5.2 and 5.3. Step 1, testing for a zero quotient, is not shown in the two examples.

Figure 5.19 shows a flowchart of the algorithm. Flowcharts are often used to represent algorithms. A more detailed flowchart would separate some of the steps, such as "shift the accumulator right $M + 1$ times," into single shifts performed in a loop which is controlled by a counter. Often, when algorithms are reasonably complicated, as this algorithm is, it is convenient to draw a flowchart of the algorithm before attempting to implement the control circuitry.

During division, the sign bits are handled in much the same way as during multiplication. The first step is to convert both the divisor and the dividend to positive magnitude form. The value of the sign bit for the quotient must be stored while the division is taking place. The rule is that if the signs of the dividend and divisor are both either 0s or 1s, the quotient will be positive. If either but not both of their signs are a 1, the quotient will be negative. The relationship of the sign bit of the quotient to the sign bit of the divisor and dividend is, therefore, the quarter-adder, or exclusive OR, relationship, that is, $S = X\overline{Y} + \overline{X}Y$. The value for the correct sign of the quotient may be read into a flip-flop while the division is taking place, and this value may then be placed in the sign bit of the register containing the quotient after the division of magnitudes has been completed.

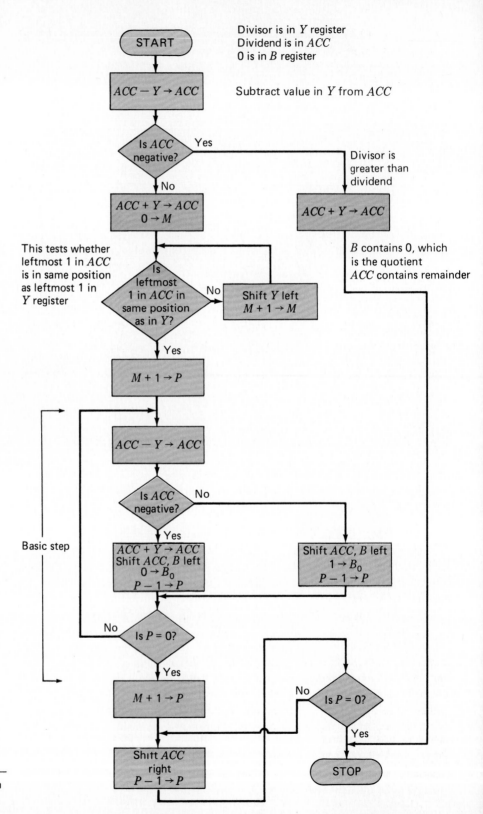

5

THE ARITHMETIC-
LOGIC UNIT

FIGURE 5.19

Flowchart of division
algorithm.

There are several techniques for nonrestoring division. One widely used algorithm employs a procedure in which the divisor is alternately subtracted and added. Another uses a technique in which the divisor is compared to the dividend at each trial division. This material is covered in detail in the Bibliography.

LOGICAL OPERATIONS

5.19 In addition to the arithmetic operations, many logical operations are performed by ALUs. Three logical operations are described here: logical multiplication, logical addition, and *sum modulo 2* addition (the exclusive OR operation). Each of these will be operations between registers, where the operation specified will be performed on each of the corresponding digits in the two registers. The result will be stored in one of the registers.

The first operation, logical multiplication, is often referred to as an *extract, masking,* or AND *operation*. The rules for logical multiplication are defined in the chapter on logical algebra. The rules are $0 \cdot 0 = 0$, $0 \cdot 1 = 0$, $1 \cdot 0 = 0$, and $1 \cdot 1 = 1$. Suppose that the contents of the accumulator register are "logically multiplied" by another register. Let each register be five binary digits in length. If the accumulator contains 01101 and the other register contains 00111, the contents of the accumulator after the operation will be 00101.

The masking, or extracting, operation is useful in "packaging" computer words. To save space in memory and keep associated data together, several pieces of information may be stored in the same word. For instance, a word may contain an item number, wholesale price, and retail price, packaged as follows:

S	1→6	7→15	16→24

item   wholesale   retail
number   price   price

To extract the retail price, the programmer will simply logically multiply the word above by a word containing 0s in the sign digit through digit 15 and 1s in positions 16 through 24. After the operation, only the retail price will remain in the word.

The logical addition operation and the sum modulo 2 operation are also provided in most computers. The rules for these operations are as follows:

LOGICAL ADDITION   MODULO 2 ADDITION

$$0 + 0 = 0 \qquad 0 \oplus 0 = 0$$
$$0 + 1 = 1 \qquad 0 \oplus 1 = 1$$
$$1 + 0 = 1 \qquad 1 \oplus 0 = 1$$
$$1 + 1 = 1 \qquad 1 \oplus 1 = 0$$

Figure 5.20 shows how a single accumulator flip-flop and B flip-flop can be gated so that all three of these logical operations can be performed. The circuit in Fig. 5.20 would be repeated for each stage of the accumulator register.

There are three control signals: LOGICAL MULTIPLY, LOGICAL ADD, and MOD 2 ADD. If one of these is a 1, when a clock pulse arrives, this operation

5

THE ARITHMETIC-LOGIC UNIT

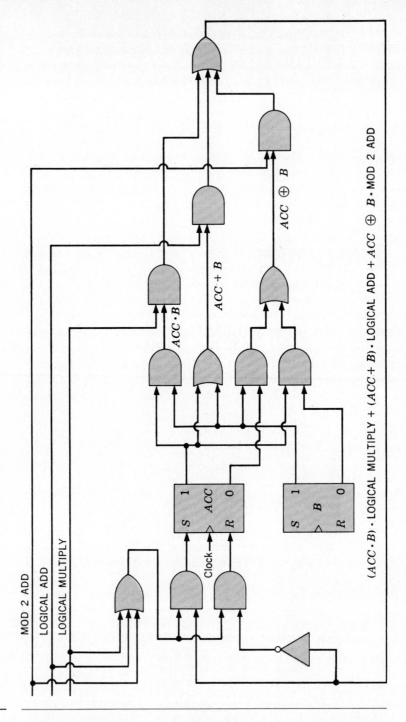

FIGURE 5.20

Circuit for gating logic operations into accumulator flip-flop.

is performed and the result placed in the ACC (accumulator) flip-flop. If none of the control signals is a 1, nothing happens, and the ACC remains as it is.

The actual values desired are formed by three sets of gates; that is, ACC·B, ACC + B, and ACC ⊕ B are all formed first. Each is then AND-gated with the appropriate control signal. Finally the three control signals are ORed, and this signal is used to gate the appropriate value into the ACC flip-flop when one of the control signals is a 1.

Figure 5.20 shows how a choice of several different function values can be gated into a single flip-flop using control signals. We could include an ADD signal and a SHIFT RIGHT and a SHIFT LEFT by simply adding more gates.

Figure 5.21 shows an example of the logic circuitry used to form sections of an ALU. All the gates are contained in a single chip (package) with 24 pins. There is a 7-ns maximum delay through the package.

This chip is called a *4-bit arithmetic-logic unit* and can add, subtract, AND, OR, etc., two 4-bit register sections. Two chips could be used for the logic in an 8-bit accumulator, four chips would form a 16-bit accumulator, etc.

The function performed by this chip is controlled by the mode input M and four function select inputs S_0, S_1, S_2, and S_3. When the mode input M is low (a 0), the 74S181 performs such arithmetic operations as ADD or SUBTRACT. When the mode input M is high (a 1), the ALU does logic operations on the A and B inputs ''a bit at a time.'' (Notice in Fig. 5.21 that the carry-generating gates are disabled by $M = 1$.) For instance, if M is a 0, S_1 and S_2 are also 0s, and S_0 and S_3 are 1s, then the 74S181 performs arithmetic addition. If M is a 1, S_0 and S_3 are 1s, and S_1 and S_2 are 0s, the 74S181 chip exclusive-ORs (mod 2 adds) A and B. (It forms $A_0 \oplus B_0$, $A_1 \oplus B_1$, $A_2 \oplus B_2$, and $A_3 \oplus B_3$.)

The table in Fig. 5.21 further describes the operation of this chip. Questions at the end of the chapter develop some operational characteristics of this 4-bit ALU section.

MULTIPLEXERS

5.20 The function of a *multiplexer* is to select from several inputs a single input. Control lines are used to make this selection.

Figure 5.22 shows an eight-input multiplexer on a single IC chip. The eight inputs are labeled I_0, I_1, . . . , I_7. There are three control wires, S_2, S_1, and S_0. These three control lines can take eight different values (from 000 to 111), and for each value a different input is selected. The value of the input selected appears on Z. An examination of this multiplexer shows that if $S_2S_1S_0$ are all 0s, then input I_0 is selected. If $S_2S_1S_0$ are 001, then I_1 is selected; if $S_2S_1S_0$ are 010, then I_2 is selected; etc.

For example, if $S_2S_1S_0 = 010$, then the output Z will be 0 if I_2 is a 0 and a 1 if I_2 is a 1. In this case, the input values on I_0, I_1, I_3, I_4, I_5, I_6 and I_7 will not affect the output value on Z. The E input enables the multiplexer.

Multiplexers are useful in many ways. Suppose we are to select as inputs to a gate network a single register from four flip-flop registers with two flip-flops in each register. Figure 5.23 shows a dual four-input multiplexer which will accomplish this. The two multiplexers each have four inputs, and the inputs selected from each are in the same respective position. There are two control inputs, S_1 and S_0. If S_1 and S_0 are both 0s, then A_0 and B_0 are selected and placed on the A and B outputs; if S_1 is a 0 and S_0 is a 1, then the values of A_1 and B_1 are placed on the A and B outputs; etc.

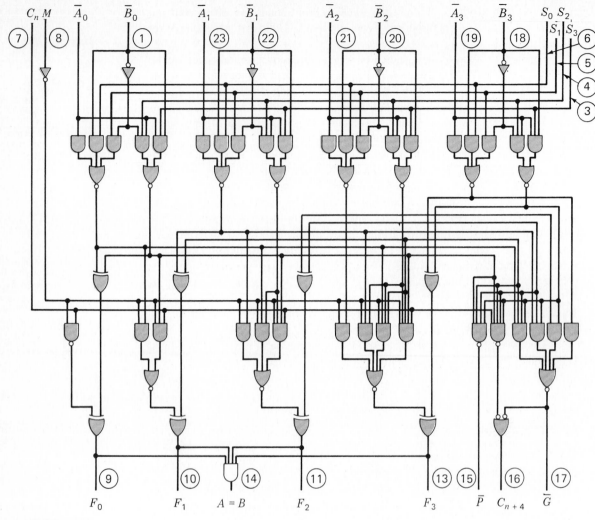

FIGURE 5.21

A 4-bit arithmetic
logic unit.

The $\overline{\text{ENABLE}}$ input is used to enable or disable both multiplexers. A 0 on the $\overline{\text{ENABLE}}$ enables the outputs, but a 1 on $\overline{\text{ENABLE}}$ forces both outputs to 0.

Figure 5.24 shows four flip-flop registers W, X, Y, and Z, each with two flip-flops. The control lines S_0 and S_1 select from each of the four sets of inputs a single two-flip-flop register whose outputs are then placed on the output lines. This shows how multiplexers can be used to select a single register from a set of registers.

If each register contained more than two flip-flops, then another dual four-input multiplexer would be needed for each additional two flip-flops.

Multiplexers are useful in many ways, and Figs. 5.22 and 5.23 should be examined carefully.

| MODE SELECT INPUTS | | | | ACTIVE LOW INPUTS & OUTPUTS | |
S_3	S_2	S_1	S_0	LOGIC $(M = H)$	ARITHMETIC $(M = L)\ (C_n = L)$
L	L	L	L	$\overline{A}$	$A - 1$
L	L	L	L	$\overline{AB}$	$AB - 1$
L	L	H	L	$\overline{A} + B$	$A\overline{B} - 1$
L	L	H	H	Logical 1	-1
L	H	L	L	$\overline{A + B}$	$A \mp (A + \overline{B})$
L	H	L	H	$\overline{B}$	$AB \mp (A + \overline{B})$
L	H	H	L	$\overline{A \oplus B}$	$A - B - 1$
L	H	H	H	$A + \overline{B}$	$A + \overline{B}$
H	L	L	L	$A\overline{B}$	$A \mp (A + B)$
H	L	L	H	$A \oplus B$	$A \mp B$
H	L	H	L	B	$AB \mp (A + B)$
H	L	H	H	$A + B$	$A + B$
H	H	L	L	Logical 0	$A \mp A$
H	H	L	H	$A\overline{B}$	$AB \mp A$
H	H	H	L	AB	$AB \mp A$
H	H	H	H	A	A

*L = 0; H = 1.

Note:

is the symbol for a mod 2 adder (exclusive OR gate)
$z = x \oplus y$

$\mp$ is the sign for arithmetic addition

FIGURE 5.21 (Cont.)

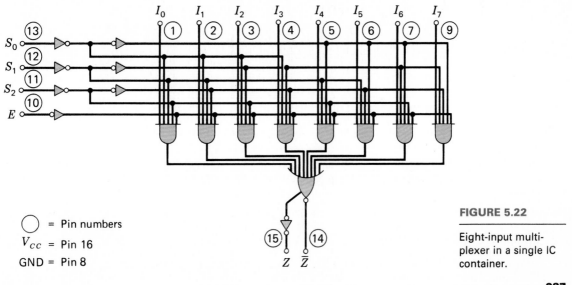

= Pin numbers
V_{cc} = Pin 16
GND = Pin 8

FIGURE 5.22

Eight-input multiplexer in a single IC container.

237

5

THE ARITHMETIC-LOGIC UNIT

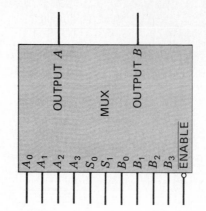

(b)

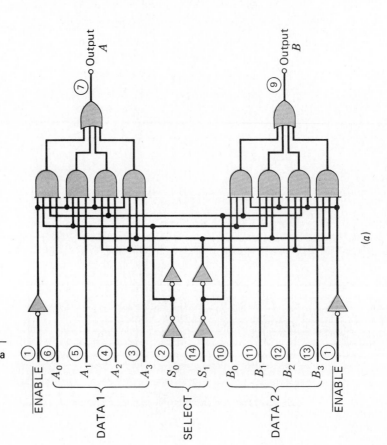

(a)

FIGURE 5.23

Two multiplexers in a single IC container (SN54153 and SN74153). (a) Block diagram showing gates. (b) Block diagram symbol.

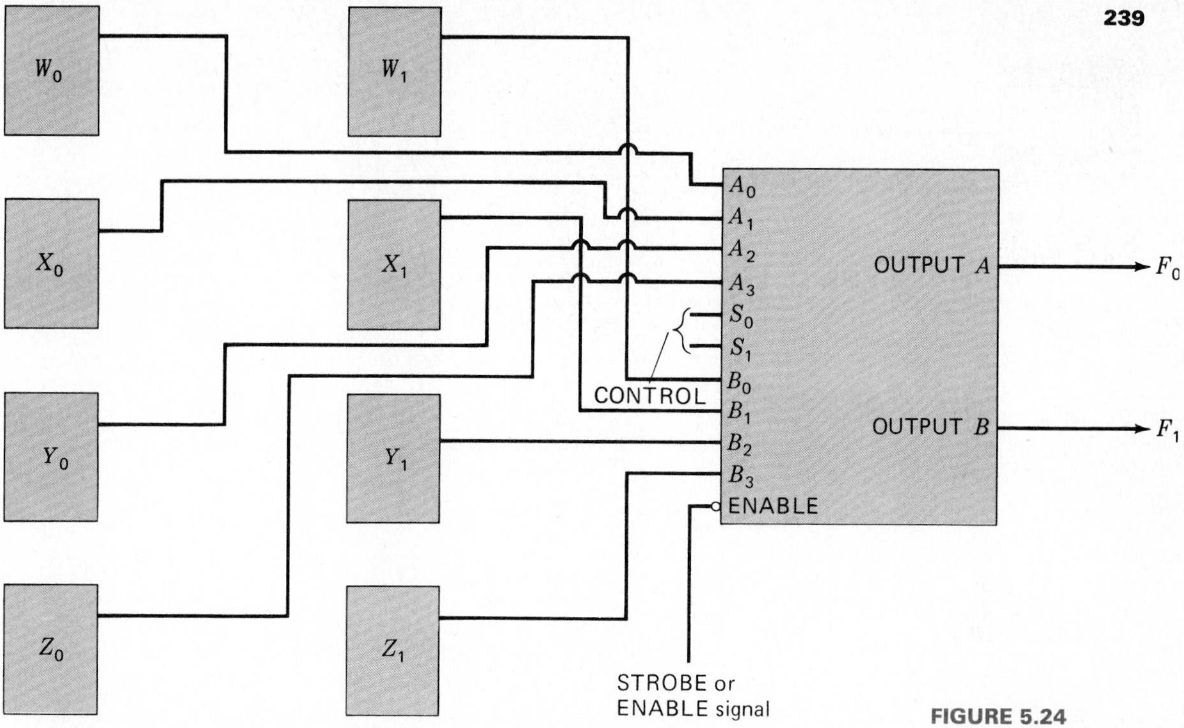

FIGURE 5.24

Using a dual four-input multiplexer IC to select from two four-input flip-flop registers.

HIGH-SPEED ARITHMETIC—SPEEDING UP ADDITION

*5.21   Since additions and subtractions are often performed in computers, it is desirable to perform them quickly. In this section we describe how the time required may be shortened. This also will speed up multiplication and division since in most cases these involve a number of additions or subtractions.

Figure 5.25 shows a set of full-adders as they might be interconnected to form a 16-bit full-adder for two registers of 16 flip-flops each (for two 16-bit numbers). Note that a carry arising in the rightmost adder (if X_0 and Y_0 are both 1s) will propagate all the way through the leftmost adder (for X_{15} and Y_{15}) if there is a 1 input at each adder in the chain.

Each gate in a network delays a signal by some time period. Thus if a set of new inputs is placed on the inputs to the adder configuration, it is necessary to wait until the signals have passed through all gates before the outputs, in this case S_{15} through S_0, can be safely used. If each gate has a delay of D ns, then for Fig. 5.25 it is necessary to wait for $32 \times D$ ns from the time the inputs are changed before we can be sure the value of S_{15} is correct.

This is called the carry propagation delay. This delay can be considerable for long registers if the configuration in Fig. 5.25 is used without modification. Fortunately, there are several ways to shorten the carry propagation delay, as we show.

Figure 5.26 shows an IC chip layout which contains gates to add two 4-bit inputs plus a carry to the group. Note here that the C_o, or carry output, has a

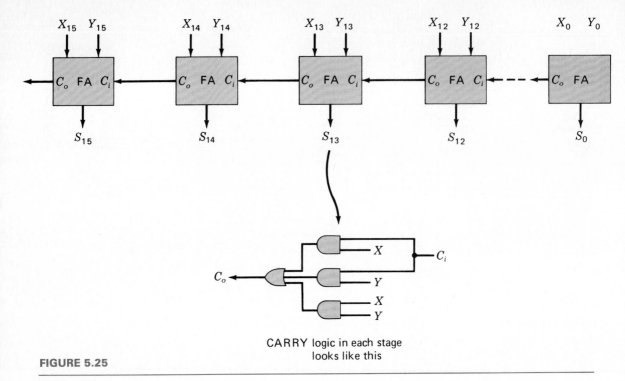

CARRY logic in each stage
looks like this

FIGURE 5.25

Chain of full-adders.

maximum delay path of three gates for any input. That is, the maximum delay path from any input to the output C_o is a three-gate delay.

Figure 5.27 shows how four of these IC containers can be interconnected to form an adder which will handle 16-bit inputs. The maximum delay through this network is shorter than that for the layout in Fig. 5.25 because of the shorter carry delays. The maximum path length in number of gates for the C_i input to the leftmost four-adder package is nine gates, or $9 \times D$ ns if a gate delay is D ns. The delay through the final package, to S_{15}, for example, is four gate delays, however, because a carry input to C_i must pass through an AND gate, a NOR gate, and exclusive OR gates to reach S_{15}; and exclusive OR gates require two delays. (Exclusive OR gates are often made from a two-level network of conventional gates.)

The reduction of adder carry propagation delay using the adder in Fig. 5.26 is due to the development of the C_o output directly from the eight inputs A_1, $B_1, \ldots, A_4, B_4,$ and C_i. For example, if we wish to put a 3-bit adder in a single container, with inputs $A_1, B_1, A_2, B_2, A_3, B_3,$ and C_i, then the C_o output can be written[15] as follows:

$$C_o = C_i(A_3 + B_3)(A_2 + B_2)(A_1 + B_1)$$
$$+ A_3B_3(A_2 + B_2)(A_1 + B_1) + A_2B_2(A_1 + B_1) + A_1B_1$$

---

[15]This is the expression for a "carry look-ahead" or "carry bridging" net. Placing carry look-aheads every few adders will speed up adder operation.

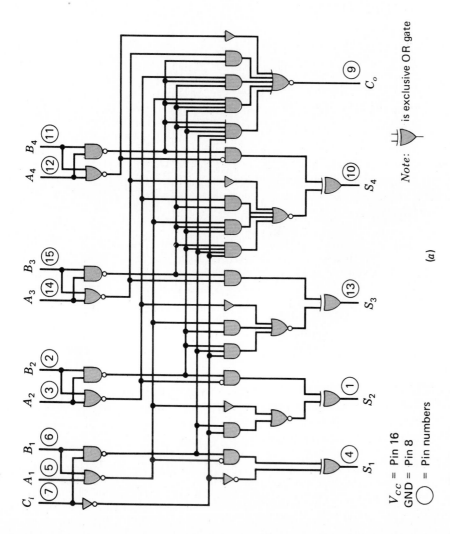

Note: ⟶ is exclusive OR gate

V_{CC} = Pin 16
GND = Pin 8
◯ = Pin numbers

FIGURE 5.26

Full adders with carry
bridge. (a) A 745283
chip with four full-
adders. (b) Block dia-
gram for (a).

THE ARITHMETIC-
LOGIC UNIT

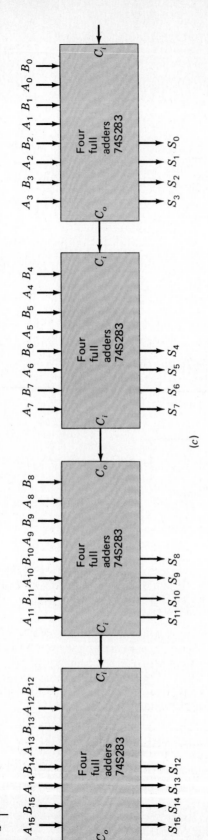

(c)

FIGURE 5.27

A 16-bit adder made
from IC chips.

Turning this expression directly into a gate network results in a three-level network and thus three-gate delays, but the expression can be "multiplied out" and a two-level net will result.

The amount of reduction of delay in adders depends on the complexity (and therefore cost) of the gating network used. As an example, Fig. 5.21 has a reasonably fast carry, but this chip also develops a P and G output which can be used with another chip, shown in the Questions, to further speed up adder operation.

HIGH-SPEED ARITHMETIC—PARALLEL MULTIPLIERS

*5.22 The multiplication technique described earlier is called the *add-and-shift algorithm*. This technique is used in most smaller computers because it is direct to implement. Also it is often used in programs which implement multiplication because many smaller computers (microcomputers, in particular) have no multiplication instruction.

In larger computers and in signal-processing computers, there is a need for high-speed multiplication. To achieve this, arrays of gates are used which multiply several binary digits at the same time. These arrays are of various sizes and range from moderately inexpensive to quite expensive. Their use is based on economic considerations and the requirements for the system.

We illustrate how two binary numbers can be multiplied in a gating network. Suppose the numbers are a_1a_0 and b_1b_0, two binary 2-bit numbers. For example, if $a_1 = 1$ and $a_0 = 0$, then $a_1a_0 = 10$, which is 2 in decimal. Similarly, if $b_1 = 1$ and $b_0 = 1$, then $b_1b_0 = 11$, which is 3 in decimal.

If these numbers are multiplied using our familiar technique, this array is formed:

$$
\begin{array}{rcrr}
 & & b_1 & b_0 \\
 & \times & a_1 & a_0 \\
\hline
 & a_0b_1 & a_0b_0 & \\
a_1b_1 & a_1b_0 & & \\
\hline
p_3 & p_2 & p_1 & p_0
\end{array}
$$

where

$$
\begin{aligned}
p_0 &= a_0b_0 \\
p_1 &= a_0b_1 \oplus a_1b_0 \\
p_2 &= a_1b_1 \oplus a_0b_1a_1b_0 \\
p_3 &= a_1b_1a_0a_1b_1a_0b_0
\end{aligned}
$$

Here

$$
\begin{array}{ll}
0 \oplus 0 = 0 & 1 \oplus 0 = 1 \\
0 \oplus 1 = 1 & 1 \oplus 1 = 1
\end{array}
$$

Figure 5.28 shows the boolean algebra expression for the product bits p_3, p_2, p_1, and p_0 realized in gate network form. If inputs for a_1a_0 and b_1b_0 are input to

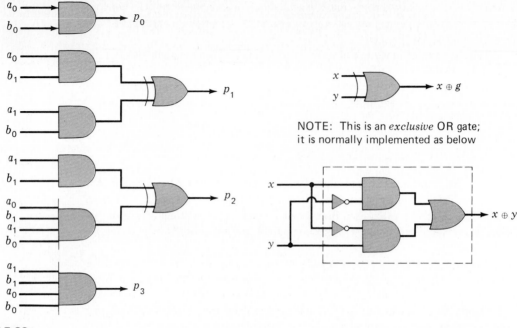

NOTE: This is an *exclusive* OR gate; it is normally implemented as below

FIGURE 5.28

A two-digit parallel binary multiplier.

the network, then $p_3p_2p_1p_0$ will give the product in binary integer form. The net in Fig. 5.28 is called a *parallel multiplier*.

The above technique for deriving boolean algebra expressions for the product bits can be used for multiplications involving more digits. Unfortunately, for 8-bit or even 16-bit multipliers and multiplicands, the expressions become very large and costly to implement. However, this technique works well for small numbers.

To make parallel multipliers for larger numbers of inputs and outputs, often an array of full-adders is used. Consider the multiplication of two 3-bit numbers shown in Fig. 5.29(*a*). The partial products are written with the product bits $p_5p_4p_3p_2p_1p_0$ immediately below. In Fig. 5.29(*b*) a set of nine AND gates is used to produce all the a_ib_j terms in the multiplier in Fig. 5.29(*a*). In Fig. 5.29(*c*) an arrangement of full-adders is shown which have as inputs the outputs from the AND gates in Fig. 5.29(*b*) and which will implement the multiplication shown in Fig. 5.29(*a*). It is instructive to see how the multiplication is performed by the full-adders. The operation of this circuit should be carefully examined.

The maximum length of carry path for Fig. 5.29(*b*) is along the top row to the p_5 output. If the full-adders have two-gate delays for each carry, then Fig. 5.29(*c*) has a worst-case delay of eight-gate delays and another delay arises from the AND gates in Fig. 5.29(*b*). As the number of bits in the numbers being multiplied increases, so does the size of the array of full-adders and so does the delay through the array. There are several ways to rearrange the adders slightly and to add more gates to reduce this delay, which are covered in the Bibliography. [The paper "High-Speed Monolithic Multipliers for Real-Time Digital Signal Processing" by S. Waser in the October 1979 issue of *Computer* is very instructive. The array in Fig. 5.29(*c*) is fundamental, however.]

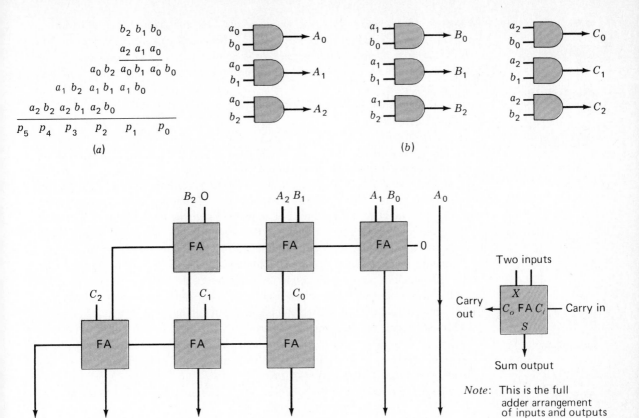

$$\begin{array}{ccccccc}
 & & & b_2 & b_1 & b_0 \\
 & & & a_2 & a_1 & a_0 \\
\hline
 & & a_0 b_2 & a_0 b_1 & a_0 b_0 \\
 & a_1 b_2 & a_1 b_1 & a_1 b_0 \\
a_2 b_2 & a_2 b_1 & a_2 b_0 \\
\hline
P_5 & P_4 & P_3 & P_2 & P_1 & P_0
\end{array}$$

(a)

(b)

(c)

Note: This is the full adder arrangement of inputs and outputs

FIGURE 5.29

A parallel multiplier. (a) Multiplication of 3-bit numbers. (b) Forming prevalent terms. (c) Parallel multiplier made of full-adders.

Parallel multiplier arrays are packaged in IC containers by several manufacturers. The largest array in a single IC container now multiplies two 16-bit numbers. The delay through this package is about 100 ns. Eight-bit parallel multipliers are common. Several of these multipliers can be grouped along with some full-adders to form multipliers for even larger numbers. Parallel multipliers also can be used to shorten multiplication time by using an add-and-shift algorithm and multiplying several bits at each step.

FLOATING-POINT NUMBER SYSTEMS

5.23   Earlier we described number representation systems in which positive and negative integers are stored in binary words. In the representation system used, the binary point is "fixed" in that it lies at the end of each word, and so each value represented is an integer. When computers calculate with binary numbers in this format, the operations are called *fixed-point arithmetic*.

In science it is often necessary to calculate with very large or very small numbers. So scientists have adopted a convenient notation in which a *mantissa* and an *exponent* represent a number. For instance, 4,900,000 may be written as

THE ARITHMETIC-
LOGIC UNIT

0.49×10^7, where 0.49 is the mantissa and 7 is the value of the exponent; or 0.00023 may be written as 0.23×10^{-3}. The notation is based on the relation $y = a \times r^p$, where y is the number to be represented, a is the mantissa, r is the base of the number system ($r = 10$ for decimal and $r = 2$ for binary), and p is the power to which the base is raised.

It is possible to calculate with this representation system. To multiply $a \times 10^n$ and $b \times 10^m$, we form $a \times b \times 10^{m+n}$. To divide $a \times 10^m$ by $b \times 10^n$, we form $a/b \times 10^{m-n}$. To add $a \times 10^m$ to $b \times 10^n$, we must first make m equal to n. If $m = n$, then $a \times 10^m + b \times 10^n = a + b \times 10^m$. The process of making m equal to n is called *scaling* the numbers.

Considerable bookkeeping can be involved in scaling numbers, and there can be difficulty in maintaining precision during computations when numbers vary over a very wide range of magnitudes. For computer usage these problems are alleviated by means of two techniques whereby the computer (not the programmer) keeps track of the radix (decimal) point, automatically scaling the numbers. In the first, programmed *floating-point routines* automatically scale the numbers used during the computations while maintaining the precision of the results and keeping track of the scale factors. These routines are used with small computers having only fixed-point operations. A second technique lies in building what are called *floating-point operations* into the computer's hardware. The logic circuitry of the computer is then used to perform the scaling automatically and to keep track of the exponents when calculations are performed. To effect this, a number representation system called the *floating-point system* is used.

A floating-point number in a computer uses the exponential notation system described, and during calculations the computer keeps track of the exponent as well as the mantissa. A computer number word in a floating-point system may be divided into three pieces: the first is the sign bit, indicating whether the number is negative or positive; the second part contains the exponent for the number to be represented; and the third part is the mantissa.

As an example, let us consider a 12-bit word length computer with a floating-point word. Figure 5.30 shows this. It is common practice to call the exponent part of the word the *characteristic* and the mantissa section the *integer part*.

The integer part of the floating-point word shown represents its value in signed-magnitude form (rather than 2s complement, although this has been used). The characteristic is also in signed-magnitude form. The value of the number expressed is $I \times 2^C$, where I is the value of the integer part and C is the value of the characteristic.

Figure 5.31 shows several values of floating-point numbers both in binary form and after they are converted to decimal. Since the characteristic has 5 bits and is in signed-magnitude form, the C in $I \times 2^C$ can have values from -15 to

FIGURE 5.30

A 12-bit floating-point word.

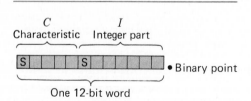

One 12-bit word

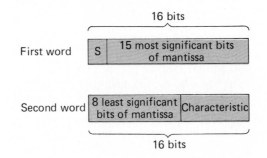

FIGURE 5.31

Values of floating-point numbers in 12-bit all-integer systems.

$+15$. The value of I is a sign-plus-magnitude binary integer of 7 bits, and so I can have values from -63 to $+63$. The largest number represented by this system would have a maximum I and would be 63×2^{15}.

This example shows the use of a floating-point number representation system to store "real" numbers of considerable range in a binary word.

One other widely followed practice is to express the mantissa of the word as a fraction instead of as an integer. This is in accord with common scientific usage since we commonly say that 0.93×10^4 is in "normal" form for exponential notation (and not 93×10^2). In this usage a mantissa in decimal normally has a value from 0.1 to 0.999. . . . Similarly, a binary mantissa in normal form would have a value from 0.5 (decimal) to less than 1. Most computers maintain their mantissa sections in normal form, continually adjusting words so that a significant (1) bit is always in the leftmost mantissa position.

When the mantissa is in fraction form, this section is called the *fraction*. For our 12-bit example, we can express floating-point numbers with characteristic and fraction by simply supposing the binary point to be to the left of the magnitude (and not to the right, as in integer representation). In this system a number to be represented has value $F \times 2^C$, where F is the binary fraction and C is the characteristic.

For the 12-bit word considered before, fractions would have values from $1 - 2^{-6}$, which is 0111111, to $-(1 - 2^{-6})$, which is 1111111, where the leftmost bit in each number is the sign bit. Thus numbers from $(1 - 2^{-6}) \times 2^{15}$

to $- (1 - 2^{-6}) \times 2^{15}$ can be represented, or about $+32,000$ to $-32,000$. The smallest value the fraction part could have is now the fraction 01000000, which is 2^{-1}, and the smallest characteristic, which is 2^{-15}, so the smallest positive number representable is $2^{-1} \times 2^{-15}$, or 2^{-16}. Most computers use this fractional system for the mantissa, although Burroughs and NCR use the integer system.

The Univac series of computers represents single-precision floating-point numbers in this format:

1	2	9	10	36	bit number
S	C		F		

↑	↑	↑
sign bit	characteristic 8 bits	fraction part 27 bits

For positive numbers, the characteristic C is treated as a binary integer, the sign bit is a 0, and the fraction part is a binary fraction with value $0.5 \leq F < 1$. The value of the number represented is $2^{C-128} \times F$. This is called an *offset system* because the value of the characteristic is simply the integer value in that portion of the word minus an offset, which in this case is 128. So the exponent can range from -128 to $+127$, since the integer in the characteristic section is 8 bits long.

As an example, the binary word

$$0 \quad 1 0 0 0 0 0 0 1 \qquad 1 \ 1 \ 0 \ 0 \ . \ . \ . \ 0$$

sign   characteristic   fraction

has value $2^{129-128} \times \frac{3}{4} = 2 \times \frac{3}{4} = 1.5$. The representation for a negative number can be derived by forming the representation for the positive number with the same magnitude and then forming the 1s complement of this representation (considering all 36 bits as a single binary number).

Another example of computers with internal circuitry which performs floating-point operations and uses a single computer word representation of floating-point numbers is the IBM series.

IBM calls the exponent part the *characteristic* and the mantissa part the *fraction*. In the IBM series, floating-point data words can be either 32 or 64 bits in length. The basic formats are as follows:

Short or single-word floating-point number:

S	characteristic	fraction
0	1→7	8→31

Long or double-word floating-point number:

S	characteristic	fraction
0	1→7	8→63

In both cases, the sign bit S is in the leftmost position and gives the sign of the number. The characteristic part of the word then comprises bits 1 to 7 and is simply a binary integer, which we call C, ranging from 0 to 127. The actual value of the scale factor is formed by subtracting 64 from this integer C and raising 16 to this power. Thus the value 64 in bits 1 to 7 gives a scale factor of $16^{C-64} = 16^{64-64} = 16^0$; a 93 (decimal) in bits 1 to 7 gives a scale factor of $16^{C-64} = 16^{93-64}$, which is 16^{29}; and a 24 in bits 1 to 7 gives a 16^{-40}.

The magnitude of the actual number represented in a given floating-point word is equal to this scale factor times the fraction contained in bits 8 to 31 for the short number or 8 to 63 for a long number. The radix point is assumed to be to the left of bit 8 in either case. So if bits 8 to 31 contain 1000 . . . 00, the fraction has value $\frac{1}{2}$ (decimal); that is, the fraction is .1000 . . . 000 in binary. Similarly, if bits 8 to 31 contain 11000 . . . 000, the fraction value is $\frac{3}{4}$ decimal, or .11000 . . . 000 binary.

The actual number represented then has magnitude equal to the value of the fraction times the value determined by the characteristic. Consider a short number:

	sign	characteristic	fraction
Floating-point number:	0	1 0 0 0 0 0 1	1 1 1 0 0 . . . 0
Bit position:	0	1 2 3 4 5 6 7	8 9 10 11 12 . . . 31

The sign bit is a 0, and so the number represented is positive. The characteristic has binary value 1000001, which is 65 decimal, and so the scale factor is 16^1. The fraction part has value .111 binary or $\frac{7}{8}$ decimal, and so the number represented is $\frac{7}{8} \times 16$, or 14 decimal.

Again, consider the following number:

	sign	characteristic	fraction
Floating-point number:	1	1 0 0 0 0 0 1	1 1 1 0 0 . . . 0
Bit position:	0	1 2 3 4 5 6 7	8 9 10 11 12 . . . 31

This has value -14 since every bit is the same as before, except for the sign bit. (The number representation system is signed magnitude.)

As further examples:

sign	characteristic	fraction	
0	1 0 0 0 0 1 1	1 1 0 . . . 0	$16^3 \times \frac{3}{4} = 3072$
0	0 1 1 1 1 1 1	1 1 0 . . . 0	$16^{-1} \times \frac{3}{4} = \frac{3}{64}$

Clearly a number of floating-point number systems exist, and each manufacturer has virtually a unique system. This can present a problem to system users

THE ARITHMETIC-
LOGIC UNIT

since programs in high-level languages may yield different results on one computer versus another. To alleviate this and several other problems, there is now a movement underway to standardize on a floating-point number system which will be made available by all manufacturers. The major effort in this area has resulted in the IEEE Proposed Standard for Binary Floating-Point Arithmetic. This standard is the result of work by several organizations (not just IEEE) and is widely supported, particularly by microcomputer manufacturers, several of which already provide actual systems conforming to the standard.

The principal feature of the standard probably is the "hidden 1" principle. Floating-point numbers generally have their fraction (magnitude) part stored with a leading 1 in the leftmost position. This is called *normalized form;* it ensures that the maximum number of significant bits is carried in the number. The reasoning behind the hidden 1 principle is that if the leftmost bit in the fraction (magnitude) section is always a 1, why carry it? Instead, this section of the floating-point number is shifted left one more bit and the 1 is discarded. However, in any reconstruction of the number for external use or during calculations, the 1 is replaced.

The IEEE standard for floating point uses the hidden 1 principle. There is a single and double format. Here is the single format.

Single format:

	1	←8→	←23 bits→
	S	E	F

where S is the sign bit, E is a binary integer, and F is a binary fraction of length 23. However, the value of F is formed by adding 1 to this fraction. Thus, if F in this format is stored as $11000\ .\ .\ .\ 00$, the value of F is $1.11000\ .\ .\ .\ 00$, which is $1\frac{3}{4}$ in decimal. The value of a floating-point number in this system is

$$V = (-1)^S \times 2^{E-127} \times 1.F$$

Notice that this system uses an offset of 127 for the exponent (characteristic) value.

Here are three examples of the system:

FLOATING-POINT FORMAT (HEXADECIMAL)	$(-1)^S \times 2^{E-127} \times 1.F$	DECIMAL VALUE
3F800000	$1 \times 2^0 \times 1.0$	$+1$
BF800000	$-1 \times 2^0 \times 1.0$	-1
40400000	$1 \times 2^1 \times 1.5$	$+3$

Note that fraction values for F range from 1 to slightly less than 2 ($1 \leq$ value of $F < 2$).

Double format:

	1	←11→	←52 bits→
	S	E	F

where S is the sign bit, E is an 11-bit binary integer, and F is a 52-bit binary fraction with binary point to the far left. However, the value for F is formed by adding 1 to the left of this fraction. So if F is stored as $101000 \ldots 00$, then the value of F is $1.10100 \ldots 00$, or $1\frac{5}{8}$ decimal. The value of the number stored is then

$$V = (-1)^S \times 2^{E-1023} \times F$$

Here are examples:

FLOATING-POINT FORMAT (HEXADECIMAL)	$(-1)^S \times 2^{E-1023} \times 1.F$	DECIMAL VALUE
$3FD0000 \ldots 00$	$1 \times 2^2 \times 1.0$	0.25
$C03E000 \ldots 00$	$-1 \times 2^4 \times 1.875$	-30
$401C000 \ldots 00$	$1 \times 2^2 \times 1.75$	7

Since a 1 is assumed to be "invisibly" stored with each number, the representation for 0 must be special. The standard 0 is represented by all 0s in the E and F sections (there is a $+0$ and a -0). Further, infinity is represented by all 1s in the E section and all 0s in the F section. There is, therefore, also a plus infinity and a minus infinity.

When numbers are so small that they cannot be represented in normalized form because E would need to be less than 1, then the F part is handled in denormalized form and the 1 is not added when the numbers are evaluated.

The results of invalid operations are signaled by making E all 0s; S can be anything; and if F is nonzero, the 1s in F signal an illegal operation.

Other formats are less used than the two shown here. A good complete introduction to this standard can be found in Jerome T. Coonen's "An Implementation Guide to a Proposed Standard for Floating-Point Arithmetic," *Computer,* January 1980.

PERFORMING ARITHMETIC OPERATIONS WITH FLOATING-POINT NUMBERS

5.24 A computer obviously requires additional circuitry to handle floating-point numbers automatically. Some machines come equipped with floating-point instructions. (For computers such as DEC PDP-11/45 and others, floating-point circuitry can be purchased and added to enable them to perform floating-point operations.)

To handle the floating-point numbers, the machine must be capable of extensive shifting and comparing operations. The rules for multiplying and dividing are

$$(a \times r^p) \times (b \times r^q) = ab \times r^{p+q}$$
$$(a \times r^p) \div (b \times r^q) = \frac{a}{b} \times r^{p-q}$$

The computer must be able to add or subtract the exponent sections of the floating-point numbers and to perform the multiplication or division operations on the mantissa sections of the numbers. In addition, precision is generally maintained by

251

PERFORMING
ARITHMETIC
OPERATIONS WITH
FLOATING-POINT
NUMBERS

shifting the numbers stored until significant digits are in the leftmost sections of the word. With each shift the exponent must be changed. If the machine is shifting the mantissa section left, for each left shift the exponent must be decreased.

For instance, in a BCD computer, consider the word

$$\underset{\text{sign}}{0} \qquad \underset{\text{exponent}}{10} \qquad \underset{\text{mantissa}}{0064}$$

To attain precision, the computer shifts the mantissa section left until the 6 is in the most significant position. Since two shifts are required, the exponent must be decreased by 2, and the resulting word is 0.08 6400. If all numbers to be used are scaled in this manner, maximum precision may be maintained throughout the calculations.

For addition and subtraction the exponent values must agree. For instance, to add 0.24×10^5 to 0.25×10^6, we must scale the numbers so that the exponents agree. Thus

$$0.024 \times 10^6 + 0.25 \times 10^6 = 0.274 \times 10^6$$

The machine must also follow this procedure. The numbers are scaled as described, so that the most significant digit of the computer mantissa section of each word contains the most significant digit of the number stored. Then the larger of the two exponents for the operands is selected, and the other number's mantissa is shifted and its exponent adjusted until the exponents for both numbers agree. The numbers may then be added or subtracted according to these rules:

$$a \times r^p + b \times r^p = (a + b) \times r^p$$
$$a \times r^p - b \times r^p = (a - b) \times r^p$$

SUMMARY

5.25 The binary full-adder forms the backbone of most arithmetic-logic units. Full-adders can be used to both add and subtract 2s or 1s complement numbers, and the layouts for these operations were shown.

Binary full-adders are often packaged in IC packages with several per package. Several examples were shown, including one which can also perform a number of logical operations.

Binary multiplication and binary division are generally performed by using three registers and a sequence of additions and/or subtractions and shifts. The control circuitry sequences these operations. Parallel multiplication can be performed by using gate networks consisting of full-adders correctly arranged. This technique makes very high-speed multipliers.

Binary-coded-decimal addition and subtraction units use special BCD adders and complementers. Examples were shown, and their use in serial-parallel systems was explained.

Floating-point number systems make it possible to represent very large and very small numbers using fewer bits than would be required for straight binary.

Often calculations are not exact since numbers are approximated in many cases, but floating-point number systems are almost always used for large scientific computations and by higher-level languages. Several examples of floating-point number systems were explained, including the new ANSI standard.

QUESTIONS

5.1 Draw a block diagram of circuitry for two registers X and Y of three flip-flops each, so that Y can be transferred into X, or the 1s complement of Y can be transferred into X.

5.2 Two parallel binary registers, designated register X and register Y, both consist of three flip-flops. Draw a block diagram of the registers and the necessary logic circuitry so that (*a*) register X can be cleared, or 1s complemented, and (*b*) the 1s complement of the contents of register Y can be transferred into register X.

5.3 If a binary computer handles numbers in the sign-plus-magnitude integer system and numbers are 5 bits (sign plus 4 bits) each, how would the following decimal numbers be represented? For example, $+5 = \underline{0}0101$.
  (*a*) $+6$ (*b*) $+10$ (*c*) -12 (*d*) -16

5.4 If a binary computer represents numbers in a sign-plus-magnitude form with 5 bits per number, how would the following decimal numbers be represented.
  (*a*) $+8$ (*b*) $+11$ (*c*) -7
  (*d*) -4 (*e*) -15 (*f*) -12

5.5 If a binary machine handles negative numbers in the true magnitude form, how would -4 be stored in a register with a sign bit and 4 bits representing magnitude? If the same machine stored numbers in the 1s complement system, how would -4 be stored?

5.6 If a register contains five flip-flops as in Fig. 5.1(*b*) and the register contains $X_0 = 1, X_2 = 1, X_3 = 0, X_4 = 0, X_5 = 1$, give the decimal value of the number in the register if the 1s complement number system is used. What is the value if 2s complement is used?

5.7 The inputs to the full adder in Fig. 5.3 are as follows: $X = 1, Y = 1$, and $C = 1$. What will the output on the S and C lines represent?

5.8 If we use the $\oplus$ symbol to mean exclusive OR and define it as $X \oplus Y = \overline{X}Y + X\overline{Y}$, then the output S from a full-adder can be written as $S = X \oplus Y \oplus C_i$. Show why this is the case.

5.9 If we load the binary number $\underline{1}0011$ into the flip-flops in Fig. 5.1(*b*), that is, if $X_4 = 1, X_3 = 0, X_2 = 0, X_1 = 1$, and $X_0 = 1$, what will the value of the register be in the 1s complement number system? Give the answer in decimal. What will the value of this number be if the 2s complement number system is used?

5.10 If register X contains $\underline{0}0111$ and register Y contains $\underline{1}1011$, what do the two numbers represent in decimal if 1s complement is used? If 2s complement is used?

Add the two numbers in 1s complement, then in 2s complement, and give the results in decimal.

5.11 Register X contains $\underline{0}1100$, and register Y contains $\underline{0}1101$ (where the underscored 0s designate that the number stored is positive). If the two registers are added, what will the result be?

5.12 If 1s complement is used, for which of the following expressions will an overflow or end-around carry be generated? Why? Assume 5-bit registers, including a sign bit.

(a) $+ 5 + (-7)$ (b) $+ 5 + (-4)$
(c) $+ 12 + (-13)$ (d) $+ 12 + 3$

5.13 Add a stage to the load-and-shift register in Fig. 5.17. Copy only D in your drawing, omitting A, B, and C.

5.14 A binary register consists of five binary storage devices; one stores the sign bit, and the other four store the magnitude bits. If the number stored is $\underline{0}0110$ and this number is then shifted right one binary place, what will be the result? Assume a 0 goes into the sign bit.

5.15 Design a half-adder, using only NOR gates.

5.16 Design a half-adder, using only NAND gates.

5.17 A binary half-subtracter has two inputs x and y and two outputs, which are the "difference" value $x - y$ and a "borrow" output that is 1 if the value of $x - y$ is negative ($x - y$ is then given the value 1). Draw a block diagram for a half-subtracter, using NAND gates and assuming x, $\bar{x}$, y, and $\bar{y}$ are all available as inputs.

5.18 Design a half-subtracter, using only NOR gates.

5.19 If a borrow input is added to the half-subtracter in Questions 5.17 and 5.18, a full-subtracter is formed. Design a full-subtracter, using only NAND gates.

5.20 Design a full-subtracter, using only NOR gates.

5.21 Design a full-adder, using only NAND gates.

5.22 Can an overflow occur during multiplication in a binary machine with numbers stored in fixed-point sign-plus-magnitude form? Assume a double-length product.

5.23 Explain how the 2s complement of the subtrahend is formed when we subtract, using the configuration in Fig. 5.6. How is the 1 added in to form this complement?

5.24 Show how the configuration in Fig. 5.6 adds and subtracts by adding and subtracting $+21$ and $+3$ in binary, showing what each output will be.

5.25 Using the configuration in Fig. 5.6, add and subtract $+6$ and -4, showing what each output will be and checking the correctness of the sum and difference.

5.26 Draw a multiplexer using only NAND gates which selects from four inputs I_0 to I_3, using two select inputs S_0 and S_1.

5.27 Design a multiplexer for four inputs, using a two-level NOR gate combinational network. The inputs are to be X_0, X_1, X_2, and X_3. The output is to be called W. The X_0, X_1, X_2, and X_3 are "selected" by S_0 and S_1. If S_0 and $S_1 = 0$, then W should equal X_0. If S_1 and $S_0 = 01$, then W should equal X_1. If S_0 and $S_1 = 10$, then W should equal X_2. If S_0 and $S_1 = 11$, then W should equal X_3.

5.28 Add a control line NAND and circuitry to Fig. 5.20 so that the NAND of ACC and B can be transferred into AOC.

5.29 If a register containing $\underline{0}110011$ is logically added to a register containing $\underline{0}101010$, what will the result be? What will be the result if the registers are logically multiplied? If the registers are exclusive ORed?

5.30 Find a sequence of logical operations which will cause the ACC to have value 0 regardless of how ACC and B start in Fig. 5.20.

5.31 Referring to Fig. 5.20, show that a logical multiplication followed by a logical addition will transfer the contents of B to ACC.

5.32 Add a control line NOR and circuitry to Fig. 5.20 so that the NOR of ACC and B can be transferred into ACC.

5.33 Demonstrate by means of a table of combinations that two half-adders plus an OR gate do make a full-adder, as shown in Fig. 5.4.

5.34 Add gates and a flip-flop X_{m+2} so that we can shift left and right into X_{m+1} in Fig. 5.16.

5.35 Add gates to the following drawing so that if the control input signal C is made a 1, the value $\overline{XY}$ will appear on the output line. If A is a 1, then $X + Y$ appears on the output; if B is a 1, then $X \cdot Y$ appears on the output; if A, B, and C are 0s, then the output is to be a 0; and only one of A, B, or C can be a 1 at a given time.

FIGURE 5.35

LOGIC DIAGRAM

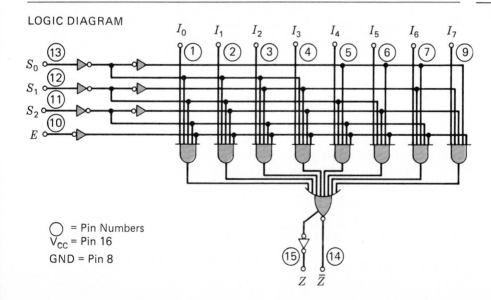

$\bigcirc$ = Pin Numbers
V_{CC} = Pin 16
GND = Pin 8

THE ARITHMETIC-
LOGIC UNIT

5.36 In what case will subtracting a negative number from 0 cause an overflow in the 2s complement system?

5.37 Design a *parallel multiplier* gate network with two inputs A_1A_0 and $B_2B_1B_0$, where A_1A_0 are two binary digits forming a binary number (with decimal values for 0 to 3) and $B_2B_1B_0$ is a 3-bit binary number (with values 0 to 7). Use only AND gates and OR gates, and see that no signal passes through more than four levels of gates. (Assume input complements are available.)

5.38 Write the boolean algebra expressions for the four least significant bits in a parallel multiplier which multiplies two 4-bit binary numbers.

5.39 Design a gating network for a module in an ALU that will add two 2-bit binary inputs A_j, A_{j-1} and B_j, B_{j-1} and an input carry-in C_{j-1}. The network is to generate the two sum digits and a carry-out C_{j+2}. Use only AND or OR gates and inverters, but assume that both complemented and uncomplemented inputs are available. The output carry C_{j+2} should have a delay of no more than three-gate delays (that is, a change in an input must pass through no more than three gates in any path to an output).

5.40 (*a*) Give the IBM floating-point representation for decimal 27.25 and -27.25.
(*b*) Give the IEEE standard format representation for $+12$ and -12.

5.41 (*a*) Give the IBM floating-point representation for $+55.4$ and -53.4.
(*b*) Give the IEEE standard single-precision floating-point representation for $+29$ and -29.
(*c*) Compare the ranges, accuracy, and other system design considerations for the above two computer floating-point number systems.

5.42 If numbers are represented in a 2s complement, 7-bit magnitude plus 1 sign-bit integer system, and we ignore overflow (that is, any result will be stored, even if it requires more magnitude bits), then the largest positive integer which can result from the addition of two numbers is _____, and the largest positive integer which can result from the subtraction of one number from another is _____. The least negative numbers which can result from an addition and subtraction are _____ and _____. As a result, any sum or difference can be stored in _____ bits.

5.43 Write all 4-bit 2s complement numbers (that is, sign plus 3-bit numbers) and their decimal values. Show that there is one more negative number than positive number. Consider 0 to be neither negative nor positive.

5.44 When addition is performed in a binary machine using the 2s complement number system to represent negative numbers, an overflow may occur in a register only when two positive or two negative numbers are added. Show that the addition of a positive number and a negative number cannot result in an overflow condition.

5.45 Show that there are as many negative as positive numbers in a 1s complement system.

5.46 The boolean algebra expressions on the output lines from the gates in Fig. 5.8 are not filled in. Develop the boolean algebra expressions for the $S1$, $S2$, and $C2$ outputs from the network.

5.47 Which of the following number systems has two 0s?

(*a*) Sign plus magnitude   (*b*) 1s complement

(*c*) 2s complement

5.48 When the 2s complement number system is used and addition is performed, let us designate the carry-out of the full-adder connected into the full-adder for the sign digits as C_3 (refer to Fig. 5.6). The rule for overflow is that two numbers cause an overflow when they are added either if both numbers are positive and C_3 equals a 1 or if both numbers are negative and C_3 does not equal a 1. Therefore, by examining the sign digits of the two numbers being added and the carry-out of the full-adder which adds the two most significant digits of the magnitude of the numbers, we can form a logic network whose output will be a 1 when an overflow condition arises and a 0 if the addition is legitimate. Let X_4 store the sign digit of the addend, let Y_4 store the sign digit of the augend, and let C_3 again be the carry-out of the full-adders connected to the X_3 and Y_3 flip-flops, as in Fig. 5.6. Show that the logic equation for an overflow condition is $X_4Y_4\overline{C}_3 + \overline{X}_4\overline{Y}_4C_3 = $ overflow.

5.49 Modify Fig. 5.16 so that the complement of X can be shifted into X_m, that is, so that SHIFT LEFT causes $\overline{X}_{m-1}$ to go into X_m.

5.50 Show that when we add 7 to 9 in the BCD system using the series-parallel BCD adder in Fig. 5.10, the answer will be correct. Do this by tracing the outputs of the circuit, filling in the binary value for each X and Y shown in the figure, and by showing the values of Z_8, Z_4, Z_2 and Z_1.

5.51 Show how the BCD adder in Fig. 5.11 adds $+6$ to $+5$ by calculating each output from the gates and then the final outputs.

5.52 Check how the gates in Fig. 5.12 form a 9s complement by trying 5 and 3 in BCD at the inputs.

5.53 Explain the operation of Fig. 5.15 by explaining how 234 can be added to or subtracted from 523 in this configuration.

5.54 What is the function of the D flip-flop in Fig. 5.15?

5.55 Explain how to load the input values on $W, X, Y,$ and Z into the flip-flops in Fig. 5.17.

5.56 Explain how to cause the flip-flops in Fig. 5.17 to shift right three times. Suppose we (1) make the *reset* input a 0 then a 1, (2) hold J and K at 1 and shift at 1, and (3) apply three clock pulses to the CLOCK line. Draw the output waveforms for $A, B, C,$ and D for this sequence of inputs.

5.57 What is the result if we multiply $\underline{0}1101$ times $\underline{0}0011$ in our generalized machine in Fig. 5.18? Give the values in each X and B flip-flop.

5.58 What is the binary number that represents -3 in the 2s complement fractional number system if we represent the number by using a sign digit plus four magnitude digits?

5.59 Using the 8,4,2,1 BCD system with a single digit for the sign digit, write

the following numbers, using a sign-plus-magnitude number system:

(*a*) $+0014$ (*b*) $+0291$

(*c*) -2346 (*d*) -0364

5.60 Using the 8,4,2,1 BCD system, write in binary form the following decimal numbers. Use a single digit for the sign digit, and express the numbers as magnitude plus sign.

(*a*) $+0043$ (*b*) -0222 (*c*) $+1234$ (*d*) -1297

5.61 Using the 8,4,2,1 code as in Question 5.59, give the same numbers but use 9s complement for the negative numbers.

5.62 Express each of the numbers in Question 5.60, using the 9s complement and the 8,4,2,1 BCD system. For example, $-1024 = \underline{1}1000\ 1001\ 0111\ 0101$.

5.63 Write the binary forms of the numbers in Question 5.60, using 8,4,2,1 but 10s complements for negative numbers.

5.64 Write the decimal numbers in Question 5.60, using the 10s complement number system and again the 8,4,2,1 BCD system. For example, $-1420 = \underline{1}1000\ 0101\ 1000\ 0000$.

5.65 If we add two 20-digit binary numbers, using the full-adders shown in Fig. 5.8, and if 3 ns is required for a signal to pass through a gate, what is the maximum time it will require a CARRY signal to propagate from the lowest-order bits to the highest-order bits, assuming a full-adder which is parallel as in Fig. 5.6?

5.66 Explain how you would add gates and inputs to Fig. 5.17 so that the flip-flop register could be shifted left as well as right.

5.67 If we multiply 6×11 in the registers in Fig. 5.18, show the placement of binary digits at the start and end of the multiplication.

5.68 Show how 7×9 and 5×5 would be multiplied in the registers in Fig. 5.18.

5.69 Draw a flowchart (as in Fig. 5.19) for the binary multiplication procedure described.

5.70 If we divide 23 by 6 in the registers in Fig. 5.18, show the beginning positioning of the numbers (in binary) and the result at the end. (Show where the quotient and the remainder are placed.)

5.71 Explain how to divide 14 by 4 by using the registers in Fig. 5.18 and showing how the quotient and the remainder are placed after the division.

5.72 Go through the division of 14 by 3, using the technique shown in the text.

5.73 Using the algorithm shown in Fig. 5.19, show how to divide 11 by 4.

5.74 Show how to represent $+6$ in the 12-bit floating-point word in Fig. 5.31.

5.75 Show how to represent -14 in the 12-bit floating-point word in Fig. 5.31.

5.76 (*a*) Give the IBM floating-point representation for 57.5 and 54.5.

(*b*) Give the IEEE standard format floating-point representation for $+25.0$ and -25.0.

(c) Compare the ranges, accuracy, and other system design considerations for the above two computer floating-point number systems.

5.77 Show two decimal numbers which, when converted to the IBM 370 floating-point number system, will have .0011 in bits 8, 9, 10, and 11.

5.78 Can you give any reasons that might be behind the decision of the systems architects at IBM to use hexadecimal as the base for the IBM series floating-point number system instead of conventional base 2? That is, in system 370 a floating-point fullword of 32 bits has as characteristic a 7-bit integer with value C and as fraction a binary signed-magnitude fraction 25-bit number with value F. The value of the number represented is then $(16^{C-64})F$. Why 16^{C-64} rather than 2^{C-64}? Give system design considerations.

5.79 Give the value of a positive nonzero *integer* less than 16^{62} which cannot be represented in the IBM 370 floating-point number system (using a single 32-bit word). Do not be afraid to use an expression such as $2^{16} + 3$ for your answer, but explain why you think your answer is correct.

5.80 A binary computer with a basic 16-bit code uses an integer 2s complement number system. The arithmetic element contains an accumulator and MQ register, each containing 16 flip-flops (or bits). When a multiplication is performed, the 16-bit word taken from the memory is multiplied by the 16-bit word in the accumulator, and the product is stored in the combined ACC-MQ with the least significant bit in the rightmost bit of the MQ. The sign bit of the MQ is set the same as the sign of the ACC and is not used to store a magnitude bit. In what bit of the ACC does the most significant bit of a product appear for numbers of maximum magnitude?

5.81 For the 74S181 chip in Fig. 5.21, write the boolean algebra expression for $\overline{F}_0$ in terms of A_0, B_0, and C_n if M, S_3, S_1, S_0 are 1s and S_2 is a 0.

5.82 For the 74S181 chip in Fig. 5.21, how would you set M and S_0, S_1, S_2, and S_3 to subtract B from A?

5.83 For the 74S181 chip in Fig. 5.21, if we set $M = 1$, $S_3 = S_1 = S_0 = 1$, and $S_2 = 0$, the chip will add A to B. Write the boolean algebra expression for F_1 in terms of the A, B, C_{n+4} inputs.

5.84 How would you set the M, S_0, S_1, S_2, S_3 inputs to the 74S181 chip in Fig. 5.21 to form the AND of A and B?

5.85 How would you set the M, S_0, S_1, S_2, S_3 inputs to perform an OR of the A and B inputs for the chip in Fig. 5.21?

5.86 Explain how the carry output C_n is formed for the chip in Fig. 5.21.

5.87 The statement was made that the maximum delay through the 74S181 chip in Fig. 5.21 is 11 ns. This means, for instance, that if all the inputs are held in the same state except for $\overline{A}_0$, then from the time $\overline{A}_0$ is changed, the maximum time for C_{n+4} to change will be 11 ns. Find the maximum number of gates through which this delay must propagate. Then determine typical single-gate delays.

5.88 The inputs to the 74S181 chip in Fig. 5.21 are each complemented, as are

THE ARITHMETIC-
LOGIC UNIT

the outputs. Suppose we connect the A and B inputs to the uncomplemented outputs of the A and B flip-flops, also changing the diagram by removing the bars over the A and B inputs and the F outputs. Now if M is a 1, the functions yielded by each S_0, S_1, S_2, and S_3 state (input combination) will be different from those shown in Fig. 5.21. For instance, $M = S_3 = S_2 = S_1 = 1$ and $S_0 = 0$ will cause the circuit to form $A + B$. Give three more different output functions and their S_0, S_1, S_2, and S_3 values.

5.89 Repeat the setup with Question 5.88 and give three more functions.

5.90 The following is the block diagram for a 74S182 chip in the TTL series. This works with four 74S181 chips as shown in Fig. 5.21. The $\overline{G}_0$, $\overline{P}_0$, $\overline{G}_1$, $\overline{P}_1$, . . . inputs here are connected to the $\overline{G}$ and $\overline{P}$ outputs for the four 74S181 chips to be used. The 74S182 chip forms a carry-look-ahead generator for all four chips, forming high-speed carries for inputs to these chips. A complete 16-bit addition can be performed in 22 ns. Explain how this works.

FIGURE 5.90

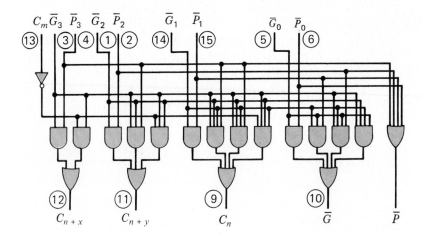

5.91 For the carry generator in Question 5.90 and four 74S181 chips as in Fig. 5.21, find the longest carry propagation path and determine how many gates are in it.

5.92 Develop the boolean algebra expression for the carry output in Fig. 5.29.

5.93 Convert the boolean algebra expression for the carry-out in a 3-bit adder to two-level AND-to-OR gate form.

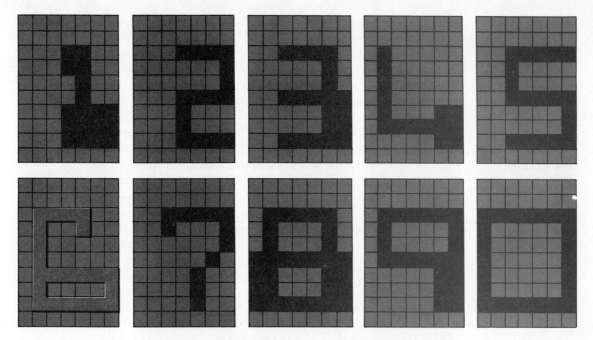

THE MEMORY ELEMENT

The memory of a computer is not actually concentrated in one place; storage devices are scattered throughout the machine. For instance, the *operation registers* are flip-flop registers which are used in the arithmetic and control units of the computer. Arithmetic operations including additions, multiplications, shifts, etc., are all performed in these registers of the machine. The actual processing of information is performed in, and at the direction of, these registers.

Looking outward, the next category of storage device encountered is called the *high-speed memory, inner memory,* or *main memory.* This section of the computer's memory consists of a set of storage registers, each of which is identified with an address that enables the control unit either to write into or read from a particular register.

It is desirable that the operating speed of this section of the computer's memory be as fast as possible, for most of the transfers of data to and from the information processing section of the machine will be via the main memory. For this reason, storage devices with very fast access times are generally chosen for the main memory; unfortunately the presently available devices which are fast enough to perform this function satisfactorily do not possess the storage capacity that is sometimes required. As a result, additional memory, which is called the *auxiliary memory,* or *secondary memory,* is added to most computers. This section of the computer's memory is characterized by low cost per digit stored, but it generally has an operating speed far slower than that of either the operation registers or the main memory. This section of the memory is sometimes designated the *backup memory,* for its function is to handle quantities of data in excess of those that may be stored in the inner memory.

**THE MEMORY
ELEMENT**

The final and outermost storage devices are used to introduce information to the computer from the "outside world" and to store results from the computer to the computer user. The storage media in this case generally consist of such input media as punched cards or perforated paper tape, and the outputs from the machine generally consist of printed characters. Again, the cost per bit is low, but the operating speeds of the tape and card readers, printers, etc., are liable to be on the order of 1000 times slower than the speeds of the operation registers. These devices are described in Chap. 8 under input-output devices. This chapter is limited to the *internal storage* of the machine, which is defined as those storage devices that form an integral part of the machine and are directly controlled by the machine.

Each division of memory has certain characteristics. For instance, the premium on speed is very high for the operation registers. These registers generally must perform operations at several times the speed of the main memory. The main memory also requires high operating speeds, but because it is desirable to store larger quantities of data (perhaps 10^5 to 10^9 bits) in this section, a compromise between cost and speed generally must be made. Often the same sort of compromise must be made in the case of the auxiliary memory. In a large machine, the auxiliary memory may have to store from 10^8 to 10^{14} binary digits, and in these instances it might prove too expensive to use devices such as those employed in the main memory.

An important point to note when operating speed is considered is that, before a word can be read, it is necessary to locate it. The time required to locate and read a word from memory is called the *access time*. The procedures for locating information may be divided into two classes, random access and sequential access. A *random-access* storage device is one in which any location in the device may be selected at random, access to the information stored is direct, and approximately equal access time is required for each location. A flip-flop register is an example of a random-access storage device, as are the IC memories, which will be described. A *sequential-access* device is one in which the arrival at the location desired may be preceded by sequencing through other locations, so that access time varies according to location.[1] For instance, if we try to read a word stored on a reel of magnetic tape and the piece of tape on which the word is stored is near the center of the reel, it is necessary to sequence through all the intervening tape before the word can be read.

Another way to subdivide storage devices is according to whether they are static or dynamic. A *static* storage device is one in which the information does not change position; flip-flop registers and even punched cards or tape are examples of static storage devices. *Dynamic* storage devices are devices in which the information stored is continually changing position. Circulating registers utilizing charge-coupled device (CCD) delay lines are examples of dynamic storage devices.

This chapter will concentrate on the three most frequently used devices for storing digital information in the internal memory sections of computers: IC memo-

---

[1]Sequential-access devices are further separated into *direct-access storage devices* (DASD) and *serial-access devices*. Direct-access storage devices have addresses, but the access time to reach the data at a given address may vary. For instance, the time to locate on a movable-head disk (to be explained) depends on the head position and disk position when the address is given. Serial-access devices are truly serial in their access properties; magnetic tape is the classic example.

ries, which are high speed and of moderate cost; magnetic disk memories, which are direct-access storage devices generally used for auxiliary storage; and magnetic-tape memories, which are used almost exclusively as an auxiliary, or backup, storage but which are capable of storing large quantities of information at low cost. Following the sections on disk and magnetic-tape devices, the techniques used to record digital information on a magnetic surface are described.

OBJECTIVES

1 Memory cells are distributed throughout a computer. The faster memory devices are in the central processing unit which uses flip-flops. The main memory then uses IC circuits (or cores), but in arrays which are slower than the very high-speed flip-flops used in the CPU. The backup, or secondary, memory uses magnetic devices such as disks or tape. All these are discussed from a general organizational viewpoint.

2 IC memories are now used in the main high-speed memory in most computers. The selection of specific cells from an array of memory cells is an important factor in memory design, and this subject is treated first. Then, how IC memory chips are organized into a memory is described. Finally, the types of IC memories now in active use are discussed.

3 Disk and tape memories are the most used large memories, and the organization and construction of these are explained along with some of their operating and cost characteristics. Bubble memories and CCD memories are also discussed.

RANDOM-ACCESS MEMORIES

6.1 The main memory of a computer is organized in a way which is particularly desirable. Figure 6.1 shows that a high-speed main memory in a computer is organized into words of fixed lengths. As the figure indicates, a given memory is

FIGURE 6.1

Words in high-speed memory.

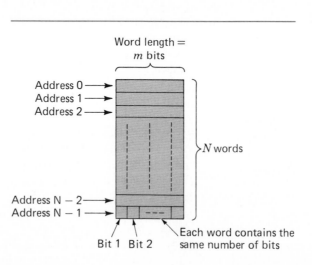

**THE MEMORY
ELEMENT**

divided into *N* words, where *N* generally is some power of 2, and each word is assigned an *address,* or *location,* in the memory. Each word has the same number of bits, called the *word length.* And if we read, for instance, the word at location 72, we receive a word from the memory with this word length.

The addresses, or address numbers, in the memory run consecutively, starting with the address 0 and running up to the largest address. Thus at address 0 we find a word, at address 1 a second word, at address 2 a third word, and so on up to the final word at the largest address.

Generally, the computer can read a word from or write a word into each location in the memory. For a memory with an 8-bit word, if we write the word 01001011 into memory address 17 and later read from this same address, we shall read the word 01001011. If we again read from this address at a later time (and have not written another word in), then the word 01001011 will be read again. This means the memory is a *nondestructive read,* in that reading does not destroy or change a stored word.

It is important to understand the difference between the *contents* of a memory address and the address itself. A memory is like a large cabinet containing as many drawers as there are addresses in memory. In each drawer is a word, and the address of each word is written on the outside of the drawer. If we write or store a word at address 17, it is like placing the word in the drawer labeled 17. Later, reading from address 17 is like looking in that drawer to see its contents. We do not remove the word at an address when we read. We change the contents at an address only when we store or write a new word.

From an exterior viewpoint, a high-speed main memory looks very much like a "black box" with a number of locations or addresses into which data can be stored or from which data can be read. Each address, or location, contains a fixed number of binary bits, the number being called the *word length* for the memory. A memory with 4096 locations, each with a different address and with each location storing 16 bits, is called a *4096-word 16-bit memory,* or, in the vernacular of the computer trade, a *4K 16-bit memory.* (Since memories generally come with a number of words equal to 2^n for some *n,* if a memory has $2^{14} = 16,384$ words, computer literature and jargon would refer to it as a 16K memory, because it is always understood that the full 2^n words actually occur in the memory. Thus, a 2^{15}-word 16-bit memory is called a 32K 16-bit memory.)

Memories can be read from (that is, data can be taken out) or written into (data can be entered into the memory). Memories which can be both read from and written into are called *read-write memories.* Some memories have programs or data permanently stored and are called *read-only memories.*

A block diagram of a read-write memory is shown in Fig. 6.2. The computer places the address of the location into which the data are to be read into the *memory address register.* This register consists of *n* binary devices (generally flip-flops), where 2^n is the number of words that can be stored in the memory. The data to be written into the memory are placed in the *memory buffer register,* which has as many binary storage devices as there are bits in each memory word. The memory is told to write by means of a 1 signal on the WRITE line. Then the memory will store the contents of the memory buffer register in the location specified by the memory address register.

Words are read by placing the address of the location to be read from into

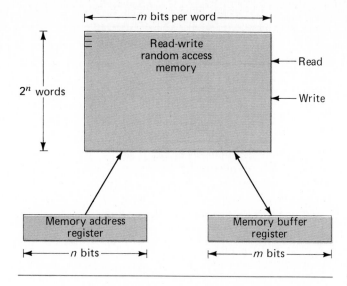

FIGURE 6.2

Read-write random-access memory.

the memory address register. Then a 1 signal is placed on the READ line, and the contents of that location are placed by the memory in the memory buffer register.

As can be seen, the computer communicates with the memory by means of the memory address register, the memory buffer register, and the READ and WRITE inputs. Memories are generally packaged in separate modules or packages. It is possible to buy a memory module of a specified size from a number of different manufacturers. For instance, a 64K 16-bit memory module can be purchased on a circuit board ready for use. Similarly, if a computer is purchased with a certain amount of main memory, generally more memory can be added later by purchasing additional modules and "plugging them in."

If it is possible to read from or write into any location "at once," that is, if there is no more delay in reaching one location than another, the memory is called a *random-access memory* (RAM). Computers almost invariably use random-access read-write memories for their high-speed main memory and then use backup or slower-speed memories to hold auxiliary data.

LINEAR-SELECT MEMORY ORGANIZATION

6.2 The most used random-access memories are IC memories. To present the basic principles, an idealized IC memory is shown, followed by details of several actual commercial memories.

In any memory there must be a basic memory cell. Figure 6.3 shows a basic memory cell consisting of an *RS* flip-flop with associated control circuitry. To use this cell in a memory, however, a technique for selecting those cells addressed by the memory address register must be used, as must a method to control whether the selected cells are written into or read from.

Figure 6.4 shows the basic memory organization for a *linear-select* IC memory. This is a four-address memory with 3 bits per word. The memory address register (MAR) selects the memory cells (flip-flops) to be read from or written into through

**THE MEMORY
ELEMENT**

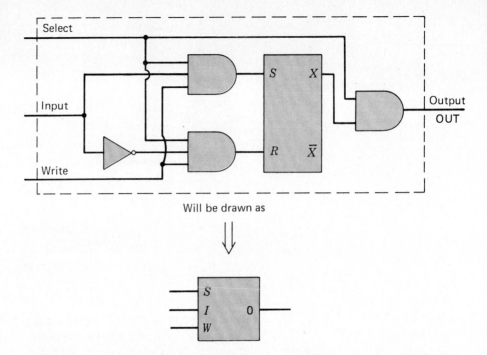

Will be drawn as

FIGURE 6.3

Basic memory cell.

a *decoder* which selects three flip-flops for each address that can be in the memory address register.

Figure 6.5(a) shows the decoder in expanded form. It has an input from each flip-flop (bit) to be decoded. If there are 2 input bits as in Fig. 6.5(a), then there will be four output lines, one for each state (value) the input register can take. For instance, if the MAR contains 0 in both flip-flops, then the upper line of the decoder will be a 1 and the remaining three lines a 0. Similarly, if both memory cells contain a 1, the lowest output line will be a 1 and the remaining three lines a 0. Similar reasoning will show that there will be a single output line with a 1 output for each possible input state, and the remaining lines will always be a 0.

Figure 6.5(b) shows a decoder for three inputs. The decoder has eight output lines. In general, for n input bits a decoder will have 2^n output lines.

The decoder in Fig. 6.5(b) operates in the same manner as that in Fig. 6.5(a). For each input state the decoder will select a particular output line, placing a 1 on the selected line and a 0 on the remaining lines.

Returning to Fig. 6.4, we now see that corresponding to each value that can be placed in the MAR, a particular output line from the decoder will be selected and carry a 1 value. The remaining output lines from the decoder will contain 0s, not selecting the AND gates at the inputs and outputs of the flip-flops for these rows. (Refer also to Fig. 6.3.)

The memory in Fig. 6.4 is organized as follows: There are four words, and each row of three memory cells comprises a word. At any given time the MAR selects a word in memory. If the READ line is a 1, the contents of the three cells in the selected word are read out on the O_1, O_2, and O_3 lines. If the WRITE line is a 1, the values on I_1, I_2, and I_3 are read into the memory.

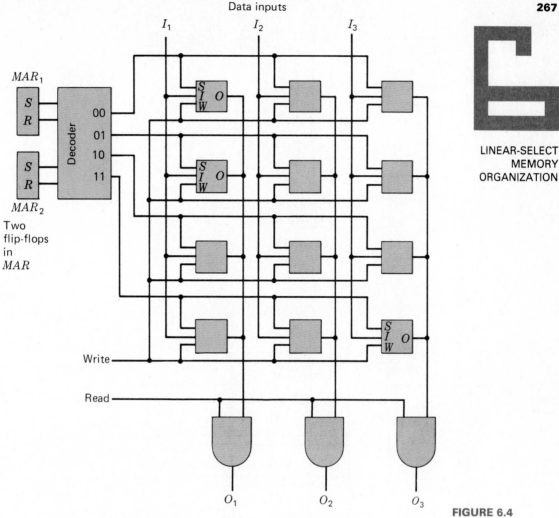

LINEAR-SELECT
MEMORY
ORGANIZATION

FIGURE 6.4

Linear-select IC
memory.

The AND gates connected to the OUT lines on the memory cells in Fig. 6.3 must have the property that when a number of AND gate output lines are connected, the output goes to the highest level. (If any OUT is a 1, the line goes to 1; otherwise, it is a 0.) This is called a *wired OR*. In Fig. 6.4 all four memory cells in the first column are wire-ORed; so if any output line is a 1, the entire line will be a 1. (Memory cells in IC memories are constructed in this manner.)

Now if the READ line is a 1 in Fig. 6.4, then the output values for the flip-flops in the selected row will all be gated onto the output line for each bit in the memory.

For example, if the second row in the memory contains 110 in the three memory cells, and if the MAR contains 01, then the second output line from the decoder (marked 01) will be a 1, and the input gates and output gates to these three memory cells will be selected. If the READ line is a 1, then the outputs from the

THE MEMORY
ELEMENT

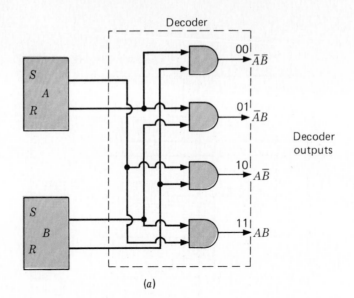

(a)

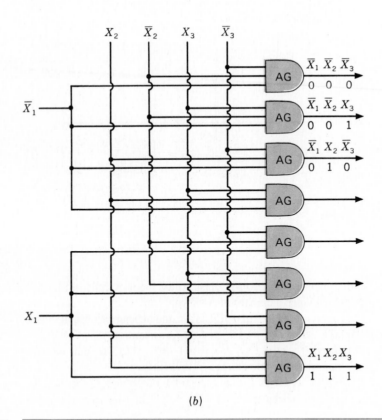

(b)

FIGURE 6.5

(a) Four-output de-
coder. (b) Parallel de-
coder.

three memory cells in the second row will be 110 to the AND gates at the bottom of the figure, which will transmit the value 110 as an output from the memory.

If the WRITE line is a 1 and the MAR again contains 01, the second row of flip-flops will have selected inputs. Then the input values on I_1, I_2, and I_3 will be read into the flip-flops in the second row.

As may be seen, this is a complete memory, fully capable of reading and writing. The memory will store data for an indefinite period and will operate as fast as the gates and flip-flops will permit. There is only one problem with the memory—its complexity. The basic memory cell (the flip-flop with its associated circuitry) is complicated, and for large memories the decoder will be large.

To further explore memory organization, we examine decoder construction in more detail, the selection schemes that are commonly used, and finally some examples of IC memories now in production.

DECODERS

6.3 An important part of the system which selects the cells to be read from and written into is the decoder. This particular circuit is called a *many-to-one decoder,* a *decoder matrix,* or simply a decoder. It has the characteristic that for each of the possible 2^n binary input numbers which can be taken by the n input cells, the matrix will have a unique one of its 2^n output lines selected.

Figure 6.5(*b*) shows a decoder which is completely parallel in construction and designed to decode three flip-flops. There are $2^3 = 8$ output lines; and for each of the eight states which the three inputs (flip-flops) may take, a unique output line will be selected. This type of decoder is often constructed by using diodes (or transistors) in the AND gates. The rule is: the number of diodes (or transistors) used in each AND gate is equal to the number of inputs to each AND gate.[2] For Fig. 6.5(*b*) this is equal to the number of input lines (flip-flops which are being decoded). Further, the number of AND gates is equal to the number of output lines, which is equal to 2^n (n is the number of input flip-flops being decoded). So the total number of diodes is equal to $n \times 2^n$. And for the binary decoding matrix in Fig. 6.5(*b*), 24 diodes are required to construct the network. As may be seen, the number of diodes required increases sharply with the number of inputs to the network. For instance, to decode an eight-flip-flop register, we would require $8 \times 2^8 = 2048$ diodes if the decoder were constructed in this manner.

As a result, several other types of structures are often used in building decoder networks. One such structure, called a *tree-type* decoding network, is shown in Fig. 6.6. This tree network decodes four flip-flops and so has $2^4 = 16$ output lines, a unique one of which is selected for each state of the flip-flops. An examination will show that 56 diodes are required to build this particular network, while $2^4 \times 4 = 64$ diodes would be required to build the parallel decoder type shown in Fig. 6.5.

Still another type of decoder network is shown in Fig. 6.7. It is called a *balanced multiplicative decoder network*. Notice that this network requires only 48

---

[2]The rule for transistors is the same: The number of transistors required equals the number of inputs.

**THE MEMORY
ELEMENT**

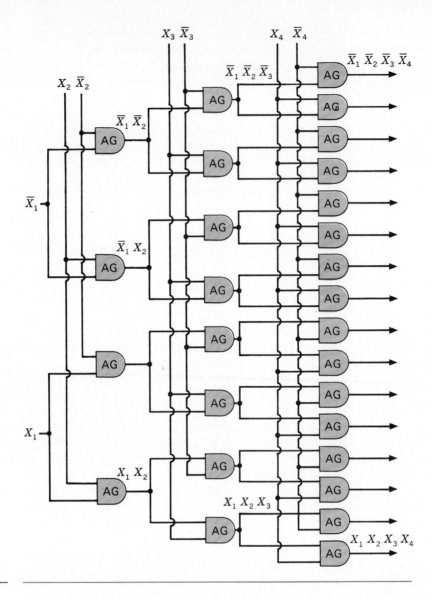

FIGURE 6.6

Tree decoder.

diodes. It can be shown that the type of decoder network illustrated in Fig. 6.7 requires the minimum number of diodes for a complete decoder network. The difference in the number of diodes, or decoding elements, to construct a network such as shown in Fig. 6.7, compared with those in Figs. 6.5 and 6.6, becomes more significant as the number of flip-flops to be decoded increases. The network shown in Fig. 6.5, however, has the advantage of being the fastest and most regular in construction of the three types.

Having studied the three types of decoding matrices now used in digital machines, we simply draw the decoder networks as a box with n inputs and 2^n outputs, with the understanding that one of the three types of circuits shown in Figs. 6.5 to 6.7 will be used in the box. Often only the uncomplemented inputs

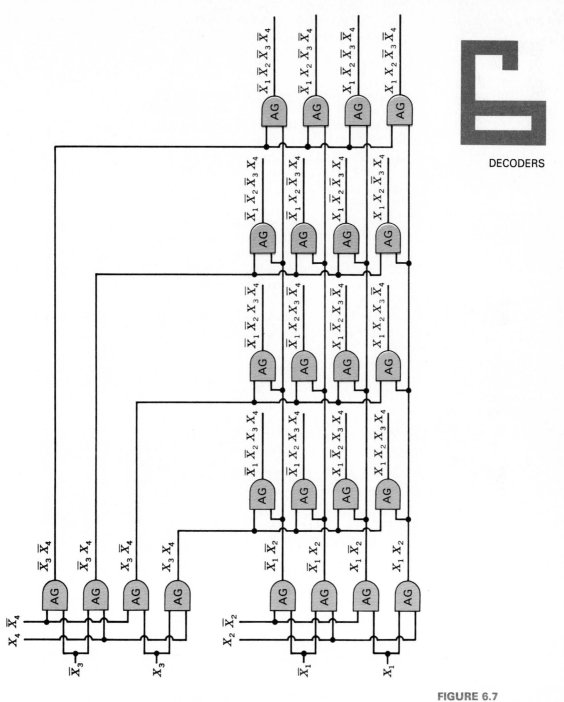

FIGURE 6.7

Balanced decoder.

THE MEMORY
ELEMENT

are connected to decoders, and inverters are included in the decoder package. Then a three-input (or three-flip-flop) decoder will have only three input lines and eight outputs.

DIMENSIONS OF MEMORY ACCESS

6.4 The memory organization in Fig. 6.4 has a basic linear-select (one-dimensional) selection system. This is the simplest organization. However, the decoder in the selection system becomes quite large as the memory size increases.

As an example, we assume a parallel decoder as shown in Fig. 6.5(*b*). These are widely used in IC packages because of their speed and regular (symmetric) construction.

Consider now a decoder for a 4096-word memory, a common size for an IC package. There will be 12 inputs per AND gate, and 4096 AND gates are required. If a diode (or transistor) is required at each AND gate's input, then $12 \times 4096 = 49,152$ diodes (or transistors) will be required. This large number of components is the primary objection to this memory organization.

Let us now consider a *two-dimensional selection system*. First we need to add another SELECT input to our basic memory cell. This is shown in Fig. 6.8. Now both the SELECT 1 and the SELECT 2 must be 1s for a flip-flop to be selected.

FIGURE 6.8

Two-dimensional memory cell.

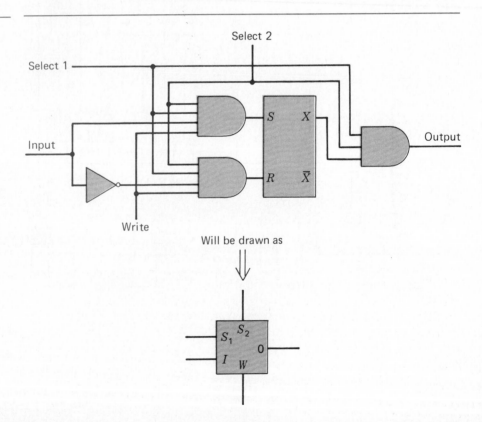

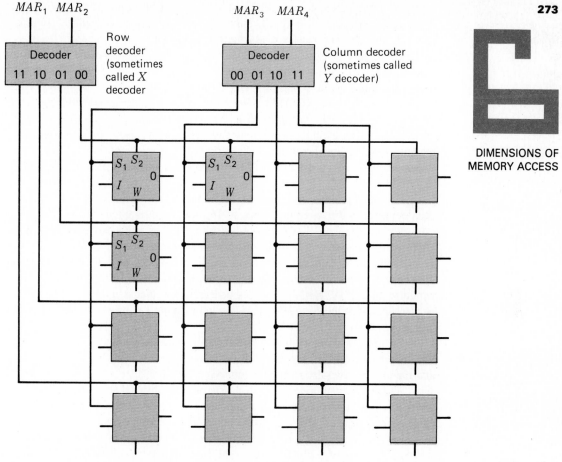

MAR_1 MAR_2

Decoder

11 10 01 00

Row decoder (sometimes called X decoder)

MAR_3 MAR_4

Decoder

00 01 10 11

Column decoder (sometimes called Y decoder)

DIMENSIONS OF
MEMORY ACCESS

WRITE— (All W inputs on cells are connected to this input)

INPUT— (All I inputs on cells are connected to this input line)

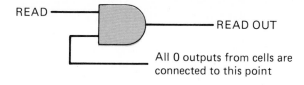

READ

READ OUT

All 0 outputs from cells are connected to this point

FIGURE 6.9

Two-dimensional IC memory organization.

Figure 6.9 shows a two-dimensional memory selection system using this cell. Two decoders are required for this memory, which has 16 words of only 1 bit per word (for clarity of explanation). The MAR has 4 bits and thus 16 states. Two of the MAR inputs go to one decoder and two to the other.

To illustrate the memory's operation, if the MAR contains 0111, then the value 01 goes to the left decoder and 11 goes to the upper decoder. This will select the second row (line) from the left decoder and the rightmost column from the top decoder. The result is that only the cell (flip-flop) at this intersection of the second

row and the rightmost column will have both its SELECT lines (and as a result its AND gates) enabled. As a result, only this particular single cell will be selected, and only this flip-flop can be read from or written into.

As another example, if the MAR contains 1001, then the line for the third row of the left decoder will be a 1, as will be the second column line. The memory cell at the intersection of this row and column will be enabled, but no other cell will be enabled. If the READ line is a 1, the enabled cell will be read from; if the WRITE line is a 1, the enabled cell will be written into.

Now let us examine the number of components used. If a 16-word 1-bit memory were designed by using the linear-select, or one-dimensional, system, then a decoder with 16×4 inputs and therefore 64 diodes (or transistors) would be required.

For the two-dimensional system, 2 two-input four-output decoders are needed, each requiring 8 diodes (transistors); so 16 diodes are required for both decoders.

For a 4096-word 1-bit-per-word memory, the numbers are more striking. A 4096-word linear-select (one-dimensional) memory requires a 12-bit MAR. This decoder therefore requires $4096 \times 12 = 49{,}152$ diodes or transistors. The two-dimensional selection system would have two decoders, each with six inputs. Each would require $2^6 \times 6 = 384$ diodes or transistors, that is, a total of 768 diodes or transistors for the decoders. This is a remarkable saving and extends to even larger memories.

To make a memory with more bits per word, we simply make a memory like that shown in Fig. 6.9 for each bit in the word (except that only one MAR and the original two decoders are required).

The above memory employs a classic two-dimensional selection system. Figure 6.10 shows a small high-speed (bipolar) IC memory with 256 bits on a single chip. As can be seen, this is a two-dimensional select memory.

In a two-dimensional memory, however, simplification in decoder complexity is paid for with cell complexity. In some cases this extra cell complexity is inexpensive, but it can be a problem, and so a variation of this scheme is used. The most used variation on the basic two-dimensional selection system is illustrated in Fig. 6.11. This memory uses two decoders, as in the previous scheme; however, the memory cells are basic memory cells, as shown in Fig. 6.3.

The selection scheme uses gating on the READ and WRITE inputs to achieve the desired two-dimensionality.

Let us consider a WRITE operation. First assume that the MAR contains 0010. This will cause the 00 output from the upper decoder to be a 1, selecting the top row of memory cells. In the lower decoder the 10 output will become a 1, and this is gated with an AND gate near the bottom of the diagram, turning on the W inputs in the third column. As a result, for the memory cell in the top row and third column, the S input and the W input will be a 1. For no other memory cell will both S and W be a 1, and so no other memory cell will have its RS flip-flop set to the input value. (Notice that all I inputs on the memory cells are connected to the input value D_I.)

Consideration of other values for the MAR will indicate that for each value a unique memory cell will be selected for the write operation. Therefore, for each MAR state only one memory cell will be written into.

The read operation is similar. If the MAR contains 0111, then the upper

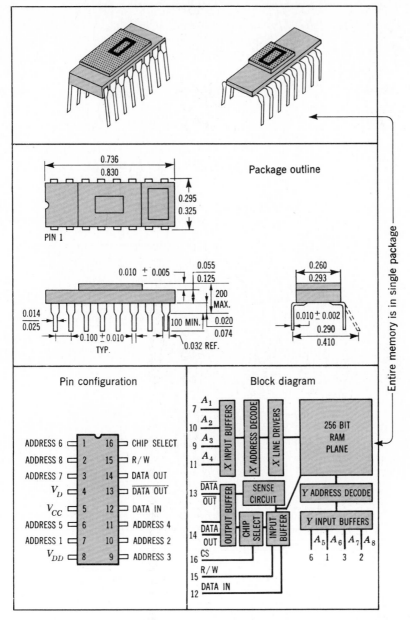

DIMENSIONS OF
MEMORY ACCESS

FIGURE 6.10

Single-chip 256-bit
memory. (*Intel Corp.*)

decoder's 01 line will be a 1, turning on the *S* inputs in the second row of memory cells. As a result only these four cells in the entire array are capable of writing a 1 on the output lines. (Again, the memory cells are wire-ORed by having their outputs connected, this time in groups of four.)

The lower decoder will have input 11, and so its lowest output line will carry a 1. This 1 turns on the rightmost AND gate in the lowest row, which enables the output from the rightmost column of memory cells. Only the second cell down has

**THE MEMORY
ELEMENT**

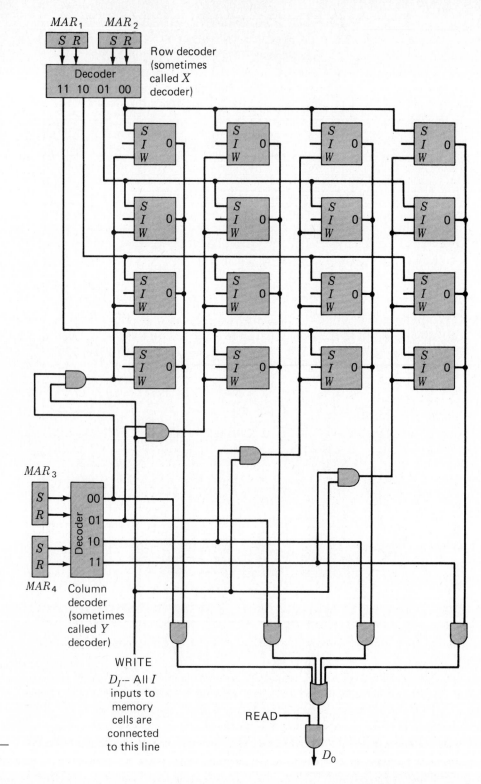

FIGURE 6.11

IC memory chip lay-
out.

its output enabled, however, and so the output from the rightmost AND gate will have the value in the cell. This value then goes through the OR gate and the AND gate at the bottom of the diagram, the AND gate having been turned on by the READ signal.

Examination will show that each input value from the MAR will select a unique memory cell to be read from, and that cell will be the same as would have been written into if the operation were a write operation.

This is basically the organization used by most IC memories at this time. The chips contain up to 256K bits. The number of rows versus the number of columns in an array is determined by the designers who choose the numbers that will reduce the overall component count.

All the circuits necessary for a memory are placed on the same chip, except for the MAR flip-flops which sometimes are not placed on the chip; the inputs go directly to the decoders. This will be clearer when interfacing with a bus has been discussed.

CONNECTING MEMORY CHIPS TO A COMPUTER BUS

6.5   The present trend in computer memory connection is to connect the computer central processing unit (CPU), which does the arithmetic, generates control, etc.,[3] to the memory by means of a *bus*. The bus is simply a set of wires which are shared by all the memory elements to be used.

Microprocessors always use a bus to interface memory. In this case the memory elements will be IC chips, which are in IC containers just like those described in Chap. 4 and shown in Fig. 6.10.

The bus used to connect the memories generally consists of (1) a set of *address lines* to give the address of the word in memory to be used (these are effectively an output from a MAR on the microprocessor chip); (2) a set of *data wires* to input data from the memory and output data to the memory; and (3) a set of *control wires* to control the read and write operations.

Figure 6.12 shows a bus for a microcomputer. To simplify drawings and clarify explanations, we use a memory bus with only three address lines, three output data lines, two control signals, and three input data lines. So the memory to be used is an 8-word 3-bit-per-word memory.

The two control signals work as follows. When the read-write ($R/\overline{W}$) line is a 1, the memory is to be read from; when the $R/\overline{W}$ line is a 0, the memory is to be written into.[4] The MEMORY ENABLE signal ME is a 1 when the memory is either to be read from or to be written into; otherwise, it is a 0.

The IC memory package is shown in Fig. 6.13. Each IC package has three address inputs A_0, A_1, and A_2, and $R/\overline{W}$ input, an output bit D_O, an input bit D_I, and a CHIP SELECT $\overline{CS}$. Each package contains an 8-word 1-bit memory.

The IC memory chip works as follows. The address lines A_0, A_1, and A_2

---

[3] A CPU includes the arithmetic and control sections of a computer.

[4] This is quite similar to the READ and WRITE signals used in prior memory description. An AND gate connected to ME and $R/\overline{W}$ will generate a READ signal, and an inverted $R/\overline{W}$ which is ANDed with ME will give a WRITE signal.

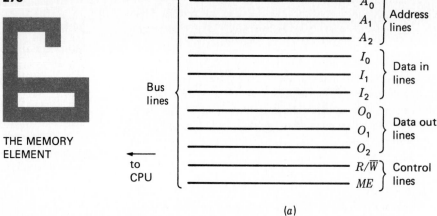

THE MEMORY
ELEMENT

(a)

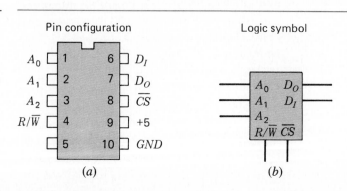

(b)

FIGURE 6.12

Bus for computer
system. (a) Bus lines.
(b) Bus, CPU, and
memory organization.

must be set to the address to be read from or written into (refer to Fig. 6.13). If the operation is a read, the $R/\overline{W}$ line is set to a 1 and the $\overline{CS}$ line is brought to 0 (the $\overline{CS}$ line is normally a 1). The data bit may then be read on line D_O. Certain timing constraints must be met, however, and these will be supplied by the IC manufacturer. Figure 6.14 shows several of these. The value T_R is the minimum cycle time a read operation requires. During this period the address lines must be stable. The value T_A is the access time, which is the minimum time from when the address lines are stable until data can be read from the memory. The value T_{C0} is the minimum time from when the $\overline{CS}$ line is made a 0 until data can be read.

FIGURE 6.13

IC package and block
diagram symbol for
RAM chip. (a) Pin
configuration. (b)
Logic symbol.

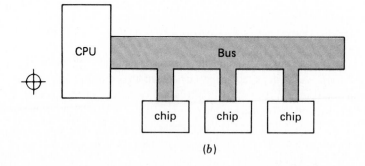

(a)   (b)

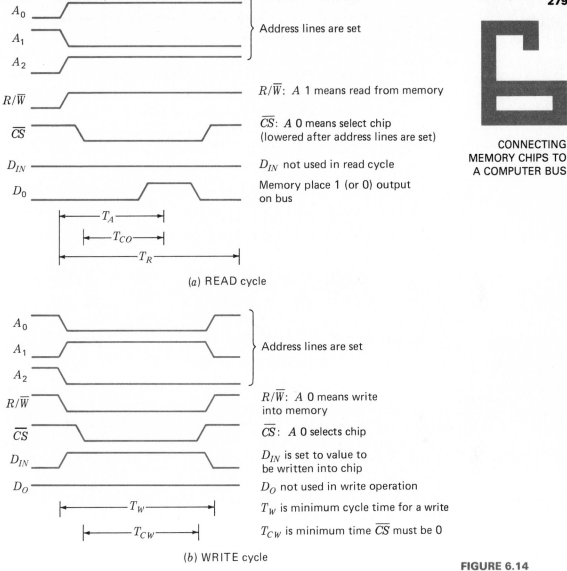

A_0

A_1

A_2
} Address lines are set

$R/\overline{W}$ $R/\overline{W}$: A 1 means read from memory

$\overline{CS}$ $\overline{CS}$: A 0 means select chip
(lowered after address lines are set)

D_{IN} D_{IN} not used in read cycle

D_0 Memory place 1 (or 0) output
on bus

T_A

T_{CO}

T_R

(a) READ cycle

A_0

A_1

A_2
} Address lines are set

$R/\overline{W}$ $R/\overline{W}$: A 0 means write
into memory

$\overline{CS}$ $\overline{CS}$: A 0 selects chip

D_{IN} D_{IN} is set to value to
be written into chip

D_O D_O not used in write operation

T_W T_W is minimum cycle time for a write

T_{CW} T_{CW} is minimum time $\overline{CS}$ must be 0

(b) WRITE cycle

FIGURE 6.14

Timing for bus IC
memory. (a) READ
cycle. (b) WRITE
cycle.

The bus timing must accommodate the above times. It is important that the bus not operate too fast for the chip and that the bus wait for at least the time T_A after setting its address lines before reading and wait at least T_{CO} after lowering the $\overline{CS}$ line before reading. Also, the address line must be held stable for at least the period T_R.

For a write operation, the address to be written into is set up on the address lines, the $R/\overline{W}$ line is made a 0, $\overline{CS}$ is brought down, and the data to be read are placed on the D_{IN} line.

The time interval T_W is the minimum time for a WRITE cycle; the time T_H is the time the data to be written into the chip must be held stable. Different types

THE MEMORY
ELEMENT

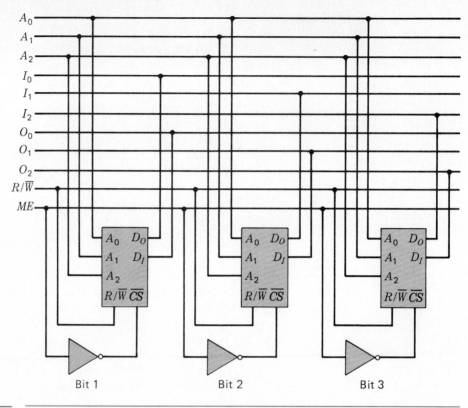

FIGURE 6.15

Interfacing chips to a
bus.

of memories have different timing constraints which the bus must accommodate. We assume that our bus meets these constraints.[5]

To form an 8-word 3-bit memory from these IC packages (chips), the interconnection scheme in Fig. 6.15 is used. Here the address line to each chip is connected to a corresponding address output on the microcomputer bus. The CHIP SELECT input $\overline{CS}$ of each chip is connected to the MEMORY ENABLE output ME from the microprocessor via an inverter, and the R/$\overline{W}$ bus line is connected to the R/$\overline{W}$ input on each chip.

If the microprocessor CPU wishes to read from the memory, it simply places the address to be read from on the address lines, puts a 1 on the R/$\overline{W}$ line, and raises the ME line. Then each chip reads the selected bit onto its output line, and the CPU can read these values on its I_1, I_2, and I_3 lines. (Notice that a chip's output is a bus input.)

Similarly, to write a word into the memory, the CPU places the address to be written into on the address lines, the bits to be written on the O_1, O_2, O_3 lines, lowers R/$\overline{W}$, and then raises ME.

In practice, for microprocessors the memory words now generally contain 8 bits each. (Some new large microprocessors have 16-bit words.) There are generally

---

[5]On the other hand, if a specific microprocessor is used, the memory must be fast enough to accommodate the bus.

16 address lines, and so 2^{16} words can be used in the memory. However, memory chips tend to have from 8 to 14 (at most) memory address lines. Fortunately there is a simple way to expand memories, and this is shown for our small system in Fig. 6.16.

In this example the chips again have three address lines, but the microprocessor bus has five lines. To enable connection, a two-input decoder is connected to the two most significant bits of the address section of the bus, while the three least significant bits are connected to the chip address buses as before.

Now the decoder outputs are each gated with the ME control signal by a NAND gate; so when ME is raised, a single CHIP SELECT line is lowered (the outputs from the NAND gates are normally high). The decoder therefore picks the chip that is enabled, and the address lines on the enabled chip select the memory cell to be written into or read from. The decoding on the chip then selects the particular memory cell to be read from or written into.

The principle shown in Fig. 6.16 is widely used in computers. Memory chips almost invariably have fewer address inputs than buses, and so this expansion technique is necessary to memory usage. Notice that only 1 bit of the memory word is completely drawn in Fig. 6.16. (One chip from the second bit is also shown.) An entire 32-word 3-bit memory would require 12 chips of the type shown here. Most buses combine the input and output data lines into a single set of lines in a way to be explained in the section on buses.

As may be seen, a microcomputer or minicomputer (or any computer) can be purchased with a minimal memory, and then the memory can be expanded by adding more chips, up to the size that the bus address lines can accommodate.

The remainder of this chapter is structured as follows. Read-only memories are explained; then disk, drum, and tape memories are covered. Finally, some information on recording techniques is presented.

RANDOM-ACCESS SEMICONDUCTOR MEMORIES

6.6 The ability to fabricate large arrays of electronic components using straightforward processing techniques and to make these arrays in small containers at reasonable prices has made semiconductor memories the most popular at this time.

Although a number of different schemes and devices are available, at present there are six main categories of IC memories:

1 *Bipolar memories* These are essentially flip-flop memories with the flip-flops fabricated using standard *pn*-junction transistors. These memories are fast but tend to be expensive.

2 *Static MOS memories* These are fabricated by using MOS field-effect devices to make flip-flop circuits. These memories are lower in speed than the bipolar memories, but cost less, consume less power, and have high packing densities.

3 *Dynamic MOS memories* These are fabricated using MOS devices. But instead of a flip-flop being used for the basic memory cell, a charge is deposited on a capacitor fabricated on the IC chip, and the presence or absence of this charge determines the state of the cell. The MOS devices are used to sense and deposit

**THE MEMORY
ELEMENT**

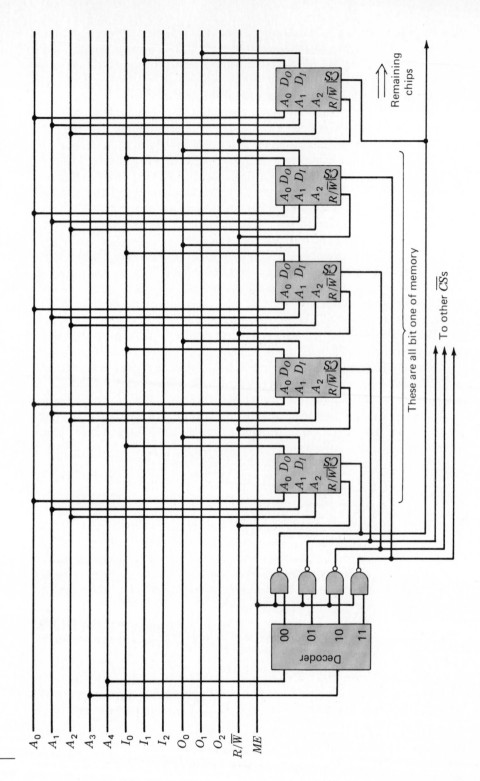

FIGURE 6.16

Layout for adding
memory to a bus.

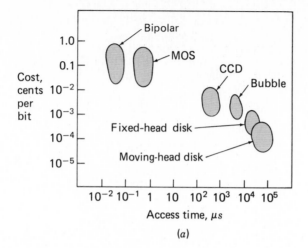

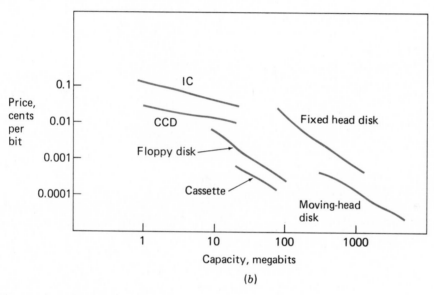

FIGURE 6.17

Characteristics of memory devices. (*a*) Access time versus cost for some memory devices. (*b*) Cost versus capacity in megabits.

the charge on the capacitors used. Since the charge used will slowly dissipate in time, it is necessary to periodically refresh this charge, and so the memories are called dynamic memories. (MOS or bipolar flip-flop memories are called static memories.) These memories tend to be slower than the other types, but they are also less expensive, consume less power, and have a high packing density.

4   *CMOS memories*   CMOS utilizes both *p*- and *n*-channel devices on the same substrate. As a result, it involves a more complex manufacturing process. CMOS has improved speed and power output figures over *n*- and *p*-channel MOS, but it costs more.

5   *Silicon-on-sapphire (SOS) memories*   SOS is similar to CMOS. Devices are formed on an insulating substrate of sapphire. This reduces the device capacitance and improves speed. However, SOS is costly.

THE MEMORY ELEMENT

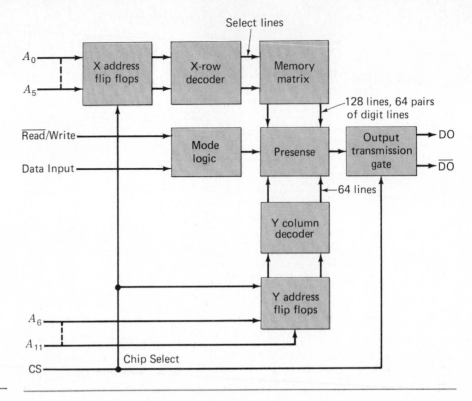

FIGURE 6.18

Block diagram of MOS static memory. (*Electronic Memories and Magnetics Corp.*)

6 *Integrated injection logic (IIL) memories* The IIL circuits eliminate the load resistors and current sources of TTL circuits. This reduces power consumption over bipolar memories, giving greater packing density than bipolar devices. As a result, IIL mixes the speed of bipolar memories with the packing density of MOS. It is medium-cost.

Figure 6.17 shows the characteristics of the basic memory devices in this chapter. Figure 6.17(*a*) shows cost per bit versus access time for these devices, and Fig. 6.17(*b*) shows price versus storage capacity. Notice the semiconductor memories are faster but more expensive than the disk devices. Magnetic-tape devices provide still slower operation but at a still lower cost per bit.

STATIC RANDOM-ACCESS MEMORIES

6.7 If we compare bipolar and MOS technologies, bipolar offers a speed advantage, although, until recently, limitations imposed by the need for isolation between transistors have limited packing density and hence per-chip storage capacity. Bipolar components can provide access times of under 10 ns, in contrast with 300 ns or more for PMOS and 20 ns for NMOS. MOS devices have relatively high internal capacitance and impedance, leading to longer time constants and access times.

The operation of a typical 4096-bit static NMOS memory chip is detailed in Figs. 6.18 through 6.20. The 4096 bits of memory are organized in an array of 64

Top view

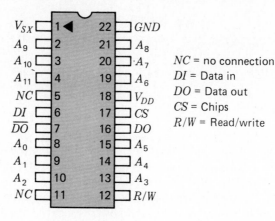

Pin assignment

NC = no connection
DI = Data in
DO = Data out
CS = Chips
R/W = Read/write

FIGURE 6.19

MOS static memory pin assignment for Fig. 6.18. (*Electronic Memories and Magnetics Corp.*)

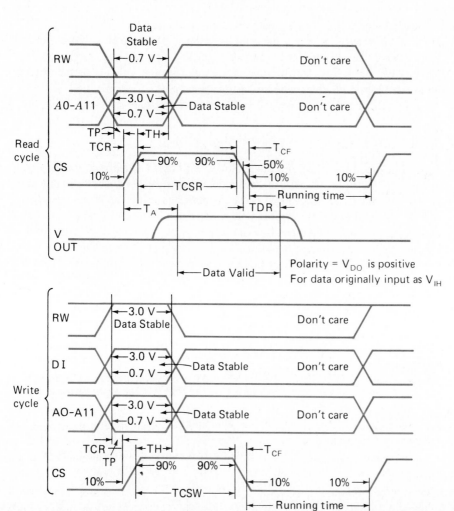

FIGURE 6.20

Timing diagrams. (*Electronic Memories and Magnetics Corp.*)

| TABLE 6.1 | | | | | STATIC MEMORY CHARACTERISTICS |

MANUFACTURER AND PART NUMBER	ORGANIZATION	ACCESS TIME, ns	POWER, MW	PINS	TYPE
Signetics 825400	4K × 1	50	500	18	Bipolar (TTL)
Fairchild F10480	16K × 1	35	936	16	Bipolar (ECL)
National Semiconductor DM1041Y	256 × 1	10	728	16	Bipolar (ECL)
TI TM S4070	16K × 1	100	720	16	NMOS

rows by 64 columns. The memory bits are accessed by simultaneously decoding the X address A_0–A_5 for the rows and the Y address A_6–A_{11} for the columns.

The basic organization is the same as that in Fig. 6.11.

The CHIP SELECT (CS) input controls the operation of the memory. When CS is low, the input address buffers, decoders, sensing circuits, and output stages are held in the off state, and power is supplied only to the memory elements. When the CS goes high, the memory is enabled. The CS pulse clocks the TTL level addresses, READ-WRITE, and DATA input into D flip-flops and enables the output stage. When a cell is read from, one of the two outputs will be a 1 (DO for data originally input as a 1, $\overline{\text{DO}}$ for data originally input as a 0).

As shown in Fig. 6.19, this memory chip is packaged in a 22-pin dual-in-line package. By assembling a number of these chips, a large, moderately fast memory can be constructed. Memory cycle times for this chip are on the order of 30 ns, and Fig. 6.20 shows the timing for the chips.

The characteristics of several static memory chips are shown in Table 6.1.

DYNAMIC RANDOM-ACCESS MEMORIES

6.8 The preceding memories have all used flip-flops for the basic memory cells in an array. There is another class of random-access memory called *dynamic random-access memories* (DRAMs). These memories have individual cells composed of from one to three MOS transistors plus a capacitor. The cell's state is determined by placing or not placing a positive charge on the capacitor. Thus, if the capacitor has no charge, the cell may represent a 0, and with a positive charge the cell may represent a 1. The advantage of this kind of memory is that the individual cells are simpler than flip-flops, requiring less area on the chips and having lower power consumption. The disadvantages are that DRAMs are slower and the charge slowly leaks from the capacitor. Thus the contents of each cell must be rewritten into each cell periodically. This is called refreshing the memory. Despite the difficulties in refreshing dynamic memories and their relatively slow speed (100-ns access times are representative), the memory costs are enough lower than for static memories for dynamic memories to be widely used in present-day systems.

Dynamic random-access memories are organized in the same manner as flip-flop memories (the organization in Fig. 6.11 is the most frequently used except that some circuit "tricks" enable the combining of each column input line and output line into a pair of lines called *bit lines*).

Two-dimensional selection with decoders is standard. Dynamic memory chips now contain up to 256K of memory per chip; however, 16K and 64K chips are more widely used.

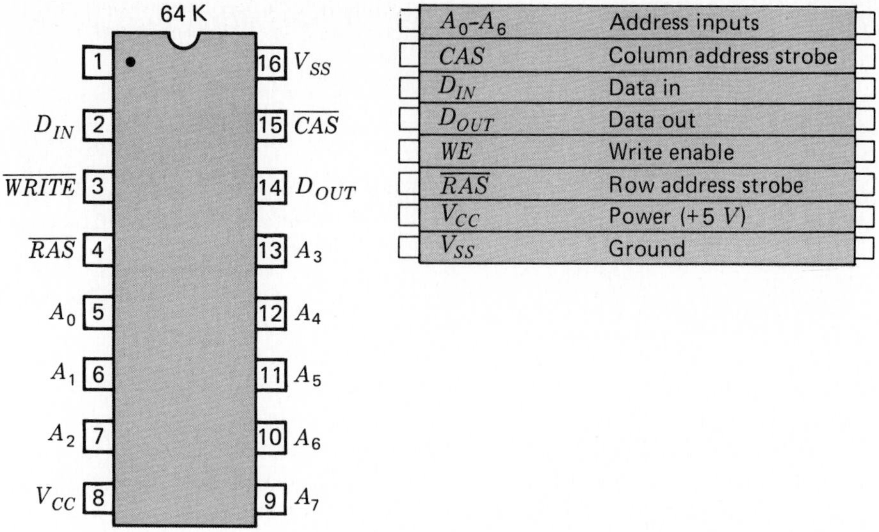

64 K

Pin layout (DIP):

Pin	Signal		Pin	Signal
1	(•)		16	V_{SS}
2	D_{IN}		15	$\overline{CAS}$
3	$\overline{WRITE}$		14	D_{OUT}
4	$\overline{RAS}$		13	A_3
5	A_0		12	A_4
6	A_1		11	A_5
7	A_2		10	A_6
8	V_{CC}		9	A_7

A_0–A_6	Address inputs
CAS	Column address strobe
D_{IN}	Data in
D_{OUT}	Data out
WE	Write enable
$\overline{RAS}$	Row address strobe
V_{CC}	Power (+5 V)
V_{SS}	Ground

DYNAMIC RANDOM-ACCESS MEMORIES

FIGURE 6.21

Pin-out for dynamic memory chip.

Figure 6.21 shows the standard pin layout for a 64K-bit dynamic RAM. There are not enough address lines into this chip, and so the addresses are time-multiplexed (that is, put on in two sections, one right after the other). This is shown in Fig. 6.22. First the row address[6] is placed on A_0–A_7 and $\overline{RAS}$ is lowered; then the column address is placed on A_0–A_7 and $\overline{CAS}$ is lowered. To use RAMs of this kind, extra circuitry for multiplexing address lines and to generate the REFRESH signal must be used.[7] Nevertheless because of their high packing density and low cost, the extra complexity of these specialized circuits is compensated for, and these memories are widely used.

As was stated, the primary advantages of dynamic MOS memories lie in the simplicity of the individual cells. There is a secondary advantage in that power

---

[6]The row address is the first half of the field 16-bit address, and the column address is the second half.
[7]IC manufacturers make special chips for this purpose. For these particular memories, refresh is done a column at a time so only the rows must be sequenced through. To refresh a row, the row address is placed on the address lines and the $\overline{RAS}$ is lowered. Each row must be refreshed in a 2-ms period.

FIGURE 6.22

Pin layout and address timing for 64K dynamic memory.

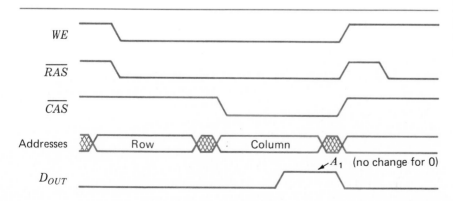

TABLE 6.2			DYNAMIC RANDOM-ACCESS MEMORY CHARACTERISTICS		
MANUFACTURER AND PART NUMBER	ORGANIZATION	ACCESS TIME, ns	POWER, MW		REFRESH RATE
			ACTIVE	STANDBY	
TI TM SY164	64K × 1	150	200	27	128 cycles/2 ms
Motorola MCM 6664	64K × 1	120	275	30	128 cycles/2 ms
TI TMS S4416	16K × 4	150	125	18	256 cycles/4 ms
Mostek MK4332	32K × 1	200	482	40	128 cycles/2 ms
Hitachi	8K × 8	120	170	100	256 cycles/4 ms
Fujitsu MB8264	64K × 1	150	300	28	256 cycles/4 ms
TI	8K × 8	100	200	100	128 cycles/2 ms

need not be applied to the cells when they are not being read from or written into, and so the power is conserved. This makes for higher packing densities per chip. The obvious disadvantage lies in the need to refresh these cells every few milliseconds since charge continually leaks from the capacitors. External circuitry to control the refresh rewrite is generally required, or sometimes the memories may include special circuits to refresh when commanded. As a result, extra refresh memory cycles are required, but these occupy only a small percentage of the overall operating time.[8] Table 6.2 lists some of the characteristics of dynamic memories.

Memory controller chips are used to control several dynamic memory chips assembled into a memory. These controller chips handle the sequencing of the row and column addresses into the individual chips during a normal memory access and also control necessary refreshing of the memory. The refreshing generally involves a counter which sequences through all possible states during a 2-ms period. The memory controller chip(s) places the counter outputs on the address lines of the dynamic memory chips and lowers the $\overline{RAS}$ inputs, loading the counter addresses into the row select latches (flip-flops). The controller attempts to perform refresh operations between memory accesses when this is possible, thus reducing the time lost to memory refreshes. (These are called ''hidden'' refreshes.)

Use of dynamic memory controller chips simplifies dynamic memory design and optimizes memory operation.

READ-ONLY MEMORIES

6.9 A type of storage device called a *read-only memory* (ROM) is widely used. ROMs have the unique characteristic that they can be read from, but not written into. Thus the information stored in these memories is introduced into the memory in some manner such that the information is semipermanent or permanent. Sometimes the information stored in a ROM is placed in the memory at the time of construction, and sometimes devices are used in which the information can be changed. In this section we study several types of ROMs. These are characteristic of this particular class of memory devices, and most devices are variations on the principles presented.

---

[8]There are even some interesting internal refresh mechanisms called *charge pumps* which require application of a sine wave on one of the inputs and make refreshing transparent (invisible) to the user. Other refresh strategies rewrite entire rows by using a single REFRESH pulse.

TABLE 6.3			BINARY-TO-GRAY CODE VALUES				
INPUT				OUTPUT			
X_1	X_2	X_3	X_4	Z_1	Z_2	Z_3	Z_4
0	0	0	0	0	0	0	0
0	0	0	1	0	0	0	1
0	0	1	0	0	0	1	1
0	0	1	1	0	0	1	0
0	1	0	0	0	1	1	0
0	1	0	1	0	1	1	1
0	1	1	0	0	1	0	1
0	1	1	1	0	1	0	0
1	0	0	0	1	1	0	0
1	0	0	1	1	1	0	1
1	0	1	0	1	1	1	1
1	0	1	1	1	1	1	0
1	1	0	0	1	0	1	0
1	1	0	1	1	0	1	1
1	1	1	0	1	0	0	1
1	1	1	1	1	0	0	0

Basically a ROM is a device with several input and output lines such that for each input value there is a unique output value. Thus a ROM physically realizes a truth table, or table of combinations. A typical (small) table is shown in Table 6.3. This list of input-output values is actually a list of binary-to-Gray code values. (The Gray code is discussed in the next chapter.) It is important to see that the list can be looked at in two ways: (1) as a table for a gating network with four inputs and four outputs and (2) as a list of addresses from 0 to 15, given by the X values, and the contents of each address, given by the values of Z. Thus we might construct a gating network as in Fig. 6.23 which would give the correct Z output for each X input. (The boxes with $\oplus$ are mod 2 adders.)

Table 6.2 could also be realized by a 16-word 4-bit-per-word IC memory into which we had read 0000 at address 0; 0001 at address 1; 0011 in the next address; and so on until 1000 at the last address. If we never wrote into this memory

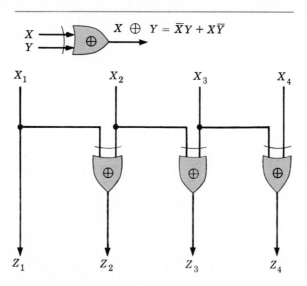

FIGURE 6.23

Combinational network for binary-to-Gray code.

THE MEMORY
ELEMENT

afterward, it would be a ROM memory and would serve the same purpose as the gating network in Fig. 6.23.

Figure 6.24(a) shows a scheme for implementing Table 6.2 by using a decoder network with four inputs X_1, X_2, X_3, and X_4 and four OR gates. With a given input combination (or address), a single output line from the decoder will be high. Let us assume that the input value is $X_1 = 0$, $X_2 = 1$, $X_3 = 1$, $X_4 = 1$. This corresponds to 0111 on the decoder output in Fig. 6.24(a). OR gates are connected to this line for outputs which are 1s, and no OR gates are placed where 0s are to appear. Thus for the input 0111 we have a single OR gate connected to output line Z_2, since the desired output is 0100. Similarly, for the input 0110 we connect OR gates to Z_2 and Z_4 since the output is to be 0101.

The entire scheme outlined above realizes the ROM with OR gates. By using LSI techniques, arrays of this sort can be inexpensively fabricated in small containers at low prices. The 4K-word 8-bit memories are of about average size for the large-scale integration ROMs; these memories effectively store 32K bits in all.

Figure 6.24(b) shows how Fig. 6.24(a) might be implemented by using diodes to form the OR gates. The diodes OR the inputs to which they are connected. The manufacturer of a conventional ROM will have an IC layout in which diodes can be placed between every input and output line; then only the specified diodes would be actually used, the remainder being omitted during manufacture.

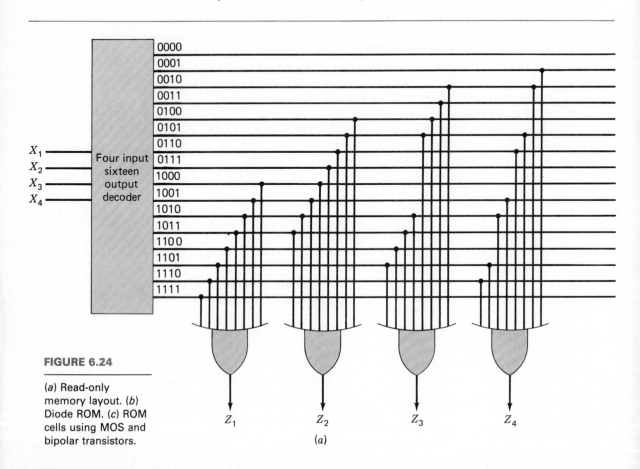

FIGURE 6.24

(a) Read-only memory layout. (b) Diode ROM. (c) ROM cells using MOS and bipolar transistors.

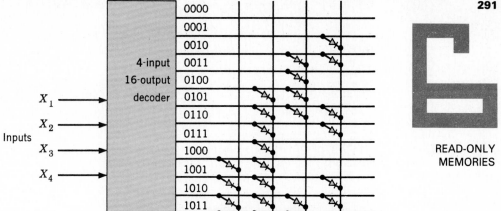

READ-ONLY MEMORIES

(b)

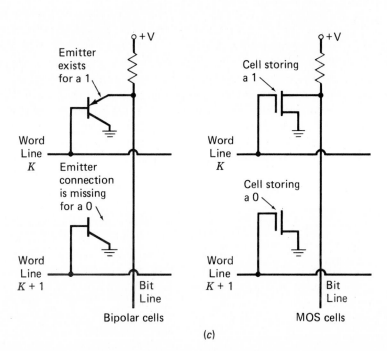

(c)

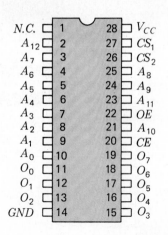

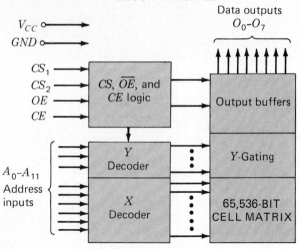

PIN NAMES

A_0-A_{12}	Addresses
$\overline{OE}$	Output enable
$\overline{CE}$	Chip enable
CS	Chip select
N.C.	No connection

FIGURE 6.25

A 64K ROM. (*Intel Corp.*)

The diodes in Fig. 6.24(*b*) are often transistors, and the manufacturing processes are of various types. Both one- and two-dimensional selection is used in ROMs. Generally MOS ROMs have 10- to 200-ns access times; access times of bipolar memories range from 10 to 100 ns.

When a ROM is constructed so that the user can electrically (or by using other techniques) write in the contents of the memory, the memory is called a *programmable ROM,* or *PROM.*[9] Often a scheme is used in which a memory chip is delivered with 1s in every position, but 0s can be introduced at given positions by placing an address on the input lines and then raising each output line which is to be a 0 to a specified voltage, thus destroying a connection to the selected cell. (Sometimes the memories contain all 0s, and 1s are written in by the user.) Devices are also manufactured which program PROMs by reading paper tapes, magnetic tapes, punched cards, etc., and placing their contents into the PROM.

Custom ROM manufacturers provide forms in which a user can fill 1s and 0s and then they will produce a custom-made mask and LSI chips which will realize the memory contents specified by the user. A single chip may cost more for such a memory, but with large production runs generally the cost per chip is less. These devices come with up to 256K bits per IC package.

Figure 6.25 shows a block diagram of a 64K-bit MOS memory which is organized as a 4096-word 8-bit-per-word memory. The user places the address on

[9]These memories are also called *field-programmable ROMs.*

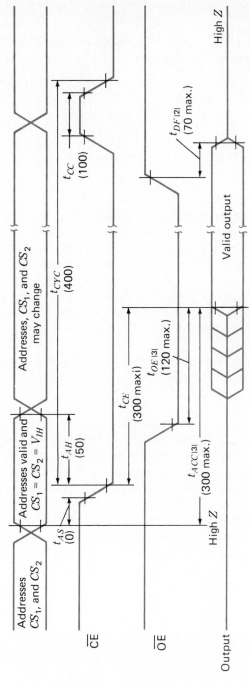

Notes

1. All times shown in parentheses are minimum times and are nanoseconds unless otherwise specified.

2. t_{DF} is specified from $\overline{OE}$ or $\overline{CE}$, whichever occurs first.

3. t_{ACC} may be delayed up to 180 ns after the falling edge of $\overline{CE}$ without impact on t_{ACC}.

FIGURE 6.25 (*Cont.*)

TABLE 6.4	CHARACTERISTICS OF READ-ONLY MEMORIES		
MANUFACTURER AND PART NUMBER	ORGANIZATION	TYPE	ACCESS TIME, ns
Monolithic Memories 6280	$1K \times 8$	ROM	100
National Semiconductor DM85529	$1K \times 8$	ROM	90
Intel 2732	$4K \times 8$	EPROM	200
TI 2532	$4K \times 8$	EPROM	400
NITRON NC7714	$256K \times 4$	EAROM	450
GI ER2805	$2K \times 4$	EAROM	500
RCA 1842	$256K \times 8$	EEPROM	250
NEC D458	$1K \times 8$	EEPROM	450

the 13 input lines A_0 to A_{12} and then raises CS_1 and CS_2 ($\overline{CE}$ must be low). This will enable the output, and the desired word will appear on lines O_0 to O_7. This is a custom-made memory in which the desired memory contents are supplied to the manufacturer by the user on a form. Then the manufacturer makes a mask to create the desired bit patterns on an IC chip and manufactures ROMs with this pattern to order. The delay time for the memory is on the order of 75 ns.

When a ROM is manufactured so that the memory's contents can be set as desired by the user and the memory can later have the contents erased and new values written in, the ROM is said to be *erasable and reprogrammable* and is often called an *EPROM*.

For example, some memory chips are made with a transparent lid. Exposing the semiconductor chip (through the lid) to ultraviolet light[10] will erase the pattern on the chip, and a new pattern can be written in electrically. This can be repeated as often as desired.

Table 6.4 shows characteristics of some bipolar ROMs and of several electrically programmable ROMs (EPROMs) which can have their contents erased by exposure to ultraviolet light and can be programmed (written into) by placing designated voltages on inputs. Also shown in Table 6.4 are some characteristics for electrically alterable ROMs (EAROMs) which can have selected contents rewritten while in place in a circuit by means of properly applied input voltages and EEPROMs (electrically erasable programmable ROMs). The difference between EAROMs and EEPROMs is that EAROMs can have their contents altered while in place in the circuit and EEPROMs must be removed to be erased and rewritten.

Several companies make devices for programming PROMs and EPROMs. Some of these devices are operated from a keyboard, others from tape, and still others from external inputs such as microprocessors.

When an EPROM, EEPROM, EAPROM, or a PROM chip is to be programmed, there is generally a write enable to be raised, which makes output lines able to accept data. Then address lines are set to the location to be written into. Next, for some chips, the output lines to have 1s are raised to high voltages (or a sequence of large-amplitude pulses are applied to them); or, for some chips, the normal logic levels are placed on the output lines, and a special program input is placed with a sequence of high-voltage (25-V) pulses. In either case, each memory

---

[10]Standard ultraviolet lamps can be used to erase the memory. About a 20- to 30-min exposure is required.

location must be written into by setting the address lines and then writing the desired contents into the output lines. Applying an erase (for example, applying an ultraviolet light to the lid for some specified time) generally erases all the contents of the memory except for EAROMs, in which the individual locations can be changed.

MAGNETIC DISK MEMORIES

6.10 The magnetic disk memory provides large storage capabilities with moderate operating speeds. Quite a number of different types of magnetic disk memories are now on the market. Although they differ in specific details, all are based on the same principles of operation.

Magnetic disk memories store information on one or more circular platters, or disks, which are continually spinning. These rotating disks are coated with a magnetic material and stacked with space between them (refer to Fig. 6.26). Information is recorded on the surface of the rotating disks by magnetic heads such

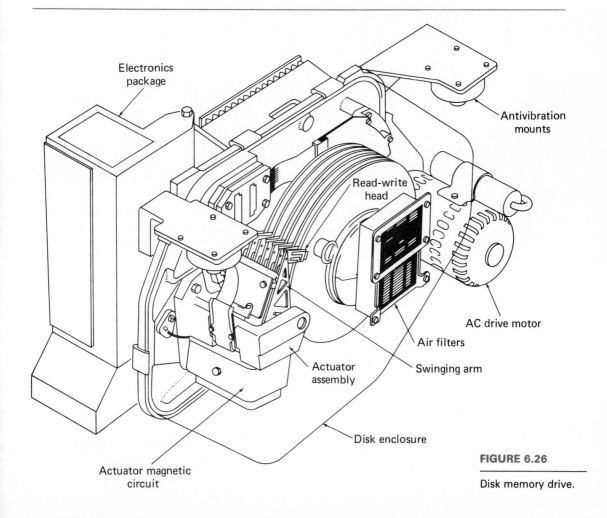

FIGURE 6.26

Disk memory drive.

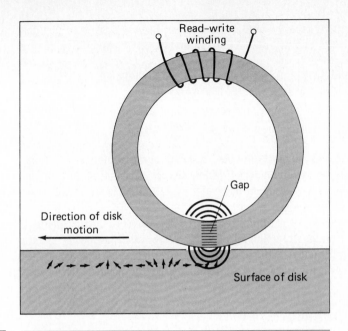

Read–write winding

Gap

Direction of disk motion

Surface of disk

FIGURE 6.27

Read-write head for a magnetic disk memory. *Note*: Passing a film of magnetic material by a head while passing current through the read-write winding will magnetize the surface of the material, forming simple magnets. Passing this same area by a head at a later time will induce currents in the read-write winding.

as that in Fig. 6.27. These heads are mounted on *access arms*. (Information is recorded in bands rather than on a spiral.) Each band of information on a given disk is called a *track*. On one side of a typical disk there can be several thousand data tracks. Bits are recorded along a track at a density of 500 to 24,000 bits/in. In some systems the outer tracks contain more bits than the inner tracks, because the circumference of an outer track is greater than that of an inner track; but many disks have the same number of bits around each track. The rotational speed of the disks varies, of course, with the manufacturer, but typical speeds are on the order of 3600 rpm.

Since each disk contains a number of tracks of information and there may be several disks in a given memory, several techniques have evolved for placing a magnetic read-write head in the correct position on a selected track. Since the same head is generally used for reading and for writing, the problem becomes that of placing this head accurately and quickly on the selected track.

There are two basic types of disk head placement systems. In the first type, the heads are fixed in position on each track. These are called *fixed-head systems*. In the second kind of system, one or more pairs of read-write heads exist for each pair of adjacent disk surfaces (because information is generally written on both the top and the bottom of each disk). These read-write heads are mounted on arms which can be moved in and out. These are called *movable-head systems*.[11]

The positioning of the heads by means of the mechanical movement of arms is a difficult and tricky business, particularly since the tracks are often recorded

[11]A few systems have been made with only one pair of read-write heads for the entire memory. In these systems, the two recording heads are positioned on an arm which first is moved between the correct pair of disks and then selects the correct surface of the adjacent surfaces (again because information is written on both the top and the bottom of each disk). The read-write head is finally placed upon the correct selected track.

thousandths of an inch apart on the disk. Clearly disk memories with many heads can locate and record on or read from a selected track faster than the ones with only a few heads, since the amount of mechanical movement before the track is reached will be less for the multihead system.

The total time it takes to begin reading selected data or to begin writing on a selected track in a particular place is called the *access time*.

The time it takes to position a head on the selected track is called the *seek time,* and it is generally several milliseconds. The other delay in locating selected data is the *latency,* or rotational, delay, which is the time required for the desired data to reach the magnetic head once the head is positioned. Thus the total access time for a disk is the seek time plus the latency.

For a rotational speed of 2400 rpm, for example, latency is a maximum of 25 ms and averages 12.5 ms. Latency represents a lower limit in systems using fixed heads. As a result, for minimum access time, fixed heads are used. In fixed-head systems, typically heads are arranged in groups of eight or nine, perhaps including a spare, and are carefully aligned in fixed positions with respect to the disk. Although head spacing in each group is typically 8 to 16 per inch, track densities of 30 to 60 per inch can be achieved by interlacing groups.

Although they are faster, fixed-head systems provide less storage capacity than moving-head systems with comparable disk recording areas because the moving-head systems have more tracks per inch. Further, the large number of heads required can increase cost for a given capacity, and fixed-head systems are used only in special applications.

An important advantage of moving magnetic heads concerns their alignment with very closely spaced data tracks. Although track spacing is limited by *crosstalk* between adjacent tracks and mechanical tolerances, spacing of 3 mils between adjacent tracks is common. Further, track widths of approximately 0.5 mil are consistent with head-positioning accuracies of 0.25 mil.

The read-write heads used on magnetic disk memories are almost invariably of the type called *flying heads*. A simplified diagram of a flying head is shown in Fig. 6.28. When a disk rotates at a high speed, a thin but resilient boundary layer of air rotates with the disk. The head is shaped so that it rides on this layer of rotating air, which causes the disk to maintain separation from the head, thus

FIGURE 6.28

Flying head in a disk memory. *Note*: The loading force is applied by the access arm pressing down, using a springlike mechanism. The flying height is determined by the amount of loading force.

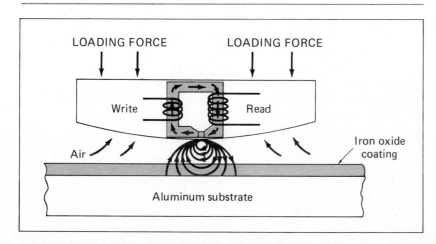

preventing wear on the disk surface. In effect, the layer of air rotating with the disk acts like a spring with a stiffness exceeding several thousand pounds per inch, thus forcing the head away from the surface of the disk. To force the head into correct proximity with the disk, a number of mechanisms have been used, but current memories use a spring-loading system based on a flexible arm on which the read-write head is mounted. These floating heads are normally about 10 microinches (μin.) from the disk surface.

There are many sizes and speeds of disk memories. Because of the large market for these memories and the seemingly infinite variety of configurations in which they can be manufactured, the system user is afforded a wide choice.

Some disk memories have changeable disk packs (or modules[12]). Each disk pack contains a set of disks which rotate together. These disk packs can be changed and are inexpensive enough that a user can store records or programs on them and keep them in files. The cost per bit is much higher than for tape, however, and so disk packs are used most in applications requiring high operating speeds.

In the mid-1970s, disk units with changeable packs, or modules, were the most used devices. At that time, however, an IBM unit with fixed disks, the 3350,[13] brought in a new disk technology with greater recording density, more tracks per data surface, and a faster transfer rate. This disk technology is referred to as *Winchester* technology and features a low head loading force [10 versus 300 grams (g) on earlier devices] and a low-mass head. Also, since these disks are generally not changeable, alignment and other tracking problems are reduced. Further, the disks are lubricated so that the lightweight heads can "crash" without damage, and they are stored with power off against the disk. Winchester disk drives require clean air and are sealed and have circulating air which is filtered. This is because the heads float so close to the disk (10 to 20 μin.). A particle of smoke, for instance, is 50 μin., and if one got between the disk and head, it could cause an error. The original Winchester disk drives were used for large storage systems. However, the technology was quickly picked up by manufacturers of smaller drives, and so now Winchester drives are made by many companies. Winchester fixed-disk systems are the most popular with minicomputer and microcomputer systems as well as with large systems. Some data on Winchester drives is given in Tables 6.5 and 6.6.

The Winchester disk drives manufactured by most concerns use 14-, 8-, $5\frac{1}{4}$-, or 3.5-in. disks. Capacities range from 5 megabytes (Mbytes) for several 3.5-in. drives to 2500 Mbytes for the Storage Technologies 8380 and the IBM 3380. Bit densities along a track range from 200 to 300 bits/in. for the less expensive drives up to 20,000 bits/in. for large thin-film disks. Track densities vary from 400 (for stepper motor access arms) to 1000 per inch for voice-coil-type access arms.

Some Winchester drives have both fixed disk(s) and a removable cartridge.

Some general data on Winchester-type tape drives follow. The head-to-disk spacing is generally 10 to 20 μin. The magnetic material on the surface of the

---

[12]A module is a disk pack which has the read-write heads and positioning arms all packaged together with the disks. These modules are costly, but enable a higher performance system.

[13]The 3350 improved an earlier Winchester technology with changeable disk packs (the 3340).

TABLE 6.5	LARGE FIXED-DISK DRIVE CHARACTERISTICS FOR CDC 9776†
CHARACTERISTIC	SPECIFICATION
Number of spindles per cabinet	2
Capacity per spindle	400 Mbytes (movable head)
	1.72 Mbytes (fixed head)
Data rate	9.6 MHz
Average access time	25 ms
Rotational speed	3600 rpm

†Courtesy CDC Corp.

TABLE 6.6	TYPICAL FIXED-DISK WINCHESTER DRIVE CHARACTERISTICS (FOR SMALL TO MEDIUM SYSTEMS)
CHARACTERISTIC	SPECIFICATION
Number of disks	1 to 4
Data surfaces	1 to 7
Bit density	8400 bits/in.
Track density	500 tracks/in.
Tracks per surface	1200
Surface capacity	7.6 Mbytes
Rotational speed	3600 rpm
Four-disk capacity	30.2 Mbytes

disks is about 0.075 in. thick except for some new thin-film disks. The access arms on inexpensive drives are positioned by using stepper motors and on more expensive drives by using servo (voice-coil-like) motors. The head type plays a large role in determining bits per inch along a track. Most heads are ferrite, but thin-film heads fabricated by using vacuum disposition through masks or through photolithography increase the number of bits per inch possible.

Because of the relative inexpensiveness per bit of information stored in disk memories and because of the relatively low access times and the high transfer rates attainable when data are read from or written into a disk file, magnetic disk memories have become one of the most important storage devices in modern digital computers.

FLEXIBLE-DISK STORAGE SYSTEMS—THE FLOPPY DISK

6.11 An innovation in disk storage, originally developed at IBM, uses a flexible, "floppy" disk with a plastic base in place of the more conventional rigid, metal-based disk. This storage medium is approximately the size and shape of a 45-rpm record (or smaller) and can be "plugged in" about as easily as a tape cartridge.

The floppy disks are changeable, and each disk comes in an envelope, as shown in Fig. 6.29. The disks are mounted on the disk drive with the envelope in place, and information is written and read through an aperture in the envelope. (A

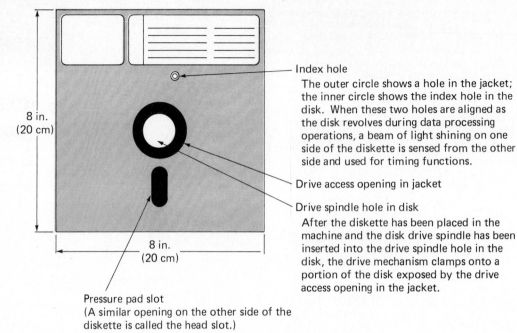

8 in.
(20 cm)

8 in.
(20 cm)

Index hole

The outer circle shows a hole in the jacket; the inner circle shows the index hole in the disk. When these two holes are aligned as the disk revolves during data processing operations, a beam of light shining on one side of the diskette is sensed from the other side and used for timing functions.

Drive access opening in jacket

Drive spindle hole in disk

After the diskette has been placed in the machine and the disk drive spindle has been inserted into the drive spindle hole in the disk, the drive mechanism clamps onto a portion of the disk exposed by the drive access opening in the jacket.

Pressure pad slot
(A similar opening on the other side of the diskette is called the head slot.)

The head slot exposes the recording surface of the disk as the disk turns in its jacket in the machine. The data recording and sensing unit of the disk drive, which is called a *read-write head* and is similar to the record/playback head in a tape recorder, moves to specified positions along the length of the slot. Moving to a specified position is called *accessing a track*. (Data are recorded only ·on the side of the diskette that contains the head slot.)

FIGURE 6.29

Floppy disk with envelope.

few systems require removing the envelope.) Several manufacturers now provide complete systems for well under $300 for use with these disks. Convenience in use and low prices have broadened the use of floppy-disk memories in many applications.

On most floppy-disk drives, the read-write head assembly is in actual physical contact with the recording material. (For increased life, head contact is generally maintained only during reading or writing.) Track life on a diskette is generally on the order of 3 to 5 million contact revolutions. There are three standard sizes for floppy disks. The original-size flexible disk is enclosed in an 8-in. square jacket, and the disk has a diameter of 7.88 in. The recording surface is a 100-in.-thick layer of magnetic oxide on a 0.003-in.-thick polyester substrate. The jacket gives handling protection; in addition, it has a special liner that provides a wiping action to remove wear products and other dirt which would be abrasive to the media and head if left on the surface.

In the original IBM version, there is a single 0.100-in.-diameter index hole 1.5 in. from the center of the disk to indicate the start of a track. A written track

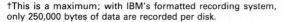

TABLE 6.7	CHARACTERISTICS FOR AN IBM-COMPATIBLE FLEXIBLE-DISK DRIVE	
CHARACTERISTIC	SPECIFICATION	
Capacity	400,000 bytes†	
Rotational speed	360 rpm	
Transfer rate	250,000 bits/s	
Track-to-track access time	16–20 ms	
Average access time	176 ms	
Bit density		
Inner track	3268 bits/in.	
Outer track	1836 bits/in.	
Track density per inch	48	
Number of tracks	77	

†This is a maximum; with IBM's formatted recording system, only 250,000 bytes of data are recorded per disk.

is 0.012 in. wide, and standard track spacing is 48 per inch. The number of tracks is 77. The capacity of a surface using standard code and a bit density of 3268 bits/in. on the innermost track is about 400,000 bytes of 8 bits each. Table 6.7 shows some characteristic of this kind of flexible-disk system.

Disks are also made in $5\frac{1}{4}$- and $3\frac{1}{2}$-in. sizes, and these minidisks are now the most popular. Several companies offer floppy-disk systems using adaptations of the flying-head concept, so the disk surface is not worn when used. Some floppy disks use an address system (like regular disks) in which the disk drive, track, and sector are given. However, other systems write *headers* on each block of recorded data on a track, and the header information is specified for each access.

The ''IBM standard'' system uses one complete track for formatting information. Sync bits and headers as well as check bits are interlaced with data on the remaining tracks. A complete description of IBM's formatting can be found in The IBM Diskette for Standard Data Interchange, IBM document GA21-9182-01.

To increase disk capacity, manufacturers now supply two-sided double-track-density (100 tracks per inch) and double-density (7 kbits/in.) drives. Less expensive drives normally have fewer tracks.

Table 6.8 shows some typical characteristics for small systems.

TABLE 6.8	FLOPPY-DISK CHARACTERISTICS		
CHARACTERISTIC	8-IN. DISK DRIVE	5.25-IN. DISK DRIVE	3.5-IN. DISK DRIVE
Capacity (unformatted)			
Single density, kbytes	800	220	218.8
Double density, kbytes	1600	440	437.5
Average access time, ms	200	300	200
Transfer rates			
Single density, kbits/s	250	250	250
Double density, kbits/s	500	500	500
Number of tracks	154	100	70
Rotational speed, rpm	360	300	600
Track density per inch	130	130	145

**THE MEMORY
ELEMENT**

6.12   At present, the most popular medium for storing very large quantities of information is magnetic tape. Although magnetic tape is not a desirable medium for the main high-speed storage of a computer because of its long access time, modern mass-production techniques have made the cost of tape very low. Thus vast quantities of information may be stored inexpensively. Furthermore, since it is possible to erase and rewrite information on tape, the same tape may be used again and again. Another advantage of magnetic tape is that the information stored does not "fade away," and therefore data or programs stored one month may be used again the next.

Another advantage of using magnetic tape for storing large quantities of data derives from the fact that the reels of tape on a tape mechanism may be changed. In this way the same magnetic-tape handling mechanism and its associated circuitry may be used with many different reels of tape, each reel containing different data.

There are four basic parts of a digital magnetic-tape system:

1   *Magnetic tape*   This is generally a flexible plastic tape with a thin coating of some ferromagnetic material along the surface.

2   *Tape transport*   This consists of a mechanism designed to move the tape past the recording heads at the command of the computer. Included are the heads themselves and the storage facilities for the tape being used, such as the reels on which the tape is wound.

3   *Reading and writing system*   This part of the system includes the reading and writing amplifiers and the *translators,* which convert the signals from the tape to digital signals that may be used in the central computing system.

4   *Switching and buffering equipment*   This section consists of the equipment necessary to select the correct tape mechanism if there are several, to store information from the tape and also information to be read onto the tape (provide buffering), and to provide such tasks as manually directed rewinding of the tape.

The tape transports used in most digital systems have two unique characteristics: the ability to start and stop very quickly and a high tape speed. The ability to start and stop the tape very quickly is important for two reasons. First, since the writing or reading process cannot begin until the tape is moving at a sufficient speed, a delay is introduced until the tape gains speed, slowing down operation. Second, information is generally recorded on magnetic tape in *blocks,* or *records.* Since the tape may be stopped between blocks of information, the tape which passes under the heads during the stopping and starting processes is wasted. This is called the *interblock,* or *interrecord, gap.* Fast starting and stopping conserves tape.[14]

Figure 6.30(*a*) shows a typical tape system. To accelerate and decelerate the tape very quickly, an effort is made to isolate the tape reels, which have a high inertia, from the mechanism that moves the tape past the recording heads. Figure

---

[14]There is a type of tape drive called a *streaming tape drive* which does not start or stop quickly but has a high tape speed. This is described in a later section.

Capstan and read-write heads are here

Control buttons

Magnetic tape reel

Vacuum columns

(a)

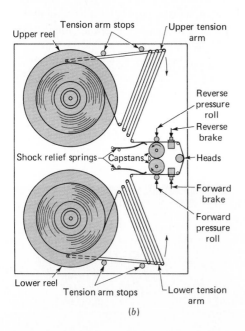

Upper reel

Tension arm stops

Upper tension arm

Reverse pressure roll

Reverse brake

Shock relief springs

Capstans

Heads

Forward brake

Forward pressure roll

Lower reel

Tension arm stops

Lower tension arm

(b)

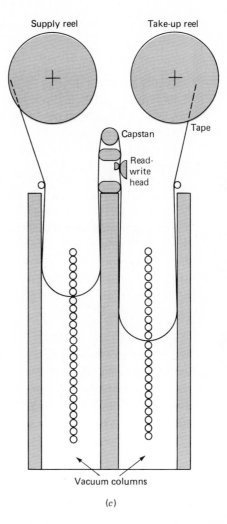

Supply reel

Take-up reel

Capstan

Read-write head

Tape

Vacuum columns

(c)

FIGURE 6.30

(a) IBM 3420 tape system. (b) Magnetic-tape mechanism using tension arms. (c) Magnetic-tape mechanism using vacuum columns.

TABLE 6.9	TYPICAL TENSION ARM TAPE DRIVE CHARACTERISTICS				
REEL SIZE, in.	bits/in.	DATA RATE, kbits	START-STOP TIME, ms	CAPACITY, Mbytes	COST OF A TYPICAL REEL OF TAPE, $
7	1600	40	15	11.5	7.50
8.5	1600	60	10	23	8.50
10.5	1600	72 kbits/s at 45 in./s; 120 kbits/s at 75 in./s	8.33 (5 ms at 75 in./s)	46	11.00

6.30(*b*) shows a high-speed start-stop tape mechanism which uses a set of tension arms around which the tape is laced. The upper and lower tension arms in Fig. 6.30(*b*) are movable, and when the tape is suddenly driven past the heads by the capstan, the mechanism provides a buffering supply of tape. A servomechanism is used to drive the upper and lower reels, maintaining enough tape between the capstan and the tape reels to keep the supply of tape around the tension arms constant. Table 6.9 shows some characteristics of this kind of system.

Another arrangement for isolating the high-inertia tape reels from the basic tape drive is shown in Fig. 6.30(*c*). This system isolates the tape from the capstan drive by means of two columns of tape held in place by a vacuum. A servosystem then maintains the correct length of tape between the reel and the capstan drive. Both this and the previous systems use continuously rotating capstans to actually drive the tape and *pressure rolls* to press the tape against the capstan when the transport is activated. Brakes are also provided for fast stopping. Table 6.10 shows some typical figures on this kind of system.

When systems of this sort are used, the start and stop times can be less than 5 ms. These are, respectively, the times required to accelerate a tape to a speed suitable for reading or writing and the time required to fully stop a moving tape. The speeds at which the tapes are moved past the heads vary greatly, most tape transports having speeds in the range of 12.5 to 250 in./s.

Some systems have changeable cartridges with a reel of tape in each cartridge. The manufacturers of these systems feel that this protects the tape and facilitates changing the reels. These are discussed in a following section.

Most tape systems have two-gap read-write heads. The two gaps (refer to Fig. 6.31) are useful because, during writing, the read gap is positioned after the write gap and is used to check what has been written by reading and comparing.

TABLE 6.10		TYPICAL VACUUM COLUMN TAPE DRIVE CHARACTERISTICS FOR 10.5-IN. TAPE REEL SYSTEMS		
SPEED, in./s	bits/in.	MAXIMUM DATA RATE, kbytes/s	START-STOP TIMES, ms	CAPACITY, Mbytes
50	1600	80	7.5	46
75	1600	120	5	46
200	1600	320	3	62
200	6250	1250	1.2	350

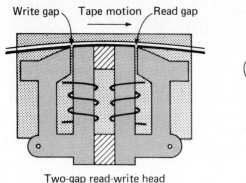 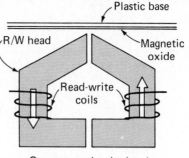

Write gap Tape motion Read gap

Two-gap read-write head

Plastic base

R/W head

Magnetic oxide

Read-write coils

One-gap read-write head

MAGNETIC TAPE

FIGURE 6.31

One- and two-gap tape heads.

Tapes vary from $\frac{1}{4}$ to 3 in. in width; however, most tape is $\frac{1}{2}$-in.-wide 1.5-mil-thick Mylar tape. A 10.5-in. reel typically has 2400 or 3600 ft of tape. Generally about nine channels or tracks are used for $\frac{1}{2}$ in. of width. The surface of the tape is usually in contact with the read-write heads. Output signals from the read heads are generally in the 0.1- to 0.5-V range. The recording density varies; however, 200, 556, 800, 1600, 6250, and even 12,500 bits/in. per channel are standard.

Data are recorded on magnetic tape by using some coding system. Generally one character is stored per row (refer to Fig. 6.32) along the tape. The tape in Fig. 6.32 has seven tracks, or channels; one of these is a parity bit, which is added to make the number of 1s in every row odd (we study this in the next chapter as well as the codes used for magnetic tape). Data are recorded on magnetic tape in blocks, with gaps between the blocks and usually with unique start and stop characters to signal the beginning and the end of a block.

A small piece of metallic reflective material is fastened to the tape at the beginning and end of the reel, and photoelectric cells are used to sense these markers and prevent overrunning of the tape [refer to Fig. 6.33(c)].

FIGURE 6.32

Basic layout of magnetic tape.

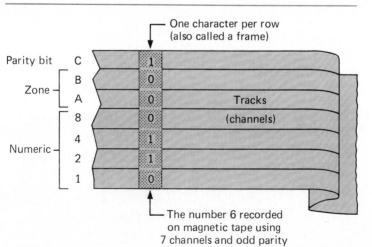

One character per row (also called a frame)

Parity bit C

Zone B A

Numeric 8 4 2 1

Tracks (channels)

The number 6 recorded on magnetic tape using 7 channels and odd parity

305

THE MEMORY
ELEMENT

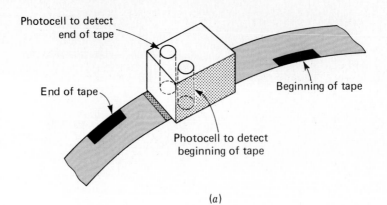

(a)

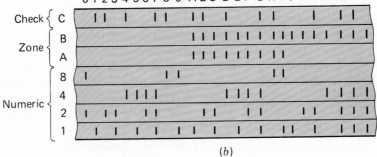

(b)

FIGURE 6.33

Magnetic-tape coding. (a) Beginning and end of tape marking. (b) Magnetic recording of seven-track BCD code on tape. (c) Nine-track (EBCDIC) and seven-track tape data format comparison.

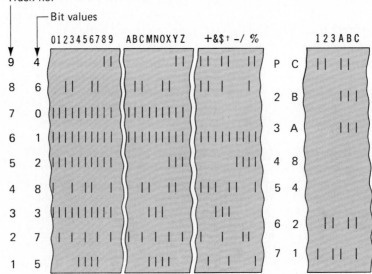

† The P bit position produces odd parity.

(c)

TABLE 6.11	VACUUM COLUMN DIGITAL TAPE TRANSPORT CHARACTERISTICS FOR THE IBM 3420-8
CHARACTERISTIC	SPECIFICATION
Data density	7 or 9 tracks, 1600 or 6250 characters/in.
Tape velocity	200 in./s
Start-stop time	3 ms at 200 in./s
Start-stop displacement	0.8214 in.
Reel diameter	10.5 in.
Tape	
Length	2400 ft
Width	0.5 in.
Thickness	1.5 mils
Rewind speed	300 in./s nominal

The codes used to record on tape vary, but two commonly used IBM codes are shown in Fig. 6.33(b) and (c). IBM standard tape is $\frac{1}{2}$ in. wide and 1.5×10^{-3} in. thick, with either seven or nine tracks. The seven-track code is shown in Fig. 6.33(b), where the 0s are simply blank and 1s are indicated by a vertical line. Figure 6.33(c) shows the nine-track code. Recording densities are 200, 556, 800, 1600, or 6250 bits (or rows) per inch [which means 200, 556, 800, 1600, or 6250 characters (or bytes) per inch, since a character is recorded in each row].

Some characteristics of a medium-priced vacuum column tape system are shown in Table 6.11. Table 6.12 gives the characteristics for an inexpensive tension arm Hewlett-Packard system.

TAPE CASSETTES AND CARTRIDGES

6.13 The changeable tape cassette used in the familiar home recorder is an attractive means for recording digital data. The cassettes are small, changeable, and inexpensive; they are frequently used in small and "home" computers. Unfortunately, the tape-moving mechanism in the conventional home tape cassette

TABLE 6.12	HEWLETT-PACKARD 7090E TAPE SYSTEMS
CHARACTERISTIC	SPECIFICATION
Number of tracks	9
Read-write speed	
2100-based systems	25, 37.5, 45 in./s
3000 system	4 in./s
Density	1600 characters/in. (8 bits/character)
Data transfer rate	72,000 characters/s maximum
Reel diameter	10.5 in. maximum
Tape (computer grade)	
Width	0.5 in.
Thickness	1.5 mils
Rewind speed	160 in./s
Start-stop time	8.33 ms (read after write) at 45 in./s
End of tape and beginning of tape reflective-strip detection	IBM-compatible

often used for small systems is not of sufficient quality for larger business and scientific computer usage. However, a number of high-quality digital cassettes with prices in the dollar region ($2 to $15 in general) have been developed. These are small—on the order of the familiar audio cassette—and have a similar appearance.

There are also larger tape cartridges which contain long strips of magnetic tape and which resemble large cassettes. These cartridges provide a more convenient way to package tape and greatly simplify the mounting of tape reels (which can be a problem with conventional reels of tape where the tape must be manually positioned on the mechanism). The tape cartridges also provide protection against dirt and contamination, since the tape is sealed in the cartridges.

A number of different digital cassettes and cassette drives are now in production, and each has different characteristics.[15] For example, TEAC offers a cassette drive with a tape speed of 15 in./s, 282 ft 0.15 in. of magnetic tape per cassette, and 1600-bits/in. tape density. The cassette can rewind in 48 s. A 22-in. reflective leader and trailer are used to mark the beginning and the end of the tape (a photodiode senses this strip).

Cartridges are a high-performance magnetic-tape storage medium. Several cartridge designs are available. These vary not only in performance capabilities, but also in the division of hardware between cartridge and transport.[16] The 3M cartridge and drive shown in Fig. 6.34 are representative. The cartridge contains 300 ft of $\frac{1}{4}$-in. tape capable of recording up to four tracks at 1600 bits/in. for a

---

[15]Standards organizations have attempted to develop standards for cassettes. The Phillips cassette is such a standard.

[16]For instance, the heads may or may not be included in each cartridge.

FIGURE 6.34

Digital cartridge and interface. (*3M Co.*)

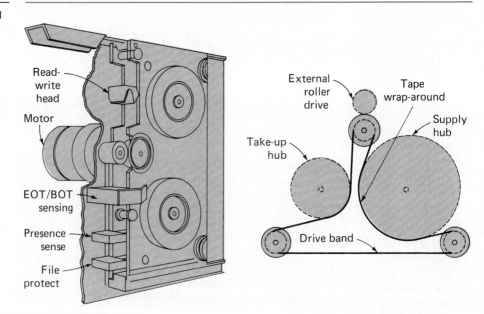

TABLE 6.13	SPECIFICATIONS OF 3M CARTRIDGE AND DCD-3 CARTRIDGE DRIVE
CHARACTERISTIC	SPECIFICATION
Operating speed	
Read-write	30 in./s forward and reverse
Fast forward, rewind, gap search	90 in./s forward and reverse
Packing density	6400 bits/in.
Transfer rate	48 kbits/s maximum
Interrecord gap	1.33 in. typical; 1.2 in. minimum per proposed ANSI standard
Maximum recommended start-stop rate	Three operations per second without forced-air cooling
Total speed variation	±4% maximum
Tape head	1-, 2-, 4-channel read-while-write heads available
Interface logic	TTL-compatible
Power	5 V dc ± 5%, ±18 V dc ± 5%

TAPE CASSETTES
AND CARTRIDGES

maximum storage capacity of more than 2×10^7 bits. The 3M transport operates at 30 in./s during reading or writing and at 90 in./s in the search mode. A novel elastic-band drive moves the tape and also supplies tape tension. Tape drive, hub, and guide components are referenced to the base of the cartridge and require no external guidance. Several new cartridge systems have been designed to back up Winchester disk drives.

Table 6.13 gives some specifications of the 3M cartridge and the 3M cartridge drive. The great popularity of the Winchester disk drives has led to the development of a new type of tape drive called a *streaming tape drive*. Because most Winchester drives have fixed disks, there is a need to *back up,* that is to write and store elsewhere, the contents of Winchester disks. This can be done with floppy disks, but they are expensive per bit and somewhat slow; with disk cartridges, but they do not have great capacity per cartridge; or with standard 0.5-in. tape drives, but these are liable to be expensive for small systems. Thus a small, inexpensive type of drive, the streaming tape drive, competes in the market for the Winchester backup function.

The streaming tape drive is small and uses 0.25-in. tape in a cartridge. An important design characteristic is that the tape is moved past the read-write heads by driving the reels, not by using a capstan as in most tape systems. This leads to fast tape movement, but starts and stops are slow and so interrecord gaps are long. As a result, a streaming tape drive can be used to transfer (or read) large quantities of data once the tape is in motion. Tape speeds of 90 in./s are common, and the tape lengths are about 450 ft per cartridge. Transfer rates can be as high as 100 kbytes/s. A single tape can store up to 67 Mbytes per cartridge. Densities of 6400 bits/in. along a track are common, and four or five tracks are generally used.

Table 6.14 compares some of the standard memory devices just described. Notice that these are standard systems, and some newer devices may exceed these characteristics. Table 6.15 gives some data on the newer low-cost devices suitable for minicomputers and microcomputers as opposed to more expensive devices. These are again representative figures for the latest systems.

TABLE 6.14

CHARACTERISTIC	5-in. REEL	PHILLIPS CASSETTE	3M-TYPE CARTRIDGE	FLOPPY DISK	LARGE HARD DISK FIXED MEDIA
Capacity, kbytes	18,500	550	2500	1600	571,000
Transfer rate, kbits/s	180	9.6	48	500	14,000
Number of tracks	9	2	4	200	600
Density, bits/in.	880	880	1600	3200	1600
Interrecord gap, in.	0.6	0.8	1.3	Not applicable	Not applicable
Mechanism cost, $	1000	400	500	100	30,000
Media cost, cents/byte	0.06×10^{-4}	1.2×10^{-3}	0.6×10^{-4}	2.6×10^{-4}	0.185×10^{-4}

Table title (top of table): **STORAGE MEDIA COMPARISONS**

TABLE 6.15 — LOW-COST STORAGE SYSTEM CHARACTERISTICS

CHARACTERISTIC	CAPACITY	COST, cents/byte
Floppy disk	2.4 Mbits	2.6×10^{-4}
High-performance cassette	1 Mbyte	0.5×10^{-4}
Phillips cassette	1.44 Mbytes	1.2×10^{-4}
Low-performance cassette	200 kbits	20×10^{-4}
3M cartridge	11.5 Mbytes	0.6×10^{-3}
7-in. tape reels	40 Mbits	0.5×10^{-4}

MAGNETIC BUBBLE AND CCD MEMORIES

6.14 The secondary, or backup, memory devices that have been really successful so far have all been electromechanical devices (drums, disks, tape, etc.) which store bits as magnetic fields on a surface and rely on mechanical motion to locate the data. However, two devices for secondary storage having no moving parts are now being developed and have started to appear in some commercial applications. These are magnetic bubble and CCD memories.

Magnetic bubble memories are primarily competing with floppy disks, small disks, cartridges, and small tape devices. Bubble memories are more reliable (having no moving parts), consume less power, are smaller, and cost less per unit. However, disks have higher transfer rates, and the cost per bit is lower except for very small systems.

Bubble memories trace their history to research at the Bell Laboratories, which showed that bits can be stored as "bubbles" in a thin magnetic film formed on a crystalline substrate. A bubble device operates as a set of shift registers. The storage mechanism consists of cylindrically shaped magnetic domains, called *bubbles*. These bubbles are formed in a thin-film layer of single-crystal synthetic ferrite (or garnet) when a magnetic field is applied perpendicular to the film's surface. A separate rotating field moves the bubbles through the film in shift register fashion. The presence of a bubble is a 1; no bubble is a 0. The bubbles move along a path determined by patterns of soft magnetic material deposited on the magnetic epitaxial film.

To the user, the physics of the bubble memory's operation are less important than its operating characteristics. The memories appear as long shift registers which can be shifted under external control. Storage is permanent since if shifting is stopped, the bits in the memory will remain indefinitely.

To utilize the shift register characteristics better and reduce access time, the shift registers are generally made of only modest lengths of perhaps 50 to 100 bits. A memory package is liable to contain from a few hundred kilobits to several megabits.

The shift rate is relatively slow, perhaps 400 MHz, so access times are on the order of a few milliseconds. (Reading and writing are performed only at the ends of the shift register.)

Bubble memories require relatively complex interface circuitry, but IC manufacturers have produced reasonable IC packages for this purpose.

Charged-coupled devices (CCDs) are constructed by using IC technology. The bits are stored on capacitors as charges similar to the dynamic IC memories, except that the storage is arranged in a shift register configuration with the charge ''packets'' being shifted from cell to cell under clock control.

Since the storage mechanism is a charge on a capacitor, if shifting stops for very long (a few milliseconds), the charges will leak from the capacitors and the memory's contents will be lost.

CCD memories generally have from 500 kbits to several megabits of storage. The shift registers are read from and written into from the ends, so access time is dependent on shift register lengths. The shift rate is generally 200 to 500 kHz, and so for reasonable-length shift registers access times are in the milliseconds.

Since CCD memories use IC technology, they require less interface circuitry than bubble memories. The strategy involved in determining how long the shift registers should be for both bubbles and CCDs is based on a cost/performance analysis. A greater number of shorter loops results in faster access times, but more interface circuits and more complicated system usage strategies. Long loops give economy but long access times.

Both bubble and CCD technologies are in the early stages, but they are already considered competitive with the smaller, more conventional disk memories.

DIGITAL RECORDING TECHNIQUES

*6.15[17]   Although the characteristics and construction of such storage devices as tape recorders and magnetic disk storage devices may vary greatly, the fundamental storage process in each consists of storing a binary 0 or 1 on a small area of magnetic material. Storage in each case is dynamic, for the medium on which the information is recorded is moved past the reading or writing device.

Although the process of recording a 0 or a 1 on a surface may appear straightforward, considerable research has gone into both the development of the recorded patterns used to represent 0s and 1s and the means for determining the value recorded. There are two necessities here: (1) The packing density should be made as great as is possible; that is, each cell or bit should occupy as little space as possible, thus economizing, for instance, on the amount of tape used to store a given amount of information. (2) The reading and writing procedure should be

---

[17]Sections with asterisks can be omitted on a first reading without loss of continuity.

THE MEMORY
ELEMENT

made as reliable as possible. These two interests are conflicting because when the recorded bits are packed more and more closely together, the distortion of the playback signal is greatly increased.

In writing information on a magnetic surface, the digital information is supplied to the recording circuitry, which then codes this information into a pattern that is recorded by the write head. The techniques used to write information on a magnetic medium can be divided into several categories: the *return-to-zero* (RZ) technique, the *return-to-bias* (RB) technique, and the *nonreturn-to-zero* (NRZ) technique. The methods for reading information written by using these techniques also vary. The basic techniques are described below, along with the recorded waveshapes and the waveshapes later read by the read heads and translated by the reading system.

RETURN-TO-ZERO AND RETURN-TO-BIAS RECORDING TECHNIQUES

*6.16   Figure 6.35 illustrates the return-to-zero recording technique. In Fig. 6.35(*a*) no current goes through the winding of the write head, except when a 1 or a 0 is to be recorded. If a 1 is to be recorded, a pulse of positive polarity is applied to the winding on the write head; and if a 0 is to be written, a negative pulse is applied to the winding. In either case, the current through the write-head winding is returned to zero after the pulse and remains there until the next bit is recorded. The second set of waveforms on this drawing illustrates the remanent flux pattern on the magnetic surface after the write head has passed. There is some distortion in this pattern because of the fringing of flux around the head.

If this pattern of magnetization is passed under a read head, some of the magnetic flux will be coupled into the core of the head. The flux takes the lower reluctance path through the core material of the head instead of bridging the gap in the head (Fig. 6.27). And when the amount of flux through the core material changes, a voltage will be induced in the coil wound around the core. Thus a change in the amplitude of the recorded magnetic field will result in a voltage being induced in the coil on the read head. The waveforms in Fig. 6.35(*a*) and (*b*) illustrate typical output signals on the read-head windings for each technique. Note that the waveform at the read head is not a reproduction of the input current during the write process, nor of the pattern actually magnetized on the magnetic material.

The problem is, therefore, to distinguish a 1 or a 0 output at the sense winding. Several techniques have been used. One consists in first amplifying the output waveform from the read winding in a linear amplifier. Then the output of this amplifier is strobed to determine whether a 1 or 0 was written. If the output from the read amplifier is connected to an AND gate and the strobe pulse is also connected as an input to the same AND gate, then the output will be a positive pulse when the recorded signal represents a 1.

It is important that the time pulse be very sharp and occur at the right time relative to the reading and writing of the bits.

A fundamental characteristic of RZ recording [Fig. 6.35(*a*)] is this: For a 1, the output signal during the first half of each bit time will be positive with regard to the second half; for a 0, the first half of the output signal during each bit time

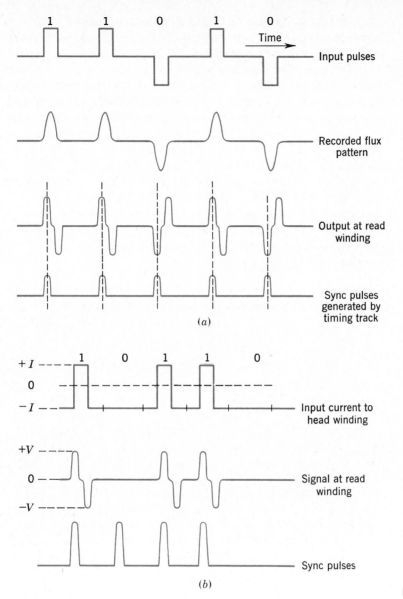

(a)

(b)

FIGURE 6.35

Recording techniques. (a) Return-to-zero recording. (b) Return-to-bias technique.

will be negative with regard to the second half of the signal. This fact is sometimes exploited in translating the signal read-back.

In the RZ system in Fig. 6.35(a), the magnetic field returns to zero flux when a 1 or a 0 pulse is not present. This makes it impossible to write over information which has previously been written unless the position of each cell is very accurately located. If a 0 pulse is written directly over a previously recorded 1, the flux generated will reverse the polarity of the recorded field only if the write head is in exactly the right position when the 0 is recorded. So the timing of the writing of information is very critical for this system, and it is rarely used.

The second method for recording information is the *return-to-bias system,* illustrated in Fig. 6.35(*b*). In this case, the current through the winding maintains the head saturated in the negative direction unless a 1 is to be written. When a 1 is written, a pulse of current in the opposite direction is applied to the winding at the center of the bit time. The outputs at the sense winding are also illustrated in the figure. In this case, there will be an output at the sense winding only when a 1 is written. This output may be amplified and strobed just as in the previous case. The timing here is not so critical when information is being written over, because the negative flux from the head will magnetize the surface in the correct direction, regardless of what was previously recorded. The current through the winding in this case, and in all those which follow, is assumed to be sufficient to saturate the material on which the signals are being recorded. A primary problem here concerns sequences of 0s. For magnetic tape, either a clock track must be used or the code used must be such that at least one 1 occurs in each line of the tape. Notice that this is because only 1s generate magnetic flux changes and, therefore, output signals at the read head.

NONRETURN-TO-ZERO RECORDING TECHNIQUES

*6.17 Figure 6.36 illustrates three recording techniques, each of which is classified as a nonreturn-to-zero system. In the first, the current through the winding is negative through the entire bit time when a 0 is recorded and is positive through the entire bit time when a 1 is recorded. So the current through the winding will remain constant when a sequence of 0s or 1s is being written and will change only when a 0 is followed by a 1 or when a 1 followed by a 0 is written. In this case, a signal will be induced in the sense winding only when the information recorded changes from a 1 to a 0, or vice versa.

The second technique illustrated is sometimes referred to as a *modified nonreturn-to-zero,* or *nonreturn-to-zero mark* (NRZI), technique. In this system the polarity of the current through the write winding is reversed each time a 1 is recorded and remains constant when a 0 is recorded. If a series of 1s is recorded, then the polarity of the recorded flux will change for each 1. If a series of 0s is recorded, no changes will occur. Notice that the polarity has no meaning in this system; only changes in polarity matter. Therefore, a signal will be read back only when a 1 has been recorded. This system is often used for tape recording when, in order to generate a clock or strobe, a 1 must be recorded somewhere in each cell along the tape width. That is, if 10 tracks are recorded along the tape, then one of these must be a timing track which records a sequence of 1s, each of which defines a different set of cells to be read; or the information must be coded so that a 1 occurs in each set of 10 cells which are read. Alphanumeric coded information[18] is often recorded on tape, and the code may be arranged so that a 1 occurs in each code group.

The third nonreturn-to-zero technique in Fig. 6.36 is sometimes called a *phase encoded, biphase-mark, Harvard, Manchester,* or *split-frequency* system. In this case a 0 is recorded as a $\frac{1}{2}$-bit-time negative pulse followed by a $\frac{1}{2}$-bit-time

---

[18]Alphanumeric codes are described in Chap. 7.

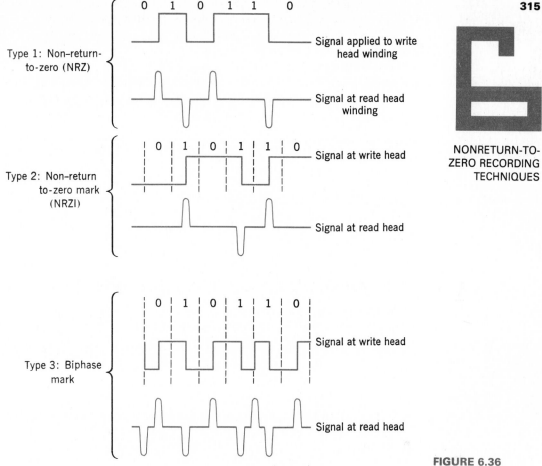

FIGURE 6.36

Three types of non-return-to-zero recording.

positive pulse, and a 1 is recorded as a $\frac{1}{2}$-bit-time positive pulse followed by a $\frac{1}{2}$-bit-time negative pulse. This technique is often used in high-speed systems.

The reading of information which has been recorded consists of two steps. First the output from the read head is amplified, and then the amplified signals are translated by logic circuitry. Figure 6.37 shows a translation technique for the first nonreturn-to-zero system illustrated in Fig. 6.36. The output signals may be either from the output flip-flop or from serial pulses. The sync pulses occur each time a cell passes under the read heads in the system.

The flip-flop (Fig. 6.37) responds to positive pulses only. Positive-pulse signals at the recording head will therefore "set" the flip-flop to 1. The inverter at the c input will cause negative pulses to be made positive. These positive pulses then will clear the flip-flop. The output of the flip-flop may be used directly by the computer; or pulse outputs can be generated by connecting an AND gate to the 1 output, delaying the sync pulses, and connecting them to the AND gate. Also, a serial representation of the number stored along the surface may be formed.

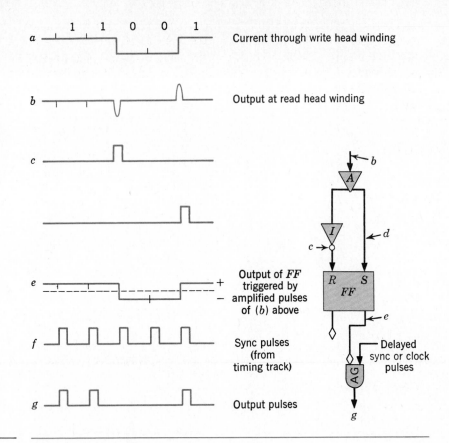

a — Current through write head winding

b — Output at read head winding

c

e — Output of FF triggered by amplified pulses of (b) above

f — Sync pulses (from timing track)

g — Output pulses

FIGURE 6.37

Nonreturn-to-zero
recording.

SUMMARY

6.18 The memory devices in a computer are organized according to their speed. The fastest are in the central processor, the next fastest are in the main memory, and the slower but less expensive devices are used as backup, or secondary, memories.

IC memories are generally organized by some variation of a two-dimensional selection scheme. They can use static (flip-flop) or dynamic memory cells. Large IC memories can be formed from a number of IC chips by using decoders and select inputs to organize the selection process. IC memories can be readily connected to the buses now used to interface memory drives to a central processing unit, and examples of this were shown.

Read-only memories are similar to read-write memories in organization but provide permanent or semipermanent storage of their contents. Some ROMs have these contents built in by the manufacturers while others can be changed by the user as desired.

Disk memories have many desirable properties. Fixed-disk Winchester memories are now very popular as are changeable floppy-disk memories. The principles, operating characteristics, and organization of these memories were discussed.

Magnetic-tape memories provide low cost per bit with longer access times than disk memories. Tape memories range from small, low-cost, entertainment-type cassette memories to large, high-speed tape drives with large reels of tape. New cassette-type streaming tape drives are often used to back up Winchester disks. The operating characteristics and recording formats for tape memories were presented along with costs and their comparison with disk memories.

QUESTIONS

6.1 Determine the number of AND gates and OR gates used in a two-dimensional and a one-dimensional IC memory by using the techniques in Figs. 6.4 and 6.9. The memory is to have 1 bit per word and 16 words. (Show how you got your numbers.)

6.2 Determine the complete OR gate and AND gate decoder count for an IC memory with 4096 words of 1 bit each, using the selection schemes in Figs. 6.4 and 6.9. (Show how your numbers are derived.)

6.3 The interface circuitry for dynamic memories is more complicated than for static memories. However, the cost per bit of actual memory is less for dynamic memories. As a result, for small memories static devices are less expensive and for larger memories dynamic devices are less expensive. If the interface for a static memory costs $1.00 and for a dynamic memory $10.00, and static memory bits cost $0.005 per bit while the dynamic memory bits cost $0.002 per bit, determine how many bits must be in a memory before the dynamic memory is less expensive.

6.4 Consider decoder matrices which are rectangular, but not square. For instance, to encode a 256-bit memory, we might use a "square" 16×16 matrix in two-dimensional form or an 8×32 two-dimensional rectangular array. Show that keeping the array "as square as possible" will reduce the number of AND gates in the decoders.

6.5 What are the sizes of the decoders in Fig. 6.18?

6.6 As the size of the memory goes up, the advantage of using a two-dimensional selection scheme increases with regard to the number of AND gates used for the decoders. The two-dimensional memory, however, requires more complicated memory cells. For a 4096-bit memory with a single output bit, compare the number of AND gates in the decoder for linear and for two-dimensional memories and also the number of gates in the linear memory cells versus the two-dimensional memory cells. Try to draw some conclusion regarding which is more economical.

6.7 Does the two-dimensional selection system in any way slow down operation compared to the linear selection scheme?

6.8 A 64K-word memory is to be assembled with chips having 4096 bits each, using the chip in Figs. 6.18 and 6.19. Explain how a memory bus can be connected so that the full 64K-word memory can be implemented (showing only 1 bit in the memory word).

6.9 There is a scheme whereby as the power declines, the contents of the IC

memory are read into a secondary (disk or tape) memory. When the power is returned, the data are reentered into the IC memory. It is important that the power not decline too much before the transfer of information can be made. As a result, it is generally necessary to have some sort of backup power to carry the memory through until the contents of the IC memory can be read out. Calculate how long this would take for a 256K memory with a cycle time of 500 ns.

6.10 Question 6.9 concerned dumping an IC memory on a disk in case of power failure. It is also necessary to find a spare area on the disk and to transfer the contents of the memory onto the disk. For one of the disk memories described in the chapter, discuss this problem for the preceding 256K 500-ns IC memory.

6.11 Several microcomputers come with a basic 256K-word 8-bit memory. How many flip-flops are in (a) the memory address register and (b) the memory buffer register?

6.12 Draw the waveforms for recording the binary sequence 101, showing the signal applied to the write-head winding and the signal at the read-head winding for the type 1, type 2, and type 3 nonreturn-to-zero recording techniques.

6.13 A block diagram of an INTEL MOS LSI memory chip is shown in Fig. 6.10. Lines A_1 through A_8 are for the 256 addresses, and R/W tells whether to read or to write (a 0 on this line is READ, a 1 is WRITE). The CHIP SELECT disables the memory for a 1 input and enables the memory with a 0 output. Discuss the construction of a 256-word 8-bit memory using these packages. How many packages are required? Each flip-flop in the address register (external) would have its 1 output connected to how many chips?

6.14 Draw the schematic for a many-to-one decoder matrix with inputs from 4 flip-flops and 16 output lines. Use the same basic configuration as is illustrated in Fig. 6.5(a).

6.15 The INTEL package in Fig. 6.10 is representative of several IC manufacturers' products. Show how the CHIP SELECT can be used to add words to a memory.

6.16 What are the primary advantages of bipolar memory over MOS memory?

6.17 Explain the operation of the digit line in a linear-select core memory.

6.18 Explain the difference between a dynamic and a static MOS memory.

6.19 Contrast the parallel tree and balanced decoder networks for a 32-output decoder. Figure the number of diodes used for each and the delay incurred because of the number of gates a signal must pass through for each, assuming diode AND gates are used.

6.20 Given eight 8-bit registers $A, B, C, \ldots, H$, show how a transfer circuit can be made by using multiplexers so that the contents of any register can be selected by a 3-bit register S and transferred to an 8-bit register X.

6.21 In larger machines, when the ac power drops below a certain level, the contents of the control unit and arithmetic-logic unit are dumped on tape or disks so that the computer can be restarted with no loss of data. If IC memories are used, their contents must be dumped also. Explain why.

6.22 Explain the operation of the memory cell in Fig. 6.3.

6.23 Explain the operation of the memory cell in Fig. 6.8.

6.24 When linear selection is used for IC memories, individual cells tend to be simpler than for two-dimensional cell select systems, but the decoders tend to be more complicated. Explain why.

6.25 Why are floppy disks more used than hard disks in microcomputers?

6.26 The memory in Fig. 6.19 uses the organization in Fig. 6.11 and has linear-select memory cells. This simplifies individual memory cell complexity while increasing sense and write circuitry. Explain why this is cost-effective for a memory of this type.

6.27 Dynamic memories that require external refreshing introduce extra complexity into computer operation. Why?

6.28 Explain the advantages and disadvantages of dynamic IC memories.

6.29 In designing a 256-word 8-bit memory, pin 1 is connected to pin 1 for each container of the chip shown in Fig. 6.10. This applies to all A inputs and to chip-select bits and R/W, but not to data out or data in. Why?

6.30 Show how to expand the 256-word 1-bit memory in Fig. 6.10 to a 2048-word 1-bit memory by using the CHIP SELECT and a three-input, eight-output decoder.

6.31 Which of the tape units described will transfer data fastest, and how fast can characters and bits be read or written?

6.32 Make up a formula to calculate how many bits a second can be read from a disk memory that revolves at a rate of r revolutions per second and has b bits per track. What will the average latency time be?

6.33 Assuming that a disk with 1500 bits/in. rotates at a speed of 2400 rpm and that we read from eight tracks simultaneously, how many bits per second can be read from one of these disks?

6.34 Explain seek time and latency for disk memories.

6.35 A magnetic-tape system has seven tracks for each $\frac{1}{2}$-in. width of tape. The packing density per track is 1280 bits/in., and the tape is moved at a speed of 75 in./s. If the tape width is 0.5 in., how many bits may be read per second?

6.36 Fixed-head disk memories reduce total access time by avoiding either seek time or latency. Which is avoided and why?

6.37 Contrast the floppy-disk figures for the 5- and the 8-in. systems.

6.38 Tape cassettes and tape cartridges have advantages and disadvantages compared to conventional tape systems. Cite several of each.

6.39 The table comparing storage media brings out some of the contrasts in price and performance for memory systems. What devices would you choose for the following kinds of computers and why?

(*a*) Microcomputers   (*b*) Minicomputers   (*c*) Large computer systems

6.40 Draw a diode ROM as in Fig. 6.24 which translates from excess-3 code to BCD.

6.41 An IC memory could be made three-dimensional by breaking the MAR into three pieces and having three decoders. The memory cell would be more complex, however. Design a 4096-word memory of this type, comparing it with the two-dimensional memory.

6.42 Design four locations in a ROM by adding gates to the following diagram. The signal C_1 is to be a 1 in locations 01111 and 11110 and a 0 otherwise; the signal C_2 is to be a 1 in locations 01111 and 10000 and a 0 otherwise; the signal C_3 is to be a 1 in 01101, 11110, and 01111 and a 0 otherwise. A given decoder output line is high when selected.

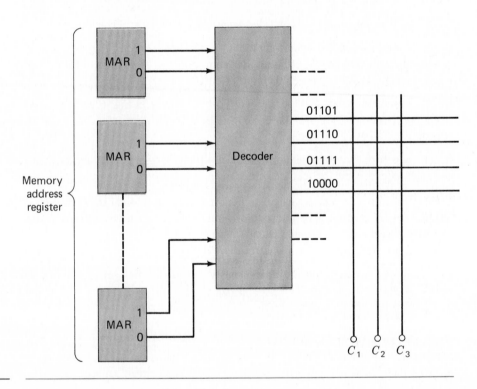

FIGURE 6.42

6.43 Here are some data on a PDP-11 disk pack:

Number of cylinders: 203	Seek time S to move N cylinders
Tracks per cylinder: 2	For $N = 0$ to 8, $S = 6 + 2N$
Bytes per track: 6144	For $N = 9$ to 24, $S = 16 + 3N/4$
Disk rotation time: 40 ms	For $N > 24$, $S = 26 + N/3$

Discuss the total search time for finding a specific piece of data, considering the heads to be positioned in the center cylinder when the search order is given. A cylinder is the set of all tracks which can be read from or written on for a given position of the head-positioning mechanism.

6.44 Compare a conventional disk memory with the floppy-disk memory with regard to operating characteristics and costs.

6.45 Memory systems, disk packs, tape drives, cassettes, and floppy disks all have different characteristics. However, in general the units with lower entry prices (that is, lower unit prices) have higher bit prices. Explain this and give examples, using figures in the text.

6.46 *Hard sectoring* refers to a disk system in which sectors are determined by some mechanical technique. For instance, sectors on some floppy disks are determined by punching a number of holes around the disk, and a sector begins when a hole occurs in the disk. *Soft sectoring* refers to a technique in which headers are written at the beginning of sectors, and so the reading circuitry locates sectors and information without the use of mechanical devices. Whta are the advantages and disadvantages of these systems?

6.47 The very high-speed high-bit-packing-density tape drives use an encoding technique in which bits are encoded in groups. For instance, in one commonly used technique 4 input bits are encoded into 5 bits. Since the 16 possible combinations of the 4 bits which can occur in the data are mapped into only 16 of the 32 possible combinations of 5 bits, these sixteen 5-bit patterns can be carefully selected so that the recording characteristics are optimal. When the 5 bits are read back, they are changed back to the original input data. This plus the use of powerful error-correcting codes allows a packing density of 6250 bits/in. (and sometimes more). Give some advantages and disadvantages of a complicated encoding and decoding scheme such as this one with regard to tape drive mechanisms and user characteristics.

6.48 Formulate a memory system for a microprocessor which has 64K of ROM, 256K of RAM, and an initial backup memory of 0.5 Mbyte with a possibility of expanding to 5 Mbytes. Choose the memory devices you think would be reasonable and justify your choice economically and from a performance viewpoint.

6.49 Bubble and CCD memories are generally considered to be competitive with floppy disk and small disk packs and are useful in replacing these devices, because disks require mechanical motion for reading and writing and are thus less reliable than straight integrated circuitry or nonmoving media. In what applications might bubble or CCD memories be particularly useful?

6.50 A dynamic memory must be given a refresh cycle 128 times each 2 ms. Each refresh operation requires 150 ns, and a memory cycle is 250 ns. What percentage of the memory's total operating time must be given to memory refreshes?

6.51 If a memory is made up of dynamic memory chips, then the time lost to refreshing can be reduced by breaking the memory into sections, or banks, and when one bank is addressed, refreshing another bank. Sketch how this might be arranged by a memory controller chip.

INPUT-OUTPUT DEVICES

In order to use a computer, it is first necessary to insert the program and the data via the input devices. The input devices to a personal computer consist of keys on a keyboard. Numeric and alphabetic data are introduced via these keys. Figure 7.1 shows a keyboard for a personal computer.

When the program and data have been read and the necessary operations completed, it is necessary for the computer to deliver the results. A great variety of output devices are available. Business applications generally require that the results be printed in tabular form or perhaps on a series of checks, as in a payroll accounting operation. Scientific results are more likely to consist of numeric data which must be clearly printed with little chance of error (such accuracy is also of prime importance in computers used to compute payroll checks) or graphs showing the results of the calculations. For any of these applications, one type of output device may be more desirable than another. However, a great many applications require that the outputs from the computer be printed on a piece of paper. This requires printers, ranging from electromechanical typewriters, which print one letter or digit at a time, to high-speed printers capable of printing a hundred or more characters at a time. Figure 7.1 shows a small printer and an oscilloscope display, the two output devices used most. There are several important input-output devices in addition to keyboards, printers, and oscilloscopes, however, and these are introduced in this chapter.

This chapter is organized as follows. First, input devices are discussed, followed by output devices. Then digital-to-analog (D-to-A) and analog-to-digital (A-to-D) converters are described, followed by a section on data collection.

FIGURE 7.1

Personal computer.

OBJECTIVES

1   Input-output devices provide for communication between computers and humans, computers and computers, and computers and external sensors and effectors (robots, for example). The various devices such as tape, cards, keyboards, oscilloscopes, and printers are discussed along with their characteristics.

2   Alphanumeric codes provide for machine interfaces with humans where keyboards and printers can be used to input and output information. Error-detecting codes provide for protection against errors. Both these subjects are discussed, and examples are given.

3   Digital-to-analog and analog-to-digital converters provide important interfaces between the outside world and computers. The principles of operation of these devices, examples, and general characteristics are presented along with a discussion of data collection from analog inputs.

PUNCHED TAPE

7.1   Punched tape was one of the first popular media for storing the programs and data to be read into a digital machine. When the first large computers were designed, telegraph systems had been using perforated paper tapes for some time, and so devices for punching and reading paper tapes already had been fairly well developed. The tape comes in many types and sizes. A medium-thickness tape has been used a great deal, and oiled tapes and plastic tapes are employed also. The widths of the tapes have varied from $\frac{1}{2}$ to 3 in. Information is punched into the

Channels

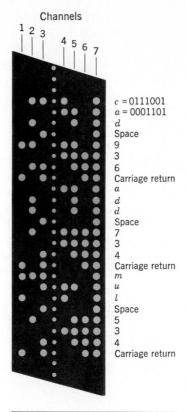

$c = 0111001$
$a = 0001101$
d
Space
9
3
6
Carriage return
a
d
d
Space
7
3
4
Carriage return
m
u
l
Space
5
3
4
Carriage return

PUNCHED TAPE

FIGURE 7.2

Punched paper tape.

tape a line at a time. Figure 7.2 illustrates a section of a punched tape. Multiple channels are used (just as on magnetic tape, a channel runs lengthwise along the tape), and a single character or code is punched as a pattern of bits in each lateral line.

The preparation of these paper input tapes is sometimes referred to as *keyboarding*. In this step the operator of a tape punch is presented with a copy of a program or input data. The operator then punches a number of holes into the tape. The holes represent, in coded form, the input information to the machine. The tape punch may be one of a number of types. The more popular devices resemble a typewriter, and the keyboards of these tape punches contain conventional symbols, similar to those on an ordinary typewriter.

When a key on the tape-punch keyboard is depressed, the binary-coded symbol for the character selected is punched into the tape, and then the tape advances to the next line. In most cases, the tape punch also prints on a separate piece of paper, in the same manner as a typewriter, the character that was punched, as well as printing the characters along the rows of the tape. There is then a typewritten copy of the program, which may be checked for errors, in addition to the paper tape punched with the coded symbols. This printed copy of the program is referred to as the *hard copy*. Many tape punches are able to read a perforated tape and to type printed copy from this tape. A punched section of tape may be placed in the

tape reader attached to the tape punch, and a typed copy of the information which was punched in the tape may be made.

Figure 7.3 shows a code which has been used frequently for paper tape systems. In the eight-channel code shown in Fig. 7.3, eight channels run lengthwise along the tape. A hole in a given one of these channels represents a 1, and the absence of a hole a 0. The 1, 2, 4, and 8 channels are used to represent the digits for 0 to 9. Thus 0s, or no holes, in positions EL, X, and 0 indicate that the encoded character is a digit with the value given by the sum of the positions 8, 4, 2, 1, in which there are holes. The check position is used for an *odd-parity check*. Its value is determined so that the number of 1s, or holes, in each character is odd. The 0 and X positions are used in conjunction with the 8, 4, 2, 1 positions to encode alphabetic and special characters.

The code has two special features. A punch in the end-of-line position indicates the end of a record on the tape. When there are punches in all seven of the positions, this indicates a blank character called *tape feed,* and the tape reader skips over such positions. This is useful for correcting mistakes in keyboarding or in editing tapes, because an erroneous character can be eliminated by simply punching in the nonpunched positions.

TAPE READERS

7.2 The function of the paper tape reader is to sense the coded information punched in the tape and deliver this information to the computer. Most tape readers used in teletype and office equipment are electromechanical devices. In many of these devices, mechanical *sensing pins* are used to determine the symbol punched ino each line of the tape. In a system of this type, there will be a sensing pin for each information channel, plus a means of moving the tape and positioning it for reading. The tape is not moved continuously, but only a single line at a time; is stopped while the coding is sensed; and then is moved to the next line. The motion of the sensing pins operates a switch, the contacts of which are opened or closed, depending on whether there is a hole in the tape. Another type of reader uses a *star wheel* to sense the absence or presence of holes in the tape, as shown in Fig. 7.4.

When the input is to a digital machine, the motion of the tape through the reader generally is controlled by the computer. Each time the tape is to be advanced and a new character read, the computer will supply the reader with a pulse which will cause it to advance the tape to the next character. To read characters as fast as possible, generally a line will be read at the same time as the advancing pulse is transmitted. Since there will be a delay owing to inertia before the tape is actually moved, the reading of the state of the sensing relays will occur during this delay period. In this case, when a stop character is sensed, the reader will proceed to the next character before actually stopping.

To speed up the reading process, tape readers use photoelectric cells or photodiodes to read the characters punched into the tape. In this case, a light-sensitive cell is placed under each channel of the tape, including the tape feed hole, or sprocket channel. A light source is placed above the tape, so that the light-sensitive element beneath the hole in the tape will be energized and will produce

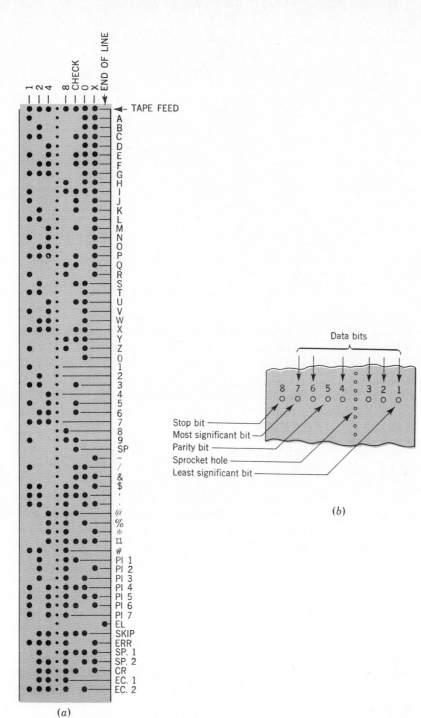

(a)

TAPE READERS

Data bits

Stop bit
Most significant bit
Parity bit
Sprocket hole
Least significant bit

(b)

FIGURE 7.3

(a) Punched tape with eight-channel code. *(b)* Format for eight-channel tape.

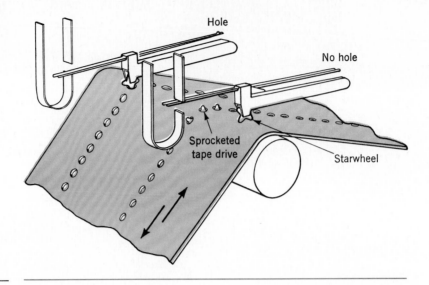

Hole

No hole

Sprocketed
tape drive

Starwheel

FIGURE 7.4

Star-wheel mechanism for reading perforated tape.

a signal indicating the presence of the hole. The signals from the light-sensitive elements are then amplified and supplied to the computer as input information.

The tape feed hole is used in this case to determine when the outputs of the light-sensitive elements are to be sensed. The tape in a reader of this type is generally friction-driven and is moved continuously until a stop character is sensed. Extremely fast starting and braking of the tape are very desirable features, and most readers are capable of stopping the tape on any given character.

PUNCHED CARDS

7.3 A widely used input medium has been the punched card. While there are a number of sizes of punched cards, the most frequently used card at present is a 12-row 80-column card $3\frac{1}{4}$ in. wide and $7\frac{3}{4}$ in. long (see Fig. 7.5). The thickness of the cards varies, although at one time most cards were 0.0067 in. thick. There is now a tendency to make the card somewhat thinner.

Just as with tape, there are numerous ways in which punched cards may be coded. The most frequently used code is the *Hollerith code,* an alphanumeric code in which a single character is punched in each column of the card. The basic code is illustrated in Fig. 7.5. As an example, the symbol A is coded by means of a punch in the top row and in the 1 row of the card, and the symbol 8 by a punch in the 8 row of the card. There are other types of cards with different hole positions, just as there are many ways of preparing the cards to be read into the computer. The most common technique is very similar to that for preparing punched tape, in that a card-punch machine with a keyboard like that of a typewriter is used, as shown in Fig. 1.8. The card punch usually also makes a hard copy of the program as it is punched into the cards. Generally, the card punch also prints the characters punched into a card on the face of the card itself. In this way, a card may be identified without examining the punches. Each character is usually printed at the top of the card directly above the column in which the character is punched.

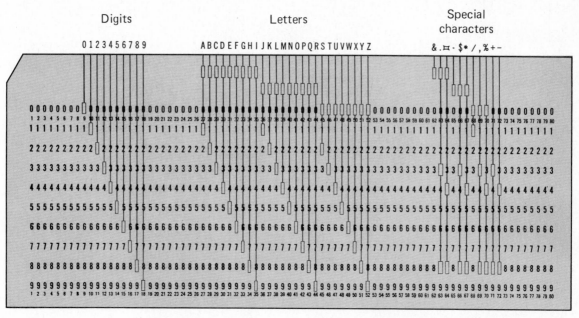

FIGURE 7.5

Punched card with
Hollerith code.

The card punch contains a hopper in which the blank cards are stacked. The operator of the card punch then causes a card to enter the punching area, and the program's list of instructions or the data to be processed are punched into the card. The card punch punches the card laterally, a column at a time, starting at the left. If a key of the card punch is depressed, the code for the character is punched into a column of the card, and then the card is moved so that the next column on the right is under the punch.

Figure 7.6 shows IBM card punches, widely used devices. These have a small memory capable of holding all the data that can be punched into two 80-column records and six program cards. The key-punch operator keyboards the data into the small memory and can backspace and change characters until the data keyboarded are correct. After all the data are in the small memory, an *enter data* key is depressed, and the card is punched from the characters in the memory. Facilities for controlling the format of the card are included by means of IC logic.

CARD READERS

7.4 Most card readers are electromechanical devices which read the information punched into a card, converting the presence or absence of a hole to an electric signal representing a binary 0 or 1. The punched cards are placed in a hopper, and when the command to read is given, a lever pushes a card from the bottom of the stack. Generally, the card is moved lengthwise over a row of 80 *read brushes*. These brushes read the information punched along the bottom row of the card. If a hole is punched in a particular row, a brush makes electric contact through the hole in the card, providing a signal which may be used by the computer. Then the

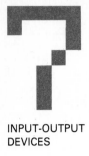

INPUT-OUTPUT
DEVICES

FIGURE 7.6

IBM 929 card
punches.

next row up is read, and this process continues until all rows have been read, after which the next card is moved into position on the brushes.

Faster card readers are constructed by using photoelectric cells under the 12 punch positions along a column and an illuminating source above the card. As each column on the card is passed over the 12 photoelectric cells, whether a given position is punched is determined by the presence or absence of light on the corresponding cell. Card readers operate at speeds of 12 to 1000 cards per minute.

Notice that when cards are read a row at a time, programs must "decipher" the characters punched in the card. Often "binary" decks are used, particularly for programs, where the computer words are distributed along rows rather than in columns and data may be loaded directly as the rows are read.

ALPHANUMERIC CODES

7.5 Data and programs are almost invariably entered in alphanumeric form, and the internal operation of computers, particularly those which involve business records, makes extensive use of alphanumeric codes. Because of the diversity of applications

	000	001	010	011	100	101	110	111
0000	NULL	DC₀ ①	ƀ	0	@	P		
0001	SOM	DC₁	!	1	A	Q		
0010	EOA	DC₂	''	2	B	R		
0011	EOM	DC₃	#	3	C	S		
0100	EOT	DC₄ (Stop)	$	4	D	T		
0101	WRU	ERR	%	5	E	U		
0110	RU	SYNC	&	6	F	V		
0111	BELL	LEM	'	7	G	W		
1000	FE₀	S₀	(	8	H	X	Unassigned	
1001	HT / SK	S₁	)	9	I	Y		
1010	LF	S₂	*	:	J	Z		
1011	V_TAB	S₃	+	;	K	[		
1100	FF	S₄	(Comma) ,	<	L	\		ACK
1101	CR	S₅	–	=	M	]		②
1110	SO	S₆	.	>	N	↑		ESC
1111	SI	S₇	/	?	O	←		DEL

Example: **100** 0001 = A

b_7 ---------------- b_1

ALPHANUMERIC
CODES

FIGURE 7.7

American Standard
Code for Information
Interchange.

and the many viewpoints on codes and code construction, many different alphanumeric codes have been suggested and used.

Fortunately, there has been an attempt to standardize on an alphanumeric code which will be agreeable to both manufacturers and users, and the American National Standards Institute has published an American Standard Code for Information Interchange (ASCII). This code is now the most used, and most major manufacturers are using the code so that their equipment will be compatible with that of other manufacturers. This code is shown in Fig. 7.7. Notice that the decimal digits are represented by the normal 8, 4, 2, 1 code preceded by the three binary digits 011. So decimal 1 becomes 0110001, decimal 2 is 0110010, decimal 7 is 0110111, etc. To expand the code, the letter A is 1000001, B is 1000010, etc. There are various codes such as "end of messages," "who are you," "skip," "carriage return," etc., which are very useful in communications systems and in editing data processes in computers. These are shown in Fig. 7.8. As a result, this is the most frequently used code for intercomputer communications systems.

Many IBM computers, and a number of other manufacturers' computer systems, use the extended BCD interchange code (EBCDIC) shown in Fig. 7.9. This code is the second most used code after the ASCII.

The abbreviations used in the figure mean:			
NULL	Null Idle	*CR*	Carriage return
SOM	Start of message	*SO*	Shift out
EOA	End of address	*SI*	Shift in
EOM	End of message	*DC$_0$*	Device control ① Reserved for data Link escape
EOT	End of transmission	*DC$_1$-DC$_3$*	Device control
WRU	"Who are you ?"	*ERR*	Error
RU	"Are you . . . ?"	*SYNC*	Synchronous idle
BELL	Audible signal	*LEM*	Logical end of media
FE	Format effector	*S$_0$-S$_7$*	Separator (information)
HT	Horizontal tabulation		Word separator (blank, normally non-printing)
SK	Skip (punched card)	*ACK*	Acknowledge
LF	Line feed	②	Unassigned control
V/TAB	Vertical tabulation	*ESC*	Escape
FF	Form feed	*DEL*	Delete Idle

FIGURE 7.8

Special characters in ASCII.

CHARACTER RECOGNITION

7.6 Techniques for data entry extend in many directions. The reading of handwritten or typewritten characters from conventional paper appears to offer an ideal input system for many applications. The systems currently in use are primarily as follows:

1 *Magnetic ink character reading (MICR)* The recording of characters by using an ink with special magnetic properties and with characters having special forms was originally used in quantity by banks. The American Banking Association settled on a type font, and several of their characters are shown in Fig. 7.10. A *magnetic character reader* "reads" these characters by examining their shapes, using a 7 × 10 matrix; it determines, from the response of the segments of the matrix to the magnetic ink, which of the characters has passed under the reader's head. This information is thus transmitted to the system. The determination of the character which is read is greatly facilitated by the careful design of the characters and the use of the magnetic ink.

2 *Optical character reading (OCR)* This area takes one of two forms. In the first, a special type font (or fonts) is used to print on conventional paper with conventional ink. The printed characters are examined by passing them under a strong light and a lens system, which differentiates light (no ink) from inked areas, and a logical system which attempts to determine which of the possible characters is being examined. The systems in actual use depend heavily on the fact that only a limited number of characters in a particular font are used, but such systems are still quite useful. The standard type font agreed on by the ANSI optical character committee is shown in Fig. 7.11.

Of course, the ideal system would be able to adapt to many different type fonts. Some systems, particularly one developed by the post office, even read handwritten characters. The limited success of these systems is due to the many

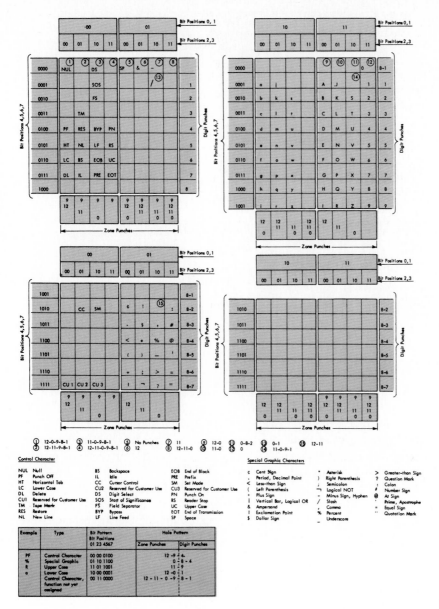

CHARACTER
RECOGNITION

FIGURE 7.9

Extended BCD inter-
change code
(EBCDIC).

shapes that a given character can have. Consider the ways you can write an *a* and
the similarity between a handwritten *a* and an *o* or a *b* and an *f*. These problems
are increased by the optical reader's difficulty with the porosity of paper, ink
smearing at the edges of lines, etc. Much work continues in this area, and much
more is needed, but the advantages of such systems continue to cause this work to
be sponsored and performed.

INPUT-OUTPUT
DEVICES

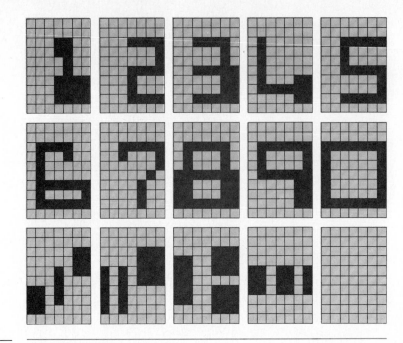

FIGURE 7.10

A magnetic reader
character set.

OUTPUT EQUIPMENT

7.7   Although many types of output equipment are used in the computer industry, the most popular form of output from a computer is undoubtedly the printed word, and printers and oscilloscopes are the most used output devices. There are many other output devices, however. For instance, loudspeakers and other audio devices are used to generate music and voices. Banks commonly use computer-driven audio to give balances and other information to tellers.

Lights are sometimes used to indicate the states of the storage devices of the principal registers of the machine (the accumulator, selected in-out registers, etc.). Such lights are generally used as troubleshooting aids, often to troubleshoot the operation of the machine. Figure 7.12 shows the lights on the console of an IBM

FIGURE 7.11

Type font for optical
character recognition.

```
ABCDEFGHIJKLM
NOPQRSTUVWXYZ
0123456789
•⌐:⌐=+/≑*″&|
'-{}%?ſꟼꟹ
ÜÑÅØÒÆ£¥
```

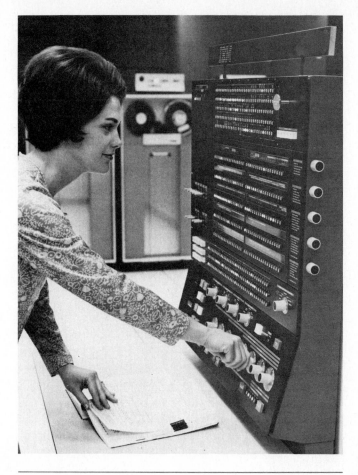

PRINTERS

FIGURE 7.12

Console of a large
computer system.
(*IBM Corp.*)

computer. Each light is connected to a flip-flop output (via a light driver). The outputs of most of the important flip-flops are monitored by using the lights. Various sets of flip-flops can be selected by using the rotary switches at the bottom of the panel, and the toggle switches and pushbuttons can be used to enter data into flip-flop registers and to sequence operations of the computer (as well as to start and stop the computer). The lights can often be driven by the same logic line used in the system.

PRINTERS

7.8 A most convenient and useful method by which the computer can deliver information is by means of printed characters. For the sake of convenience, the printer should have the ability to print alphabetic characters, decimal digits, and common punctuation marks.

The process in printing is the inverse of the encoding procedure in which a key corresponding to an alphanumeric character is depressed, causing a coded binary character to be punched into a tape or card. In this case, coded groups of

INPUT-OUTPUT
DEVICES

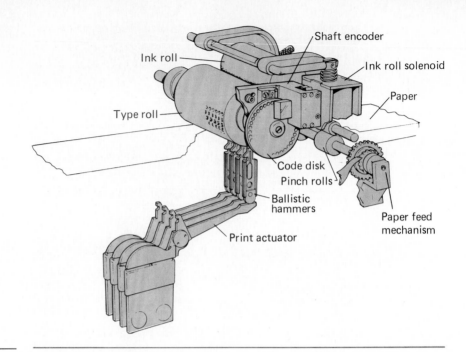

FIGURE 7.13

Line-at-a-time drum
printer.

binary bits are delivered to the printer, which decodes them and then prints the
correct characters. The basic binary-code groups may contain 7 through 9 bits,
depending on the coding for alphanumeric characters that the printer provides.

The information delivered to a printer operated online will be in the form of
electronic signals directly from the computer. If the printer is operated offline, the
reading and decoding of data stored on punched tape, punched cards, or magnetic
tape may be a part of the printing operation. Since the electronic circuitry of a
computer is able to operate at speeds much higher than those of mechanical printing
devices, it is desirable that a printer operated online be capable of printing at a
very high speed. Even if the printer is operated offline, speed is highly desirable,
since the volume of material to be printed may be quite large.

An example of a fast printer in which the raised characters are distributed
around a *print wheel* that revolves constantly is shown in Fig. 7.13. In this case
the print wheel does not contain moving parts, but consists of a motor-driven drum
with a number of bands equal to the number of characters printed per line. A set
of all the characters which are used is distributed around each band. The print
wheel is revolved continuously. When the selected character is in position, the
print hammer strikes the ribbon against the paper and thus against the raised character on the print wheel located behind the paper. A printer of this type requires a
decoder and a memory for each character position along the line as well as a
character-timing encoder for each position, which determines when the selected
character is in position. Printers of this type can print up to 1250 lines per minute
with 160 characters per line.

In Fig. 7.13 the print wheel is continually revolving, and when a selected
character passes by the position where it is to be printed, the print actuator pushes

the chosen ballistic hammer against the paper, forcing the paper against the selected character on the print wheel. The print wheel is continually inked by an ink roll, and no ribbon is used. In this system a code disk and shaft encoder are used to tell which character is currently in a position to be printed. Shaft encoders are discussed in a later section. Figure 7.13 shows that the paper is moved horizontally after each line is printed.

Figure 7.14 shows an IBM printer in which the paper is moved vertically in front of a chain of raised characters of type. This chain is continually moving in the horizontal direction so that each of the 48 different characters continually passes by each of the 100 printer's positions in each line. (Other numbers of characters per line are availble.) When a character to be printed passes the position where it is to be printed, the armature hammer magnet is energized, striking a hammer and forcing the paper against the type at that position. An inked ribbon is placed between paper and type so that the character is impressed on the paper in ink.

To provide inexpensive printers for minicomputers and microcomputers, lower-speed "character at a time" printers are used. Consider the print wheel or drum type of printer shown in Fig. 7.13. The drum can be reduced to a small cylinder with only one set of characters. This single rotating cylinder can be moved across the paper along with a single hammer, making an inexpensive character-at-a-time printer [see Fig. 7.15(c)]. Sometimes the characters are distributed around a "daisy wheel," as shown in Fig. 7.15(b). A hammer then drives the selected character against the paper when it is in position.

The use of pins which are driven against the paper to print characters also provides low-cost printing. Sometimes the pins are arranged in a complete dot matrix, but generally only a single column of seven pins is provided, and this is moved across the paper, requiring five positions per character [see Fig. 7.15(a)]. Character generator logic must sequence the striking of the pins as the print head is moved across the paper.

Microprocessors are used to control the timing and other functions required in printers. Character buffering also can be provided by microprocessors.

Many inexpensive printers use thermal or electrostatic papers (see below). The printers are inexpensive; but since the paper is not "ordinary" paper, its costs are generally greater than for regular paper. However, because of the volume of production, the special papers required are quite reasonable in price.

The natural limitations of speed in electromechanical devices and cost considerations have led to the development of printers called *nonimpact printers*. These printers fall primarily in the following categories:

1　*Electromagnetic*　By using magnetic recording techniques, a magnetic image of what is to be printed can be written on a drum surface. Then this surface is passed through magnetic powder which adheres to the charged areas. The powder is pressed onto the paper. Speeds of up to 250 characters per second are obtained in such systems.

2　*Electrostatic*　For electrostatic printers the paper is coated with a nonconducting dielectric material which holds charges when voltages are applied with writing "nibs" (heads). These heads write dots on the paper as it passes, as shown in Fig. 7.15(a). Then the paper passes through a toner which contains material

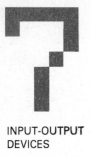

INPUT-OUTPUT
DEVICES

(a)

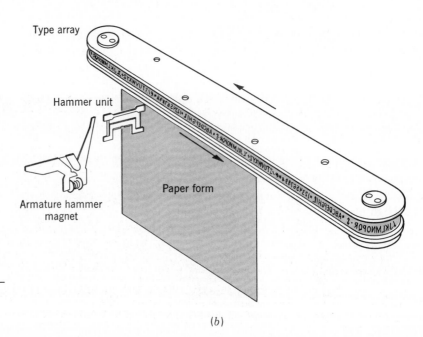

Type array

Hammer unit

Armature hammer
magnet

Paper form

(b)

FIGURE 7.14

(a) High-speed line
printer. (b) Type
chain for the printer.

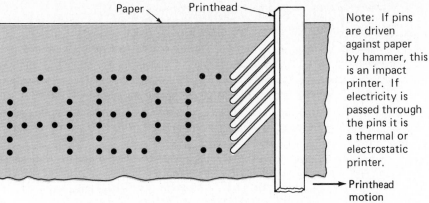

Paper — Printhead —

Note: If pins are driven against paper by hammer, this is an impact printer. If electricity is passed through the pins it is a thermal or electrostatic printer.

→ Printhead motion

Matrix printhead moves across page. The correct pins are forced against the paper in the proper sequence to form characters as shown. A 5 × 7 matrix is illustrated here; 7 × 9 is also used.

(a)

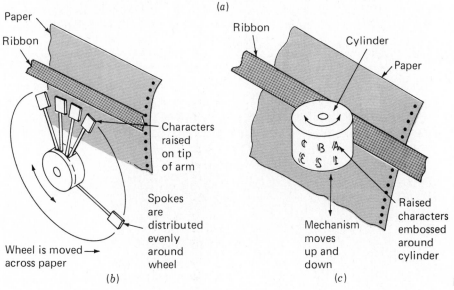

Paper
Ribbon

Characters raised on tip of arm

Spokes are distributed evenly around wheel

Wheel is moved → across paper

(b)

Ribbon
Cylinder
Paper

Mechanism moves up and down

Raised characters embossed around cylinder

(c)

PRINTERS

FIGURE 7.15

Impact printer mechanisms. (a) Matrix printhead. (b) Daisy wheel printer. (c) Cylinder printer.

with colored particles carrying an opposite charge to that written by the nibs; as a result, particles adhere to the magnetized areas, forming printed characters.

3   *Thermal printers*   An electric pulse can be converted to heat on selected sections of a printing head or on wires or nibs. When this heat is applied to heat-sensitive paper, a character is printed, as shown in Fig. 7.15(a).

4   *Ink jets*   Some printers direct a high-velocity stream of ink toward the paper. This stream is deflected, generally by passing it through an electrostatic field such as that used to deflect beams in oscilloscopes. In some systems the ink stream is broken into droplets by an ultrasonic transducer.

The wide variety of printers available and the continuing development of new ideas make the printer field a fascinating area. The cost-performance tradeoffs often make selection of a satisfactory printer difficult.

7

INPUT-OUTPUT
DEVICES

7.9 Cathode-ray tubes (CRTs) are often used as output devices. The CRT is a very fast and inexpensive output device, but it does not deliver permanent copy.

The cathode-ray tubes used in computer displays are the same type as those used in oscilloscopes and television sets, and entire television sets are sometimes used. For these display systems, the displayed points are made by positioning and turning on an electron beam in the tube, just as in television sets or oscilloscopes. The displays are called *CRT, oscilloscope,* or *scope,* displays. Figure 7.16 shows a cathode-ray-tube display with a keyboard.

Many systems have been used to encode data for transmission to oscilloscope displays. The simplest system consists of simply sending the coordinates of each point to be displayed. The oscilloscope electronics then position the beam.

The above system is simple but very inefficient, in that many points must be transmitted, which takes considerable computer time. (In most of these oscilloscope displays, the points must be illuminated at least 30, and generally 60, times each second. There are, however, *storage oscilloscopes,* which hold displayed points and do not require refreshing. These must be erased, however, before rewriting, and are relatively expensive at present.)

FIGURE 7.16

Cathode-ray-tube display. (*Computek, Inc.*)

Because of the problem of repeatedly sending data points to the display device, generally the display-device electronics are independent of the computer and on separate boards which include a memory which stores the data and then generates the display from the last data transmitted, changing or updating the display only when the computer so directs.

Complicated but efficient techniques for data transmission to oscilloscope display electronics are generally used in inexpensive displays. If only alphanumeric data are to be displayed, the ASCII code is used for the transmission of each character to be displayed. The display electronics then converts from each 8-bit coded ASCII character to the sequence of points required to display the character.[1] A memory capable of storing the alphanumeric character codes for the entire oscilloscope face is then included in the display electronics, so that the computer proper must send characters only once, and the oscilloscope electronics refreshes the oscilloscope from the memory. Typically the displays have about 25 lines of 40 to 80 characters per line. Lines for graphic displays such as that shown in Fig. 7.16 are often drawn using a technique in which the computer sends the difference in coordinates between the electronic beam's present location and line segment to be drawn.

Microcomputers generally include display electronics which generate CRT displays using the standard television scanning procedure (or that for television monitors). If only alphanumeric characters are displayed, a memory of about 16K bits (for 25 lines of 80 characters) is required to store the information to be displayed. When a special graphics feature is included so the microcomputer user can make graphics drawings, the display memory must be on the order of 128K to 900K bits (for color).

The individual points in a graphics display are called *pixels*. IBM uses 320 or 640 pixels per line on the scope face and 200 lines. Two or four bits are required for each pixel in a color mode of operation. The memory size required to store a display can be calculated from numbers such as these. From these calculations the additional memory and complexity required for graphics displays versus alphanumeric displays becomes clear.

MAGNETIC-TAPE OUTPUT OFFICE OPERATION

7.10 Magnetic tape is often used as an intermediate storage medium for offline output equipment operation in large systems.

The advantage is in the speed-to-cost ratio attainable. A high-speed magnetic-tape recorder will be much faster than a high-speed printer so the computer will be less slowed down in recording results. The final printing may then take place on a printer, which interprets the recorded tape and prints the final result. This is another case of offline operation, in which the final computer operation is performed at the speed of a faster output device, and the computer is, therefore, not slowed down as much as it would be if a printer were used. Even the magnetic-tape recorder devices, however, are inherently much slower than the computer's internal circuitry.

---

[1]Oscilloscopes are quite often scanned a line at a time, as in television sets, and so some conversion electronics is required. IC packages to generate characters for CRT displays are made by several companies.

INPUT-OUTPUT
DEVICES

7.11 The process of transferring information into the machine and from the machine is especially liable to error. Although card and tape readers are constructed with the highest possible regard for correct operation, and the occurrence of errors is relatively infrequent, still errors occur, and it is desirable to detect them whenever possible. To facilitate the detection or correction of errors, two classes of codes have been invented: error-detecting codes and error-correcting codes. The first type of code enables the equipment to detect the errors which occur in the coded groups of bits, and the second type of code corrects the errors automatically.

Both error-detecting and error-correcting codes require that redundant information be sent along with the actual information being processed. The most commonly used type of error-detecting code is undoubtedly the parity-check code. Parity-check codes are commonly used for card and tape readers and for the storage of information on magnetic tape.

Parity checking

The parity check is based on the use of an additional bit, known as a *parity bit,* or *parity-check bit,* in each code group. The parity bit associated with each code group in an *odd-parity-bit* checking system has such a value that the total number of 1s in each code group plus the parity bit is always odd. (An *even-parity-bit* checking code has a parity bit such that the sum of the 1s in the code group plus the parity bit is always an even number.) The example shown in Table 7.1, which uses an 8, 4, 2, 1 code, has an odd parity bit which makes the sum of the 1s in each code group an odd number.

If a single error occurs in transmitting a code group—for instance, if 0011, 1 is erroneously changed to 0010, 1—the fact that there is an even number of 1s in the code group plus the parity bit will indicate that an error has occurred. If the values of the parity bits had been selected so that the total sum of the 1s in each code group plus the parity bit were even instead of odd, each parity bit would be the complement of the parity bit shown above, and the code would be an even-parity-bit checking code.

The technique of parity checking is doubtless the most popular method of detecting errors in stored code groups, especially for storage devices such as magnetic tape, paper tape, and even core-and-drum systems.

TABLE 7.1		
DECIMAL	BCD	ODD PARITY BIT
0	0000	1
1	0001	0
2	0010	0
3	0011	1
4	0100	0
5	0101	1
6	0110	1
7	0111	0
8	1000	0
9	1001	1

If the parity-bit system is used, an additional bit must be sent with each code group. As another example, if the 7-bit ASCII is used, each line of a punched tape will have an additional hole position which will contain a 1 or a 0. When the tape is read by the tape reader, each code group will be examined, together with the parity bit; and in an odd-parity-bit system, an alarm will be generated if the number of 1s in a group is even.

This type of checking will detect all odd numbers of errors. Suppose that an even-parity check is used as in Table 7.1 and the code group to be sent is 0010; the parity bit in this case will be a 1. If the code group is erroneously read as 0110, the number of 1s in the code group plus the parity bit will be odd, and the error will be detected. If, however, a double error is made and 0010 is changed to 0111, the error will not be detected since the number of 1s will again be even. A parity-bit check will only detect odd numbers of errors. (The above rule will also apply when the parity bit is in error. For instance, consider an odd-parity-bit checking system where 0010 is to be sent and the parity bit is 1. If the parity bit is changed to 0, the number of 1s in the code group plus the parity bit will be even, and the error will be detected.)

There are many types of error-correcting codes, and some very clever and sophisticated coding schemes are used in both communications and computer systems. For instance, magnetic tape is a memory device that is especially prone to errors. Most errors are due to either imperfections in the tape or foreign matter which gets between reading head and the tape, causing the tape to be physically pushed away from the reading head and the recorded signal to be incorrectly interpreted. Such errors are said to be caused by *dropout*. These errors tend to lie in a single track, and several clever codes have been used to detect and correct such errors.[2]

KEYBOARDS

7.12 The important data entry device is the keyboard. In some cases keyboards are used to enter data into punched cards or punched tape, for example; in other cases keyboards enter data directly into a computer. The most familiar keyboards are on terminals which include either a printer or an oscilloscope (CRT) display. Sometimes small keyboards with only a few keys (similar to touch-tone telephone dialing keyboards) are used in industrial applications. These small assemblies of keys are generally called *keypads*.

When an operator depresses a key, electric signals must be generated which will enable the computer (or other device) to determine which key was depressed. This is called *encoding*. The encoding process is dependent on the mechanism used to make the individual keys in the keyboard.

The most direct method for encoding is based on the use of keyboard switches, which contain a switch similar to the pushbutton switch used in many electric devices. Figure 7.17 shows such a switch. When the plunger is depressed, the contacts of the switch in the housing are closed, and the two terminals at the output

---

[2]A study of error-correcting and error-detecting codes in some depth may be found in W. W. Peterson, *Error Correcting Codes,* and in G. Birkhoff and T. C. Bartee, *Modern Applied Algebra.*

**INPUT-OUTPUT
DEVICES**

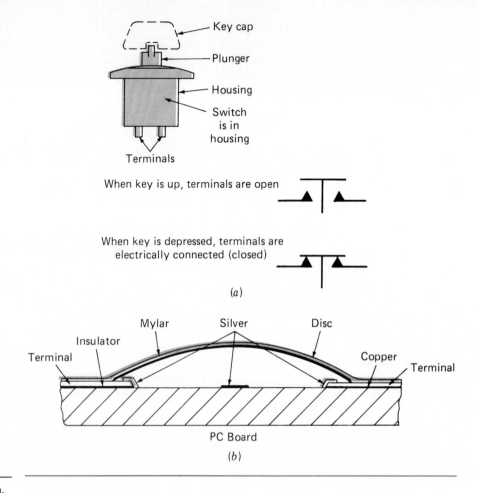

Key cap

Plunger

Housing

Switch
is in
housing

Terminals

When key is up, terminals are open

When key is depressed, terminals are
electrically connected (closed)

(a)

Mylar   Silver   Disc

Insulator   Copper

Terminal   Terminal

PC Board

(b)

FIGURE 7.17

(a) Keyboard switch.
(b) Keypad switch.

are effectively connected. When the plunger is up (key is not depressed), the switch in the housing is open, and the terminals are not electrically connected.

To encode a keyboard by means of electromechanical switches, diodes (or transistors) can be used. Figure 7.18 shows the layout for encoding three keys into the ASCII illustrated in Fig. 7.8. An odd-parity-check bit has been added at the right end to make an 8-bit character. Each of the horizontal wires on the drawing is normally at a 0 logic level. When a key is depressed, however, the switch in its housing is closed, and this connects the wire to a logic level of 1. Thus if the *A* key is depressed, the value 10000011 will appear on the output lines, for example, because a diode connects the horizontal wire to the *A* switch to the leftmost and two rightmost vertical wires. This is the ASCII for *A* with a parity bit on the right end.

It is a good idea to load the values on the output lines into a flip-flop register before the computer reads the outputs. This has the advantage of storing the values until the computer can read them, particularly if the keyboard operator raises the key before the computer can respond. Figure 7.19 shows a scheme in which a flip-flop is used on each output, and a strobe is generated to load the flip-flops, by

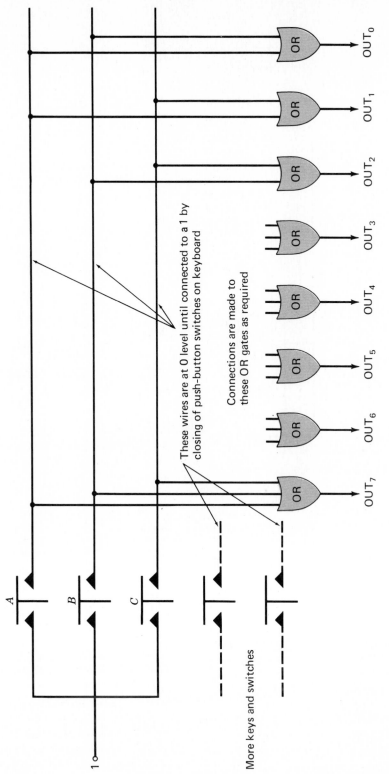

These wires are at 0 level until connected to a 1 by closing of push-button switches on keyboard

Connections are made to these OR gates as required

More keys and switches

FIGURE 7.18

Encoding a keyboard.

INPUT-OUTPUT
DEVICES

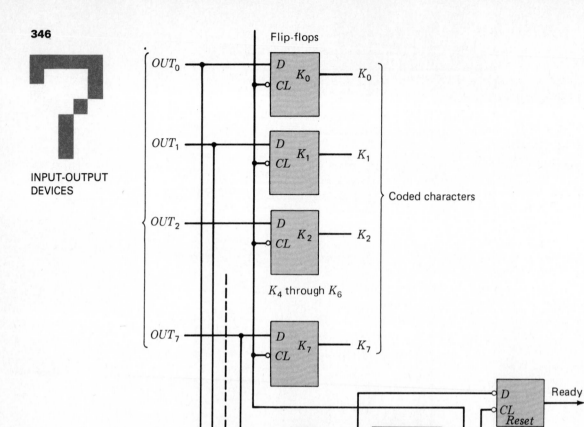

Flip-flops

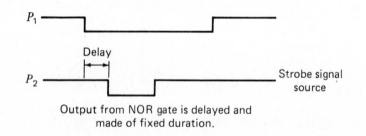

Output from NOR gate is delayed and
made of fixed duration.

FIGURE 7.19

Keyboard buffer for
interface.

using a delayed inverted pulse signal generated whenever any one of the output
lines from the encoder goes high. The delay is inserted to compensate for signal
skewing, where signals arrive at the output lines at different times because of
differing delays through the wires in the system. The delay must be adequate to
accommodate the largest delays that may occur. Also, the length of the strobe pulse
should be short compared to the shortest time a key might be depressed. (A delay
of 1 ms and a pulse of 1 ms would be reasonable.)

Here we are assuming that the switch contacts do not bounce, as is the case with some switches. If the contacts do bounce, the output signals must be "smoothed," and various circuits are available. When reed relays are used (and these are sometimes used), there is little need for this. (The switches are often momentary-contact switches which generate a closure of relatively fixed duration.)

In Fig. 7.19 the strobe signal is also used to load a flip-flop, called *ready,* which will be used in an interface design in the next chapter. Notice that the encoding scheme shown here requires that there be a 1 in the code for each character (so that the strobe pulse will be generated).

The keyboard market is very large, and so many kinds of keyboards are now made as manufacturers compete to see who can produce a lower-cost, more reliable, more durable keyboard. The basic division of keyboards is (1) the electromechanical keyboard, which includes the switch type just explained and (2) the solid-state keyboard.

There are several basic mechanisms for solid-state keyboards. Capacitor types have mechanisms which vary the capacity of a capacitor when a key is depressed. These are low-cost keys, often used in keypads and other cost-conscious keyboards. Hall-effect keyboards are more expensive, but have long life and good key feel, as do ferrite-core and photooptic keyboards. Each of the basic mechanisms has different problems with regard to encoding the keyprinters' output into a coded form usable by a computer. (The references include discussions of the encoding techniques.)

The encoding technique is often based on a two-dimensional array of keys and wires instead of the "linear" array shown in Fig. 7.18 for reasons of economy. (This is discussed in the Questions.) IC packages for encoding are made by several manufacturers and can include *smoothing* or *debouncing* for contacts and sometimes *key rollover* protection, which protects against two keys being depressed at the same time. (This can happen when an adjacent key is inadvertently depressed or when the next character is struck before a key is released.)

Chapter 8 discusses interfacing keyboards and printers in some detail. However, the overall physical setup for interfacing a mini- or microcomputer is discussed now.

Figure 7.20 shows the general layout for a microcomputer. Printed-circuit boards contain the logic for the CPU, which consists of the arithmetic-logic unit (ALU), the control section, and the high-speed (IC) memory. The high-speed memory is connected to the bus, and the control section controls the high-speed memory by using signals it places on the bus. (The bus in Fig. 7.20 consists of a set of wires running under the printed-circuit boards. Printed-circuit-board connectors are mounted to these wires, and the printed-circuit boards are plugged into these connectors, thus making connection to the logic on the boards.)

To interface input-output devices with the CPU section boards, *interface boards* are connected to the bus. The boards contain the logic gates and flip-flops to read from and write onto the bus and to control and interface the input-output devices.

In a typical system, in order to interface a keyboard, a keyboard interface board is connected to the bus, by a connector, and then a cable runs from this board to the keyboard. Similar boards are used to interface a tape unit, a disk drive, etc.

INPUT-OUTPUT
DEVICES

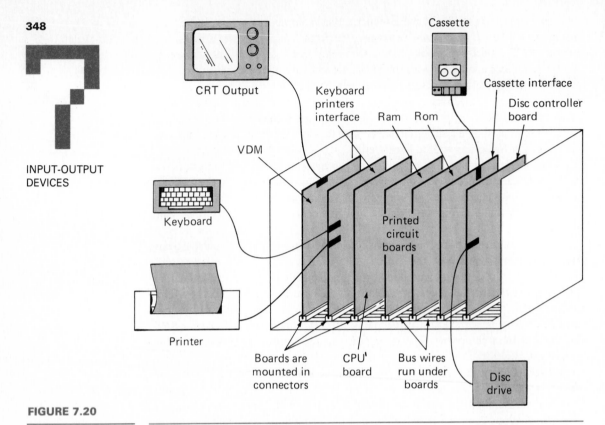

FIGURE 7.20

Microcomputer inter-
face layout for input-
output devices.

Notice that communication between input-output devices and the CPU utilizes the interface boards and the bus. In very small systems the CPU and one, two, or more interface chips may be placed on a single board, with the bus on the same board. Cables then connect this board to the input-output devices.

TERMINALS

7.13   When a keyboard is combined and packaged together with an oscilloscope display or a printing mechanism and suitable electronics is provided so that characters struck on the keyboard can be entered into a computer and the computer can also have the ability to print on the oscilloscope or printing mechanism, the keyboard and printer or keyboard oscilloscope are called a *terminal*. Terminals are widely used to input programs and data to computers.

Figure 7.16 shows a terminal consisting of an oscilloscope and a keyboard. Characters struck on the keyboard will appear on the oscilloscope face, and output signals are also provided which are suitable for computer usage. A computer can print on the oscilloscope providing for two-way communications. The primary disadvantage is that no hard copy, or record of what is typed by the terminal operator or printed by the computer, remains when the terminal is turned off.

Terminals range from minimal systems containing almost no memory to *smart* terminals in which a small microcomputer or minicomputer is included. Smart terminals provide many facilities for the user, sometimes including text editing, input formatting, and checking for typing errors made by operators.

Oscilloscope-keyboard combinations almost always contain a small memory in which the present contents of the screen are stored, so that the screen can be refreshed by the terminal electronics instead of requiring the computer to continually rewrite data on the screen. In this case, a small memory and some electronics are required, and microprocessors are often used to control the terminal's operation. By enlarging the memory capabilities and program in the microprocessor, a smart terminal can be formed without too much additional cost.

Terminals generally generate output data in serial form and accept input data in serial form. The formats, coding, and electrical properties of the signals generated vary from terminal to terminal, but there are now strong movements to standardize the interface designs.

Most of the terminals in present-day use generate an 11-bit output in serial form whenever a key on the keyboard is depressed. This same stream is generally used to activate the printer mechanism or oscilloscope. In most cases, when a key is struck, the code for the character is read by the computer, which must then write this character back into the terminal. This is called *echoing* the character. Microcomputers generally echo characters.

Figure 7.21 shows how the present standard character transmission operates. The output line from the keyboard is normally in the high[3] state, but when a key is depressed, a *start bit* at a low level is generated. This start bit is followed by

[3]Communications people call this a *mark* value and the other level a *space*.

FIGURE 7.21

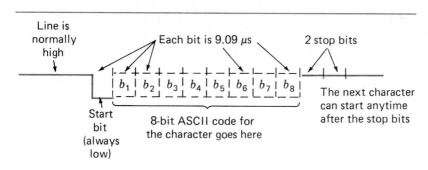

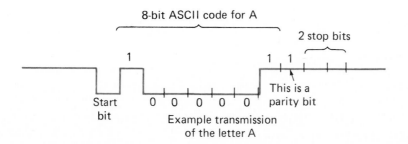

Sending a character using the standard code.

the proper 8-bit ASCII character, and then two *stop bits* at the high level are inserted before another character can be started (that is, before another start bit can be generated). The start bit, each stop bit, and the bits in the ASCII character are each of the same time duration. For most current systems this is $\frac{1}{110}$ s for each; and since 11 such time periods, or *bit times,* are required, a single character requires $\frac{11}{110}$, or $\frac{1}{10}$, s.

Several other speeds are currently used, including 300, 600, and 1200 bits/s. In each case, the same character construction with start and stop bits is used, and so character rates of $\frac{11}{300}$, $\frac{11}{600}$, and $\frac{11}{1200}$ s are attainable.

The character transmission system described here is called *asynchronous transmission,* for the character and start bits can occur at any time. *Synchronous transmission* systems have the bits clocked into fixed time periods, and characters are placed in fixed positions in the bit stream. These systems require both bit timing and character timing to be established between the transmitting device and receiver and thus are more complicated. Character transmission can be at higher rates, however. (Since start and stop bits are not required, the character beginnings and ends are established by the system.) As a result, high-speed data communication is generally in synchronous form.

The output levels and interface requirements for the coded characters are explained in the Questions, and several standards are noted.

When terminals are operated at some distance from a computer, the telephone system is often used to provide the necessary communications link. If a terminal is to be operated into the telephone system, special devices are needed to translate logic levels produced by the terminal into signals acceptable for telephone-line transmission.

Figure 7.22 shows a terminal with an *acoustic coupler.* The handset from the telephone is placed in this acoustic coupler. When a key is depressed, the bits comprising the character are converted to audio tones by a small loudspeaker in the coupler. Generally one frequency is used for a 0 and another for a 1. These signals enter the transmitter part of the handset and are transmitted into the telephone line. At the computer end these frequencies are received by a microphone connected to a handset and then converted back to 1s and 0s in electrical form. The electrical logic levels output at the receiver are therefore replicas of the signals originally generated at the terminal.

The computer "talks" back to the terminal by using an acoustic coupler at its end of the telephone line, and the acoustic coupler at the terminal converts the computer's signals back to logic levels which are used to drive the display.

When output signals in logic-level form are converted directly to electric signals suitable for telephone transmission by electronic circuitry (instead of acoustic coupling), the converting device is called a *modem.* A modem can convert logic levels to electric signals for the telephone system and can convert received signals from the telephone line back into logic levels. This means, of course, that the connections to the telephone line are made electrically (generally into a telephone jack) and directly into the telephone line, and a handset is not used. It also means that the electric signals must comply with telephone system regulations. The design of modems which will (1) send bits through telephone lines at high speeds, (2) make few errors in transmission, and (3) comply with telephone company regulations is a highly developed and interesting scientific area.

Telephone
receiver

When telephone receiver is placed in
acoustic coupler, terminal can
communicate (both ways) with a computer

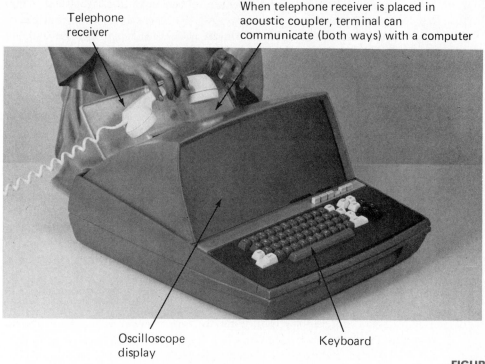

Oscilloscope
display

Keyboard

FIGURE 7.22

Oscilloscope display
and terminal with
acoustic coupler.

Like acoustic couplers, modems generally use a different frequency for a 1
and a 0. As an example, the Bell 103 modem sends data through telephone lines
at either 110 or 300 bits/s. The modem at one end of a telephone line uses 1070
Hz (for 1s) and 1270 Hz (for 0s) to send, while the modem at the other end uses
2025 Hz (for 1s) and 2225 Hz (for 0s). The reason for the two sets of frequencies
is that transmission can be in either direction, and while one modem is transmitting
a character, the other will still be sending its high (mark) frequency. (A single
telephone line handles communications in both directions. Both ends can talk at
the same time. You can, for instance, interrupt someone who is talking.)

INPUT-OUTPUT DEVICES FOR SYSTEMS
WITH ANALOG COMPONENTS

7.14 Not all the inputs to digital machines consist of alphanumeric data. Computers used in data collection systems or in real-time control systems often must
measure the physical position of some device or must process electric signals which
are analog in nature. Consider a real-time control system in which a computer is
used automatically to point a telescope. If, by some system of gears, the position
of the telescope along an axis is related to the position of a shaft, the position of
this shaft may have to be read into the computer, giving the telescope's pointing
angle. This will involve the translation of the shaft position into a binary-coded
number which can be read by the computer.

**INPUT-OUTPUT
DEVICES**

Changing a physical displacement or an analog electric signal to a digital representation is called *analog-to-digital (A-to-D) conversion*. Two major types of A-to-D converters are (1) those that convert mechanical displacements to a digital representation and (2) those that convert an electric analog signal to digital-coded signals.

Suppose that an analog device has as its output a voltage which is to be used by a digital machine. Let us assume that the voltage varies within the limits of 0 to 63 V dc. We can then represent the voltage values with a set of 6-bit numbers ranging from 000000 to 111111. For each integer value the input voltage may assume we assign a corresponding value of the 6-bit number. If the input voltage is 20 V, the corresponding digital value will be 010100, and if the input voltage is 5 V, the corresponding number will be 000101. If, however, the input signal is 20.249 V dc, the 6-bit binary number will not completely describe the input voltage, but will only approximate the input value. The process of approximating the input value is called *quantizing*. The number of bits in the binary number which represents the analog signal is the *precision* of the coder, and the amount of error which exists between the digital output values and the input analog values is a measure of the *accuracy* of the coder.

Not only are the inputs to a computer sometimes in analog form, but it is often necessary for the outputs of a computer to be expressed in analog form. An example lies in the use of a cathode-ray tube as an output device. If the output from the computer is to be displayed as a position on an oscilloscope tube, then in some systems the binary-coded output signals from the computer must be converted to voltages or currents, which may be used to position the electron beam and which are proportional to the magnitude of the output binary number represented by the computer's output signals. This involves D-to-A conversion, and a device that performs this conversion is called a *D-to-A converter*. When digital computers are used in control systems, it is generally necessary to convert the digital outputs from the machine to analog-type signals, which are then used to control the physical system.

DIGITAL-TO-ANALOG CONVERTERS

7.15 The most used digital-to-analog converters (DACs) convert a binary unsigned number to either an electric voltage or an electric current. DACs which convert from binary inputs to a voltage are discussed first.

A block diagram for a DAC is shown in Fig. 7.23(*a*). There are three input lines X_0, X_1, and X_2, each of which will carry a binary 0 or 1. The number of binary inputs is called the *resolution* of the DAC.[4] The output from this DAC ranges from 0 to 7 V. A list of input-output relations for this DAC is shown in Fig. 7.23(*b*). For each input value there is a corresponding analog output voltage which in this case is equal to the value of the input as a binary integer. Examination of this input-output relation will show that the output value can be calculated by giving the input value X_0 a *weight* of 1 V, X_1 the weight of 2 V, and X_2 the weight of 4 V. Then the output value is equal to the sum of the weights for which the X_i

---

[4]Appendix G shows circuits for IC realization of DACs.

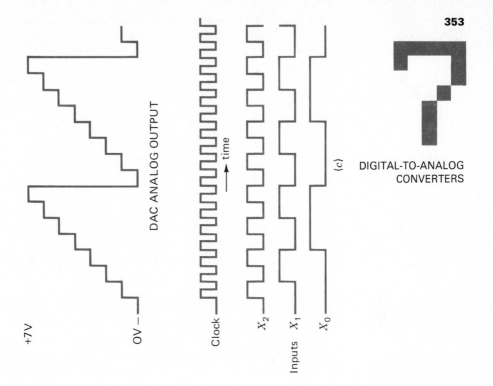

DIGITAL-TO-ANALOG
CONVERTERS

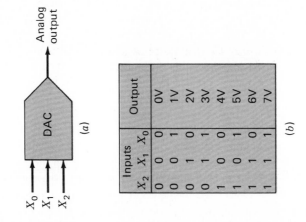

FIGURE 7.23

DAC operation. (a)
Block diagram. (b)
List of input-output
values. (c) Staircase
DAC output.

are equal to 1. This is a general principle for DACs: Each input has a *weight*, and the output voltage is the sum of the weights for which the binary inputs are 1s.

In this DAC, X_2 is the *most significant bit* (MSB) and X_0 the *least significant bit* (LSB).

If a three-flip-flop counter with positive-edge triggering were connected to the DAC's three inputs with X_0 connected to the counter's LSB and the counter were clocked, the input-output relation would be as in Fig. 7.23(*c*). The analog waveform shown here is called a *staircase*.

The minimum and maximum values which the analog output of a DAC can take vary for different DACs. Some manufacturer's DACs have only a single built-in minimum and maximum while others allow users to introduce reference signals which will control the minimum and maximum output voltages. In most cases the minimum output voltage for a DAC will be 0 V.

If the maximum output voltage of a DAC is V volts[5] and if the resolution is R bits, then the weight of the least significant bit will be $V/(2^R - 1)$. [For our 3-bit resolution 7-V maximum output, this gives $7/(2^3 - 1) = 7/7 = 1$ V.] The weight of the second least significant bit will be $2V/(2^R - 1)$, the next least significant bit has weight $4V/(2^R - 1)$, and so on up to the most significant bit which has weight $(2^{R-1})V/(2^R - 1)$. [For our example this is $(2^{3-1})7/(2^3 - 1) = 4$.]

As a further example, if a DAC had a maximum output voltage of 10 V and a resolution of 8 bits, the least significant bit would have weight.

$$\frac{10}{2^8 - 1} = \frac{10}{255} \simeq 0.0392157$$

This means that if an 8-bit counter is connected to the DAC's input, the staircase at the output will have steps of $\frac{10}{255}$ V from 0 to $+10$ V, and there will be 256 steps (counting the 0 step).

Since actual DACs are made of physical devices, they are imperfect and will have analog outputs which will not exactly be at the output for a "perfect" DAC. To give the user some idea of the size of the DAC's errors, the manufacturers of DACs generally specify the accuracy of the converter. The *absolute accuracy* is defined as the maximum difference between the actual DAC's outputs and a perfect DAC's outputs divided by the maximum analog output value.

For example, if the maximum output for a 6-bit DAC is $+10$ V, then the "perfect" output for a binary input of 000011 is $3 \times 10/(2^6 - 1) \simeq 0.4761905$. If the actual output is 0.465, then an error of 0.0111905 will exist; and if this is the maximum error for all possible inputs, the absolute accuracy will be $0.0111905/10 = 0.111905$ percent.

Sometimes manufacturers will simply specify the absolute value in general terms such as "less than $\frac{1}{2}$ LSB," meaning that the maximum error between perfect and actual values will never exceed half the weight of the least significant bit.

If the maximum error in a DAC is less than half the weight of the least significant bit, then the output will be *monotonic*, which means the output voltage will always

---

[5]In all these examples the DAC is assumed to have outputs ranging from 0 to V volts. DACs with nonzero minimum values are dealt with later.

increase when the input value to the converter increases. For DACs with many bits of resolution, the manufacturer will sometimes only specify that the DAC is monotonic instead of giving an accuracy figure.

Some DACs can be set to have analog outputs which do not range from 0 to a positive voltage, but rather are in an interval from V_1 to V_2. (For instance, V_1 might be -5 V and V_2 might be $+10$ V.) The same principles exist except that the voltage V in the formulas for the weights is obtained by subtracting V_1 from V_2 and weights are added to V_1 to obtain output values. This would give 15 for the -5- to $+10$-V example, and the weight of the LSB for a 4-bit DAC with lower voltage -5 V and maximum $+10$ V would be 1 V. The outputs would then be $-5, -4, -3, \ldots, 9, 10$.

When DACs have the ability to be set to some interval, the manufacturer will generally specify two input lines to which the user can connect two input voltages which will control the DAC's upper and lower output limits.

ANALOG-TO-DIGITAL CONVERTERS—SHAFT ENCODERS

7.16   The most used type of an analog-to-digital converter which directly converts a physical position to a digital value is the *shaft encoder*. The shaft encoder is connected to a rotating shaft and reads out the angular position of the shaft in digital form.

In the A-to-D converter in Fig. 7.24(*a*), a coded-segment disk which can rotate is coupled to a shaft. A set of brushes is attached so that a single brush is positioned in the center of each concentric band of the disk. Each band is constructed of several segments made of either conducting material (the darkened areas) or some insulating material (the unshaded areas). A positive voltage is connected to the conducting sections. If a given brush makes contact with a segment of conducting material, a 1 signal will result; but if the brush is over the insulating material, the output from the brush will be a 0. The four output lines of the coder shown represent a 4-bit binary number. There are 16 distinct intervals around the

FIGURE 7.24

Shaft-position encoder disks. (*a*) Binary-coded disk. (*b*) Unit-distance code disk.

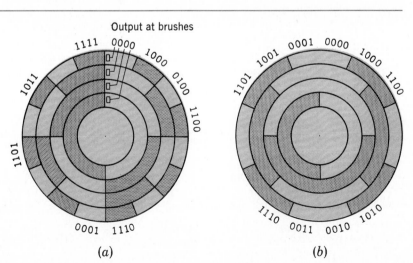

(*a*)   (*b*)

coder disk, each corresponding to a different shaft-position interval, and each causes the coder to have a different binary number output.

Photoelectric coders are constructed by using a coder disk with bands divided into transparent segments (the shaded areas) and opaque segments (the unshaded areas). A light source is put on one side of the disk, and a set of photoelectric cells on the other side, arranged so that one cell is behind each band of the coder disk. If a transparent segment is between the light source and a light-sensitive cell, a 1 output will result; and if an opaque area is in front of the photoelectric cell, there will be a 0 output. By increasing the number of bands around the disk, more precision may be added to the coder. The photoelectric type of coder has greater resolution than the brush type, and even greater resolution may be obtained by using gears and several disks. The state of the art is about 18 bits or 2^{18} positions per shaft revolution, but most commercial coders have 14 bits or fewer.

There is one basic difficulty with the coder illustrated: If the disk is in a position where the output number is changing from 011 to 100, or in any position where several bits are changing value, the output signal may become ambiguous. Since the brushes are of finite width, they will overlap the change in segments; and no matter how carefully it is made, the coder will have erroneous outputs in several positions. If this occurs when 011 is changing to 100, several errors are possible; the value may be read as 111 or 000, either of which is a value with considerable error. To circumvent this difficulty, a number of schemes have been devised, generally involving two sets of brushes with one set displaced slightly from the other. By logically choosing from the outputs available, the ambiguity may be eliminated at a slight cost in accuracy.

Another scheme for avoiding ambiguity involves the use of a *Gray,* or *unit-distance, code* to form the coder disk [Fig. 7.24(*b*)]. In this code, 2 bits never change value in successive coded binary numbers. By using a Gray-coded disk, a 6 may be read for a 7 or a 4 for a 5, but larger errors will not be made. Table 7.2 shows a listing of a 4-bit Gray code.

If the inputs to the machine are from a coder using a Gray code, the code groups must be converted to conventional binary or BCD before use.

TABLE 7.2	
DECIMAL	GRAY CODE $a_3a_2a_1a_0$
0	0000
1	0001
2	0011
3	0010
4	0110
5	0111
6	0101
7	0100
8	1100
9	1101
10	1111
11	1110
12	1010
13	1011
14	1001
15	1000

There are straightforward ways to convert from Gray to binary or binary to Gray code. The conversion from binary to Gray code is as follows:

1 The leftmost digit of the binary number is also the leftmost digit of the Gray code.

2 The mod 2 sum ($0 \oplus 0 = 1 \oplus 1 = 0$ and $1 \oplus 0 = 0 \oplus 1 = 1$) of the two leftmost digits in the binary number will give the second leftmost digit in the Gray code.

3 The mod 2 sum of the second and third digits of the binary number give the third leftmost digit of the Gray code. This rule continues until the mod 2 sum of the two rightmost digits of the binary number give the rightmost Gray code digit.

Here is an example of conversion of 0111 binary to Gray code:

$$
\begin{array}{rl}
\text{0111 binary} & \\
0 & \text{leftmost digit} \\
0 \oplus 1 = 1 & \text{2d leftmost digit} \\
1 \oplus 1 = 0 & \text{next digit} \\
1 \oplus 1 = 0 & \text{rightmost digit}
\end{array}
$$

So Gray code for 0111 binary is 0100.

Here is an example of conversion from 1010 binary to Gray code:

$$
\begin{array}{rl}
\text{1010 binary} & \\
1 & \text{leftmost digit} \\
1 \oplus 0 = 1 & \text{2d leftmost digit} \\
0 \oplus 1 = 1 & \text{next digit} \\
1 \oplus 0 = 1 & \text{rightmost digit}
\end{array}
$$

Thus Gray code for 1010 binary is 1111.

Here is a five-digit example of converting 10111 to Gray code:

$$
\begin{array}{rl}
\text{10111 binary} & \\
1 & \text{leftmost digit} \\
1 \oplus 0 = 1 & \text{next digit} \\
0 \oplus 1 = 1 & \text{next digit} \\
1 \oplus 1 = 0 & \text{next digit} \\
1 \oplus 1 = 0 & \text{rightmost digit}
\end{array}
$$

So 10111 binary is 11100 in Gray code.

ANALOG-TO-DIGITAL CONVERTERS

7.17 When an analog voltage must be converted to a digital number, an analog-to-digital converter (ADC) is used. Figure 7.25(a) shows the block diagram symbol for a small ADC with a single analog input and 3 binary bits of output. The CONVERT input is normally a 0 and is changed to a 1 signal when a conversion

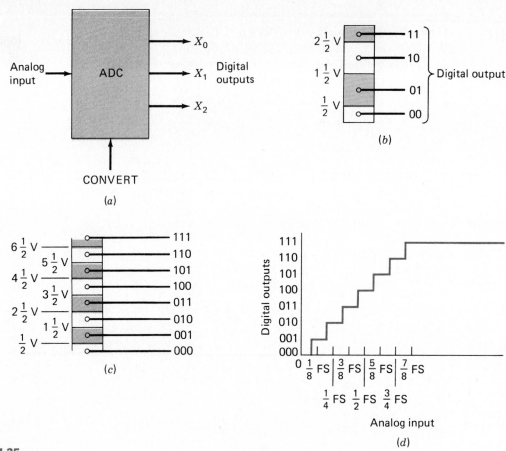

FIGURE 7.25

ADC operation and conversion intervals. (*a*) Block diagram (*b*) Two-output converter intervals. (*c*) Three-output converter intervals. (*d*) Graph of intervals.

is to occur. The ADC responds to the position transition on CONVERT by measuring the input voltage on the analog input and then outputting a binary number on the X outputs which represents the input voltage in digital form.

Converting an analog input signal such as a voltage to a digital number is called *quantizing* the input. Since the input can take infinitely many different voltage values and the digital representations will have only some finite number of values, each digital number at the output actually covers an interval of input values.

Figure 7.25(*b*) shows a graph of the input signal versus digital output numbers for a 2-bit ADC. The input voltage range is to be from 0 to 3 V, and the digital numbers at the outputs will range from 00 to 11. The output number 00 indicates the input voltage is in the interval from 0 to 0.5 V, the output number 01 indicates an input voltage value from 0.5 to 1.5 V, the number 10 indicates an input from 1.5 to 2.5 V, and the number 11 indicates an input of greater than $2\frac{1}{2}$ V.

This is the normal and most used system for ADCs. In this case, for example, the input voltage interval for the output number 01 has its center at 1 V, the interval for 10 has its center at 2 V, etc. This means when the ADC reads out a 10, for example, the input is 2 V plus or minus $\frac{1}{2}$ V, as we would expect.

Figure 7.25(c) shows the intervals for a 3-bit converter which has a normal input voltage range from 0 to 7 V. In this example, the output 011 indicates the input voltage is 3 V $\pm \frac{1}{2}$ V.

The final graph in Fig. 7.25(d) shows an analog input along the horizontal axis and digital values along the vertical axis. This graph is included in many manufacturers' manuals and specification sheets and again shows that the 0 interval is half the size of the other intervals which are of the same size (except that the final interval extends on).

In many converters there is an *overrange* feature to handle inputs outside the normal interval. This generally consists of an output line which indicates the input is "out of range" when it is 1.[6]

FLASH CONVERTERS

7.18 The fastest ADCs are called *simultaneous*, or *flash*, converters. Figure 7.26(a) shows a flash converter with two digital output lines X_0 and X_1. This converter realizes the converter input-output relations for Fig. 7.25(b).

The converter uses an analog circuit called a *comparator*. The block diagram symbol for a comparator is a triangle on its side. When the voltage at the upper $(+)$ input to a comparator is relatively positive with respect to the lower $(-)$ input, the comparator outputs a digital 1; when the upper input is negative with respect to the lower input, the comparator outputs[7] a digital 0. As an example, the lowest comparator in Fig. 7.26 has a lower $(-)$ input of $\frac{1}{2}$ V. If the INPUT is at $\frac{1}{4}$ V, the comparator will have a 0 output; but if the INPUT is at $\frac{3}{4}$ V, the comparator will have a 1 output.

Analysis of the operation of this flash converter is as follows. (1) If the INPUT is at 0 to $\frac{1}{2}$ V, the three points A, B, and C will all be 0s and the X_0 and X_1 outputs will also be 0s. (2) If the input is from $\frac{1}{2}$ to $1\frac{1}{2}$ V, then points A and B will be 0s but point C will be a 1, and the X_0 output will be a 1 and the X_1 output a 0. (3) If the INPUT is between $1\frac{1}{2}$ and $2\frac{1}{2}$ V, points B and C will be 1s and A a 0, giving $X_0 = 1$ and $X_1 = 1$. (4) If the INPUT is greater than $2\frac{1}{2}$ V, then A, B, and C will be 1s and the output will be $X_0 = 1$ and $X_1 = 1$.

This example of a small flash converter shows the basic parts: the reference voltages, the comparators, and a gate network to connect the outputs from the comparators to the proper binary number.

Figure 7.27(a) shows a block diagram of a 6-bit flash converter which is packaged in a single IC container. This ADC operates at up to 100 million conversions per second. The resistor chain at the left provides the correct reference voltages for the inputs to the comparators. The CONV and $\overline{\text{CONV}}$ inputs which

---

[6]The overrange feature reduces the size of the first highest output interval to half the size of the other interval.

[7]The output of a comparator is unspecified when both inputs are equal (it can be a 0 or 1).

INPUT-OUTPUT
DEVICES

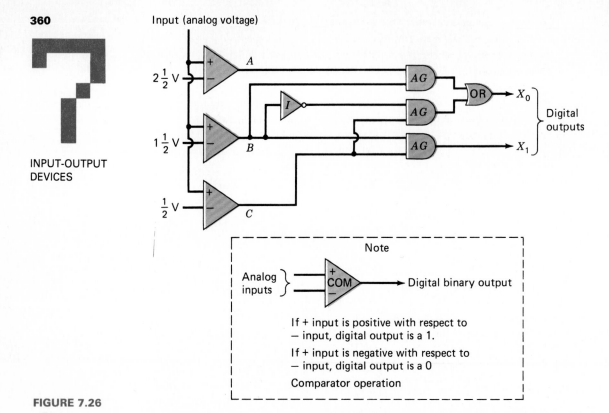

Input (analog voltage)

FIGURE 7.26

A 2-bit flash converter.

control conversions operate as follows: When the CONV is made a 1, the outputs from the 63 comparators go into the 63 latches (flip-flops) to their right. The C on the latches is the clock input which works on a positive 1 level. When $\overline{\text{CONV}}$ goes to 0, this transfers the outputs from these latches into the latches to their right. The ROM contains the conversion codes for the inputs from the latches, converting these inputs to the correct binary number. This ROM replaces the gate network shown in the preceding figure and provides an example of how ROMs and gate networks are sometimes interchangeable. When $\overline{\text{CONV}}$ is next a 1, the outputs from the ROM are transferred into the latches to its right. These latches now contain the correct conversion number. Finally, when $\overline{\text{CONV}}$ is made a 1, the output latches take the six output values for the ADC. (The triangles to the right of these latches are simply amplifiers or buffers providing drive for chip output; they do not shift 0 and 1 output levels from the latches.) Notice the upper and lower voltages which establish the interval through which the ADC converters are set by connecting the desired voltages to the RT and RB inputs to the ADC's container.

FIGURE 7.27

A high-speed flash A-to-D converter. (*Courtesy TRW, LSI Products Division*) (*a*) Block diagram of 6-bit 100-MHz flash converter. (*b*) Waveforms for flash converter in (*a*).

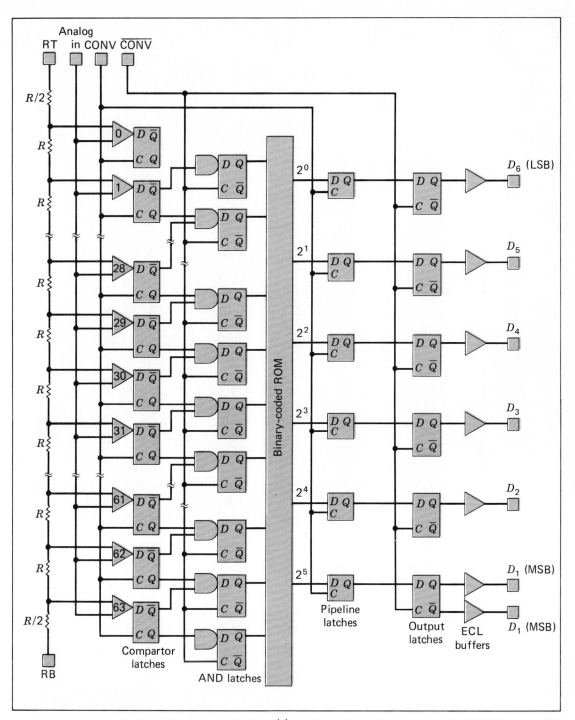

(a)

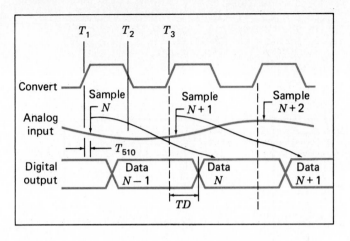

(b)

FIGURE 7.27 (Cont.)

Figure 7.27(b) shows the waveforms for conversion.

Flash converters come in many sizes and speeds. The fastest single-chip converters now perform 8-bit conversions at a 100 million conversions per second rate, but smaller, slower, less expensive devices are readily available.

The principal problem with flash converters is the large number of comparators required as the number of output bits increases. For an n-bit converter, $2^n - 1$ comparators are needed, and this involves considerable circuitry if n is very large.

COUNTER AND SUCCESSIVE-APPROXIMATION CONVERTERS

7.19   Quite often ADCs are made from a DAC and some flip-flops and other logic. These ADCs are generally slower than the flash ADCs but are less expensive and ordinarily have more output bits (resolution) and thus greater accuracy. (Flash converters can be combined to give more bits, but more logic and one or more DACs are required.)

The most conceptually straightforward nonflash ADC involves a binary counter, a DAC, and a comparator and is called a *counter* ADC. The block diagram for a counter ADC is shown in Fig. 7.28(a). This uses a 3-bit counter, a 3-bit input DAC, and a comparator.

A conversion by this ADC is initiated by lowering the $\overline{\text{CONVERT}}$ line and then raising it (this line is normally a 1, so making it a 0 tells the ADC to convert). The actual conversion begins when the $\overline{\text{CONVERT}}$ line is returned to the 1 state which "frees" the counter that has been reset. The CLOCK input is supplied with clock signals continuously, and the three-flip-flop counter then begins to count. Also while the $\overline{\text{CONVERT}}$ is down, the CONVERSION COMPLETE flip-flop is set to 0 ($\overline{\text{CONVERT}}$ must be a 0 long enough for this flip-flop to be set).

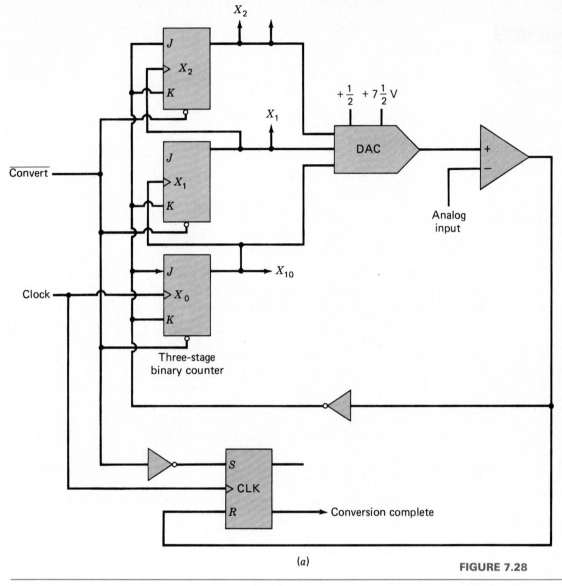

(a)

FIGURE 7.28

Counter ADC.
(a) Block diagram.
(b) Waveforms.

As the counter counts, the output from the DAC begins to increase in voltage[8] as shown in Fig. 7.28(b). Until the output from the DAC exceeds the analog input voltage, the comparator output will be a 0 and the JK inputs to the counter will be 1s (notice the inverter) and so the counter will count. When the DAC's output exceeds the analog input, the counter will be stopped and the CONVERSION COMPLETE signal will go to 1, indicating the conversion is complete.

---

[8]Note the DAC is biased $+\frac{1}{2}$ V positive. That is, a 0 input to the DAC would give a $+\frac{1}{2}$ V output. The DAC then increases its output voltages in 1-V steps as the counter is incremented.

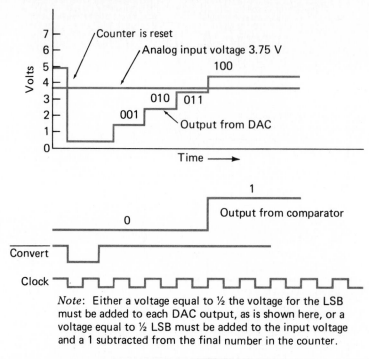

Counter is reset

Analog input voltage 3.75 V

100

010 011

001

Output from DAC

Time →

1

0   Output from comparator

Convert

Clock

Note: Either a voltage equal to ½ the voltage for the LSB
must be added to each DAC output, as is shown here, or a
voltage equal to ½ LSB must be added to the input voltage
and a 1 subtracted from the final number in the counter.

(*b*)

FIGURE 7.28 (*Cont.*)

As can be seen, the counter ADC is less expensive but slower than the flash
converter. Another type of ADC, called a *tracking* ADC, simply follows the analog
input up and down continuously, giving a continuous output of its value. This is
formed by connecting the flip-flops in an up-down counter and then connecting the
comparator's output to the DOWN input and the inverted comparator's output to
the UP input. In this way the counter-DAC combination will continually track the
analog input signal.

The most used ADC of this general type is the *successive-approximation*
ADC. Figure 7.29(*a*) shows an ADC similar to the counter ADC but with control
logic where the counter logic was. This ADC works as follows. First, all flip-flops
are set to 0. Then the most significant bit (MSB) is set to 1. The output of the
comparator is examined by the control logic: if it is a 1, the MSB flip-flop (the
flip-flop connected to the MSB of the DAC) is turned off; if it is a 0, the flip-flop
is left on. Next the second least significant bit's flip-flop is turned on. Again, if
the comparator's output is a 1, the flip-flop is turned off; if the comparator's output
is a 0, then the flip-flop is left on. This continues for each flip-flop up to and
including the LSB flip-flop. Thus the final number in the flip-flop will represent
the input voltage.

Figure 7.29(*b*) shows the waveform for a 3-bit successive-approximation
ADC.

The important thing to notice is that a counter ADC with n binary outputs
can take up to $2^n - 1$ clock signals to convert an input and will take $(2^n - 1)/2$

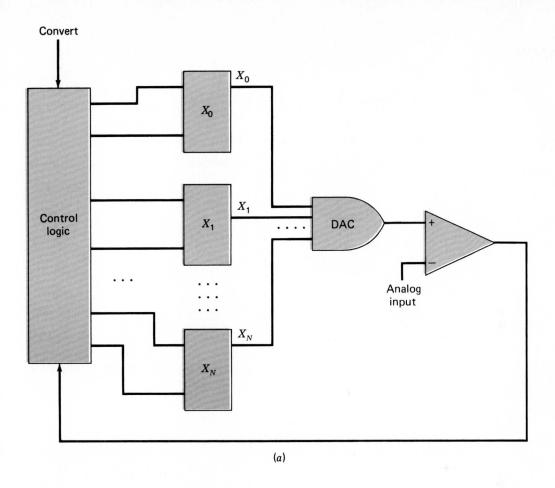

(a)

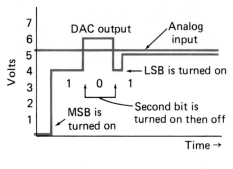

Note: Either a voltage equal to ½ LSB must be added to the analog input voltage or the output from the DAC must biased down ½ LSB

(b)

FIGURE 7.29

Successive-approximation ADC.

**INPUT-OUTPUT
DEVICES**

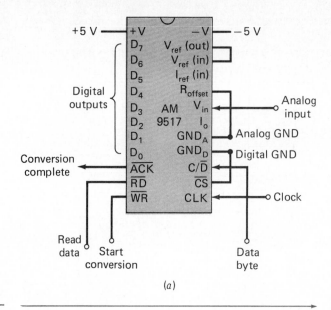

+5 V ——— +V   −V ——— −5 V

D_7 V_{ref} (out)

D_6 V_{ref} (in)

D_5 I_{ref} (in)

Digital D_4 R_{offset}

outputs D_3 AM V_{in} ——o Analog input

D_2 9517 I_o

D_1 GND_A ——• Analog GND

D_0 GND_D ——• Digital GND

Conversion
complete ◄—— $\overline{ACK}$ $C/\overline{D}$ ◄—

$\overline{RD}$ $\overline{CS}$ ◄—

$\overline{WR}$ CLK ◄——o Clock

Read data o   Start conversion   Data byte

(a)

FIGURE 7.30

A successive-approxi-
mation A-to-D con-
verter. (*Courtesy Ad-
vanced Micro Devices
Inc.*) (a) Pin-out for
AM 9517 showing in-
put-output signals.
(b) Waveforms for (a)
and (c) showing how
$C/\overline{D}$ controls multiplexing of digital out-
put. (c) Block diagram
of successive-approx-
imation ADC in (a)
and (b).

steps on the average. The successive-approximation ADC requires only n clock signals or steps to make each conversion. For a 12-bit ADC then, the successive-approximation ADC would require 12 steps while the counter ADC would require 4095/2 steps on average and could require up to 4095.

ADCs are packaged in IC containers or on printed-circuit boards when several IC chips are used; they are also sold in instrument cabinets. The block diagram and input-output signal lines for a 12-bit ADC which uses the successive-approximation technique and has a 3-μs conversion time are shown in Fig. 7.30(a) and (c). Waveforms for this device are seen in Fig. 7.30(b). Lowering $\overline{WR}$ to 0 initiates a conversion. At this time the $\overline{ACK}$ line goes high (a 1), and it goes back to 0 when the conversion is complete. Data are read from the chip in two steps.[9] (In order to conserve on in/out connections, the data output lines are time-multiplexed.) When RD is low, the ADC outputs appear on D_0 to D_7. If $C/\overline{D}$ is low, when RD is low, the 8 least significant bits are output on D_0 to D_7. If $C/\overline{D}$ is high, the 4 most significant bits appear on D_0 to D_3. $\overline{CS}$ is a chip select input (as in memories) which enables the ADC when low (a 0); holding this line high disables the chip (this permits easy connection to microcomputer buses). GND_A is analog ground, and GND_D is digital ground.

The outputs and inputs are TTL levels; approximately 0 V = 0 and 3.5 V = 1.

COMPUTER DATA ACQUISITION SYSTEMS

7.20 Computer data acquisition and computer control systems are important areas in computer technology. Computers have long been used to make measurements in laboratories and to monitor and control manufacturing processes. Machine

---

[9]These outputs utilize three-state drivers which are explained in Chap. 8.

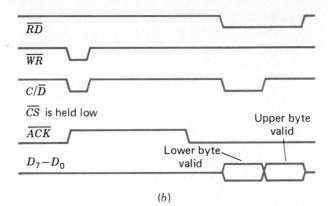

(b)

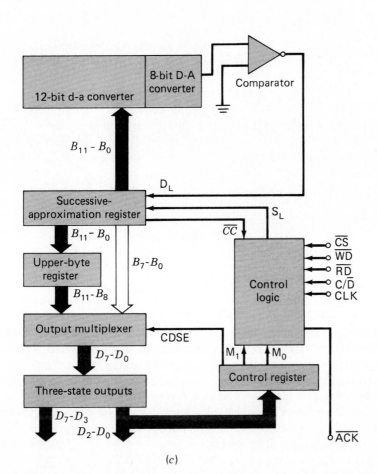

(c)

tools are often controlled by computers as are plastic forming machines and other industrial devices. Now the advent of microprocessors is moving the level of control down to consumer items such as automobiles, stoves, temperature control of houses, etc. For example, for some time the automobile industry has used computers to test motors and perform other manufacturing operations. Now cars themselves have computer controls. Some Ford models use a microcomputer-based logic control system with inputs from six sensors. A vane airflow meter in the air induction system outputs a voltage proportional to the amount of air drawn into the engine. The temperature of this air is also measured by a second sensor while still another gives engine temperature. The amount of free oxygen in the exhaust gas is measured, too, as is the crankshaft position. By using data from these sensors as input, the ignition spark timing is set, and the amount of fuel discharged through the injector nozzles is controlled, as is the exhaust-gas recirculation system. Other manufacturers use computers to control transmissions, shock absorber pressure, fuel pumps, etc.

All the above applications rely on the measuring of analog inputs by computer, which involves extensive use of ADCs. As may be seen, in these and in laboratory data systems, blood processing laboratories, computer patient monitoring, and many other such systems, different sensors must be monitored by the computer continuously. This general area is called *data acquisition* and is rapidly expanding.

Figure 7.31(*a*) shows a section of a waveform to be monitored by a computer. This waveform is to be sampled periodically, and the value at sample points input to the computer.

The sampling process is not perfect, however. If counter or successive-approximation types of ADCs are used, the conversion times are liable to be long; and if the signal is changing during the conversion process, the output from the ADC can represent almost any point in the sampling interval. Figure 7.31(*b*) shows an expanded section of waveform, and clearly the output from the ADC could be from any point on this curve.

The indeterminacy in output value caused by the change of input during the sample interval may or may not be important. However, if the analog signal changes rapidly so that a significant change can occur during the sample interval, then mathematical analyses of the digital inputs, or attempts to reconstruct the original input signal from the sample values, can be severely degraded.

To alleviate this problem, a device called a *sample-and-hold amplifier* is often used. Figure 7.31(*c*) shows a functional representation of this device (it is an electronic circuit on a chip) and a block diagram symbol. The sample-and-hold amplifier works as follows: When a positive pulse is placed on the SAMPLE input, the current value at the input is placed on the OUTPUT and the value remains there until the SAMPLE input again is given a positive pulse. The functional representation shows a relay whose contacts are closed by the positive edge on the SAMPLE input and then opened by the negative edge of the positive pulse. (In actual practice, a high-speed semiconductor switch is used—not a relay.) When the contacts of the relay are closed, the leftmost amplifier charges the capacitor to the INPUT value. When the contacts are opened, the capacitor stores this value until the contacts are again closed.

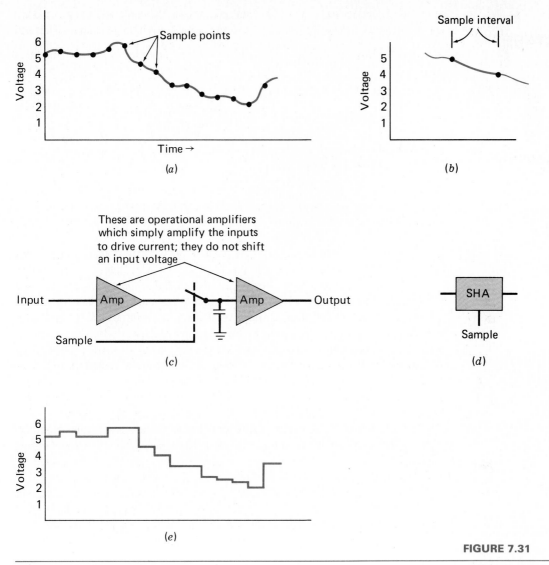

Sample points

Sample interval

Voltage

Time →

(a)

Voltage

(b)

These are operational amplifiers
which simply amplify the inputs
to drive current; they do not shift
an input voltage

Input — Amp — Amp — Output

Sample

(c)

SHA

Sample

(d)

Voltage

(e)

FIGURE 7.31

Sampling an analog
signal. (*a*) Waveform
to be sampled. (*b*)
Typical sample inter-
val. (*c*) Functional
representation. (*d*)
Block diagram sym-
bol for sample-and-
hold amplifier. (*e*)
Output of sample-
and-hold amplifier
sampling waveform
in (*a*).

Figure 7.31(*e*) shows the output from a sample-and-hold amplifier with input
the waveform in (*a*) and sample points the same. Now, if an ADC is connected to
the sample and holds output and told to convert, then the analog output from the
sample-and-hold amplifier will be constant in the interval between the sample points
and the ADC will have a constant input to convert. Then the output of the ADC
will represent the value of the analog input at the time the sample-and-hold amplifier
was told to sample.

There are important considerations concerning the operation of a sample-and-
hold amplifier:

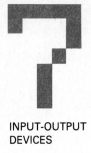

1   The *aperture time* is the time elapsing between the command to hold and the actual opening of the hold switch. (This can be as low a 1 ns for some switches.)

2   The *settling time* is the time required for the output to reach the input value when the switch is closed. If the switch is closed by the positive edge of a pulse, as in our example, and opened by the negative edge, then the time between positive and negative edges (pulse width) must be long enough for the output value to change from the prior to the new value. [This will involve charging the capacitor in Fig. 7.31(e).] The manufacturer's specification will give the settling time. Reasonable figures might be a 10-ns aperture delay, 0.25-ns aperture jitter (variation in delay), and 100-ns settling time.

3   *Droop* is the amount or rate of drift in the output between samples. A typical figure would be 100 $\mu V/\mu s$, which means a maximum change of 100 μV might occur during 1 μs.

Another important device in data acquisition systems is the *analog multiplexer,* or AMUX. This is shown in Fig. 7.32(a). An AMUX has several analog inputs [four are shown in Fig. 7.32(a)], enough digital *select inputs* to select one of the analog inputs, and a single analog output. The function of the AMUX is to select one of the analog inputs from several possible inputs by using the digital select inputs and to output only this particular input. Figure 7.32(a) shows this in the functional diagram by a rotary switch where the position of the wiper arm on the switch selects and connects one of the four inputs to the output. In practice, AMUXs are made of semiconductors and are often packaged in a single IC container. The inputs and outputs are generally connected to amplifiers, and the switch is a semiconductor switch.

As can be seen, each select value will cause a particular input to be output. In Fig. 7.32(a), $S_0, S_1 = 00$ would cause A_0 to be output, $S_0 S_2 = 01$ would output A_1, etc.

Figure 7.33 shows a typical *data acquisition system*. There are four analog signals, A_0, A_1, A_2, and A_3. Each is connected to the AMUX; the computer selects from these inputs the one it wants to be sampled and places its number on $S_0 S_1$. Then the selected analog signal is connected to the sample-and-hold amplifier. When the correct time for a sample occurs, the computer raises and lowers the SAMPLE input, thereby causing the selected input voltage to be held at its value

**FIGURE
7.32**

Analog multiplexer. (a) Functional diagram of four-input analog multiplexer. (b) Block diagram.

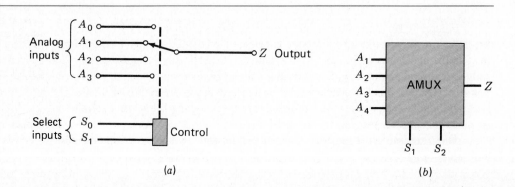

(a)   (b)

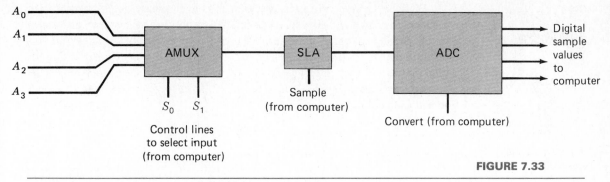

FIGURE 7.33

Data acquisition system.

at this particular time. Next the CONVERT signal to the ADC is raised, causing the ADC to measure and output the value of the selected analog signal. The computer can now read the output signal from the ADC and proceed to the sampling of another signal.

With the above data acquisition system, the analog inputs can be sampled at varying rates in case some signals change more rapidly than others or are more critical than the others. Also, the exact time at which the sample was taken will be known by the computer since it issues the SAMPLE signal (generally this signal is combined with some precise timing source).

AMUXs are produced with more than four analog inputs to handle large systems. Sometimes several sample-and-hold amplifiers are used, and these are connected to the analog inputs rather than the AMUX's output. This makes it possible to sample two or more imputs at the same time and to then read them by addressing one and then the other, using the AMUX.

Sometimes the analog signals have voltage amplitudes which are outside the normal range of the ADC. The sample-and-hold amplifiers (and sometimes the AMUX) contain amplifiers which often can be set to accommodate these inputs, increasing or decreasing signal values and even inverting (converting from negative to positive) input values. There are also circuits for *offsetting,* or *translating,* input signals which consists of adding a selected voltage to them, thereby changing their range. This area is called *signal conditioning* and generally involves the use of operational amplifiers. Some material on this can be found in the Questions and more in the Bibliography.

SUMMARY

7.21 This chapter presented an introduction to punched tapes, punched cards, and the punches and readers for these input-output media.

Alphanumeric codes are widely used in computer-human interfaces, and these were discussed and tables of the most used codes given.

Printers are the most used output devices, and they come in many kinds. The general operating characteristics of these and their principles of operation were presented. Oscilloscope displays were also discussed.

A typical keyboard and its operation were discussed as was the operation of terminals.

Digital-to-analog converters are used to convert binary output signals from computers to analog signals which can be used to position mechanical (and other) devices. Analog-to-digital converters are used to convert inputs from physical systems to digital form. The basic principles of both digital-to-analog and analog-to-digital converters were presented followed by examples of each, including flash and successive-approximation converters. The use of these devices in data collection and sampled data systems was discussed.

QUESTIONS

7.1 Using the code in Fig. 7.3, an operator keyboards the following:

> ADD 641
> CAD 932
> SUB 841

How many lines will be punched in the paper tape? How many holes will be punched in the tape?

7.2 The code in Fig. 7.3 is a parity-checking code. Is the parity check odd or even?

7.3 Write out in binary form the first line of the program in Question 7.1, using the code in Fig. 7.3.

7.4 The code in Fig. 7.3 has at least one punch or hole for each character. This makes it possible for the reader to detect when to read. Explain the tape feed character.

7.5 If the short program in Question 7.1 is punched into cards according to the code in Fig. 7.5 by using normal procedures, how many holes will be punched into the cards used? If a mistake is made during keyboarding, will it be easier to correct if cards or tape are used? Explain why.

7.6 In EBCDIC, when the first 4 bits are 1s, the remaining 4 bits represent a digit. Is the code for these bits BCD or straight binary? Give a reason for your answer.

7.7 Generally, programs are punched into cards with an instruction word per card. The first line of the program in Question 7.1 would go on one card. How many holes will be punched in the first card for the code in Fig. 7.5?

7.8 The tape feed character can be used to take out any character in the code in Fig. 7.3 except one. Which character and why? *Hint:* Remember the parity checks.

7.9 List the binary-code groups for each decimal digit in the excess-3 BCD code in Chap. 3, and assign a parity bit for an even-parity-bit checking system to each code group. List the values of the parity bits for the same excess-3 code for an odd-parity-bit checking system.

7.10 Discuss any problems you can foresee in attempting to read characters optically which would not occur for magnetic characters. Do these reasons somewhat explain why banks adopted magnetic readers before optical readers?

7.11 Each of the following rows of digits consists of a code group in ASCII. A single parity check has been added as the rightmost bit in each row, and a single row of parity checks has been added at the end, as explained in Question 7.15. In addition, errors have been added so that the data are not correct at present. Correct these groups of data, and then convert each seven-digit character to the alphanumeric character it represents. The parity checks are odd-parity checks.

(a) 10101000
10010001
10000011
10101000
01001111
10100111
01100000
10000100
10110010
10001111
10010001
10101000
11000101   parity-check row

(b) 10001001
10011110
10011101
01001111
10101000
01001000
10100111
10101000
10011110
10100001
01011011
10111001   parity-check row

7.12 Using the error-detecting and error-correcting scheme in Question 7.11, a message has been sent. It arrives as below. Determine whether errors have occurred and correct any you find in the following message:

10100100
10000010
10001101
10010001
10101000
01111111

7.13 How many bands must a coder disk similar to that shown in Fig. 7.24 have for an A-to-D converter that has a precision of 10 binary digits? List the successive code groups for a 5-bit unit-distance Gray code which counts from 0 to 31_{10}.

7.14 A 3, 3, 2, 1 code for encoding the 10 decimal digits into 4 binary digits can be made so that no more than two positions change each time a single digit is increased by 1. Write this code down.

7.15 More powerful parity-check systems can be formed by adding columns with the number of 1s in each column written at the end as a binary number. For instance, if we wish to encode

1011
1101
1100
1110

we add

$$
\left.\begin{array}{c}
0 \\
0 \\
1 \\
0
\end{array}\right\} \text{parity checks}
$$

$$
\left.\begin{array}{c}
01001 \\
01110 \\
10000
\end{array}\right\} \text{number of 1s in each column}
$$

└────indicates two 1s

└indicates four 1s

Adding this to the data forms this encoded block of data:

$$
\begin{array}{c}
10110 \\
11010 \\
11001 \\
11100 \\
\left.\begin{array}{c}
01001 \\
01110 \\
10000
\end{array}\right\} \text{check digits}
\end{array}
$$

Now if one or more errors occur in the same column, they can be corrected by simply noting that the column does not agree with the number of 1s recorded at the end, and that there are parity checks in the rows of the block of data containing errors. By simply changing these errors, we convert the message back to its original form.

Here are two other blocks of data which include errors. Correct the errors in these blocks of data, and write the alphanumeric code for each set of seven digits in a row to the right of the rows. The code is that of Fig. 7.7, so the parity checks are as indicated in the figure, and not in the rightmost column.

(a)
```
00100011
01101010
01100011
00100001
00110010
00010000
01110110
01111001
01000101
01110101
```
$$
\left.\begin{array}{c}
00010100 \\
01001101 \\
01010011 \\
00100000
\end{array}\right\} \text{check digits}
$$

(b)
```
01100010
01000001
01000100
00010000
00100011
01100001
01010111
01110101
00110010
00010000
```
$$
\left.\begin{array}{c}
00110101 \\
01100100 \\
01110011 \\
00000000
\end{array}\right\} \text{check digits}
$$

7.16 If the ASCII code in Fig. 7.7 is transmitted serially in binary, draw the waveform for the character 6, assuming a 1 is $+4$ V and a 0 is -4 V.

7.17 Put errors into the message in Question 7.12 which the coding will neither correct nor detect.

7.18 Characters are generally read from punched paper tape a line at a time. When the code in Fig. 7.3(a) is used, the computer will be supplied with information bits each time a line is read. If the computer used is a serial computer, the bits will arrive in parallel and must be changed to serial form. By loading a seven-place shift register in parallel and then shifting the register at the machine's pulse-repetition frequency, the bits representing the character can be converted to serial form. Draw a block diagram of a seven-flip-flop shift register, along with the input lines necessary to load the register. (Assume that there are seven input lines—one to each flip-flop—from the tape reader and that a given input line will contain a pulse if a hole is in the respective position of the tape.)

7.19 Explain why, in large computer systems, output data to be printed are generally recorded on magnetic tape for offline printing and not printed at once.

7.20 Which of the sets or errors in Question 7.11 would have been detected if the error-catching system in Question 7.15 had been used? Which of these sets of errors in Question 7.15 could have been corrected by the error-detecting and error-correcting scheme in Question 7.11 and which would only have been detected?

7.21 Is it possible to invent a 7-binary-bit code which includes an odd-parity-check bit and which contains 70 characters? Give a reason for your answer.

7.22 The code in Question 7.15 is not generally able to correct double errors in a row or errors in the checking numbers at the end, but will almost always detect each of these. Explain this statement.

7.23 Show how a teletypewriter would read out the character B if this key were depressed. Draw the output waveform.

7.24 What is ASCII for "line feed," which is also LF?

7.25 What is EBCDIC for E?

7.26 Notice that the characters in the magnetic reader character set in Fig. 7.10 are "blocked," not curved. Why might this be a good idea?

7.27 Notice the difference in a 0, a Q, and an O in Fig. 7.11. Find other letters that have similar printed shapes and have been altered to make them more machine-readable.

7.28 What is the difference between an acoustic coupler and a modem?

7.29 Why might it be a good idea for a computer to echo a character struck on a keyboard it is to read from instead of having the character printed immediately.

7.30 Why are start bits and at least one stop bit necessary for the teletypewriter code transmission explained for terminals?

7.31 Explain the difference between synchronous and asynchronous transmission of digital data.

7.32 Explain how the Bell 103 modem described would send the ASCII character G on a line in a chosen direction. How would it send in the other direction? Use the teletypewriter scheme to encode, using start and stop bits.

7.33 Design an A-to-D converter that converts using the successive-approximation technique.

7.34 Show how long it would take an A-to-D converter using the successive-approximation technique to convert 7 bits. Assume that it takes 10 ms for the D-to-A converter-resistor network to stabilize its output. Explain by showing how conversions are made for three specific input voltages.

7.35 Again assuming that it takes 10 ms for the D-to-A converter network to stabilize, show how a 6-bit converter uses the successive-approximation technique for three voltages $+9$, $+1$, and $+7$ V, assuming a 0- to 10-V range for inputs (0 and $+10$ V as voltage levels for the level converter outputs).

7.36 Show how the converter in Fig. 7.28 converts the three voltages in the preceding question and compare the conversion times.

7.37 Using the information in the preceding three questions, can you compare the average time for conversion for an A-to-D converter as shown in Fig. 7.28 with that of a successive-approximation converter? Assume 6 bits.

7.38 Show how a flash converter works for a 3-bit 0 to $+7$ volt system. Draw the gates from the comparator outputs to the binary numbers.

7.39 Explain how the converter in Figure 7.28 converts $+0.5$, $+3.2$, and $+5.4$ V.

7.40 Discuss resolution and quantizing error. Can the quantizing error be less than the resolution? Why or why not?

7.41 Discuss A-to-D converters, bringing out the important characteristics which must be considered in choosing a converter. What is the primary advantage of a flash A-to-D converter, and what is its primary disadvantage? Can a flash converter convert an analog input directly to digital form, using a Gray code instead of binary? Justify your answer.

7.42 Design a gating network that converts a 3-bit Gray code to a 3-bit conventional binary number. Use only NOR gates in your design.

7.43 A straightforward technique for encoding a keyboard is shown in this chapter. Several other methods are sometimes used, and these are primarily intended to either reduce the number of semiconductors in the decoder mechanism or simplify the wiring.

One technique involves a two-dimensional array similar to the selection systems used in memories. The following figure shows a two-dimensional array. The horizontal wires are connected to the vertical wires by switches which are activated by keys on the keyboard. Thus depressing a key closes a switch which connects a single X wire to a single Y wire. Each key which is depressed produces a unique X wire, or Y wire, combination. Determining which key has been closed, however, is nontrivial. A common technique is to raise one of the X or horizontal wires and then scan (i.e., sample) each of the Y wires. If one of the wires is high and the other wires are low, then the particular intersection of the X and Y wires which are connected can be determined. Sometimes a microprocessor is programmed to generate the X wire sequence and sample the Y wires, but special *keyboard encoding chips* are also made for this process. In each case the X wires are normally low except that, one at a time, the microprocessor, or scanner, raises a single X wire and then examines each of the Y wires to see whether one is high. If it is, a key has been depressed, and since the microprocessor is aware of which X wire has been raised and also which Y wire was raised, it can determine the unique key that has been depressed. By encoding the X wires with a unique 3-bit code on each wire and the Y wires with a unique 2-bit code, a unique pair of 5-bit combinations can be arranged. For larger keyboards the ASCII code can be used by proper choice of the X and Y values. Draw a simple 8-character encoder which encodes only 8 of the ASCII characters shown in Fig. 7.7, assigning values to the X and Y access wires.

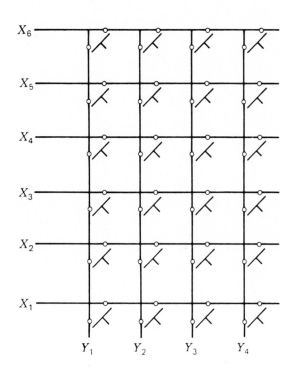

7.44 What is the weight of the least significant bit in a DAC with a resolution of 6 bits and an output voltage in the range of 0 to $+10$ V?

7.45 What is the weight of the most significant bit for a DAC with 5 bits of resolution and an output voltage range of 0 to $+5$ V?

7.46 If a 6-bit DAC has a 0- to $+5$-V output range, what is the expected output for an input of 010101?

7.47 A 7-bit DAC has an output range of 0 to $+10$ V. The manufacturer specifies that the DAC has a monotonic output with perfect values of 0 and $+10$ V. In terms of voltage, what is the maximum error that can occur?

**INPUT-OUTPUT
DEVICES**

7.48 What is the Gray code for 10111 binary? If the Gray code is 11011, what is the corresponding binary code?

7.49 Derive a rule for converting from Gray code to binary.

7.50 Draw the waveform from the DAC and input voltage for a 4-bit counter converter converting the input voltage of $+2\frac{3}{4}$ V. The conversion range for the ADC is 0 to $+5$ V.

7.51 Draw the DAC output waveform for a 5-bit successive-approximation ADC converting the input voltage of $+3\frac{1}{3}$ V. The ADC voltage has an input voltage range of 0 to $+7$ V.

7.52 Design a 4-bit ADC which uses the successive-approximation technique, showing gates, flip-flops, etc.

7.53 Design a 4-bit tracking ADC using an up-down counter as in Chap 4. The input voltage range should be 0 to $+15$ V.

7.54 Lay out the block diagram for a data acquisition system which samples the output from four DACs connected to temperature-measuring devices and a DAC connected to an accelerometer in a jet sled. Use sample-and-hold amplifiers, multiplexers, and an ADC. Have a computer control the sampling.

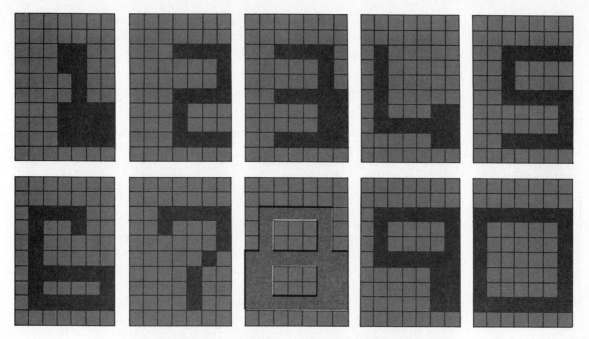

BUSES AND INTERFACES

A computer can be conveniently broken into five sections, as explained in Chap. 1. It is necessary to interconnect these sections so that they will operate as a system. That is the subject of this chapter.

To interconnect memories, I/O devices, and other sections of a computer, most often a bus is used. Several examples of buses were given in Chap. 6, and buses are covered in greater depth in this chapter. When a given I/O device or memory is connected to a bus, an *interface* is required. This interface consists of the logic necessary for the I/O device or memory to successfully communicate with the bus. Since each device must be interfaced, there are at least as many interfaces in a system as there are devices. In general, whenever one part of a digital system is connected to another, the logic which effects the interconnection is called the interface.

To describe both buses and interfaces, examples from actual computers and buses are used. Also, interfaces are developed for a keyboard and printer, and a program to drive these interfaces is shown.

OBJECTIVES

1 There are several ways to interconnect system components in a computer, but the most used is a bus. The characteristics of buses are described followed by the overall organization of several computers and their interconnection strategies.

2   When lines on a bus are shared, special circuits are used. These are discussed, followed by a description of the operational considerations. Then hand shaking for a bus and synchronous and asynchronous bus data transfers are discussed.

3   A design for a keyboard and printer interface for a microcomputer is presented. Program control of this interface is also described, and program sections are presented.

4   Input-output interrupts and other bus strategies are described for several systems. The general-purpose interface bus IEEE Standard 488-1978 is presented.

INTERCONNECTING SYSTEM COMPONENTS

8.1   The components of a computer system, that is, the memories, input-output devices, etc., must be interconnected to form a computer system. The way these components are put together and how they communicate with each other profoundly affect the system's performance characteristics.

The arithmetic-logic unit and control unit are generally placed physically together and called the central processing unit (CPU). The CPU is then "in charge" of the system's operation, directing the operation of the other parts of the system.

In the earlier computers the CPU was connected directly to each input-output device and memory unit by a separate cable for each connection.[1] This is shown in Fig. 8.1. Then, if a card is to be read from a card reader, the CPU must accept the information; and if it is to be stored in memory, the CPU must store it. The CPU is therefore central and involved directly in each transaction.

The above system has the disadvantage of many different cables and considerable interface logic (at each end of each cable).

To make interconnection of the system components less expensive and to standardize the interface logic used, a very popular technique involves interconnecting all components by using a single *bus*. This bus consists of a number of

---

[1]A cable is a set of electric conductors (wires). Connections are made to a cable only at each of the two ends, while a bus has connections made along the conductors.

FIGURE 8.1

Individual connections between computer system units.

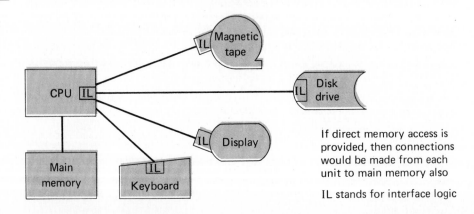

If direct memory access is provided, then connections would be made from each unit to main memory also

IL stands for interface logic

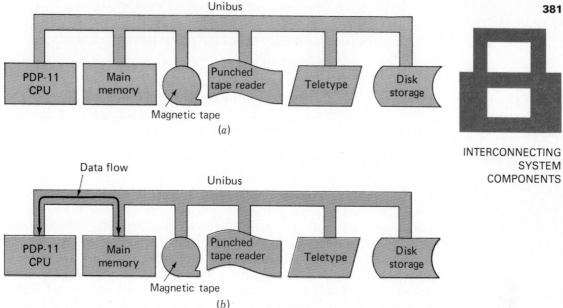

Unibus

PDP-11 CPU | Main memory | Magnetic tape | Punched tape reader | Teletype | Disk storage

(a)

Data flow

Unibus

PDP-11 CPU | Main memory | Magnetic tape | Punched tape reader | Teletype | Disk storage

(b)

INTERCONNECTING
SYSTEM
COMPONENTS

FIGURE 8.2

Bus for DEC PDP-11.
(*a*) CPU, memory,
and other devices are
connected by a single
bus. (*b*) CPU controls
transfers of data in
normal use. (*Digital
Equipment Corp.*)

wires, or connections, and in the bus are provisions for addressing the components and transferring data from or to each component.

Figure 8.2 shows the organization for the DEC PDP-11 bus, which DEC calls a *unibus*. Notice that the same wires are used to transfer data from the CPU to the high-speed main memory as from the CPU to a tape punch or other input-output device.

In the simplest systems, the CPU is the director of all traffic on the bus. If a transfer of data must be made from, for instance, a disk pack to the core memory, then the CPU, under program control, will read each piece of data into its CPU general registers and then store each piece of data in the core memory.

There is a problem here in the computer's ability to know when a *peripheral device*[2] has performed a given operation. Suppose we wish to find some data on a magnetic tape and are unwilling to wait for the tape to be searched, desiring to perform other calculations while waiting. If the computer must continually look to see whether the tape drive now has the data available, then time is lost and programming complexity is increased. To alleviate this, the computer bus is generally provided with control lines[3] which are called *interrupt lines,* and a peripheral device can raise one of these lines when it has completed an action and is ready for attention.

The computer must be provided with some kind of interrupt facility so that

---

[2]*Peripheral devices* are the input-output devices, disk packs, tape drives, and other devices not including the main (IC) memory.

[3]The lines are normally 0; to raise a line means to place a 1 on it. In microcomputers and minicomputers there may be only one line. The word *lines* is often used for the conductors (wires) on a bus. Physically the lines are electric conductors.

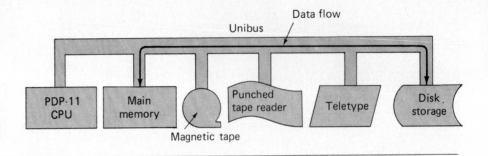

FIGURE 8.3

DEC bus in DMA
mode. (*Digital Equip-
ment Corp.*)

it can "service" the interrupt without losing its place in the program being executed. This problem becomes serious in systems where a number of input-output
devices (such as A-to-D converters) must be serviced frequently, and computers
are designed to service these interrupts as efficiently as possible.

Even with a good interrupt facility, the computer is still involved in every
data transfer, and this can be very time-consuming. It is possible to add a *direct
memory access* (DMA) feature to most systems where a disk pack or tape reader
transfers data directly into high-speed main memory using the bus but without
passing the data through the CPU (see Fig. 8.3). This is done by "stealing"
memory cycles, called *cycle stealing*. The CPU is simply held in its present state
for one or more memory cycles while data are transferred from the disk pack
directly into the main memory. The CPU does not "see" each transfer when it
occurs, but simply continues executing its program, which is slowed down a little
because of the cycle stealing, but not nearly as much as if the CPU had to make
each transfer itself. The CPU must, of course, originate these DMA transfers by
telling where in the disk pack the data are to be read from and into which locations
in the main memory the data are to be read. (Transfers generally can be made in
either direction when the DMA feature is added to a system, that is, for example,
tape to main memory or main memory to tape.)

Because of the economy of operation, a bus is now the most used way to
interconnect components of a microcomputer or minicomputer system.

Large systems have quite different problems from very small systems, and
so different interconnection configurations are used. Since large systems contain
many components, they are quite expensive, and it is important to utilize the CPU
and other components to the maximum. Thus the cost of more expensive interconnection configurations is warranted.

As a result, in order to keep large processor configurations such as that shown
in Fig. 8.4 working at their maximum speeds, the systems are operated in *multi-
programming mode*. This means that several programs are kept in memory at the
same time. A given program is executed until it demands an input-output device
or perhaps a disk drive. Since these devices are slow compared to the CPU, the
device is started in its function, but then the CPU begins executing another different
program until this program asks for input-output. When this happens, the CPU
begins executing a third program, and this process continues.

When a program completes execution, another program is read in. As can
be seen, the CPU must keep track of where it is in each program and must control

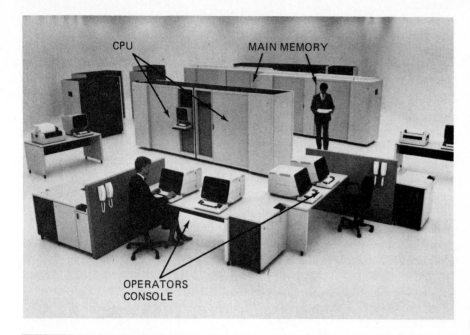

FIGURE 8.4

Parts of a large gen-
eral-purpose com-
puter. (*IBM Corp.*)

all the data transfers between system components, but would be hopelessly held up if it had to participate in each transfer.

One way to configure a large system of this sort is shown in Fig. 8.5, which illustrates the IBM 3081 configuration. It shows a single CPU and two input-output processors, one of which IBM calls a *multiplexer channel* and the other a *selector channel*.[4] Some systems have more input-output processors, and others even have more than one CPU, in which case the system is called a *multiprocessor*.

The system operates as follows: All transfers to and from peripheral devices (such as card readers, printers, tape drives, etc.) are initiated by the CPU telling an input-output processor what is to be done. The actual transfers are then made by the special-purpose processors, which work independently of the CPU. To initiate a data transfer, the CPU tells the input-output processor where in memory to put (or find) the data, which input-output device to use, and (if necessary) where in that device the data are located. The actual transfer of data is guided by a *channel program* executed by the input-output processor which has been written in advance, and the CPU also sees that the correct channel program is used.

Once an input-output data transfer has been initiated by the CPU, the CPU can go about executing other programs. When the input-output processor completes its work, the CPU is notified so that it can return and continue where it was in the program which called for the input-output transfer.

Another large computer configuration is that in Fig. 8.6, which shows the

---

[4] A multiplexer channel has logic particularly suited to relatively slow devices with random characteristics. Selector channels are for fast bursts of data generated by disk packs and tape drives, for instance.

BUSES AND
INTERFACES

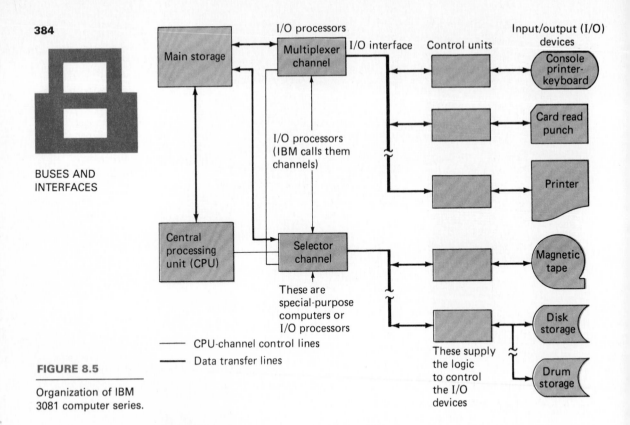

FIGURE 8.5

Organization of IBM
3081 computer series.

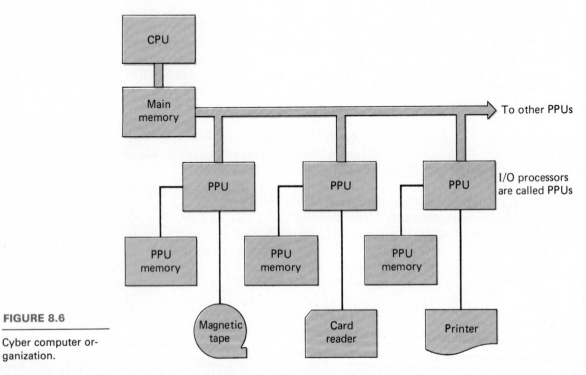

FIGURE 8.6

Cyber computer or-
ganization.

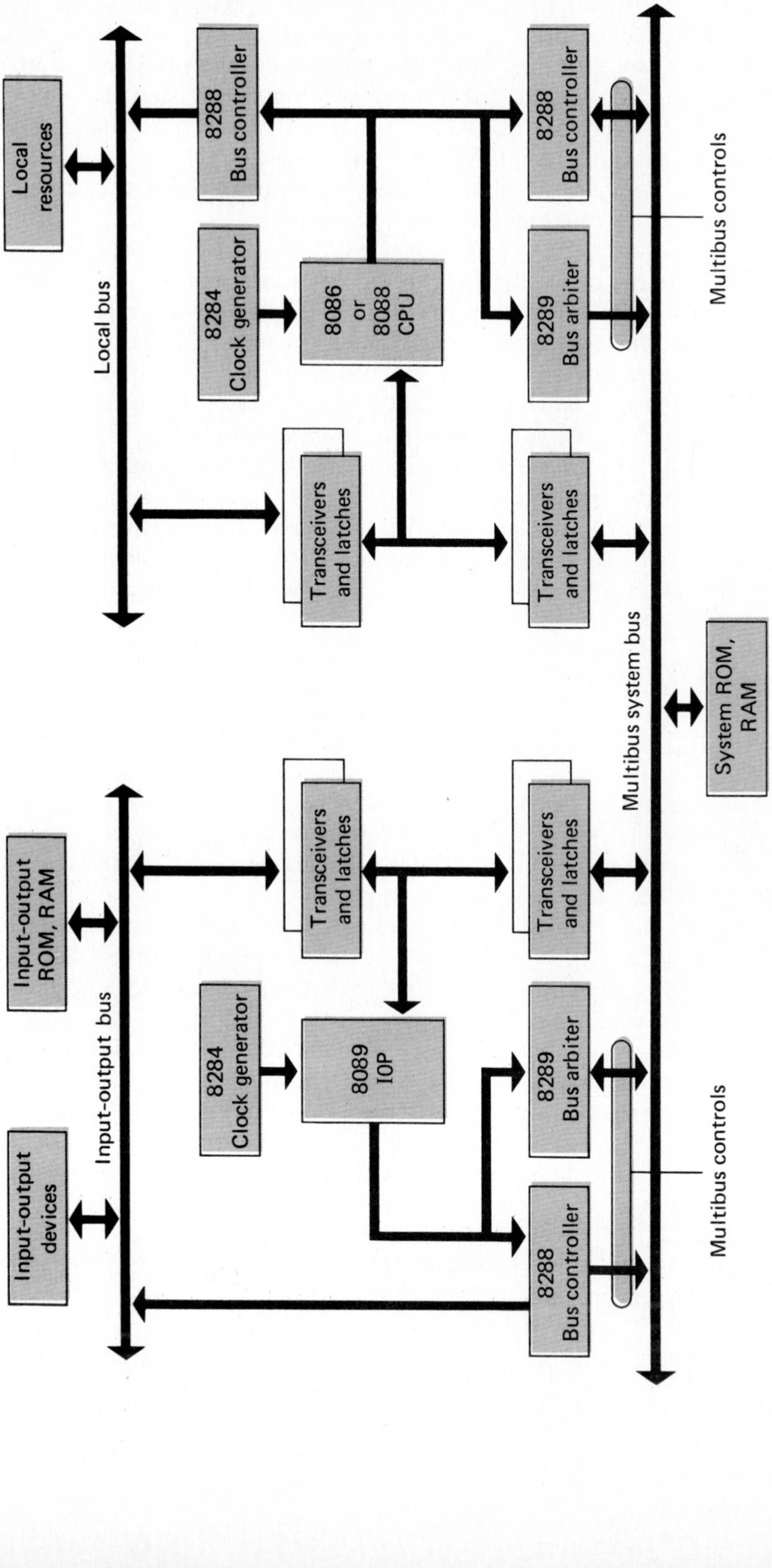

INTERCONNECTING
SYSTEM
COMPONENTS

FIGURE 8.7

Multiprocessor configuration using 8086 and 8088 microprocessors.

organization of the CDC Cyber computer. In this case the input-output operations are all handled by small "computers" called *peripheral processing units* (PPUs). The PPUs have their own memories and programs and work independently of the Cyber CPU. The way the Cyber commands input-output operations is to "plant" messages in a specified area in its memory, telling what it would like. The PPUs then search this memory, looking for orders; when they find one, they execute the necessary operations and plant a message telling the CPU that its orders have been fulfilled and the necessary operations performed.

Complex structures such as the IBM 3081 and Cyber make good sense because a number of peripheral or input-output devices can be operating simultaneously at the relatively low speeds they can maintain, while the CPU races from job to job. In this way the overall throughput for the computer system can be increased because of the parallel operation of all parts of the system.

The idea of providing several CPUs which execute programs in parallel is an attractive one. As just mentioned, such systems are called *multiprocessor systems*. Again, they have high throughput and make good usage of both large memories and the several input-output devices.

Figure 8.7 shows how the 8086, 8088, and 8089 microprocessor chips can be combined with a number of support chips to produce a multiprocessor system. More 8086 or 8088 CPUs can be added to the multiprocessor as desired, each using the same configuration.

INTERFACING—BUSES

8.2 When input-output devices, memory devices, the arithmetic-logic unit, and the control unit are all combined to form a computer system, all these must be connected. When one device or unit is connected to another, an interface is required which includes the necessary logic.

The primary disadvantages of using a large number of individual cables to interconnect parts of a system are cost and complexity. The necessary interface logic must be repeated for each connection along with cable-driving circuits and receiving circuits.

As has been stated, a widely used technique to interface modules efficiently at low cost employs a single bus to interconnect all the units. This is shown in Fig. 8.8, where the several lines or conductors which form the bus pass through and connect to a number of units, or modules. In general, each module can read from or write onto the bus. The bus interface is usually standardized since the same bus connects all units. Since each unit connects only once to the bus, the amount of interface circuitry and logic required tends to be lower than for separate connections between units. As a result, buses are widely used in microcomputers and minicomputers and even in large computer systems for modules where the data flow is not excessive.

Often the modules which are bused together share the same data lines. Then it is necessary for each module to be able to both write onto and read from a given line.

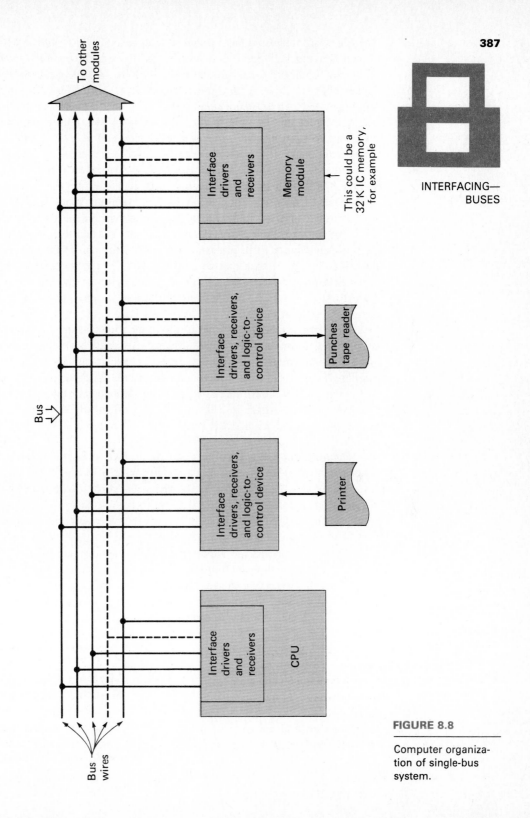

INTERFACING—
BUSES

FIGURE 8.8

Computer organization of single-bus system.

To share lines on a bus,[5] a logic circuit called a *three-state* or *tristate driver* is used. The block diagram for the three-state driver is shown in Fig. 8.9(*a*). There are IN and ENABLE inputs and a single OUT line. A table showing the operation of the three-state driver is also given. The three-state driver has three output states: a 0 output, a 1 output, and a state in which the circuit is effectively disconnected from the output. In Fig. 8.9(*a*), where the ENABLE is a 0, the circuit is effectively disconnected from the OUT line; where ENABLE is a 1, the output is the same as the input on IN.

Figure 8.9(*c*) shows a way of looking at the operation of the three-state driver in Fig. 8.9(*a*). When the ENABLE is a 0, the relay is open and so the IN is disconnected from the output; when the ENABLE is a 1, the relay is closed and the output is connected to the input, and so the logic values are the same.

The important thing to understand is that if several three-state drivers have their outputs connected to the same line and if only one of the drivers has as its ENABLE input a 1, then that particular driver will control the state of the line. When three-state drivers are used for interfaces, only one interface on a line (conductor) must have its ENABLE input a 1 at a given time, and this interface will control the state of the line.

Inverters or other logic gates can have their inputs connected to a line which is controlled by several three-state drivers. Generally, manufacturers arrange so that the three-state driver will drive a line of considerable length and with several gate inputs connected to it, which is often the case for a bus line.

Figure 8.9(*b*) shows a three-state driver that inverts its input. The table shows this: When the ENABLE is a 0, the driver is effectively disconnected from the output; and when the ENABLE is a 1, the OUT value is the complement of the IN value.

Figure 8.9(*d*) shows a functional representation of (*b*) showing the driver operates much like an inverter and a relay connected.

Sometimes manufacturers make three-state drivers with a DISABLE input instead of an ENABLE input [see Fig. 8.9(*e*)]. In this case the driver is disconnected when the DISABLE input is a 1 and the output, which is inverted in this case, is the complement of the input when the DISABLE is a 0.

Three-state drivers are widely used in the interfaces for buses. They enable control of bus lines to pass from interface to interface as is appropriate.

Figure 8.10 shows a tristate octal *D*-type latch IC package with eight latches equipped with tristate drivers. Each latch reads the input at *D* when the clock input is high. The outputs from the latches are forced on the outputs from the chip when the ENABLE is a 1. When the ENABLE is a 0, the outputs represent "high impedances" (and another chip can drive the lines as they are connected to a desired state).

Figure 8.11 shows an octal tristate buffer with positive-edge-triggered flip-flops in which the outputs are forced to the input state only when the ENABLE input is high (a 1).

Since several units are sharing the same bus lines, the interface procedures for bused modules must be carefully worked out so that, for instance, two modules

---

[5]Three-state drivers are used in many applications other than on buses, but the sharing of a line is always the reason for their use.

In	Enable	Out
0	0	—
1	0	—
0	1	0
1	1	1

— indicates driver is
electrically disconnected

In	Enable	Out
0	0	—
1	0	—
0	1	1
1	1	0

In ⟶ Out

Enable

(a)

Enable

(b)

In	Enable	Out
0	0	Relay open
1	0	Relay open
0	1	0
1	1	1

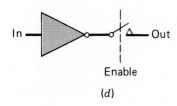

(d)

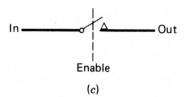

(c)

In	Disable	Out
0	0	1
1	0	0
0	1	—
1	1	—

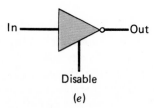

In ⟶ Out

Disable

(e)

FIGURE 8.9

Three-state driver
operation. (*a*) Three-
state driver. (*b*)
Three-state driver
with inverted output.
(*c*) Functional repre-
sentation of (*a*). (*d*)
Functional represen-
tation of (*b*). (*e*)
Three-state driver
with disable input.

**BUSES AND
INTERFACES**

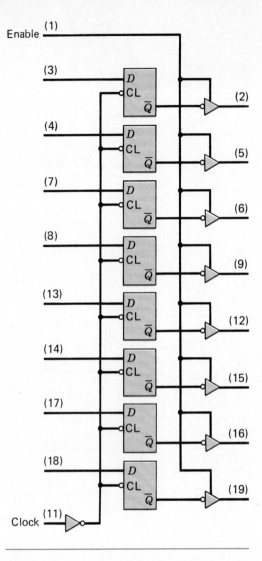

FIGURE 8.10

Octal latches with
tristate drivers.

do not attempt to write data on the bus at the same time and the module for which
the data are intended knows it is the selected module, etc.

BUS FORMATS AND OPERATION

8.3 A number of different types and several different standards for buses exist.
All buses can be divided into three major sections, however: the *address, data,*
and *control* sections. This is shown in Fig. 8.12 as are two commonly used ways
to represent multiple lines on a bus. Figure 8.12(*a*) shows the three sections, using
a wide, ribbonlike representation for the multiple lines (wires). Figure 8.12(*b*)
shows that sometimes a single printed line is used with a starting slash through the
printed line to indicate that there are actually a number of lines (wires). For both

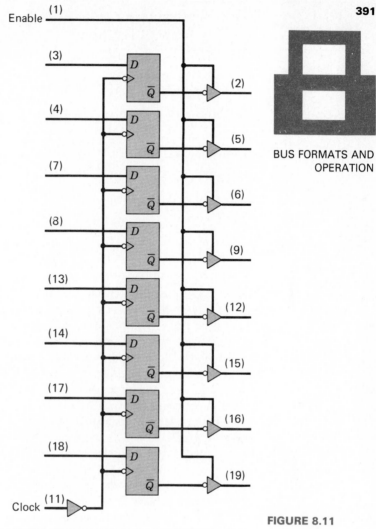

**BUS FORMATS AND
OPERATION**

FIGURE 8.11

Octal flip-flop chip
with tristate drivers.

Fig. 8.12(*a*) and (*b*) there are 16 address lines, 8 data lines, and 4 control lines. Both representations in (*a*) and (*b*) are frequently used.

Most buses now use tristate drivers to write data on the data lines. In the most straightforward systems, the address lines are completely controlled by the *bus master* which is generally a miniprocessor or microprocessor CPU. If there is a single bus master, the remaining devices connected to the bus are called *slaves*. Each slave then has an address number, and the bus master uses the address lines to control who is to use the bus. In some systems, however, devices other than the CPU can take control of the bus. In this case, a controlling device is called the bus master only when it has control, and at that time the responding devices are called slaves. For buses in which control is shared among several devices (that is, more than one device can take control of the bus), the address lines also are driven by tristate drivers.

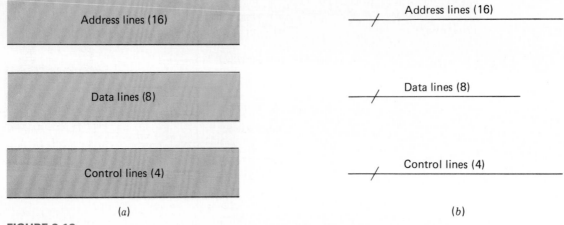

FIGURE 8.12

Address, data, and control sections of a bus. (a) The three sections of a bus. (b) Alternative representation for (a).

Some of the control lines may be permanently controlled by the CPU, and others may be used by several devices and thus require tristate drivers (or wired OR or wired AND drivers).

Note that any device can read from a line driven by a tristate driver and conventional inverters or gates can be connected to these lines. (The only restriction is that the gates connected to the lines not load the lines unduly.)

Buses transfer information over data wires by using either a *synchronous* or an *asynchronous* technique. Different manufacturers and bus designers have different philosophies about which is better, with the result that there is no standard.

For synchronous transfers, the bus works as follows. Let us assume a CPU wishes to read and write from peripheral devices. Each device is given a separate number, and a device is selected by the CPU placing that number on the address lines.[6]

Figure 8.13 shows the timing of synchronous data transfers involving a set of address wires, data wires, and a READ and WRITE control line. All transfers are controlled by the CPU. Note that the convention is that the meaning of READ and WRITE is always relative to the master or CPU on buses. Therefore, a READ means the CPU (master) reads data from the bus, and a WRITE means the CPU (master) writes data on the bus.

Figure 8.13 shows that in order to read, the CPU places the number of the device to be read from on the address lines. Then the CPU lowers[7] the $\overline{\text{READ}}$ line, and the selected device must place data on the DATA lines, which means enabling its tristate drivers connected to the bus DATA wires. When the $\overline{\text{READ}}$ line goes back to a 1, the device must disable its tristate drivers.

When the CPU desires to write data (to give data to a device), the device's number is placed on the address line and then the data are placed on the DATA lines. The CPU lowers the $\overline{\text{WRITE}}$ line to 0, and the device must read the data at

---

[6] A disk drive might be given the number 1, a keyboard the number 3, etc.

[7] It is common practice to use a 0 signal to activate devices on a bus. This is indicated by the bar over the name of the line $(\overline{\text{READ}})$. If a device is activated by a 1 signal, no bar is used.

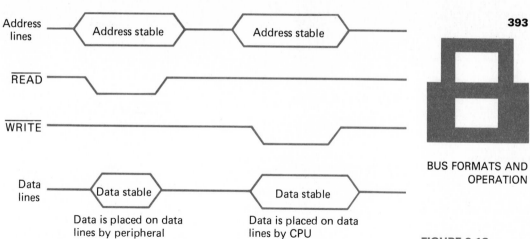

Address
lines — Address stable — Address stable —

READ ‾‾‾‾‾‾‾‾

WRITE ‾‾‾‾‾‾‾‾

Data
lines — Data stable — Data stable —

Data is placed on data
lines by peripheral

Data is placed on data
lines by CPU

FIGURE 8.13

Timing signals for
synchronous trans-
fers.

that time. The data must have been read when the $\overline{\text{WRITE}}$ line goes back to a 1. The interface designer must know how long the $\overline{\text{WRITE}}$ will be a 0 so that the data can be read safely during the time the $\overline{\text{WRITE}}$ line is a 0.

Note here that the device being written into or read from must respond during the fixed time period permanently established by the CPU. If a READ is performed, the device must place data on the data lines at once and keep them there while the $\overline{\text{READ}}$ line is down. Similarly, for a WRITE the device must have already read the data by the time that the $\overline{\text{WRITE}}$ line goes high.

Synchronous transfers are generally thought to be the fastest way to transfer data and are used for memory data transfers and sometimes for transferring data to other types of devices. The problem is that all devices must be able to respond at the same speed unless the CPU has READ and WRITE signals of different durations for different devices.[8] To alleviate this problem (that is, to accommodate devices with differing response times), the asynchronous transfer technique is often used.

When an asynchronous bus transfer technique is used, another control line is required, called DATA VALID OR RECEIVED (see Fig. 8.14). This line is controlled by the devices and not the CPU, however. And if there is more than one device on the bus, a tristate driver will be required for each device using this line.[9]

The sequence of timing steps performed in Fig. 8.14 is as follows. To read from the bus, the CPU sets the number of the device on the ADDRESS lines and then lowers the $\overline{\text{READ}}$ line. The device which is selected then places data on the DATA lines and a 1 on the DATA VALID OR RECEIVED line. This tells the CPU that the data are on the lines and can be read. The CPU cannot read from the DATA lines until the DATA VALID OR RECEIVED line is a 1. If the device is slow in preparing its data, the CPU must wait until the data are on the DATA lines

---

[8]This would be a complicated strategy. Another bad alternative is for all devices to operate at the speed of the slowest devices.

[9]A driver which wire-ORs its output could also be used.

BUSES AND INTERFACES

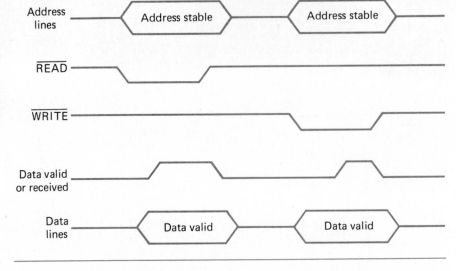

FIGURE 8.14

Timing signals for asynchronous transfers.

and the DATA VALID OR RECEIVED line is raised. Next the CPU reads the data and raises the $\overline{\text{READ}}$ line to a 1. This means the selected device must keep its data on the DATA line until $\overline{\text{READ}}$ goes to a 1. The selected device then turns off its tristate drivers to the DATA lines and lowers the DATA VALID OR RECEIVED line.

A write operation is performed similarly. First the CPU places the number of the selected device on the ADDRESS line and the data on the DATA lines. Then the CPU lowers the $\overline{\text{WRITE}}$ line. The selected device now reads the data and raises the DATA VALID OR RECEIVED line. The CPU must keep its DATA and ADDRESS lines stable until it receives this signal, so the device can be "slow to read" and still get the data. After the CPU receives the DATA VALID OR RECEIVED high signal, it removes the address and data from the bus and then raises the $\overline{\text{WRITE}}$ line; this allows the selected device to lower the DATA VALID OR RECEIVED lines.

The asynchronous procedure involves what is called a *handshake*. The effect is that the CPU tells which is selected if it is reading or writing and then waits for the selected device to respond (with a handshake) before continuing. Thus means fast and slow devices can be accommodated on the same bus. This is the reason for the wide use of asynchronous buses.

For both synchronous and asynchronous buses, there are several variations on Figs. 8.13 and 8.14. Often, instead of separate READ and WRITE lines, a single $R/\overline{W}$ line is used (1 for read, 0 for write) and a separate ADDRESS VALID line is used to indicate when the address is on the address lines. Sometimes the DATA VALID and DATA RECEIVED lines are separate. The principles of synchronous and asynchronous data transfers remain, and the combining or splitting of control lines can be figured out easily if the general principles are understood.

ISOLATED AND MEMORY-MAPPED INPUT-OUTPUT

8.4 Two general techniques for identifying input-output (I/O) devices have been the most used for bus operation. The first separates the I/O devices from the

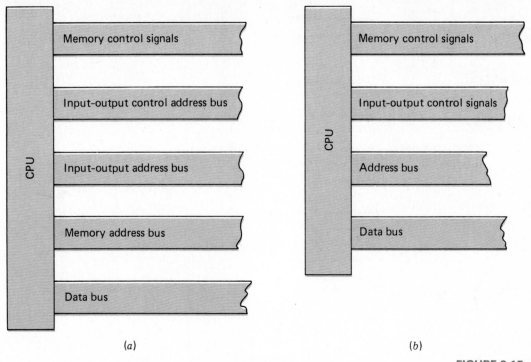

Memory control signals

Input-output control address bus

Input-output address bus

Memory address bus

Data bus

CPU

(a)

Memory control signals

Input-output control signals

Address bus

Data bus

CPU

(b)

FIGURE 8.15

Bus structure for input-output and memory. (a) Separate memory and input-output address lines. (b) Shared memory and input-output address bus.

memory and addresses (or numbers), for I/O devices are separate from memory addresses; this is often called *isolated I/O*. The second, called *memory-mapped I/O,* mixes memory addresses with I/O device numbers.

In the isolated I/O technique, the I/O devices are each given a separate number on the bus. For instance, a printer would be assigned device number 3, a keyboard device number 4, a disk drive device number 5, etc. These numbers are placed in binary on the address section of the bus when an I/O device is to be read from or written into by the CPU. The I/O devices may even have a separate I/O address bus, as shown in Fig. 8.15(a), or the I/O devices may share the address section of the bus with memory, as in Fig. 8.15(b). In either case, the I/O device number is placed on the bus by the CPU, and then the control lines tell the I/O device whether to place data on the lines, to read data, etc. If the I/O devices share bus lines with the main (IC) memory, the control signals must tell whether an address on the bus is for I/O devices or for memory.

The 8080 microprocessor is an example of an I/O system which has device numbers on the address lines that are shared with memory, as in Fig. 8.15(b). Figure 8.16 shows the sections of the 8080 bus. To read from a memory device, the 8080 places the memory address to be read from on A_0 to A_{15} and then lowers $\overline{\text{MEMR}}$; next the memory places the contents at this address on data wires DB_0 to DB_7. To write into memory, the 8080 places the address to be written into on A_0 to A_{15} and the data to be written on DB_0 to DB_7 and lowers $\overline{\text{MEMW}}$; the data are then written at the selected location.

The 8080 uses only eight of the address lines A_0 to A_{15} to select I/O devices. These lines are A_0 to A_7. As a result, only 256 I/O devices can be used. Suppose

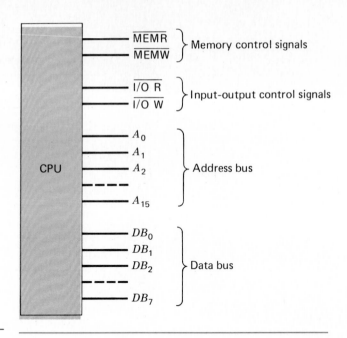

FIGURE 8.16

8080 memory and intput-output bus sections.

a keyboard has device number 3_{10}. Then to read from the keyboard, the CPU[10] places 00000011 on A_7 to A_0 and then lowers $\overline{I/O\ R}$; next the keyboard places an 8-bit character (data) on DB_0 to DB_7.

As another example, if a printer has device number 5 and the CPU wishes to print a character, the CPU places 00000101 on A_7 to A_0, the character on DB_0 to DB_7 and then lowers $\overline{I/O\ W}$. This bus is synchronous, and so the devices must read or write data at the specified time because the $\overline{I/O\ W}$ and $\overline{I/O\ R}$ lines are lowered only for a time determined by the clock rate of the 8080.

The 8080 is only the original member of a line of 8-bit microprocessors produced by Intel. Other processors have numbers such as 8085, 8089, etc. Each has particular features. The bus interfaces for each are compatible; however, the speed of transfer is determined by the clock rate of the particular chip which varies from device line to device line. (A memory or I/O device which responds in 100 ns could interface any of the current devices.)

The second general technique for addressing I/O devices is called *memory-mapped I/O*. When this is used, the I/O devices are assigned addresses in memory. These locations must not conflict with addresses given to memory devices such as ROM and RAM chips. Then the I/O devices are read from and written into by using the same control lines as for the IC memory chips.

The memory-mapped I/O technique requires making a map of memory showing which locations are devoted to IC memory and which to I/O devices. Figure 8.17 shows a memory map for a bus with 16 address bits and 8 data bits. The computer has a 4K-word read-only memory, a 4K-word random-access memory, a printer, and a keyboard. The ROM is connected to addresses 0 to 4095 and the

---

[10]The most significant bit is A_7; the least significant bit is A_0. For numbers on DB_7 to DB_0, the sign bit goes on DB_7 and the least signficant bit is DB_0.

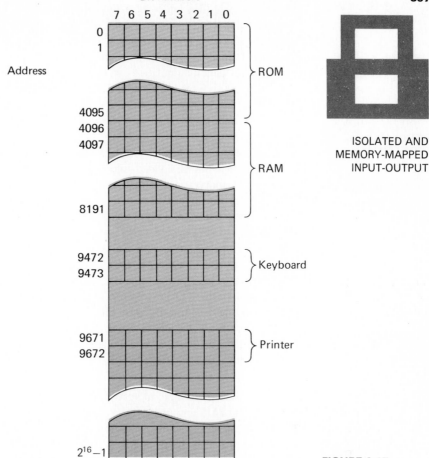

Bit numbers

Address

ISOLATED AND
MEMORY-MAPPED
INPUT-OUTPUT

FIGURE 8.17

Map of memory layout for memory-mapped I/O.

RAM to addresses 4096 to 8191; the keyboard is given locations 9472 and 9473, and the printer is given locations 9671 and 9672. (The keyboard and printer are each given two locations because each requires a status register, we discuss later.)

The programmer for this system must know where the RAM, ROM, keyboard, and printer are located. To print a character, the particular address allocated to the printer must be used; to read a character from the keyboard, the address given to the keyboard must be employed.

Memory-mapped computers have no I/O instructions in their list of instructions. To read a character from a keyboard, the keyboard address is simply used; any instruction which reads from memory can read from that address. Data from a keyboard would be added to or ANDed with the current contents of an accumulator by using a single instruction, for example; or a character from the keyboard could be simply transferred into an accumulator. The PDP-11 series and 6800 and 68000 microprocessors are examples of memory-mapped computers.

In systems having separate I/O control lines and device numbers, the CPU will have specific I/O instructions. For example, the 8080 has IN and OUT in-

structions, and these specifically cause transfers to and from I/O devices. The programmer must then know the I/O device numbers and the memory addresses.

Advocates of separate I/O point out that interfaces may be simpler and that programmers' use of I/O instructions seems more natural. Advocates of memory-mapped I/O claim that the CPU is simpler as is the bus and that the instructions in the CPU for data manipulation can be used for I/O data, simplifying programs.

The 68000 is a memory-mapped and asynchronous microcomputer. A section of the 68000 bus is shown in Fig. 8.18(a). This is a large bus with 23 address lines and 16 data lines. There are a number of control signals, five of which are shown.

The 68000 has a 16-bit word, which is the normal unit for data transfer. However, each word is divided into two 8-bit bytes, called the *upper byte* and *lower byte*. Memory and I/O reads and writes can transfer either a complete 16-bit word or an upper or lower byte. To indicate to an I/O device or memory whether 1 or 2 bytes are to be transferred, two control signals $\overline{UDS}$ (upper data strobe) and $\overline{LDS}$ (lower data strobe) are used [Fig. 8.18(a)]. If $\overline{LDS}$ is low, data are placed on lines D_0 to D_7; if $\overline{UDS}$ is low, data lines D_8 to D_{15} are used. If both are low, an entire 16-bit word is transferred.

Figure 8.18(b) shows the timing for both a read and write. Since the 68000 is memory-mapped, I/O devices use addresses in memory and data transfers to and from I/O devices use the same timing signals as memory transfers.

Let us assume the 68000 wants to read a 16-bit word from a disk drive interface which uses location $000FF6_{16}$. The timing would be as follows [refer to Fig. 8.18(b)]:

1 The 68000 places the address 000FF6 on the address lines and then lowers $\overline{AS}$, $\overline{UDS}$, and $\overline{LDS}$ and makes R/$\overline{W}$ a 1. A 0 on $\overline{AS}$ tells the devices on the bus that the address on the address lines is valid, both $\overline{UDS}$ and $\overline{LDS}$ low indicates all 16 data lines are to be used, and R/$\overline{W}$ indicates a read operation.

2 The disk drive interface places 16 bits of data on D_0 to D_{15} and then lowers $\overline{DTACK}$ (for data acknowledge), which indicates the data are on lines D_0 to D_{15}.

3 The 68000 reads the data from D_0 to D_{15}.

4 The 68000 raises $\overline{AS}$ to indicate the disk interface can release the data because they have been read.

5 The disk interface turns off its tristate drivers to lines D_0 to D_{15} and raises $\overline{DTACK}$.

A write is performed similarly. Assume a tape drive interface accepts data on address $00076F4_{16}$. When data are written into the tape drive interface, the following occurs:

1 The 68000 places 00076F4 on address lines A_1 to A_{23}; places the data to be transferred on D_0 to D_{15}; and then lowers $\overline{AS}$, $\overline{UDS}$, $\overline{LDS}$, and R/$\overline{W}$. This indicates that the address is valid, all of D_0 to D_{15} is to be used, and the operation is a write operation.

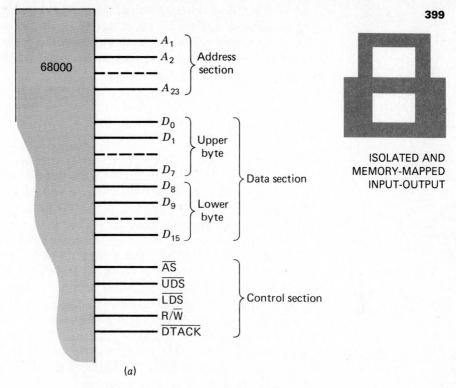

ISOLATED AND
MEMORY-MAPPED
INPUT-OUTPUT

(a)

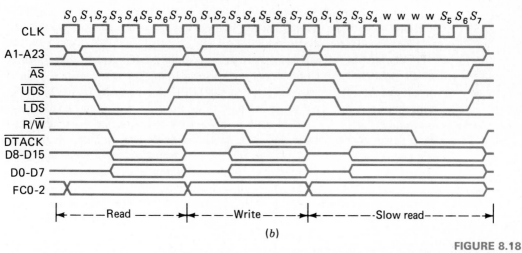

(b)

FIGURE 8.18

68000 bus signal. (a)
Bus layout. (b) Read-
write timing.

2   The tape drive interface reads the data from D_0 to D_{15}.

3   After it has the data, the tape drive interface lowers $\overline{\text{DTACK}}$, to indicate the data transfer is complete.

4   The 68000 releases its address from the address bus and the data from the data bus and then raises $\overline{\text{AS}}$, R/$\overline{\text{W}}$, $\overline{\text{UDS}}$, and $\overline{\text{LDS}}$.

Note that these transfers are asynchronous because the I/O device or memory must signal the acceptance of data or the placing of data on D_0 to D_{15} by using $\overline{\text{DTACK}}$. The 68000 will not proceed until $\overline{\text{DTACK}}$ is lowered. This is shown by "slow read" shown where $\overline{\text{DTACK}}$ is not lowered quickly, resulting in a longer read time.

INTERFACING A KEYBOARD

8.5 Section 7.12 described keyboards. In this section we describe the interfacing of a keyboard with a bus. The bus to be used is that for the 8080 microprocessor. The interface developed will be a straightforward typical design.

Figure 8.19 shows the basic bus for an 8080 microprocessor. The 8080 CPU chip requires a separate chip to generate the clock and several other timing signals. It will not affect the interface design, but for completeness we show a chip developed for this purpose, the 8224 clock generator driver.

An 8228 bidirectional bus driver chip is also used in this design.[11] The 8080 output lines have limited drive capabilities, and the 8228 bus driver has TTL levels and drive capabilities which are useful for interfacing. Also, and more importantly, the 8080 bus uses its data lines D_0 to D_r for transmitting several control signals (status bits) during an early section of each cycle. These status bits are considered a part of the bus for the 8080. The 8228 driver strobes these values into flip-flops and then outputs them as $\overline{\text{INTA}}$, $\overline{\text{MEMR}}$, I/O R, $\overline{\text{I/O W}}$, etc., which are then considered to be a part of the 8080 system bus.

Notice that the 8080 bus has three basic classes of input-output lines: address lines A_{15} to A_0, data lines D_7 to D_0, and control lines such as $\overline{\text{WR}}$, DBIN, and $\overline{\text{I/O R}}$.

The address signals are used both to address the IC memory and to select which input device is to be written into or read from. The data lines are bidirectional; that is, data are written into the 8080 CPU chip by using D_7 to D_0. These same lines are also used to output data to memories, input-output devices, etc. Bidirectional lines are widely used in buses for computers, the main advantage being fewer connections to and from chips and fewer pins on chips. If the data wires D_7 to D_0 were not bidirectional, a set of both eight input wires and eight output wires would be required instead of the eight bidirectional wires.[12]

Using bidirectional data lines means that the various system components such as memories and keyboards must be carefully controlled and timed in their operations so that only one device writes on a wire at a time and so that system components know exactly when to examine wires with signals on them.

Each input and output device which interfaces an 8080 system is given a unique *device number*. The numbers given devices can have up to 8 bits. Thus 256 different devices can be handled directly.

---

[11]This is a chip developed by Intel to facilitate interfacing with input-output devices. Often microprocessor chips have limited power output lines and require extra chips for interfacing.

[12]Three-state drivers are normally used to drive these lines.

**INTERFACING A
KEYBOARD**

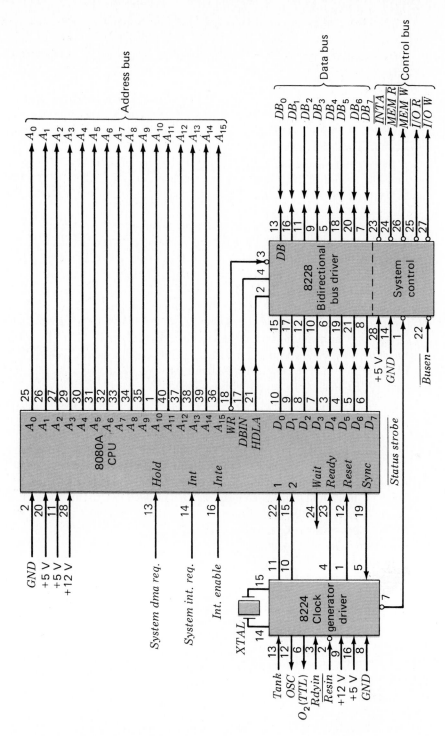

FIGURE 8.19

8080 bus. (*Intel Corp.*)

The 8080 system selects an input-output device as follows:

1 The device number of the selected device is placed on address lines A_7 to A_0.

2 If the device is to be read from by the 8080 bus, $\overline{\text{I/O R}}$ (which is normally 1) is made a 0. While $\overline{\text{I/O R}}$ is a 0, the selected device to be read from places its data on D_7 to D_0. When $\overline{\text{I/O R}}$ goes back to its normal 1 state, the selected device removes the data from lines D_7 to D_0.[13]

If the 8080[14] wishes to output data to a device, it places the device's number on A_7 to A_0. Then it places the data to be output on D_7 to D_0 and makes $\overline{\text{I/O W}}$, which is normally 1, a 0. The selected device then reads these data from the bus.

The reading and writing operations for the 8080 are under program control. An OUT instruction executed by the 8080 causes the outputting of data to a device. Executing an IN instruction causes a device to be read from. The accumulator register in the 8080 system receives data during an IN instruction and sends data during an OUT instruction. If an IN instruction is executed, the data from the selected device are read onto D_7 to D_0 and from there into the accumulator. If an OUT instruction is executed, the data are read from the 8080 system's accumulator onto D_7 to D_0, and then the selected device accepts the data on D_7 to D_0. (This accumulator is the same accumulator used for arithmetic operations such as those described in Chap. 5. The internal operation of the 8080 microprocessor is covered in Chap. 10. Section 10.11 covers program operation.)

An interface design for the keyboard of Fig. 7.18 is shown in Fig. 8.20. The keyboard is given the device number 1, or binary 00000001. Therefore the lines A_7 to A_1 are 0s and A_0 is a 1 when the keyboard is selected. The NAND gate in Fig. 8.20 shows these inputs to be NANDed along with I/O R. Now, when I/O R is a 1($\overline{\text{I/O R}}$ a 0), the 8080 bus is saying, "Place the selected device's data on D_7 to D_0." In this design, if A_7 to A_0 contain 00000001 and $\overline{\text{I/O R}}$ is a 0, then the output of the NAND gate becomes a 0. This enables the tristate drivers connected to K_7 to K_0, the keyboard output from the flip-flops in Fig. 7.19. As a result, the values of K_7 to K_0 are placed on bus lines D_7 to D_0 where the 8080 bus can read them (into its accumulator).

Notice that the output of the NAND gate is normally a 1, which disables the tristate drivers so that they have high impedance and write nothing on bus lines D_7 to D_0.

A major question now arises: At any given time the operator of the keyboard may or may not have depressed a key, so that the keyboard may or may not have new information for the 8080. If the keyboard is simply read, the 8080 cannot tell whether the character supplied is new or old. (The same key could be pressed twice in succession.) To compensate for this, a system is used in which a *keyboard status word* can be read by the 8080 bus which will tell whether a new character

---

[13]This $\overline{\text{I/O R}}$ line corresponds to the $\overline{\text{READ}}$ line in Fig. 8.13; the $\overline{\text{I/O W}}$ line corresponds to the $\overline{\text{WRITE}}$ line in that figure.

[14]We refer to the 8080 microprocessor chips as simply the 8080, as is common practice.

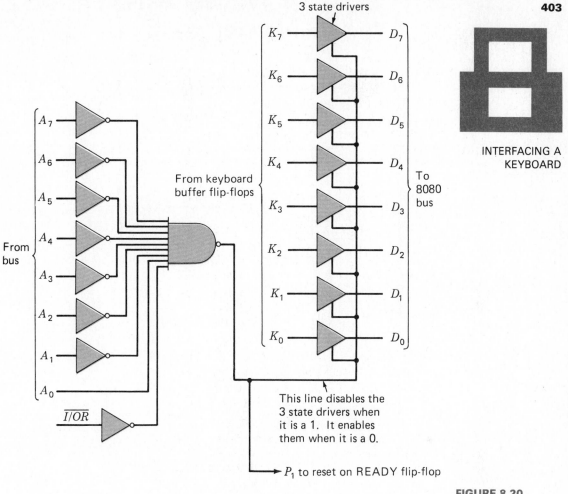

3 state drivers

K_7 D_7

K_6 D_6

K_5 D_5

From keyboard
buffer flip-flops

K_4 D_4 To
8080
bus

K_3 D_3

K_2 D_2

K_1 D_1

K_0 D_0

A_7

A_6

A_5

A_4

From
bus

A_3

A_2

A_1

A_0

$\overline{I/OR}$

This line disables the
3 state drivers when
it is a 1. It enables
them when it is a 0.

P_1 to reset on READY flip-flop

INTERFACING A
KEYBOARD

FIGURE 8.20

Interfacing a key-
board to the 8080
microprocessor.

is ready to be read from the keyboard. The scheme used here is the one most used for this kind of interface.

Figure 8.21 shows the *status word generator* interface for the keyboard. We have given this keyboard status word generator the device number 2. The keyboard status word is used as follows. If a new character is available from the keyboard, the keyboard status word will have a 1 in the D_7 position. If there is no new keyboard character, a 0 will be in the D_7 position. The remaining D_0 to D_6 of the keyboard status word will always be 0s.

The interface operates as follows. The program in the 8080 system reads the status word (an IN instruction is executed). The accumulator now contains the status word, and the program sees whether it has a 1, in which case the keyboard should be read. If the status word is all 0s, the program goes on to other programs or devices or, if it has nothing else to do, simply continues to read the status word until a 1 is found.

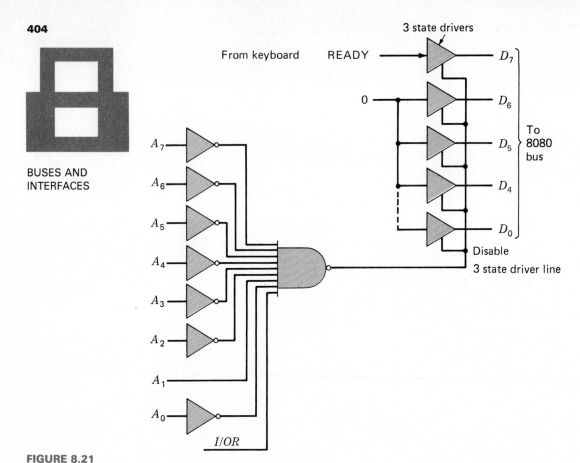

BUSES AND
INTERFACES

FIGURE 8.21

Keyboard status word
generator.

The operation of the keyboard status word interface is shown in Fig. 8.21. When a key is depressed, the READY flip-flop is set to a 1, as shown in Fig. 7.19. Therefore when the $\overline{I/O\ R}$ is made a 0, indicating a device read, and the device number on A_7 to A_0 is 00000010, the NAND gate output in Fig. 8.21 goes to a 0, enabling the tristate devices so that a 10000000 is placed on D_7 to D_0, indicating that the keyboard is ready to be read.

When the keyboard is read, the READY flip-flop is cleared (reset) by the signal generated in Fig. 8.20. Therefore, if keyboard status words are read in the interval between when the keyboard has been read and when a key is depressed, the output on D_7 to D_0 will be all 0s.

The described use of a status register in the interface circuitry to give the status of an input-output device to the CPU is the most widely used technique for interfacing of this sort. In more complicated input-output devices, such as disk memories, there are more status bits in the status word which have a meaning, and these bits are set and reset by the processor and disk controller as operations are sequenced.

*8.6[15] The interface design for the keyboard is intended to be under program control. Thus a section of the program in the microprocessor will examine the keyboard status register to see whether the keyboard has data, if it does, data are read from the keyboard.

Table 8.1 shows a section of program for the 8080 microprocessor which will read from a keyboard. The 8080 system has an 8-bit *byte* at each address in memory. Each OP (operation) code, which tells what the instruction is to do, is a single byte in memory. There is an IN instruction with OP code 11011011 (binary), which tells the microprocessor to read from an input-output device. The number of the device (device code) immediately follows the IN instruction's OP code in the next byte.

In Table 8.1 the presentation of the program listing is arranged as follows. The program in assembly language is to the right. The program as actually stored is in the two left columns, which lists addresses in memory followed by the contents of each address in hexadecimal. The Label column lists names for locations in the memory, enabling programs to use names in memory instead of actual numeric addresses.

For example, this program starts at location 030 in memory. At this location is the value DB, the OP code for the IN instruction. The comments (to the right) are always preceded by a slash; the assembler ignores these comments.

The location 030 in memory is given the name KEYSTAT in the Label column.

In location 031 there is the device number 2; therefore, the microprocessor will read location 030, find the IN instruction OP code, and read location 031, finding in it the device number 2. The microprocessor will then place the value 2 on the address lines and issue an input-output device read sequence on the bus.

This will result in the status register interface placing 00000000 on the data lines if there is no character to be read from the keyboard and placing 10000000

---

[15]Sections with asterisks can be omitted without loss of continuity.

TABLE 8.1

LOCATION IN MEMORY	CONTENTS	ASSEMBLY LANGUAGE			
		LABEL	OP CODE	OPERAND	COMMENTS
030	DB	KEYSTAT	IN	2	/READ STATUS WORD
031	02				/INTO ACCUMULATOR
032	E6		ANI	80H	/AND ACCUMULATOR BITS
033	80				
034	CA		JZ	KEYSTAT	/JUMP BACK IF ZERO
035	30				
036	00				
037	DB		IN	1	/READ KEYBOARD
038	01				

if there is a character. This value will be read by the microprocessor into its accumulator, completing the instruction.

The next instruction is an ANI instruction with OP code E6. The ANI instruction performs a bit-by-bit AND of the byte following the instruction, in this case 10000000 (binary), with the accumulator. If the keyboard is ready to be read, this will result in a 1 in the leftmost position; if not, a 0.

The ANI instruction also sets a flip-flop called Z (for zero) in the 8080 to a 1 if the results of the AND contain a 1 and a 0 if not. Therefore, if a character is ready to be read, Z will contain a 1; if not, it will contain a 0.

The JZ is the OP code for a "jump-on-zero" instruction in the 8080. If the Z flip-flop is a 0, the microprocessor will take its next instruction word from the address given in the bytes[16] following the JZ; if Z is a 1, the instruction following these 2 bytes will be executed. As a result, if a character is ready to be read, the microprocessor will read the IN instruction 037 next; if no character is ready, the microprocessor will jump back to location 030. Notice that the programmer has used the label KEYSTAT instead of giving the numeric value in the address part of the instruction, but the actual address appears in the Contents column. (The assembler determined the location.) Also, note that a complete address in the 8080 requires 2 bytes (2^{16} words can be used in memory). The lower-order (least significant) bits come first in an instruction word, followed by the higher-order bits.

When the keyboard is to be read, the instruction word beginning at location 037 will be executed. This is an IN instruction, but the device number is 1, so the keyboard itself will be read from.

When the instruction is executed, the 8080 will place the device number 1 on its address lines and then generate a device read sequence of control signals. As a result, the keyboard interface will place the character in the keyboard buffer register on the data lines, and this character will be read into the 8080 accumulator, ending the read process.

INTERFACING A PRINTER

8.7 The preceding sections have detailed the reading of data from a keyboard into a microprocessor (CPU). We now examine outputting characters from a microprocessor into a printer.

We assume that the printer uses an ASCII character in 8-bit parallel form to cause the printing of a single character. In 8080 interfacing, first the printer is selected. To do this, since different output devices may be connected to the microprocessor, the printer is given a unique device number, and we assume that the number is 3 (decimal). When the printer is selected, this number will appear on the microprocessor address lines A_7 to A_0 in binary.

Figure 8.22 shows an interface design. A NAND gate and six inverters are connected so that the NAND gate will have a 0 output only when the number 3 appears on A_7 to A_0 and $\overline{\text{I/O W}}$ is a 0. This NAND gate's output is used as a GO signal, which ultimately causes the printer to print the character on data lines D_7 to D_0. The $\overline{\text{I/O W}}$ signal is pulled negative (to a 0) when the character to be printed

---

[16]The 8080 system address has 2^{16} words of memory; thus 2 bytes are required for a complete address.

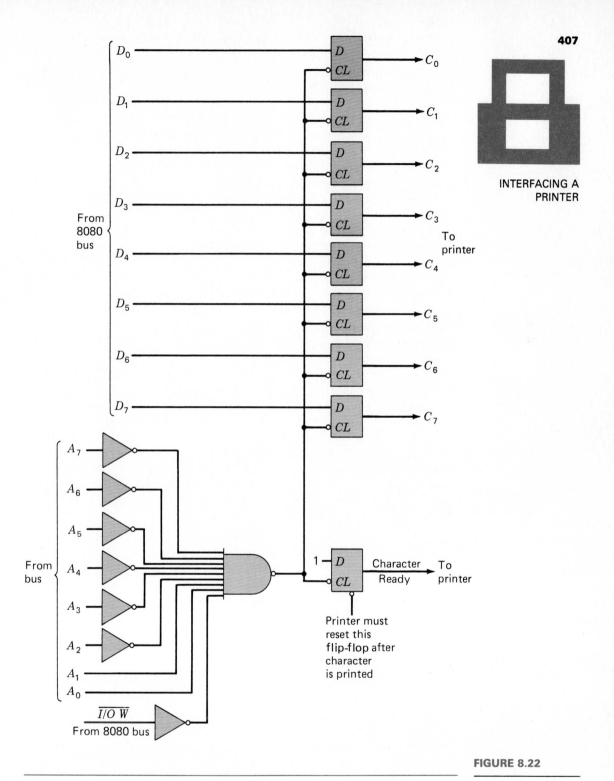

INTERFACING A
PRINTER

FIGURE 8.22

Interfacing a printer.

is available on D_0 to D_7 and the device address (3 in this case) is on lines A_7 to A_0.

A flip-flop called *character ready* is used to signal the printer that a character is ready to be printed. The printer must read this flip-flop and then print the character.

The program instruction which causes this character transfer in the 8080 is called an OUT instruction. The OUT instruction occupies two 8-bit bytes in memory, with the second byte containing the device number. When the OUT instruction is executed, the contents of the accumulator are placed on D_0 to D_7. Execution of the OUT instruction causes the printer to print a character corresponding to whatever code was stored in the accumulator.

The above implies that the computer program in the 8080 memory has previously stored the ASCII character for the character to be printed in the accumulator. (A load-accumulator instruction, described in Chap. 10, will effect this. For now we restrict our discussion to the interface strategy.)

There is a basic problem with the above scheme. A printer is a very slow electromechanical device, and the microprocessor, because of its high speed, is capable of flooding the printer with characters which it cannot possibly print. An attempt to print only after a pause between each character will be difficult to implement because the printer may require different time intervals to respond to different characters.

There are two basic solutions to this problem. One is to have the microprocessor examine the printer at regular intervals to see when a new character can be printed. If the printer can print, it "raises a flag" (turns on a flip-flop) which the microcomputer reads. If the flag is a 1, the microcomputer outputs a character to be printed; if the flag is a 0, the microcomputer goes back to what it was doing and then examines the printer again at a later time. (The computer may simply continue to examine the flag until it goes on.)

The other solution is to have the printer signal the computer with an INTERRUPT line whenever it is able to print. The computer then services this interrupt by feeding the printer a character.

We use the first technique in our example and explain interrupts in the following section.

All that is required to respond to a query from the 8080 microprocessor is shown in Fig. 8.23. When the printer is clear and able to handle a character, it sets the flag flip-flop on. The flag is then made a bit in a status register of 8 bits.

The program step to read the flag involves transferring an entire 8-bit character placed on the data lines from the status registers into the accumulator. The status register is given device number 4. When an IN instruction with device number 4 is executed by the microprocessor, the number 4 comes up on A_7 to A_0, and finally the $\overline{\text{I/O R}}$ line is brought low. This causes the transfer of the flag and its associated 0s into the microprocessor accumulator. Another instruction must then examine the accumulator to see whether it is all 0s or contains a 1. If the accumulator sign bit is a 1, the printer is ready for a character; if not, the computer must wait.

The above interfacing technique is widely used because of its simplicity of implementation. Using a flag (or several flags) to determine an output device's status, placing the flag(s) in a status register, and then reading the status register using a program are a standard computer interface technique.

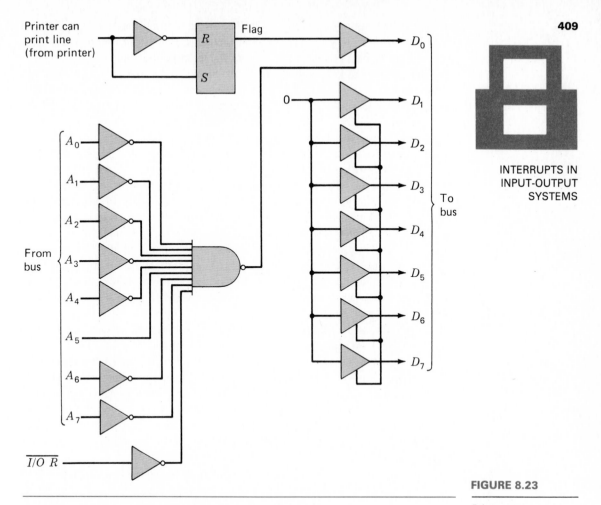

FIGURE 8.23

Printer status generator.

INTERRUPTS IN INPUT-OUTPUT SYSTEMS

8.8   The preceding examples showing how to interface a keyboard and a printer demonstrated a technique in which the program was used to examine flags in status registers to see whether an input-output device either had information or could accept information. This technique is widely used, particularly in microcomputer and minicomputer systems where not too many external devices are to be interfaced and sufficient time is available that the program can continually test the devices to see whether they are ready. Stepping from status register to status register by using a program to see which device is ready is called *polling* the I/O devices.

In many cases, however, there will be too many devices for this scheme to be successful. Or there will be a great amount of computation to be performed, so that continually taking time out to examine the status of input-output devices cannot be tolerated.

To deal with this problem, computers have *interrupt systems* for input-output devices, in which a given device can cause the program operation to be interrupted long enough for the input-output device to be serviced.

The operation of such a system can best be shown by an example. Suppose

that we have a computer system with a keyboard, a printer, and an input from an A-to-D converter (ADC) measuring temperature in a physics experiment. A great deal of computation is required to process the temperature reading from the ADC. The operator of the keyboard examines the results of the computation, which are printed on the printer, and occasionally the operator comments, using the keyboard. These comments are to be printed by the printer along with the temperature and the results of the calculation.

In this case the keyboard inputs are made infrequently, the printer is kept quite busy, and we assume that the A-to-D inputs are read at fairly frequent intervals.

The interrupt system works as follows. The computer normally is processing the inputs from the ADC. Each time a key on the keyboard is depressed, however, an interrupt signal is generated by the keyboard, the program in operation is interrupted, the keyboard is serviced, and the program which was interrupted is returned to. Similarly, a short list of characters to be printed may be stored in the computer, and the program adds to this list as it gathers results. Whenever the printer can print, it generates an interrupt, current program operation is interrupted long enough to service the printer by giving it another character to print, and the original program operation then continues at the point at which it had been interrupted.

The ADC will also generate interrupts which must be serviced by reading the output, and the readings are processed as soon as time is available.

To effect the above, there are some features an interrupt system should have. For instance, it may be necessary to turn off the interrupt feature of the printer, since when there is nothing to print, the printer would simply generate many time-consuming interrupts. (It can always print when there is nothing to print.) It might be necessary to turn off the entire interrupt system for a short time, since during servicing of the keyboard, an interrupt from the printer might cause an interrupt of an interrupt.

In order to examine the interrupt feature more closely, we note that the following things must be done each time an interrupt is generated:

1　The state of the program in operation when the interrupt is executed must be saved. Then the program can be reentered when the interrupt servicing program is finished.

2　The device that generated the interrupts must be identified.

3　The CPU must jump to a section of the program that will service the interrupt.

4　When the interrupt has been serviced, the state of the program which was interrupted must be restored.

5　The original program's operation must be reinitiated at the point at which it was interrupted.

Discussion of how the interrupted program is handled and how returns are made to this program is deferred to Chap. 10 since more information is required about program execution. The mechanism for interrupt generation and identifying the device that wishes to be serviced can be dealt with here, however.

The interrupts are initiated by a device placing a 1 on an interrupt wire in the bus. This notifies the CPU that a device wishes to be serviced. The CPU then completes the instruction it is executing and transfers control to a section of program designed to service the interrupt.

In the 6800 microprocessor and in the 6150, for example, the various devices are polled by examining the status registers, each in turn, until the interrupting device is located. This device is then serviced.

In the 8080 microcomputer and in the PDP-11 minicomputer, for example, the place in memory where the service program is located for the particular device that generated the interrupt is read into the CPU by the interrupting device. This is called a *vectored interrupt*. In effect, the device tells the CPU "who did it" and does not wait to be asked.

There can be a problem when several devices generate a 1 signal on the interrupt wire at the same time. If the devices are polled, the polling order determines who gets serviced first, and a device not serviced will continue to interrupt until it is serviced. For the vectored interrupt, however, if two devices attempted to write their identifier into the CPU at the same time, they might overwrite each other, so a scheme must be devised by which only one device tells the CPU whom to service. This is accomplished by chips[17] external to the CPU, which set a priority on the devices that can interrupt and handle only the highest priority device with its interrupt on.

More details on interrupts are given in the sections on particular computers in Chap. 10.

When microcomputer systems become larger and more peripheral devices are used, the interface design problem increases. To be efficient and use the microprocessor CPU chip to its utmost ability, it is necessary to use an interrupt system for peripheral devices so that the CPU is not burdened with polling peripherals continuously. To remove the load of servicing peripherals from the CPU, several microprocessor manufacturers produce separate chips that are I/O processors and that work closely with the CPU in handling peripheral servicing. Other important chips now produced to facilitate peripheral handling convert serial input signals (like the ASCII signals in Fig. 7.21) to parallel and place the parallel form on the bus as well as converting from parallel to serial (to drive some printers and modems). Chips are also produced to aid in interrupt processing, including the selection of the highest-priority peripheral demanding service, etc.

Figure 8.24 shows a block design of a system based on the 8086 microprocessor chip.[18] (This system is similar to IBM's personal computer system which uses the 8088.) Examination of this layout reveals how chips are assembled to interface devices in larger systems.

Figure 8.24 shows the parts of the 8086 microprocessor: (1) An 8234 clock generator generates the clock signal for the 8086 and is involved in resets. (2) The 8081 I/O processor (IOP) handles interrupts for the 8086 (the 8086 can be interfaced without this chip, it simply takes some I/O processing load from the 8088).

---

[17]The IC packages used range from gate arrays which examine and allocate priority to programmable interface controllers which contain ROMs with programs for the specific interfaces to be implemented.

[18]Intel (and others) also make an 8086 microprocessor chip which would interface like this chip except that the 8086 handles data 16 bits at a time while the 8088 has 8-bit data paths, and so a 16-bit data bus would be used for the 8086.

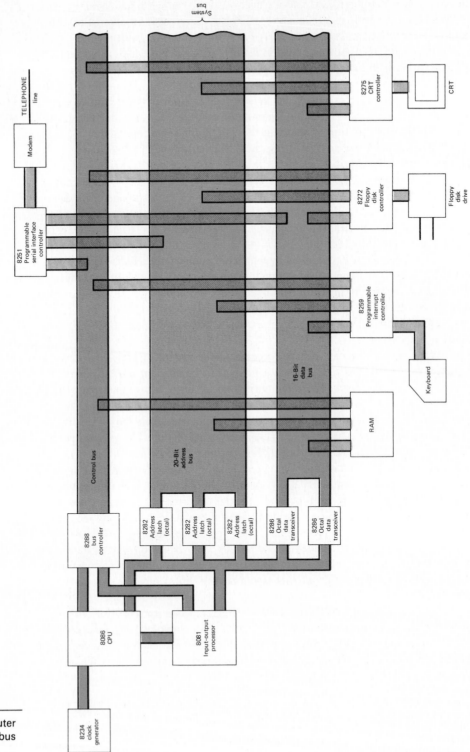

FIGURE 8.24

8086 microcomputer
system showing bus
layout.

(3) The 8288 bus controller buffers control signals and handles the time multiplexing of the control signals (the 8086 uses the same lines for address lines and control lines, producing control signals to tell which is being output at a given time). (4) The 8282 latches simply hold the address information and provide tristate drivers for the bus. This is necessary for two reasons: First, the 8086 outputs are not capable of driving many other circuits; second, the 8086 time-multiplexes its address signals, and the latches are used to hold the address while control signals are output on the same lines. (5) The 8286 transceivers simply provide tristate drivers and considerable drive capability for the data bus and receivers to read from the Data bus. (6) The 8259 is a programmable interrupt handler which examines demands for service from the peripherals, determines the highest-priority demand, and then interrupts the 8086-8089 combination and outputs a "vector" telling which peripheral requires service. (7) The 8259 programmable parallel interface controller handles keyboard interrupts. The term *programmable* means that the input-output configuration and data-handling functions of the chip are set up by means of data transfers from the 8086 under program control. (8) The 8251 programmable serial interface controller is used to handle serial data and to provide control signals for modems. This chip is programmable and such parameters as (*a*) the number of stop bits in a character transmission (refer to Fig. 7.21, the RS.232C interface it supports), (*b*) the speed of transmission and reception (controlled by a clock and a divide action), (*c*) whether parity is odd or even, etc., are all controlled by a register in the 8251 which is loaded from a program over the data lines by the 8086. (9) The floppy disk and CRT controllers are special interface chips made to service particular devices.

A STANDARD BUS
INTERFACE

A STANDARD BUS INTERFACE

8.9 There has been some attempt to standardize on buses, particularly by such organizations as the IEEE and the National Bureau of Standards. Most buses which have become standards have been developed by computer and electronic concerns and have been used and adopted by several manufacturers before the standards organization have developed an official document.

Note that these bus standards do not simply have pin connections and line operation procedures, but also specify connectors and printed-circuit board sizes. Thus a system built around one of the buses can add printed-circuit boards containing more memory, interfacing for I/O devices, etc., as long as the board and bus operation for the board meet the standard specifications. So when the organization in Fig. 7.20 is used, the connectors, and boards, and interfaces are all prescribed by the standard.

A widely used bus and its protocol, which has been developed for interfacing instruments and microcomputers, are briefly outlined here. This bus, often called the *general-purpose interface bus* (GPIB), is described in IEEE Standard 488-1978, which is a microcomputer bus standard.

Figure 8.25 shows the basic interface and bus lines which can be used to interconnect a number of modules. Each bus line performs at least one interface function, depending on the interface capabilities. The specifications for cable construction and connectors are given in the standard.

**BUSES AND
INTERFACES**

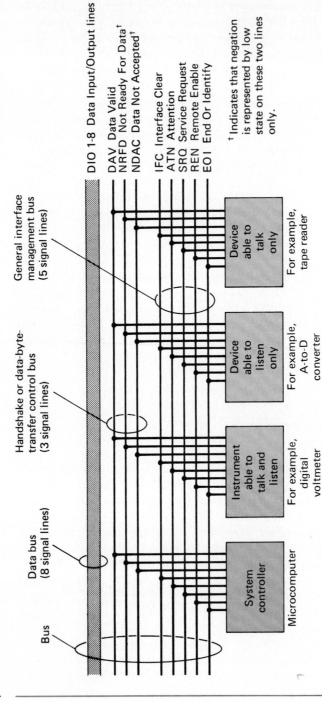

FIGURE 8.25

International standard
bus.

At a given time, any particular module connected to the bus may be idle, monitoring the activity on the bus or functioning as (1) a talker, (2) a listener, or (3) a controller. As a talker, a module sends data over the bus to a listener (or listeners). As a listener, a module receives such data. As a controller, it directs the flow of data on the bus, mainly by designating which modules are to send data and which are to receive data.

Notice that the bus consists of 16 signal lines, grouped functionally into three component buses. The *data bus* (eight lines) is used to transfer data in parallel from talkers to listeners; it also transfers certain commands from the controller to subordinate modules. The *transfer bus* (three lines) is used for the handshaking process by which a talker or controller can synchronize its readiness to receive data. The *general interface management bus* (five lines), as its name suggests, is used principally by the controller.

Each system must have one module to designate listeners and talkers, and this module is called a *controller*. The controller uses a group of commands, referred to as *interface messages,* to direct the other modules on the bus in carrying out their functions of talking and listening.

Normally the controller would be the CPU of a computer, and this unit would generate the command signals on the bus to the other modules, which would then respond. Because this interface is designed to handle a large number of different types of modules, the specification is reasonably complicated and general. The basic procedure for generating a transfer of data on this bus is as follows. First, the controller designates a listener by placing the listener's address (each listener is given a 5-bit address) on the data bus and raising the appropriate control lines. Then a talker is designated by placing the talker's address on the data lines and raising the appropriate control lines. Finally, the talker and listener are told to proceed, and the talker places data, 8 bits at a time, in parallel on the data lines.

In the transfer of data from talker to listener, certain basic problems arise in the operation of every bus.[19] These problems are solved by a handshaking procedure whereby talker and listener interact using the control lines. It is convenient to describe this procedure with a flowchart, as shown in Fig. 8.26. This diagram shows that three control lines, called DAV, NRFD, and NDAC (defined in Fig. 8.25), are used to control each data byte transfer. The talkers and receivers each raise and lower the control signals, as shown by the flowchart, and the talker places data on the data bus at the appropriate time.

The necessary control circuitry to implement this handshaking and the other required functions must be provided by each module's interface circuitry. It is possible to design a line of input-output equipment including instruments, tape punches, etc., and to interface each to the same bus by using the interface specification. IC manufacturers often furnish single chips made to provide the necessary logic for an interface.

---

[19]These problems concern how the listener knows when data are on the bus and how the talker knows when the listener has received the data. The bus described here is an *asynchronous bus.* Microprocessors and minicomputers often use synchronous buses where one wire in the bus contains a clock and the clock signal is used to time data transfers. In these systems, the talker must place the data on the data wires, and the listener must be ready to receive data when the clock edge arrives. A synchronous system is faster and simpler but less flexible.

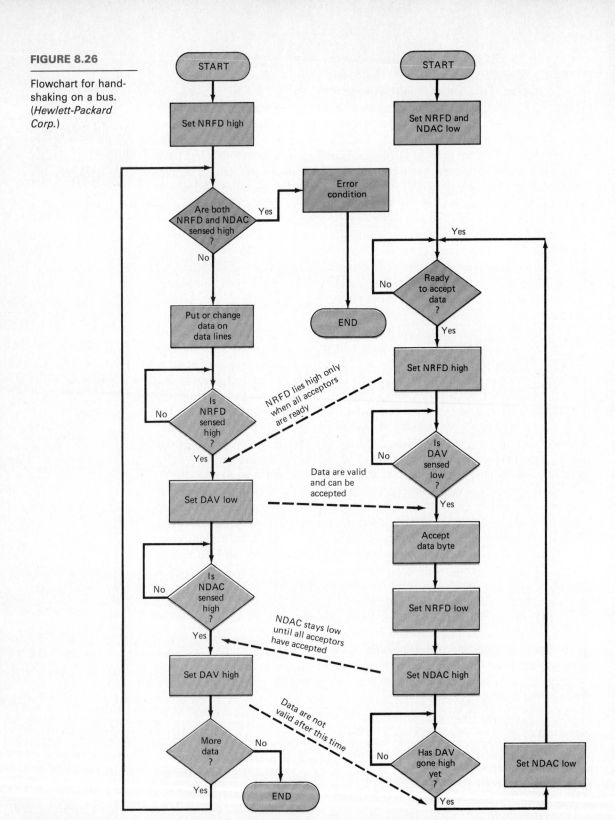

FIGURE 8.26

Flowchart for hand-shaking on a bus. (*Hewlett-Packard Corp.*)

START

Set NRFD high

Are both NRFD and NDAC sensed high ? — Yes → Error condition → END

No

Put or change data on data lines

Is NRFD sensed high ? — No (loop back)

Yes

NRFD lies high only when all acceptors are ready

Set DAV low

Data are valid and can be accepted

Is NDAC sensed high ? — No (loop back)

Yes

NDAC stays low until all acceptors have accepted

Set DAV high

Data are not valid after this time

More data ? — No → END

Yes

START

Set NRFD and NDAC low

Ready to accept data ? — No (loop back)

Yes

Set NRFD high

Is DAV sensed low ? — No (loop back)

Yes

Accept data byte

Set NRFD low

Set NDAC high

Has DAV gone high yet ? — No (loop back)

Yes → Set NDAC low

The DAV line is controlled by the talker, NRFD and NDAC by the listeners.

Even connector types and electrical loading and driving rules are called out so that circuit designers can proceed with the necessary details. Minicomputer and microcomputer manufacturers also provide bus specifications for the buses they use so that peripheral manufacturers can comply with their interface specifications and purchasers of these computers can design their own equipment when necessary. Large computer manufacturers provide similar specifications for their buses and other interfaces.

The bus shown is adequate for most instrument computer purposes. A higher-speed bus could be designed by adding more control lines and address lines in parallel with the data lines; many computers have buses with 50 or more lines.

SUMMARY

8.10 The interfacing of I/O devices to a computer is an important subject. Small and large computers use different strategies with large computers often having separate I/O processors to relieve the CPU from the pressure of I/O operations.

Buses are widely used to interconnect both memories and I/O devices to a CPU. The three basic ways of sharing a line on a bus were shown, followed by an explanation of synchronous and asynchronous bus operations. Examples of bus operations for several microcomputers were presented.

A design for an interface to a keyboard for a microcomputer bus was shown and its operation described. A typical program section to interact with the keyboard was presented and explained. The need for and use of status registers were explained, and examples were given.

Interrupt strategies make it possible to reduce the time spent by the CPU in servicing I/O devices. An overview of this area was presented (more is said on this subject in Chap. 10).

There are several "standard" bus designs in existence, and these were noted. A particular bus, the IEEE Standard 488 general-purpose interface bus, which is widely used to interface instruments to a CPU, was described.

QUESTIONS

8.1 Discuss the extra complexity of interface logic for a disk drive if DMA is used instead of the CPU to handle each data transfer.

8.2 How would you convert a three-state driver with a DISABLE input to one with an ENABLE input?

8.3 Discuss the problems that might be encountered when several devices connected to the same bus can each become the bus master for a time.

8.4 If the high-speed memory for a microcomputer were assembled from a collection of IC memories including 100-, 200-, and 500-ns memories, would a synchronous or an asynchronous data bus be better? Explain your reasoning.

8.5 Cite some advantages of memory-mapped I/O versus specific I/O instructions.

BUSES AND
INTERFACES

8.6 Explain how a keyboard with an 8-bit output would be interfaced to the 68000 bus.

8.7 Draw waveforms for the 68000 bus for an 8-bit transfer of data to a printer.

8.8 The 8086 configuration in Fig. 8.24 is fairly complex. Discuss the benefits of such a configuration for a personal computer, and contrast it with a microprocessor used as a traffic light controller or an automobile ignition control system.

8.9 Explain the handshake on an asynchronous bus.

8.10 Design an interface for a 256-word 8-bit memory using the chip in Fig. 6.10 for the bus timing in Fig. 8.14.

8.11 Design an interface for a 256-word 8-bit memory using the chip in Fig. 6.10 for the bus timing in Fig. 8.13.

8.12 In the status register scheme used to interface a microprocessor to a keyboard, only 1 bit is used to determine the status of the keyboard. A status register could have several status bits, however, each with a different meaning. Discuss the use of the AND instruction to test various bits in conjunction with the JUMP instruction for the 8080.

8.13 The single status bit used in the printer interface status register is set on and off by the printer. It could be controlled by the printer and the interface. Explain how the interface would work in this case.

8.14 In an interface such as a printer there is a question as to how the interface should notify the printer when the character to be printed is on the signal wires, and how long the signal should be held there. There are two approaches:

(1) The printer must read the information within a stipulated time. In this case signals with data are placed on the interface wires (the interface device address having already been placed there) and are always held for some fixed time which is acceptable to all the interface circuitry used.

(2) The device being read into notifies the interface when it has received the characters. In this case another interface wire is used, and a signal is placed on this wire by the device being read into when it has accepted the input data. This is a handshake procedure where the interface device address is placed on the wires, data are then placed on the wires, and a wire to the device is raised which says, ''The data are on the lines.'' The interface device then raises another wire, saying, ''The data have been accepted.''

IBM uses the first technique in its 3081 interfaces, whereas the IEEE (and several other standards organizations and computer manufacturers) use the handshaking technique. Discuss the advantages and disadvantages of each technique.

8.15 With the IEEE 488 interface it is possible to read into several devices at the same time. In this case the system controller places the data on the wires and then raises the wire, showing that the data are there. In responding, the devices accepting data use the *open-collector* circuit shown in Appendix C so that if any single device has not yet accepted the data, the response wire will be set to low.

Show how the open-collector circuit in Fig. C.5(*a*) ANDs and can only indicate acceptance of data by moving the line to 1.

8.16 Show how the circuitry in Fig. 8.20 can be modified to interface a keyboard with address 6 (device number 6).

8.17 Show how the program in Table 8.1 would be modified to service a keyboard with device number 8 and status register number 7.

8.18 Write a sequence of instructions which will read a keyboard and then print the characters read on a printer. Give the keyboard device number 5 and the printer device number 7. Number the status registers as you please.

8.19 Design an interface that will accept serial bit strings using ASCII and the teletypewriter serial format shown in Fig. 7.21. The interface should buffer this bit string of characters into the 8080 microprocessor.

8.20 Design an interface that will take a parallel data byte from an 8080 microprocessor bus and convert it to serial for a teletypewriter.

8.21 Explain handshaking on a bus when data are transferred from a sender to a receiver. How can this be used to prevent errors due to signal skew caused by signals on different wires arriving at different times (skewed) because of the differences in line length and characteristics and differences in delays through IC line drivers, etc.?

8.22 For the standard instrument interface, draw the signals DAV, NRFD, and NDAC for a data transfer from a talker to a listener. Assume that there are no problems in transferring data, and indicate who is raising and lowering each signal.

8.23 For the standard instrument interface, indicate how the controller selects a talker and a listener.

8.24 How is signal skew handled on the standard instrument interface?

8.25 Explain how peripheral devices interrupt a computer with a single bus organization.

8.26 Explain the meaning of *direct memory access* (DMA) and why it is desirable in some cases.

8.27 Can you think of any problems that might arise in multiprocessor systems?

8.28 If devices and status registers are numbered 1, 2, 4, 8, . . . and only a few are used (less than or equal to the number of address wires), the gate to determine which device is selected in an interface can be simplified (or omitted). Show why.

8.29 Show in flowchart form the procedure for testing and finding which switch is closed, if any, for the encoding scheme described in Question 7.43.

8.30 How many steps would it take to scan an entire keyboard for the ASCII given in Fig. 7.7, using the two-dimensional keyboard scheme?

8.31 When the encoding scheme in the preceding questions is used, if the switches bounce, that is, if a closure of the switch is not constant but goes on and off when

**BUSES AND
INTERFACES**

a key is depressed, this complicates the encoding. Explain some problems that might arise from contact bounce if the above technique is used.

8.32 How would you suggest smoothing the bounce from the contacts for the encoding scheme from Question 8.31

8.33 Draw an encoder matrix for three ASCII characters (not shown in the chapter) as in the section on keyboards.

8.34 The signal that strobes the values into the flip-flops which read from the encoder of Fig. 7.18 must be slightly delayed. Explain why.

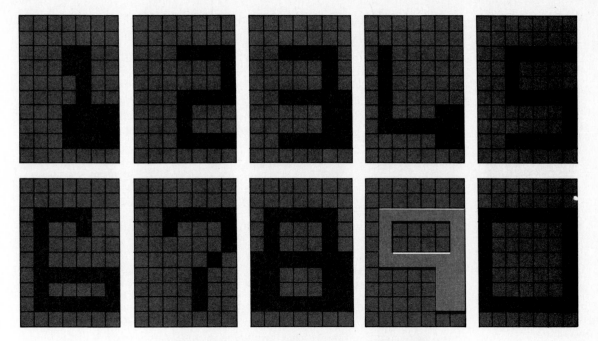

THE CONTROL UNIT

This chapter describes the control sections of digital computers. Preceding chapters illustrated techniques whereby arithmetic and logical operations may be performed and information read into and from various memory devices. To utilize the speeds and information handling capabilities of these techniques and devices, it is necessary to sequence automatically the various operations which occur at speeds compatible with those of the rest of the machine. The control element, therefore, must be constructed of high-speed circuitry. The basic elements used in the control element of a digital computer are described in Chaps. 3 and 4, and most of the concepts underlying the functioning of the control element are presented in Chaps. 3 through 5.

The *control unit* may be defined as "the parts that effect the retrieval of instructions in proper sequence, the interpretation of each instruction, and the application of the proper signals to the arithmetic unit and other parts in accordance with this interpretation."[1]

The function of the control circuitry in a general-purpose computer is to interpret the instruction words and then sequence the necessary signals to those sections of the computer that will cause it to perform the instructions. Previous chapters have shown how the application of the correct sequence of control signals to the logic circuitry in the arithmetic element enables the computer to perform arithmetic operations, and how binary words may be stored and later read from

---

[1]From *IEEE Standard Dictionary of Electrical and Electronics Terms,* IEEE Standard 100–1977, Institute of Electrical and Electronics Engineers, Inc.

several types of memory devices. For the computer to function, the operation of its sections must be directed, and the control circuitry performs that function.

This chapter first presents some introductory material concerning computer instruction-word execution. Two general-purpose computers are used as examples. Then a small general-purpose computer's control circuitry is described. The basic ideas in the design of control circuitry are presented in these sections. Register transfer concepts are emphasized. The final sections describe microprogrammed computer control concepts, giving the basic ideas used in this class of computers.

OBJECTIVES

1   Instruction word formats and instruction repertoires for two general-purpose binary computers are presented.

2   The design of the control section for a small computer is shown with a description of overall design procedures for large and small computers.

3   The use of register transfer language in designing and maintaining computers is presented. The control section designs in the chapter are based on this language and associated procedures. These are the most widely used techniques for digital computer system descriptions.

4   The control structure of a computer can be implemented by using a ROM, and then the computer is said to be microprogrammed. The subject is explained along with how register operations are sequenced when microprogramming is used.

CONSTRUCTION OF INSTRUCTION WORD

9.1   A computer word is an ordered set of characters handled as a group. Basically all words consist of a set of binary digits, and the meaning of the digits depends on several factors. For instance, the bits 01000100 could represent the decimal number 68 in a pure binary computer and the decimal number 44 in a BCD computer which uses an 8, 4, 2, 1 code. Thus the meaning of a set of digits is sometimes determined by its usage. In addition, other interpretations are possible, for instruction words are stored just as are data words, and the digits could represent an instruction to the computer. Since memory locations can store either instruction words or data words, the programmers and system operators must see that the instruction words are used to determine the sequence of operations which the computer performs, and that reasonable meanings are assigned to the data words.

If we assume that each memory location can contain a single instruction word, then a computer will start with the word stored in some specified address, interpret the contents of this location as an instruction, and then continue taking instruction words from the memory locations in order, unless a HALT or BRANCH instruction is encountered. The data to be used in the calculations will be stored in another part of the memory. Since the computer can store either instructions or data in the same memory addresses, considerable flexibility of operation results.

An instruction word in a digital machine generally consists of several sections. The number of divisions in the word depends on the type of computer. Because of its wide usage and simplicity, we describe what are called *single-address instruction words* in this and the following sections, leaving more complicated formats for later. The single-address instruction word is widely used in microcomputers and minicomputers, as well as in many of the larger computers; it serves as a good basis for introducing control unit operations. Basically each single-address instruction word contains two sections: the *operation code* (OP code), which defines the instruction to be performed, such as addition, subtraction, etc.; and the *address part*, which contains the location of the number to be added or subtracted or otherwise used (the operand).

As an example, we now examine the Harris 6100 microprocessor. This microprocessor IC chip is used in the DEC word processors, one of their personal computers, and several other items including disk drive controllers, printer controllers, etc. The instruction word format, instruction repertoire, and general architecture originated in the DEC PDP-8 series, which was DEC's first "big winner" in the minicomputer area and the largest-selling minicomputer for some years. The Harris 6100 is widely used in DEC products, among others, and is generally available.

The 6100 has a basic memory word and instruction word of 12 bits.[2] The instruction word comprises two sections, an OP-code part and an address part, as shown in Fig. 9.1(*a*). There are only 3 bits in the OP-code part, and so only eight basic instruction types are possible. In this section we describe only three of these, leaving the remainder for Chap. 10. The instructions we study are the TAD (2s complement add), the DCA (deposit and clear), and the JMP (jump) instructions.

The TAD instruction [Fig. 9.1(*b*)] has an OP code of 001 (in binary). It tells the computer to add the number located in memory at the address given in the address part of the instruction to the number currently in the accumulator and to place the sum in the accumulator. Thus if the address part of the instruction were 000100110, this would reference the number at address 38 (decimal) in memory. The computer instruction word that will cause the 12-bit number at address 38 (decimal) memory to be added to the number in the accumulator will be 001000100110. Words are generally written in octal in the 6100, and this word would be 1046 in octal.

The DCA instruction has OP code 011 in binary. This instruction tells the CPU to deposit or store the present contents of the accumulator at the address given by the address part of the instruction. Thus the instruction word 011000001101 tells the CPU to store the current contents of the accumulator at location 13 in the memory. The DCA instruction also clears the accumulator to all 0s.

Let us now examine two program steps, a DCA followed by a TAD. Let these two instruction words be at memory locations 41 and 42 (octal). Let the DCA refer to location 50 (octal) and the TAD to location 51. The arrangement is as follows:

---

[2]This is a good size for a word processor because a character plus underscore, overbar, and other options in word processors can be stored in the 12 bits at each location.

THE CONTROL UNIT

```
 11 10  9  8  7  6  5  4  3  2  1  0
┌──────┬──────────────────────────┐
│  OP  │        Address           │
│ code │         part             │
└──────┴──────────────────────────┘
```
(a)

```
┌──────┬──────────────────────────┐
│ 001  │        Address           │
│      │         part             │
└──────┴──────────────────────────┘
```
OP code for
TAD instruction
is 001

001000000111 Example: This instruction
word tells computer to
add word at location 7
in memory into
the accumulator

(b)

```
┌──────┬──────────────────────────┐
│ 011  │        Address           │
│      │         part             │
└──────┴──────────────────────────┘
```
OP code for DCA
instruction is 011

011000001101 Example: This instruction
word tells computer to
deposit the contents of
the accumulator at
the address in memory
given in the address
section which is 13_{10}

(c)

FIGURE 9.1

6100 instruction
words. (a) Instruction
word format. (b) TAD
instruction format.
(c) DCA instruction
format.

LOCATION IN MEMORY (OCTAL)	MEMORY CONTENTS (OCTAL)	MEMORY CONTENTS (BINARY)
--	----	------------
41	3050	011000101000
42	1051	001000101001
--	----	------------
50	0222	000010010010
51	0243	000010100011

We now analyze the action of the computer as it executes these two instructions. Suppose that the accumulator contains 0102 (octal) when the instruction at 41 is executed. Then the value 0102 will be deposited (stored) at location 50, overwriting or destroying the value 0222 which was in location 50. The accumulator will be cleared to all 0s.

Next, the instruction at location 42 in memory will be executed. This instruction will add the value at location 51, which is 0243 (octal), to the current value in the accumulator.

Therefore, when execution is begun on the instruction word at location 43 (not shown), the accumulator will contain 0243, and the contents of memory location 50 will be 0102.

TABLE 9.1			SECTION OF 6100 PROGRAM		
ADDRESS IN MEMORY (OCTAL)	CONTENTS (OCTAL)	ASSEMBLY LANGUAGE			
		LABEL	OP CODE	ADDRESS	COMMENTS
0041	3051		DCA	LOC1	/CLEARS ACC
0042	1052		TAD	LOC2	/LOADS 0200
0043	1053		TAD	LOC3	/ADDS 212
0044	3054		DCA	LOC4	/STORES AT 54
0045	5071		JMP	71	/GO TO 71
. . .	. . .		. . .		
0051	0600	LOC1	0600		
0052	0200	LOC2	0200		
0053	0212	LOC3	0212		
0054	0310	LOC4	0310		

INSTRUCTION CYCLE
AND EXECUTION
CYCLE
ORGANIZATION OF
CONTROL
REGISTERS

Another instruction in the 6100's repertoire is the JMP instruction with OP code 101. This instruction causes a jump in memory to the address (location) given in the address part of the instruction word. For example, suppose the value at location 71 (octal) in memory is 101001000011 (binary) or 5103 (octal). When the CPU reads this as the instruction word JMP 0103, it will cause the next instruction to be taken from location 103 in memory and not from location 72.

Table 9.1 shows the three instructions so far introduced, combined into a five-instruction-word section of program. Assembly language and octal values are both shown in this table.

The operation of these instructions by a CPU would be as follows. When location 41 is read, the DCA instruction stores the current contents of the accumulator, which is then cleared to 0s. The next instruction word is TAD LOC2, which causes the number 0200 at location 52 to be added to the accumulator, giving 0200 in the accumulator.

When the TAD LOC3 instruction is read, it causes the number 0212 at location 53 in memory to be added to the number 0200 in the accumulator, giving 0412 in the accumulator. The CPU then executes the instruction DCA LOC4, causing the value in the accumulator, which is 0412, to be stored at address 54 in the memory. The CPU then reads the JMP 71 instruction, causing it to fetch the next instruction word from location 71 in the memory (and not from location 46).

After this section of the code has been executed, the sum of the numbers at locations 52 and 53 is stored in location 54, and the CPU jumps to location 71 in memory.

The 6100 has several addressing features which are discussed in the next chapter. Also, because of the short OP code (3 bits), several of the other instructions are very clever (and somewhat tricky). More details of this also are given in Chap. 10.

INSTRUCTION CYCLE AND EXECUTION CYCLE
ORGANIZATION OF CONTROL REGISTERS

9.2 A digital computer proceeds through the execution of a program with a basic rhythm or pattern in its sequence of operation which is produced by the necessity of drawing both instructions and operands from the same memory.

THE CONTROL UNIT

The basic sequence of operations for most instructions in a digital computer of the single-address type consists of an alternation of a time period called the *instruction cycle* and a period called the *execution cycle*. During the instruction cycle, an instruction word is obtained from the memory and interpreted, and the memory is given the address of the operand to be used. During the execution cycle, the memory obtains the operand to be used (for instance, the multiplier if the instruction is a multiplication or the augend if the instruction is an addition), and then the operation called for by the instruction word is performed upon this operand.

Most computers now being made use an IC memory for the storing of both instruction words and operands or data. The cycle time for the memory is fixed. Once we tell the memory that we wish to read from it or write into it, a certain time will elapse before we can instruct the memory that we are again ready to read or write. If we are reading from the memory, the selected word will be delivered a short time after the memory has been given the address of the word to be read and has been instructed to read.

If the memory is to be written into, the word to be written as well as the address at which we wish to write it must be given to the memory. A WRITE signal also must be given to write this word at the location or address which we have given. As discussed in Chap. 6, the address which we write into or read from in the memory will be put into a *memory address register* and the word to be written into the memory put into the *memory buffer register*. When we read from the memory, the word read from the memory is delivered to the memory buffer register.

During each instruction cycle, the instruction word is transferred by the memory into the memory buffer register. To obtain this word, we must tell the memory to read and give the memory the address to read from. During the instruction cycle, the instruction word which was read into the memory buffer register is interpreted, and the address of the operand to be used is delivered to the memory address register. For many instructions this will be the address part of the instruction word which was read from the memory during the instruction cycle. During the execution time or execution cycle, an operand is obtained from or written into the memory, depending on the instruction word which was interpreted during the previous instruction time period.

For example, if the instruction being interpreted is an ADD instruction, the location of the augend is given in the address part of the instruction word, and this address must be given the memory address register. The memory then obtains the desired word and puts it into the memory buffer register. The computer must add this word to the word already in the accumulator. Afterward the computer must give to the memory the address of the next instruction word to be used and command the memory to read this word.

Note that the machine alternates between instruction cycles and execution cycles. Also note that during an execution cycle we must store somewhere in our control circuitry the OP code of the instruction word which was read from the memory, the address of the operand to be used (which was a part of the instruction word read from the memory), and the address of the next instruction word to be read from the memory and used.

As a result, there are several registers which are basic to almost every digital computer. These are shown in Fig. 9.2 and are described as follows:

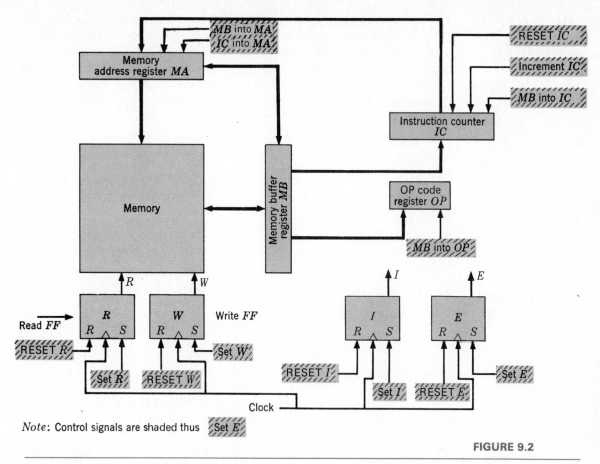

FIGURE 9.2

Control registers.

1 *Instruction counter*[3] This counter is the same length as the address section of the instruction word. The counter can be either reset or incremented. A typical logic diagram for the instruction counter could consist of the counter shown in Fig. 4.14(*a*), having a RESET line and an INCREMENT or ENABLE line. This counter keeps track of the instructions to be used in the program, so that normally, during each instruction time, the counter is incremented by 1, which will give the location of the next instruction word to be used in the program. If, however, the instruction is a BRANCH or JUMP instruction, we may wish to place part of the *B* register's contents into this counter, and the MB INTO IC line does this. The counter can be reset to 0 when a program is started.[4]

It must also be possible to transfer the contents of this counter into the memory address register, which is used to locate a word in memory. Normally the instruction counter is increased by 1 during the performance of each instruction, and the contents of the counter are transferred into the memory address register at the beginning of each instruction time.

---

[3]In some computers the instruction counter is called the *program counter*.
[4]Most computers make it possible to load a selected address into the operation counter and thereby start the machine at that selected address.

2   *OP-code register*   When an instruction word is read from the memory, the OP-code section of this word must be stored in order to determine what instruction is to be performed. If the computer has an OP code with a length of five binary digits, the operation register will be five binary digits in length and will contain the OP-code part of the instruction word which is read from the memory. Therefore we must be able to transfer a section of the memory buffer register into the OP-code register during the instruction time period.

3   *Memory address register*   This register contains the location of the word in memory to be read or the location to be written into.

4   *R flip-flop*   When this flip-flop is turned on, it tells the memory to read a word. (The flip-flop can be turned off shortly afterward, for it need not be on during the entire memory cycle.)

5   *W flip-flop*   Turning on this flip-flop tells the memory to write the word located in the memory buffer register at the location given by the memory address register.

6   *I flip-flop*   When this flip-flop is on, the computer is in an instruction cycle.

7   *E flip-flop*   The computer is in an execution cycle when this flip-flop is on.

SEQUENCE OF OPERATION OF CONTROL REGISTERS

9.3   Let us consider further the construction of the control circuitry of a digital computer, again using the block diagram of the control registers, memory, memory address register, and memory buffer register shown in Fig. 9.2.

The control signals necessary to the operation of this small single-address computer are shown on the diagram and are as follows. There is a RESET IC line which clears the instruction counter to 0. (This is often connected to a pushbutton which clears the counter when the program is to be started.) There is an MB INTO IC control signal which causes the contents of the memory buffer register to be transferred into the instruction counter, and an INCREMENT IC control signal causes the instruction counter to be incremented by 1. Another control signal is MB INTO OP, which transfers the first five digits of the memory buffer register that contains the OP code of an instruction word into the five flip-flops in the operation register. The memory address register has two control signals. The IC INTO MA control signal causes the contents of the instruction counter to be transferred into the memory address register, and the MB INTO MA control signal causes the last 16 digits of the memory buffer register (which constitute the address part of an instruction word) to be transferred into the memory address register.

During each instruction cycle of the computer, we must turn on the READ flip-flop and at the same time (or earlier) transfer the contents of the instruction counter into the memory address register. The memory will now read an instruction word into the memory buffer register, after which time we can enable the MB INTO OP line, transferring the OP-code section of the instruction word into the OP-code register. The next actions that the computer will take are now dependent upon the contents of the OP-code register.

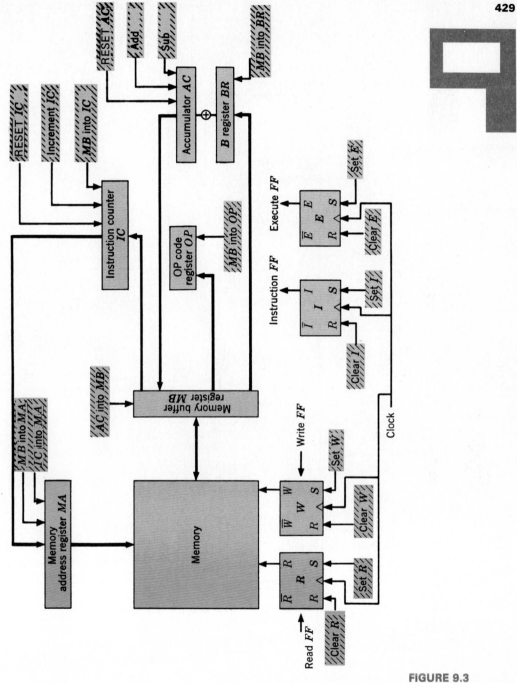

FIGURE 9.3

Control registers and arithmetic registers.

THE CONTROL UNIT

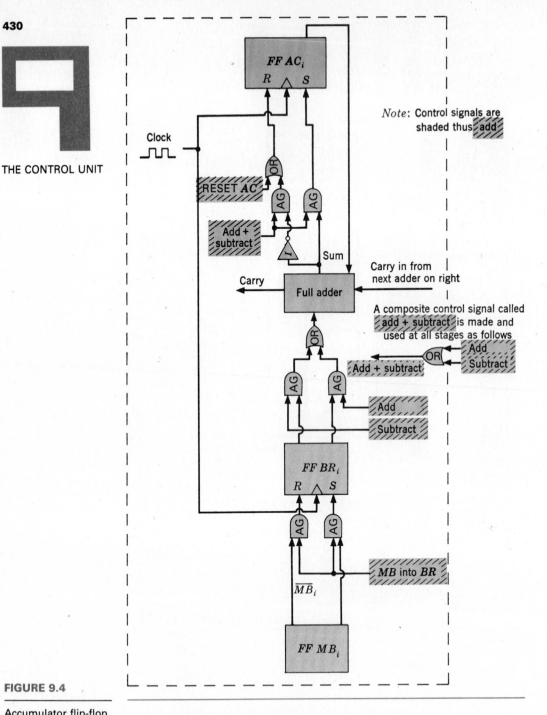

FIGURE 9.4

Accumulator flip-flop
and *B* register flip-
flop with control sig-
nals.

CONTROLLING ARITHMETIC OPERATIONS

9.4 Consider the problem of directing the arithmetic element as it performs an instruction word. Let us add an accumulator and a *B* register to the registers shown in Fig. 9.2, thus forming the block diagram shown in Fig. 9.3. Five more control signals are required to perform such instructions as ADD, SUBTRACT, CLEAR AND ADD, and STORE:

1 *RESET ACC*   This signal sets all the flip-flops in the accumulator to 0.

2 *ADD*   This signal causes the B register to be added to the accumulator and the sum transferred into the accumulator.

3 *SUBTRACT*   This signal causes the B register to be subtracted from the accumulator and the difference to be placed in the accumulator.

4 *MB INTO BR*   This signal transfers the memory buffer register into the B register.

5 *AC INTO MB*   This causes the contents of the accumulator to be transferred into the memory buffer register.

Figure 9.4 shows a single accumulator flip-flop and a single B register flip-flop, along with the control signals and gates required for these operations. The accumulator and B register are basically composed of as many of these blocks as there are bits in the basic computer word. (The carry into the least significant bit is connected to the SUBTRACT signal when 2s complement addition is used and to the carry-out of the sign digit when the 1s complement system is used.)

One further thing is needed. We must distribute our control signals in an orderly manner. Some sort of a time base, which will indicate where we are in the sequence of operations to be performed, is required. To do this, each memory cycle is broken into four equal time periods, the first of which we call T_0, the second T_1, the third T_2, and the fourth T_3. If we are in the first time period, we need a signal which will tell us that it is now time T_0; during the second period, we need a signal which will tell us that it is time T_1; etc.

Figure 9.5 shows a way of generating such timing signals. There is a clock signal input, and the clock is assumed to be running so that during a memory cycle

FIGURE 9.5

Timing-signal distributor.

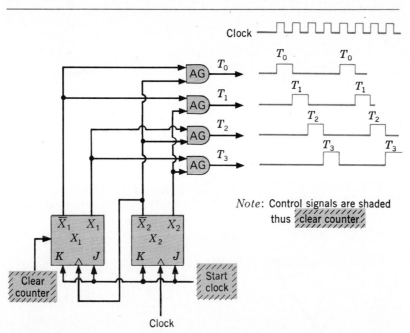

Note: Control signals are shaded thus ⁄clear counter⁄

THE CONTROL UNIT

TABLE 9.2   SEQUENCING OF CONTROL SIGNALS

INSTRUCTION	LIST OF CONTROL SIGNALS TO BE TURNED ON	COMMENTS
ADD		
I and T_0	SET R	Tells memory to read instruction word.
I and T_1	MB INTO OP, RESET R	Transfers OP-code part of instruction word into OP-code register; turns off READ flip-flop.
I and T_2	INCREMENT IC	Adds 1 to the instruction counter, preparing for the next instruction.
I and T_3	MB INTO MA, RESET I, SET E	Transfers the address part of the instruction word (which is in the memory buffer register) into the memory address register. Puts the computer in the execution cycle.
E and T_0	SET R	Turns on the READ flip-flop telling the memory to read a word.
E and T_1	MB INTO BR, RESET R	Transfers the contents of the memory buffer register into the B register. Since the memory buffer register now contains what was read from the memory, the addend is transferred into the B register; also turns off READ flip-flop
E and T_2	ADD	The contents of the B register are added to the accumulator, and the sum is placed in the accumulator.
E and T_3	IC INTO MA, SET I, RESET E	The contents of the instruction counter are transferred into the memory address register, giving the location of the next instruction word to the memory. The instruction cycle flip-flop is turned on, and the execution cycle flip-flop turned off.
CLEAR AND ADD		
I and T_0	SET R	Tells memory to read instruction word.
I and T_1	MB INTO OP, RESET R	Transfers OP-code part of instruction word into OP-code register; turns READ flip-flop off.
I and T_2	INCREMENT IC	Adds 1 to the instruction counter, preparing for the next instruction.
I and T_3	MB INTO MA, RESET I, SET E	Transfers the address part of the instruction word (which is in the memory buffer register) into the memory address register.
E and T_0	SET R	Turns on the READ flip-flop, telling the memory to read a word.
E and T_1	MB INTO BR, RESET AC, RESET R	Transfers the memory buffer register into the B register and also clears the accumulator, so if the B register is now added to the accumulator, the accumulator will contain the word read from memory.
E and T_2	ADD	The contents of the accumulator are added to the B register, and the sum is placed in the accumulator.
E and T_3	IC INTO MA, SET I, RESET E	The contents of the instruction counter are transferred into the memory address register, giving the location of the next instruction word to the memory. The instruction cycle flip-flop is turned on, and the execution cycle flip-flop is turned off.

CONTROLLING
ARITHMETIC
OPERATIONS

INSTRUCTION	LIST OF CONTROL SIGNALS TO BE TURNED ON	COMMENTS
SUBTRACT		
I and T_0	SET R	Tells memory to read instruction word.
I and T_1	MB INTO OP, RESET R	Transfers OP-code part of instruction word into OP-code register; turns off READ flip-flop.
I and T_2	INCREMENT IC	Adds 1 to the instruction counter, preparing for the next instruction.
I and T_3	MB INTO MA, RESET I, SET E	Transfers the address part of the instruction word (which is in the memory buffer register) into the memory address register. Puts the computer in the execution cycle.
E and T_0	SET R	Turns on the READ flip-flop, telling the memory to read a word.
E and T_1	MB INTO BR, RESET R	Transfers the contents of the memory buffer register into the B register. Since the memory buffer register now contains what was read from the memory, the subtrahend is transferred into the B register; also turns off READ flip-flop.
E and T_2	SUB	The contents of the B register are subtracted from the accumulator, and the difference is placed in the accumulator.
E and T_3	IC INTO MA, SET I, RESET E	The contents of the instruction counter are transferred into the memory address register, giving the location of the next instruction word to the memory. The instruction cycle flip-flop is turned on, and the execution cycle flip-flop is turned off.
STORE		
I and T_0	SET R	Tells memory to read instruction word.
I and T_1	MB INTO OP, RESET R	Transfers OP-code part of instruction word into OP-code register; turns off READ flip-flop.
I and T_2	INCREMENT IC	Adds 1 to the instruction counter, preparing for the next instruction.
I and T_3	MB INTO MA, RESET I, SET E	Transfers the address part of the instruction word (which is in the memory buffer register) into the memory address register.
E and T_0	SET W, AC INTO MB	Transfers word to be read into memory from accumulator into the memory buffer register.
E and T_1	RESET W	Turns off WRITE flip-flop.
E and T_2		Contents of memory buffer register are written into memory.
E and T_3	IC INTO MA, SET I, RESET E	The contents of the instruction counter are transferred into the memory address register, giving the location of the next instruction word to the memory. The instruction cycle flip-flop is turned on, and the execution cycle flip-flop is turned off.

we obtain four clock pulses. If it requires 1 μs to read into or write from the memory, a clock pulse should be generated every $\frac{1}{4}$ μs. Therefore the clock will run at a rate of 4 MHz.

The circuit has four output lines, designated T_0, T_1, T_2, and T_3. When the computer is in time period T_0, the output line T_0 will carry a 1 signal, and T_1, T_2, and T_3 will be 0s; at time T_1 only, line T_1 will have a 1 signal on it, etc.

Let us now write, in a short table, the sequence of operations which must occur during each of the ADD, SUBTRACT, CLEAR AND ADD, and STORE instructions. Notice that when the instruction cycle flip-flop is on, the operations during times T_0 and T_1 are always the same. In Table 9.2 the control signal to be turned on (or made a 1) is listed to the left, and what the signal does is listed to the right.

From this table of operations it is possible to design the control section of this small computer. The inputs are the OP code stored in the OP-code register, the timing-signal distributor, and the I and E flip-flops.

Notice, for instance, that when it is time T_0 and we are in an instruction cycle, we always turn on the READ flip-flop, telling the memory to read the instruction word located at the address in the memory address register. Then we assume that the memory places this word in the memory buffer register before time T_1, so at time T_1 we transfer the OP-code part of the instruction word into the OP-code register. These two facts tell us that we should logically AND the output line T_0 from the timing-signal distributor with the 1 output of the I flip-flop and then connect the $T_0 \cdot I$ signal to the set input of the READ flip-flop. Next we should connect a $T_1 \cdot I$ signal to the control line that transfers the first 5 bits of the memory buffer register into the OP register. This is shown in Fig. 9.6.

What happens next is always dependent on the OP-code register. We now connect a decoder with $2^5 = 32$ outputs to that register (assuming that we will use all the combinations by adding more instructions). We then have a set of signal lines, so that line 00000 = ADD will carry a 1 signal when we are adding (since the operation code for ADD is 00000); 00001 = SUB will carry a 1 if and only if we are subtracting, since the OP code for subtract is 00001; and 00010 = CLA will be a 1 only when we clear and add. We combine these lines and the timing-signal distributor lines and the I and E flip-flop lines to give us all the control signals needed to run the computer. Figure 9.6 shows the complete control circuitry required. A comparison of this figure with the timing and control signal chart in Table 9.2 will show how the control circuitry works and signals are manufactured when they are needed.

More instructions can be added by adding to the timing and control signal chart and by adding the required gates to the control circuitry. Analyzing the computer in this way, we can readily see how the control circuitry directs the operations performed in the machine, alternating the acquisition of instructions from the memory and the performance of the instructions.

TYPICAL SEQUENCE OF OPERATIONS

9.5 It is instructive to analyze the control circuitry in Fig. 9.6 during both an ADD instruction and a STORE instruction. Each instruction is started with the I (instruction cycle) flip-flop on and with the timing-signal distributor having an

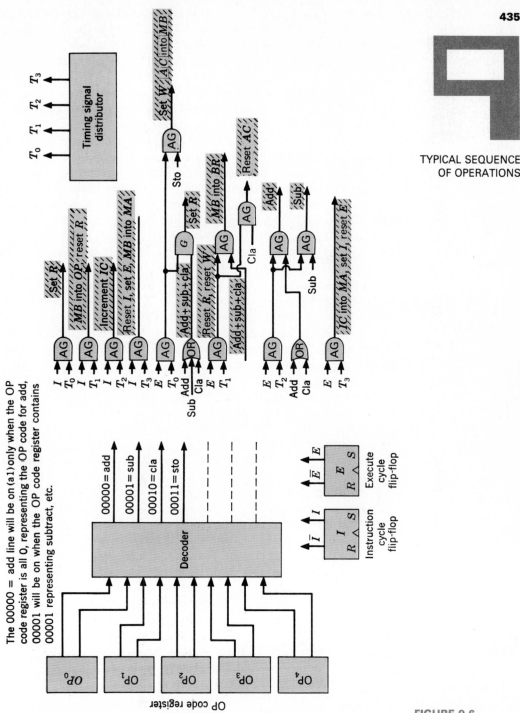

TYPICAL SEQUENCE
OF OPERATIONS

FIGURE 9.6

Control circuitry for
four-instruction com-
puter.

output on line T_0. The AND gate at the upper right of the figure will therefore be turned on by I and T_0, thus setting the READ flip-flop to the 1 state and initiating a READ from the memory. At this time, the memory address register is assumed to have the address of the instruction that will be read into the memory buffer register.

By time T_1 the word read from the memory will have been read into the memory buffer register, so that when we have the control state I and T_1, the contents of the memory buffer register which constitute the OP-code section of the instruction will be transferred into the OP-code register, and the computer will be in a position to decode the OP code and determine what instruction is to be performed.

At time I and T_2 the instruction counter is incremented by 1, so that the instruction counter now contains the address of the next instruction to be read from the memory. The AND gate connected to the I and T_2 input signals is used in turn on the INCREMENT IC control signal, and its output is designated by the name of the control signal.

Similarly, at time I and T_3 the memory buffer register is transferred into the memory address register by the MB INTO MA signal, thus transferring the address part of the instruction word into the memory address register. The next word read from or written into the memory will then be at the address designated by the address part of the instruction word which was just read from the memory.

At the same time, the instruction cycle flip-flop is cleared by the RESET I signal, and the execution cycle flip-flop is set on by the SET E signal, thus changing the state of the computer from an instruction cycle to an execution cycle.

At time E and T_0, then, during an ADD instruction, we set the R flip-flop on, thus telling the memory to read the word at the address currently in the memory address register. In this case, this address is the address part of the instruction word that is being executed. Then at time E and T_1 we transfer the contents of the memory buffer register into the B register. The memory buffer register at that time contains the word which has been read from the memory, so that we now have the word which has been addressed by the instruction word in the B register for the addition. At the same time we reset the READ flip-flop.

Notice that the RESET R and RESET W lines are used to reset both the READ and the WRITE flip-flops simultaneously. There is no harm in resetting both flip-flops, since only one will be on at any given time.

If the instruction is an ADD instruction at time E and T_2, we add the contents of the B register to the contents of the accumulator. The B register contains the word which has been read from the memory, and the accumulator has not been changed; so their sum will be transferred into the accumulator. Thus the sum of the word read from the memory and the previous contents of the accumulator will be placed in the accumulator. Then, at time E and T_3, we transfer the instruction counter into the memory address register (thus giving the address of the next instruction to be performed to the memory), at the same time clearing the EXECUTE flip-flop, setting the instruction cycle flip-flop on, and changing the computer from an execution cycle to an instruction cycle.

Since the I flip-flop is on and it is time T_0, the SET R control line will go high, thus telling the memory to read a word. The next instruction word will be read from the memory and can then be interpreted.

Let us now examine the operation of the STORE instruction. When the instruction flip-flop is on and we are in an instruction cycle, the R flip-flop will be set on when time T_0 arrives, telling the memory to read just as for an addition, subtraction, or clear and add. Since at time I and T_1 the memory buffer register flip-flops contain the OP code of the instruction these will be transferred into the OP-code register.

At time I and T_2 we increment the instruction counter so that the address of the next instruction in memory now lies in the instruction counter; and at time I and T_3 we reset the instruction flip-flop and turn on the execution cycle flip-flop, thus putting the computer in an execution cycle.

At time E and T_1, if the instruction is a STORE instruction, we set the WRITE flip-flop on, thus initiating a WRITE into the memory. We also transfer the contents of the accumulator into the memory buffer register, so that the word written into the memory will be the current contents of the accumulator register, and so that after the WRITE cycle has been terminated, the accumulator will have been written into the memory at the address that was given by the instruction word.

At time E and T_1 we reset the WRITE flip-flop, since we have already told the memory to write, nothing need be done at E and T_2, for we are now writing the word into the memory. At time E and T_3 the instruction counter is transferred into the memory address register by the IC INTO MA control signal, thus giving the address of the next instruction to the memory. The instruction cycle flip-flop is turned on and the execution cycle flip-flop turned off, thus turning the computer to the instruction cycle state. The machine will now execute an instruction cycle by reading the next instruction word from the memory, interpreting it, and continuing the program.

The preceding example demonstrates how it is possible to design a computer that will execute a given sequence of operations and thereby cause it to perform each instruction word that is read from the memory. Although only four instructions are demonstrated in this particular example, more instructions can be added in exactly the same manner by simply writing what must be done when an instruction word is read from the memory, listing the operations that must be performed, and providing gates which will generate the control signals necessary to the performance of each instruction. Subsequent sections discuss shifting instructions and branching instructions. All these may be incorporated into the computer shown by simply adding gates to the control circuitry and providing for the additional gates necessary for the transfers and operations between registers.

The general form of the control signal generating scheme is shown in Fig. 9.7. It shows a timing-pulse distributor with eight different time divisions, in which case each time period is one-eighth of the memory cycle time.

BRANCH, SKIP, OR JUMP INSTRUCTIONS

9.6 The BRANCH, SKIP, or JUMP instruction varies from the normal instruction in several ways.[5] For single-address machines only one word, the instruction word, must be located in memory. Also, the contents of the instruction counter may be modified instead of being simply increased by 1. There are two types of

---

[5]A survey indicates that some manufacturers call these instructions BRANCH instructions, others call them TRANSFER instructions, and still others call them SKIP or JUMP instructions. All are the same thing.

THE CONTROL UNIT

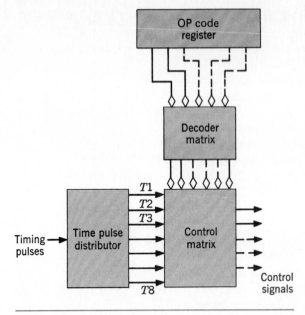

FIGURE 9.7

General configuration
of control circuitry.

BRANCH instructions: conditional and unconditional. For an *unconditional* BRANCH instruction, the contents of the address portion of the memory buffer register are always transferred into the instruction counter. The next instruction performed will be the instruction at the location indicated by the address section of the instruction word. In a *conditional* branch instruction the branch may or may not occur depending on some condition. For example, in single-address computers the *conditional* BRANCH-ON-MINUS instruction will cause the machine to branch only if the number stored in the accumulator register of the arithmetic element is negative. If the number in the accumulator is positive, the contents of the instruction counter will simply be increased by 1, and the next instruction will be taken in the normal order.

As can be seen, during a conditional BRANCH-ON-MINUS instruction, the sign bit of the accumulator of the arithmetic element must be examined by control circuitry. If the sign bit is a 1, the number stored is negative, and so the number in the address part of the instruction word is transferred into the instruction counter. If the sign bit is a 0, a 1 is added to the instruction counter, and the computer proceeds.[6]

To demonstrate how a typical BRANCH-ON-MINUS (BRM) instruction operates in a single-address computer, we modify the control circuitry shown in Fig. 9.6 so that the small machine will include a BRM instruction. Let us give the OP code 00100 to BRM, so that the line beneath the 00011 = STO line will be high from the decoder attached to the OP-code register in Fig. 9.6 when a BRM instruction is in the register.

---

[6]Many computers have a set of *status bits* (flip-flops) which are set and reset depending on the results of operations performed. Jumps or transfers are then taken based on these flip-flops. The Questions and Chap. 10 cover this in detail.

TABLE 9.3

BRANCH ON MINUS	LIST OF CONTROL SIGNALS TO BE TURNED ON	COMMENTS
I and T_0	SET R	Tells memory to read instruction word.
I and T_1	MB INTO OP, RESET R	Transfers OP-code part of instruction word into OP-code register; turns off READ flip-flop.
I and T_2 and $\overline{AC_N}$	INCREMENT IC	If the sign digit of the accumulator AC_N is a 0, we want to increment the instruction counter and use its contents as the address of the next instruction.
I and T_2 and AC_N	MB INTO IC	If the sign digit of the accumulator is a 1, the accumulator is negative, and we want to use the address in the instruction word as the address of the next instruction word.
I and T_3	IC INTO MA	This transfers the instruction counter into the memory address register. Notice that the E flip-flop is not turned on as we are ready to read another instruction word; an EXECUTE cycle is not needed.

BRANCH, SKIP, OR JUMP INSTRUCTIONS

The first two time periods of the instruction cycle are the same for all instructions. First the memory is told to read, and then the instruction word is read from memory into the memory buffer register. The OP-code part is transferred into the OP-code register, so that, after time T_1 and the beginning of time T_2, the line $00100 =$ BRM will be high and all the other output lines from the decoder will be low. Now let us make a small table for a BRM instruction, showing what must be done to carry out this instruction. Table 9.3 shows the steps that must be taken.

If at time T_2 during the instruction cycle a BRM instruction OP code is in the OP-code register, one of two things must happen. Either we wish to increment the instruction counter and give this number as the address of the next instruction to be taken from the memory, or we wish to transfer the contents of the address portion of the instruction word into the instruction counter. Which choice we make depends on the sign bit of the accumulator, called AC_N. If the accumulator contains a negative number, it will have a 1 in AC_N; and if it contains a positive number, it will have a 0 in flip-flop AC_N. Therefore, if I AND T_2 AND $\overline{AC_N}$, we want to increment the instruction counter. If I AND T_2 AND AC_N happens to be the case, we wish to transfer the memory buffer register into the instruction counter. This is shown in the table. During time T_3 of this instruction cycle we want to transfer the instruction counter into the memory address register. We do not need to put the machine in an execution cycle, but can simply continue to another instruction cycle, taking the word at the address which has been transferred into the memory address register as the next instruction. Therefore, we do not clear the instruction cycle flip-flop or put a 1 in the execution cycle flip-flop; we simply transfer the instruction counter into the memory address register.

The control circuitry which will implement these operations is shown in Fig. 9.8. This means that the two particular AND gates in Fig. 9.6, which are connected to the I, T_2 and I, T_3 inputs, will be replaced with the two circuits shown in Fig.

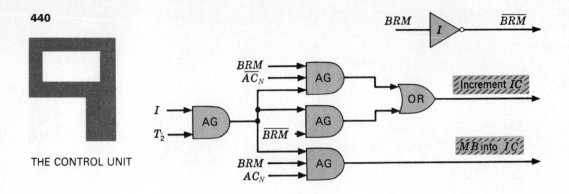

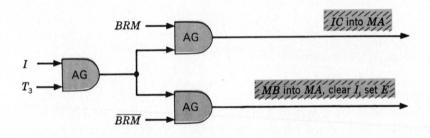

THE CONTROL UNIT

FIGURE 9.8

Modification of control circuitry for BRANCH instruction.

9.8. Notice that this logical circuitry, plus the circuitry in Fig. 9.6, is all that is needed to generate the control signals required for the BRM instruction.

Notice that the BRM instruction requires only one access to memory and thus only one instruction cycle for its execution.

SHIFT INSTRUCTIONS

9.7 The instructions we have examined to date were always performed within a basic fixed number of memory cycles. That is, the ADD, SUBTRACT, CLEAR AND ADD, and STORE instructions were performed within exactly two memory cycles, and the TRANSFER and BRANCH instructions required only one memory cycle. Several types of instructions may require more time than two memory cycles. Typical of these are multiplication and division, which generally require more time than two memory cycles. Similarly, an instruction such as SHIFT RIGHT or SHIFT LEFT could conceivably be performed in a single memory cycle, since the operand is in the accumulator when the instruction word is obtained. However, if the instruction calls for a large number of shifts, more than one memory cycle may be needed. In this case we could not initiate another memory cycle until we had finished shifting the requisite number of times. Similarly, for multiplication and division we could not initiate another memory cycle until we had finished our multiplication and division process.

To implement these types of instructions, we turn over our control of the computer to a simple control element which is dominated by a counter. This counter will sequence and count the number of steps that must be performed until the instruction has been completed, and then it will put the computer in an instruction cycle and tell the memory to read the next instruction word. We illustrate with a shift right instruction.

The SHIFT RIGHT instruction word consists of two parts: an OP code and an address part. The OP code of 00101 tells the machine to shift the word in the accumulator to the right the number of times given in the address part. So if we write 00101 for the OP code in an instruction word and then write 8 in binary form in the address part, the computer has been instructed to shift the binary number in the accumulator to the right 8 binary digits.

Assuming that we have an accumulator with gates so that we can shift the accumulator digits to the right, as explained in Chap. 5, all we need is to apply eight consecutive SHIFT RIGHT control signals to the accumulator and we will have shifted the number to the right eight places. Since there are only four pulses per memory cycle, we will not want to use the memory until we have completed our shifting. If, for instance, the instruction said SHIFT RIGHT 1, we could finish in one pulse time and start the next instruction cycle immediately after. But if the instruction word said SHIFT RIGHT 4, 5, or 15 or more times, we would have to wait until we had completed shifting before we could initiate another instruction cycle and fetch the next instruction word from the memory.

To do this, we first prepare the computer for the shifting operation by incrementing the instruction counter so that the next word obtained will contain the address of the next instruction word. To count the number of shifts that we perform, we add another register, called a *step-counter register,* which counts downward from a given number to 0. We then transfer the address part of the memory buffer register into the step counter, so the step counter contains the number of shifts to be performed. Then each time we shift, we decrement the counter by 1; so when the counter reaches 0, we will have performed the requisite number of shifts.

Figure 9.9 shows two stages of a decrementing counter and the gates necessary to transfer the memory buffer register contents into the step counter, designated SC. The two rightmost, or least significant, digits of the counter are shown (SC_1 and SC_0), as are the two rightmost digits of the memory buffer register (MB_1 and MB_0).

The actual number of stages in the step counter is determined by the maximum number of shifts which the machine must ever make and, since we will also use the same counter for multiplication and division, by the maximum number of steps that will ever be required to multiply or divide. For a computer containing 21 binary digits in the basic computer word, the counter might well contain five flip-flops. For a computer with a basic computer word of perhaps 35 or 36 binary digits, the step counter might well contain six or even seven flip-flops:

Consider a sequence of operations for a SHIFT instruction. Times I AND T_0 and I AND T_1 are as usual. At I AND T_2 we increment the instruction counter and transfer the count into the step counter. At I AND T_3, we set a flip-flop called SR (shift right) on, which tells the computer to start shifting. At the same time we clear the I flip-flop, so that the machine is in neither an instruction nor an execution cycle, although it is actually executing an instruction. Thus we do not initiate

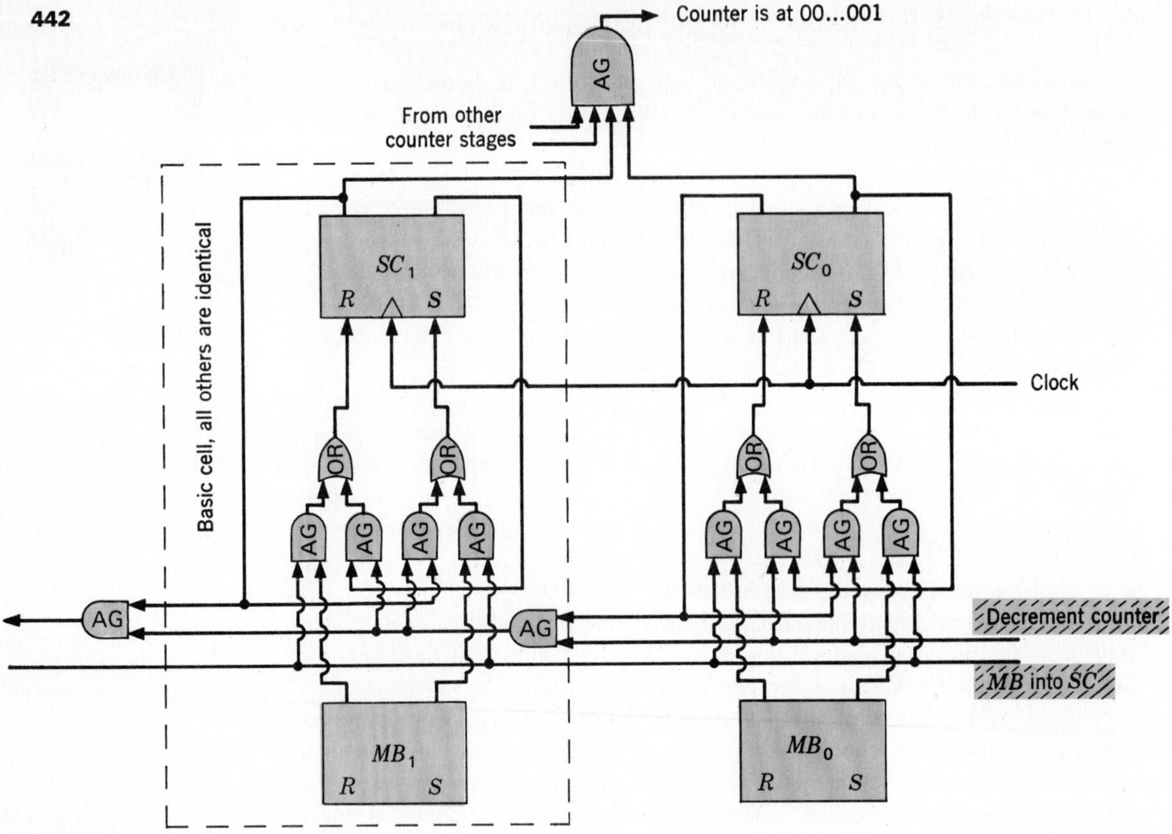

FIGURE 9.9

Two stages of decrementing counter and transfer network.

subsequent memory cycles, and the machine effectively freezes in the shifting state until the step counter has counted to 0, indicating that the requisite number of shifts has been performed. (Actually the step counter counts only to binary 1 rather than to 0 before the order to stop counting is given, for counting when the counter is at 0 would introduce an extra shift.) If we turn off the counter SR flip-flop when the output of the counter is at the 00 . . . 001 signal, and if at the same time we turn on the I or instruction cycle, the computer will proceed to the next instruction cycle, fetching the next instruction word from the memory and performing it. Table 9.4 shows this.

When the SR flip-flop is on, it will be necessary to stop the timing-signal distributor. Thus we arrange to disable this circuit, using the SR flip-flop's output for this purpose.

Implementation of the above procedure is straightforward. A three-input AND gate with inputs I, T_3, and $00101 = $ SHR (the output from the decoder in Fig. 9.6) can be used to turn on an SR flip-flop, the STOP output from the step counter to turn it off, also turning on I. The input to the clock can be turned off when SR is on.

TABLE 9.4

SHIFT RIGHT	CONTROL SIGNAL TURNED ON	COMMENTS
I and T_0	SET R	Tells memory to read.
I and T_1	MB INTO OP, RESET R	OP code of instruction word is transferred into OP-code register. READ flip-flop is turned off.
I and T_2	INCREMENT IC, MB INTO SC	The instruction counter is prepared to obtain the next instruction word. The address part of the instruction word is transferred into the step counter.
I and T_3	RESET I, SET SR	The instruction cycle flip-flop is turned off. The SHIFT RIGHT flip-flop is turned on.

REGISTER TRANSFER
LANGUAGE

REGISTER TRANSFER LANGUAGE

9.8   The preceding design showed how to generate a sequence of control signals which would cause instruction words read from a memory to be executed. The control signals were named so that the function of each was indicated. For example, the control signal INCREMENT IC causes the IC (instruction counter) to be incremented; RESET W causes W to be reset; MB INTO BR causes the contents of MB to be transferred into the BR register, etc.

To document a design, it is convenient to have a notational technique for representing these operations on and between registers. The most used way to organize and write register operations is called *register transfer language,* and was invented by I. S. Reed.[7] Currently, manufacturers' design efforts and their manuals documenting computer designs all use some version of register transfer language.

An example of a transfer between registers in register transfer language is

$$A \rightarrow B$$

This says, "Transfer the contents of register A into register B." A control signal to effect this might be conveniently called A INTO B.

Another example of register transfer language is

$$0 \rightarrow D$$

This says, "Set D to a 0." If D is a flip-flop, this simply means to reset D, and an appropriate control signal name might be RESET D.

---

[7]The book *Theory and Design of Digital Machines* by T. C. Bartee, I. L. Lebow, and I. S. Reed, McGraw Hill, New York, first presented this design technique in detail.

THE CONTROL UNIT

Here is another example:

$$A + B \rightarrow A$$

This says, "Add the numbers in A and B and place the sum in A." A control signal for this might well be called ADD or ADD AB.

The above operations on and between registers are sometimes called *micro-operations,* particularly if the computer is microprogrammed, as will be discussed.

An interesting statement in register transfer language is

$$A + 1 \rightarrow A$$

This says, "Add 1 to A and place the sum in A." A name for the corresponding control signal might be INCREMENT A.

In some cases, register transfers or operations affect only parts of registers. An example was shown in preceding sections where the first 5 bits in the memory buffer register MBR were transferred into the OP register. Subscripts are generally used to indicate specific bits, and an example transfer can be written

$$B_{0-4} \rightarrow P_{0-4}$$

This assumes that the B register flip-flops have been named $B_0, B_1, \ldots, B_N$; and this means $B_0, B_1, B_2, B_3,$ and B_4 will be transferred into $P_0, P_1, P_2, P_3,$ and $P_4,$ respectively.

A specific bit in a register also can be transferred. Consider

$$A_3 \rightarrow B_2$$

This transfers A_3 of register A into B_2 of register B.

Sometimes operations and transfers are dependent on certain conditions. This is indicated as follows:

$$R = 0 : A \rightarrow B$$

This statement means, "If R has value 0, transfer A into B." Here is another example:

$$R \cdot T_2 : IC + 1 \rightarrow IC$$

This statement says, "If R is a 1 and T_2 is a 1, then increment the IC register." The colon is used to indicate a conditional operation.

Here is the CLEAR AND ADD instruction in Table 9.2 rewritten in register transfer language. We will use the CLEAR AND ADD control signal CLA from the decoder in Fig. 9.6.

$$I \cdot T_0 : 1 \to R$$
$$I \cdot T_1 : MB_{19-23} \to OP_{0-4},$$
$$0 \to R$$
$$CLA \cdot I \cdot T_2 : IC + 1 \to IC$$
$$CLA \cdot I \cdot T_3 : MB_{0-18} \to MA_{0-18},$$
$$0 \to I, 1 \to E$$
$$CLA \cdot E \cdot T_0 : 1 \to R$$
$$CLA \cdot E \cdot T_1 : MB \to BR,$$
$$0 \to AC, 0 \to R$$
$$CLA \cdot E \cdot T_2 : A + B \to A$$
$$CLA \cdot E \cdot T_3 : IC \to MA$$
$$1 \to I, 0 \to E$$

REGISTER TRANSFER
LANGUAGE

The above assumes 24 bits in the A and MB registers and 19 bits in the memory address register. So MB_{0-18} is the address part of an instruction word and gets transferred into MA_{0-18}.

Also notice that the entire circuitry for generating the gates for control signals can be read directly from the table. The final statement,[8] for example, says this: "If you AND CLA, E, and T_3, then the output from the AND gate can be used to initiate the transfer IC $\to$ MA and $1 \to I$ and $0 \to E$." This means the output from the AND gate can be connected to (perhaps being ORed with other signals) the control signals IC INTO MA, SET I, and RESET E.

Many register transfer languages have been designed and used by different individuals and companies. One frequent variation is in making transfers move from right to left (which is more like programming practice). In this variation, we find

$$B \leftarrow A$$

instead of

$$B \to A$$

Sometimes equals signs are used. Then

$$B = A$$

says to transfer A into B. Occasionally we see

$$B := A$$

This also says to transfer A into B in some variations.

---

[8]Notice the control signal CLA from the decoder in Fig. 9.6 can be used after time T_1 because the OP code is in OP after that time.

It is generally not hard to read one of the register transfer languages once a basic one has been understood.

The wide success and usage of register transfer languages to describe the internal operations of a computer is primarily due to the facility with which a design can be organized and the direct way a design can be translated from register transfer language into the control gating structure once the control signals have been named. Register transfer language is also widely used in giving the details of instruction repertoires, as we will see in Chap. 10.

MICROPROGRAMMING

*9.9   In the preceding sections, the control signals which sequence the operations that are performed to execute computer instructions were generated by using gates. There is another method, called *microprogramming,* which is also used to generate the control signals in an orderly fashion. This method generally involves use of a ROM to effectively store the control signals in a manner that will be described.

When a computer is microprogrammed, the individual operations between and on registers are called *microoperations*. For instance, transferring the program counter's contents into the memory address register is a microoperation. Similarly, incrementing the program counter is a microoperation, as is transferring the accumulator's contents into the memory buffer register.[9] In each case a microoperation is initiated by raising a single control signal and sequencing microoperations involves sequencing the appropriate control signals.

Figuring out a sequence of microoperations to do something is called *microprogramming*. The microprogrammer generally writes the list of operations, or *microprogram,* using a special language. Quite often a computer program is used to translate this microprogram into a listing describing the appropriate contents for a ROM, which will be used to store the microprogram. The statements that the microprogrammer writes are in a microprogramming language. This language can be very primitive or very complex.

To explain microprogramming, we use the computer layout and instructions given in the previous sections and redo the design, using a ROM to store the control signals. Therefore, the registers and control signals in Fig. 9.3 are used in the design. First we note that the basic list of microoperations needed is shown in Table 9.5. Each microoperation is described by using a symbolic notation (in effect, a microprogramming or register transfer language), and the corresponding control signal which will cause this operation to occur is also shown.

For instance, the microoperation MB $\rightarrow$ BR, which says to transfer the contents of the memory buffer register (MB) into the B register (BR), is made to occur by raising the control signal MB INTO BR. Notice the considerable similarity between the description in the microprogramming language and the control signal's name. This is a convenient practice, although the control signals could be named X_1, A_1, or anything desired. A 16-bit instruction word is assumed.

---

[9]Microoperations are just the same as register operations. The term *microoperations* is used in this area along with *microprogramming* for historical reasons. Microoperations and register transfers and operations are physically realized using the same control signals and associated gating structures.

TABLE 9.5 MICROOPERATIONS **447**

MICROOPERATION	CONTROL SIGNAL NAME	BIT IN READ-ONLY CONTROL MEMORY
$0 \to IC$	RESET IC	C_7
$IC + 1 \to IC$	INCREMENT IC	C_8
$MB \to IC$	MB INTO IC	C_9
$0 \to AC$	RESET AC	C_{10}
$AC + BR \to AC$	ADD	C_{11}
$AC - BR \to AC$	SUBTRACT	C_{12}
$1 \to W$	SET W	C_{13}
$0 \to W$	RESET W	C_{14}
$1 \to R$	SET R	C_{15}
$0 \to R$	RESET R	C_{16}
$0 \to AC$	CLEAR AC	C_{17}
$MB_{10-0} \to MA$	MB INTO MA	C_{18}
$IC \to MA$	IC INTO MA	C_{19}
$AC \to MB$	AC INTO MB	C_{20}
$MB_{15-11} \to OP$	MB INTO OP	C_{21}
$MB \to BR$	MB INTO BR	C_{22}
$IAR + 1 \to IAR$	INCREMENT IAR	C_{23}
$C_{0-6} \to IAR$	C INTO IAR	C_{24}
$OP + IAR + 1 \to IAR$	ADD OP TO IAR	C_{25}
$0 \to IAR$	RESET IAR	C_{26}

MICROPROGRAMMING

Figure 9.10 shows a block diagram for the control system as it will be implemented. There is a ROM with 64 locations and 30 bits per address and an address register for this memory called *IAR* (microinstruction address register). Each output bit from the ROM is a control signal which will generate a microoperation, and these control signals are named C_0 to C_{26}. Seven of these outputs are special because they are *next addresses* which can be loaded into the IAR and which will be used to sequence the IAR in several cases. (This ROM is often called a *control memory*.)

FIGURE 9.10

Block diagram for control system.

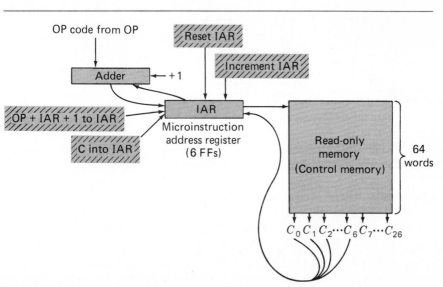

THE CONTROL UNIT

The following operations can be performed on this control unit. A 1 can be added to the IAR (in microprogramming language, IAR + 1 → IAR, the control signal is called INCREMENT IAR), and the output bits from the control memory labeled C_0 to C_6 can be transferred into the IAR. It is also possible to add the value in OP (see Fig. 9.3) plus 1 to the current contents of the IAR.

Now the basic scheme is this: The control signals to generate a given computer instruction, say ADD, are stored in a section of the control memory. The IAR sequences through this section, and at each location the outputs from the control memory will comprise the control signals. These ROM outputs then replace the control signals generated by the gates in Fig. 9.6.

The first problem is that the IAR must be set to the correct address at the beginning of that section in control memory which contains the bits storing the control signals for the instruction to be executed. To do this, we must examine the OP-code register's contents after we have read the instruction word from memory and then moved the OP-code section from the memory buffer register into the OP-code register. The complete microprogram for the control memory is shown in Table 9.6. Notice that the first microoperations performed are as follows:

LOCATION IN CONTROL MEMORY	MICROPROGRAM
0	$1 \rightarrow R$ IAR + 1 → IAR
1	$MB_{15-11} \rightarrow OP$ IAR + 1 → IAR
2	OP + IAR + 1 → IAR
3	$C_{0-6} \rightarrow$ IAR
4	$C_{0-6} \rightarrow$ IAR
5	$C_{0-6} \rightarrow$ IAR
6	$C_{0-6} \rightarrow$ IAR

The operation here is as follows. First the memory is told to read. (The prior instruction has loaded the memory address register with the location of the instruction word.) The instruction word is then in the memory buffer register when the next microoperation is performed. This microinstruction loads the OP-code register with the first 5 bits in the memory buffer register. Next this value is added to the IAR register plus 1. Now if the instruction is an ADD instruction with OP code 00000, then 1 will be added to the current IAR's contents (which will give 3 decimal). Thus the next word in the control memory to be accessed will be at location 3, and in location 3 the value for C in the first 7 bits is 20. When C is loaded into the IAR, the next microinstruction word addressed will be that at address 20 in the ROM, which contains the first microinstruction in the ADD section. If the instruction in OP was a SUBTRACT, the OP code will be 00001, and so the next word in the control memory to be used will be at location 4 decimal, which will cause a transfer to location 25, which in turn contains the microinstructions for the SUBTRACT instruction.

Therefore, an ADD instruction will cause a jump to location 20 (decimal) in the control memory, and a SUBTRACT will cause a branch to location 25. In each case these locations begin the section of memory containing the microinstructions which will cause the instruction to be executed.

At the end of each microprogram section which causes an instruction to be

LOCATION IN CONTROL MEMORY	MICROPROGRAM	COMMENTS
0	$1 \to R$, IAR $+ 1 \to$ IAR	Tell memory to read, increment IAR.
1	$MB_{15-11} \to$ OP, IAR $+ 1 \to$ IAR	Place OP code in instruction in OP.
2	OP $+$ IAR $+ 1 \to$ IAR	Add OP code to 3; this gives next address in IAR to be used.
3	$C_{0-6} \to$ IAR, C_{0-6} has value 20 decimal	Instruction was ADD; go to location 20 in ROM.
4	$C_{0-6} \to$ IAR, C_{0-6} has value 25 decimal	Instruction was SUBTRACT, go to location 25 in ROM.
5	$C_{0-6} \to$ IAR, C_{0-6} has value 30 decimal	Instruction was CLA, go to location 30 in ROM.
6	$C_{0-6} \to$ IAR, C_{0-6} has value 35 decimal	Instruction was STO, go to location 35 in ROM.
7 8 9 10 11 12 13 14 15 16 17 18 19	Left blank to add more instructions NOTE: IAR$+ 1 \to$ IAR occurs in every following line except 24, 29, 34, and 39.	
20	$0 \to I$, $1 \to E$, $MB_{10-0} \to$ MA	Begin ADD instruction microoperations; place address of augend in memory address register.
21	$1 \to R$, IC $+ 1 \to$ IC	Read augend from memory, increment instruction counter.
22	MB $\to$ BR, $0 \to R$	Place augend in B register.
23	AC $+$ BR $\to$ AC	Add and place sum in accumulator.
24	IC $\to$ MA, $1 \to I$, $0 \to E$, $0 \to$ IAR	Set up for next instruction by placing instruction counter in memory address register and going to location 0 in control memory.
25	$MB_{10-0} \to$ MA, $0 \to I$, $1 \to E$	Begin SUBTRACT instruction microoperations.
26	$1 \to R$, IC $+ 1 \to$ IC	
27	MB $\to$ BR, $0 \to R$	Place subtrahend in B register.
28	AC $-$ BR $\to$ AC	Subtract and place difference in accumulator.
29	IC $\to$ MA, $1 \to I$, $0 \to E$, $0 \to$ IAR	Place address of next instruction word in memory address register and go to 0 in control memory.
30	$MB_{10-0} \to$ MA, $0 \to I$, $1 \to E$	Begin CLA instruction operations.
31	$1 \to R$	
32	MB $\to$ BR, $0 \to$ AC, $0 \to R$	Reset accumulator.
33	AC $+$ BR $\to$ AC	Add B register to accumulator.
34	IC $\to$ MA, $1 \to I$, $0 \to E$, $0 \to$ IAR	End CLA instruction; place address of next instruction in memory address register and go to 0 in control memory.
35	$0 \to I$, $1 \to E$, $MB_{10-0} \to$ MA	Begin STO instruction.
36	$1 \to W$, AC $\to$ MB	Place accumulator's contents in memory buffer register so that it can be stored; tell memory to write.
37	$0 \to W$	
38	IC $+ 1 \to$ IC	Set up for next instruction.
39	IC $\to$ MA, $1 \to I$, $0 \to E$, $0 \to$ IAR	End of instruction, place address of next instruction in memory address register and go to 0 in control memory.

executed, the IAR is set to 0, which is the starting point for the operations that lead to reading in the next instruction and branching to the correct section in the control memory to cause the instruction to be executed.

VARIATIONS IN MICROPROGRAMMING CONFIGURATIONS

9.10 Figure 9.11 shows the microprogram of Table 9.6 stored in a memory. The implementation here has the control memory in Fig. 9.10 with its contents, as shown in Fig. 9.11. This basic configuration is used in most modern microprogrammed computers. There are many variations on this idea, however, and there are many microprogramming languages. The references contain further descriptions and information in this area.

The microprogramming configuration shown in Fig. 9.11 has an output bit from the memory for each control signal. This is called *horizontal microprogramming*. For larger computers there may be many control signals, and thus there would be many bits in the control memory. (In general, the number of control signals varies from about 60 for small computers to about 3000 for the largest machines.) Since this would involve too large a control memory, the control signals are examined, and an attempt is made to reduce the number of outputs from the

FIGURE 9.11

Microprogram in memory. Control address C_0 has 0s in all positions.

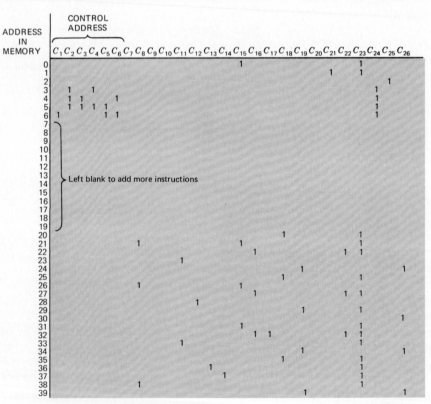

Note: Only 1s are shown; remaining positions are 0s.

memory. After this is done, the resulting configuration is said to use *vertical microprogramming*.

As an example of how the number of outputs might be reduced, consider that in some cases when one control signal is raised, another is always raised, and so these two signals could be combined into a single signal.

In some cases different control signals are never turned on at the same time. If N such signals can be found, then only M control lines, where $2^M > N$, will be required, and a decoder can be used to provide the necessary control signals. For instance, the ADD, SUB, RESET AC, and MB INTO BR signals are never turned on at the same time. Thus two control output lines with a four-output decoder could be used to generate these signals.

VARIATIONS IN
MICROPROGRAMMING
CONFIGURATIONS

When vertical microprogramming is used, the system becomes less flexible, since if a microprogram is to be changed or enlarged, fewer options in control signal generation will be available. As a result most commercial computers are arranged so they are somewhere between horizontal and vertical in their construction. (Many schemes have been used, and several are described in the Questions.)

Microprogramming is widely used in the new computer lines. Since the instruction repertoire for the computer is effectively stored in the ROM, the instructions provided can be changed or added to by changing or adding to the ROM.

Further, microprogramming is useful in simulating one computer on another. Suppose that we have a computer which has a basic set of registers and operations between registers, and we have the ability to microprogram this computer. Further, we have a second computer with a certain set of instructions and a set of programs written to run on this second computer. We now wish to make the first computer run these programs and deliver the same results as the second computer would have delivered. This is called *simulation,* and the first computer is said to *simulate* the second computer. To do this, we microprogram the simulator computer so that a given instruction has the same effect as the same instruction in the second machine.[10]

As can be seen, a computer which is microprogrammed can be made to simulate another computer. Clearly some computers have architectures which are much better suited for simulation than others.

The microprograms provided by a manufacturer (or anyone else) to be used on its microprogrammed computer are generally called *firmware*. The instructions that a microprogrammed computer provides can be very complex and can be carefully designed to satisfy the programmer's needs. The primary objections to microprogramming are (1) speed, because the logic gates used in a "conventional" computer will be faster than the ROM in most cases, and so the conventional machine may run faster; (2) the gates can be minimized in number since the instructions are to be fixed, and thus the total amount of equipment can often be made smaller. (This is not always the case; however, ROMs are quite compact and inexpensive so that the advantage of gates decreases as time passes.) As a result, most large, fast "super" computers tend to use logic gates for control, while the medium and smaller computers now tend to be microprogrammed.

---

[10]This is often called *emulation* when microprogramming is used, it is necessary to rename registers and arrange for other changes to really effect this, but the principle is essentially given here.

9

THE CONTROL UNIT

SUMMARY

9.11 The instruction word formats and instruction repertoires for two single-address computers were discussed. A design for a single-accumulator computer's control section was then presented. This design is based on register operations which can be described by using register transfer language. The most used general procedures for control design and computer description were presented including timing operation and the use of tables of operations to implement instructions.

When a computer is microprogrammed, a ROM is used to store the control signals needed to sequence register operations. The preparation of the sequence of operations to be performed by the computer is called microprogramming and is often performed by using a register transfer language to describe these register microoperations.

If each control signal has a bit in the ROM output word dedicated to it, the microprogramming is said to be horizontal. When the size of the ROM is reduced by encoding ROM outputs and then decoding them by gates, the microprogramming is said to be vertical.

QUESTIONS

9.1 A single-address, one-instruction-per-word computer has a word length of 22 binary digits. The computer can perform 32 different instructions, and it has three index registers. The inner memory is a 16,000-word magnetic core memory. Draw a diagram of the computer word, allocating space for each part of the basic instruction word (OP-code part, address part, index register part). Do not use the sign digit (leftmost digit) of the word.

9.2 Design a single stage of an accumulator and B register which will add and shift left in one operation (step) or will simply shift left in one step. Use SHIFT LEFT and ADD AND SHIFT LEFT as control signals, a full-adder, AND and OR gates, and RS flip-flops.

9.3 Make out a timing table and modify the control circuitry in Fig. 9.6, including the modification in Fig. 9.8, so that the machine has an unconditional BRANCH instruction BRA, as well as a conditional BRANCH instruction BRM, generating the necessary control signals.

9.4 Discuss how you would expand or perhaps improve the register transfer language in Table 9.5. Do you think that microprogramming in a higher-level language, such as Pascal or one of its variations, would yield an efficient microprogram in the control memory? Discuss this.

9.5 Show how to modify Fig. 9.8 so that the BRM instruction becomes a BRP instruction, meaning that the computer jumps or branches when the ACC is positive instead of negative.

9.6 Show how to generate timing signals (such as T_0, T_1, T_2, and T_3 in Fig. 9.5) by using a shift register with the rightmost stages' outputs connected to the leftmost stages' inputs. This is called a *ring counter*. In what states would you set the flip-flops to start?

9.7   Why is the instruction counter always placed in the memory address register at time T_3 during the execution part of an instruction in Table 9.2?

9.8   Explain why some instructions require both execution and instruction cycles and others require only instruction cycles. Give examples of both kinds of instruction.

9.9   Why can the SET W and AC INTO MB control signals be combined in Fig. 9.6?

9.10   Why can the IC INTO MA, SET I, and CLEAR E control signals be combined in Fig. 9.6?

9.11   Show how to add a pushbutton connected to a reset and start wire which will (using DC SETs and DC RESETs on the flip-flops) cause the computer in Fig. 9.6 to start executing a program beginning at location 0 in the memory when it is depressed.

9.12   Add a BRANCH ON ZERO instruction similar to that in Table 9.3 and Fig. 9.8, except that the computer branches when the accumulator value is all 0s.

9.13   Add a SHIFT LEFT instruction to the example computer control, using a technique as shown in Table 9.4 and Figs. 9.8 and 9.9.

9.14   When microprogramming is used to generate control signals and a ROM is used, how can the instruction repertoire of the computer be changed?

9.15   In Fig. 9.10 the control signals could be loaded into D flip-flops and the flip-flops' outputs used as the actual control signals. Give advantages and disadvantages of this arrangement.

9.16   Explain the difference between a microoperation and the control signal which implements it.

9.17   To implement BRANCH or JUMP ON ACCUMULATOR NEGATIVE instructions, another control signal C_{27} can be added which, when it is a 1, causes a test of the sign bit of the accumulator and a jump in the control memory to a section of microoperations which cause the desired change in the computer sequence of operations. Design this instruction.

9.18   In writing microprograms it is convenient to have an IF microoperation. For instance, to write a microprogram to implement a branch instruction, we might like an IF ($AC_0 = 1$) THEN $C_{0-6} \rightarrow$ IAR ELSE IAR + 1 $\rightarrow$ IAR microoperation. This says if AC_0 is a 1, then place the current value of C_0 to C_6 in IAR, which means that the next microinstruction will be from the address given in C_0 to C_6. If AC_0 is a 0, the next microinstruction will be from the next location in the control store. Write a microprogram for the branch-register-minus (BRM) instruction, using this microoperation.

9.19   Write a microprogram for a BRP (branch or positive) instruction, using the information in Question 9.18.

9.20   Show how to implement the instruction in Question 9.19.

9.21   Write a microprogram for a SHIFT RIGHT instruction, using the IF type of statement just described. (You will also need a counter.)

9.22 Show how to implement the microprogram in Question 9.21.

9.23 Write a microprogram to implement a multiplication instruction.

9.24 Show how to implement the multiplication instruction in Question 9.23.

9.25 Write a microprogram to implement a DIVIDE instruction.

9.26 Show how to implement your DIVIDE instruction from Question 9.25.

9.27 Reduce the number of control signals used in Fig. 9.11.

9.28 Explain what features you might like in a computer, which is to be microprogrammed to simulate several other computers.

9.29 Discuss some of the advantages and disadvantages of microprogramming.

9.30 Some computers now use a branch or jump scheme where status bits stored in flip-flops are continually being set during arithmetic and logic operations. For instance, status bits Z and N are commonly used to indicate if the result of an operation is "all zero" or "negative." Show how to add such status bits to the arithmetic section of the computer shown in Fig. 9.6.

9.31 When status bits are used, jump instructions are of the form "jump on zero," meaning jump if the Z flip-flop is a 1, or "jump negative," meaning jump if the N flip-flop is a 1. Design these two instructions, using the Z and N circuitry from Question 9.30.

9.32 Discuss the advantages and disadvantages of *random logic* (gate-generated logic) versus microprogramming for a computer control section. Assume that the computer is a minicomputer.

9.33 Compare the microprogramming and conventional random logic techniques for generating the control signals in a general-purpose digital computer. Assume that the computer is to be sold in a large market where both business and scientific programs are to be run. Give the advantages and disadvantages of both techniques for implementing control logic.

9.34 The control of a single-address small computer normally passes through two major phases in executing an instruction which fetches a single operand from memory (an ADD or SUBTRACT instruction, for example). We call these the *instruction cycle* and the *execution cycle*. In order for control to know which phase or cycle it is in, a conventional random logic control unit uses an E flip-flop and an I flip-flop.

(*a*) Why are two flip-flops used instead of one?

(*b*) Why does a microprogrammed version of the same computer not require an E and an I flip-flop?

9.35 Write the transfer in Table 9.3 in register transfer language. Write the transfers for a SUBTRACT instruction (as in Table 9.2) in register transfer language.

9.36 Write a register transfer statement to transfer every other bit (starting with bit X_0) from a register X with 10 flip-flops into a register Y with 5 flip-flops.

COMPUTER ORGANIZATION

Computers are available in a wide range of sizes and capabilities. The smallest computers are called microcomputers, the next largest are minicomputers, followed by small, medium-sized, and finally the large, super, or "maxi" computers. The prices range from a few dollars (for a chip set for a microcomputer) to several million dollars. Speeds are from microseconds per instruction to hundreds of instructions per microsecond.

A microcomputer generally consists of several integrated-circuit (IC) chips, including a central processing unit (CPU) chip (or chips), called a *microprocessor chip* (or chips); several memory chips; and one or more input-output interface chips. These sets of chips can be quite inexpensive (a few dollars in large quantities) or fairly expensive (several hundred dollars for high-speed chip sets). Hand calculators are often assembled from IC chips including one of the lower-priced microprocessor chips. Personal computers also use microcomputer chip sets.

Microprocessor chips also are widely used in so-called original equipment manufacturer (OEM) devices or systems. Traffic lights, printers, communications controllers, automatically controlled instrument complexes, cash registers, and automatic checkout facilities in grocery and department stores, for example, all make wide use of microprocessors.

Similarly, minicomputers, which generally have prices from a thousand to tens of thousands of dollars (including memory and input-output devices), are widely used in control systems and OEM systems as well as in scientific applications and business data processing for small businesses, schools, laboratories, etc. The minicomputer preceded the microcomputer, and it continues to be widely used

COMPUTER ORGANIZATION

since computers in this price range provide many users with enough additional capabilities to warrant the extra cost.

The small- and medium-scale computer market finds applications in businesses and laboratories of all kinds as well as in hospitals, warehouses, small banks, etc. The largest computers are to be found in large corporations such as insurance companies, banks, scientific laboratories, and universities. These "super" computers range from scientific application oriented "number crunchers" to large complexes of input-output devices and memories used in businesses where emphasis is on maintaining large files of data, producing management reports, billing, automatic ordering, inventory control, etc.

The characteristics of these different kinds of computers differ considerably from category to category and from design to design. Computers for business data processing have different system features than those for scientific work. There is also considerable variation in opinion as to how computers for the same application area should be configured, which leads to differing computer designs. The general subject of how computers should be configured and what features should be included is called *computer architecture*.

The subject of *computer architecture* ranges through almost every aspect of computer organization. Included are the lengths of the instruction words, whether the length is variable or there are several different lengths, and how many addresses in memory are referenced by an instruction word. Other architectural considerations concern the number of bits in each memory word, whether instructions and data words are of the same size as the memory words, whether numbers are handled in 1s or 2s complement form or in BCD or some combination of these. What are the instructions provided, how are the memories organized, and how are input-output devices interfaced? As can be seen, computer architecture is a large and rich subject which deals with most aspects of computer design and organization and interacts with every aspect of the computer.

OBJECTIVES

1 The addressing techniques used in computers are explained, and examples from existing computers used to illustrate these techniques.

2 Good programming practice calls for breaking programs into subprograms. A single subprogram can be used several times in an overall program. Computer instruction repertoires have special instructions to go to and return from subprograms, and these are described along with how they work.

3 Interrupts from I/O devices are handled differently by various computers. The general principles involved are discussed, and examples from computers presented.

4 The architectures and instruction repertoires for several present-day computers are described. Examples of sections of programs for these computers and explanations for their operation are included.

10.1 A given computer has one or more basic formats for its instruction words. We have emphasized the single-address instruction word, which is popular for microcomputers. There are also several other formats in use.

Two-address instructions

The number of divisions in the basic computer instruction word is determined primarily by the number of addresses which are referred to. The single-address instruction has been covered. Many computers, however, have two-address instruction words with three sections (Fig. 10.1), the first consisting of the OP code and the second and third sections each containing the address of a location in the memory.

Different computers use these addresses differently. Generally, both addresses in a two-address machine specify operands, and the result is stored at the first address.[1] The Minneapolis-Honeywell 200 and the IBM 370 and 1801 series have two-address instructions that provide examples in which each address refers to an operand in the memory.

In many computers, instead of a single accumulator, there are two or more registers which are called either *multiple accumulators* or *general-purpose registers*. An instruction word will have the first address section (the "address of operand A" section in Fig. 10.1) tell which general register contains one of the operands. The second address section of the instruction word will then give the address in memory of the second operand. If only two accumulators or general registers are provided, only 1 bit is needed for the address section; if 16 general registers are used, then 4 bits will be needed for the first address. Results are generally stored in the general register (accumulator) specified by the first address.

In some computers instruction words are provided in which each of the two addresses refers to general registers. Thus, for instance, in a computer with 16 general registers, an instruction word would consist of the OP code plus two 4-bit address sections.

---

[1]In several computers the result of the calculation is stored at the second of the two addresses.

FIGURE 10.1

Formats for instructions.

Operation code	Address of operand

Single address instruction

Operation code	Address of operand (A)	Address of operand (B)

Two address instruction

Two-address instruction words in which one or both addresses refer to general registers are shorter than two-address instruction words where both addresses refer to the memory, and this format is popular in microcomputers and minicomputers.

Zero-address instructions—stacks

There is a type of instruction word that does not specify any location in memory for an operand, but which relies on what is called a *stack* to provide operands. Basically a stack is a set of consecutive locations in a memory into which operands can be placed. The name *stack* is derived from the fact that the memory is organized like a stack of plates in a cafeteria. (Each operand can be thought of as a plate.) The first operand placed on the stack is said to be at the *bottom* of the stack. Placing an operand on the stack is called *pushing*, and removing an operand is called *popping* the operand. The operand most recently placed on the stack is said to be on the *top* of the stack. Only this top operand is immediately available.

If we push operands *A*, *B*, and *C* onto an empty stack and then pop an operand, *C* will be removed. If we push *A*, *B*, and *C* in order and then pop three operands, first *C* will be popped, then *B*, and finally *A*. (This last-in first-out principle leads to stacks sometimes being called *LIFO lists*.)

Figure 10.2 shows the operation of a stack. Stacks are generally maintained as a set of words in a memory. Each word therefore has a fixed length (number of bits) and an address. The *stack pointer* is a register that contains the address of the top operand in the stack. The stack pointer is incremented or decremented when an operand is pushed or popped.

If an ADD instruction is given to a computer using a stack architecture, the top two operands in the stack will be removed; added and then the sum is placed on the top of the stack. Similarly, a MULTIPLY instruction would cause the top two operands to be multiplied and the product placed on the stack.

Since only the OP-code section of an arithmetic instruction need be given to specify an arithmetic operation, these instruction words can be very short. It is still

FIGURE 10.2

Stack operations.

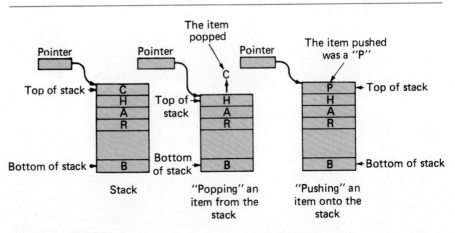

Note: In this case each item in the stack is a single character. The stack items could be numbers, words, records, etc. The pointer contains the address of the "top of the stack."

necessary, however, to move operands from memory onto the stack and from the stack back into the memory, and the instruction words for this will be longer since memory addresses must be specified. (These instruction words will be like single-address instruction words, except that the operands are moved to and from the stack instead of to and from the accumulator.)

The advocates of stacked computer architecture have some convincing arguments, but problems do exist. Stacked computers include the Burroughs 5500 and 1700 and the Hewlett-Packard 3000. Stacks are widely used in other sections of computers we show.

REPRESENTATION OF INSTRUCTIONS AND DATA

10.2 Important features of a computer's architecture concern the number of bits in instruction words, the size of memory words, and the way data are represented in the computer. In most early computers and in some present-day computers, the high-speed memory contains the same number of bits at each address (in each location) as the instruction words. Similarly, numbers are represented by using the same number of bits. This makes for straightforward implementation. An example of a computer with this structure can be found in the 6100, which has a 12-bit/word memory, 12-bit instruction words with a 3-bit OP code, and numbers represented by using a 12-bit signed 2s complement number system. Most of the large scientific number-crunching machines also use this structure, and CDC produces a number of 64-bit/word large computers with this basic structure as well as some smaller 24-bit/word computers. CRAY also makes computers of this type.

There is a desire to be efficient with the length of instruction words. Also, business data processing involves much manipulation involving character strings (names, addresses, text, etc.). The desire to create computer architectures that conserve on instruction word length and also permit storing of strings of characters of arbitrary length efficiently has led to a number of computer architectures with (1) only 8 bits at each address in memory, so a single alphanumeric character can be stored at each address, and (2) instruction words with variable lengths (each word length is some multiple of 8 bits).

As a result, most small computers now have memory words of 8 bits per word. Instruction words are then of variable length with each being some multiple of 8 bits. Data words are also multiples of 8 bits with many microprocessors having 8-, 16-, and 32-bit words.

ADDRESSING TECHNIQUES

10.3 When an address in memory is given in an instruction word, the most obvious technique is simply to give the address in binary form. This is called *direct addressing,* and the instruction words in the examples in Chap. 9 all use direct addressing.

Although direct addressing provides the most straightforward (and fastest) way to give a memory address, several other techniques are also used. These techniques are generally motivated by one of the following considerations:

1 *Desire to shorten address section* For instance, if we have a computer with a 256K memory, 18 bits will be required for each direct address, some addressing techniques are used to reduce this number.

2 *Programmer convenience* Several addressing techniques (such as index registers, which are described) provide a convenience to the programmer in writing programs.

3 *System operation facilities* In many computer systems, the computer will have several different programs in memory at a given time and will alternate the running of these programs. To efficiently load and remove these programs from memory in differing locations, addressing techniques are provided which make the program *relocatable,* meaning that the same program can be run in many different sections of memory. The operating systems in microcomputers use this facility.

The following sections describe the basic addressing techniques now in use: direct addressing, immediate addressing, paging, relative addressing, indirect addressing, and indexed addressing. Examples of these techniques are given for actual computers and enough are given so the principle can be clearly understood. Knowing how real computers use these techniques is important.

DIRECT ADDRESSING

10.4 Simply giving the complete binary address in memory is the most direct way to locate an operand or to give an address to jump to. As a result, most computers have some form of *direct addressing.* The following examples are for computers that will also be used in the sections on more complex addressing strategies.

Example

The 8080 microprocessor has a single 8-bit accumulator. The 8080's memory is organized into words of 8 bits each which are called *bytes.* An OP code for this microprocessor occupies 8 bits, or 1 byte, an entire memory location. The address bits are then located in the following memory locations. Since 2^{16} words can be used in a memory, 2 bytes are required for a direct address. As a result, a direct-address instruction requires 3 bytes in memory—one for the OP code and two for the direct address.

In executing an instruction, the 8080 CPU[2] always obtains the OP code from memory first, and this tells how many bytes are required for the address. The 8080 CPU then reads the necessary bytes from memory and assembles a complete instruction word in its registers, which it then proceeds to execute.

A typical direct-access instruction in the 8080 is the LDA (load accumulator) instruction with OP code 00111010 (3A hexadecimal). This OP code is followed

---

[2]The 8080 CPU is constructed on a single chip. This chip, which is sometimes called the *8080 microprocessor chip,* interprets and executes instructions. Memory is on separate chips, as are input-output interface circuits.

by 2 bytes giving the address in memory of the 8-bit word to be loaded into the accumulator. The low-order (least significant) bits of the address are given in the first byte of the address and the high-order bits in the second byte.

Assume that the memory contains these values:

ADDRESS (HEXADECIMAL)	CONTENTS (HEXADECIMAL)
0245	3A
0246	49
0247	03
. . .	. . .
0349	23

DIRECT ADDRESSING

The 3 bytes in locations 245, 246, and 247 contain a single LDA instruction which, when executed, will cause the value 23_{16} to be transferred into the accumulator of the 8080 microprocessor.

Example

The 6800 microprocessor has two 8-bit accumulators which are referred to as accumulator A and accumulator B. The microprocessor has 8 bits per memory word. The OP code of an instruction occupies 8 bits and therefore a complete memory word. The address bits for an instruction word are in the memory location(s) following the OP code. The memory can be up to 2^{16} locations in size. As an example of direct addressing, the OP code for ADDA, which causes the contents of the address referenced to be added to and then stored in accumulator A, is BB (hexadecimal), or 10111011 (binary). If the microprocessor reads this OP code, it knows that the address is given in the following 16 bits. As a result, if the 6800 CPU reads an OP code of BB, it then reads the next 2 bytes in memory to obtain the address. The microprocessor reads from this address and performs the required addition. The next OP code is read from the memory location following the two locations that contained the address.[3]

The OP code for an ADDB instruction, which causes the number stored in the memory location referenced by the next 16 bits to be added to accumulator B, is FB (hexadecimal). Now examine Fig. 10.3. If the microprocessor reads the two instruction words shown, it will cause addition into first accumulator A, then accumulator B, and will take the next instruction word from location 17 in the memory.

In the 6800 microprocessor, instruction words can have addresses with 1 byte or 2 bytes, as will be seen. [Some instructions have only "implied addresses" (no address bits); HALT is such an instruction.] The microprocessor must therefore read the OP code before it can determine how many more locations from the memory need to be read to form the instruction word.

One note is necessary here. The 6800 microprocessor also has instructions with only 8-bit addresses. In this case an address has only 8 bits, and thus only

---

[3]Notice that the 6800 places the most significant bits in the address in the second byte and the least significant bits in the third byte. (The 8080 does the reverse.)

ADDA OP code is *BB* for direct addressing

ADDB OP code is *FB* for direct addressing

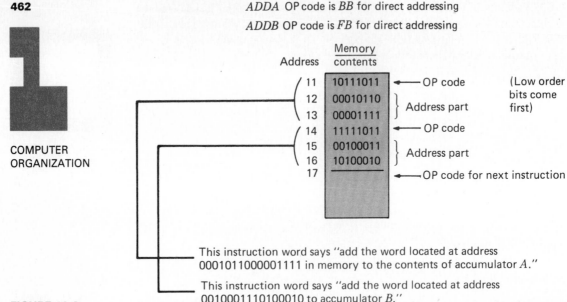

FIGURE 10.3

6800 microprocessor
instruction execution.

the first 256 bytes in the memory can be referenced. As an example, an instruction
to add the number at the location given in the following 8 bits to accumulator *A*
has OP code 9B. An instruction to add to accumulator *B* the number at the location
given in the following byte has OP code DB. The OP code tells whether a complete
16-bit address or an 8-bit address is to be read from the memory. (In its manuals
Motorola calls the 8-bit address instruction words *direct-addressing instructions*
and the 16-bit address instruction words *extended direct-addressing instructions*.)
The 16-bit addresses have been used to illustrate the direct-addressing technique
because they are more natural and all the memory can be reached.

Example

The PDP-11 is a DEC minicomputer and microcomputer series with sizes ranging
from small to large. A particular size is designated by the model number, so that
a PDP-11/05 is a small computer, the PDP-11/45 is a medium-sized machine, and
the PDP-11/70 is a fairly large system. This series of computers is typical of what
is offered by DEC and other manufacturers.

   The PDP-11 has eight 16-bit general registers (accumulators). It is common
practice to name these general registers R_0 to R_7, and we follow this practice.

   The PDP-11 memory is organized into 8-bit words, so 1 byte is in each
memory location. The PDP-11 has a number of addressing modes and, as a result,
a fairly complex instruction word format.

   A typical direct-address instruction in the PDP-11 involves adding the numbers in two general registers and storing the sum in one of the registers. The
instruction word to do this has three sections: the OP code, the source address,
and the destination address. (In an ADD, the number in the source register is added

to that in the destination register, and the sum is placed in the destination register.) Since the source and destination are each general registers and there are eight general registers, 3 bits are required to give each address. However, since the PDP-11 has a number of addressing modes, 3 extra bits are included in each of the source and destination addresses to tell which addressing mode is to be used. The instruction word format is as follows:

OP code	Source address	Destination address
15 12	11 6	5 0

The first (leftmost) 3 bits in the source and destination addresses give the mode, and for direct addressing these will be all 0s. The next 3 bits give the register number. The OP code for ADD in the PDP-11 is 0110, and so the instruction word which will add register 3 to register 5 and store the sum in register 5 is

0110	000011	000101

Another example of direct addressing is the increment instruction, which simply adds 1 to a selected general register. The instruction word to accomplish this has two sections: an OP code and an address section. The address section has 3 bits to tell the mode and 3 bits to designate the register. The OP code for an INC (increment) instruction is 0000101010. Thus an instruction that will increment general register 5 is

0000101010	000101

OP code   address part

Notice that this OP code is larger than the ADD OP code, because only one operand is required here. (The first 4 bits are not duplicated in any of these larger OP codes; they tell the class of operation.)

IMMEDIATE ADDRESSING

10.5 A straightforward way to obtain an operand is simply to have it follow the instruction word in memory. Suppose that we want to add the number 7 to the accumulator in a single accumulator computer, and suppose that the memory is organized in 8-bit bytes. A direct way to cause this addition would be to have an 8-bit OP code which says to ADD and that the augend follows "immediately" in memory (the next byte). The computer would then read the OP code, get the byte to be added from memory (which would contain 7), add it into the accumulator, and take the next instruction word's OP code from the byte following the byte containing the augend. This is essentially how the 8080 (and 6800) computers operate.

COMPUTER
ORGANIZATION

In general, immediate addressing simply means that an operand immediately follows the instruction word in memory.

Example

For the 8080 microprocessor, the instruction ADI (add immediate) has OP code 11000110 and tells the CPU to take the byte following this OP code and add it into the accumulator. Consider the following:

ADDRESS	CONTENTS
16_{16}	11000110
17_{16}	00001100
. . .	. . .

When the computer reaches address 16_{16} in memory, it reads the OP code, sees that this instruction is an ADI instruction, takes the next byte from the memory which is 00001100, adds this into the accumulator, and takes the next OP code from location 18_{16} in memory.

Example

The 6800 microcomputer has two accumulators, and so the OP code must tell which accumulator to use. The instruction ANDA with OP code 84_{16} will cause the byte following the OP code to be ANDed bit by bit with accumulator A, while the instruction ANDB with OP code $C4_{16}$ will cause the byte following the OP code to be ANDed bit by bit with accumulator B.

Suppose that accumulator A contains 01100111 and accumulator B 10011101. Then consider this in memory:

ADDRESS	CONTENTS
10_{16}	10000100
11_{16}	11010101
12_{16}	11000100
13_{16}	10100101
14_{16}	. . .

The 6800 will read the ANDA at location 10_{16} and AND the next byte with accumulator A, giving 01000101, which will be placed in accumulator A. It will then read the ANDB in location 12_{16}, AND the next byte with B to give 10000101, place this in accumulator B, and read the next OP code for an instruction from location 14_{16}.

Example

The PDP-11 has eight accumulators and so must tell which accumulator to use when an addition instruction uses immediate addressing. The OP code for ADD is 0110, and an instruction word for an immediate add looks like this:

0110	010111	000011

OP code   source   destination

The source bits say that the add is an immediate add and that the augend is in the 2 bytes (since the accumulators have 16 bits) following this word. The destination section here refers to general register 3, so the next 16 bits will be added into general register 3. (Placing 101 in the rightmost bits instead of 011 will cause an addition into general register 5, etc.)

Now consider that general register 4 contains 000061_8, and the memory is as follows (all these numbers are in octal, which is DEC's practice):

ADDRESS	CONTENTS
1020–1021	062704
1022–1023	000012
. . .	. . .

Execution of these by the CPU will result in 12_8 being added into general register 4, giving 73_8 in that register.

Notice in the PDP-11 that the ADD instruction OP code is the same for immediate and for direct addressing. It is the first 3 bits in the source and destination address sections that tell the addressing mode, not the OP code.

PAGING

10.6 Microcomputers and minicomputers sometimes alleviate the problem of addressing a large memory with a short word by using a technique that actually arose in a large computer called Atlas. This technique is called *paging*. When paging is used, the memory is divided into pages, each of a fixed length. An instruction word then designates a page and a location on that page.

Example

For the 6100 microprocessor mentioned in Chap. 9, the basic memory of 4096 words of 12 bits each is divided into 32 *pages* of 128 words each. Thus page 0 contains the memory locations from 0 to 127 (decimal), page 1 refers to the memory locations from 128 to 255, . . . , and finally page 31 refers to the locations from 3968 to 4095, as shown in Fig. 10.4. Then 5 bits are required to reference a page, and 7 bits to reference a location within a page.

The addressing of data in a computer with paging varies from computer to computer. Generally the address given in the instruction word can refer either to the page in which the instruction word lies or possibly to some other particular page previously specified.

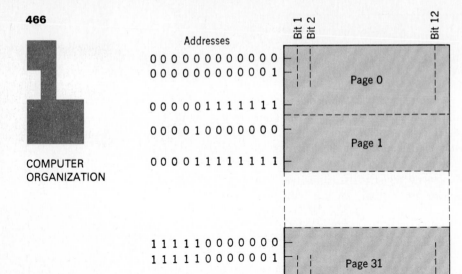

FIGURE 10.4

Layout of 32-page
memory with 4096
words of 12 bits.

Example

For the 6100 the seventh bit in a 12-bit instruction word is called the *page bit*. This bit tells whether the 7-bit address in the instruction word refers to the page in which the instruction lies (in which case the bit is a 1) or to the first page in the memory (in which case the bit is a 0).

Figure 10.5 shows the page bit in the instruction word for the 6100. If this bit is a 0 in a TAD (2s complement ADD) (or other) instruction, the address given by bits 6 to 0 refers to an address on page 0 (see Fig. 10.4). Therefore the instruction word 001000001110 refers to location 14_8 in memory, regardless of where in memory the instruction is placed. (The first 3 bits are 001, the OP code for TAD.)

If the instruction word has a 1 in the page bit position and if the final bits give the number 14_8, then the address to be used is the 15_8th address on the page in which the instruction lies. This is shown in Fig. 10.5 where the instruction word 001010001100, when located at address 000100110000 in memory, points to location 000100001100 in memory; and the augend for the TAD would be fetched from that address.

Paging shortens the length of the address part. For the 6100, a 4096-word memory, which would require 12 address bits if a direct address were used, is addressed by using a page bit and 8 more bits. Some addresses are not reachable from a given instruction word, however. To reach addresses not on page 0 or the page containing the instruction word, a technique called *indirect addressing* is used, as will be shown.

RELATIVE ADDRESSING

10.7 *Relative addressing* is quite similar to paging, except that the address referred to is relative to the instruction word. In general, when relative addressing is used, the address part of the instruction word gives a number to be added to the

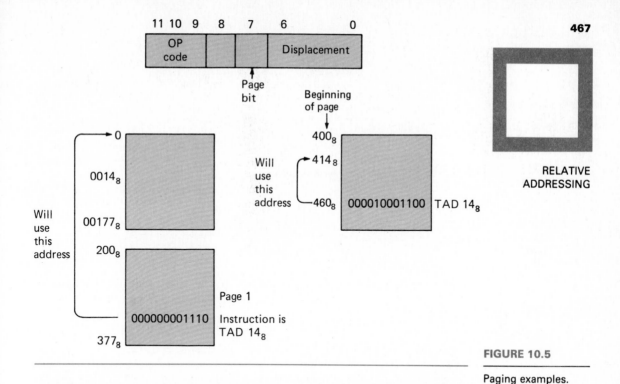

FIGURE 10.5

Paging examples.

address following the instruction word. Thus in relative addressing, the address section contains a displacement from the instruction word's location in the memory. Giving only a displacement reduces the number of address bits but makes only a part of the memory available. For instance, if the instruction word uses relative addressing and the address part contains 8 bits, then only 256 memory locations are available to a given instruction.

Relative addressing is best explained by using examples.

Example

The 6800 microprocessor can have up to 2^{16} memory words. So 16 bits are required to address the entire memory in a direct mode. When relative addressing is used, this address is reduced to an 8-bit displacement, shortening the instruction word.

In the 6800 a relative-address instruction word contains only the OP code and an 8-bit address, so only two locations in memory (bytes) are required. (The OP code tells what kind of addressing to use.) When the addressing is relative, the address in the second byte of the instruction is added to the address at which the OP code lies plus 2. The address in the second byte is considered as a signed 2s complement number, however, so the address referenced can be at a higher or lower address in memory than the instruction word. In fact, the address can be from -125 to $+129$ memory words from the address of the OP code.

Figure 10.6 shows this. The OP code for a BRA (branch) instruction with relative addressing is 20 (hexadecimal). The microprocessor would read the OP code at location 10, see that it is a BRA instruction, get 00000101 from the next memory location, add this 5 (decimal) to 2 plus 10 (where the OP code lies), giving 17. The next OP code would then come from location 17. In Fig. 10.6 this OP

COMPUTER
ORGANIZATION

FIGURE 10.6

Relative addressing
in 6800 micro-
processor.

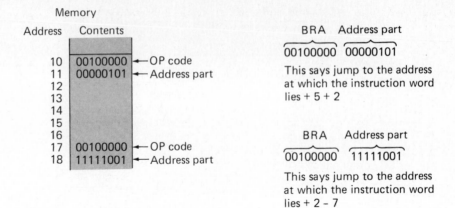

code is again BRA, and location 18 contains 11111001, which is -7 decimal. Since $17 + 2 - 7 = 12$, the next OP code would come from location 12.

Example

In the PDP-11, a relative addressing mode can be used for the INC (increment) instruction. The OP code for INC in the PDP-11 is 0052_8, and 27_8 in the address part indicates a relative addressing mode.

Assume that we have the following situation in memory:

ADDRESS (OCTAL)	CONTENTS (OCTAL)
1020	005627
1022	000012
1024	. . .

The relative addressing feature operates as follows. The displacement, 12_8 in this example, is added to the address following the instruction word, in this case 1024. This gives 1036, and so the number at location 1036 in memory would be incremented.

INDIRECT ADDRESSING

10.8 Another widely used variation in addressing is called *indirect addressing*. Indirect addressing causes the instruction word to give the address, not of the operand to be used, but of the address of the operand. For example, if we write ADD 302 and the instruction is a conventional direct-addressing addition instruction, the number at location 302 will be added to the word currently in the accumulator.

If the addition instruction is indirectly addressed and we write IAD 302 (indirect add), then the number stored at address 302 will give the *address* of the operand to be used. As an example, when the instruction word at address 5 in the memory in the following program is performed, it will cause the number 164 to be added to the current contents of the accumulator.

MEMORY ADDRESS	CONTENTS
5	IAD 302
. . .	. . .
302	495
. . .	. . .
495	164

**INDIRECT
ADDRESSING**

Example

The 6100 has a 12-bit instruction word, as shown in Fig. 10.7. The instruction word contains a 3-bit OP code, a page bit, an indirect bit, and a 7-bit unsigned binary number. The page bit has been explained. There is also an indirect bit. A 0 in the indirect bit says, "This is not an indirect address." However, a 1 in the indirect bit indicates the address referenced is indirect.

As an example refer to Fig. 10.7. The TAD instruction with OP code 001 is used again. The figure shows a case in which the instruction word is TAD with the page bit a 0, so the address is on page 0 in the memory, and the indirect bit is a 1. Since the 7 address bits point to location 62_8, that location contains the address of the operand. Again, referring to the figure, at location 62_8 we find a 3432_8, and it is this location, at which the operand 3255, is located, that is added to the accumulator.

Notice that the entire 4096-word memory is accessible to an instruction word through the use of indirect addressing because each memory word contains 12 bits. Placing an address on page 0 where it can be reached from anywhere in the memory makes that address always available in programming.

FIGURE 10.7

Indirect addressing in 6100 microprocessor.

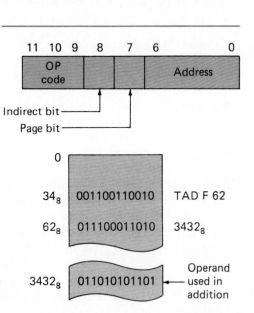

**COMPUTER
ORGANIZATION**

Example

In the 8080 microprocessor there are several registers in the CPU in addition to the accumulator. These are called *scratchpad registers* and may be used in several types of instructions. The scratchpad registers are named *B, C, D, E, H,* and *L.* The registers are each 8 bits in length. Sometimes they can be handled in pairs with a resultant length of 16 bits, thus forming a complete address. Then an indirect-address mode can be used where the number in the register pair points to the address where the operand lies.

For example, in the 8080 there is a MOV (move) instruction which moves an 8-bit word from the memory into a designated register. The format for this instruction word is as follows:

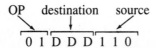

$$OP \quad destination \quad source$$
$$0\ 1\ D\ D\ D\ 1\ 1\ 0$$

The DDD section here is 3 bits,[4] which simply call out the register into which the 8-bit word from memory is to be moved. The accumulator has number 111, register *B* has number 000, scratchpad register *C* has number 001, etc. The location in the memory from which the word to be moved is taken is always given by the register pair *H, L.* Thus if register pair *H, L* contains $45A2_{16}$ (*H* contains 45, *L* contains A2), then the address in memory used will be $45A2_{16}$.

If the instruction word is 01111110 and register pair *H, L* contains 3742_{16}, then the word at location 3742_{16} will be moved into the accumulator. If the instruction word is 01001110 and the *H, L* pair contains 2379_{16}, then the word at location 2379_{16} in memory will be moved into scratchpad register *C*.

Moving an address into the *H, L* registers in the CPU makes the word at that address available to an instruction word through the use of indirect addressing. Complete details and how to load the *H, L* pair are given in Sec. 10.11.

INDEXED ADDRESSING

10.9   There is a variation on conventional direct memory addressing which facilitates programming, particularly the programming of sequences of instructions that are to be repeated many times on sets of data distributed throughout the machine. This technique is called *indexing*.

Indexing was first used in a computer developed at the University of Manchester. A register named the *B box* was added to the control section.[5] The contents of the B box could be added to the contents of the memory address register when desired. When the B box was used, the address of the operand located in memory would be at the address written by the programmer plus the contents of the B box. The U.S. term for B box is *index register,* and we use this term. Index registers are so useful that computers sometimes provide several.

---

[4]Each D stands for a single destination bit that can be either a 0 or a 1.
[5]The idea was so useful that several B boxes were later used.

Use of index registers eases writing programs that process data in tables, such as those described in Chap. 1, greatly reducing the number of instructions required in an iterative program. The index registers permit the automatic modification of the addresses referred to without altering the instructions stored in memory.

When index registers are included in a computer, a section of the instruction word tells the computer whether an index register is to be used and, if so, which one. So the basic instruction word is broken, for a single-address computer, into three parts instead of two. A typical division is shown in Fig. 10.8.

Generally two additional instructions are also added. One is used to load the index register, and the other modifies the number stored in the specified index register or causes the computer to branch.

If an index register is not to be used, the programmer places 0s in the index register designation section of the word. If there are three index registers, there will be two binary digits in the index register section of the word, and the index register desired can be selected by placing the correct digits in the index register designation section.

To describe the operation of the index registers, two instructions are introduced. We designate one of these by the mnemonic code SIR (set index registers), and this instruction will cause the address section of the instruction word to be transferred into the index register designated by the index register designation bits in the word. For instance, 01 SIR 300 will load the number 300 into index register 01. Since the address section normally contains the address section of the computer word, all that is required is that the contents of the address register be transferred into the index register designated.

We designate the second instruction with the mnemonic code BRI (branch on index). This instruction will cause the contents of the index register designated to be decreased by 1 if the number stored in the index register is positive. At the same time, the computer will branch to the address in the address section of the instruction word, taking its next instruction from that address. If the index register designated contains a 0, the computer will not branch but instead will perform the next instruction in normal order.

The index registers may be used during any normal instruction by simply placing the digits indicating the index register to be used in the index register designation section of the computer word. For instance, if index register 01 contains 300 and we write a CAD (clear and add) instruction

01 CAD 200

then the computer will add the contents of index register 01 to the contents of the address section, and the address used will be the total of these two. Since index

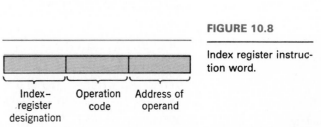

FIGURE 10.8

Index register instruction word.

Index–
register
designation

Operation
code

Address of
operand

TABLE 10.1

ADDRESS IN MEMORY	INSTRUCTION WORD			COMMENTS
	INDEX REGISTER DESIGNATION	OP CODE	ADDRESS SECTION	
0	01	SIR	99	The number 99 is placed in index register 01.
1	01	CAD	201	Picks up number to be added.
2	00	ADD	301	Adds to total thus far.
3	00	STO	301	Stores the current sum.
4	01	BRI	1	Subtracts 1 from index register 01 and then branches to first instruction until index register 01 contains 0, then proceeds to next instruction.
5	00	HLT	0	
201 to 300	Contain numbers to be added.			
301	Location at which sum is stored.			

register 01 contains 300 and the address section contains 200, the address from which the operand will be taken will be address 500 in memory.

An example of the use of an index register may be found in the short program shown in Table 10.1, which will add all the numbers stored in memory addresses 201 to 300 and store the sum in address 301.

The program repeats the instructions at addresses 1 to 4 until index register 01 is finally at 0. Then the computer does not branch and is halted by the next instruction.

Example

The 6800 microprocessor mentioned before has a single 16-bit index register. For the ADDA instruction, when indexing is used, the OP code is AB (hexadecimal). This instruction has only one 8-bit address part, so an entire instruction word requires only 16 bits (two memory locations).

Figure 10.9 shows an example for the 6800 microprocessor. The instruction word is at locations 68 and 69 in memory and is an indexed ADDA instruction. The 8-bit address part contains 14 (hexadecimal), and the index register in the CPU contains 0102. This results in the number at location 116 in memory being added into accumulator A.

The 6800 has instructions to load, increment, or decrement the index register, and these are covered in Sec. 10.12.

SINGLE-ADDRESS COMPUTER ORGANIZATION

10.10 A straightforward example of a single-address computer is the Harris 6100, which is widely used in word processors and also personal computers and I/O device interfaces. This computer is used to point out some basic principles in computer architecture.

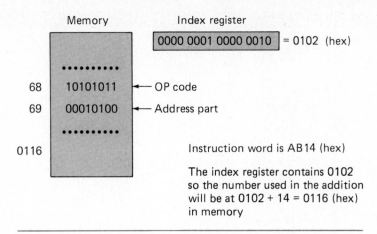

Memory

Index register

0000 0001 0000 0010 = 0102 (hex)

. . . .

68   10101011 ← OP code

69   00010100 ← Address part

. . . .

0116

Instruction word is AB14 (hex)

The index register contains 0102 so the number used in the addition will be at 0102 + 14 = 0116 (hex) in memory

FIGURE 10.9

Index register in the 6800 microprocessor.

The basic organization of the 6100 is shown in Fig. 10.10. It has a 12-bit instruction word as shown in Fig. 10.11. The memory is also organized in 12-bit words, and a basic memory block consists of $2^{12} = 4096$ words. Since the instruction word is very short, the designers have allowed only 3 bits for the OP-code part; thus, as shown in Fig.10.11, there are only eight basic classes of instruction words.

Several of the basic instructions are very straightforward. For instance, the TAD instruction (for 2s complement ADD) simply performs a 2s complement addition of the operand addressed in memory to the operand currently in the 12-bit single accumulator and places the sum in this accumulator. There is an extra flip-flop called the *link,* or *L, bit* which receives any overflow from this addition. The OP code for TAD is 001_2, or 1_8.

Similarly, the AND instruction simply performs a bit-by-bit AND on the operand addressed in memory and the contents of the accumulator, placing the result in the accumulator. The OP code for AND is 000_2, or 0_8.

The addressing techniques used in the 9 bits to form addresses have been described. The eight bit in an instruction word is a 0 if the address is direct and a 1 if indirect (the address of the address). The seven bit is a 0 if the remaining 7 bits (bits 0 to 6) give the actual address on page 0 of the memory and a 1 if the address is on the same page as the instruction word.

An ISZ (increment and skip if zero) instruction simply increments the word addressed and returns it to memory. However, if this word becomes a 0, the next instruction following the ISZ instruction is not executed. Instead, the computer next executes the word in memory following this word. This particular instruction is very useful in indexing through tables when indirect addressing is used and is provided as a substitute for index registers.

The DCA (deposit and clear accumulator) instruction stores the accumulator in the memory at the address specified and also clears the accumulator to all 0s. The OP code for DCA is 011_2, or 3_8.

The JMS (jump to subroutine) instruction brings up an important feature in instruction repertoires for computers. It is good form in writing a computer program to break the program into as many subprograms (separable pieces) as possible.

473

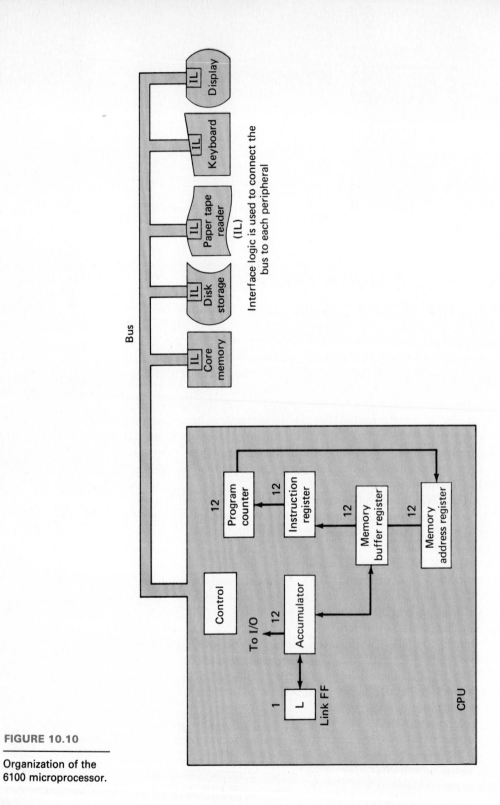

FIGURE 10.10

Organization of the 6100 microprocessor.

Interface logic is used to connect the bus to each peripheral (IL)

BASIC INSTRUCTIONS

AND	0000	Logical AND
TAD	1000	2s complement add
ISZ	2000	Increment, and skip if zero
DCA	3000	Deposit and clear AC
JMS	4000	Jump to subroutine
JMP	5000	Jump
IOT	6000	In/out transfer
OPR	7000	Operate

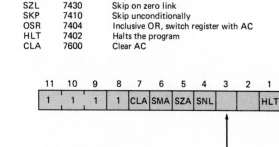

Memory Reference Instruction Bit Assignments

GROUP 1 OPERATE MICROINSTRUCTIONS

			Sequence
NOP	7000	No operation	—
CLA	7200	Clear AC	1
CLL	7100	Clear link	1
CMA	7040	Complement AC	2
CML	7020	Complement link	2
RAR	7010	Rotate AC and link right one	4
RAL	7004	Rotate AC and link left one	4
RTR	7012	Rotate AC and link right two	4
RTL	7006	Rotate AC and link left two	4
IAC	7001	Increment AC	3
BSW	7002	Swap bytes in AC	4

Logical sequences
1 CLA, CLL
2 CMA, CML
3 IAC
4 RAR, RAL, RTR, RTL, BSW

GROUP 2 OPERATE MICROINSTRUCTIONS

SMA	7500	Skip on minus AC
SZA	7440	Skip on zero AC
SPA	7510	Skip on plus AC
SNA	7450	Skip on nonzero AC
SNL	7420	Skip on nonzero link
SZL	7430	Skip on zero link
SKP	7410	Skip unconditionally
OSR	7404	Inclusive OR, switch register with AC
HLT	7402	Halts the program
CLA	7600	Clear AC

Logical sequences
1 (Bit 8 is zero) Either SMA or SZA or SZA or SNL
1 (Bit 8 is one) Both SPA and SNA and SZL
2 CLA
3 OSR, HLT

INTERNAL IOT MICROINSTRUCTIONS
PROGRAM INTERRUPT AND FLAG (1.2 μs)

SKON	6000	Skip if interrupt ON, and turn OFF
ION	6001	Turn interrupt ON
IOF	6002	Turn interrupt OFF
SRQ	6003	Skip on interrupt request
GTF	6004	Get interrupt flags
RTF	6005	Restore interrupt flags
SGT	6006	Skip on Greater Than flag
CAF	6007	Clear all flags

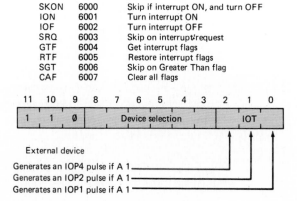

FIGURE 10.11

Instruction repertoire
for the 6100. (*Harris
Semiconductor.*)

IOT Instruction Bit Assignments

475

These subprograms or subroutines[6] are then jumped to whenever the function they perform is required [refer to Fig. 10.12(a)].

The problem confronting the computer designer is that a given subprogram can be jumped to from several different locations in the program. This is shown in Fig. 10.12(b). For instance, in minicomputers and microcomputers no square root instruction is provided. If many square roots are called for in a program, the programmer writes a single square root subprogram (or subroutine), and whenever the program must find a square root, a jump is made to this subprogram. After the square root has been formed, the subprogram then causes a jump back to the instruction following the JMS subprogram instruction in the original program section. The subprogram is said to be *called,* and it exits by returning to the *calling program*.

The problem is to arrange for a smooth jump to the called subprogram and to make it easy for the subprogram to return to the original program. To implement this, it is necessary to "plant" the address of the instruction to be returned to when the subprogram is finished in some convenient place for the subprogram. Since the program counter (instruction counter) contains this address when the jump is made, most computers provide a "jump to subroutine" instruction that will store the program counter before the jump is made.

The JMS instruction in the 6100 operates as follows. The program counter is stored at the address given in the address portion of the JMS instruction. The computer then jumps to the next address in memory. That is, if we write JMS 50_8 (where 50_8 is the 50th location in memory) and if our instruction word is at 201_8 in the memory, then when the JMS 50_8 instruction is executed, the value 202_8 will be stored at location 50_8 in the memory, and the computer will actually jump to or execute the word at location 51_8 next.[7]

Planting the program counter's contents at location 50_8 in the above example enables the writer of the subroutine to exit from the subprogram by placing a JMP (jump) instruction at the end of the subprogram, using address 50_8 in the address section but making the address an indirect address. Therefore, the computer will actually jump to the address stored at location 50_8, which will be 202_8, and the next instruction executed will be that at location 202_8.

Notice that a subprogram set up in this way can be jumped to by a JMS and exited by using a JMP indirectly from any place in memory, and the return will always be correct.

The above scheme is a good one and has been used (with variations) in several computers. But it has the problem that if a subprogram calls another subprogram which calls the first subprogram, then the return address for the original return will be wiped out. While this may seem unlikely, programs can become very complicated, and this must be avoided.

If a subprogram can call itself or can call another program which calls it without damage, then the subprogram is said to be *recursive*.

A scheme whereby jumps to subprograms can be made so that a subprogram can call itself is given in a later section.

---

[6]We use the words *subroutine* and *subprogram* to mean the same thing. Different manufacturers use different words.
[7]DEC uses octal numbers almost exclusively in 6100 programming.

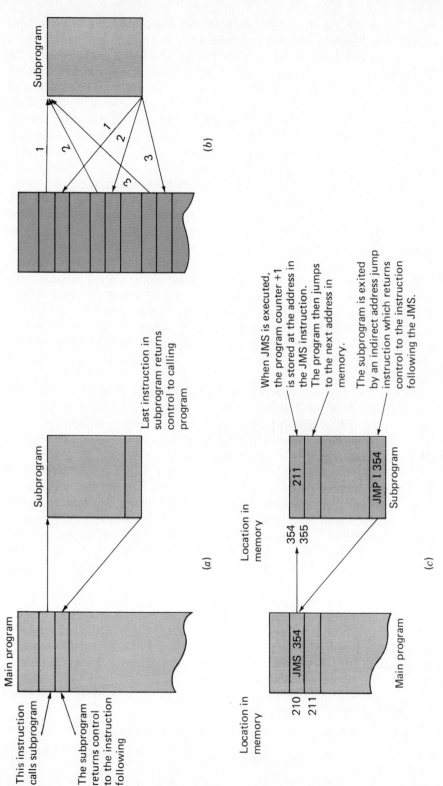

Subprogram

Main program

This instruction
calls subprogram

The subprogram
returns control
to the instruction
following

Last instruction in
subprogram returns
control to calling
program

(a)

Subprogram

1
2
3
1
2
3

(b)

Location in
memory

Main program

JMS 354

210
211

Location in
memory

211

354
355

JMP I 354

Subprogram

When JMS is executed,
the program counter +1
is stored at the address in
the JMS instruction.

The program then jumps
to the next address in
memory.

The subprogram is exited
by an indirect address jump
instruction which returns
control to the instruction
following the JMS.

(c)

FIGURE 10.12

(a) Calling a subpro-
gram. *(b)* The same
subprogram may be
called several times.
(c) How the 6100
handles subprogram
calls and returns.

The 6100 is bused, and input-output devices are connected to this bus. Input-output in the 6100 is provided by the IOT (input-output transfer) instruction. The input-output devices are each assigned a number from 0 to $2^6 - 1$. When an IOT instruction is given, the number in bits 3 to 8 of the IOT is placed on six wires in the bus which each input-output device inputs to see whether it is being addressed. The remaining 3 bits are also transmitted on the bus and tell the input-output device what to do (read, write, rewind, etc.). The selected input-output device responds to the bus signals generated by the IOT instruction, using logic circuits in its interface to interpret the instruction and to place data on the data section of the bus, read from it, etc.

The input-output devices are allowed to interrupt the processor and demand service during program operation, by using the computer's interrupt facility. The ION (interrupt on) instruction raises a bus wire called ION to the input-output devices, telling them it is their right to raise the INTERRUPT line on the bus and demand service.

If an input-output device raises its INTERRUPT line while the computer is operating a program, the address of the next instruction word which would normally be executed is placed in location 0 in the memory, and the next instruction executed is at location 1 in the memory. (This is generally a jump to the subprogram which services input-output devices.) Since the address of the next instruction word in the program which was interrupted is in location 0, the interrupt service program[8] can exit, using that address to return to the original program. This is shown in Fig. 10.13.

Again, an interrupt of an interrupt will cause the original return address (at 0 in the memory) to be destroyed. The programmer must see that this does not occur, and the right of devices to interrupt is revoked as soon as an interrupt occurs. (The bus line for ION is lowered.) The program must issue another ION to restore the interrupt privilege to input-output devices.

The 6100 has a number of features which have helped to make it attractive, but which are outside the context of this description. For instance, since there is only a single arithmetic instruction, TAD, it is necessary to complement an operand and then add in order to subtract. To perform this complement and to provide ROTATE or SHIFT instructions, some SKIP instructions, and some other logic operations, the OP code 111 is a "no address" instruction class where the remaining 9 bits tell which of a number of different possible operations can be made to occur.

Table 10.2 shows a section of an assembler listing[9] for a 6100. The leftmost two columns (or digits) list the addresses in memory and their contents. The columns to the right of these were written by the programmer. The programmer fed the assembler-language statements to the assembler program, which then generated the complete listing shown here. All material to the right of the slashes is comments and is ignored by the assembler program.

The purpose of this subroutine, or subprogram, is to read from a keyboard

---

[8]The program (or subprogram) which handles the peripheral that generates the interrupt is called an *interrupt service program.*

[9]This listing is in octal. Each digit is an octal digit.

Address in
memory

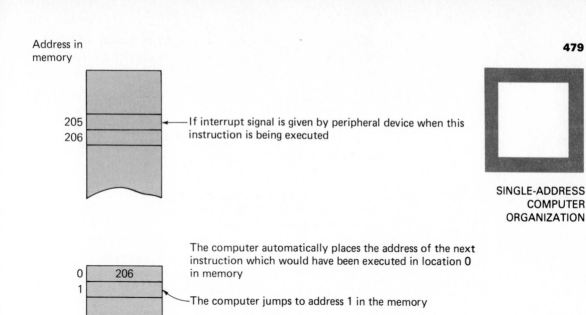

205 — If interrupt signal is given by peripheral device when this
206   instruction is being executed

**SINGLE-ADDRESS
COMPUTER
ORGANIZATION**

The computer automatically places the address of the next
instruction which would have been executed in location 0
in memory

0   206

1   — The computer jumps to address 1 in the memory

JMP I   0 — After the interrupt has been serviced, a jump instruction
with indirect address 0 will cause a jump back to the
next instruction which would have been executed

FIGURE 10.13

Interrupts in the 6100
microprocessor.

into the 6100's accumulator. Another program enters this subprogram with a JMS
statement, which deposits the address of the next instruction to be operated when
the subroutine is completed in the first address of the subprogram. The address to
be returned to will be stored at location 251 in the memory when the subroutine
is entered, and the first statement executed will be the statement at location 252 in
the memory.

The statement at 252 in the memory is a KSF statement, which is a special
input statement that reads from the keyboard's status register (see Chap. 7 for
details). If the status bit is a 1 in this register, the program skips over the next
instruction. As a result, when the KSF statement is executed, if there is a character
to be read from the keyboard, the next statement read will be at location 254. If
the status word is all 0s, then the statement executed after the KSF will be the
JMP instruction at 253 in the memory.

TABLE 10.2				6100 SUBPROGRAM
ADDRESS	CONTENTS	LABEL	OP CODE	COMMENTS
Ø251	ØØØØ	LISN,	Ø	/INPUT SUB
Ø252	6Ø31		KSF	
Ø253	5252		JMP #252	
Ø254	6Ø36		KRB	
Ø255	5651		JMP I LISN	

The JMP instruction causes the computer to jump to location 252 in the memory. Notice that the OP code for JMP is 5, and the instruction has assembled into a word as follows:

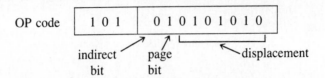

This instruction word says, "Jump to the word at location 52 on the same page as the instruction lies." The first address on this page is 200 (octal), so the final address for the jump is 252 (octal).

When a character is to be read, the KRB instruction selects the keyboard. Using the bus, the keyboard places its character on the data wires in the bus, and the character is read by the 6100 into its accumulator. After this instruction is read, the accumulator contains the character from the keyboard. (The status bit in the status word is also turned off.)

The JMP I LISN instruction causes a jump to the address given at the location LISN. This will return control to the location in the memory after the JMS which called this subroutine.

The JMP I LISN instruction word is as follows:

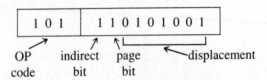

This instruction word says, "Since the page bit is a 1, use the location on the same page, which is the 51st location on that page." Since the beginning of the page is location 200, the address generated is 251. Now the indirect bit is a 1, so the number at location 251 is the actual address to be used for the jump, as desired.

Another short segment of a 6100 program is shown in Table 10.3. This first calls the subroutine just described by using a JMS LISN instruction. Therefore, when the DCA STORE instruction is executed, the accumulator contains the character from the keyboard. The purpose of this section of program is to see whether the character read is a period.

First, the DCA STORE deposits the character at an address with label (name) STORE. In another section of the program, STORE has been located at 264 in the memory, so the DCA STORE instruction is to store the accumulator at 264. The assembled instruction looks like this:

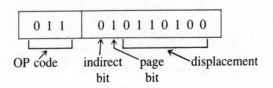

TABLE 10.3		SECTION OF 6100 PROGRAM			
ADDRESS IN MEMORY	CONTENTS	LABEL	OP CODE	ADDRESS	COMMENTS
0200	6032	START,	KCC		/CLEAR KB
0201	4251		JMS	LISN	/ENTER SUB
0202	3264		DCA	STORE	/
0203	1265		TAD	PD	/GET NEG PD
0204	1264		TAD	STORE	/ADD INPUT
0205	7440		SZA		/SKIP IF EQ
0206	5213		JMP	A	/

A SINGLE-ADDRESS
MICROPROCESSOR

The indirect bit is a 0, the page bit is a 1, so the address is on the same page as the instruction word. This page begins with location 200, so the actual address will be 200 plus the displacement, which is 64, or 264.

The next instruction, TAD PD, loads the accumulator with the negative (2s complement) of the keyboard code for a period. This has already been loaded by the program at location 265, so the function of the TAD PD is to read from location 265. As an examination of the assembled value 1265 will indicate, the page bit is a 1, and so 65 is added to 200, the first address of the page on which the instruction lies, giving 265.

The value in STORE, which is that of the character read, is now added to the negative of the character code for a period. If the resulting value in the accumulator is a 0, the character just read is a period. The SZA instruction is a special 6100 instruction which tests the accumulator for "all zeros" and skips the next instruction if it is 0, but does not skip otherwise. (The 6100 uses skip instructions instead of conditional jump instructions with addresses.) As a result, if the character is a period, the instruction at location 207 will be executed next. If not, control will jump to location A because the JMP A will be executed.

This section of the program shows some good and bad features of the 6100. Since there is no subtract instruction, a 2s complement of the period character value had to be formed and added. Since there is no conditional jump instruction, a skip and then a jump instruction were required. On the other hand, the code is very compact and reasonably clear.

A SINGLE-ADDRESS MICROPROCESSOR

10.11 The Intel 8080[10] is an example of a microprocessor chip series. A basic 40-pin IC chip is used to package the 8080 CPU. Other chips available include RAMs, ROMs, interface chips, etc. The chips are interconnected by a bus which contains 8 data lines, 16 address lines, and 6 control lines. This microprocessor has been so successful that various "upward-compatible" microprocessors have grown out of it, including the 8085 and the Z-80. Even the 16-bit 8086 uses much of its design.

---

[10]The microprocessor chip generally called the 8080 is actually the 8080A. Because of production problems the 8080 was made for only a short time. A replacement, the 8080A, was released, and it is this chip which is described here and elsewhere.

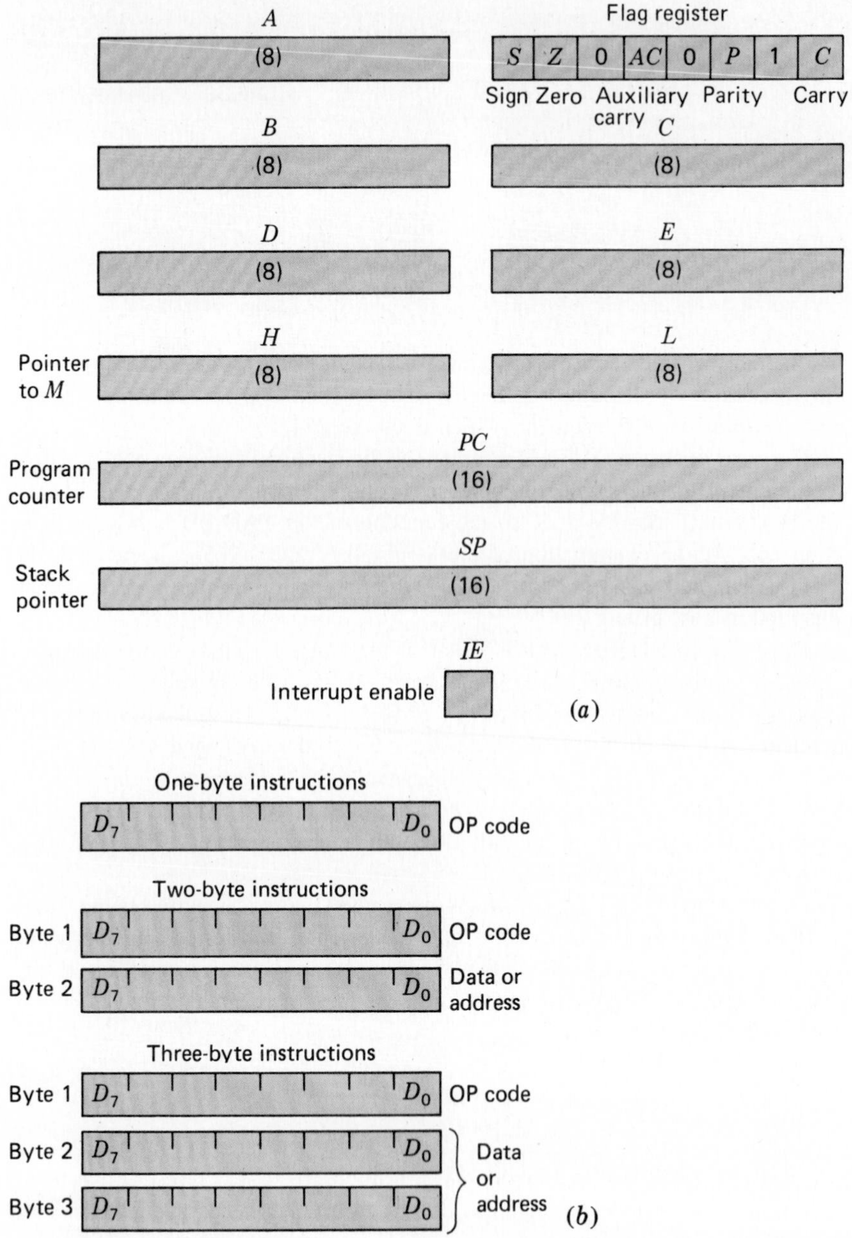

COMPUTER
ORGANIZATION

A
(8)

Flag register

| S | Z | 0 | AC | 0 | P | 1 | C |

Sign Zero Auxiliary Parity Carry
carry

B
(8)

C
(8)

D
(8)

E
(8)

H
(8)

L
(8)

Pointer
to M

Program
counter

PC
(16)

Stack
pointer

SP
(16)

Interrupt enable

IE

(a)

One-byte instructions

D_7 .... D_0 OP code

Two-byte instructions

Byte 1 D_7 .... D_0 OP code

Byte 2 D_7 .... D_0 Data or
address

Three-byte instructions

Byte 1 D_7 .... D_0 OP code

Byte 2 D_7 .... D_0 } Data
Byte 3 D_7 .... D_0 } or
address (b)

FIGURE 10.14

(a) 8080 CPU regis-
ters. (b) Instruction
word formats for
8080 CPU.

The 8080 CPU is basically a single-accumulator organization, but a number
of other scratchpad registers are provided, as illustrated in Fig. 10.14(a). The
instruction word formats are shown in Fig. 10.14(b), and a functional block diagram of the 8080 is shown in Fig. 10.15.

The Intel 8080 has a good set of addressing modes (see Table 10.4). At the
beginning of each instruction cycle, the 8-bit OP code is read by the 8080 CPU,
and this determines how many more fetches from memory the CPU must make to

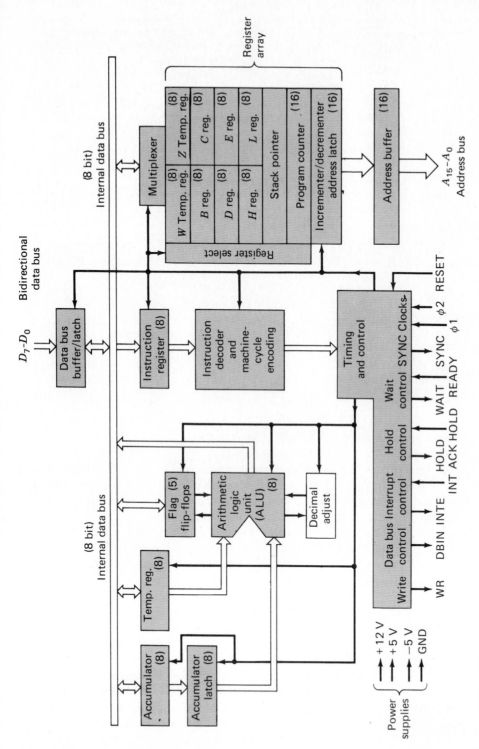

A SINGLE-ADDRESS
MICROPROCESSOR

FIGURE 10.15

8080 CPU functional
block diagram. (*Intel
Corp.*)

TABLE 10.4	ADDRESSING MODES FOR THE 8080 CPU

When multibyte numeric data are used, the data, like instructions, are stored in successive memory locations, with the least significant byte first, followed by increasingly significant bytes. The 8080 has four different modes for addressing data stored in memory or in registers:

1 *Direct* Bytes 2 and 3 of the instruction contain the exact memory address of the data item (the low-order bits of the address are in byte 2, the high-order bits in byte 3).

2 *Register* The instruction specifies the register or register pair in which the data are located.

3 *Register indirect* The instruction specifies a register pair that contains the memory address where the data are located (high-order bits of the address are in the first register of the pair, low-order bits in the second).

4 *Immediate* The instruction contains the data. This is either an 8- or a 16-bit quantity (least significant byte first, most significant byte second).

Unless directed by an INTERRUPT or a BRANCH instruction, the execution of instructions proceeds through consecutively increasing memory locations. A BRANCH instruction can specify the address of the next instruction to be executed in one of two ways:

1 *Direct* The BRANCH instruction contains the address of the next instruction to be executed. (Except for the RST instruction, byte 2 contains the low-order address and byte 3 the high-order address.)

2 *Register indirect* The BRANCH instruction indicates a register pair that contains the address of the next instruction to be executed (high-order bits of the address are in the first register of the pair, low-order bits in the second).

execute the instruction. Some instructions require only the 8-bit OP code, while others require 8-bit and some 16-bit addresses or operands, and so the CPU must make the necessary accesses to perform the instruction.

Since 8 bits are used for the OP code, a large instruction repertoire has been provided. A short list of the instructions used in examples is presented in Tables 10.5 and 10.6. Table 10.7 shows the complete instruction set.

The 8080 has conditional JUMP instructions which jump or do not jump, depending on the values in the *condition flags*. These consist of five flip-flops (see Table 10.8) which are set to 0 or 1 by the results of arithmetic instructions. For instance, if an addition is performed and the result is 0, then the Z flag will be set to 1 and the S, P, and C flags to 0 (provided no carry was generated). A conditional JUMP instruction which tests the Z flag for a 1 state would then cause a jump, whereas a conditional JUMP instruction which tests the S, P, or C flags would not cause a jump. (Refer to the BRANCH instructions in Table 10.6.)

In programming the 8080, considerable use is made of the scratchpad registers B, C, D, E, H, and L as well as accumulator A. In some instructions the scratchpad registers are used in pairs. For instance, the INR M instruction, a 1-byte instruction, uses the two 8-bit registers H and L to form a 16-bit address. The 8-bit number in the memory at this address is then incremented by the instruction. The Z, S, P, and AC flags are all set and reset by the instruction, so a 0 result at that location will set the Z flag, a negative result will set the S flag, etc.

SYMBOL	MEANING
Accumulator	Register A
Addr	16-bit address quantity
Data	8-bit data quantity
Data 16	16-bit data quantity
Byte 2	Second byte of the instruction
Byte 3	Third byte of the instruction
Port	8-bit address of an input-output device.
r, r1, r2	One of the registers A, B, C, D, E, H, L
DDD, SSS	Bit pattern designating one of the registers A, B, C, D, E, H, L (DDD = destination, SSS = source):

DDD or SSS	Register Name
111	A
000	B
001	C
010	D
011	E
100	H
101	L

rh	First (high-order) register of a designated register pair
rl	Second (low-order) register of a designated register pair
rp	One of the register pairs:
	B represents the B, C pair with B as the high-order register and C as the low-order register.
	D represents the D, E pair with D as the high-order register and E as the low-order register.
	H represents the H, L pair with H as the high-order register and L as the low-order register.
	SP represents the 16-bit stack pointer register.
RP	Bit pattern designating one of the register pairs B, D, H, SP:

RP	Register pair
00	B, C
01	D, E
10	H, L
11	SP

PC	16-bit program counter register (PCH and PCL are used to refer to the high-order and low-order 8 bits, respectively)
SP	Stack pointer
r_m	Bit m of register r (bits are numbered 7 through 0 from left to right)
Z, S, P, CY, AC	Condition flags: zero, sign, parity, carry, and auxiliary carry, respectively.
( )	Contents of memory location or registers enclosed in the parentheses
$\leftarrow$	"Is transferred to"
$\wedge$	Logical AND
$\veebar$	Exclusive OR
$\vee$	Inclusive OR
$+$	Addition
$-$	2s complement subtraction
$*$	Multiplication
$\leftrightarrow$	"Is exchanged with"
$-$	Is complement [e.g., $(\overline{A})$]
n	Restart numbers 0 to 7
NNN	Binary representation 000 to 111 for restart numbers 0 to 7, respectively

A SINGLE-ADDRESS
MICROPROCESSOR

MOV r1, r2   (move register)

(r1) ← (r2)

    Content of register r2 is moved to register r1.

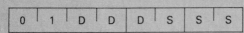

0	1	D	D	D	S	S	S

Addressing: register   Flags: none

MOV r, M   (move from memory)

(r) ← ((H)(L))

    Content of memory location, whose address is in registers H and L, is moved to register r.

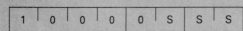

0	1	D	D	D	1	1	0

Addressing: register indirect   Flags: none

MOV M, r   (move to memory)

((H)(L)) ← (r)

    Content of register r is moved to memory location whose address is in registers H and L.

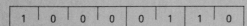

0	1	1	1	0	S	S	S

Addressing: register indirect   Flags: none

ADD r   (add register)

(A) ← (A) + (r)

    Content of register r is added to content of accumulator. Result is placed in accumulator.

1	0	0	0	0	S	S	S

Addressing: register   Flags: Z, S, P, CY, AC

ADD M   (add memory)

(A) ← (A) + ((H)(L))

    Content of the memory location, whose address is contained in registers H and L, is added to content of accumulator. Result is placed in accumulator.

1	0	0	0	0	1	1	0

Addressing: register indirect

Flags: Z, S, P, CY, AC

ADI data   (add immediate)

(A) ← (A) + (byte 2)

    Content of second byte of instruction is added to content of accumulator. Result is placed in accumulator.

1	1	0	0	0	1	1	0
Data							

Addressing: immediate

Flags: Z, S, P, CX, AC

INR M   (increment memory)

((H)(L)) ← ((H)(L)) + 1

    Content of the memory location, whose address is contained in registers H and L is incremented by 1. *Note:* All condition flags except *CY* are affected.

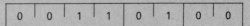

0	0	1	1	0	1	0	0

Addressing: register indirect

Flags: *Z, S, P, AC*

LDA addr   (load accumulator direct)

(A) ← ((byte 3)(byte 2))

    Content of memory location, whose address is specified in byte 2 and byte 3 of instruction, is moved to register A.

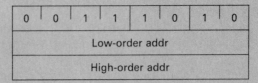

0	0	1	1	1	0	1	0
Low-order addr							
High-order addr							

Addressing: direct   Flags: none

STA addr   (store accumulator direct)

((byte 3)(byte 2)) ← (A)

    Content of accumulator is moved to memory location whose address is specified in bytes 2 and 3 of instruction.

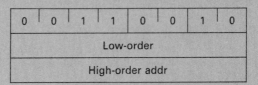

0	0	1	1	0	0	1	0
Low-order							
High-order addr							

Addressing: direct   Flags: none

SUB M   (subtract memory)

(A) ← (A) − ((H)(L))

    Content of memory location, whose address is contained in registers H and L, is subtracted from content of accumulator. Result is placed in accumulator.

1	0	0	1	0	1	1	0

Addressing: register indirect

Flags: *Z, S, P, CY, AC*

SUI data   (subtract immediate)

(A) ← (A) − (byte 2)

    Content of second byte of instruction is subtracted from content of accumulator. Result is placed in accumulator.

TABLE 10.6   **INSTRUCTION REPERTOIRE FOR 8080 CPU (continued)**

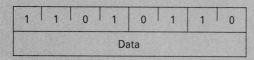

Addressing: immediate
Flags: *Z, S, P, CY, AC*

SBB r (subtract register with borrow)
(A) ← (A) − (r) − (CY)
   Content of register *r* and content of *CY* flag are both subtracted from accumulator. Result is placed in accumulator.

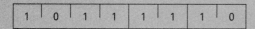

Addressing: register   Flags: *Z, S, P, CY, AC*

CMP M (compare memory)
(A) − ((H)(L))
   Content of memory location, whose address is contained in registers *H* and *L,* is subtracted from accumulator. Accumulator remains unchanged. Condition flags are set as a result of subtraction. *Z* flag is set to 1 if (A) = ((H)(L)). *CY* flag is set to 1 if (A) < ((H)(L)).

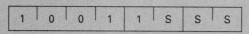

Cycles: 2   States: 7
Addressing: register indirect
Flags: *Z, S, P, CY, AC*

INX rp (increment register pair)
(rh)(rl) ← (rh)(rl) + 1
   Content of register pair *rp* is incremented by 1. *Note:* No condition flags are affected.

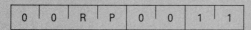

Cycles: 1   States: 5
Addressing: register   Flags: none

DCX rp (decrement register pair)
(rh)(rl) ← (rh)(rl) − 1
   Content of register pair *rp* is decremented by 1. *Note:* No condition flags are affected.

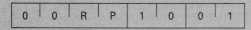

Cycles: 1   States: 5
Addressing: register   Flags: none

RST n (restart)
((SP) − 1) ← (PCH)   ((SP) − 2) ← (PCL)
(SP) ← (SP) − 2   (PC) ← 8* (NNN)
   The high-order 8 bits of next instruction address are moved to memory location whose address is 1 less than content of register *SP.* The low-order 8

bits of next instruction address are moved to memory location whose address is 2 less than content of register *SP.* Content of register *SP* is decremented by 2. Control is transferred to instruction whose address is eight times the content of NNN.

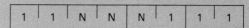

Cycles: 3   States: 11
Addressing: register indirect   Flags: none

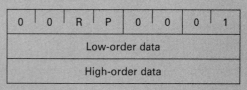

Program counter after restart

LXI rp, data 16 (load register pair immediate)
(rh) ← (byte 3)   (rl) ← (byte 2)
   Byte 3 of instruction is moved into high-order register *rh* of register pair *rp.* Byte 2 of instruction is moved into low-order register *rl* of register pair *rp.*

0	0	R	P	0	0	0	1
Low-order data							
High-order data							

Addressing: immediate   Flags: none

BRANCH GROUP
   This group of instructions alters normal sequential program flow. *Condition flags are not affected by any instruction in this group.*
   The two types of branch instructions are unconditional and conditional. Unconditional transfers simply perform the specified operation on register *PC* (the program counter). Conditional transfers examine the status of one of the four processor flags to determine whether the specified branch is to be executed. The conditions that may be specified are as follows:

CCC		Condition
000	NZ	Not zero (*Z* = 0)
001	Z	Zero (*Z* = 1)
010	NC	No carry (*CY* = 0)
011	C	Carry (*CY* = 1)
100	PO	Parity odd (*P* = 0)
101	PE	Parity even (*P* = 1)
110	P	Plus (*S* = 0)
111	M	Minus (*S* = 1)

JMP addr (jump)
(PC) ← (byte 3)(byte 2)
   Control is transferred to instruction whose address is specified in byte 3 and byte 2 of current instruction.

TABLE 10.6 **INSTRUCTION REPERTOIRE FOR 8080 CPU (continued)**

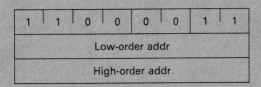

1	1	0	0	0	0	1	1

Low-order addr

High-order addr

Addressing: immediate   Flags: none

Jcondition addr   (conditional jump)
If (CCC), (PC) ← (byte 3)(byte 2)
    If specified condition is true, control is transferred to instruction whose address is specified in byte 3 and byte 2 of current instruction; otherwise, control continues sequentially.

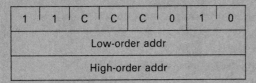

1	1	C	C	C	0	1	0

Low-order addr

High-order addr

Addressing: immediate   Flags: none

DCR r   (decrement register)
(r) ← (r) − 1
Content of register r is decremented by 1. *Note:* All condition flags except CY are affected.

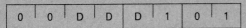

0	0	D	D	D	1	0	1

Addressing: register   Flags: *Z, S, P, AC*

LDAX rp   (load accumulator indirect)
(A) ← ((rp))
Content of memory location, whose address is in register pair *rp,* is moved to register *A. Note:* Only register pairs *rp* = *B* (registers *B* and *C*) or *rp* = *D* (registers *D* and *E*) may be specified.

0	0	R	P	1	0	1	0

Addressing: register indirect   Flags: none

STAX rp   (store accumulator indirect)
((rp)) ← (A)
Content of register *A* is moved to memory location whose address is in register pair *rp. Note:* Only register pairs *rp* = *B* (registers *B* and *C*) or *rp* = *D* (registers *D* and *E*) may be specified.

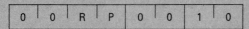

0	0	R	P	0	0	1	0

Addressing: register indirect   Flags: none

XCHG   (exchange H and L with D and E)
(H) ↔ (D)   (L) ↔ (E)

Contents of registers *H* and *L* are exchanged with contents of registers *D* and *E*.

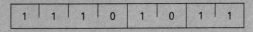

1	1	1	0	1	0	1	1

Addressing: register   Flags: none

INR r   (increment register)
(r) ← (r) + 1
Content of register *r* is incremented by 1. *Note:* All condition flags except *CY* are affected.

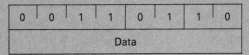

0	0	D	D	D	1	0	0

Addressing: register   Flags: *Z, S, P, AC*

MVI M, data   (move to memory immediate)
((H)(L)) ← (byte 2)
Content of byte 2 of instruction is moved to memory location whose address is in registers *H* and *L*.

0	0	1	1	0	1	1	0

Data

Addressing: immediate register indirect
Flags: none

CALL addr   (call)
((SP) − 1) ← (PCH)   (SP) ← (SP) − 2
((SP) − 2) ← (PCL)   (PC) ← (byte 3)(byte 2)
The high-order 8 bits of next instruction address are moved to memory location whose address is 1 less than content of register *SP*. The low-order 8 bits of next instruction address are moved to memory location whose address is 2 less than content of register *SP*. Content of register *SP* is decremented by 2. Control is transferred to instruction whose address is specified in byte 3 and byte 2 of current instruction.

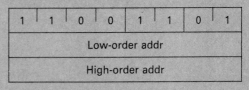

1	1	0	0	1	1	0	1

Low-order addr

High-order addr

Addressing: immediate/register indirect
Flags: none

RET   (return)
(PCL) ← ((SP))   (PCH) ← ((SP) + 1))
(SP) ← (SP) + 2
Content of memory location, whose address is specified in register *SP,* is moved to low-order 8 bits of register *PC*. Content of memory location, whose address is 1 more than content of register *SP*, is moved

TABLE 10.6   **INSTRUCTION REPERTOIRE FOR 8080 CPU (continued)**

to high-order 8 bits of register *PC*. Content of register *SP* is incremented by 2.

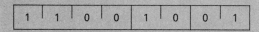

| 1 | 1 | 0 | 0 | 1 | 0 | 0 | 1 |

Addressing: register indirect   Flags: none

STACK, INPUT-OUTPUT, AND MACHINE CONTROL GROUP

This group of instructions performs input-output, manipulates the stack, and alters internal control flags.

Unless otherwise specified, *condition flags are not affected by any instruction in this group.*

PUSH rp   (push)
$((SP) - 1) \leftarrow (rh)$ $((SP) - 2) \leftarrow (rl)$
$(SP) \leftarrow (SP) - 2$

Content of high-order register of register pair *rp* is moved to memory location whose address is 1 less than content of register *SP*. Content of low-order register of register pair *rp* is moved to memory location whose address is 2 less than content of register *SP*. Content of register *SP* is decremented by 2. *Note:* Register pair *rp* = *SP* may not be specified.

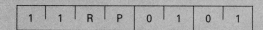

| 1 | 1 | R | P | 0 | 1 | 0 | 1 |

Addressing: register indirect   Flags: none

PUSH PSW   (push processor status word)
$((SP) - 1) \leftarrow (A)$
$((SP) - 2)_0 \leftarrow (CY),$ $((SP) - 2)_1 \leftarrow 1$
$((SP) - 2)_2 \leftarrow (P),$ $((SP) - 2)_3 \leftarrow 0$
$((SP) - 2)_4 \leftarrow (AC),$ $((SP) - 2)_5 \leftarrow 0$
$((SP) - 2)_6 \leftarrow (Z),$ $((SP) - 2)_7 \leftarrow (S)$
$(SP) \leftarrow (SP) - 2$

Content of register *A* is moved to memory location whose address is 1 less than register *SP*. Contents

of condition flags are assembled into a processor status word, and word is moved to memory location whose address is 2 less than content of register *SP*. Content of register *SP* is decremented by 2.

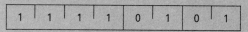

| 1 | 1 | 1 | 1 | 0 | 1 | 0 | 1 |

Addressing: register indirect   Flags: none

POP rp   (pop)
$(rl) \leftarrow ((SP))$ $(rh) \leftarrow ((SP) + 1)$
$(SP) \leftarrow (SP) + 2$

Content of memory location, whose address is specified by content of register *SP*, is moved to low-order register of register pair *rp*. Content of memory location, whose address is 1 more than content of register *SP*, is moved to high-order register of register pair *rp*. Content of register *SP* is incremented by 2. *Note:* Register pair *rp* = *SP* may not be specified.

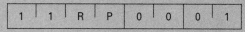

| 1 | 1 | R | P | 0 | 0 | 0 | 1 |

Addressing: register indirect   Flags: none

POP PSW   (pop processor status word)
$(CY) \leftarrow ((SP))_0$ $(P) \leftarrow ((SP))_2$ $(AC) \leftarrow ((SP))_4$
$(Z) \leftarrow ((SP))_6$ $(S) \leftarrow ((SP))_7$ $(A) \leftarrow ((SP + 1))$
$(SP) \leftarrow (SP) + 2$

Content of memory location, whose address is specified by content of register *SP*, is used to restore condition flags. Content of memory location, whose address is 1 more than content of register *SP*, is moved to register *A*. Content of register *SP* is incremented by 2.

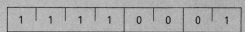

| 1 | 1 | 1 | 1 | 0 | 0 | 0 | 1 |

Addressing: register indirect
Flags: *Z, S, P, CY, AC*

Parentheses are used to indicate "the contents of" in Tables 10.5 and 10.6. For example, the notation (H) ↔ (D) used in the XCHG instruction means, "The contents of register *H* and register *D* are exchanged." Similarly, ((H)(L)) ← (byte 2) in the description of the MVI instruction means, "The contents of byte 2 of the instruction word are transferred into the location in memory whose address is formed by writing the contents of register *H* to the left of the contents of register *L*." This notation is widely used and worth examining in some detail.

Table 10.9 shows an 8080 program in assembly language and a listing of the hexadecimal values for memory location and contents as generated by the assembler. The programmer wrote the columns: Label, OP Code, Operand, and Comments. The assembler generated the two leftmost columns.

COMPUTER
ORGANIZATION

TABLE 10.7   8080 INSTRUCTION REPERTOIRE

MNEMONIC	DESCRIPTION	D_7	D_6	D_5	D_4	D_3	D_2	D_1	D_0
MOV r1, r2	Move register to register	0	1	D	D	D	S	S	S
MOV M, r	Move register to memory	0	1	1	1	0	S	S	S
MOV r, M	Move memory to register	0	1	D	D	D	1	1	0
HLT	Halt	0	1	1	1	0	1	1	0
MVI r	Move immediate register	0	0	D	D	D	1	1	0
MVI M	Move immediate memory	0	0	1	1	0	1	1	0
INR r	Increment register	0	0	D	D	D	1	0	0
DCR r	Decrement register	0	0	D	D	D	1	0	1
INR M	Increment memory	0	0	1	1	0	1	0	0
DCR M	Decrement memory	0	0	1	1	0	1	0	1
ADD r	Add register to A	1	0	0	0	0	S	S	S
ADC r	Add register to A with carry	1	0	0	0	1	S	S	S
SUB r	Subtract register from A	1	0	0	1	0	S	S	S
SBB r	Subtract register from A with borrow	1	0	0	1	1	S	S	S
ANA r	AND register with A	1	0	1	0	0	S	S	S
XRA r	Exclusive-OR register with A	1	0	1	0	1	S	S	S
ORA r	OR register with A	1	0	1	1	0	S	S	S
CMP r	Compare register with A	1	0	1	1	1	S	S	S
ADD M	Add memory to A	1	0	0	0	0	1	1	0
ADC M	Add memory to A with carry	1	0	0	0	1	1	1	0
SUB M	Subtract memory from A	1	0	0	1	0	1	1	0
SBB M	Subtract memory from A with borrow	1	0	0	1	1	1	1	0
ANA M	AND memory with A	1	0	1	0	0	1	1	0
XRA M	Exclusive-OR memory with A	1	0	1	0	1	1	1	0
ORA M	OR memory with A	1	0	1	1	0	1	1	0
CMP M	Compare memory with A	1	0	1	1	1	1	1	0
ADI	Add immediate to A	1	1	0	0	0	1	1	0
ACI	Add immediate to A with carry	1	1	0	0	1	1	1	0
SUI	Subtract immediate from A	1	1	0	1	0	1	1	0
SBI	Subtract immediate from A with borrow	1	1	0	1	1	1	1	0
ANI	AND immediate with A	1	1	1	0	0	1	1	0
XRI	Exclusive-OR immediate with A	1	1	1	0	1	1	1	0
ORI	OR immediate with A	1	1	1	1	0	1	1	0
CPI	Compare immediate with A	1	1	1	1	1	1	1	0
RLC	Rotate A left	0	0	0	0	0	1	1	1
RRC	Rotate A right	0	0	0	0	1	1	1	1
RAL	Rotate A left through carry	0	0	0	1	0	1	1	1
RAR	Rotate A right through carry	0	0	0	1	1	1	1	1
JMP	Jump unconditional	1	1	0	0	0	0	1	1
JC	Jump on carry	1	1	0	1	1	0	1	0
JNC	Jump on no carry	1	1	0	1	0	0	1	0
JZ	Jump on zero	1	1	0	0	1	0	1	0
JNZ	Jump on no zero	1	1	0	0	0	0	1	0
JP	Jump on positive	1	1	1	1	0	0	1	0
JM	Jump on minus	1	1	1	1	1	0	1	0
JPE	Jump on parity even	1	1	1	0	1	0	1	0
JPO	Jump on parity odd	1	1	1	0	0	0	1	0
CALL	Call unconditional	1	1	0	0	1	1	0	1
CC	Call on carry	1	1	0	1	1	1	0	0
CNC	Call on no carry	1	1	0	1	0	1	0	0
CZ	Call on zero	1	1	0	0	1	1	0	0
CNZ	Call on no zero	1	1	0	0	0	1	0	0
CP	Call on positive	1	1	1	1	0	1	0	0
CM	Call on minus	1	1	1	1	1	1	0	0
CPE	Call on parity even	1	1	1	0	1	1	0	0
CPO	Call on parity odd	1	1	1	0	0	1	0	0

INSTRUCTION CODE†

TABLE 10.7   **8080 INSTRUCTION REPERTOIRE (continued)**   **491**

MNEMONIC	DESCRIPTION	INSTRUCTION CODE†							
		D_7	D_6	D_5	D_4	D_3	D_2	D_1	D_0
RET	Return	1	1	0	0	1	0	0	1
RC	Return on carry	1	1	0	1	1	0	0	0
RNC	Return on no carry	1	1	0	1	0	0	0	0
RZ	Return on zero	1	1	0	0	1	0	0	0
RNZ	Return on no zero	1	1	0	0	0	0	0	0
RP	Return on positive	1	1	1	1	0	0	0	0
RM	Return on minus	1	1	1	1	1	0	0	0
RPE	Return on parity even	1	1	1	0	1	0	0	0
RPO	Return on parity odd	1	1	1	0	0	0	0	0
RST	Restart	1	1	A	A	A	1	1	1
IN	Input	1	1	0	1	1	0	1	1
OUT	Output	1	1	0	1	0	0	1	1
LXI B	Load imediate register pair *B, C*	0	0	0	0	0	0	0	1
LXI D	Load immediate register pair *D, E*	0	0	0	1	0	0	0	1
LXI H	Load immediate register pair *H, L*	0	0	1	0	0	0	0	1
LXI SP	Load immediate stack pointer	0	0	1	1	0	0	0	1
PUSH B	Push register pair *B, C* on stack	1	1	0	0	0	1	0	1
PUSH D	Push register pair *D, E* on stack	1	1	0	1	0	1	0	1
PUSH H	Push register pair *H, L* on stack	1	1	1	0	0	1	0	1
PUSH PSW	Push *A* and flags on stack	1	1	1	1	0	1	0	1
POP B	Pop register pair *B, C* off stack	1	1	0	0	0	0	0	1
POP D	Pop register pair *D, E* off stack	1	1	0	1	0	0	0	1
POP H	Pop register pair *H, L* off stack	1	1	1	0	0	0	0	1
POP PSW	Pop *A* and flags off stack	1	1	1	1	0	0	0	1
STA	Store *A* direct	0	0	1	1	0	0	1	0
LDA	Load *A* direct	0	0	1	1	1	0	1	0
XCHG	Exchange *D, E* and *H, L* registers	1	1	1	0	1	0	1	1
XTHL	Exchange top of stack, *H, L*	1	1	1	0	0	0	1	1
SPHL	*H, L* to stack pointer	1	1	1	1	1	0	0	1
PCHL	*H, L* to program counter	1	1	1	0	1	0	0	1
DAD B	Add *B, C* to *H, L*	0	0	0	0	1	0	0	1
DAD D	Add *D, E* to *H, L*	0	0	0	1	1	0	0	1
DAD H	Add *H, L* to *H, L*	0	0	1	0	1	0	0	1
DAD SP	Add stack pointer to *H, L*	0	0	1	1	1	0	0	1
STAX B	Store *A* indirect	0	0	0	0	0	0	1	0
STAX D	Store *A* indirect	0	0	0	1	0	0	1	0
LDAX B	Load *A* indirect	0	0	0	0	1	0	1	0
LDAX D	Load *A* indirect	0	0	0	1	1	0	1	0
INX B	Increment *B, C* registers	0	0	0	0	0	0	1	1
INX D	Increment *D, E* registers	0	0	0	1	0	0	1	1
INX H	Increment *H, L* registers	0	0	1	0	0	0	1	1
INX SP	Increment stack pointer	0	0	1	1	0	0	1	1
DCX B	Decrement *B, C*	0	0	0	0	1	0	1	1
DCX D	Decrement *D, E*	0	0	0	1	1	0	1	1
DCX H	Decrement *H, L*	0	0	1	0	1	0	1	1
DCX SP	Decrement stack pointer	0	0	1	1	1	0	1	1
CMA	Complement *A*	0	0	1	0	1	1	1	1
STC	Set carry	0	0	1	1	0	1	1	1
CMC	Complement carry	0	0	1	1	1	1	1	1
DAA	Decimal adjust *A*	0	0	1	0	0	1	1	1
SHLD	Store *H, L* direct	0	0	1	0	0	0	1	0
LHLD	Load *H, L* direct	0	0	1	0	1	0	1	0
EI	Enable interrupt	1	1	1	1	1	0	1	1
DI	Disable interrupt	1	1	1	1	0	0	1	1
NOP	No operation	0	0	0	0	0	0	0	0

A SINGLE-ADDRESS
MICROPROCESSOR

Note: DDD or SSS is numbered as follows: 000, B; 001, C; 010, D; 011, E; 100, H; 101, L; 110, memory; 111, A. For example, 01010001 instructs the computer to move the contents of register *C* into register *D*.

TABLE 10.8

FLAGS USED IN 8080 CPU

Flag word

D_7	D_6	D_5	D_4	D_3	D_2	D_1	D_0
S	Z	O	AC	O	P	1	CY

There are five condition flags associated with the execution of instructions on the 8080: zero, sign, parity, carry, and auxiliary carry. Each is represented by a 1-bit register in the CPU. A flag is "set" by forcing the bit to 1 and "reset" by forcing the bit to 0.

Unless indicated otherwise, when an instruction affects a flag, it affects it in the following manner:

1 *Zero* If the result of an instruction has the value 0, this flag is set; otherwise, it is reset.

2 *Sign* If the most significant bit of the result of the operation has the value 1, this flag is set; otherwise, it is reset.

3 *Parity* If the modulo 2 sum of the bits of the result of the operation is 0 (i.e., if the result has even parity), this flag is set; otherwise, it is reset (i.e., if the result has odd parity).

4 *Carry* If the instruction resulted in a carry (from addition) or a borrow (from subtraction or a comparison) out of the high-order bit, this flag is set; otherwise, it is reset.

5 *Auxiliary carry* If the instruction caused a carry out of bit 3 and into bit 4 of the resulting value, the auxiliary carry is set; otherwise, it is reset. This flag is affected by single-precision additions, subtractions, increments, decrements, comparisons, and logical operations.

The purpose of the program is to find the larger of two 8-bit numbers in locations 50 and 51 in the memory and to store this number at location 52.

The first instruction, LXI H, 50H, loads 50_{16} into registers H and L. When the 8080 assembler is used, writing an H to the right of a number means the number is hexadecimal. Therefore 50H means 01010000_2, or 50_{16} to the assembler. So LXI loads 00000000 into register H and 01010000 into register L. (Notice that the least significant byte is first in the memory in an instruction word in the 8080.)

The MOV A, M instruction[11] moves the byte in the memory pointed to by the address in registers H and L into accumulator A. Since H and L point to location 50, the byte at that location will be moved into the accumulator.

The INX H instruction adds 1 to the register pair H, L, giving 51 in H and L.

The CMP M instruction compares the byte in the memory pointed to by the H, L pair with the contents of accumulator A and sets the status flags accordingly. In effect, the flags are set as if the byte in memory had been subtracted from accumulator A. However, neither memory nor accumulator is changed. As a result, if the byte in the memory equals that in A, the Z bit will be set to 1; if A is less than the byte in the memory, the C flag will be set to 1.

The JNC FINIS instruction causes a jump to FINIS if the C flag is a 0. (In this case the content of A is larger than or equal to that in location 51 in the

---

[11]M is used in assembler language to indicate the byte in the memory pointed to by the H, L pair of registers. These must have been properly set before such an instruction is used.

TABLE 10.9   8080 PROGRAM TO FIND LARGEST NUMBER

MEMORY ADDRESS	CONTENTS	LABEL	OP CODE	OPERAND	COMMENTS
00	21		LXI	H, 50H	LOAD H AND L
01	50				
02	00				
03	7E		MOV	A, M	GET 1ST OPERAND
04	23		INX	H	
05	BE		CMP	M	IS 2D OPERAND LARGER?
06	D2		JNC	FINIS	
07	0A				
08	00				
09	7E		MOV	A, M	2D OPERAND IS LARGER
0A	23	FINIS	INX	H	
0B	77		MOV	M, A	

memory.) If no jump is taken, the MOV A, M instruction moves the byte at location 51 (now pointed to by H, L) into the accumulator.

The INX H instruction adds 1 to the H, L register pair, giving 52, and the MOV M, A instruction moves the contents of the accumulator into location 52 in the memory.

This computer employs what is now becoming the most used technique for subroutine calls and for servicing interrupts. For a subroutine jump a CALL instruction is used. The address of the subroutine is in the 16 bits (two memory addresses) following the CALL OP code. This instruction first increments the program counter to the address of the next instruction in sequence and then places (pushes) the contents of the program counter on a stack in the memory. The stack pointer (see Fig. 10.16) is adjusted to point to this address on the stack. The jump to the subroutine is then made.

At the end of the subroutine a RETURN instruction is used. This instruction specifies no address but simply causes a return to the address currently on top of the stack and then pops this address.

An investigation of this scheme will show that if a subroutine calls another subroutine which calls another subroutine which then calls the first subroutine, the successive addresses needed are stacked one on the other, and the subprograms will finally work their way back to the original calling program without loss of any of the necessary address links.

In preparing subroutines, some method must be agreed on for "passing parameters" into the subroutine. For example, if the subroutine's function is to find the square root of a number, then the original number must be passed to the subroutine, and the square root calculated by the subroutine must be passed back to the calling program. In this case the accumulator is a logical place to use for passing the number involved. Then each time the subroutine is to be used, the number whose square root is to be formed will be placed in the accumulator, the subroutine will be called, and at the end of the subroutine the square root will be in the accumulator.

In this computer interrupts are handled in a way similar to subroutine calls. The program being executed is interrupted, and the address of the next instruction which was to be executed is placed on top of the stack maintained by the stack

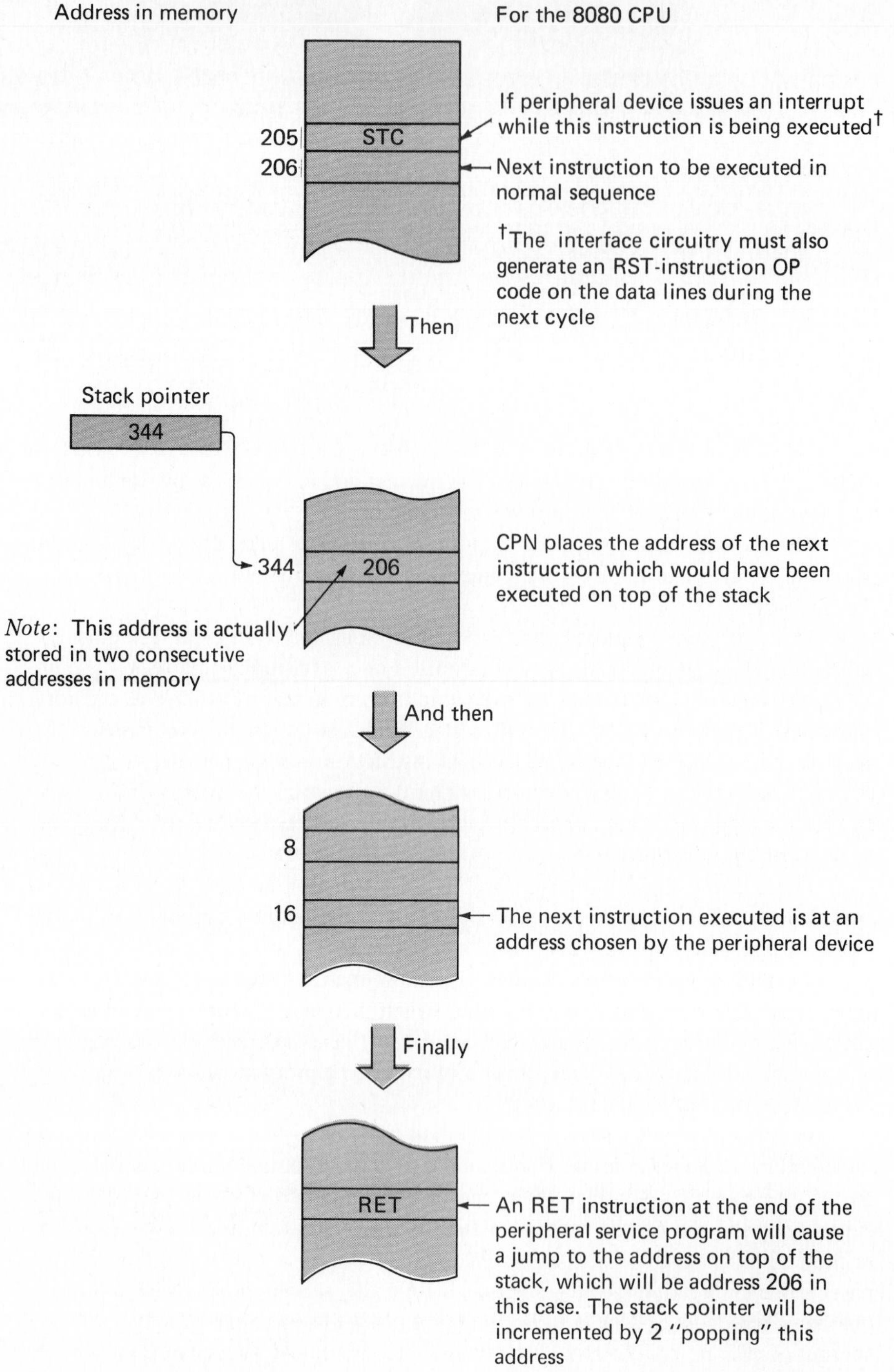

Address in memory   For the 8080 CPU

**COMPUTER
ORGANIZATION**

205   STC   ← If peripheral device issues an interrupt
206   ← while this instruction is being executed[†]
                Next instruction to be executed in
                normal sequence

[†]The interface circuitry must also
generate an RST-instruction OP
code on the data lines during the
next cycle

Then

Stack pointer

344

344   206   CPN places the address of the next
               instruction which would have been
               executed on top of the stack

Note: This address is actually
stored in two consecutive
addresses in memory

And then

8
16   ← The next instruction executed is at an
                address chosen by the peripheral device

Finally

RET   ← An RET instruction at the end of the
                peripheral service program will cause
                a jump to the address on top of the
                stack, which will be address 206 in
                this case. The stack pointer will be
                incremented by 2 "popping" this
                address

FIGURE 10.16

Interrupt servicing
using a stack.

pointer. The interrupting device places an RST instruction on the data lines of the bus, and the 8080 next performs this instruction. The address section (NNN in Table 10.6) of this instruction contains the address in memory where the subroutine to service the interrupt is located. Returns from the interrupt servicing subroutine can then use the RETURN instruction to return to the original program. This is shown in Fig. 10.16.

When this kind of stacking of subprogram and interrupt addresses is used, it is possible to have subroutines interrupted, interrupts interrupted, and so on, and still return to each strip of instructions correctly as long as the stack does not overflow the area in memory allocated for it.

It is also necessary to save the registers in the CPU when interrupts occur if they are changed by the interrupt servicing subroutine. (The same applies for subroutine calls.) The interrupt program must take care of this saving and restoring of registers. Some idea of how this is done by using a stack can be gathered by examining the PUSH and POP instructions, and the Questions treat this in more detail.

We now examine a program using a subroutine call. The subroutine is to search a table for a specific character. If the character is found, the position of the character in the table is to be passed back to the calling routine.

Examination of the problem indicates that the following information must be passed to the subroutine: the location of the table in the memory, the length of the table (number of characters in the table), and the character to be searched for. To pass these three parameters, we choose registers H and L to point to the ending location of the table, put the number of characters into register B, and place the character to be searched for in the accumulator. The subroutine is then entered; its job is to find the character, place its position in the table in register B, and then return to the calling program. If the character is not in the table, B is made a 0.

A subroutine to perform this function is shown in Table 10.10. When the subroutine is entered, the register pair H, L points to the table's last location in memory, B gives the number of characters, and A contains the character to be located.

The name of the subroutine is SRCH. The ORG 30H statement, which occurs first, is an *assembler directive* which tells the assembler to "locate this subroutine beginning at location 30_{16} in memory."

The label SRCH identifies the subroutine. The CMP M instruction compares the last entry in the table (which is pointed to by the H, L pair) with the accu-

A SINGLE-ADDRESS MICROPROCESSOR

TABLE 10.10			A SEARCH SUBROUTINE
LABEL	OP CODE	OPERAND	COMMENTS
	ORG	30H	
SRCH	CMP	M	; IS CHAR = TABLE ENTRY?
	JZ	FINIS	; YES
	DCX	H	; GO TO NEXT ENTRY
	DCR	B	; DECREMENT B
	JNZ	SRCH	; IS SEARCH OVER?
FINIS	RET		; RETURN

TABLE 10.11		CALLING PROGRAM FOR SEARCH SUBROUTINE	
LABEL	OP CODE	OPERAND	COMMENTS
	LXI	H, TBEND	; LOAD TABLE END ADDRESS
	MVI	B, 20H	; LOAD NO. OF CHARS
	LDA	CHAR	; LOAD CHARACTER
	CALL	SRCH	; CALL SUBROUTINE
	LDR	40H	; RETURN IS TO HERE
	. . .	. . .	

mulator. If they are equal, the Z status flag will be set, and the JZ instruction will cause a jump to FINIS. If they are not equal, the DCX H instruction subtracts 1 from the H, L pair, and then the DCR B subtracts 1 from B. When the DCR B instruction is executed, if B becomes 0, the Z flag will be set. The JNZ instruction tests this, and if another location is to be checked, it jumps back to SRCH; otherwise, the subroutine ends.

A possible calling sequence is shown in Table 10.11. The location of the end of the table is at TBEND in the memory, and the number of items is 20_{16}. These are loaded into the H, L pair and B, and the character to be searched for, here called CHAR, is loaded into the accumulator. Finally the subroutine is entered, by using a CALL SRCH instruction.

When the RET instruction in the subroutine is executed, the return will be to the LDR 40H instruction, which would be executed next. (This statement is placed in the program only for completeness and does not affect any operation discussed.)

6800 MICROPROCESSOR

10.12 Another widely used example of a microcomputer is the 6800 microprocessor-microcomputer system first developed by Motorola. (Chips for this system are also available from a number of other manufacturers.) The basic CPU is on a single 40-pin IC chip, as shown in Fig. 10.17. The 6800 has an 8-bit data bus and a 16-bit address bus (see Fig. 10.17). From a programming viewpoint, the CPU chip contains six basic registers, shown in Fig. 10.18.

1   *Accumulator A*   This is an 8-bit accumulator.

2   *Accumulator B*   This is an 8-bit accumulator.

3   *Index register*   This is a single 16-bit index register.

4   *Stack pointer*   This is a 16-bit register which points to a stack in memory.

5   *Program counter*   This is the instruction counter or program counter and contains 16 bits.

6   *Status register*   This is a 6-bit register containing six flip-flops, H, I, N, Z, V, and C. The results of arithmetic and other operations are stored in these bits.

The instruction repertoire for this CPU chip includes over 100 different instructions. The operation code is 8 bits, the size of a word in memory. There are

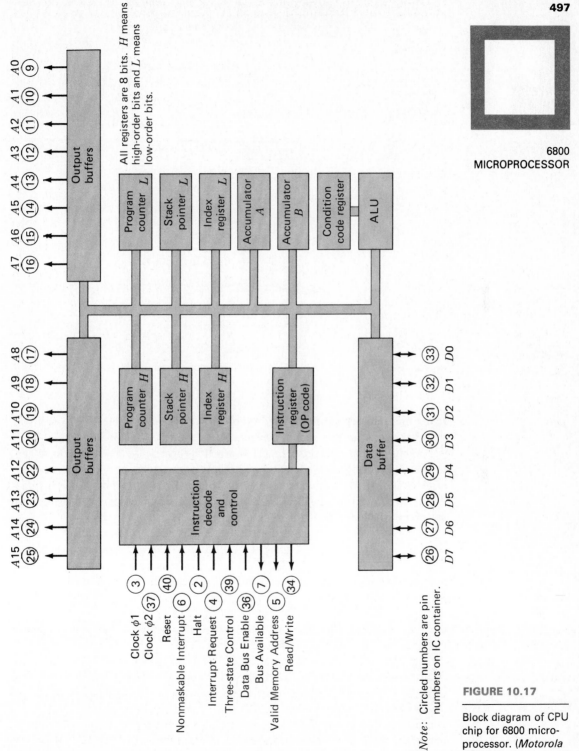

6800
MICROPROCESSOR

FIGURE 10.17

Block diagram of CPU chip for 6800 microprocessor. (*Motorola Corp.*)

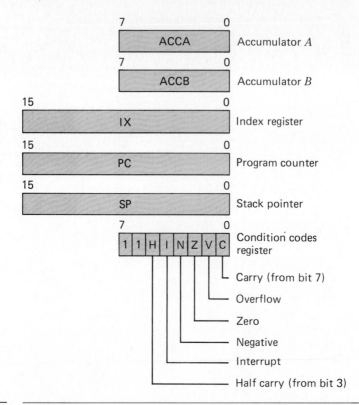

FIGURE 10.18

Basic registers used in programming the 6800.

seven different addressing modes, which are described in Table 10.12. A list of the instructions for this microprocessor chip is shown in Tables 10.13 to 10.15.

The way that conditional branch instructions operate deserves mention. When an arithmetic or boolean operation is performed, the status bits are set according to the result of this operation. Tables 10.16 and 10.17 show the status bits and detail their function. The BRANCH instructions use the values of these bits to determine whether a branch is to be made.

For instance, let us assume accumulator A is added to accumulator B. Then if the sum is negative, the N bit will be set to a 1. We also assume no overflow, so V will be set to a 0. Now if a BLT (branch if less than 0) instruction follows, the computer will branch to the address given in the address part of the instruction. If the result of the addition had been 0 or positive, no branch would have occurred, and the next instruction in sequence would be taken.

The *interrupt mask bit (I)* in the status register is set on when external input-output devices are allowed to interrupt the computer. When an interrupt occurs, the computer jumps to an interrupt servicing routine (program) which is stored in the memory. To simplify and shorten the interrupt servicing program, this microprocessor automatically transfers the values in all the CPU registers into a stack in the memory and places the address of these stored register contents in the stack pointer. The interrupt servicing program can then simply service the printer, reader, or whatever generated the interrupt and can later return the contents of the CPU

TABLE 10.12	ADDRESSING MODES FOR MICROPROCESSOR
MODE	OPERATION
Accumulator (ACCX) addressing	In accumulator-only addressing, either accumulator A or accumulator B is specified. These are 1-byte instructions.
Immediate addressing	In immediate addressing, the operand is contained in the second byte of instruction, except LDS and LDX, which have operands in second and third bytes of instruction. These are 2- or 3-byte instructions.
Direct addressing	In direct addressing, the address of the operand is contained in second byte of instruction. Direct addressing allows user to directly address lowest 256 bytes in machine, i.e., locations 0 through 255. Enhanced execution times are achieved by storing data in these locations. In most configurations it would be a random-access memory. These are 2-byte instructions.
Extended addressing	In extended addressing, the address contained in second byte of instruction is used as higher 8 bits of address of the operand. Third byte of instruction is used as lower 8 bits of address for the operand. This is an absolute address in memory. These are 3-byte instructions.
Indexed addressing	In indexed addressing, the address contained in second byte of instruction is added to index register's lowest 8 bits. Any carry generated is then added to higher-order 8 bits of index register. This result is then used to address memory. The modified address is held in a temporary address register so there is no change to index register. These are 2-byte instructions.
Implied addressing	In the implied addressing mode, the OP code gives the address (i.e., stack pointer, index register, etc.). These are 1-byte instructions.
Relative addressing	In relative addressing, the address contained in second byte of instruction is added to program counter's lowest 8 bits plus 2. The carry or borrow is then added to high 8 bits. This allows user to address data within a range of -125 to $+129$ bytes of present instruction. These are 2-byte instructions.

6800
MICROPROCESSOR

registers to their status when interrupted and restart the program where it was interrupted.

Maintaining these stored registers in a stack also enables the interrupt servicing program to be interrupted, since the contents of the registers are again placed in the stack. In this way several interrupts can follow one another, and the program can still service each interrupt in turn and then return to the original program, which was operating when the first interrupt occurred.

Details of the operating features of this microprocessor can be found in the manufacturers' manuals listed in the Bibliography.

Table 10.18 shows a short program for the 6800 microprocessor. Its purpose is to add a table of 8-bit bytes located in the memory starting at address 51_{16}. The number of bytes in the table is in location 50_{16}. The sum of the numbers is to be stored at location 0F in the memory. Carries from the addition are ignored.

TABLE 10.13

ACCUMULATOR AND MEMORY INSTRUCTIONS*

OPERATIONS	MNEMONIC	IMMED OP	DIRECT OP	INDEX OP	EXTND OP	IMPLIED OP	BOOLEAN/ARITHMETIC OPERATION† (ALL REGISTER LABELS REFER TO CONTENTS)
Add	ADDA	8B	9B	AB	BB		$A + M \rightarrow A$
	ADDB	CB	DB	EB	FB		$B + M \rightarrow B$
Add accumulators	ABA					1B	$A + B \rightarrow A$
Add with carry	ADCA	89	99	A9	B9		$A + M + C \rightarrow A$
	ADCB	C9	D9	E9	F9		$B + M + C \rightarrow B$
And	ANDA	84	94	A4	B4		$A \cdot M \rightarrow A$
	ANDB	C4	D4	E4	F4		$B \cdot M \rightarrow B$
Bit test	BITA	85	95	A5	B5		$A \cdot M$
	BITB	C5	D5	E5	F5		$B \cdot M$
Clear	CLR			6F	7F		$00 \rightarrow M$
	CLRA					4F	$00 \rightarrow A$
	CLRB					5F	$00 \rightarrow B$
Compare	CMPA	81	91	A1	B1		$A - M$
	CMPB	C1	D1	E1	F1		$B - M$
Compare accumulators	CBA					11	$A - B$
Complement 1s	COM			63	73		$\overline{M} \rightarrow M$
	COMA					43	$\overline{A} \rightarrow A$
	COMB					53	$\overline{B} \rightarrow B$
Complement 2s (negate)	NEG			60	70		$00 - M \rightarrow M$
	NEGA					40	$00 - A \rightarrow A$
	NEGB					50	$00 - B \rightarrow B$
Decimal adjust, A	DAA					19	Converts binary addition of BCD characters into BCD format
Decrement	DEC			6A	7A		$M - 1 \rightarrow M$
	DECA					4A	$A - 1 \rightarrow A$
	DECB					5A	$B - 1 \rightarrow B$
Exclusive OR	EORA	88	98	A8	B8		$A \oplus M \rightarrow A$
	EORB	C8	D8	E8	F8		$B \oplus M \rightarrow B$
Increment	INC			6C	7C		$M + 1 \rightarrow M$
	INCA					4C	$A + 1 \rightarrow A$
	INCB					5C	$B + 1 \rightarrow B$
Load accumulator	LDAA	86	96	A6	B6		$M \rightarrow A$
	LDAB	C6	D6	E6	F6		$M \rightarrow B$
Inclusive OR	ORAA	8A	9A	AA	BA		$A + M \rightarrow A$
	ORAB	CA	DA	EA	FA		$B + M \rightarrow B$

Operations	Mnemonic	Immed	Direct	Index	Extend	Implied	Boolean/Arithmetic Operation
Push data	PSHA					36	$A \rightarrow M_{SP},\ SP - 1 \rightarrow SP$
	PSHB					37	$B \rightarrow M_{SP},\ SP - 1 \rightarrow SP$
Pull data	PULA					32	$SP + 1 \rightarrow SP,\ M_{SP} \rightarrow A$
	PULB					33	$SP + 1 \rightarrow SP,\ M_{SP} \rightarrow B$
Rotate left	ROL			69	79		M — $\boxed{C}\,\boxed{b_7\cdots b_0}$ rotate left
	ROLA					49	A
	ROLB					59	B
Rotate right	ROR			66	76		M — $\boxed{C}\,\boxed{b_7\cdots b_0}$ rotate right
	RORA					46	A
	RORB					56	B
Shift left, arithmetic	ASL			68	78		M — $\boxed{C}\,\boxed{b_7\cdots b_0}\leftarrow 0$
	ASLA					48	A
	ASLB					58	B
Shift right, arithmetic	ASR			67	77		M — $\boxed{b_7\cdots b_0}\,\boxed{C}$
	ASRA					47	A
	ASRB					57	B
Shift right, logic	LSR			64	74		M — $0\rightarrow\boxed{b_7\cdots b_0}\,\boxed{C}$
	LSRA					44	A
	LSRB					54	B
Store accumulator	STAA		97	A7	B7		$A \rightarrow M$
	STAB		D7	E7	F7		$B \rightarrow M$
Subtract	SUBA	80	90	A0	B0		$A - M \rightarrow A$
	SUBB	C0	D0	E0	F)		$B - M \rightarrow B$
Subtract accumulator	SBA					10	$A - B \rightarrow A$
Subtract with carry	SBCA	82	92	A2	B2		$A - M - C \rightarrow A$
	SBCB	C2	D2	E2	F2		$B - M - C \rightarrow B$
Transfer accumulators	TAB					16	$A \rightarrow B$
	TBA					17	$B \rightarrow A$
Test, zero or minus	TST			6D	7D		$M - 00$
	TSTA					4D	$A - 00$
	TSTB					5D	$B - 00$

*Courtesy Motorola Corp.
†OP code (hexadecimal)
+ Arithmetic plus
− Arithmetic minus
· Boolean AND
+ Boolean inclusive OR
⊕ Boolean exclusive OR
$\overline{M}$ Complement of M
→ Transfer into
0 Bit = zero
00 Byte = zero
M_{SP} Contents of memory location pointed to by stack pointer
Note: Accumulator addressing mode instructions are included in the column for implied addressing.

COMPUTER
ORGANIZATION

TABLE 10.14 INDEX REGISTER AND STACK MANIPULATION INSTRUCTIONS

| POINTER OPERATIONS | MNEMONIC | ADDRESSING MODES | | | | | BOOLEAN ARITHMETIC OPERATION† |
		IMMED OP	DIRECT OP	INDEX OP	EXTND OP	IMPLIED OP	
Compare index register	CPX	8C	9C	AC	BC		$X_H - M, X_L - (M + 1)$
Decrement index register	DEX					09	$X - 1 \rightarrow X$
Decrement stack pointer	DES					34	$SP - 1 \rightarrow SP$
Increment index register	INX					08	$X + 1 \rightarrow X$
Increment stack pointer	INS					31	$SP + 1 \rightarrow SP$
Load index register	LDX	CE	DE	EE	FE		$M \rightarrow X_H, (M + 1) \rightarrow X_L$
Load stack pointer	LDS	8E	9E	AE	BE		$M \rightarrow SP_H, (M + 1) \rightarrow SP_L$
Store index register	STX		DF	EF	FF		$X_H \rightarrow M, X_L \rightarrow (M + 1)$
Store stack pointer	STS		9F	AF	BF		$SP_H \rightarrow M, SP_L \rightarrow (M + 1)$
Index register $\rightarrow$ stack pointer	TXS					35	$X - 1 \rightarrow SP$
Stack pointer $\rightarrow$ index register	TSX					30	$SP + 1 \rightarrow X$

†See footnotes to Table 10.13

TABLE 10.15   JUMP AND BRANCH INSTRUCTIONS

OPERATIONS	MNEMONIC	ADDRESSING MODES				BRANCH TEST†
		RELATIVE OP	INDEX OP	EXTND OP	IMPLIED OP	
Branch always	BRA	20				None
Branch if carry clear	BCC	24				$C = 0$
Branch if carry set	BCS	25				$C = 1$
Branch if $= 0$	BEQ	27				$Z = 1$
Branch if ≥ 0	BGE	2C				$N \oplus V = 0$
Branch if > 0	BGT	2E				$Z + (N \oplus V) = 0$
Branch if higher	BHI	22				$C + Z = 0$
Branch if ≤ 0	BLE	2F				$Z + (N \oplus V) = 1$
Branch if lower or same	BLS	23				$C + Z = 1$
Branch if < 0	BLT	2D				$N \oplus V = 1$
Branch if minus	BMI	2B				$N = 1$
Branch if not equal to 0	BNE	26				$Z = 0$
Branch if overflow clear	BVC	28				$V = 0$
Branch if overflow set	BVS	29				$V = 1$
Branch if plus	BPL	2A				$N = 0$
Branch to subroutine	BSR	8D				
Jump	JMP		6E	7E		
Jump to subroutine	JSR		AD	BD		
No operation	NOP				02	Advances program counter only
Return from interrupt	RTI				3B	
Return from subroutine	RTS				39	
Software interrupt	SWI				3F	
Wait for interrupt	WAI				3E	

†See footnotes to Table 10.13.

TABLE 10.16	CONDITION CODE REGISTER BITS

Condition code register The condition code register indicates the results of an ALU operation: negative (*N*), zero (*Z*), overflow (*V*), carry from bit 7 (*C*), and half-carry from bit 3 (*H*). These bits of the condition code register are used as testable conditions for the conditional branch instructions. Bit 4 is the interrupt mask bit (*I*). The unused bits of the condition code register (b_6 and b_7) are 1s.

The programmer wrote the columns from Label to the right. The assembler generated the leftmost two columns.

The first instruction, CLRA, simply clears accumulator *A*. The LDAB instruction gets the number of bytes in the table from location 50_{16} in the memory and stores that number in register *B*. Notice that in 6800 assembly language a hexadecimal number is designated by placing a $ in front of the number. Also notice that the 50 occurs in the second memory address of the instruction word, and the addressing mode is immediate.

The LDX #$01 loads the value 1 in the index register. The symbol # tells the assembler to use this as an actual number, not as an address. The resulting immediate address operand requires 2 bytes since the index register contains 16 bits. Also note that the least significant byte is the last byte in the 3-byte instruction word.

The ADDA $50, X is an addition instruction in *indexed* addressing mode. In the 6800 the indexed mode is indicated by the X in the statement. The $50 (for hexadecimal 50) gives the offset. The actual address used is formed by adding the offset to the contents of the index register. In this case, the first time through the loop, the address will be the offset 50_{16} plus 1, or 51_{16}. Notice that the offset is loaded in the memory following the OP code and is a single byte. (A check of the OP codes will indicate that AB is the OP code for an indexed-mode addition.) After this instruction is executed, accumulator *A* will contain the number at location 51.

The INX adds 1 to the index register, which will now contain 2. The DECB decrements register *B* and also sets the status bits. In particular, if *B* becomes 0, the *Z* status bit will be set to a 1, and this will indicate that the entire table has been processed.

The BNE LOOP instruction tests the *Z* bit and branches if *Z* is *not* a 1. When *Z* becomes 1, the program control "falls through" the BNE to the STAA instruction.

TABLE 10.17			CONDITION CODE REGISTER MANIPULATION INSTRUCTIONS
OPERATIONS	MNEMONIC	OP CODE	BOOLEAN ARITHMETIC OPERATION
Clear carry	CLC	0C	$0 \rightarrow C$
Clear interrupt mask	CLI	0E	$0 \rightarrow 1$
Clear overflow	CLV	0A	$0 \rightarrow V$
Set carry	SEC	0D	$1 \rightarrow C$
Set interrupt mask	SEI	0F	$1 \rightarrow I$
Set overflow	SEV	0B	$1 \rightarrow V$
Accumulator $A \rightarrow$ CCR	TAP	06	$A \rightarrow$ CCR
CCR $\rightarrow$ accumulator A	TPA	07	CCR $\rightarrow A$

TABLE 10.18				A 6800 PROGRAM	
MEMORY ADDRESS	CONTENTS	LABEL	OP CODE	OPERAND	COMMENTS
0000	4F		CLRA		CLEAR A
0001	D6		LDAB	$50	GET NO. OF ENTRIES
0002	50				
0003	CE		LDX	#$01	LOAD INDEX REGISTER
0004	00				
0005	01				
0006	AB	LOOP	ADDA	$50, X	
0007	50				
0008	08		INX		INCREMENT IR
0009	5A		DECB		DECREMENT B
000A	26		BNE	LOOP	
000B	FA				
000C	97	⸱	STAA	$0F	
000D	0F				

6800
MICROPROCESSOR

When the program control loops back the first time, the index register plus the offset now equals 52, so the number at that address will be added into accumulator A by the ADDA $50, X instruction. This process continues with numbers at successive locations being added into A until the table end is reached. Then the STAA $0F instruction stores the sum at location F in the memory.

Subroutine calls for the 6800 are made by a JSR (jump subroutine) instruction which pushes the program counter's contents (2 bytes)[12] on top of the stack (also adjusting the stack pointer). When an RTS (return from subroutine) instruction is given, the address (2 bytes) on top of the stack is placed in the program counter, causing return to the instruction after the initial JSR.

An example of a subroutine is shown in Table 10.19. The ORG $30 is an *assembler directive* which tells the assembler to place the subroutine starting at location 30_{16} in the memory. The purpose of this subroutine is to find where in a table in the memory a character lies. The parameters are passed[13] as follows: (1) the address of the end of the table must be in the index register before the subroutine is entered, (2) the number of entries in the table is placed in accumulator B, (3) the character to be searched for must be in accumulator A.

---

[12]After the program counter has already been updated to point to the next instruction.
[13]See description of the 8080 for a discussion of parameter passing.

TABLE 10.19		6800 SUBROUTINE FOR TABLE LOOKUP	
LABEL	OP CODE	OPERAND	COMMENTS
	ORG	$30	SET ORIGIN
SRCH	CMPA	0,X	CHAR = TABLE ENTRY?
	BEQ	FINIS	YES QUIT
	DEX		INCREMENT IR
	DECB		DECREMENT B
	BNE	SRCH	TEST FOR END
FINIS	RTS		RETURN TO CALLER

TABLE 10.20			CALLING 6800 SUBROUTINE
LABEL	OP CODE	OPERAND	COMMENTS
	LDX	#ENDTA	LOAD IR WITH TABLE END
	LDAB	#20	LOAD B WITH NO. OF ENTRIES
	LDAA	CHAR	LOAD A WITH CHAR
	JSR	SRCH	
	STAA	MABEL	

The subroutine is entered at SRCH, where the CMPA 0, X instruction causes the byte at the memory address given by the index register (notice that the offset is 0) to be compared with accumulator A. If they are equal, the Z status bit will be set to 1, and the BEQ FINIS instruction will test this instruction and branch to FINIS. Otherwise, the index register will be decremented so that it points to the next lowest entry in the table. Accumulator B will then be decremented by the DECB, and if this sets the Z flag to 1, indicating a 0 in B, the search will be ended. Otherwise, the return to SRCH will cause the next entry in the table to be compared with the character in accumulator A. This will be repeated until all table entries have been examined.

The RTS will cause a return to the calling program with accumulator B containing the number in the table at which the matched character lies.

A possible calling program segment is shown in Table 10.20. LDX loads the index register with the address of the end of the table, which is assumed to be at ENDTA. The number of table entries is assumed to be 20_{10}, and LDAB loads B with that value. (No $ symbol means decimal.) JSR causes a jump to the subroutine, and the jump back from the subroutine using RTS will cause the STAA instruction to be executed.

When a set of chips for a microprocessor of this kind is used with a fixed program, such as in an industrial controller, the program is generally developed by using system software which is provided by the chips' manufacturer and software vendors and placed in a ROM memory. A ROM memory can be addressed and used just like a RAM memory when it is connected to a microprocessor CPU (except, of course, that we cannot write into a ROM). It is common practice to write the program for the microprocessor and assemble this program using another computer. The program is sometimes tested using this larger computer, which runs it on a simulator. The larger computer then produces a tape which is used to set up the ROM in which the program will be stored.

Considerable effort is made by the manufacturers of the microprocessor chips to facilitate programming the microprocessor, preparing the ROMs, and loading the RAMs, when required. Sometimes higher-level languages are provided, enabling programs to be written in Fortran, PL/M, or other compiler languages, which are then translated into the program for the microcomputer.

PDP-11

10.13 The PDP-11 series includes minicomputers and microcomputers. These computers have 16-bit words, each containing two 8-bit bytes (see Fig. 10.19). Notice, however, that each address in memory contains 1 byte. The eight general registers are 16 bits each, and a computer word normally has 16 bits.

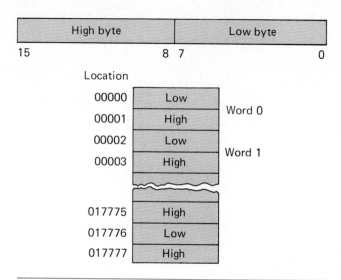

PDP-11

FIGURE 10.19

Memory organization
of PDP-11.

The PDP-11 reads from and writes into external input-output devices in the same manner that it reads from and writes into high-speed memory. Each input-output device is simply given an address in memory. To read from an address, and in turn an input-output device, the computer uses not a special input-output instruction, but a MOVE instruction, an ADD instruction, or whatever is desired. This means that status registers must be used by the CPU (as in Chap. 8) to determine whether a device can be written into, has something to read, etc.

There is a complex interrupt structure in the PDP-11 where the CPU continually puts a status number on three wires of its bus. Each external device has a status number, and if that status number is greater than the CPU status number, it has the right to interrupt. Setting a CPU's status number to its maximum stops all interrupts. The CPU's status number is set under program control and can be changed as the program operates.

Interrupts are "vectored" (see Chap. 8 and the description of the 8080, Sec. 10.11) in that an interrupting device places data (an interrupt vector) on the bus lines which enable the CPU to transfer control directly to a service program for the interrupting device.

The general registers of the PDP-11 are shown in Fig. 10.20(a). Notice that register R_6 is a stack pointer and R_7 is the program counter. These can be used and addressed just as the other general-purpose registers, making for interesting instruction variations.

The CPU in the PDP-11 includes a status register, as shown in Fig. 10.20(b). This status register contains the priority number just discussed, which is placed on the bus in bits 5 to 7. Bits 11 to 15 in Fig. 10.20(b) are used by the operating system to control program operations in the 11/45, one of the larger PDP-11 models, and are not discussed here. (Details are given in the manuals listed in the Bibliography.)

The N, Z, V, C bits in the status word are set and reset as instructions are operated. For example, the N bit indicates when a result is negative. If an ADD instruction is performed and the result is negative, the N bit will be set to a 1;

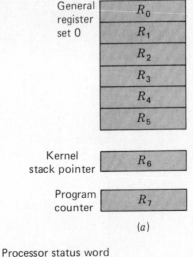

General
register
set 0

R_0

R_1

R_2

R_3

R_4

R_5

Kernel
stack pointer R_6

Program
counter R_7

(a)

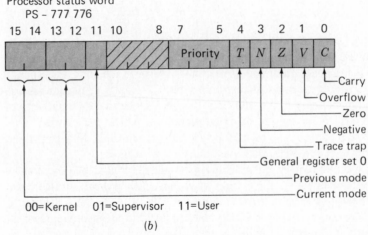

Processor status word
PS – 777 776

| 15 | 14 | 13 | 12 | 11 | 10 | 8 | 7 | 5 | 4 | 3 | 2 | 1 | 0 |

Priority T N Z V C

Carry
Overflow
Zero
Negative
Trace trap
General register set 0
Previous mode
Current mode

00=Kernel   01=Supervisor   11=User

(b)

FIGURE 10.20

PDP-11 organization.
(a) General registers.
(b) Processor status
word.

otherwise, it will be a 0. Similarly, the Z bit indicates a zero result and will be set on if an instruction's result is zero. (V is for overflow and C is for carry.)

The conditional jump or branch instructions in the PDP-11 use these bits to determine whether a jump is to be taken. For instance, BNE (branch on negative) will cause a branch only if the N bit is a 1. As another example, BEQ (branch on equal) causes a branch only if the Z bit is a 1.

Table 10.21 lists the addressing modes for the PDP-11. The addressing mode number is placed before the register number in an instruction word and indicates how the designated register is to be used. Table 10.22 gives the instructions for the computer.

Table 10.23 shows a sample section of a program for a PDP-11. This is a subroutine, or subprogram, which reads from a teletypewriter keyboard. There is a status byte (interface register) at address 177030 in the memory which tells when the keyboard has a new character. The subprogram places characters in a table until a period is typed, at which time control is transferred to another subprogram.

PDP-11

TABLE 10.21

ADDRESSING MODES FOR PDP-11 MINICOMPUTER

ADDRESS	MODE	NAME	SYMBOLIC	DESCRIPTION
General register Mode R	0	Register	R	(R) is operand [e.g., R_2 = %2]
	1	Register deferred	(R)	(R) is address
	2	Auto increment	(R)+	(R) is address; (R) + (1 or 2)
	3	Auto increment deferred	@(R)+	(R) is address of address; (R) + 2
	4	Auto decrement	−(R)	(R) − (1 or 2); (R) is address
	5	Auto decrement deferred	@−(R)	(R) − 2; (R) is address of address
	6	Index	X(R)	(R) + X is address
	7	Index deferred	@X(R)	(R) + X is address of address
Program counter, Reg = 7 Mode 7	2	Immediate	#n	Operand n follows instruction
	3	Absolute	@#A	Address A follows instruction
	6	Relative	A	Instruction address + 4 + X is address
	7	Relative deferred	@A	Instruction address + 4 + X is address of address

COMPUTER ORGANIZATION

TABLE 10.22   PDP-11 INSTRUCTION REPERTOIRE

LEGEND

OP CODES		OPERATIONS		BOOLEAN		CONDITION CODES
■	0 for word/1 for byte	( )	Contents of	$\wedge$ = AND		*Conditionally set/cleared
SS	Source field (6 bits)	s	Contents of source	$\vee$ = Inclusive OR		— Not affected
DD	Destination field (6 bits)	d	Contents of destination	$\veebar$ = Exclusive OR		0 cleared
R	General register (3 bits) 0 to 7	r	Contents of register	$\sim$ = Not		1 Set
XXX	Offset (3 bits) + 127 to − 128	←	Becomes			
N	Number (3 bits)	X	Relative address			
NN	Number (6 bits)	%	Register definition			

SINGLE OPERAND: OPR dst

15	6	5	0
OP CODE		DD	

				dst RESULT		N	Z	V	C
MNEMONIC	**OP CODE**	**INSTRUCTION**				N	Z	V	C
General									
CLR(B)	■050DD	Clear		0		0	1	0	0
COM(B)	■051DD	Complement (1s)		~d		*	*	0	1
INC(B)	■052DD	Increment		d + 1		*	*	*	—
DEC(B)	■053DD	Decrement		d − 1		*	*	*	—
NEG(B)	■054DD	Negate (2s complement)		− d		*	*	*	*
TST(B)	■057DD	Test		d		*	*	0	0
Rotate and Shift									
ROR(B)	■060DD	Rotate right		→ C, d ↓		*	*	*	*
ROL(B)	■061DD	Rotate left		C, d ↓		*	*	*	*
ASR(B)	■062DD	Arithmetic shift right		d/2		*	*	*	*
ASL(B)	■063DD	Arithmetic shift left		2d		*	*	*	*
SWAB	0003DD	Swap bytes				*	*	0	0
Multiple Precision									
ADC(B)	■055DD	Add carry		d + C		*	*	*	*
SBC(B)	■056DD	Subtract carry		d − C		*	*	*	*
▲SXT*	0067DD	Sign extend		0 or − 1		—	*	0	—

DOUBLE OPERAND: OPR src, dst   OPR src, R or OPR R, dst

15	12	11		6	5		0
OP CODE		SS			DD		

15		9	8	6	5		0
OP CODE			R		SS OR DD		

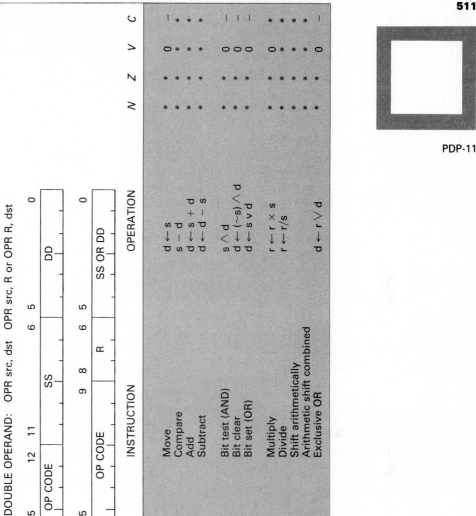

MNEMONIC	OP CODE	INSTRUCTION	OPERATION	N	Z	V	C
General							
MOV(B)	■1SSDD	Move	$d \leftarrow s$	*	*	0	—
CMP(B)	■2SSDD	Compare	$s - d$	*	*	*	*
ADD	06SSDD	Add	$d \leftarrow s + d$	*	*	*	*
SUB	16SSDD	Subtract	$d \leftarrow d - s$	*	*	*	*
Logical							
BIT(B)	■3SSDD	Bit test (AND)	$s \wedge d$	*	*	0	—
BIC(B)	■4SSDD	Bit clear	$d \leftarrow (\sim s) \wedge d$	*	*	0	—
BIS(B)	■5SSDD	Bit set (OR)	$d \leftarrow s \vee d$	*	*	0	—
▲*Register*							
MUL	070RSS	Multiply	$r \leftarrow r \times s$	*	*	0	*
DIV	071RSS	Divide	$r \leftarrow r/s$	*	*	*	*
ASH	072RSS	Shift arithmetically		*	*	*	*
ASHC	073RSS	Arithmetic shift combined		*	*	*	*
XOR	074RDD	Exclusive OR	$d \leftarrow r \vee d$	*	*	0	—

PDP-11

TABLE 10.22   PDP-11 INSTRUCTION REPERTOIRE (continued)

LEGEND

BRANCH: B—location
If condition is satisfied:
Branch to location,
New PC ← updated PC + (2 × offset)

$\overline{\text{address of branch instruction} + 2}$

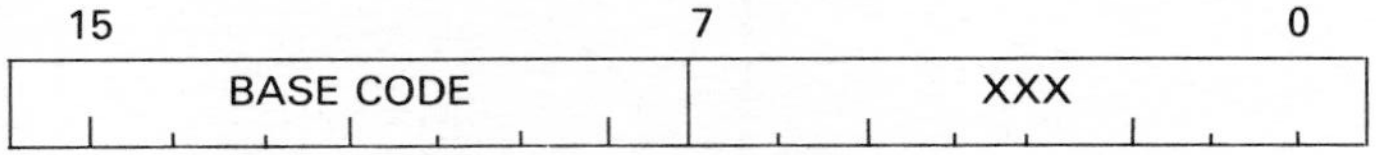

15			BASE CODE	7			XXX	0

OP code = base code + XXX

MNEMONIC	BASE CODE	INSTRUCTION	BRANCH CONDITION	
Branches				
BR	000400	Branch (unconditional)	(always)	
BNE	001000	Branch if not equal (to 0)	$\neq 0$	$Z = 0$
BEQ	001400	Branch if equal (to 0)	$= 0$	$Z = 1$
BPL	100000	Branch if plus	$+$	$N = 0$
BMI	100400	Branch if minus	$-$	$N = 1$
BVC	102000	Branch if overflow is clear		$V = 0$
BVS	102400	Branch if overflow is set		$V = 1$
BCC	103000	Branch if carry is clear		$C = 0$
BCS	103400	Branch if carry is set		$C = 1$
Signed Conditional Branches				
BGE	002000	Branch if greater than or equal (to 0)	≥ 0	$N \veebar V = 0$
BLT	002400	Branch if less than (0)	< 0	$N \veebar V = 1$
BGT	003000	Branch if greater than (0)	> 0	$Z \vee (N \veebar V) = 0$
BLE	003400	Branch if less than or equal (to 0)	≤ 0	$Z \vee (N \veebar V) = 1$
Unsigned Conditional Branches				
BHI	101000	Branch if higher	$>$	$C \vee Z = 0$
BLOS	101400	Branch if lower or same	$\leq$	$C \vee Z = 1$
BHIS	103000	Branch if higher or same	$\geq$	$C = 0$
BLO	103400	Branch if lower	$<$	$C = 1$

JUMP AND SUBROUTINE

MNEMONIC	OP CODE	INSTRUCTION	NOTES
JMP	0001DD	Jump	PC ← dst
JSR	004RDD	Jump to subroutine	Use same R
RTS	00020R	Return from subroutine	
▲MARK	0064NN	Mark	Aid in subroutine return
▲SOB	077RNN	Subtract 1 and branch (if $\neq 0$)	$(R) - 1$, then if $(R) \neq 0$: PC ← updated PC $- (2 \times NN)$

TRAP AND INTERRUPT

MNEMONIC	OP CODE	INSTRUCTION	NOTES
EMT	104000 to 104377	Emulator trap (not for general use)	PC at 30, PS at 32
TRAP	104400 to 104777	Trap	PC at 34, PS at 36
BPT	000003	Break-point trap	PC at 14, PS at 16
IOT	000004	Input-output trap	PC at 20, PS at 22
RTI	000002	Return from interrupt	
▲RTT	000006	Return from interrupt	Inhibit T bit trap

CONDITION CODE OPERATIONS

15					5	4	3	2	1	0
	OP CODE BASE = 000240						H	Z	V	C

0 = CLEAR SELECTED CONDITION CODE BITS
1 = SET SELECTED CONDITION CODE BITS

MNEMONIC	OP CODE	INSTRUCTION	N	Z	V	C
CLC	000241	Clear C	—	—	—	0
CLV	000242	Clear V	—	—	0	—
CLZ	000244	Clear Z	—	0	—	—
CLN	000250	Clear N	0	—	—	—
CCC	000257	Clear all condition code bits	0	0	0	0
SEC	000261	Set C	—	—	—	1
SEV	000262	Set V	—	—	1	—
SEZ	000264	Set Z	—	1	—	—
SEN	000270	Set N	1	—	—	—
SCC	000277	Set all condition code bits	1	1	1	1

MISCELLANEOUS

MNEMONIC	OP CODE	INSTRUCTION
HALT	000000	Halt
WAIT	000001	Wait for interrupt
RESET	000005	Reset external bus
NOP	000240	(No operation)
●SPL	00023N	Set priority level (to N)
▲MFPI	0065SS	Move from previous instruction space
▲MTPI	0066DD	Move to previous instruction space
●MFPD	1065SS	Move from previous data space
●MTPD	1066DD	Move to previous data space

Note: ▲ Applies to 11/35, 11/40, 11/45 computers. ● Applies to 11/45 computer.

TABLE 10.23

A PDP-11 PROGRAM SEGMENT

MEMORY ADDRESS	CONTENTS	LABEL	OP CODE	ADDRESS PART	COMMENTS
000524	105767 177030	READ:	TSTB	KSR	; READY
000530	100375		BPL	READ	; NO
000532	116710 177024		MOVB	KSB, @R0	; MOVE IT INTO THE TABLE
000536	005267 000200		INC	COUNT	; INCREASE COUNT
000542	122027 000256		CMPB	(R0) +, #256	; IS IT A PERIOD?
000546	001366		BNE	READ	; NO

The section shown in Table 10.23 is from an actual assembler listing for a PDP-11, and all numbers are in octal. The programmer writes all text from the Label column to the right. Semicolons indicate comments, and everything to the right of a semicolon is a comment and is ignored by the assembler.

The listing was prepared by the programmer who wrote the assembly-language program and then fed it into the assembler program which generated this listing.

The leftmost column lists locations in the memory, and the next column the contents of these locations. For instance, TSTB (test byte) has OP code 105767, and the assembler has read the programmer's TSTB instruction and converted it into octal value.

The statement TSTB tests the byte at the address given. If the value there is negative, it places a 1 in the N bit; if it is zero, a 1 is placed in the Z bit. KSR designates the address in memory, 177030, where the status byte for the keyboard is located. The programmer has (in an earlier section of the program) told the assembler the value of KSR. If the keyboard has a character ready, the sign bit of the KSR byte will be a 1, causing the N bit to go on.

The next instruction, BPL READ, says branch to READ if $N = 0$. This means that if no character is available, the program goes back to READ and looks again. This continues until a character is ready and $N = 1$.

The BPL has an OP code of 100. The next byte contains the displacement, or offset, for the branch in 2s complement form. The address for the branch is equal to two times the offset byte's value (375) added to the address of the next instruction. In this case the offset value is negative, and a branch would go back to location 524.

When $N = 1$, the instruction word at location 532 will be executed. This is a MOVB (move byte) instruction which causes a byte to be moved from KSB, which is 177024 (the address of the keyboard's buffer, the value of which the program has already given to the assembler), to the value pointed to by R_0. This is an example of indirect addressing, where R_0 is used to point to the actual address. Prior to this section of the program the programmer has loaded R_0 with the starting location of the table in the memory where the input characters are to be stored.

The program now checks to see whether the input character is a period, which has octal code 256, by comparing it with the character just loaded in the memory. Notice that indirect addressing is again used. The plus sign causes the value in R_0 to be incremented. Only if the character pointed to is equal to 256 will the Z bit be set to 1.

The BNE (branch on not equal) instruction checks this. If the character is a period, it transfers control to another program; otherwise, control is transferred back to the READ, where another character is then read from the keyboard.

The variety and complexities of the PDP-11's instruction repertoire can be appreciated only through a study of the manuals for this computer. The preceding example should point out the kind of efficient programs which can be written for this computer.

8086 AND 8088 MICROPROCESSORS

10.14   The 8086 and 8088 microprocessors are extensions of Intel's earlier 8080 microprocessor series. There are a number of changes in the 8086/8088, the most obvious being the fact that computations can be performed using 16-bit data versus 8-bit data for the 8080. There are a number of other advantages, however, including multiplication and division instructions, instruction queuing to improve operation speed, the ability to address a million bytes of memory, more general registers, and more instructions and addressing modes.

The 8086 and 8088 chips are part of a series which include the clock generator and interface chips shown in Fig. 8.22 and a floating-point arithmetic chip (the 8089).

The pin-outs for the 8086 and 8088 are shown in Fig. 10.21. As explained in Chap. 8, the address and data lines are shared by using time-division multiplexing. The principal difference between the 8086 and 8088 lies in the number of data lines output to the bus. The 8086 has 16 data lines on its bus, and the 8088 has only 8. This is shown by the number of *AD* (address/data) lines versus *A* (address) lines in the pin-out for each chip. The 8086 use 16 of the address lines for data also, so that *AD*0 to *AD*15 are used for address and data while the 8088 has only *AD*0 to *AD*7 for data and uses *A*8 to *A*19 for addresses. The internal data paths on the chips are the same, however; and each can add, subtract, multiply, or divide 16-bit binary numbers.

The result of the sharing of output lines is that several chips are required to demultiplex the address data and control lines. One possible configuration is shown in Fig. 10.22. The output from these extra chips forms the actual bus for the 8086 or 8088. The control lines from the chips are used to strobe the data address and control signals into the bus interface chips.

An important feature of the 8086 and 8088 microprocessor is the instruction queue used in each. The 8086/8088 chips read instructions in order from the memory in advance of their operation, and the instructions are placed in a queue consisting of a set of flip-flop registers. This speeds up operation because the processor can continue executing a time-consuming instruction (multiplication, for example) and at the same time read instructions from the memory of the processor. Then the processor can execute fast instructions (shift or test instructions, for example) from the queue at a speed faster than memory cycle times. Logic is supplied so that if the computer branches (jumps), the instructions in the queue are discarded if necessary.

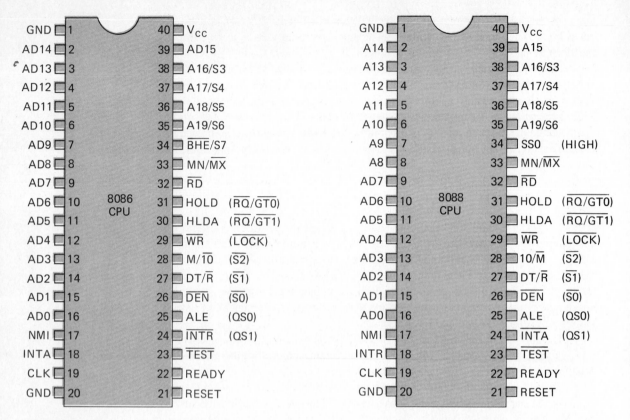

FIGURE 10.21

Pin-outs for 8086 and 8088 processors.

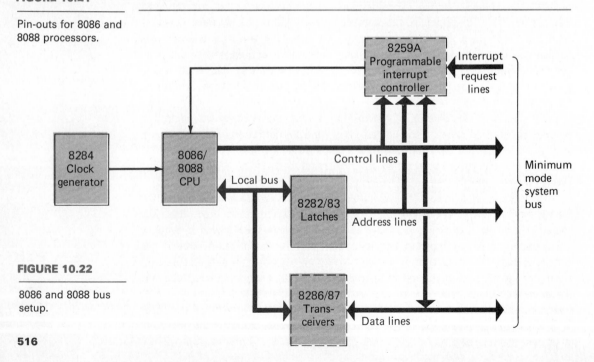

FIGURE 10.22

8086 and 8088 bus setup.

The 8086/8088 pair each have a special output pin, the *MN/MX* pin. When this pin is connected to TSV, the processor is placed in a minimum mode; when it is connected to OV, the processor is placed in a maximum mode. When in the minimum mode, the processor is used in single processor systems. In the maximum mode, several processors can be used with an 8288 bus controller which provides a special multibus architecture for multiprocessor systems. The maximum mode is for large arrays of memory, processors, and I/O devices.

A block diagram of the registers of the 8086 and 8088 is shown in Fig. 10.23. Notice eight general registers.

The 8086/8088 processors have a number of addressing modes. Addresses are 20 bits in length. Each address is formed in two sections which are then added: a *segment* address and an offset. The segment address is a full 20 bits, and the offset address is 16 bits.

There are four segment registers, *CS, DS, SS,* and *ES,* each containing 16 bits. These registers must be loaded by the program to starting values because the contents of one of these registers are *automatically* added to each address as it is generated. The contents of the 16-bit segment registers are first shifted left four binary places, however. (This is the equivalent of multiplying the contents of the registers by 16.) Loading the segment registers with 0s would simply place the program and stacks in the first 2^{16} words in memory and would effectively remove this feature for simple programs.

When a program is operated, the content of the program counter is automatically added to *CS* to form each instruction address. Data offsets are automatically added to *DS* (or *ES* in special cases), and stack offsets are automatically added to *SS.* Setting the *CS, DS,* and *SS* registers to addresses in different parts of a large memory would cause the instructions, data, and stacks to be in different parts of the memory. Setting the *CS, SS,* and *DS* registers to the same number would place everything in the same part of memory. Once the segment registers are set, the processor simply generates 16-bit offset addresses in a conventional manner from the instruction words while adding the segment register to each address to form the final 20-bit address. If a program really needed 2^{20} addresses, it would be necessary to change the segment registers from time to time to utilize the entire memory.

In effect, the 8086 and 8088 generate conventional 16-bit (offset) addresses by using instruction words and then add the contents of a 20-bit number to each of these offsets to form a 20-bit final address.

Quite a number of addressing modes are used to form the offsets in the 8086/8088 chips. Operands can be in general registers, memory, or I/O ports, and immediate addressing is provided. When 20-bit addresses are generated, the second byte in an instruction word contains the information as to how the 16-bit offset or effective address part of the address is to be calculated. (The first 3 and last 2 bits in this byte provide that information.) In general, this section of the address is formed by summing the contents of a displacement (part of the instruction word), an index register, and a base register. Any combination of these three can be used. And this implements, for example, direct addressing, register indirect addressing, and based indexed addressing (summing the base register, index register, and displacement).

The segment registers make it possible to address a 2^{20}-word memory while

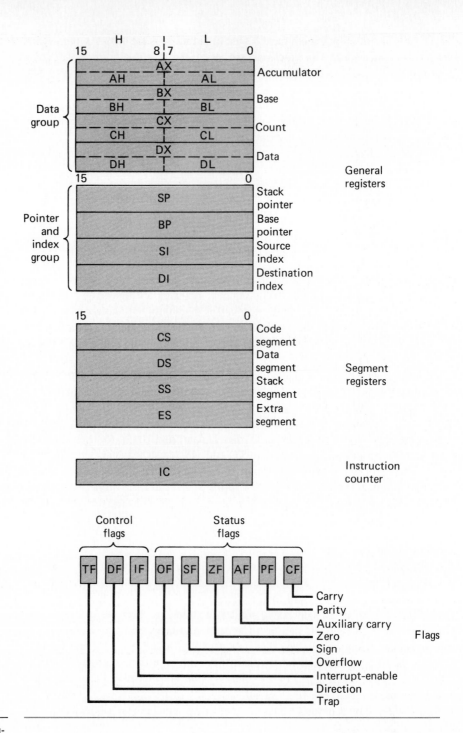

FIGURE 10.23

General-purpose registers in the 8086 and 8088.

518

DATA TRANSFER INSTRUCTIONS	
GENERAL PURPOSE	
MOV	Move byte or word
PUSH	Push word onto stack
POP	Pop word off stack
XCHG	Exchange byte or word
XLAT	Translate byte
INPUT, OUTPUT	
IN	Input byte or word
OUT	Output byte or word
ADDRESS OBJECT	
LEA	Load effective address
LDS	Load pointer using DS
LES	Load pointer using ES
FLAG TRANSFER	
LAHF	Load AH register from flags
SAHF	Store AH register in flags
PUSHF	Push flags onto stack
POPF	Pop flags off stack

BIT MANIPULATION INSTRUCTIONS	
LOGICALS	
NOT	"Not" byte or word
AND	"And" byte or word
OR	"Inclusive or" byte or word
XOR	"Exclusive or" byte or word
TEST	"Test" byte or word
SHIFTS	
SHL/SAL	Shift logical/arithmetic left byte or word
SHR	Shift logical right byte or word
SAR	Shift arithmetic right byte or word
ROTATES	
ROL	Rotate left byte or word
ROR	Rotate right byte or word
RCL	Rotate through carry left byte or word
RCR	Rotate through carry right byte or word

ARITHMETIC INSTRUCTIONS	
ADDITION	
ADD	Add byte or word
ADC	Add byte or word with carry
INC	Increment byte or word by 1
AAA	ASCII adjust for addition
DAA	Decimal adjust for addition
SUBTRACTION	
SUB	Subtract byte or word
SBB	Subtract byte or word with borrow
DEC	Decrement byte or word by 1
NEG	Negate byte or word
CMP	Compare byte or word
AAS	ASCII adjust for subtraction
DAS	Decimal adjust for subtraction
MULTIPLICATION	
MUL	Multiply byte or word unsigned
IMUL	Integer multiply byte or word
AAM	ASCII adjust for multiply
DIVISION	
DIV	Divide byte or word unsigned
IDIV	Integer divide byte or word
AAD	ASCII adjust for division
CBW	Convert byte to word
CWD	Convert word to doubleword

STRING INSTRUCTIONS	
REP	Repeat
REPE/REPZ	Repeat while equal/zero
REPNE/REPNZ	Repeat while not equal/not zero
MOVS	Move byte or word string
MOVSB/MOVSW	Move byte or word string
CMPS	Compare byte or word string
SCAS	Scan byte or word string
LODS	Load byte or word string
STOS	Store byte or word string

PROGRAM TRANSFER INSTRUCTIONS	
UNCONDITIONAL TRANSFERS	
CALL	Call procedure
RET	Return from procedure
JMP	Jump
CONDITIONAL TRANSFERS	
JA/JNBE	Jump if above/not below nor equal
JAE/JNB	Jump if above or equal/not below
JB/JNAE	Jump if below/not above nor equal
JBE/JNA	Jump if below or equal/not above
JC	Jump if carry
JE/JZ	Jump if equal/zero
JG/JNLE	Jump if greater/not less nor equal
JGE/JNL	Jump if greater or equal/not less
JL/JNGE	Jump if less/not greater nor equal
JLE/JNG	Jump if less or equal/not greater
JNC	Jump if not carry
JNE/JNZ	Jump if not equal/not zero
JNO	Jump if not overflow
JNP/JPO	Jump if not parity/parity odd
JNS	Jump if not sign
JO	Jump if overflow
JP/JPE	Jump if parity/parity even
JS	Jump if sign
ITERATION CONTROLS	
LOOP	Loop
LOOPE/LOOPZ	Loop if equal/zero
LOOPNE/LOOPNZ	Loop if not equal/not zero
JCXZ	Jump if register CX = 0
INTERRUPTS	
INT	Interrupt
INTO	Interrupt if overflow
IRET	Interrupt return

FIGURE 10.24

Instruction repertoire for the 8086 and 8088.

only generating 16-bit offset addresses in the instruction words. Another advantage is that use of the segment registers makes a program relocatable in memory. For example, consider that each segment register is set to the same number, say 0102_{16}, and then a program is run. If the segment registers are set to $FF02_{16}$ and the same program is run, the result will be the same (unless the program prints where it is located). This means that an operating system can place a program in memory where it desires. It can even place several programs in different parts of memory, while the programmer simply writes a program without concern about where it will be run.

There are many different types of instructions in the 8080/8088 processors. Figure 10.24 lists them.

In all, the 8080 and the 8086 are powerful processors with 16-bit internal operations, the ability to address a large memory, many addressing modes, and a large instruction repertoire.

COMPUTER
ORGANIZATION

10.15   The 68000 microprocessor is a semiconductor chip with a number of support chips such as I/O processors, a floating-point arithmetic chip, and bus handler chips. The 68000 has 16-bit data paths on its system bus and performs 32-bit arithmetic and logic operations internally. The 68000 microprocessor can directly address 16 Mbytes of memory, having a 24-bit address bus. There are 14 addressing modes and 56 types of instructions. The I/O is memory-mapped.

Chapter 8 showed a drawing of the 68000 bus and the timing signals for reads and writes on the bus. The bus is asynchronous in order to accommodate both slow and fast memory and I/O devices.

The basic registers in the 68000 are shown in Fig. 10.25. The registers are 32 bits, and there are eight data registers along with seven address registers and a program counter. There are actually two stack pointers. A status bit determines whether the 68000 is in the *supervisor* (operating system) *mode* or *user mode;* this bit also determines which of the two stack pointers are in use. The status register is shown in Fig. 10.25 and contains 5 bits for condition codes.

The 68000 *supervisor* and *user* modes are an important feature. There are privileged instructions which can be executed in supervisor mode, but not in user mode. When the supervisor-user mode select bit is a 1, the 68000 uses the supervisor stack pointer and the privileged instructions are available. When the select bit is a 0, the user stack pointer is employed, and certain instructions will not execute.

Figure 10.26 shows that data are organized into bits, bytes, words, and long words and shows how these are placed in the memory which has 8 bits (1 byte) at each address. Instruction words can be from one word (16 bits) to four words in length.

Stacks in the 68000 go from high memory to low memory. So the stack pointer is decremented when data are pushed into a stack and incremented when data are popped from a stack.

Let us examine a particular instruction to understand how the addressing operates. The ANDI (for AND immediate) has the following instruction word format.

15	14	13	12	11	10	9	8	7	6	5	4	3	2	1	0
0	0	0	0	0	0	1	0	Size		Mode			Address register		
Word data (16)								Byte data (8)							
Long word (32 bits)															

The OP-code part of this instruction is 02_{16}. This tells the microprocessor that the instruction is ANDI. The function of this instruction is to AND the immediate data which follow the first 16 bits of the instruction (word), which is called the source, with the destination operand and to place the result in the destination.

The number of bits in an ANDI instruction word depends on the 2 bits in the *size* section. If these are 00, the operation is a byte operation and the instruction

68000
MICROPROCESSOR

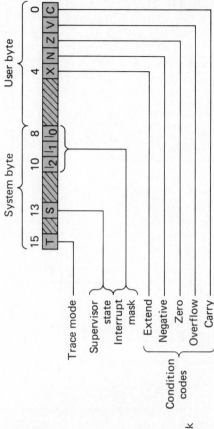

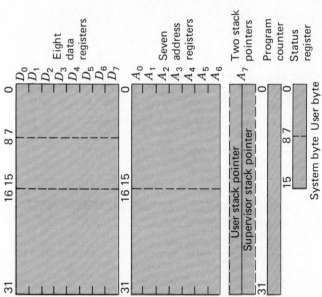

FIGURE 10.25

68000 programmable registers.

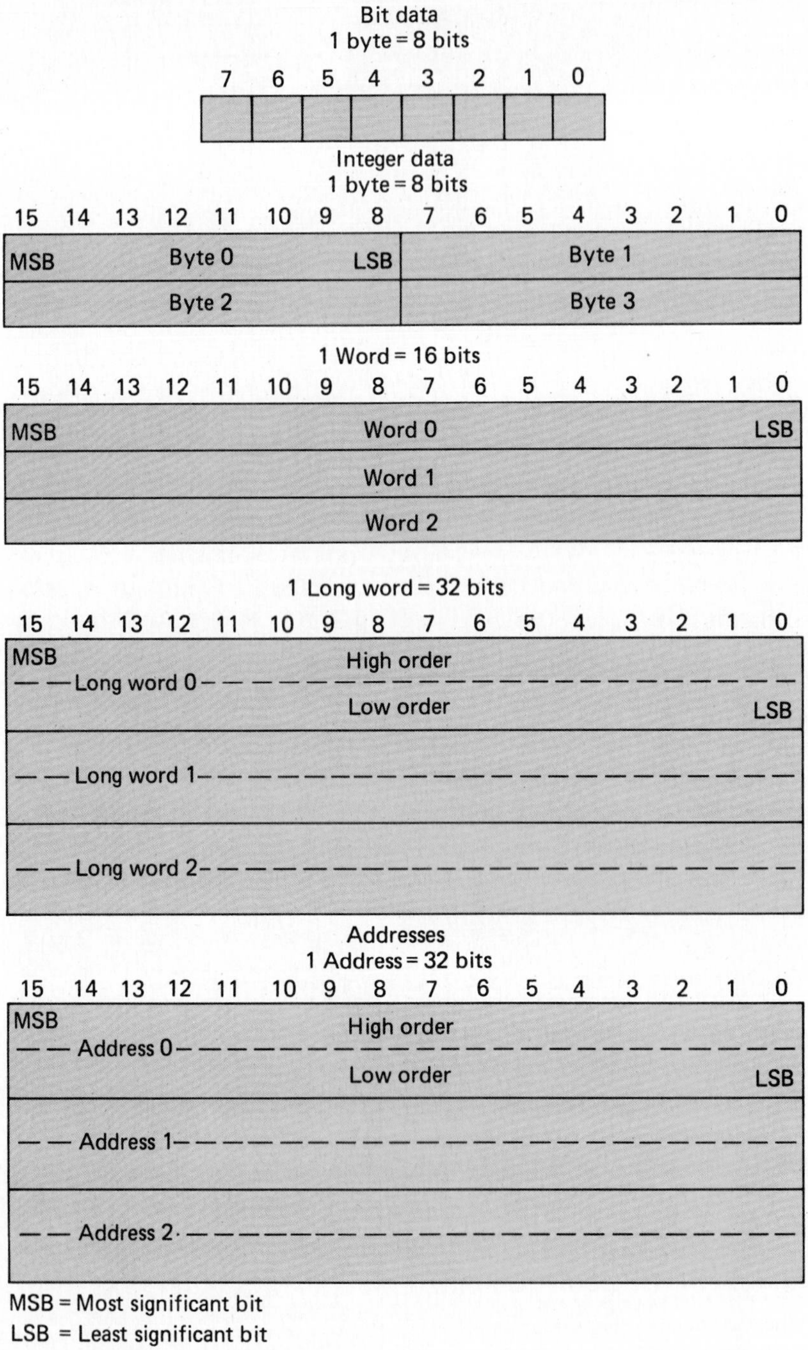

COMPUTER
ORGANIZATION

Bit data
1 byte = 8 bits

7	6	5	4	3	2	1	0

Integer data
1 byte = 8 bits

15	14	13	12	11	10	9	8	7	6	5	4	3	2	1	0
MSB		Byte 0					LSB			Byte 1					
		Byte 2								Byte 3					

1 Word = 16 bits

15	14	13	12	11	10	9	8	7	6	5	4	3	2	1	0
MSB						Word 0									LSB
						Word 1									
						Word 2									

1 Long word = 32 bits

15	14	13	12	11	10	9	8	7	6	5	4	3	2	1	0
MSB							High order								
— —Long word 0—							Low order								LSB
— — Long word 1—															
— — Long word 2—															

Addresses
1 Address = 32 bits

15	14	13	12	11	10	9	8	7	6	5	4	3	2	1	0
MSB							High order								
— — Address 0—							Low order								LSB
— — Address 1—															
— — Address 2·															

MSB = Most significant bit
LSB = Least significant bit

FIGURE 10.26

Organization of data in memory for 68000.

word is two 16-bit words in length with the immediate data in bits 7 to 0 of the second word. If the size bits are 01, the instruction word is again 32 bits in length, but the immediate operand is the entire 16 bits in the second word. If the size bits are 10, then ANDI has a 32-bit-long word for its immediate data and the instruction word is 48 bits in length.

Mode	Generation
Register direct addressing	
Data Register Direct	EA = Dn
Address Register Direct	EA = An
Absolute data addressing	
Absolute Short	EA = (Next Word)
Absolute Long	EA = (Next Two Words)
Program counter relative addressing	
Relative with Offset	EA = (PC) + d_{16}
Relative with Index and Offset	EA = (PC) + (Xn) + d_8
Register indirect addressing	
Register Indirect	EA = (An)
Postincrement Register Indirect	EA = (An), An ← An + N
Predecrement Register Indirect	An ← An − N, EA = (An)
Register Indirect with Offset	EA = (An) + d_{16}
Indexed Register Indirect with Offset	EA = (An) + (Xn) + d_8
Immediate data addressing	
Immediate	DATA = Next Word(s)
Quick Immediate	Inherent Data
Implied addressing	
Implied Register	EA = SR, USP, SP, PC

Notes:
EA = Effective Address
An = Address Register
Dn = Data Register
Xn = Address or Data Register used as Index Register
SR = Status Register
PC = Program Counter
d_8 = 8-bit Offset (displacement)
d_{16} = 16-bit Offset (displacement)
N = 1 for Byte, 2 for Words, and 4 for Long Words.
  If An is the stack pointer and the operand size byte, N = 2 to keep the stack pointer on a word boundary.
( ) = Contents of
← = Replaces

FIGURE 10.27

Addressing modes for 68000.

The destination operand is determined by the mode bits and address register bits. If the mode bits are 000, then the destination is the register given by the address register bits. If these are 010, for example, then data register 2 (refer to Fig. 10.25) will be the destination register and the part of that register used (byte word or long word) will be determined by the size section. If, for example, the data register used is 010 and the size bits are 00, bits 7 to 0 in data register 2 will be ANDed with bits 7 to 0 in the second word in the instruction, and the result is placed in bits 7 to 0 of data register 2.

If the mode bits are 010, then the address register given by the address register bits in the instruction word will contain the address of the (destination) data in memory. For example, if the mode bits are 010, the address register bits are 011; then address register 3 will contain the address of the operand. So if address register 3 contains 0143_{16}, then the operand will be at that location in memory. If the size bits are 00, then bits 7 to 0 of that location in memory will be used for the AND, and the result placed in these bits. If the size bits are 01, then the entire word in location 0143_{16} will be ANDed with the 16 bits in the second word of the instruction, and the result placed in memory location 0143_{16}.

The instruction repertoire is described in what Motorola calls its register transfer language (as in Chap. 9). In their system, (A_n) means, "The contents of A_n gives the location in memory of the operand." (The n in A_n is given by the address register bits. The register A_n is frequently called the *pointer* because it points to the operand.) The notation $A_n@+$ is called "address register indirect with post-increment" and $A_n-@$ is called "address register indirect with predecrement."

The notation (A_n-) means, "Decrement A_n and then use the result as the address of the operand." The notation $(A_n)+$ means, "Use the contents of A_n to determine the location in memory and then increment." For $(A_n)+$ and (A_n-), the number in A_n is incremented or decremented by 1, 2, or 4 depending on whether the instruction is a byte, word, or long word instruction.

The notation $A_n@$ is also used to mean, "A_n contains the address of the operand." This is the same as (A_n) but leads to the notation $(A_n)@$ which means, "Take the address in A_n, go to that address in memory, and at that address find

The following register transfer language definitions are used for the operation description in the details of the instruction set.

OPERANDS

An	address register	SSP	supervisor stack pointer
Dn	data register	USP	user stack pointer
Rn	any data or address register	SP	active stack pointer (equivalent to A7)
PC	program counter		
SR	status register	X	extend operand (from condition codes)
CCR	condition codes (low order byte of status register)	Z	zero condition code
		V	overflow condition code

Immediate Data — immediate data from the instruction
d — address displacement   Destination   destination location
Source — source location   Vector   location of exception vector

SUBFIELDS AND QUALIFIERS

< bit > OF < operand >	selects a single bit of the operand
< operand >[< bit number >:< bit number >]	selects a subfield of an operand
(< operand >)	the contents of the referenced location
< operand > 10	the operand is binary coded decimal; operations are to be performed in decimal.
< operand > @ < mode >	the register indirect operator which indicates that the operand register points to the memory location of the instruction operand. The optional mode qualifiers are −, +, (d) and (d, ix); these are explained in Chapter 2.

OPERATIONS

Operations are grouped into binary, unary, and other.

Binary   These operations are written < operand > < op > < operand > where < op > is one of the following:

→	the left operand is moved to the location specified by the right operand
↔	the contents of the two operands are exchanged
+	the operands are added
−	the right operand is subtracted from the left operand
*	the operands are multiplied
/	the first operand is divided by the second operand
Λ	the operands are logically ANDed
v	the operands are logically ORed
⊕	the operands are logically exclusively ORed
<	relational test, true if left operand is less than right operand
>	relational test, true if left operand is not equal to right operand
shifted by	the left operand is shifted or rotated by the number of positions specified
rotated by	by the right operand

UNARY

∼ < operand >	the operand is logically complemented
< operand > sign-extended	the operand is sign extended, all bits of the upper half are made equal to high order bit of the lower half
< operand > tested	the operand is compared to 0, the results are used to set the condition codes

---

MULS — Signed Multiply

Operation: (Source)*(Destination) → Destination

Assembler syntax: MULS < ea >, Dn

Attributes: Size = (Word)

Description: Multiply two signed 16-bit operands yielding a 32-bit signed result. The operation is performed using signed arithmetic. A register operand is taken from the low order word; the upper word is unused. All 32 bits of the product are saved in the destination data register.

Condition codes:

X	N	Z	V	C
—	*	*	0	0

N   Set if the result is negative. Cleared otherwise.
Z   Set if the result is zero. Cleared otherwise.
V   Always cleared
C   Always cleared
X   Not affected.

Instruction format

15	14	13	12	11 10 9	8	7	6	5 4 3	2 1 0
1	1	0	0	Register	1	1	1	Effective Mode	Address Register

Instruction fields
Register field   Specifies one of the data registers. This field always specifies the destination.
Effective address field   Specifies the source operand. Only data addressing modes are allowed as shown:

Addressing Mode	Mode	Register	Addressing Mode	Mode	Register
Dn	000	register number	d(An, Xi)	110	register number
An	—	—	Abs.W	111	000
(An)	010	register number	Abs.L	111	001
(An)+	011	register number	d(PC)	111	010
−(An)	100	register number	d(PC, Xi)	111	011
d(An)	101	register number	Imm	111	100

ANDI — AND Immediate

Operation: Immediate Data Λ (Destination) → Destination

Assembler syntax: ANDI # < data >, < ea >

Attributes: Size = (Byte, Word, Long)

Description: AND the immediate data to the destination operand and store the result in the destination location. The size of the operation may be specified to be byte, word, or long. The size of the immediate data matches the operation size.

Condition codes:

X	N	Z	V	C
—	*	*	0	0

N   Set if the most significant bit of the result is set. Cleared otherwise.
Z   Set if the result is zero. Cleared otherwise.
V   Always cleared.
C   Always cleared.
X   Not affected.

Instruction format

15	14	13	12	11	10	9	8	7 6	5 4 3	2 1 0
0	0	0	0	0	0	1	0	Size	Effective Mode	Address Register
Word Data (16 bits)								Byte Data (8 bits)		
Long Data (32 bits, including previous word)										

Instruction fields
Size field   Specifies the size of the operation:
  00   byte operation.
  01   word operation.
  10   long operation.
Effective Address field   Specifies the destination operand. Only data alterable addressing modes are allowed as shown:

Addressing Mode	Mode	Register	Addressing Mode	Mode	Register
Dn	000	register number	d(An, Xi)	110	register number
An			Abs.W	111	000
(An)	010	register number	Abs.L	111	001
(An)+	011	register number	d(PC)	—	—
−(An)	100	register number	d(PC, Xi)	—	—
d(An)	101	register number	Imm	—	—

Immediate field   (Data immediately following the instruction):
If size = 00, then the data is the low order byte of the immediate word.
If size = 01, then the data is the entire immediate word.
If size = 10, then the data is the next two immediate words.

Bcc — Branch Conditionally

Operation: If (condition true) then PC + d → PC

Assembler syntax: Bcc < label >

Attributes: Size = (Byte, Word)

Description: If the specified condition is met, program execution continues at location (PC) + displacement. Displacement is a twos complement integer which counts the relative distance in bytes. The value in PC is the current instruction location plus two. If the 8-bit displacement in the instruction word is zero, then the 16-bit displacement (word immediately following the instruction) is used. "cc" may specify the following conditions:

CC	carry clear	0100	$\overline{C}$	LS	low or same	0011	C + Z
CC	carry set	0101	C	LT	less than	1101	$N \cdot \overline{V} + \overline{N} \cdot V$
EQ	equal	0111	Z	MI	minus	1011	N
GE	greater or equal	1100	$N \cdot V + \overline{N} \cdot \overline{V}$	NE	not equal	0110	$\overline{Z}$
GT	greater than	1110	$N \cdot V \cdot \overline{Z} + \overline{N} \cdot \overline{V} \cdot \overline{Z}$	PL	plus	1010	$\overline{N}$
HI	high	0010	$\overline{C} \cdot \overline{Z}$	VC	overflow clear	1000	$\overline{V}$
LE	less or equal	1111	$Z + N \cdot \overline{V} + \overline{N} \cdot V$	VS	overflow set	1001	V

Condition codes: Not affected.

Instruction format

15	14	13	12	11 10 9 8	7 6 5 4 3 2 1 0
0	1	1	0	Condition	8-bit Displacement
16-bit Displacement if 8-bit Displacement = 0					

Instruction fields
Condition field   One of fourteen conditions discussed in description.
8-bit displacement field   Twos complement integer specifying the relative distance (in bytes) between the branch instruction and the next instruction to be executed if the condition is met.
16-bit displacement field   Allows a larger displacement than 8 bits. Used only if the displacement is equal to zero.

Note: A short branch to the immediately following instruction cannot be done because it would result in a zero offset which forces a word branch instruction definition.

Operation: (Destination) – (Source)

Assembler syntax: CMP < ea >, Dn

Attributes: Size = (Byte, Word, Long)

Description: Subtract the source operand from the destination operand and set the condition codes according to the result; the destination location is not changed. The size of the operation may be specified to be byte, word, or long.

Condition codes

X	N	Z	V	C
—	*	*	*	*

N   Set if the result is negative. Cleared otherwise.
Z   Set if the result is zero. Cleared otherwise.
V   Set if an overflow is generated. Cleared otherwise.
C   Set if a borrow is generated. Cleared otherwise.
X   Not affected.

Instruction format

15	14	13	12	11 10 9	8 7 6	5 4 3	2 1 0
1	0	1	1	Register	Op-Mode	Effective Address Mode	Register

Instruction fields
Register field   Specifies the destination data register.
Op-Mode field

Byte	Word	Long	Operation
000	001	010	(< Dn >) – (< ea >)

Effective address field   Specifies the source operand. All addressing modes are allowed as shown:

Addressing Mode	Mode	Register	Addressing Mode	Mode	Register
Dn	000	register number	d(An, Xi)	110	register number
An*	001	register number	Abs.W	111	000
(An)	010	register number	Abs.L	111	001
(An) +	011	register number	d(PC)	111	010
– (An)	100	register number	d(PC, Xi)	111	011
d(An)	101	register number	Imm	111	100

*Word and Long only.

Note: CMPA is used when the destination is an address register. CMPI is used when the source is immediate data. CMPM is used for memory to memory compares. Most assemblers automatically make this distinction.

Operation: (Destination)/(Source) → Destination

Assembler syntax: DIVS < ea >, Dn

Attributes: Size = (Word)

Description: Divide the destination operand by the source operand and store the result in the destination. The destination operand is a long operand (32 bits) and the source operand is a word operand (16 bits). The operation is performed using signed arithmetic. The result is a 32-bit result such that:
1. The quotient is in the lower word (least significant 16-bits).
2. The remainder is in the upper word (most significant 16-bits).
The sign of the remainder is always the same as the dividend unless the remainder is equal to zero. Two special conditions may arise:
1. Division by zero causes a trap.
2. Overflow may be detected and set before completion of the instruction. If overflow is detected, the condition is flagged but the operands are unaffected.

Condition codes

X	N	Z	V	C
—	*	*	*	0

N   Set if the quotient is negative. Cleared otherwise. Undefined if overflow.
Z   Set if the quotient is zero. Cleared otherwise. Undefined if overflow.
V   Set if division overflow is detected. Cleared otherwise.
C   Always cleared.
X   Not affected.

Instruction format

15	14	13	12	11 10 9	8	7	6	5 4 3	2 1 0
1	0	0	0	Register	1	1	1	Effective Address Mode	Register

Instruction fields
Register field   Specified any of the eight data registers. This field always specifies the destination operand.
Effective Address field   Specifies the source operand. Only data addressing modes are allowed as shown:

Addressing Mode	Mode	Register	Addressing Mode	Mode	Register
Dn	000	register number	d(An, Xi)	110	register number
An	—	—	Abs.W	111	000
(An)	010	register number	Abs.L	111	001
(An) +	011	register number	d(PC)	111	010
– (An)	100	register number	d(PC, Xi)	111	011
d(An)	101	register number	Imm	111	100

Note: Overflow occurs if the quotient is larger than a 16-bit signed integer.

Operation: PC → – (SP); Destination → PC

Assembler syntax: JSR < ea >

Attributes: Unsized

Description: The long word address of the instruction immediately following the JSR instruction is pushed onto the system stack. Program execution then continues at the address specified in the instruction.

Condition codes: Not affected.

Instruction format

15	14	13	12	11	10	9	8	7	6	5 4 3	2 1 0
0	1	0	0	1	1	1	0	1	0	Effective Address Mode	Register

Instruction fields
Effective address field   Specifies the address of the next instruction. Only control addressing modes are allowed as shown:

Addressing Mode	Mode	Register	Addressing Mode	Mode	Register
Dn	—	—	d(An, Xi)	110	register number
An	—	—	Abs.W	111	000
(An)	010	register number	Abs.L	111	001
(An) +	—	—	d(PC)	111	010
– (An)	—	—	d(PC, Xi)	111	011
d(An)	101	register number	Imm		

Operation: (SP) + → PC

Assembler syntax: RTS

Attributes: Unsized

Description: The program counter is pulled from the stack. The previous program counter is lost.

Condition codes: Not affected.

Instruction format

15	14	13	12	11	10	9	8	7	6	5	4	3	2	1	0
0	1	0	0	1	1	1	0	0	1	1	1	0	1	0	1

FIGURE 10.28

Selected instructions for 68000.

Operation: (Destination) − (Source) → Destination

Assembler: SUB < ea >, Dn
Syntax: SUB Dn, < ea >

Attributes: Size = (Byte, Word, Long)

Description: Subtract the source operand from the destination operand and store the result in the destination. The size of the operation may be specified to be byte, word, or long. The mode of the instruction indicates which operand is the source and which is the destination as well as the operand size.

Condition codes   X N Z V C

*	*	*	*	*

N   Set if the result is negative. Cleared otherwise.
Z   Set if the result is zero. Cleared otherwise.
V   Set if an overflow is generated. Cleared otherwise.
C   Set if a borrow is generated. Cleared otherwise.
X   Set the same as the carry bit.

Instruction format

15	14	13	12	11 10 9	8 7 6	5 4 3	2 1 0
1	0	0	1	Register	Op-Mode	Effective Mode	Address Register

Instruction fields
Register field   Specifies any of the eight data registers.
Op-Mode field

Byte	Word	Long	Operation
000	001	010	(< Dn >) − (< ea >) → < Dn >
100	101	110	(< ea >) − (< Dn >) → < ea >

Effective address field   Determines addressing mode:
(a) If the location specified is a source operand, then all addressing modes are allowed as shown:

Addressing Mode	Mode	Register	Addressing Mode	Mode	Register
Dn	000	register number	d(An, Xi)	110	register number
An*	001	register number	Abs.W	111	000
(An)	010	register number	Abs.L	111	001
(An)+	011	register number	d(PC)	111	010
−(An)	100	register number	d(PC, Xi)	111	011
d(An)	101	register number	Imm	111	100

If the location specified is a destination operand, then only alterable memory addressing modes are allowed as shown:

Addressing Mode	Mode	Register	Addressing Mode	Mode	Register
Dn	—	—	d(An, Xi)	110	register number
An	—	—	Abs.W	111	000
(An)	010	register number	Abs.L	111	001
(An)+	011	register number	d(PC)	—	—
−(An)	100	register number	d(PC, Xi)	—	—
d(An)	101	register number	Imm	—	—

Notes: 1. If the destination is a data register, then it cannot be specified by using the destination < ea > mode, but must use the destination Dn mode instead.
       2. SUBA is used when the destination is an address register. SUBI and SUBQ are used when the source is immediate data. Most assemblers automatically make this distinction.
       3. For byte size data register direct is not allowed.

FIGURE 10.28
(Cont.)

Operation: (Source) + (Destination) → Destination

Assembler: ADD < ea >, Dn
Syntax: ADD Dn, < ea >

Attributes: Size = (Byte, Word, Long)

Description: Add the source operand to the destination operand, and store the result in the destination location. The size of the operation may be specified to be byte, word, or long. The mode of the instruction indicates which operand is the source and which is the destination as well as the operand size.

Condition codes   X N Z V C

*	*	*	*	*

N   Set if the result is negative. Cleared otherwise.
Z   Set if the result is zero. Cleared otherwise.
V   Set if an overflow is generated. Cleared otherwise.
C   Set if a carry is generated. Cleared otherwise.
X   Set the same as the carry bit.

Instruction format

15	14	13	12	11 10 9	8 7 6	5 4 3	2 1 0
1	1	0	1	Register	Op-Mode	Effective Mode	Address Register

Instruction fields
Register field   Specifies any of the eight data registers.
Op-Mode field

Byte	Word	Long	Operation
000	001	010	(< Dn >) + (< ea >) → < Dn >
100	101	110	(< ea >) + (< Dn >) → < ea >

Effective address field   Determines addressing mode:
(a) If the location specified is a source operand, then all addressing modes are allowed as shown:

Addressing Mode	Mode	Register	Addressing Mode	Mode	Register
Dn	000	register number	d(An, Xi)	110	register number
An*	001	register number	Abs.W	111	000
(An)	010	register number	Abs.L	111	001
(An)+	011	register number	d(PC)	111	010
−(An)	100	register number	d(PC, Xi)	111	011
d(An)	101	register number	Imm	111	100

(b) If the location specified is a destination operand, then only alterable memory addressing modes are allowed as shown:

Addressing Mode	Mode	Register	Addressing Mode	Mode	Register
Dn	—	—	d(An, Xi)	110	register number
An	—	—	Abs.W	111	000
(An)	010	register number	Abs.L	111	001
(An)+	011	register number	d(PC)	—	—
−(An)	100	register number	d(PC, Xi)	—	—
d(An)	101	register number	Imm	—	—

Notes: 1. If the destination is a data register, then it cannot be specified by using the destination < ea > mode, but must use the destination Dn mode instead.
       2. ADDA is used when the destination is an address register. ADDI and ADDQ are used when the source is immediate data. Most assemblers automatically make this distinction.
       3. Word and Long only.

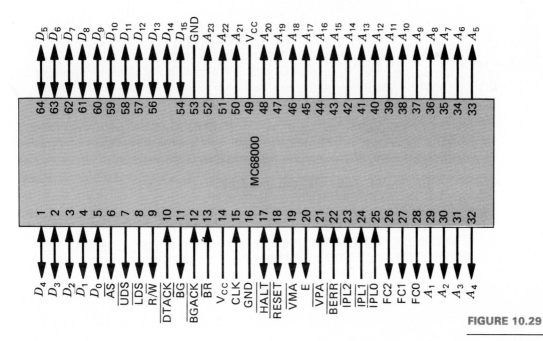

Pin Name	Description
D0–D15	Data bus
A1–A23	Address bus
$\overline{AS}$	Address strobe
$R/\overline{W}$	Read/Write control
$\overline{UDS}$, $\overline{LDS}$	Upper, lower data strobes
$\overline{DTACK}$	Data transfer acknowledge
FC0, FC1, FC2	Function code (status) outputs
$\overline{IPL0}$, $\overline{IPL1}$, $\overline{IPL2}$	Interrupt requests
$\overline{BERR}$	Bus error
$\overline{HALT}$	Halt processor
$\overline{RESET}$	Reset processor or reset external devices
CLK	Clock
$\overline{BR}$	Bus request
$\overline{BG}$	Bus grant
$\overline{BGACK}$	Bus grant acknowledge
E	Enable (clock) output
$\overline{VMA}$	Valid memory address
$\overline{VPA}$	Valid peripheral address
V_{CC}, GND	Power (+5 V) and Ground

FIGURE 10.29

Pin-out for 68000.

527

the address of the operand.'' In effect, for $(A_n)@$, the number in A_n is the address of the address of the operand.[14]

Figure 10.27 shows the addressing modes for the 68000. These cover most of the conventional modes for addressing and offer considerable options to the programmer.

Several selected instructions from the 68000's large instruction set are shown in Fig. 10.28. A large number of instructions are available, including most conventional instructions.

Notice that addresses are generated in 32-bit registers and are complete addresses. The pin-out in Fig. 10.29 shows that all 24 address lines and 16-bit data lines are externally available. And there is no multiplexing of these lines because the 68000 has a 64-pin package which provides for the necessary connections.

The 68000 microprocessor chip and its support chips provide a powerful instruction repertoire and high-speed operation of programs. They are widely used in everything from personal computers to communication and control systems.

QUESTIONS

10.1 Discuss the advantages and disadvantages of the following addressing strategies in a microcomputer: (*a*) Paging, (*b*) indirect addressing, (*c*) index registers.

10.2 Describe some advantages and disadvantages of multiple-accumulator (general-purpose registers) versus single-accumulator computer architecture. Include effects on instruction word length, convenience in programming, etc.

10.3 (*a*) The 6100 series uses the original paging scheme for addressing. The PDP-11 and other computers use a relative address or sliding page. Discuss the advantages and disadvantages of these two techniques.

(*b*) What is the obvious problem in indirect addressing of 8K or larger memories which arises in the 6100 but does not occur for 16-bit-word computers such as the NOVA, PDP-11, or Varian?

10.4 Discuss the desirability of the following computer architectural features for a microcomputer to be used as a traffic light controller: (*a*) Paging of memory, (*b*) floating-point arithmetic, (*c*) indirect addressing.

10.5 The following is a short program in assembly language for the 6100:

```
7ØØ
                CLA     CLL         /CLEARS AC AND LINK
                TAD     DAT1
        GO,     ISZ     DAT2
                JMP     GO
                RAL                 /RIGHT SHIFT AC AND LINK
                JMP     GO
        DAT1,   ØØ77
        DAT2,   Ø
        $
```

---

[14]Alternate ways to write $(A_n)@$ would be $A_n@@$ or $((A_n))$.

After this program has been assembled and loaded, it appears as follows in memory (all digits are octal), except that the contents of two addresses in memory need to be filled in:

ADDRESS NUMBER	CONTENTS
0700	
0701	
0702	2307
0703	5302
0704	7004
0705	5302
0706	0077
0707	0000

QUESTIONS

Supply the contents of (octal) locations 700 and 701 in memory.

10.6 The program in Question 10.5 rotates a sequence of 0s and 1s through the accumulator link.

(a) How many 0s and how many 1s? In what order?

(b) How many instructions must be executed for a complete cycle of a given 0 and 1 pattern?

10.7 A microcomputer has a bus with a single INTERRUPT line which an external device is to raise when it wishes to be serviced. The bus is controlled by the microcomputer's CPU chip. Explain the CPU's problem in determining which input-output device(s) generated an interrupt, and discuss two possible solutions.

10.8 The following is a short program for the 6800 which was written to compute $Y = 32(9 - 7)$ and store it. The programmer then converted the program into hexadecimal and is now prepared to enter it into the computer. There are several mistakes in the program. Find as many as possible and explain each.

#	ADDRESS	OP	OPER	LABEL	MNEMONICS	OPERAND	COMMENTS
01	0200	4F		START	CLRA		; CLEAR REGISTER A
02	0201	86	OE		LDA	X	; LOAD X INTO REGISTER A
03	0203	43			COMA		; COMPLEMENT X
04	0204	8B	09		ADDA(IM)	#09	; ADD 9
05	0206	CE	05		LDX(IM)	#05	; LOAD INDEX REGISTER WITH 5
06	0208	49		LOOP	ROLA		; ROTATE LEFT 1 BIT (MULTIPLY BY 2)
07	0209	09			DEX		; DECREMENT INDEX REGISTER
08	020A	26	FD		BNE	LOOP	; ROTATE AGAIN IF INDEX REGISTER ≠ 0
09	020C	97	OF		STAA	Y	; AFTER MULTIPLYING BY $2^5 = 32$, STORE THE RESULT IN Y
10	020E	07		X	DATA	1 BYTE	
11	020F	00		Y	DATA	1 BYTE	; DATA IN THIS LOCATION WILL BE REPLACED BY VALUE OF Y

10.9 A short program has been written for the 6800 to determine the number of bytes in a table which have 1s in their sign bits. The number of elements in the table is stored at location 50, and the table begins in location 60. The number of bytes with 1 in the sign bit is to be stored in location 51. Modify this program so that the number of nonzero bytes with a 0 in the sign bit is stored in location 55.

```
                LDX      #$60        /LOAD I REGISTER
                CLRB
LOOKN   LDAA     X           /CHECK FOR NEGATIVES
                BPL      HOUS
                INCB
HOUS    INX
                DEC      $50
                BNE      LOOKN       /DONE?
                STAB     $51
```

10.10 A two-address computer has a large IC memory with a 0.5-μs memory cycle time and a small high-speed memory with a 0.25-μs memory cycle time. An addition instruction word looks like this:

ADD	1st address	2d address

The first address refers to the small high-speed memory and the second address to the large memory. The sum is placed in the high-speed memory at the first address. How long will it take to perform an addition instruction? Why?

10.11 Using the index instructions given in Sec. 10.9, write a program that adds 40 numbers located in the memory, starting at address 200 and storing the sum in register 300.

10.12 If we use three binary digits in the instruction word to indicate which index register is used, or if one is to be used, then how many index registers can be used in the machine?

10.13 Modify the program in Sec. 10.9 so that the numbers located at memory addresses 353 through 546 are added and stored at address 600.

10.14 Modify the program in Sec. 10.9 so that the numbers located at addresses 300 through 305 are multiplied and the product is stored at address 310.

10.15 The use of paging enables the relocation of programs in the memory without extensive modification of the addresses in the program. Explain why.

10.16 Explain how paging and indirect addressing can be useful in relocating subprograms when a program is rewritten. What are some disadvantages of paging and indirect addressing?

10.17 Discuss the architecture of the 6800 versus the 8080 microprocessors.

10.18 Compare the PDP-11 addressing to the 8080 addressing modes.

10.19 Explain how paging as an addressing technique can be useful in relocating programs. Then explain how small pages can sometimes force programmers to "think in segments." Are the above characteristics desirable or undesirable?

10.20 Explain the addressing of pages in the 6100 series and the displacement-plus-instruction-location addressing technique used by the PDP-11. Why do you think systems architects have elected to use these systems?

10.21 The following is a section of program and memory contents from an assembly listing for a 6100. The programmer who wrote this contends that after the instruction at location 255_8 is executed, the location 256_8 in memory will contain the difference $A - B$ of the numbers A and B at locations 260_8 and 2053_8. Is the programmer correct? Give the reason for your answer, explaining the program operation.

25Ø

memory address	contents of memory		program written in assembly language		
Ø25Ø	73ØØ		CLA	CLL	
Ø251	1657		TAD	I	F
Ø252	7Ø4Ø		CMA		
Ø253	126Ø		TAD	A	
Ø254	3256		DCA	C	
Ø255	74Ø2		HLT		
Ø256	ØØØ4		C,	Y	
Ø257	2Ø53		F,	2Ø53	
Ø26Ø	ØØØ5		A,	5	
2Ø53	ØØØ6	2Ø53	B,	6	

10.22 Sketch, describe, and discuss the merits of one of the machine architectures that have been presented, or of any other machine with which you are familiar (or with which you would like to be familiar—including any of your own ''ideal'' designs).

10.23 A real-time system for manufacturing control is to be constructed using a computer. The system is to perform two functions:

(*a*) The computer has to automatically test cameras as they are manufactured. This involves, among other things, reading 1000 values each second from several A-to-D converters and checking to see whether the values are within prescribed limits.

(*b*) The computer has to service four terminals which run inquiries against the data base maintained on the cameras, and it also has to run some Fortran and Cobol programs.

Give an architecture for the computer to be used.

10.24 Show how a recursive subroutine call can erase the return location planted at the beginning of a subroutine when the 6100 JMS instruction is used.

10.25 Show how the 6800 microprocessor subroutine call will not destroy the return address in a recursive subroutine call because of the use of the stack.

10.26 Show how the 8080 jump to a subroutine will not destroy the return location in a recursive subroutine call because of the stack.

10.27 Write a program in assembly language for the 6800 microprocessor which will multiply Y by 16 and then subtract 15 from the result. (Ignore overflows.)

10.28 Write a program in assembly language for the 8080 microprocessor which will multiply a number X by 32 and then subtract 14 from the result. (Ignore overflows.)

10.29 Write a subroutine for the 8080 microprocessor which will double the number in the accumulator and then subtract 5. (Ignore overflows.)

10.30 Write a subroutine for the 6800 which will add accumulator A to accumulator B, store the result in accumulator A, and then subtract 12 from this result, storing that in accumulator B. (Ignore overflows.)

10.31 Write a subroutine call for the 6800 which will utilize the subroutine written in Question 10.30. Before this subroutine call, place 13 in accumulator A and 23 in accumulator B.

10.32 Discuss PDP-11 addressing [where the addressing mode (or modes) is carried in the address section] versus placing that information in the OP code.

10.33 Show the mode information in the two 3-bit fields in a PDP-11 instruction word which uses both source and destination registers in a direct addressing mode.

10.34 Write a program for the PDP-11 which will add the number in R_1 to the number in R_3 and then store this number at location 63_8 in the memory.

10.35 Why is it not a good idea to store data at location 0 in the 6100 memory?

10.36 Explain why placing often used data in the first 256 words of the memory in a 6800 will shorten some instruction words.

10.37 Explain the following sentence: The 6800 has one index register, the PDP-11 can use any general register as an index register, and the 8080 has no index register.

10.38 Explain how the auto-increment and auto-decrement instruction modes in the PDP-11 can be useful in processing tables.

10.39 In the 8080 an interrupt is serviced as follows. The device which is being serviced places on the data lines of the 8080 bus an instruction word which is a special instruction, called RST. Three bits of this instruction give the address of the next instruction to be executed. The interrupting device places the correct 3 bits in the section of the RST instruction on the bus, and the 8080 then takes the next instruction from that location. (See OP-code description of RST.) In that location is a jump to the subroutine which actually services the device generating the interrupt. Discuss the advantages and disadvantages of this procedure.

10.40 The IBM series of computers uses a priority delegation scheme where interrupt devices are interconnected as shown below. When an interrupt service is issued, the leftmost point of the "daisy-chain" wire is raised. If a device wishes to be serviced, it does not forward this 1 to the device on the right. If it does not wish to be serviced, it forwards this 1 to the device on the right. Each device in turn makes this decision, either passing the 1 to the right or passing a 0. (A 0 on

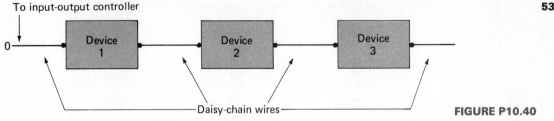

To input-output controller

Daisy-chain wires

FIGURE P10.40

the left is always passed right.) Design a logic circuit to effect this. Use an interrupt flip-flop which is turned on by the device utilizing the interface and which has a 1 output if the device wishes service and a 0 if not.

10.41 The daisy-chain interrupt scheme in Question 10.40 assigns interrupt priorities according to the position in the daisy chain. Explain this statement.

10.42 The passing of a 1 or a 0 along the daisy chain by each device must be carefully controlled with regard to time. Strict standards are given as to how long maximum delays can be for each device. Explain the advantages and disadvantages of the daisy-chain scheme in assigning priorities and determining which device has generated an interrupt.

10.43 Notice that when the daisy-chain scheme explained in Question 10.40 is used, a device can place its identity or interrupt vector on the bus without the danger of other devices placing their vectors on at the same time and overwriting at the same time. In some microcomputers combinational logic is used to determine which device is to be serviced first. Explain how this might be done, assuming that each device uses an interrupt flip-flop as in Question 10.40.

10.44 Compare the disadvantages and advantages of using combinational logic versus the daisy-chain technique for interrupt servicing.

10.45 When DMA (direct memory access) is used on a bus, a line to the CPU on the bus is raised by the device wishing to read into memory using the bus. The CPU then stops, executing instructions at the first possibility, and raises another line on the bus, indicating that it has stopped execution of instructions. The device wishing access to the bus then uses the bus, and when it is done, it lowers the wire that was used to stop the CPU. The CPU then continues to execute instructions. Explain the danger of having several devices able to generate interrupts of this kind at the same time.

10.46 The 6100 uses an input-output instruction to test and see whether a device has data ready or can accept data. Incorporated in this instruction is a jump if the device is not ready. In the 6800 and 8080 computers it is necessary to check a status bit and then use a conventional jump-on-condition instruction to see whether a device can be serviced. Discuss the advantages and disadvantages of these approaches to seeing whether the device is ready.

10.47 Show how indirect addressing can be used in the 6100 to access a word located at address 4322_8 in the memory when an instruction word is on page 1 of the memory.

10.48 Translate the following program into hexadecimal for the 6800:

	ORG	$50
	LDX	#$79
	LDAA	#$20
BLKC	NX	
	CMPA	X
	BEQ	BLKC
	STX	$55

10.49 The program in Question 10.48 stores the address of the first nonspace character in a string at location 55 in the memory. Analyze the program operation instruction by instruction.

10.50 Translate the following program into hexadecimal for the 8080, showing the contents of each memory location:

	ORG	50H
	LXI	H, 50H
	MOV	A, M
	INX	H
	ADD	M
	INX	H
	MOV	M, A

10.51 Analyze the operation of the section of program given in Question 10.50 instruction by instruction, explaining what it does.

10.52 Translate the following PDP-11 program into octal. What does this short section of program do?

READ	TSTB	KSR	; READY
	BPL	READ	; NO
	INC	R5	; INC BUFFER PTR
	MOVB	KSB; @R5	; STORE INPUT
	MOV	@R5; R4	; STORE LASCHR IN RY
	JSR	PC, PRINT	; PRINT INPUT
	BR	READ	; READ NEXT CHAR
PRINT	CMPB	R4, #212	

Place the read statement at location 500_8. KSB is at location 177562_8.

10.53 Suppose that we push A, B, D, and F on a stack, pop the stack twice, and then push M and N onto the stack. If we pop letters from the stack three times, what letters will be popped and in what order?

10.54 Explain extended addressing, implied addressing, and relative addressing in the 6800 microprocessor.

10.55 Explain how the branch-if-zero instruction works on the 6800 microprocessor.

10.56 Explain the difference in an ADD accumulator (ABA) and an ADD (ADDA or ADDB) instruction for the 6800 microprocessor.

10.57 Explain a ROTATE RIGHT instruction on the 6800 microprocessor.

10.58 What are the differences between ROTATE and SHIFT instructions on the 6800 microprocessor? Why are both useful?

10.59 Explain the branch-to-subroutine and the return-from-subroutine instructions for the 6800 microprocessor. How would they be used to enter and then exit from a subroutine?

10.60 Contrast the JMS instruction in the 6100 with the JSR instruction in the 6800.

10.61 Explain the register indirect and immediate addressing modes for the 8080 microprocessor.

10.62 Explain how two of the arithmetic-type instructions for the 8080 affect the setting of the condition flags.

10.63 How do conditional JUMP instructions work in the 8080 microprocessor?

10.64 Explain the PUSH and POP instructions in the 8080 microprocessor.

10.65 Explain the CALL and RET instructions for the 8080 microprocessor. Compare these with the JSR and RTS instructions for the 6800 microprocessor.

10.66 Explain the STA and LDA instructions for the 8080 microprocessor.

10.67 Explain the ADI instruction for the 8080 microprocessor, and contrast it to the ADM instruction.

10.68 Compare the ADM instruction for the 8080 with the ADDA and ADDB instructions for the 6800.

10.69 Contrast the PUSH and POP instructions for the 8080 with the DES and INS instructions for the 6800.

10.70 Compare the BRANCH instructions for the 6800 with those for the 8080.

10.71 Write a program to service the printer interface in Chap. 8 for the 8080 microprocessor.

10.72 Show how the BPL instruction in Table 10.23 operates by calculating the value of the offset for the branch and adding it to the program counter to see whether the branch goes to the right place.

10.73 The plus before the indirect address in Table 10.23 for the MOVB instruction indexes through the table where index characters are to be stored. Explain how this is accomplished.

10.74 How did the assembler calculate the value for the TSTB instruction in Table 10.23?

10.75 Explain how the assembler calculated the binary translation of the BNE LOOP instruction in Table 10.18.

10.76 Modify Tables 10.19 and 10.20 so that the parameter being passed from calling program to subroutine is a pointer to the beginning of the table to be searched instead of the end of the table.

10.77 Explain how the BNE LOOP instruction operates in Table 10.18, calculating the value of the jump in the computer word and seeing whether it points to the right location in the memory.

10.78 Modify the program in Table 10.10 so that the number of characters in the table is passed by using register *D* instead of register *B*.

10.79 Modify the programs so that Table 10.11 passes the lowest table address in memory instead of the end of the table. This will require modification to both Tables 10.10 and 10.11.

10.80 Explain how the JZ instruction operates in Table 10.10.

10.81 Convert the program in Table 10.10 into binary as an assembler would.

10.82 For the 8080 or 6800 microprocessor, explain how you would pass parameters if two tables should both be searched for an input character and the start or end points of each table must be given to the subroutine as well as the character to be searched for and the number of characters in each table.

10.83 Explain how the bracket notation is used for the LDA instruction in the instruction repertoire table for the 8080 (Table 10.7).

10.84 Write a program like that in Table 10.9 with the aim to find the smallest number instead of the largest.

10.85 Modify the program in Table 10.2 so that it checks for all 1s in the character transferred as well as for periods, jumping to the same section of program if all 1s are found.

10.86 What is the character code for a period in the 6100?

10.87 Change the JMP I LISN instruction in Table 10.2 so that it causes a jump to location 254 in the memory and not to 252. Change memory contents also.

10.88 Explain how the index instruction in the 6800 can be used to sequence through two tables, each of which is located at a different position in the memory, but has the same number of elements.

10.89 The MOVE instruction in the 8080 uses register pair *H, L* as a pointer to the memory. Explain how register pair *H, L* can be loaded.

10.90 Find two examples of relative addressing in the sample programs given for the computers in this chapter.

10.91 Compare paging to relative addressing as an address strategy.

10.92 Compare the pin-outs for the 8086 and 68000 microprocessors with regard to economy and interfacing considerations.

10.93 Explain how programs and data can be distributed through a memory by using the 8086 segment registers.

10.94 What are the advantages of having four segment registers versus one segment register in the 8086?

10.95 For the 68000 write in binary an AND I instruction which will AND the 01011110 with the word at location FF in memory. The value FF is in general register 3.

10.96 Write an ADD instruction in binary for the 68000 which will add two operands of your choice, explaining how the instruction works.

10.97 Explain the meaning of $(A_4)+$ in the 68000 register transfer language.

10.98 Discuss how the supervisor and user modes for the 68000 might be useful in a timeshared system.

10.99 Does a computer with I/O instructions and a bus provide all the facility of a memory-mapped system? Explain your answer.

QUESTIONS

APPENDIX A
CIRCUIT PRINCIPLES

The intent of this appendix is first to explain some of the circuit principles which relate to all digital circuits and then to examine, one at a time, the major circuit technologies. Basic facts about the general properties of each circuit technology are given, and some of the advantages and disadvantages of each type of circuit are pointed out.

Before we analyze logic circuits, the general characteristics of transistors and diodes are discussed. No attempt will be made to explain the physics of junction semiconductor devices. Semiconductor physics and a detailed analysis of the operating characteristics of junction devices are so interwoven with the manufacturing techniques, the geometry of the junctions, and many other considerations that the subject has grown into a highly specialized (and very fascinating) field, which is treated in detail in other books. For our purposes, and for the purposes of most users of circuit devices, the operational characteristics of these devices are important, and we limit our discussion to these operational characteristics.

The characteristics of diodes are first briefly noted. A semiconductor diode is made of two pieces of semiconductor material[1] of different types joined together. One type of semiconductor material is called *p-type* material, and the other *n-type* material [refer to Fig. A.1(a)].[2] When two differing types of semiconductor ma-

---

[1] A semiconductor has a conductivity roughly halfway between those of metals, which are good conductors, and insulators, which conduct poorly.

[2] *n*-type material has an excess of negative current carriers (electrons), while *p*-type material has an excess of positive current carriers (holes). Thus current flows readily when the *p*-type material is positive and the *n*-type material negative. Alternatively, very little current flows when the *p*-type material is negative and the *n*-type material is positive.

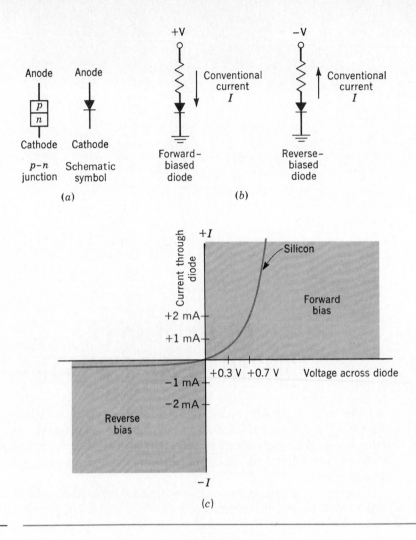

FIGURE A.1

Diode symbol and
characteristics.

terial are joined, a *semiconductor junction* is formed, and a single junction is also
called a *diode*. In Fig. A.1(*a*), the *p*-type material is referred to as the *anode* of
the diode, and the *n*-type material is called the *cathode* of the diode. Figure A.1(*a*)
also shows the schematic symbol for the diode.

A study of semiconductor, or solid-state, devices would explain the physical
internal workings of the diode. However, our sole interest here is to view the diode
as a component in electronic switching circuits; so we examine the diode from the
viewpoint of its electrical characteristics only. When we apply an electric voltage,
possibly through a resistor as in Fig. A.1(*b*), so that the anode of the diode is
positive with respect to the cathode, the diode is said to be *forward-biased*. A
diode which is forward-biased will conduct current rather freely. (*Conventional
current* is used in our discussion; conventional current flows from positive to negative.)

Figure A.1(*c*) shows a typical characteristic curve for a diode. Notice that, when forward-biased, the diode drops on the order of 0.7 V.[3] The forward-biased region on the graph lies to the right of the ordinate of the graph.

When the cathode of a diode is positive with respect to the anode, the diode is said to be *reverse-biased,* and it will present a very high resistance to current flow [refer to Fig. A.1(*b*) and (*c*)]. This ranges from tens to hundreds of megohms.[4]

A diode may, therefore, be thought of as a kind of electronic switch which is closed (freely passes current) when forward-biased and open (passes almost no current) when reverse-biased.

There are two general types of transistors used in computer circuits: bipolar and field-effect transistors (FETs). FETs are covered later. A *bipolar transistor* consists of either a piece of *n* material between two pieces of *p* material or a piece of *p* material between two pieces of *n* material. The first is called a *pnp* transistor, and the second an *npn* transistor. Figure A.2(*a*) and (*b*) shows this. The pieces of *n* and *p* material are named; for the *pnp* transistor the "middle" piece is *n* type and is called the *base,* while the two *p*-type pieces are called the *collector* and *emitter* and are further identified with the schematic symbols shown in Fig. A.2(*a*). For the *npn* transistor, the *p*-type material is the base, and the two pieces of *n*-type material are the emitter and collector.

Figure A.3 shows an *npn* transistor in a circuit with the emitter grounded. The currents and voltages in the circuit are identified as follows: The current *into* the base of the transistor is called I_b; the current *into* the collector is called I_c; the current *into* the emitter is called I_e. The voltage of the collector is called V_{ce} (this is the voltage between the collector and the emitter); the voltage at the base is called V_{be} (the voltage between base and emitter).

In this configuration the transistor can be operated in three modes: (1) *active region,* (2) *saturated,* and (3) *cutoff.* First let us define these terms, and then we examine the transistor's characteristics in each region of operation.

---

[3]Provided enough current flows.

[4]The part of the curve for silicon diodes which is below the 0 current level is somewhat distorted since a diode actually passes less than a few hundred nanoamperes when reverse-biased (1 nA $= 10^{-9}$ A).

FIGURE A.2

Transistor symbols and designations.

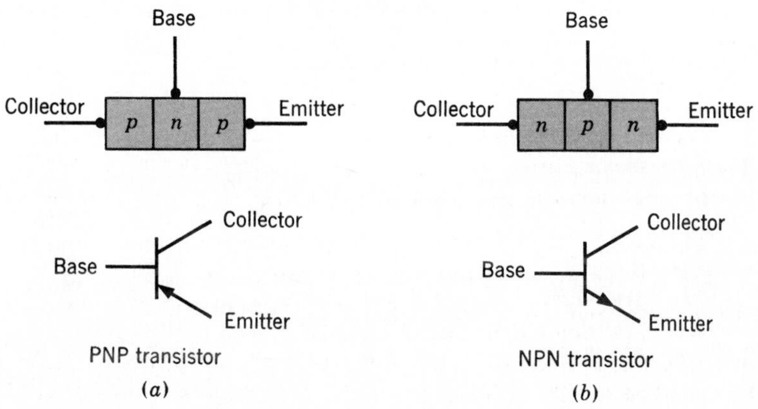

PNP transistor

(*a*)

NPN transistor

(*b*)

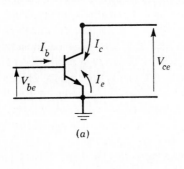

(a)

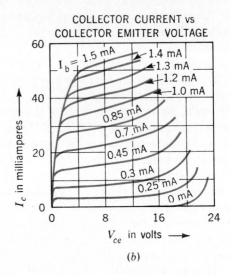

COLLECTOR CURRENT vs
COLLECTOR EMITTER VOLTAGE

(b)

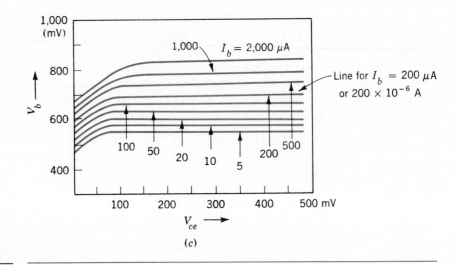

(c)

FIGURE A.3

npn-transistor common-emitter configuration and its operation.

1 *Active* The *npn* transistor in Fig. A.3(a) is in the *active region* when current flows into the base, that is, when I_b is positive and when V_{ce} is more positive than V_{be} (the collector is more positive than the base).

2 *Saturated* The *npn* transistor in Fig. A.3(a) is in the *saturated region* when positive current flows into the base (I_b is positive) and when V_{ce} is equal to or less than V_{be} (the collector is less positive than the base).

3 *Cutoff* The *npn* transistor is said to be *cut off* when either no current flows into the base or current flows out of the base (when I_b is either 0 or negative).

Active   When transistors are used in television or radio circuits, they are most often operated in the active region, because a small change in base current then causes a large change in collector current, thus making it possible to amplify the input. To examine this, a set of transistor curves is presented in Fig. A.3(*b*).

In the active region the base-emitter junction is forward-biased and the base-collector junction is reverse-biased. Thus current flows easily from base to emitter, but the base-to-collector current is small. As current is increased through the base-emitter junction, however, this stimulates current flow through the base from the collector to the emitter. The fact that a small change in base current causes a large change in current from the collector to the emitter is the "secret" of the transistor's usefulness as an amplifier. The base of a transistor is made very thin, which encourages the flow of current through the base (from collector to emitter) once the base area begins to "break down" (that is, to permit current flow) owing to the current from base to emitter. Notice that this base-emitter current also controls the collector-emitter current.

Saturated   When the input current I_b is positive but V_{ce} is less than V_{be}, both the base-collector and the base-emitter junctions will be forward-biased and the transistor will "look like" two forward-biased diodes. Current will flow freely in both the base and the base-collector junctions.[5]

Cutoff   When no current or negative current flows into the base (that is, V_{be} is negative), the transistor is cut off and virtually no current flows in the collector ($I_c = 0$). This can be seen in Fig. A.3(*b*), for with 0.25 mA into the base, less than 3 mA will flow in the collector; and for I_b equal to 0, virtually no current flows in the collector ($I_c = 0$).[6] If V_{be} is negative (the base is negative with respect to the emitter), both junctions of the transistor will be reverse-biased and virtually no current will flow in the circuit (I_c and I_b will be 0).

Let us now examine the operation of the inverter circuit in Fig. A.4(*a*). A load resistor of 500 Ω has been added to the collector circuit, and an input resistor of 2000 Ω to the base circuit. The plot of an input-output signal for this circuit is shown in Fig. A.4(*b*).

In Fig. A.4(*b*) the input starts at 0 V, so that no base current flows in the transistor and it is cut off. As a result, the output is at +5 V, since no current flows in the collector and no voltage is dropped across $R2$.

As the input starts positive, current begins to flow into the base and the transistor passes into the active region. This causes current to flow in the collector circuit, and this current flows through resistor $R2$, and so the output begins to fall. At some point the output will fall below the voltage at the base, which will be held at about 0.8 V—the base-emitter junction is well forward-biased by the current through resistor $R1$—and the transistor will be saturated.

---

[5]Some curves for a saturated transistor are shown in Fig. A.3(*c*). Notice that the collector voltages are less than the base voltages. Also the base voltages are very "flat" for wide ranges of collector voltage. For instance, with a base current I_b of 1000 μA (microamperes) (1 μA = 10^{-6} A), the base voltage will be about 0.75 V when the collector is from 0.1 to 0.5 V.

[6]The slight "turnup" in the ends of the curves in Fig. A.3(*b*) is due to junction breakdown at higher voltages. The transistor is to be operated with collector voltage of less than +10 V.

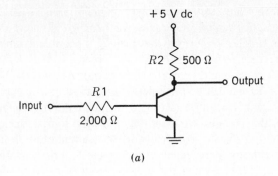

(a)

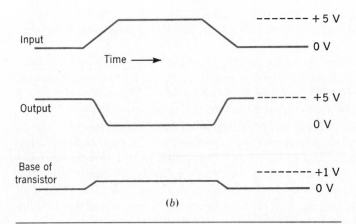

(b)

FIGURE A.4

The transfer inverter.
(a) Inverter circuit.
(b) Waveforms for inverter circuit.

When the voltage at the input goes back to 0 V, the process is reversed; the transistor passes from saturation through the active region and is again cut off.

Notice that the output from the transistor is an "inverted" near-replica of the input; so the circuit is called an *inverter*.

Note: An *npn* transistor is, strictly speaking, "cut off" when the base current is 0 or negative, which means, for our circuits, when the base voltage V_{be} is 0 or negative. In general practice, a transistor is said to be cut off when "negligible" current flows. This is, of course, not precise, nor can it be made so. What is meant is that so little current flows into the base that virtually no current flows in the collector circuit.

The operation of a *pnp* transistor is essentially the same as that of the *npn* transistor, except that all the polarities discussed are reversed. For instance, the *pnp* transistor is cut off when I_b is positive or into the base. The voltage V_{ce} is made negative for *pnp* transistors in the common-base circuit.

APPENDIX B
DIODE GATES

In most systems 0s and 1s are represented by a positive dc signal (representing a 1) or a 0-V dc signal (representing a 0). The function of the AND gate circuit is to produce a positive dc signal at its output when a positive dc signal is applied to all the inputs to the circuit simultaneously. If the inputs to the circuit are labeled X, Y, and Z the circuit will produce a positive dc signal only when a positive dc signal is simultaneously applied to X AND Y AND Z.

Figure B.1 illustrates a two-input diode AND gate. In the circuit, a 0-V dc level represents a binary 0 and a $+3$-V signal a binary 1. If both inputs are at 0 V, both diodes will be forward-biased and the output will be held at 0 V by the diodes. The total voltage drop across the resistor will be 5 V.[1]

If the X input line goes to 3 V and the Y input remains at 0 V, the diode connected to the Y input will still be forward-biased, and the output will remain at 0 V dc. (Notice that in this case the X input diode will be reverse-biased, and 3 V will be dropped across the diode.) If the input at Y goes to $+3$ V and X remains at 0 V, the output will be at 0 V dc.

When the inputs at X and Y both go to the $+3$-V level, the output level will rise to $+3$ V, and the output will represent a 1.

The responses of the diode AND gate to several types of inputs are illustrated in Fig. B.1. The circuit could have more than two inputs. In this case a diode would be required for each input, and each additional diode would be connected

---

[1] We have assumed, for simplicity of explanation, that no voltage is dropped across a forward-biased diode. In fact, for silicon diodes, the output would be at approximately $+0.7$ V and the drop across the resistor about 4.3 V.

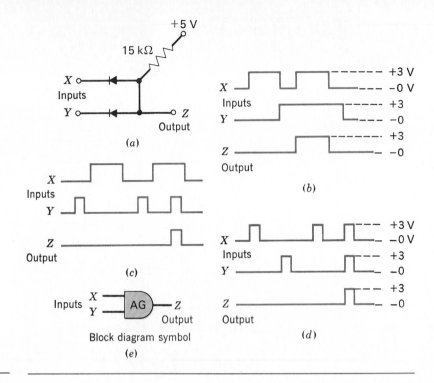

Diode AND gate.

just as the two diodes are connected in the figure. If four diodes are connected as shown in Fig. B.1, the output will rise to the $+3$-V signal level only when the input signals to all four diodes are positive. There is a practical limit to the number of diodes which can be connected in this manner, however, because the diodes do not actually have an infinite back resistance or zero forward resistance. With a large number of inputs, the finite forward and back resistances of the diodes will cause varying output levels, depending on the state of the inputs.

The diode OR gate

The OR gate has the property that a signal representing a 1 will appear at the output if any one of the inputs represents a 1. Figure B.2 illustrates a diode OR gate circuit. There are two inputs to the circuit (X and Y) and one output. The input signals to the circuit consist of 0-V signals representing 0s and $+3$-V signals representing 1s. If both inputs to the circuit are at 0 V dc, both diodes will be forward-biased and the output of the circuit will be at 0 V dc, representing a 0. If either input to the circuit rises to $+3$ V dc, the diode at this input will be forward-biased and the output will rise to $+3$ V, representing a 1. The diode at the input remaining at 0 V will then be reverse-biased by the $+3$-V signal at the output. This circuit has the property that the output level will be at the level of the most positive input.

If both inputs to the circuit rise to $+3$ V, the output will again be at $+3$ V. (This circuit is sometimes referred to as an *inclusive* OR circuit, because the output is a 1 when both inputs are 1s.)

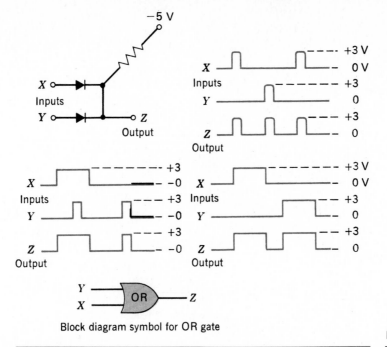

Block diagram symbol for OR gate

More inputs may be added to the circuit illustrated in Fig. B.2. A diode is then required for each input. If any one or any combination of the inputs rises to the +3-V level, the output will be at +3 V.

As in the case of the diode AND gate, it is not practical to have too many inputs to the circuit because the forward and back resistances of the diodes are finite, and different combinations of input signals will cause different signal levels at the outputs.

APPENDIX C
TRANSISTOR-TRANSISTOR LOGIC

The line of circuits called transistor-transistor logic (TTL) is now the most widely used because of the high speed of TTL circuits. The characteristic which distinguishes TTL circuits from other circuit lines is a multiple-emitter transistor at the input circuit. The schematic diagram for this kind of transistor is shown as $T1$ in Fig. C.1(a). The multiple-emitter transistor simply has a larger than normal collector area and several base-emitter junctions. The two-emitter transistor in Fig. C.1(a) functions as the two-transistor circuit because the two-emitter transistor is effectively two transistors with a common collector and base. Figure C.1(b) and (c) shows the TTL input circuit in separate transistor and multiple-emitter transistor form. The transistors, $T1A$, $T1B$, and $T1C$ are combined to form a single multiple-emitter transistor $T1$ in Fig. C.1(c). This circuit operates as follows. If one of three inputs X, Y, and Z is at 0 V, current will flow through $R1$ and the base-emitter junction of $T1$ to the input. This will hold the base of $T1$ at about 0.5 V. The base collector of $T1$ and the base emitter of $T2$ form two junctions in series with resistor $R3$ to ground, and so the base of $T2$ will not be positive more than 0.2 V, which is insufficient to turn on $T2$. Little (leakage only) current will flow in the collector circuit of $T1$, and $T2$ will be off. As a result, no current will flow through resistors $R2$ and $R3$, and the emitter of $T2$ will be at ground and the collector at $+5$ V.

If all three inputs are at a level of $+3.5$ V (the 1 level), then current will flow through $R1$ and the base-collector junction of $T1$ (which is forward-biased) into the base of $T2$, turning it on. Current will flow through $R1$ and $R2$ until the transistor $T2$ is saturated with its emitter and collector both at about 2.5 V. At this time, the three emitter-base junctions of the multiple-emitter transistor will be reverse-biased.

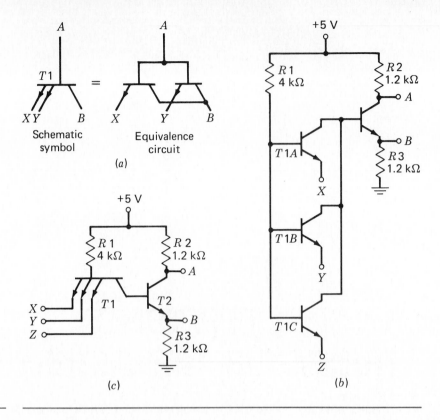

Schematic
symbol

Equivalence
circuit

(a)

(c)

(b)

FIGURE C.1

TTL gate circuit. (a) Schematic symbol and equivalent circuit. (b) Discrete version of TTL gate. (c) Multiple-emitter TTL gate.

The two outputs from the collector and emitter of $T2$ operate as scissors which close when $T2$ is on and open when $T2$ is off. That is, the emitter and collector of $T2$ will be at about the same voltage (closed) when $T2$ is on, and the emitter will be at ground and the collector at $+5$ V when $T2$ is off (open scissors).

Notice that $T2$ is on when the three inputs are high (1s) and off when any one of the three inputs is low (a 0). So the circuit operation is basically that of a NAND gate. Logic levels for TTL are that 0 to 0.2 V represents a 0 and $+2.5$ to $+5$ V represents a 1.

A complete TTL NAND gate is shown in Fig. C.2. This is a *second-generation* TTL circuit and is typical of the circuits offered by the major TTL manufacturers in their medium-speed lines.

Let us examine the operation of the circuit in Fig. C.2 by assuming that input Y is at $+3.5$ V and X is at 0 V. Therefore $T1$ has its base-emitter junction connected to Y reversed-biased, and the full current from $R1$ flows through the base-emitter junction connected to X. At this time, (1) $T2$ will be off; (2) $T4$ will be off because with no current through $R4$ its base will be at essentially ground; (3) $T3$ and $T5$ will be turned on by current flowing through $R2$. The transistors $T5$ and $T3$ are connected in what is called a *Darlington configuration* which gives large current gain. As a result, little current will be required through $R2$ to turn on $T3$, and the output will be at $+5$ V minus the base-emitter drops for $T5$ and $T3$, or about $+4$ V.

Let us consider that the input voltage at X is slowly raised positive. As a

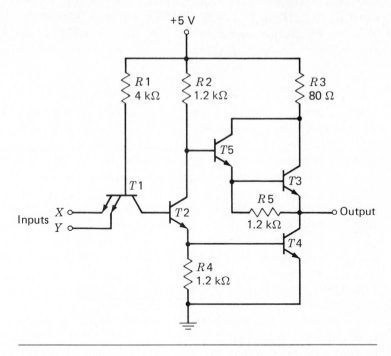

+5 V

Inputs

X

Y

Output

FIGURE C.2

Classic TTL NAND
gate.

result, the collector of $T1$ goes positive, and $T2$ begins to conduct. As the emitter of $T2$ becomes more and more positive, $T4$ begins to conduct, and as the collector of $T2$ becomse more and more negative, the $T5$ to $T3$ combination begins to turn off. Finally $T2$ will saturate and $T4$ will be saturated, and therefore about $+0.5$ V or less.

The circuit in Fig. C.2 will have about 4-ns turn-on delays and 7-ns turn-off delays and a power dissipation of about 10 mW.

The reason for the high speeds lies in the all-transistor construction of the TTL and in the fact that the final stage drives current in both directions. The standard transistor inverter has an output which is "driven down" by the turning on of the output transistor. When the transistor is turned off, however, the rising edge is formed by the resistor at the circuit's output supplying current to all the stray capacity in this circuit and any circuits connected to the output. Therefore the rise time is exponential. With TTL's two-transistor output (the circuit is called a *totem pole*), the rising edge is "driven up" by the upper transistor turning on and the lower transistor turning off. This gives a sharp edge, and the falling edge is similarly sharp.

In many aerospace, military, and industrial applications, it is desirable to have a much lower power dissipation. If the resistor values in the basic circuit design shown in Fig. C.2 are raised, the circuit will consume far lower power, and circuit manufacturers offer low-power TTL circuits. Typical resistor values are $R1 = 40$, $R2 = 20$, $R3 = 500$, $R4 = 12$, and $R5 = 5$ kΩ. Naturally there will be a decrease in speed, but low-power gates are still capable of 23-ns delays at only 1-mW power dissipation.

There is a famous problem with TTL circuits which can be illustrated by using Fig. C.2. When TTL circuits are switched, they generate large "spikes" on their outputs, and interconnections must be carefully watched to prevent ringing or even circuit damage. Sometimes, capacitors are even placed across the +5 V to ground power supply on each circuit container to prevent spikes in the power-supply voltage.

The problem develops because it is possible for both $T3$ and $T4$ to be on simultaneously when the circuit is switching. For instance, if the output is switching from a 0 to a 1 level, then $T4$ must go off and $T3$ must go on. But if $T3$ goes on before $T4$ is completely off, then both transistors will be on simultaneously, almost short-circuiting the +5 V to ground.

The TTL current spike problem has plagued the TTL family and is clearly in evidence in the circuit of Fig. C.2. While $T3$ and $T4$ can both be on during turn-on and turn-off, the turn-off case is usually worse since the storage time of $T4$ causes both transistors to be on for a greater time. Turn-on current spiking may be lowered by increasing the ratio of $R2$ to $R4$. In this way the collector of $T2$ reaches a lower voltage before $T4$ begins to conduct. There is a tradeoff involved, however, since increasing $R2$ decreases the on drive for $T4$, decreasing its turn-on time. The increased value of $R2$ also results in decreased noise immunity. So far, no perfect answer to current spiking has been found.

Although the standard TTL circuits are fast, there is always a desire to speed up circuit lines. To increase still further the speeds of TTL, a basic problem must be dealt with. When a transistor is saturated and must be turned off, before the transistor begins to go off there is a delay (caused by the minority carriers) called the *storage time delay*. This is shown in Fig. C.3(a) where a transistor inverted is turned off from saturation. While this delay is on the order of nanoseconds, it is

FIGURE C.3

Schottky clamped transistor. (*a*) Storage delay. (*b*) Schottky diode and transistor.

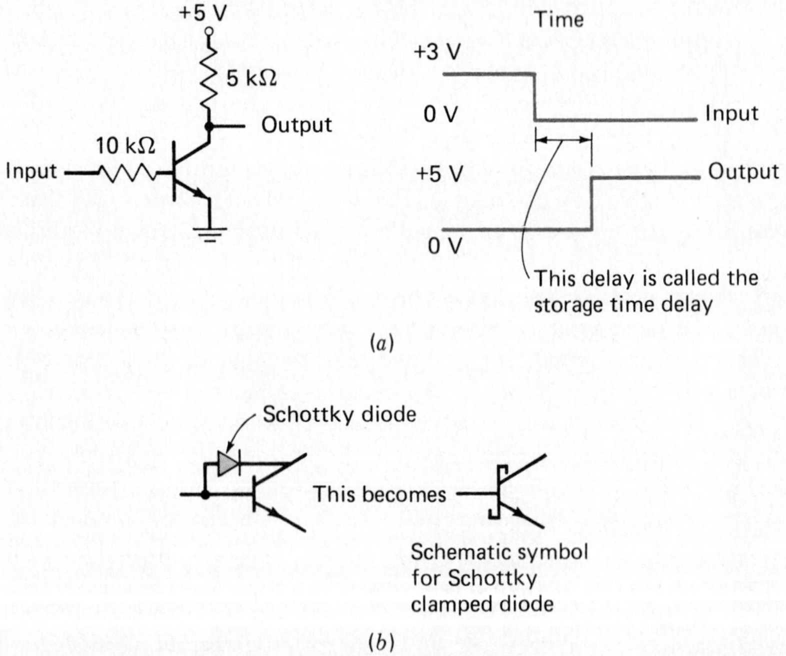

(a)

(b)

still significant since several of the TTL circuit transistors become saturated at various times.[1]

To alleviate this problem, the fastest TTL circuits use a diode clamp between base and collector. This is shown in Fig. C.3(b). The diode used is not a conventional diode, however, but a special diode (called a *Schottky diode*) formed by the junction of a metal and a semiconductor.

The Schottky diode is faster than conventional diodes because electrons which have crossed the junction and entered the metal when current is flowing are not distinguishable from the conduction electrons of the metal. Since these electrons are majority carriers, there is no delay associated with minority carrier recombination as in semiconductor diodes. As a result, reverse recovery times from Schottky diodes are generally in the low picosecond range. Further, because of the choice of materials (aluminum or platinum silicides), the forward drop of the Schottky diode is less than for a conventional diode.

The transistor with a Schottky diode connected from base to collector will switch faster because the transistor is not allowed to saturate. The minority carrier storage time normally associated with the transistor's operation when coming out of saturation is avoided and the circuit can operate faster.

When a transistor is fabricated with a Schottky diode connected from base to collector, the combination is given a special schematic diagram symbol as shown in Fig. C.3(b).

The use of Schottky clamped transistors has resulted in a series of high-speed TTL circuits with delays on the order of 1 ns (rise and fall times are on the order of 2 ns). Figure C.4(b) shows a typical circuit. Notice that the transistors which normally become saturated at some time are now Schottky clamped transistors, and so storage delays are reduced. The operation of this circuit is essentially the same as that of Fig. C.2 except that the transistors do not saturate.

The diodes connected to ground at the inputs dampen negative spikes and negative-going signals which may occur during ringing. These circuits must be carefully interconnected, however. Wire or printed-circuit connections of more than 8 in. in length should be treated with respect and terminated according to the rules given by the circuits' manufacturers.

Table C.1 gives some of the characteristics of several TTL lines. Notice that speed is associated with power consumption.

TTL circuits are also available in MSI. The MSI seven-segment decoder and BCD counters in Chap 4. were TTL. A simplified TTL gate is used internally for such MSI circuits, and this gate is shown in Fig. C.4(a).

Manufacturers make a special TTL gate which can be connected in a wired-AND circuit. Figure C.5(a) shows the basic circuit. The inputs are ANDed by the multiple-emitter input transistor and inverted by the output transistor. The output transistor has no resistor to +5, however, and so the circuit is not completed and an external resisitor must be supplied. The advantage of the circuit is that if two or more of these circuits have their outputs connected, they form a NAND-to-wired-AND configuration as in Fig. C.5(b).

Figure C.5(b) also shows that a resistor must be connected to +5 from the

---

[1]Gold doping is often used to reduce minority carrier storage times in switching transistors.

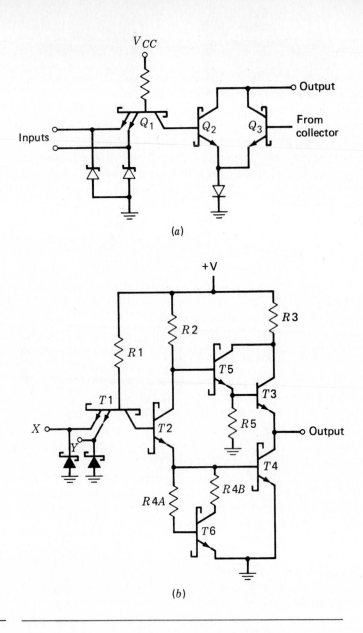

FIGURE C.4

(a) Schottky MSI circuit. (b) Schottky clamped TTL gate.

wired-AND output, but only a single resistor is required. Generally, this resistor is not shown on block diagrams, but it is included in Fig. C.5(b) to show how the circuit is connected. The AND function is performed at the outputs because if any output transistor is on (saturated), it will force all outputs to the 0 level at about 0.2 V.

Several open-collector NAND gates are packaged in a single IC container. Using this gate makes for economical, reasonably fast circuitry, and they are widely used. The gates can also be used to connect to bus wires which are normally high but which are to be forced low to indicate status.

TABLE C.1   TTL CHARACTERISTICS

	VERY HIGH SPEED 74 S (SCHOTTKY CLAMPED)	HIGH SPEED	MEDIUM SPEED 74	LOW SPEED 74 L
High-level input (minimum)	2 V	1.8 V	2 V	2 V
Low-level input (maximum)	0.8 V	0.9 V	0.8 V	0.7 V
High-level output (minimum)	2.7 V	2.5 V	2.4 V	2.4 V
Low-level output (maximum)	0.5 V	0.4 V	0.4 V	0.3 V
High-level noise margin (minimum)	700 mV	700 mV	400 mV	400 mV
Low-level noise margin (minimum)	300 mV	500 mV	400 mV	400 mV
Maximum input load current	−2 mA	−2 mA	−1.6 mA	−1.8 mA
Average power per gate	20 mW	22 mW	10 mW	1 mW
Typical delay, high to low	1.5 ns	4 ns	8 ns	31 ns
Typical delay, low to high	1.5 ns	4 ns	12 ns	35 ns
Supply voltage	5 V	5 V	5 V	5 V

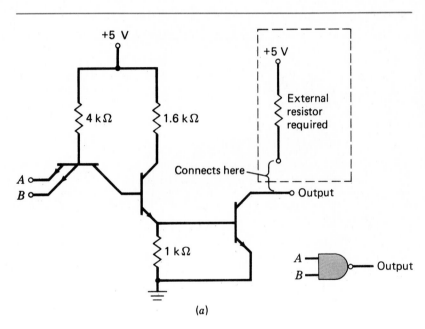

FIGURE C.5

Open collector TTL gate and wired AND connection. (*a*) Open collector TTL gate. (*b*) Open collector TTL gates connected in wired-AND configuration.

(*a*)

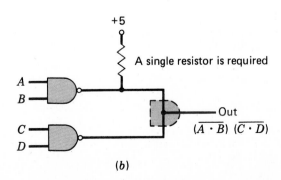

(*b*)

APPENDIX D
EMITTER-COUPLED LOGIC

Emitter-coupled logic (ECL) has several other common names: *current-mode logic* (CML), *current-steering logic,* and *nonsaturating logic*. The last term is the key to this type of circuit. When transistors are operated in a saturated condition, they turn off slowly because of the delay caused by a charge stored in the collector and base region.[1] This delay in turn-off time can be eliminated by operating transistors only in either the active or the off regions. As will be seen, in these circuits current is "steered" rather than having voltages or levels passed around.

The ECL line is the fastest currently available. Manufacturers of ECL have a number of basic circuits, each with different features and drawbacks. ECL has not proved as popular as TTL, primarily because it is more expensive, harder to cool, and more difficult to interconnect and is considered to have less noise immunity (this is debatable). Also, ECL may be faster than is necessary in many applications. On the other hand, the superfast computers use ECL as do a number of the highest speed special-purpose computers.

The basic ECL configuration can be best described by examining a particular inverter. Figure D.1 shows an ECL inverter with an input X. The logic levels in this system are as follows: Binary 0 is represented by -1.55 V and binary 1 by -0.75 V. Notice that this is "positive logic," since, although both levels are negative, the more positive level, -0.75, is the binary 1. Also, notice the small signal difference between 0 and 1.

The circuit's operation is based on a *differential amplifier* consisting of $T4$

---

[1]This was called the storage delay in the preceding section.

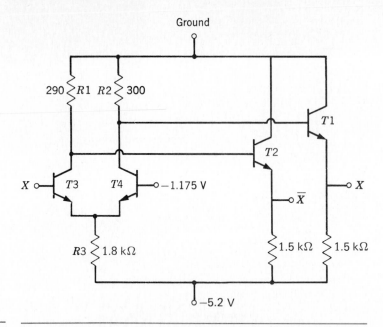

FIGURE D.1

Basic circuit of ECL gate. (*Motorola Corp.*)

and T3. When the input to T3 is at -1.55 V, T3 will be off and current will flow through R3 and R2. Calculation will indicate a drop of about 0.8 V across R2. So figuring a base-emitter drop of 0.75 V for T1, we see the X output will be at -1.55 V.

Since T2 is cut off by the -1.55-V input, very little current will flow through R1, and the output $\overline{X}$ will be at the base-emitter drop voltage across T2. So the output will be at -0.75 V.

An examination will show that if the input is at -0.75 V, transistor T3 will be on, T4 will be off, the X output will be at -0.75 V, and the $\overline{X}$ output at -1.55 V. (The key to analyzing this circuit is to notice that in a differential amplifier circuit such as the T3 to T4 form, the current through the resistor R3 shared by the two emitters will be almost constant.) Notice that the transistors are never saturated. They are either in their active region or off.

A three-input gate is shown in Fig. D.2. This is a combined NOR and OR gate, as shown by the block diagram, depending on which output connection is used.

As time has passed, several generations of ECL circuits have evolved. In general the circuits have become faster and require more power with each generation. More facilities and more complicated logic per chip are also available in the new lines, including MSI chips. Notice that the circuits in Fig. D.1 require three voltages: ground, -1.175 V, and -5.2 V. Later circuits provide a circuit on each chip to generate the intermediate voltage (in this case, -1.175 V), so that only a single power supply is required.

Figure D.3 shows the four generations Motorola has gone through with their

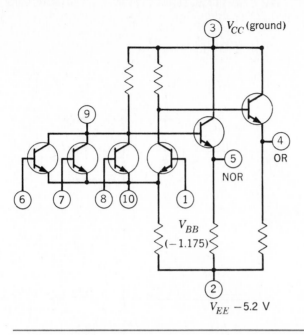

TRUTH TABLE

Inputs			Outputs	
8	7	6	5	4
0	0	0	1	0
0	0	1	0	1
0	1	0	0	1
0	1	1	0	1
1	0	0	0	1
1	0	1	0	1
1	1	0	0	1
1	1	1	0	1

FIGURE D.2

ECL three-input gate.

ECL which is called Motorola ECL, or MECL, and also Fairchild's 10,000 series. Table D.1 outlines some of the characteristics of these circuits, and the speed versus power and general noise characteristics can be deduced from the table. From Fig. D.3 it is evident which variations were employed as technology advanced. For instance, notice that the circuit to produce the third -1.175-V bias voltage for the MECL 1 line is not included on the chip, whereas all subsequent lines have this as an internal feature.

Corresponding resistor values differ among MECL lines. This is necessary to achieve the varying speed and power improvements. Of course, speed is not determined by resistor values alone; transistor geometries, while not shown on a schematic, are a major factor. The transistor geometries in conjunction with the resistor values provide the speed and power characteristics of the different families.

Notice also that Fairchild 10,000 and MECL III gates are supplied with base pull-down resistors (50 kΩ) to each of the input transistors, while the other two families are not. These resistors provide a path for base leakage current to unused input bases, causing them to be well turned off.

A final significant difference between the families is in the output circuits. MECL I circuits normally are supplied with output pull-down resistors on the chip. MECL II circuits can be obtained with or without output resistors. MECL III and Fairchild 10,000 circuits normally have open outputs. The use of on-chip output resistors has both advantages and limitations. An advantage is that fewer external components are required. However, with open outputs the designer can choose both the value and the location of the terminating resistance to meet system requirements. Finally the use of external resistors reduces on-chip heating and power dissipation, allowing more complex LSI and increasing chip life and reliability.

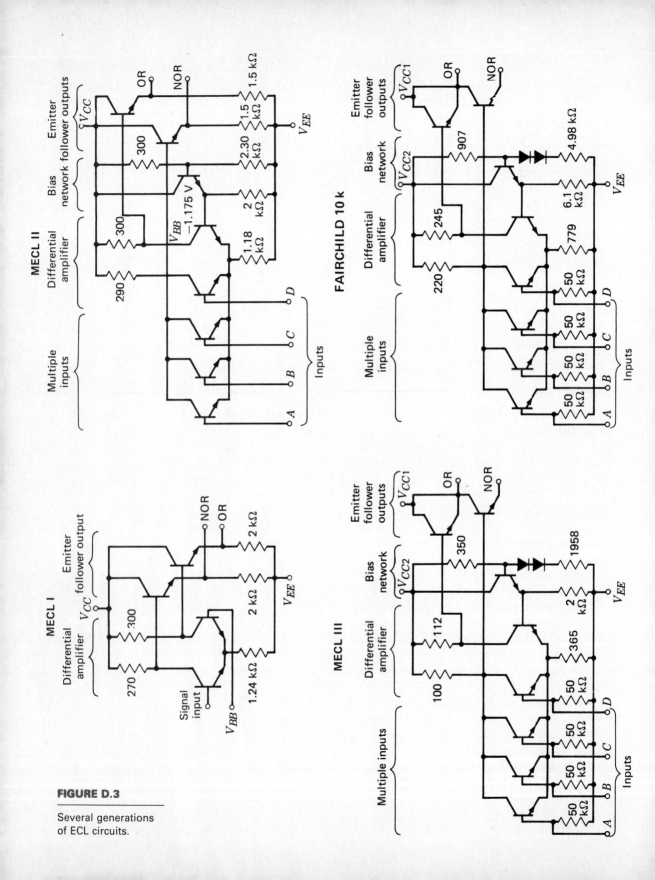

FIGURE D.3

Several generations
of ECL circuits.

FEATURE	MECL I	MECL II	FAIRCHILD 10k SERIES	100K SERIES	MECL III
Gate propagation delay, ns	8	4	2	0.75	0.75
Gate edge speed, ns	8.5	4	3.5	1.5	0.75
Flip-flop toggle speed (minimum), MHz	30	70	125	500	500
Gate power, mW	31	22	25	65	60
Input pull-down resistors, kΩ	No	No	50	50	2, 50

GENERAL CHARACTERISTICS OF ECL CIRCUITS

APPENDIX E
METAL-OXIDE SEMICONDUCTOR CIRCUITS

The circuits described so far are all termed *bipolar circuits* and use "conventional" transistors. For large-scale integration (LSI), quite often another type of transistor, called a *field-effect transistor* (FET), is used. Although the characteristics of these FETs have not proved desirable for some applications (because of their slowness, delicacy, and lack of drive characteristics), the ease of manufacture, small size, and small power dissipation have offset the negative factors and have led to FETs constructed of metal-oxide semiconductor (MOS) as the primary technology for use in large arrays. FETs constructed of MOS are called MOSFETs.

Figure E.1(*a*) shows a cross section of a FET of *p*-channel type. As shown in Fig. E.1(*b*), a substrate of *n*-type (silicon) material is first formed, and two separate low-resistivity *p*-type regions are diffused into this substrate. Then the surface of this structure is covered with an insulating oxide layer. Holes are cut into the oxide, and two metal contacts are made to the two pieces of *p* material, and a thin piece of metal called the *gate* (*G*) is placed over what is called the *channel*.

With no voltages applied, the above structure (refer to Fig. E.1) forms two diodes back to back. And if we attempt to force current from source to drain, the alternate *pn* junction followed by an *np* junction will not permit current flow (in either direction).

The gate is used to cause and control current flow in the following manner. Consider the source to be grounded and the drain connected to a negative voltage through a resistor. Figure E.2 shows this. [The schematic symbol for the FET is shown in Fig. E.1(*d*).] The metal area of the gate and the insulating oxide layer and semiconductor channel form a capacitor, with the metal gate as the top plate

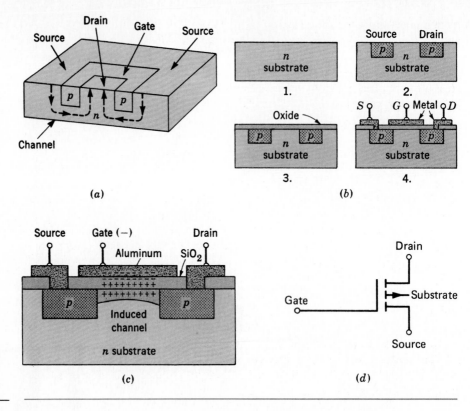

(a)

(b)

(c)

(d)

FIGURE E.1

MOSFET structure. (a) General configuration. (b) Fabrication steps. (c) Cross section with gate biased negative. (d) Schematic symbol. (*Motorola Corp.*)

and the *n*-material substrate as the lower plate. Making the gate potential negative causes a corresponding positive charge in the *n*-type semiconductor substrate along the channel, as shown in Fig. E.1(*c*). Given sufficient negative potential on the gate, the positive charge induced in the channel finally causes this section of material to become *p* type, and current begins to flow from source to drain—thus the term *current enhancement mode*.

The more negative the gate becomes, the more "*p* type" the semiconductor channel becomes, and the more current flows. As a result, this type of MOS is also called PMOS.

As a switching circuit, a FET can be used to form an inverter. With a 0, or

FIGURE E.2

Alternative schematic symbols for MOSFET resistive element.

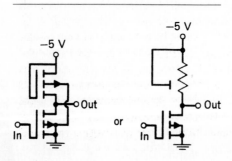

ground, input the output of the circuit shown in Fig. E.2 will have a -5-V output, and with a -2-V or more negative input, the output will go to about 0 V.

Instead of forming actual resistors for these circuits, another FET is used, thus simplifying manufacture. This is shown in Fig. E.2. The FET resistor's gate areas are controlled so that the FET represents a high resistance (perhaps 10 to 100 kΩ) when the gate is at the drain potential. Some manufacturers show this FET by using the regular symbol, and others show the resistor-plus-bar symbol, also seen in the figure.

When a p-type substrate with n doping for the source and drain is used, as in Fig. E.3, then the n-channel transistor is formed as shown. The schematic diagram symbols for the n-channel transistor and an inverter circuit are shown in Fig. E.3(a) and (b). Notice that the circuit uses a positive voltage and behaves similarly to an npn transistor inverter circuit. This type of MOS is called NMOS.

A NOR gate can be formed in NMOS as shown in Fig. E.4(a). The logic levels for this circuit are 0 to 1 V for a binary 0 and $> +1.5$ V for a binary 1. (This is positive logic.) If any of the inputs A, B, or C is a 1, the corresponding FET will conduct, causing the output to go to about $+0.8$ V or less. If all inputs are at $+0.8$ V or less, all the FETs will be off and the output will be at $+8$ V (or more).

Several different gates and flip-flops using NMOS are shown in Fig. E.4. (PMOS is the same except for negative V_{CC} voltages and negative logic.) The high resistances used in these circuits mean low power dissipation. This, combined with the small areas needed to fabricate a FET, makes it possible to fabricate large numbers of circuits on a single small chip.

CMOS logic circuits

A series of circuits using MOSFET transistors called *complementary MOS* (CMOS) was originally developed for the aerospace and oceanographic industries. These circuits have very low power consumption and considerable resistance to noise. They are, however, slow relative to the high-speed logic lines. But large numbers of circuits can be placed on a single chip, the power-supply voltage can vary over a large range, and the circuits are relatively economical to manufacture. The newest CMOS circuits have become relatively fast and are widely used for everything from electronic watches and calculators to microprocessors.

The CMOS circuits are fabricated as illustrated in Fig. E.5(a), which shows that both n- and p-channel transistors can be fabricated on the same substrate.

The simplest form of CMOS integrated circuit consists of one n-channel and one p-channel MOS transistor, with both gate contacts tied together to form the input and both drain contacts tied together to form the output. This circuit is the basic CMOS inverter [Fig. E.5(b)]. When the voltage at the input is near ground level, the gate-to-source voltage of the p-channel transistor approaches the value of the supply voltage $+V$, and the p channel is turned on. A low-resistance path is created between the supply voltage and the output, while a high-resistance path exists between the output and ground, because the n-channel transistor is off. The output voltage will approach that of the supply voltage $+V$. When the input voltage is near $+V$, the p channel turns off and the n channel turns on, causing the output voltage to approach ground.

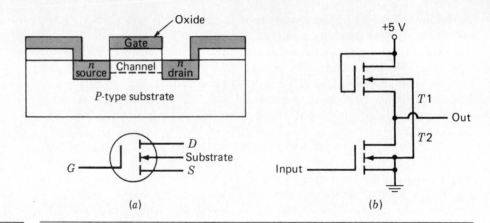

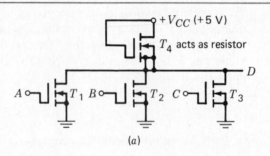

FIGURE E.3

(a) n-channel MOS-FET transistor. (b) n-channel inverter.

FIGURE E.4

FET logic circuits. (a) Three-input NOR gate. (b) Three-input NAND gate. (c) RS flip-flop.

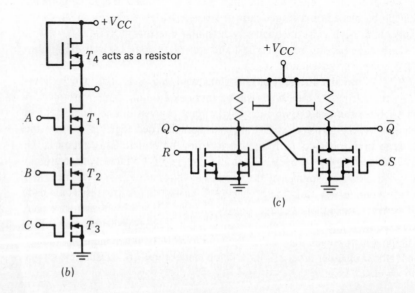

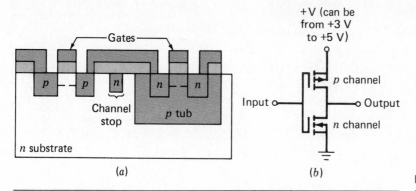

(a)

(b)

CMOS inverter.
(a) CMOS elements.
(b) Circuit that is the
basic CMOS inverter.

Notice that in either state the circuit's power consumption is extremely low because one transistor is always off and because n- and p-channel transistors exhibit very high resistance when off, permitting very low leakage current to flow through the transistor which is in the off condition.

When conventional metal- and silicon-gate technologies are used, protective channel stops are provided to minimize leakage current between separate transistors, as shown in Fig. E.5(a). All p-channel devices must be surrounded by a continuous n-channel stop, which can also act as a conducting path for the external power supply to appropriate locations. Similarly, p-channel stops surround all n-channel devices and provide a conducting path between those n-channel devices which are electrically connected to the lowest potential and the external ground contact.

A two-input NOR gate can be constructed as shown in Fig. E.6. Each additional input requires an additional p- and n-channel pair of MOS transistors.

Table E.1 gives some details of CMOS operation versus other circuit lines. Notice the low power consumption (nanowatts when they are not being switched), competitive speeds, and noise protection.

FIGURE E.6

CMOS NOR gate.

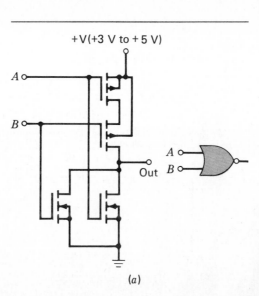

(a)

	STANDARD TTL 74	LOW-POWER TTL	DTL	SCHOTTKY CLAMPED TTL	CMOS 5-V SUPPLY	CMOS 10-V SUPPLY	ECL
Quiescent power, mW	10	1	8.5	20	10	10	60
Propagation delay, ns	4	20	20	1.5	10	7	0.3
Flip-flop toggle frequency, MHz	45	5	7	100	10	12	600
Noise immunity, V	1	1	1	0.8	2	4	0.5
Fan-out	10	10	8	10	50	50	5

APPENDIX G
DAC IMPLEMENTATION

The most straightforward digital-to-analog converter (DAC) involves the use of a resistor network. A basic type of resistor network DAC is illustrated in Fig. G.1, which shows a resistor network with four inputs. Each input is connected to a switch which connects a resistor to either 0 V or V_+. When a switch is in the position connecting to V_+, the binary bit represents a 1; when the switch connects to 0 V, the input bit is a binary 0. The output at E_0 will then be a dc voltage in the range of 0 to V_+ and will be proportional to the value of the binary number represented by the inputs.

For instance, if the input number is 0111 (leftmost switch down, other three up), the output voltage of E_0 will be $\frac{7}{15}V_+$; if the input is 1111, the output E_0 will be V_+; and if the input is 0001, the output E_0 will be at $\frac{1}{15}V_+$. For example, if V_+ were 15 V, then for an input of 0111 the output would be 7 V, for input 1000 the output would be 8, and for input 1111 (all switches up) the output would be 15 V. To achieve accuracy, all the resistors should be of the precision type. More resolution can be added by increasing the number of inputs and adding a resistor for each input. (The resistor values are halved for each input added.)

Resistor networks of this type are manufactured by several firms. The resistors are generally laser-beam-trimmed to the necessary accuracies. Often electronic (transistor-driven) switches are packaged in an IC container with the resistors, making a complete DAC.

Figure G.2 shows another type of resistor network which can be used for D/A conversion. The advantage of this network is that only two different values of resistors are used. The inputs are shown as switches, but generally semiconductor

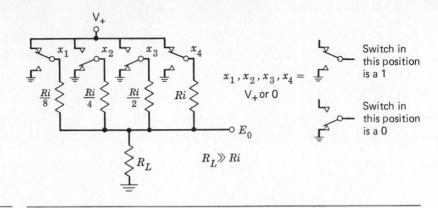

FIGURE G.1

D-to-A converter network.

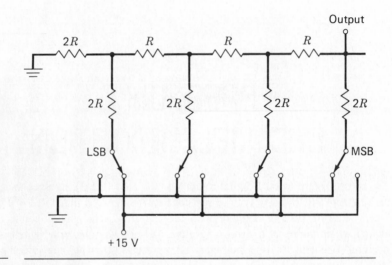

FIGURE G.2

D-to-A converter with two resistor sizes.

switches or level-setting amplifiers are used. The disadvantage of this converter is that two resistors are required per input.

There are several other circuits for DACs, and the design and construction of these devices represent a growing area in the computing field.

BIBLIOGRAPHY

Chapter 1

1 Grogano, P.: *Programming Pascal,* Addison-Wesley, Reading, MA, 1980.

2 Rauch-Hindin, W. B.: "Mainframes and Micros," *Systems and Software,* vol. 2, no. 6, June 1983.

3 Pier, K.: "A Retrospective on the Dorado, a High-Performance Personal Computer," *ACM 10th Annual Symposium on Computer Architecture, SIGARCH Newsletter,* vol. 11, no. 3, June 1983.

4 Welsh, J., and J. Elder: *Introduction to Pascal,* 2d ed., Prentice-Hall, Englewood Cliffs, NJ, 1982.

5 Clark, R., and S. Koehler: *The UCSD Pascal Handbook,* Prentice-Hall, Englewood Cliffs, NJ, 1982.

6 Tenenbaum, A. M., and M. J. Augenstein: *Data Structures Using Pascal,* Prentice-Hall, Englewood Cliffs, NJ, 1982.

Chapter 2

1 Rajeraman, V., and T. Radhakrishman: *Introduction to Digital Computer Design,* Prentice-Hall, Englewood Cliffs, NJ, 1983.

2 Iliff, S.: *Advanced Computer Design,* Prentice-Hall, Englewood Cliffs, NJ, 1982.

3 Bell, C. G., et al.: *Computer Engineering,* Digital Equipment Corp., Maynard, ME, 1976.

4   Hwang, K.: *Computer Arithmetic,* Wiley, New York, 1979.

5   Ong, S., and D. E. Atkins: "A Basis for the Quantitative Comparison of Computer Number Systems," *IEEE Trans. on Computers,* vol. C-32, no. 4, April 1983.

6   Kornerup, P., and D. W. Matula: "Finite Precision Rational Arithmetic," *IEEE Trans. on Computers,* vol. C-32, no. 4, April 1983.

Chapter 3

1   Parker, R., and S. Shapiro: "Workstations That Take the Chip's Design from End to End," *Computer Design,* vol. 22, no. 8, July 1980.

2   Agazzi, E.: *Modern Logic,* D. Reidel, Hingham, MA, 1980.

3   Marik, W., and Z. Onyszkiewicy: *Elements of Logic Foundations of Mathematics in Problems,* D. Reidel, Hingham, MA, 1982.

4   Fletcher, W. I.: *An Engineering Approach to Digital Design,* Prentice-Hall, Englewood Cliffs, NJ, 1980.

5   Bywater, R. E. H.: *Hardware/Software Design of Digital Systems,* Prentice-Hall, Englewood Cliffs, NJ, 1981.

6   Ramanatha, K. S., and N. N. Biswas: "A Design for Testability of Undetectable Crosspoint Faults in Programmable Logic Arrays," *IEEE Trans. on Computers,* vol. C-32, no. 6, June 1983.

Chapter 4

1   Bursky, D.: "New Processes, Device Structures Point to Million-Transistor IC," *Electronic Design,* vol. 31, no. 12, June 1983.

2   Fisher, A., and H. Kung: "Synchronizing Large VLSI Processor Arrays," *ACM 10th Annual Symposium on Computer Architecture, SIGARCH Newsletter,* vol. 11, no. 3, June 1983.

3   Kline, R.: *Structured Digital Design Including MSI/LSI Components and Microprocessors,* Prentice-Hall, Englewood Cliffs, NJ, 1983.

4   Marcus, M.: *Switching Circuits for Engineers,* Prentice-Hall, Englewood Cliffs, NJ, 1975.

5   McCurdy, L., and A. McHenry: *Digital Logic Design and Applications—An Experimental Approach,* Prentice-Hall, Englewood Cliffs, NJ, 1981.

6   *Integrated Fuse Logic Data Manual,* Signetics Corp., Sunnyvale, CA, 1983.

Chapter 5

1   Ling, J.: "High-Speed Binary Adder," *IBM Journal of Research and Development,* vol. 25, nos. 2 and 3, May 1981.

2   Hwang, K.: *Computer Arithmetic,* Wiley, New York, 1979.

3 "Floating Point ROM," Motorola Semiconductor MC68A39, Motorola Corp., Austin, TX, 1983.

4 Waser, S.: "High-Speed Monolithic Multipliers for Real-Time Digital Signal Processing," *Computer,* vol. 5, no. 6, October 1979.

5 Technical Staff of Monolithic Memories, Inc.: *Designing with Programmable Array Logic,* McGraw-Hill, New York, 1981.

6 Coonen, J. T.: "An Implementation Guide to a Proposed Standard for Floating Point Arithmetic," *Computer,* vol. 6, no. 7, Jan. 1980.

7 Parasuroman, B.: "Hardware Multiplication Techniques for Microprocessor Systems," *Computer Design,* vol. 18, no. 5, April 1977.

8 Watamuki, O., and M. D. Erreguvac: "Floating Point On-Line Arithmetic for Addition, Subtraction and Multiplication," *IEEE Trans. on Computers,* vol. C-32, no. 4, April 1983.

Chapter 6

1 McLeod, J.: "Data Storage Interface," *Systems and Software,* vol. 2, no. 6, June 1983.

2 Killman, P.: "Tiny Floppies Squeeze in the Bits," *Computer Design,* vol. 22, no. 6, 1983.

3 Domsky, L. D.: "Built for Speed: Quarter Inch Streaming Tape Drives," *Computer Design,* vol. 22, no. 1, May 1983.

4 Hemmerick, L. D.: "Rethinking Winchester Backups," *Computer Design,* vol. 22, no. 6, May 1983.

5 Jones, F., and A. Lancaster: "EEPROM Adapts Easily to System Change, *Electronics Design,* vol. 21, no. 17, Aug. 1983.

6 Pope, K.: "No Waiting—EEPROM at Work," *Computer Design,* vol. 22, no. 7, June 1983.

7 Bursky, D.: "Innovative Chips Designs Lead to Dense, Superfast RAMs," *Electronic Design,* vol. 21, no. 17, Aug. 1983.

8 Warren, C.: "Tape Unravels Secondary Storage Knots," *Electronic Design,* vol. 21, no. 17, Aug. 1983.

9 Ohr, S.: "Optical Disks Launching Gigabyte Data Storage," *Electronic Design,* vol. 21, no. 17, Aug. 1983.

10 Longfellow, D., and H. Sussman: "32 K-by-8 DRAM Reduces Size, Cost of Microprocessor Systems," *Electronic Design,* vol. 21, no. 17, Aug. 1983.

11 White, R. M.: "Magnetic Disks: Storage Densities on the Rise," *IEEE Spectrum,* vol. 20, no. 8, Aug. 1983.

12 Chi, C. S.: "Advances in Computer Mass Storage Technology," *Computer,* vol. 15, no. 5, May 1982.

Chapter 7

1   Davis, A., and J. Fierke: "Analog I/O Boards Bring Personal Computers into the Plant," *Computer Design,* vol. 22, no. 5, April 1983.

2   Wedding, D. K., et al.: "Mammoth Displays That Measure in Meters," *Computer Design,* vol. 22, no. 8, July 1983.

3   Morkoff, N.: "Printer Technology Quietly Advances," *Computer Design,* vol. 22, no. 10, Sept. 1983.

4   Dive, S., and M. Maniar: "Chips Set Given a Smooth Scroll in CRT Displays," *Computer Design,* vol. 22, no. 10, Sept. 1983.

5   Engibous, T., and G. Drayser: "Flat Displays, An Alternative to CRT's?" *Computer Design,* vol. 22, no. 10, Sept. 1983.

6   Oikonomon, N., and R. Y. Kain: "Code Construction for Error Control in Byte-Organized Memory Systems," *IEEE Trans. on Computers,* vol. C-32, no. 6, June 1983.

7   Sherays, R. J., and J. L. Gieser: "Experiments in Automatic Microcode Generation," *IEEE Trans. on Computers,* vol. C-32, no. 6, June 1983.

Chapter 8

1   Boxer, A.: "Designing for High Performance Data Acquisition," *Computer Design,* vol. 22, no. 10, Sept. 1983.

2   Jendro, J.: "Extending the Megabris," *Mini-Microsystems,* vol. 16, no. 10, Sept. 1983.

3   Parker, R., and S. Shapiro: "Analog I/O Boards Get Smarter," *Computer Design,* vol. 22, no. 5, April 1983.

4   Artwick, B.: *Microcomputer Interfacing,* Prentice-Hall, Englewood Cliffs, NJ, 1980.

Chapter 9

1   Warren, C.: "Supermicrocomputers," *Electronic Design,* vol. 31, no. 11, May 1983.

2   Niehaus, J.: "32-Bit Supermini Built with Bit-Slice IC Family," *Electronic Design,* vol. 31, no. 11, May 1983.

3   Dadags, A.: "System/370 Extended Architecture: Design Considerations," *IBM Journal of Research and Development,* vol. 27, no. 3, May 1983.

4   Rodis, G.: "The 801 Minicomputer," *IBM Journal of Research and Development,* vol. 27, no. 33, May 1983.

5   Wright, R. E.: "Documenting a Computer Architecture," *IBM Journal of Research and Development,* vol. 27, no. 3, May 1983.

6   Dasgupta, S.: "On the Verification of Computer Architecture Using an Architecture Description Language," *ACM 10th Annual Symposium on Computer Architecture, SIGARCH Newsletter,* vol. 11, no. 3, June 1983.

7   Kruft, G. D., and W. N. Toz: *Microprogrammed Control and Reliable Design of Small Computers,* Prentice-Hall, Englewood Cliffs, NJ, 1981.

Chapter 10

1   King, R. M.: "Research on Syntheses of Concurrent Computing Systems," *ACM 10th Annual Symposium on Computer Architecture, SIGARCH Newsletter,* vol. 11, no. 3, June 1983.

2   Giloi, W., and P. Behr: "Hierarchical Function Distribution—A Design Principle for Advanced Microcomputer Architecture," *ACM 10th Annual Symposium on Computer Architecture, SIGARCH Newsletter,* vol. 11, no. 3, June 1983.

3   Finkler, G. A.: "Full 32-Bit Microprocessors: The Next Generation," *Mini-Microsystems,* vol. 16, no. 9, April 1983.

4   Lenk, J. D.: *Handbook of Microprocessors, Microcomputers and Minicomputers,* Prentice-Hall, Englewood Cliffs, NJ, 1980.

5   Hawk, R. L.: "A Supermini for Super Maxi Tasks," *Computer Design,* vol. 22, no. 10, Sept. 1983.

6   Frailey, D. J.: "Word Length of a Computer Architecture: Definitions and Applications," *Computer Architecture News,* vol. 11, no. 2, June 1983.

7   Wilkes, M. V.: "Size, Power, and Speed," *ACM 10th Annual Symposium on Computer Architecture, SIGARCH Newsletter,* vol. 11, no. 3, June 1983.

8   Fathi, E. T., and M. Kreiger: "Multiple Microprocessor Systems: What, Why and When," *Computer,* vol. 16, no. 3, March 1983.

9   Treleaven, P. C.: "VLSI Processor Architectures," *Computer,* vol. 15, no. 6, June 1982.

ANSWERS TO SELECTED
ODD-NUMBERED QUESTIONS

Chapter 1

1.7

ADDRESS	OP CODE	ADDRESS PART
1	CLA	40
2	ADD	41
3	ADD	42
4	STO	43
5	HLT	000
40	contains	X
41	contains	Y
42	contains	Z
43	contains	0

1.9

ADDRESS	OPERATION	OPERAND
1	CLA	20
2	MUL	20
3	STO	40
4	CLA	21
5	MUL	21
6	ADD	40
7	STO	40
8	CLA	22
9	MUL	22
10	ADD	40
11	STO	40
12	HLT	
20	contains	X
21	contains	Y
22	contains	Z
40	contains	0

1.13

ADDRESS	OPERATION	OPERAND
1	CLA	20
2	STO	21
3	CLA	21
4	MUL	20
5	STO	21
6	CLA	50
7	ADD	51
8	STO	50
9	BRM	3
10	CLA	21
11	ADD	20
12	STO	40
13	HLT	
20	contains	X
21	contains	0
50	contains	-5
51	contains	1

We will store our $X^5 + X$ in the address assigned by the assembler to the variable D.

ADDRESS	OPERATION	OPERAND
A	DEC	0
B	DEC	-5
C	DEC	1
D	DEC	0
	CLA	X
	STO	D
E	CLA	D
	MUL	X
	STO	D
	CLA	B
	ADD	C
	STO	B
	BRM	E
	CLA	D
	ADD	X
	STO	D
	HLT	

1.19

If we assume that the integers are in ascending or descending order only,

ADDRESS	OPERATION	OPERAND
1	CLA	30
2	SUB	31
3	BRM	5
4	HLT	
5	HLT	

The computer stops at address 4 if the numbers are in ascending order and at 5 if the numbers are in descending order. We must check to see whether the numbers are in ascending or descending order.

ADDRESS	OPERATION	OPERAND
1	CLA	30
2	SUB	31
3	BRM	10
4	CLA	31
5	SUB	32
6	BRM	13
7	HLT	
10	CLA	31
11	SUB	32
12	BRM	15
13	HLT	
15	HLT	

This program stops at address 13 if the numbers are in neither ascending nor descending order, at address 7 if the numbers are ascending, and at address 15 if the numbers are descending.

1.23

ADDRESS	OPERATION	OPERAND
1	CLA	26
2	SUB	25
3	BRM	300
4	BRA	400

1.25

ADDRESS	OPERATION	OPERAND
P	CLA	A
	SUB	B
	BRM	M
	CLA	A
	SUB	C
	BRM	M
	CLA	A
	STO	X
	HLT	
M	CLA	B
	SUB	C
	BRM	N
	CLA	B
	STO	X
	HLT	
N	CLA	C
	STO	X
	HLT	

1.32

ADDRESS	OPERATION	OPERAND	ADDRESS	OPERATION	OPERAND
1	CLA	300	13	CLA	6
2	BRM	5	14	ADD	400
3	STO	300	15	STO	6
4	BRA	7	16	CLA	401
5	SUB	300	17	ADD	400
6	SUB	300	18	STO	401
7	CLA	3	19	BRM	1
8	ADD	400	20	HLT	
9	STO	3	300 ⎱		
10	CLA	5	329 ⎰	contains numbers	
11	ADD	400	400	contains 1	
12	STO	5	401	contains −30	

Chapter 2

2.1 (*a*) 101011   (*b*) 1000000   (*c*) 100000000000   (*d*) 0.011
(*e*) 0.11011   (*f*) 0.0111   (*g*) 1000000000.1   (*h*) 10000011.1001
(*i*) 10000000000.0001

2.3 (*a*) 13   (*b*) 27   (*c*) 23   (*d*) 0.6875   (*e*) 0.203125   (*f*) 0.212890625
(*g*) 59.6875   (*h*) 91.203125   (*i*) 22.3408203125

2.5 (*a*) 11   (*b*) 36   (*c*) 19   (*d*) 0.8125   (*e*) 0.5625   (*f*) 0.3125
(*g*) 11.1875   (*h*) 9.5625   (*i*) 5.375

2.7 (*a*) 10100.11 = 20.75   (*b*) 1001010 = 74   (*c*) 1.1 = 1.5
(*d*) 10101 = 21

2.9 (*a*)   1101.1   13.5   (*b*)   101101   45
 $\underline{1011.1}$ $\underline{11.5}$ $\underline{110110}$ $\underline{109}$
 11001.0   25 1100011   154
(*c*)   0.0011   0.1875   (*d*)   1100.011   12.375
 $\underline{0.1110}$ $\underline{0.875}$ $\underline{1011.011}$ $\underline{11.375}$
 1.0001   1.0625 10111.110   23.750

2.11 (*a*)   1000000   (*b*)   1111111
 $\underline{-100000}$ $\underline{-111111}$
 100000 1000000
(*c*)   1011101.1   (*d*)   1010100.01001
 $\underline{-101010.11}$ $\underline{-110000.01010}$
 110010.11 100011.11111

2.13 (*a*)   100101   (*b*)   10000000
 $\underline{-100011}$ $\underline{01000000}$
 000010 1000000
(*c*)   1011110.1   (*d*)   11111111
 $\underline{101011.11}$ $\underline{1111111}$
 110010.11 10000000

2.15 (*a*) 100100000   (*b*) 11111100   (*c*) 100   (*d*) 1.1   (*e*) 10100000001.101
(*f*) 10.1

2.17 (*a*)

```
      1111
      1101
      1111
     11110
     1111
  11000011
```

(*b*)

```
      1111
      1010
     11110
    11110
 10010110
```

(*c*)

```
           100
  1011)101100
          1011
           000
```

(*d*)

```
              11.1
  1100)101010.0
          1100
         10010
          1100
          1100
          1100
             0
```

(*e*)

```
    111.11
     10.1
    11111
   111110
 10011.011
```

(*f*)

```
    10110.1
    100.11
    101101
    101101
  10110100
 1101010.111
```

2.19

	9s COMPLEMENT	10s COMPLEMENT
(*a*)	4563	4564
(*b*)	8067	8068
(*c*)	54.84	54.85
(*d*)	81.706	81.707

2.21

	9s COMPLEMENT	10s COMPLEMENT
(*a*)	6345	6346
(*b*)	7877	7878
(*c*)	45.80	45.81
(*d*)	62.736	62.737

2.23

	1s COMPLEMENT	2s COMPLEMENT
(*a*)	0100	0101
(*b*)	00100	00101
(*c*)	0100.10	0100.11
(*d*)	00100.10	00100.11

2.25

	1s COMPLEMENT	2s COMPLEMENT
(*a*)	010000	010001
(*b*)	011011	011100
(*c*)	01000.01	01000.10
(*d*)	01100.00	

2.27

	9s COMPLEMENT	10s COMPLEMENT
(*a*)	948	948

9s COMPLEMENT:
```
      948
      765
    1 713
    └─→ 1
      714
```

10s COMPLEMENT:
```
      948
      766
      714
```

(b)
$$
\begin{array}{r}
347 \\
736 \\
\hline
1\ 083 \\
\end{array}
$$
$\llcorner\!\!\rightarrow 1$
$$
\begin{array}{r}
\hline
084
\end{array}
$$

$$
\begin{array}{r}
347 \\
737 \\
\hline
084
\end{array}
$$

(c)
$$
\begin{array}{r}
349.5 \\
754.6 \\
\hline
1\ 104.1 \\
\end{array}
$$
$\llcorner\!\!\rightarrow 1$
$$
\begin{array}{r}
\hline
104.2
\end{array}
$$

$$
\begin{array}{r}
349.5 \\
754.7 \\
\hline
104.2
\end{array}
$$

(d)
$$
\begin{array}{r}
412.7 \\
590.7 \\
\hline
1\ 003.4 \\
\end{array}
$$
$\llcorner\!\!\rightarrow 1$
$$
\begin{array}{r}
\hline
3.5
\end{array}
$$

$$
\begin{array}{r}
412.7 \\
590.8 \\
\hline
3.5
\end{array}
$$

2.29   9s COMPLEMENT   10s COMPLEMENT

(a)
$$
\begin{array}{r}
1024 \\
9086 \\
\hline
0110 \\
\end{array}
$$
$\llcorner\!\!\rightarrow 1$
$$
\begin{array}{r}
\hline
111
\end{array}
$$

$$
\begin{array}{r}
1024 \\
9087 \\
\hline
0111
\end{array}
$$

(b)
$$
\begin{array}{r}
249 \\
862 \\
\hline
111 \\
\end{array}
$$
$\llcorner\!\!\rightarrow 1$
$$
\begin{array}{r}
\hline
112
\end{array}
$$

$$
\begin{array}{r}
249 \\
863 \\
\hline
112
\end{array}
$$

(c)
$$
\begin{array}{r}
24.1 \\
86.5 \\
\hline
10.6 \\
\end{array}
$$
$\llcorner\!\!\rightarrow 1$
$$
\begin{array}{r}
\hline
10.7
\end{array}
$$

$$
\begin{array}{r}
24.1 \\
86.6 \\
\hline
10.7
\end{array}
$$

(d)
$$
\begin{array}{r}
239.3 \\
880.5 \\
\hline
119.8 \\
\end{array}
$$
$\llcorner\!\!\rightarrow 1$
$$
\begin{array}{r}
\hline
119.9
\end{array}
$$

$$
\begin{array}{r}
239.3 \\
880.6 \\
\hline
119.9
\end{array}
$$

2.31   1s COMPLEMENT   2s COMPLEMENT

(a)
$$
\begin{array}{r}
1011 \\
1010 \\
\hline
1\ 0101 \\
\end{array}
$$
$\llcorner\!\!\rightarrow 1$
$$
\begin{array}{r}
\hline
0110
\end{array}
$$

$$
\begin{array}{r}
1011 \\
1011 \\
\hline
0110
\end{array}
$$

(b)
$$
\begin{array}{r}
11011 \\
00110 \\
\hline
1\ 00001 \\
\end{array}
$$
$\llcorner\!\!\rightarrow 1$
$$
\begin{array}{r}
\hline
10
\end{array}
$$

$$
\begin{array}{r}
11011 \\
00111 \\
\hline
00010
\end{array}
$$

(c)
```
    10111.1        10111.1
    01100.0        01100.1
  1 00011.1         100.0
  └──────→ 1
     100.0
```

(d)
```
    11011.00       11011.00
    01100.00       01100.01
  1 00111.00        111.01
  └──────→ 1
     111.01
```

2.33 $2^6 = 64$

2.35 1000 different numbers in each case (from 0 to 999, for instance)

2.37 0, 1, 2, 3, 10, 11, 12, 13, 20, 21

2.39 0, 1, 2, 3, 4, 5, 6, 7, 8, 9, A, 10, 11, 12, 13, 14, 15, 16, 17, 18, 19, 1A, 20, 21, 22

2.41

(a)
```
   .1001
   .1001
 ┌ 0010
 └──→ 1
   .0011
```
(b)
```
   .1110
   .1001
 ┌ 0111
 └──→ 1
   .1000
```
(c)
```
   01111
   10110
 ┌ 00101
 └──→ 1
   .00110
```

(d)
```
   11011
   00110
 ┌ 00001
 └──→ 1
   00010
```
(e)
```
    1110101
    0101101
  1 0100010
  └──────→ 1
    0100011
```

2.45

(a)
```
  45,056
   1,536
     192
       7
  46,791
```
(b)
```
  24,576
   1,024
     160
      12
  25,772
```
(c)
```
  40,960
   1,024
     144
       2
  42,130
```
(d)
```
  851,968
    8,192
    1,792
       96
        3
  862,051
```

2.49 (a) 55 (b) 556 (c) 267 (d) 66.3 (e) 3.554

2.53 (a) 1644. (b) 514 (c) 1041.3 (d) 1170.76051 (e) 10515.5

2.57 (a) B7 (b) 9C (c) 5F (d) 0.7E (e) B7A

2.61

(a)
```
     1
    15₈
  + 14₈
    31₈
```
(b)
```
     1
    24₈
  + 36₈
    62₈
```
(c)
```
     1
    126₈
    347₈
    475₈
```

(d)
```
     1
    67₈
    45₈
   134₈
```
(e)
```
     1
    136₈
    636₈
   774₈
```

Chapter 3

ANSWERS TO SELECTED ODD-NUMBERED QUESTIONS

3.1 (*a*)

X	Y	Z	XYZ	$\overline{X}\overline{Y}\overline{Z}$	$XYZ + \overline{X}\overline{Y}\overline{Z}$
0	0	0	0	1	1
0	0	1	0	0	0
0	1	0	0	0	0
0	1	1	0	0	0
1	0	0	0	0	0
1	0	1	0	0	0
1	1	0	0	0	0
1	1	1	1	0	1

(*b*)

A	B	C	ABC	$A\overline{B}\overline{C}$	$\overline{A}\overline{B}\overline{C}$	$ABC + A\overline{B}\overline{C} + \overline{A}\overline{B}\overline{C}$
0	0	0	0	0	1	1
0	0	1	0	0	0	0
0	1	0	0	0	0	0
0	1	1	0	0	0	0
1	0	0	0	1	0	1
1	0	1	0	0	0	0
1	1	0	0	0	0	0
1	1	1	1	0	0	1

(*c*)

A	B	C	$B\overline{C}$	$\overline{B}C$	$B\overline{C} + \overline{B}C$	$A(B\overline{C} + \overline{B}C)$
0	0	0	0	0	0	0
0	0	1	0	1	1	0
0	1	0	1	0	1	0
0	1	1	0	0	0	0
1	0	0	0	0	0	0
1	0	1	0	1	1	1
1	1	0	1	0	1	1
1	1	1	0	0	0	0

(*d*)

A	B	C	$A + B$	$A + C$	$\overline{A} + \overline{B}$	$(A + B)(A + C)(\overline{A} + \overline{B})$
0	0	0	0	0	1	0
0	0	1	0	1	1	0
0	1	0	1	0	1	0
0	1	1	1	1	1	1
1	0	0	1	1	1	1
1	0	1	1	1	1	1
1	1	0	1	1	0	0
1	1	1	1	1	0	0

3.3 Only the values of the expressions are listed:

(*a*)

A	B	$A\overline{B} + \overline{A}B$
0	0	0
0	1	1
1	0	1
1	1	0

(b)

A	B	C	$A\overline{B} + B\overline{C}$
0	0	0	0
0	0	1	0
0	1	0	1
0	1	1	0
1	0	0	1
1	0	1	1
1	1	0	1
1	1	1	0

(c)

A	C	$A\overline{C} + AC$
0	0	0
0	1	0
1	0	1
1	1	1

(d)

A	B	C	$\overline{A}BC + AB\overline{C} + \overline{A}BC$
0	0	0	0
0	0	1	0
0	1	0	0
0	1	1	1
1	0	0	0
1	0	1	1
1	1	0	1
1	1	1	0

(e)

A	B	C	$A(\overline{A}BC + A\overline{B}C + AB\overline{C})$
0	0	0	0
0	0	1	0
0	1	0	0
0	1	1	0
1	0	0	1
1	0	1	1
1	1	0	1
1	1	1	0

3.7   (a) $\overline{B}\overline{C} + \overline{A}\overline{C} + \overline{A}\overline{B}$ (b) $\overline{C} + \overline{B} + \overline{A}$

      (c) $A(B + C)$ (d) A is a minimal expression

3.9   (a) $ABC(AB\overline{C} + A\overline{B}C + \overline{A}BC) = 0$, for no assignment of binary values will make this expression take the value 0.

      (b) $AB + A\overline{B} + \overline{A}C + \overline{A}\overline{C} = 1$, for every assignment of values will give this expression the value 1.

      (c) $XY + XYZ + XY\overline{Z} + \overline{X}YZ = XY + YZ$

      (d) $XY(\overline{X}YZ + X\overline{Y}\overline{Z} + \overline{X}\overline{Y}Z) = 0$

3.11 (a) $\overline{A}(\overline{B} + \overline{C})(\overline{A} + \overline{B}) = \overline{A}B + \overline{A}C$ or $\overline{A}(B + C)$

      (b) $\overline{A}\overline{B} + \overline{B}\overline{C} + \overline{A}\overline{C}$

(c) $(\overline{A} + \overline{B})(B + \overline{C})(\overline{C} + D) = \overline{A}B\overline{C} + \overline{A}\overline{C} + \overline{A}BD + \overline{A}CD$
$= \overline{A}\overline{C} + \overline{B}\overline{C} + \overline{A}BD$

(d) $(\overline{A} + \overline{B}) + (C + \overline{D})(B + \overline{C}) = \overline{A} + \overline{B} + BC + B\overline{D} + \overline{C}D$
$= \overline{AB} + C + \overline{D}$

(e) $\overline{A} + \overline{B}C + CD$

3.13 The important columns in these tables are as follows:

X	Y	Z	$(\overline{X + Y + Z})$	$\overline{X}\,\overline{Y}\,\overline{Z}$
0	0	0	1	1
0	0	1	0	0
0	1	0	0	0
0	1	1	0	0
1	0	0	0	0
1	0	1	0	0
1	1	0	0	0
1	1	1	0	0

X	Y	Z	$(\overline{XYZ})$	$\overline{X} + \overline{Y} + \overline{Z}$
0	0	0	1	1
0	0	1	1	1
0	1	0	1	1
0	1	1	1	1
1	0	0	1	1
1	0	1	1	1
1	1	0	1	1
1	1	1	0	0

3.15 (a) $\overline{A}BC + A\overline{B}C + AC + BC = AC + BC$

(b) $A\overline{B} + A\overline{C} + ABC + AB\overline{C} + \overline{A}BC + \overline{B}C$ (This can be simplified to $\overline{B}C$)

(c) $A\overline{B} + A\overline{B}C = A\overline{B}$

3.17 Rule 13

3.19 (a) $AB + AD + BC + CD$

(b) $AB + AD + AC + BC + CD + C + BD + D + DC = C + D + AB$

(c) $ABC + ABD + AC + BC + DC + ADC + BDC + DC = AC + BC + DC + ABD$

(d) $A\overline{B} + A\overline{C}$

3.21 $\overline{X}\,\overline{Y}Z + XY\overline{Z}$

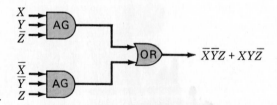

$\overline{X}\,\overline{Y}Z + XY\overline{Z}$

3.25 $XY + X\overline{Z}$

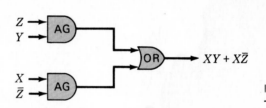

3.27

X	Y	$X + \overline{X}Y$	$X + Y$
0	0	0	0
0	1	1	1
1	0	1	1
1	1	1	1

3.29 $Y\overline{Z} + \overline{Y}Z$ is the sum-of-products expression, and $(Y + Z)(\overline{Y} + \overline{Z})$ is the product-of-sums expression.

3.35 (a)

	$\overline{X}$	X
$\overline{Y}$	1	
Y	1	

$\overline{X}\overline{Y} + \overline{X}Y$

(b)

	$\overline{X}\overline{Y}$	$\overline{X}Y$	XY	$X\overline{Y}$
$\overline{Z}$	1		1	
Z				

$\overline{X}\overline{Y}\overline{Z} + XY\overline{Z}$

(c)

	$\overline{X}\overline{Y}$	$\overline{X}Y$	XY	$X\overline{Y}$
$\overline{Z}$	1	1		
Z	1			

$\overline{X}Y\overline{Z} + \overline{X}\overline{Y}$

(d)

	$\overline{X}\overline{Y}$	$\overline{X}Y$	XY	$X\overline{Y}$
$\overline{Z}$	1	1		1
Z				

$\overline{X}\overline{Y}\overline{Z} + \overline{X}Y\overline{Z} + X\overline{Y}\overline{Z}$

(e)

	$\overline{X}\overline{Y}$	$\overline{X}Y$	XY	$X\overline{Y}$
$\overline{Z}$	1	1		1
Z				

$\overline{X}\overline{Z} + \overline{Y}\overline{Z}$

(f)

	$\overline{A}\overline{B}$	$\overline{A}B$	AB	$A\overline{B}$
$\overline{C}$				
C				

$AB(\overline{\overline{A}\overline{B}\overline{C}} + \overline{B}C)$

3.39 (a)

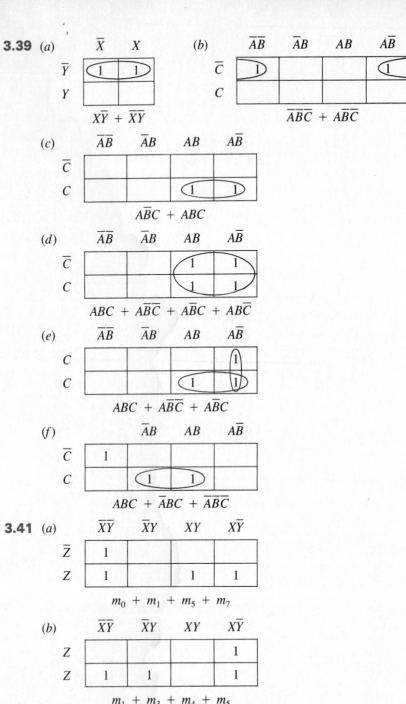

(a)

	$\overline{X}$	X
$\overline{Y}$	1	1
Y		

$X\overline{Y} + \overline{X}\,\overline{Y}$

(b)

	$\overline{A}\overline{B}$	$\overline{A}B$	AB	$A\overline{B}$
$\overline{C}$	1			1
C				

$\overline{A}\,\overline{B}\,\overline{C} + A\overline{B}\,\overline{C}$

(c)

	$\overline{A}\overline{B}$	$\overline{A}B$	AB	$A\overline{B}$
$\overline{C}$				
C			1	1

$A\overline{B}C + ABC$

(d)

	$\overline{A}\overline{B}$	$\overline{A}B$	AB	$A\overline{B}$
$\overline{C}$			1	1
C			1	1

$ABC + A\overline{B}\,\overline{C} + A\overline{B}C + AB\overline{C}$

(e)

	$\overline{A}\overline{B}$	$\overline{A}B$	AB	$A\overline{B}$
C				1
C			1	1

$ABC + A\overline{B}\,\overline{C} + A\overline{B}C$

(f)

	$\overline{A}\overline{B}$	$\overline{A}B$	AB	$A\overline{B}$
$\overline{C}$	1			
C		1	1	

$ABC + \overline{A}BC + \overline{A}\,\overline{B}\,\overline{C}$

3.41 (a)

	$\overline{X}\overline{Y}$	$\overline{X}Y$	XY	$X\overline{Y}$
$\overline{Z}$	1			
Z	1		1	1

$m_0 + m_1 + m_5 + m_7$

(b)

	$\overline{X}\overline{Y}$	$\overline{X}Y$	XY	$X\overline{Y}$
Z				1
Z	1	1		1

$m_1 + m_3 + m_4 + m_5$

(c)

	$\overline{X}\overline{Y}$	$\overline{X}Y$	XY	$X\overline{Y}$
$\overline{Z}$		1		
Z	1	1		1

$m_1 + m_2 + m_3 + m_5$

(d)

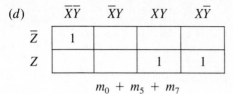

	$\overline{X}\overline{Y}$	$\overline{X}Y$	XY	$X\overline{Y}$
$\overline{Z}$	1			
Z			1	1

$$m_0 + m_5 + m_7$$

3.45 (b)

	$\overline{W}\overline{X}$	$\overline{W}X$	WX	$W\overline{X}$
$\overline{Y}\overline{Z}$	1	1	1	1
$\overline{Y}Z$			1	1
YZ				1
$Y\overline{Z}$	1			1

$m_0 = \overline{W}\overline{X}\overline{Y}\overline{Z}$ $m_{10} = W\overline{X}Y\overline{Z}$
$m_2 = \overline{W}\overline{X}Y\overline{Z}$ $m_{11} = W\overline{X}YZ$
$m_4 = \overline{W}X\overline{Y}\overline{Z}$ $m_{12} = WX\overline{Y}\overline{Z}$
$m_8 = W\overline{X}\overline{Y}\overline{Z}$ $m_{13} = WX\overline{Y}Z$
$m_9 = W\overline{X}\overline{Y}Z$

$m_0 + m_2 + m_4 + m_8 + m_9 + m_{10} + m_{11} + m_{12} + m_{13}$
$\overline{X}\overline{Z} + \overline{Y}Z + W\overline{X} + W\overline{Y}$
$\overline{Z}(\overline{X} + \overline{Y}) + W(\overline{X} + \overline{Y})$
$(\overline{Z} + W)(\overline{X} + \overline{Y})$

3.47 (a) $m_1 + m_3 + m_5 + m_7 + m_{12} + m_{13} + m_8 + m_9$

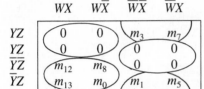

	WX	$W\overline{X}$	$\overline{W}\overline{X}$	$\overline{W}X$
YZ	0	0	m_3	m_7
$Y\overline{Z}$	0	0	0	0
$\overline{Y}\overline{Z}$	m_{12}	m_8	0	0
$\overline{Y}Z$	m_{13}	m_0	m_1	m_5

Product of sums:

$\overline{(W\overline{Y} + \overline{W}Z)} = (\overline{W} + \overline{Y})(W + Z)$

Sum of products:
$W\overline{Y} + \overline{W}Z$

(b) $m_0 + m_5 + m_7 + m_8 + m_{11} + m_{13} + m_{15}$

	WX	$W\overline{X}$	$\overline{W}\overline{X}$	$\overline{W}X$
YZ	m_{15}	m_{11}		m_7
$Y\overline{Z}$	0			0
$\overline{Y}Z$	0	m_8	m_0	0
$\overline{Y}\overline{Z}$	m_{13}			m_5

Product of sums:

$(X\overline{Z} + Y\overline{Z} + \overline{W}XZ + \overline{X}\overline{Y}Z)$
$= (\overline{X} + Z)(\overline{Y} + Z)(W + X + \overline{Z})$
$(X + Y + \overline{Z})$

don't-cares

3.49 (a) $\overline{A}\overline{B}\overline{C} + A\overline{B}\overline{C} + \overbrace{ABC + \overline{A}B\overline{C} + \overline{A}\overline{B}C}^{} = \overline{B}\overline{C}$
$\quad\quad\quad AB \quad A\overline{B} \quad \overline{A}B \quad \overline{A}B$

	AB	$A\overline{B}$	$\overline{A}B$	$\overline{A}B$
C	D		D	
C		1	1	D

don't-cares

(b) $ABC + A\overline{B}\overline{C} + \overbrace{AB\overline{C} + A\overline{B}C}^{} = A$
$\quad\quad AB \quad A\overline{B} \quad \overline{A}B \quad \overline{A}B$

	AB	$A\overline{B}$	$\overline{A}B$	$\overline{A}B$
C	1	D		
$\overline{C}$	D	1		

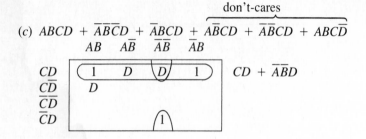

(c) $ABCD + \overline{A}\overline{B}\overline{C}D + \overline{A}BCD + A\overline{B}CD + \overline{A}\overline{B}CD + ABC\overline{D}$

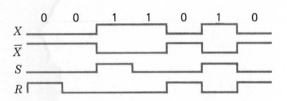

$CD + \overline{A}\overline{B}D$

Chapter 4

4.1

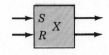

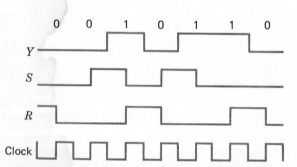

FIGURE A4.1

4.5

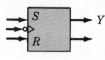

FIGURE A4.5

4.9

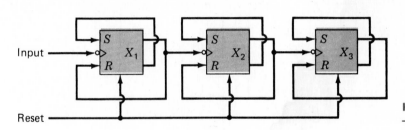

FIGURE A4.9

4.13

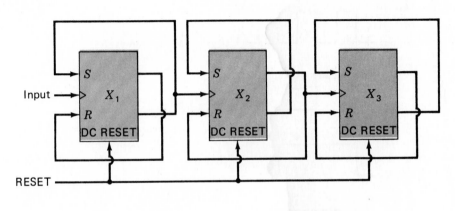

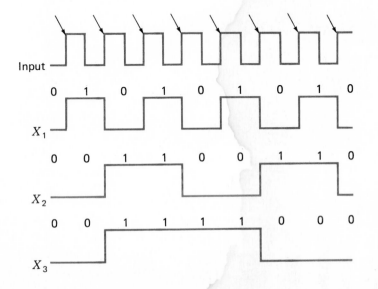

FIGURE A4.13

4.15

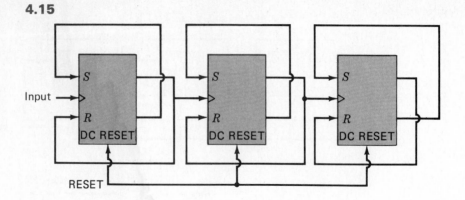

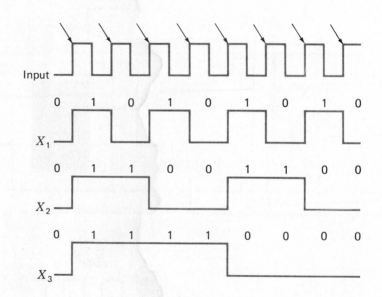

4.17

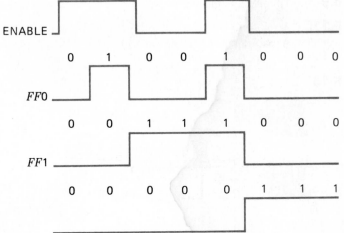

FIGURE A4.17

Chapter 5

5.1

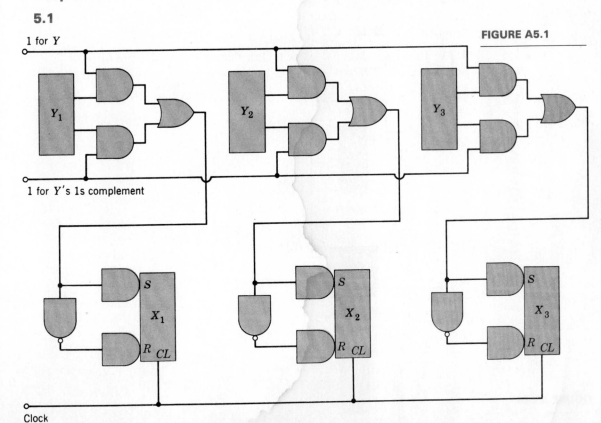

5.3   (*a*) $\underline{0}0110$ (*b*) $\underline{0}1010$ (*c*) $\underline{1}1100$ (*d*) Not representable

5.5 -4 would be stored $\underline{1}0100$ in the magnitude system, $\underline{1}1011$ in the 1s complement system, and $\underline{1}1100$ in the 2s complement system.

5.7 $S = 1$ and $C = 1$

5.9 -12 in 1s complement; -13 in 2s complement

5.11   The sum will overflow the register and cause an incorrect addition. Most machines sense for this and turn on an "addition overflow" or indicate the overflow in some manner.

5.15

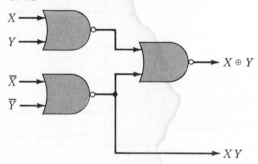

FIGURE A5.15

5.29   Logical addition, $\underline{0}111011$
Logical multiplication, $\underline{0}1000\ 10$
Exclusive OR, $\underline{0}011001$

5.31   The logical MULTIPLY will clear those digits of X where 0s occur in Y, and the logical ADD will add 1s into the places in X where 1s occur in Y.

5.48

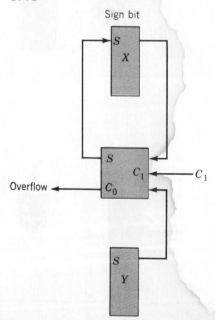

FIGURE A5.48

Overflow $= (X > \emptyset) \cdot (Y > \emptyset) \cdot (C_3 = 1) + (X < \emptyset) \cdot (Y < 0) \cdot (C_3 = \emptyset)$
Overflow $= \overline{X_4} \overline{Y_4} C_3 + X_4 Y_4 \overline{C_3}$

5.50 The general scheme is

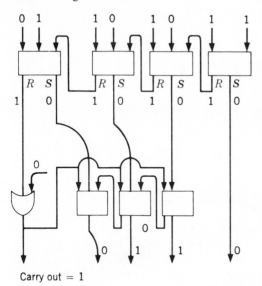

Carry out $= 1$

Chapter 6

6.12

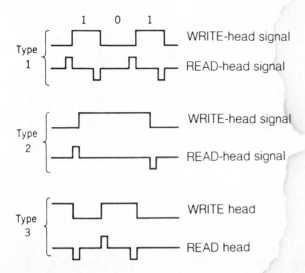

6.35 262,500 bits/s

Chapter 7

7.3 01100001
01100100
01100100
00010000
00010110
00000100
00000001
10000000 Carriage return is optional

7.5 27 holes in three cards. Easier to correct if cards are used, for erroneous cards may simply be replaced.

7.7 Nine holes

7.9

DECIMAL	EXCESS-3 CODE	EVEN-PARITY CHECK	ODD-PARITY CHECK
0	0011	0	1
1	0100	1	0
2	0101	0	1
3	0110	0	1
4	0111	1	0
5	1000	1	0
6	1001	0	1
7	1010	0	1
8	1011	1	0
9	1100	0	1

7.11 (a) The errors are in the seventh, eighth, and ninth rows; the sixth digit in each row is in error, and the message is, "That's right."

(b) The error is the fourth digit in the sixth row, and the message is, "Don't stop."

7.13 10. One such code can be formed by adding a leading 0 to each of the four-binary-digit Gray code groups listed in Chap. 8 and then adding another 16 rows with the four rightmost binary digits the same as those in Chap. 8 but with their order reversed and with a leading 1 added to each code row.

7.15 (a) Errors are in the second, third, and fourth rows, the seventh digit in. The message is, "That's fine."

(b) Errors are in the second and third rows, the third digit in, and the message is, "Bad tapes." Notice that we corrected a double error in a column.

Chapter 8

8.16 To interface a keyboard with device address 6, modify Fig. 8.20 as follows. The keyboard-to-bus data line drivers remain the same and are not shown here. The address line selection logic is changed:

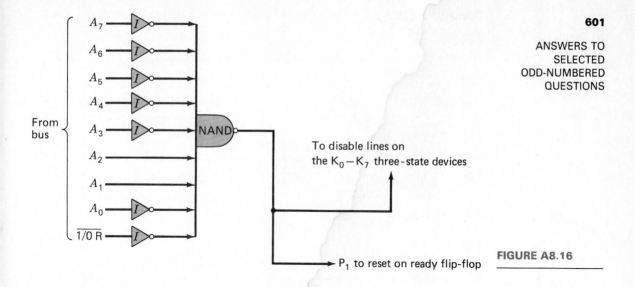

To disable lines on
the $K_0 - K_7$ three-state devices

P_1 to reset on ready flip-flop

Chapter 9

9.3 The timing table is shown in Table 9.3 with the following additions:
OPCODE 00100 = BRM

BRM (from Table 9.4)

I and T_0	Set R	Tell memory to read instruction word
I and T_1	MB into OP,	Operation portion of instruction word into the operation register.
	RESET R	Clear memory read flip-flop.
I and T_2 and AC_0	MB into IC	If sign bit of accumulator is 1 (contents as negative), then use the address portion of the instruction address as the next instruction address.
I and T_2 and AC_0	INCREMENT IC	If sign bit of accumulator is 0 (contents are not negative), then use the next sequential address in memory as the next instruction address
I and T_3	IC INTO MA	Set up to read the next instruction from memory. Leave $I = 1$ so that the next cycle will be another instruction cycle.

BRA

I and T_0	SET R	Tell memory to read instruction
I and T_1	MB INTO OP,	Operation portion of instruction word into the operation register.
	RESET R	Clear memory read flip-flop.
I and T_2	MB INTO IC	Use address portion of instruction word as the next instruction address.
I and T_3	IC INTO MA	Set up to read the next instruction from memory. Leave $I = 1$ so that the next cycle will be another instruction cycle.

The control signal generation logic in Figs. 9.6 and 9.8 should be augmented with the following:

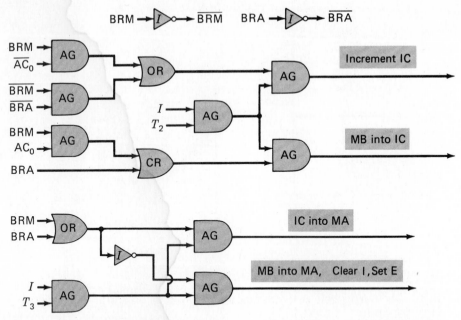

FIGURE A9.3

9.8 Instructions which require an execution cycle generally must access memory to obtain or to store an operand. Examples from the instruction set of Table 9.3 include ADD and STORE. Instructions which do not require an access to memory for an operand generally do not require an execution cycle. In such cases there may be no operand; or the operand has been obtained as part of the instruction and is manipulated solely within the central registers of the processor. Examples are BRM, BRA, and CLR.

9.18 This question says: Provide a microprogram for the BRM branch-on-minus instruction of Table 9.4. The OP code in the BRM instruction is $00100 = 4_{10}$.

MICROPROGRAM ROM LOCATION	C_0 to C_6	MICROPROGRAM C_7 to C_n
0	—	$1 \rightarrow R$; $IAR + 1 \rightarrow IAR$
1	—	$MB_{0-4} \rightarrow OP$; $IAR + 1 \rightarrow IAR$; $0 \rightarrow R$
2	—	$OP + IAR + 1 \rightarrow IAR$
3	20_{10}	$C_{0-6} \rightarrow IAR$
.	.	.
.	.	.
.	.	.
7	40_{10}	$C_{0-6} \rightarrow IAR$
.	.	.
.	.	.
.	.	.
40	42_{10}	IF $(AC_0 = 1)$ THEN $C_{0-6} \rightarrow IAR$; ELSE $IAR + 1 \rightarrow IAR$
41	43_{10}	$C_{0-6} \rightarrow IAR$; $IC + 1 \rightarrow IC$
42	—	$MB_{0-24} \rightarrow IC$
43	—	$IC \rightarrow MA$; $0 \rightarrow IAR$
.	.	.
.	.	.
.	.	.

INDEX